MERGERS, ACQUISITIONS, AND CORPORATE RESTRUCTURINGS

SECOND EDITION

MERGERS, ACQUISITIONS, AND CORPORATE RESTRUCTURINGS

SECOND EDITION

PATRICK A. GAUGHAN

JOHN WILEY & SONS, INC.

New York • Chichester • Weinheim • Brisbane • Singapore • Toronto

Copyright © 1999 by John Wiley & Sons, Inc. All rights reserved.

Published simultaneously in Canada.

Library of Congress Cataloging in Publication Data:

Gaughan, Patrick A.
    Mergers, acquisitions, and corporate restructurings / Patrick A. Gaughan. --2nd ed.
        p. cm.
    Includes bibliographical references and index.
    ISBN 0-471-31670-9 (cl. : alk. paper)
    1. Consolidation and merger of corporations. 2. Corporate reorganizations. I. Title.
    HD2746.5.G38 1999
    658.1'6--dc21   99-12056

Printed in the United States of America

10 9 8 7 6 5 4 3

CONTENTS

Preface   xi

Part One   Background   1

1 Introduction   3

Definitions   7
Types of Mergers   7
Reasons for Mergers and Acquisitions   8
Merger Financing   8
Merger Professionals   9
Leveraged Buyouts   9
Corporate Restructuring   10
Merger Approval Process   11
Merger Negotiations   12
Merger Approval Procedures   13
Short-Form Merger   14
Freezeouts and the Treatment of Minority Shareholders   15
Purchase of Assets Compared with Purchase of Stock   15
Assumption of the Seller's Liabilities   15
Advantages of Asset Acquisitions   16
Asset Selloffs   16
Holding Companies   17
Joint Ventures   18
Strategic Alliances   19
References   20

2 History of Mergers   21

The First Wave, 1897–1904   21
The Second Wave, 1916–29   26
The 1940s   29
The Third Wave, 1965–69   30
Trendsetting Mergers of the 1970s   38
The Fourth Wave, 1981–89   43
The Fifth Wave   50

Summary 59
References 59

3 Legal Framework 61

Overview 61
Laws Governing Mergers, Acquisitions, and Tender Offers 61
Securities Laws 62
Business Judgment Rule 84
Antitrust Laws 86
Changing Patterns of Antitrust Enforcement in the United States 96
Measuring Concentration and Defining Market Share 99
State Antitakeover Laws 103
Regulation of Insider Trading 109
A Company's Obligation to Disclose Merger Negotiations 112
Summary 113
References 114

4 Merger Strategy 116

Growth 116
Synergy 117
Diversification 128
Economic Motives 144
Hubris Hypothesis of Takeovers 158
Improved Management Hypothesis 161
Tax Motives 164
Summary 167
References 168

Part Two   Hostile Takeovers 173

5 Antitakeover Measures 175

Management Entrenchment Hypothesis versus Stockholder Interests Hypothesis 176
Preventative Antitakeover Measures 177
Changing the State of Incorporation 203
Active Antitakeover Defenses 204
Information Content of Takeover Resistance 236
Summary 238
References 239

6 Takeover Tactics 243

Preliminary Takeover Steps 245
Tender Offers 247
Open Market Purchases and Street Sweeps 264

Advantages of Tender Offers Over Open Market Purchases   266
Proxy Fights   268
Role of the Independent Election Corporation of America   277
Combination of a Proxy Fight and a Tender Offer   283
Proxy Fights and Takeovers in the 1990s   283
Summary   285
References   286

Part Three   Leveraged Transactions   **289**

7 Leveraged Buyouts   **291**
LBO Data   291
Costs of Being a Public Company   293
Management Buyouts   294
Leveraged Buyout Process   296
Financing for Leveraged Buyouts   299
Capital Structure of Unsecured LBO Firms   305
Sources of LBO Financing   306
LBO Funds   307
LBO Firms   307
Financial Analysis of LBO Candidates   310
Returns to Stockholders from LBOs   311
Returns to Stockholders from Divisional Buyouts   312
Efficiency Gains from LBOs   312
Reverse LBOs   314
Conflicts of Interest in Management Buyouts   317
Empirical Research on Wealth Transfer Effects   321
Protection for Bondholders   322
Summary   326
References   326

8 Junk Bonds   **330**
History   330
Investment Bankers   334
The Evolutionary Growth of the Junk Bond Market   337
Rating System for Bonds   342
Z Scores and Zeta Analysis: Credit Evaluation Alternative to Bond Ratings   346
Junk Bond Research   347
Junk Bond Returns: 1980–94   358
Diversification of Junk Bond Investments   360
Risk of a Junk Bond Portfolio   360
Underwriting Spreads   361
Bank Loan Financing versus Junk Bond Financing   365

Junk Bonds and Greenmail   365
Regulations Affecting Junk Bond Financing   366
Summary   369
References   370

9 Employee Stock Ownership Plans   372
Historical Growth of ESOPs   372
Types of Plans   374
Characteristics of ESOPs   375
Leveraged versus Unleveraged ESOPs   375
Corporate Finance Uses of ESOPs   376
Voting of ESOP Shares   376
Cash Flow Implications   377
Valuation of Stock Contributed into an ESOP   377
Eligibility of ESOPs   378
Put Options of ESOPs   378
Dividends Paid   378
ESOPs versus a Public Offering of Stock   379
Employee Risk and ESOPs   380
Securities Laws and ESOPs   380
Tax Benefits of Leveraged ESOPs   381
Balance Sheet Effects of ESOPs   381
Drawbacks of Leveraged ESOPs   382
ESOPs and Corporate Performance   383
ESOPs as an Antitakeover Defense   385
ESOPs and Shareholder Wealth   386
ESOPs and LBOs   387
Summary   390
References   392

Part Four   Corporate Restructuring   395

10 Corporate Restructuring   397
Divestitures   398
Divestiture and Spin-Off Process   404
Wealth Effects of Sell-Offs   410
Equity Carve-Outs   420
Voluntary Liquidations, or Bustups   423
Master Limited Partnerships   425
Restructuring of the 1990s   426
Summary   428
References   429

11 Restructuring in Bankruptcy   **432**

Types of Business Failure   432
Causes of Business Failure   433
Bankruptcy Data   435
Bankruptcy Laws   437
Reorganization versus Liquidation   439
Chapter 11 Reorganization Process   439
Benefits of the Chapter 11 Process for the Debtor   444
Company Size and Chapter 11 Benefits   445
Prepackaged Bankruptcy   446
Workouts   449
Corporate Control and Default   450
Liquidation   450
Investing in the Securities of Distressed Companies   452
Summary   456
References   457

Part Five   Valuation for Mergers and Acquisitions   **459**

12 Financial Analysis   **461**

Hostile versus Friendly Deals: Access to Financial Data   462
Balance Sheet   463
Income Statement   468
Statement of Cash Flows   470
Analysis of Financial Statements and Computer Programs   472
Financial Ratio Analysis   473
Summary   489
References   489

13 Valuation of a Publicly Held Company   **491**

Valuation Methods: Science or Art?   492
Managing Value as an Antitakeover Defense   493
Stock Valuation Methods   493
Marketability of the Stock   498
Defining the Earnings Base   499
Forecasting Methods   507
Financial Valuation Methodologies   512
Cost of Preferred Stock   517
Cost of Common Stock   517
How the Market Determines Discount Rates   518
Control Premium   519

Valuation of Stock-for-Stock Exchanges   529
Exchange Ratio   533
Stock Price Variability and Collar Agreements   540
Benchmarks of Value   540
Desirable Financial Characteristics of Targets   541
Summary   553
References   554

14 Valuation of Privately Held Businesses   557
Differences in Valuation of Public and Private Businesses   557
Differences in Reporting of Income   560
Recasting the Income Statement: An Example of the Addback Process   562
Most Commonly Used Valuation Methods   565
Summary   586
References   587

15 Tax Issues   589
Financial Accounting   589
Taxable versus Tax-Free Transactions   593
Tax Consequences of a Stock-for-Stock Exchange   595
Asset Basis Step-Up   598
Changes in the Tax Laws   598
Role of Taxes in the Merger Decision   600
Taxes as a Source of Value in Management Buyouts   602
Summary   604
References   604

Glossary   607

Index   615

PREFACE

The field of mergers and acquisitions continues to experience dramatic growth. Record-breaking mega-mergers have become commonplace in the 1990s. This is particularly impressive in light of the fact that the decade started off with the number and value of mergers and acquisitions being well below the lofty levels set in the fourth merger wave of the 1980s. That period featured many headline-setting hostile deals and leveraged buyouts. Many of these notable leveraged buyouts ended in bankruptcy when the economy entered the 1990–91 recession. The pressure of the heavy debt service proved too much for some of these deals that appeared questionable from a strategic point of view.

The 1990s features one of the longest economic expansions in U.S. economic history. With the expanded demand from a growing economy, companies are increasingly using mergers and acquisitions as the fastest way to take advantage of the increased market opportunities. Through mergers and acquisitions, companies can quickly expand their capacity and/or market new products.

The deals of the fifth merger wave seem to have more of a strategic focus than the transactions of the 1980s. Break-up transactions designed to provide a quick return for the dealmakers are uncommon. Rather, the deals of the 1990s claim to have more of a strategic focus.

Firms in several industries were consolidated in roll-up transactions which resulted in more of an oligopolistic market structure. Even though the number of competitors declined, the deal participants often did not appear to gain market power. Instead they sought cost reductions through scale economies and expanded market opportunities.

Although many companies are pursuing an expansion strategy that includes mergers and acquisitions, many others are relying on corporate restructuring to become more efficient. For some companies, this may mean selling off prior acquisitions or divisions that no longer pull their weight. For others, it may mean more drastic restructuring, such as through the bankruptcy reorganization process. The world of mergers and acquisitions of today includes a prominent role for corporate restructuring.

Many of the methods that applied to deals of prior years are still relevant, but new rules are also in effect. These principles consider the mistakes of prior periods along with the economic and financial conditions that are in effect in the 1990s. It is hoped that these new rules will make the mergers of the fifth merger wave sounder and more profitable than those of prior periods.

The focus of this book is decidedly pragmatic. I have attempted to write it in a manner that will be useful to both the business student as well as the practitioner. Since the world of mergers and acquisitions is clearly interdisciplinary, material from the fields of law and economics is presented along with corporate finance, which is the primary emphasis of the book. The practical skills of finance practitioners have been integrated with the research of the academic world of finance. For example, three chapters are devoted to the valuation of businesses, including the valuation of privately held firms. This is an important topic that is usually ignored by traditional finance references. Much of the finance literature tends to be divided into two camps: practitioners and academicians. Clearly, both groups have made valuable contributions to the field of mergers and acquisitions. This book attempts to interweave these contributions into one comprehensible format.

The increase in mergers and acquisition activity has given rise to the growth of academic research in this area. This book attempts to synthesize some of the more important and relevant research studies and to present their results in a straightforward and pragmatic manner. Because of the voluminous research in the field, only the findings of the more important studies are highlighted. Issues such as shareholder wealth effects of antitakeover measures have important meanings to investors who are concerned about how the defensive actions of corporations will affect the value of their investments. This is a good example of how the academic research literature has made important pragmatic contributions that have served to shed light on important policy issues.

I have avoided incorporating theoretical research that has less relevance to those seeking a pragmatic treatment of the mergers and acquisitions. However, some theoretical analyses, such as agency theory, can be helpful in explaining some of the incentives for managers to pursue management buyouts. Material from the field of portfolio theory can help explain some of the risk-reduction benefits that junk bond investors can derive through diversification. These more theoretical discussions, along with others, are presented because they have important relevance to the real world of mergers and acquisitions.

The rapidly evolving nature of mergers and acquisitions requires constant updating. Every effort has been made to include recent developments occurring just prior to the publication date. I wish the reader an enjoyable and profitable trip through the world of mergers and acquisitions.

Patrick A. Gaughan

Part One

BACKGROUND

1

INTRODUCTION

After a short hiatus, mergers and acquisitions had resumed the frantic pace that was established during the fourth merger wave of the 1980s and by the mid-1990s we were in the middle of the fifth merger wave, which featured deal volume that surpassed the level reached in the 1980s. The 1980s represented one of the most intense periods of merger activity in U.S. economic history. This period witnessed the fourth merger wave of the twentieth century. One such wave occurred at the end of the 1960s, with the two prior waves occurring in the 1920s and at the turn of the century.

The fourth wave was unique compared with the three prior waves. It specifically featured the hostile takeover and the corporate raider. In addition, in the 1980s the junk bond market grew into a tool of high finance whereby bidders for corporations obtained access to billions of dollars to finance raids on some of the largest, most established corporations in the United States. This access to capital markets allowed megamerger deals to become a reality. The resurgence of merger and acquisition activity in the 1990s quickly shifted into the fifth merger wave. The intensity of this wave is underscored by the fact that several of the ten largest deals in U.S. history took place in 1998 alone (Table 1.1).

The 1980s featured an unprecedented volume of merger and acquisition activity compared with prior historical periods. Not only did the volume of mergers and acquisitions reach an all-time high in the 1980s (Table 1.2 and Figure 1.1), but also the average price of each acquisition increased steadily (Table 1.3 and Figure 1.2). Before the 1980s larger U.S. companies had little need to worry about preserving their independence. With the advent of the hostile raid, however, they erected formidable defenses against takeovers and increasingly called on state governments to pass laws to make hostile acquisitions more difficult.

The 1980s also featured the rapid growth and decline of the leveraged buyout (LBO)—the use of debt capital to finance a buyout of the firm's stock. In an LBO, a public company goes private by purchasing its publicly outstanding shares. This financing technique was popular in the mid-1980s but became a less viable alternative toward the end of the decade as the number of good LBO targets declined. The end of the decade also signaled a dramatic decline in the junk bond market as raiders and LBO firms lost some of their access to the financing necessary to complete leveraged transactions (Figure 1.1).

The falloff in merger and acquisition activity at the beginning of the 1990s reversed in 1992 when the volume of transactions intensified. By 1993 we were once again in the throes of a full-scale merger wave. However, this wave was distinctly different from the wave that preceded it. The deals of the 1990s are not the highly leveraged hostile transactions that were common in the 1980s. Rather, the 1990s feature more strategic mergers that

Table 1.1.   Ten Largest Mergers and Acquisitions

Year	Acquirer	Target	Amount ($ Billions)
1998	Exxon Corp.	Mobil Corp.	77.2
1998	SBC Communications Inc.	Ameritech	61.4
1998	British Petroleum Co. PLC	Amoco Corp.	56.5
1999	AT&T Corp.*	MediaOne Group Inc.	55.8
1998	Bell Atlantic Corp.	GTE Corp.	52.9
1998	NationsBank Corp.	BankAmerica Corp.	43.2
1999	U.S. West*	Global Crossing	37.0
1998	AT&T Corp.	Tele-Communications Inc.	37.0
1998	Travelers Group Inc.	Citicorp.	36.0
1997	WorldCom Inc.	MCI Communications Corp.	35.3

* Preliminary by the price.

Source: Mergerstat Review, 1999.

are not motivated by short-term profits or dependent on highly leveraged capital structures. The mergers and acquisitions of the 1990s use more equity and less debt. In doing so, the 1990s dealmakers are hoping to avoid the bankruptcies that followed the collapse of some of the highly leveraged transactions of the fourth merger wave.

This book describes the growth and development of the field of mergers and acquisitions through a historical focus followed by a review of the laws or rules that govern the game of mergers and acquisitions. In addition, the strategy and motives that inspire mergers and acquisitions are examined. The offensive and defensive techniques of hostile acquisitions are also discussed. The vast array of defenses that may be implemented to thwart a hostile bid are then reviewed. Offensive and defensive methods from the viewpoints of both management and shareholder are explored. In addition, the impact on the shareholder wealth is examined through a review of the wealth effects of these different offensive and defensive tactics.

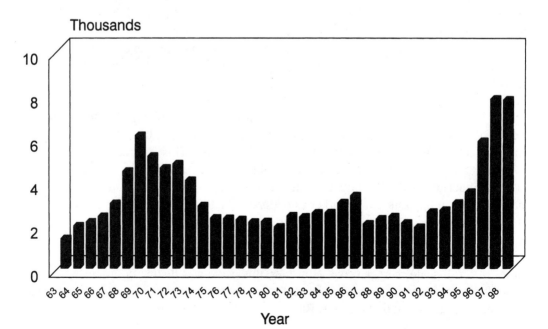

Figure 1.1.   Net mergers and acquisitions announcements.

Table 1.2.   Net Merger and Acquisition Announcements, 1963-1998

Year	Number	Percentage Change (%)	Year	Number	Percentage Change (%)
1963	1,361		1981	2,395	27
1964	1,950	43	1982	2,346	−2
1965	2,125	9	1983	2,533	8
1966	2,377	12	1984	2,543	1
1967	2,975	25	1985	3,001	18
1968	4,462	50	1986	3,336	11
1969	6,107	37	1987	2,032	−39
1970	5,152	−16	1988	2,258	11
1971	4,608	−11	1989	2,366	5
1972	4,801	4	1990	2,074	−12
1973	4,040	−16	1991	1,877	−9
1974	2,861	−29	1992	2,574	37
1975	2,297	−20	1993	2,663	3
1976	2,276	−1	1994	2,997	13
1977	2,224	−2	1995	3,510	17
1978	2,106	−5	1996	5,848	67
1979	2,128	1	1997	7,800	33
1980	1,889	−11	1998	7,809	−1

Source: Mergerstat Review, 1990 and 1999.

Table 1.3.   Average and Median Purchase Price, 1968–98 ($ millions)

Year	Total Dollar Value Paid	Base*	Total**	Number of Transactions Valued At $100 MM or More	Number of Transactions Valued At $1000 MM or More	Average Price	Median Price
1970	43.6	1,671	5,152	10	1	9.8	NA
1971	23.7	1,707	4,608	7		7.4	NA
1972	16.4	1,930	4,801	15		8.6	2.8
1973	16.7	1,574	4,040	28		10.6	3.4
1974	12.5	995	2,861	15		12.5	3.6
1975	11.8	848	2,297	14	1	13.9	4.3
1976	20.0	998	2,276	39	1	20.1	5.1
1977	21.9	1,032	2,224	41		21.3	6.6
1978	34.2	1,071	2,106	80	1	31.9	8.1
1979	43.5	1,047	2,128	83	3	41.6	8.5
1980	44.3	890	1,889	94	4	49.8	9.3
1981	82.6	1,126	2,395	113	12	73.4	9.0
1982	53.8	930	2,346	116	6	57.8	10.5
1983	73.1	1,077	2,533	138	11	67.9	16.5
1984	122.2	1,084	2,543	200	18	112.8	20.1
1985	179.8	1,320	3,001	270	36	136.2	21.1
1986	173.1	1,468	3,336	346	27	117.9	24.9
1987	163.7	972	2,032	301	36	168.4	51.3
1988	246.9	1,149	2,258	369	45	215.1	56.9
1989	221.1	1,092	2,366	328	35	202.5	36.6
1990	108.2	856	2,074	181	21	126.4	21.0
1991	71.2	722	1,877	150	13	98.6	22.7
1992	96.7	950	2,574	200	18	101.8	22.5
1993	176.4	1,081	2,663	242	27	163.2	26.0
1994	226.7	1,348	2,997	383	51	168.2	33.0
1995	356.0	1,735	3,510	462	74	205.2	30.5
1996	495.0	2,658	5,848	640	94	186.7	25.3
1997	657.1	3,013	7,827	873	120	209.2	29.2
1998	1,191.7	3,091	7,759	906	158	385.6	33.5

*Base: The number of transactions that disclosed a purchase price.
**Total: Net merger-acquisition announcements.

Source: Mergerstat Review, 1990 and 1999.

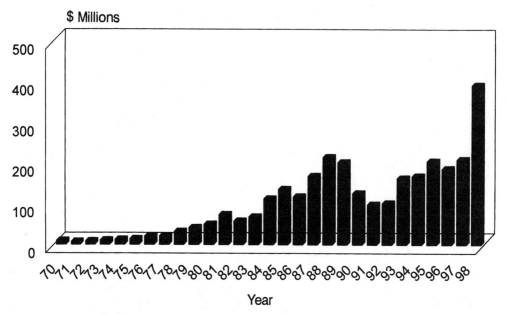

Figure 1.2. Average purchase price, 1970–98.

Also analyzed in detail are the techniques of leveraged buyouts: the junk market, which is one of the main sources of LBO financing; and employee stock ownership plans, an important financing technique for certain types of LBOs.

Leveraged transactions may rely on the utilization of tax benefits. Therefore, the various tax issues involved in both leveraged and nonleveraged transactions are reviewed. Corporate restructuring that involves a contraction, as opposed to acquisition-related expansion, is discussed in detail. Various forms of corporate restructuring, including divestitures, spinoffs, and equity carve-outs have become more commonplace in the 1990s as some firms pursued a downsizing strategy while others expanded through mergers and acquisitions. Other firms that were in a more distressed financial condition were forced to use the corporate reorganization process available under the bankruptcy laws. Having covered a thorough background of the field, the rest of the book is dedicated to valuation.

The process of valuation for mergers and acquisitions is covered in three parts:

1. A review of financial analysis to ensure that the reader has a common body of financial knowledge with which to approach the valuation process
2. An application of this financial analysis to valuing publicly held firms
3. An analysis of the methods of valuing privately held businesses

Throughout this book, the material is presented from both a pragmatic and an academic viewpoint. The pragmatic focus utilizes a "how to" approach and a detailed description of the real world of mergers and acquisitions rather than a theoretical treatment. This approach is complemented by a more traditional academic analysis of the relevant research literature in each of the areas described. This dual pragmatic and academic approach will give the reader the benefits of practitioners' experience as well as researchers' work on the frontier of the field. Research that lacks pragmatic value is not reviewed.

DEFINITIONS

A *merger* is a combination of two corporations in which only one corporation survives and the merged corporation goes out of existence. In a merger, the acquiring company assumes the assets and liabilities of the merged company. Sometimes the term *statutory merger* is used to refer to this type of business transaction. A statutory merger differs from a *subsidiary merger,* which is a merger of two companies in which the target company becomes a subsidiary or part of a subsidiary of the parent company. The acquisition by General Motors of Electronic Data Systems, led by its colorful Chief Executive Officer Ross Perot, is an example of a subsidiary merger. In a *reverse subsidiary merger,* a subsidiary of the acquirer is merged into the target.

A merger differs from a *consolidation,* which is a business combination whereby two or more companies join to form an entirely new company. All of the combining companies are dissolved and only the new entity continues to operate. For example, in 1986 the computer manufacturers Burroughs and Sperry combined to form UNISYS. In a consolidation, the original companies cease to exist and their stockholders become stockholders in the new company. One way to look at the differences between a merger and a consolidation is that with a merger A + B = A, where company B is merged into company A. In a consolidation, A + B = C, where C is an entirely new company. Despite the differences between them, the terms *merger* and *consolidation,* as is true of many of the terms in the mergers and acquisitions field, are sometimes used interchangeably. In general, when the combining firms are approximately the same size, the term *consolidation* applies; when the two firms differ significantly by size, merger is the more appropriate term. In practice, however, this distinction is often blurred, with the term *merger* being broadly applied to combinations that involve firms of both different and similar sizes.

Another term that is broadly used to refer to various types of transactions is *takeover.* This term is more vague and sometimes refers only to hostile transactions; at other times it refers to both friendly and unfriendly mergers.

TYPES OF MERGERS

Mergers are often categorized as horizontal, vertical, or conglomerate mergers. A *horizontal merger* occurs when two competitors combine. For example, in 1994 two defense firms, Northrop and Grumman, combined in a $2.17 billion merger. If a horizontal merger causes the combined firm to experience an increase in market power that will have anticompetitive effects, the merger may be opposed on antitrust grounds. In recent years, however, the government has been somewhat liberal in allowing many horizontal mergers to go unopposed.

Vertical mergers are combinations of companies that have a buyer-seller relationship. For example, in 1993 Merck, the world's largest drug company, acquired Medco Containment Services, Inc., the largest marketer of discount prescription medicines, for $6 billion. The transaction enabled Merck to go from being the largest pharmaceutical company to also being the largest integrated producer and distributor of pharmaceuticals. This transaction was not opposed by antitrust regulators even though the combination clearly resulted in a more powerful firm. Ironically, regulators cited increased competition and lower prices as the anticipated result.

A *conglomerate merger* occurs when the companies are not competitors and do not have a buyer-seller relationship. One example would be Philip Morris, a tobacco company, which acquired General Foods in 1985 for $5.6 billion. Clearly, these companies were in very different lines of business. The advisability of conglomerate acquisitions is discussed in Chapter 4.

REASONS FOR MERGERS AND ACQUISITIONS

As is discussed in Chapter 4, there are several possible motives or reasons that firms might engage in mergers and acquisitions. One of the most common motives is expansion. Acquiring a company in a line of business or geographic area into which the company may want to expand can be a quicker way to expand than internal expansion. An acquisition of a particular company may provide certain synergistic benefits for the acquirer, such as when two lines of business complement one another. However, an acquisition may be part of a diversification program that allows the company to move into other lines of business.

In the pursuit of expansion, firms engaging in mergers and acquisitions cite the pursuit of synergistic gains as one of the reasons for the transaction. Synergy exists when the sum of the parts is more productive and valuable than the individual components. There are many potential sources of synergy and they are discussed in Chapter 4.

Financial factors motivate some mergers and acquisitions. For example, an acquirer's financial analysis may reveal that the target is undervalued. That is, the value of the buyer may be significantly in excess of the market value of the target, even when a premium that is normally associated with changes in control is added to the acquisition price.

Other motives, such as tax motives, also may play a role in an acquisition decision. These motives and others are critically examined in greater detail in Chapter 15.

MERGER FINANCING

Mergers may be paid for in several ways. Transactions may use all cash, all securities, or a combination of cash and securities. Securities transactions may use the stock of the acquirer as well as other securities such as debentures. The stock may be either common stock or preferred stock. They may be registered, meaning they are able to be freely traded on organized exchanges, or they may be restricted, meaning they cannot be offered for public sale, although private transactions among a limited number of buyers, such as institutional investors, is permissible.

Stock transactions may offer the seller certain tax benefits that cash transactions do not provide. However, securities transactions require the parties to agree on the value of the securities. This may create some uncertainty and may give cash an advantage over securities transactions from the seller's point of view. For large deals, all cash compensation may mean that the bidder has to incur debt, which may carry with it unwanted adverse risk consequences. Although such deals were relatively more common in the 1980s, securities transactions became more popular in the 1990s. The various advantages and valuation effects of cash versus securities transactions are discussed in Chapters 13 and 15.

MERGER PROFESSIONALS

When a company decides it wants to acquire or merge with another firm, it typically does so by using the services of outside professionals. These professionals usually include investment bankers, attorneys, accountants, and valuation experts. Investment bankers may provide a variety of services, including helping to select the appropriate target, valuing the target, advising on strategy, and raising the requisite financing to complete the transaction. During the heyday of the fourth merger wave in the 1980s, merger advisory and financing fees were a significant component of the overall profitability of the major investment banks. Table 1.4 shows a ranking of merger and acquisition financial advisors.

Investment banks are often faced with the concern about conflicts between various departments of these large financial institutions, which may play very different roles in the merger process. Investment banks often have arbitrage departments that may accumulate stock in companies that may be taken over. If they purchase shares before the market is convinced that a company will be acquired, they may buy at a price significantly below the eventual takeover price, which usually includes a premium above the price at which that stock had been trading. This process, which is fraught with risks, is known as *risk arbitrage*. If an investment bank is advising a client regarding the possible acquisition of a company, it is imperative that a *Chinese wall* between the arbitrage department and the advisers working directly with the client be constructed so that the arbitragers do not benefit from the information that the advisers have but that is not yet readily available to the market. To derive financial benefits from this type of *inside information* is a violation of the law. This is discussed further in Chapter 3.

The role of investment banks changed somewhat in the 1990s. The dealmakers who promoted transactions just to generate fees became unpopular. Companies that were engaged in mergers and acquisitions tended to be more involved in the deals and took over some of the responsibilities that had been relegated to investment bankers in the 1980s. More companies directed the activities of their investment bankers as opposed to merely following their instructions as they did in the prior decade.

Table 1.4. Financial Advisor Rankings: 1/1/98–12/31/98

Rank	Financial Advisor	Total Invested Capital of Deals Worked ($ billions)	Total Number of Deals	Deals Reporting a Price
1	Goldman Sachs & Co.	846.4	179	161
2	Merrill Lynch & Co.	544.4	168	141
3	Morgan Stanley Dean Witter	444.4	145	136
4	Salomon Smith Barney	333.3	92	82
5	Credit Suisse First Boston	240.3	100	89
6	JP Morgan & Co.	201.5	81	63
7	Donaldson Lufkin & Jenrette	182.7	134	120
8	Lehman Brothers	166.3	84	74
9	Bear Stearns & Co.	108.8	54	45
10	Lazard Freres & Co.	97.8	67	58

Source: Mergerstat Review, 1998.

Table 1.5.   Legal Advisor Rankings: 1/1/98–12/31/98

Rank	Financial Advisor	Total Invested Capital of Deals Worked ($ billions)	Total Number of Deals	Deals Reporting a Price
1	Simpson Thacher & Bartlett	587.2	101	87
2	Skadden Arps Slate Meagher & Flom LLP	559.5	144	134
3	Wachtell Lipton Rosen & Katz	508.8	74	64
4	Sullivan & Crowell	338.4	95	83
5	Shearman & Sterling	278.1	72	65
6	Cleary Gottlieb Steen & Hamilton	253.1	36	32
7	Fried Frank Harris Shriver Jacobson	228.5	49	45
8	Debevoise & Plimpton	167.1	39	28
9	Davis Polk & Wardwell	155.1	44	42
10	Andrews & Kurth LLP	144.3	53	52

Source: Mergerstat Review, 1998.

Given the complex legal environment that surrounds mergers and acquisitions, attorneys also play a key role in a successful acquisition process. Law firms may be even more important in hostile takeovers than in friendly acquisitions because part of the resistance of the target may come through legal maneuvering. Detailed filings with the Securities and Exchange Commission (SEC) may need to be completed under the guidance of legal experts. In both private and public mergers and acquisitions, there is a legal due diligence process that attorneys should be retained to perform. Table 1.5 shows the leading legal merger and acquisition advisors in 1998.

Accountants play an important role in mergers and acquisitions. They have their own accounting due diligence process. In addition, accountants perform various other functions such as preparing pro forma financial statements based on scenarios put forward by management or other professionals.

Still another group of professionals who provide important services in mergers and acquisitions are valuation experts. These individuals may be retained by either a bidder or a target to determine the value of a company. We will see in Chapters 13 and 14 that these values may vary depending on the assumptions employed. Therefore, valuation experts may build a model that incorporates various assumptions, such as revenue growth rate or costs, which may be eliminated after the deal. As these and other assumptions vary, the resulting value derived from the value also may change.

LEVERAGED BUYOUTS

In an LBO a buyer uses debt to finance the acquisition of a company. The term is usually reserved, however, for acquisition of public companies where the acquired company becomes private. This is referred to as *going private* because all of the public equity is purchased, usually by a small group or a single buyer, and the company is no longer traded in securities markets. One version of a leveraged buyout is a *management buyout*. In a management buyout, the buyer of a company, or a division of a company, is the manager of the entity.

Most LBOs are buyouts of small and medium-sized companies or divisions of large companies. However, in what was then the largest transaction of all time, the 1989 $25.1

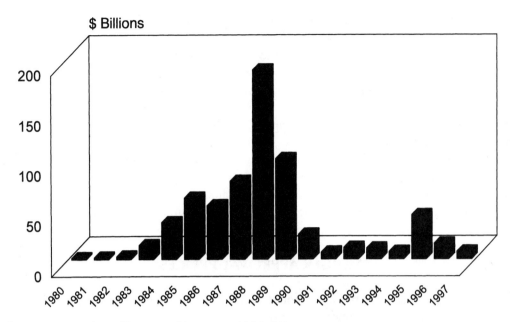

Figure 1.3.   Value of leveraged buyouts, 1980–97.

Source: Securities Data Company.

billion leveraged buyout of RJR Nabisco by Kohlberg Kravis & Roberts shook the financial world.

Leveraged buyouts, which were more common in the 1980s, have declined dramatically
in the 1990s (Figure 1.3). There are several reasons for this, including the collapse of the
junk bond market. These issues are discussed at length in Chapters 7 and 8.

CORPORATE RESTRUCTURING

Users of the term *corporate restructuring* usually are referring to asset selloffs such as *divestitures.* Companies that have acquired other firms or have developed other divisions
through activities such as product extensions may decide that these divisions no longer fit
into the company's plans. The desire to sell parts of a company may come from poor performance of a division, financial exigency, or a change in the strategic orientation of the
company. For example, the company may decide to refocus on its *core* business and sell
off noncore subsidiaries. This type of activity increased after the end of the third merger
wave as many companies that engaged in diverse acquisition campaigns to build conglomerates began to question the advisability of these combinations.

There are several forms of corporate selloffs, with divestitures being only one of them.
Spinoffs enjoyed increased popularity in the early 1990s, while equity carve-outs provided
another way that selloffs could be accomplished. The relative benefits of each of these alternative means of selling off part of a company are discussed in Chapter 10.

Other forms of corporate restructuring are cost and work force restructuring. In the
1990s we saw many companies engage in *corporate downsizing* as they strove to become
more efficient. This was encouraged by several factors, including the 1990-91 recession

and the international competitive pressure of the globalization of world markets. During the 1990s it was not unusual to see companies that were reporting increased profits announce large-scale layoffs as they reacted to actions of competitors who were also taking steps to become more efficient. The strong economy, however, provided assurance that the corporate downsizing did not cause net unemployment as a result of the growth in job opportunities in the labor market.

Another form of corporate restructuring is *financial restructuring,* which refers to alterations in the capital structure of the firm, such as adding debt and thereby increasing financial leverage. Although this type of restructuring is important in corporate finance and is often done as part of the financing activities for mergers and acquisitions, it is not treated in this text as a form of corporate restructuring. Rather, the term *restructuring* is reserved for the more physical forms of restructuring such as divestitures.

MERGER APPROVAL PROCESS

Most mergers and acquisitions are negotiated in a friendly environment. The process usually begins when the management of one firm contacts the target company's management, often through the investment bankers of each firm. The management of both firms keep the respective boards of directors up-to-date on the progress of the negotiations because mergers usually require the boards' approval. Sometimes this process works smoothly and leads to a quick merger agreement. A good example of this was the 1995 $19 billion acquisition of Capital Cities/ABC Inc. by Walt Disney Co. In spite of the size of this deal, there was a quick meeting of the minds by management of these two firms and a friendly deal was completed relatively quickly. In other instances, friendly negotiations may break down, leading to the termination of the bid or a hostile takeover. An example of a negotiated deal that failed and led to a hostile bid was the 1995 tender offer by Moore Corporation for Wallace Computer Services, Inc. Here negotiations between two archrivals in the business forms and printing business proceeded for five months before they were called off, leading to a $1.3 billion hostile bid.

MERGER NEGOTIATIONS

Except for hostile transactions, mergers usually are the product of a negotiation process between the managements of the merging companies. The bidding firm typically initiates the negotiations when it contacts the target's management to inquire whether the company is for sale and to express its interest in buying the target. This interest may be the product of an extensive search process to find the right acquisition candidates. However, it could be a recent interest that was inspired by the bidder's investment bank approaching it with a proposal that it believes would be a good fit for the bidder. For small-scale acquisitions, this intermediary might be a business broker.

Both the bidder and the target should conduct their own valuation analyses to determine what the target is worth. As is discussed in the valuation chapters, the value of the target for the buyer may be different from the value of that company to the seller. Valuations can differ due to varying uses of the target assets or different opinions on the future growth of the target. If the target believes that it is worth substantially more than what the buyer is willing to pay, a friendly deal may not be possible. If, however, the seller is interested in selling and both parties are able to reach an agreement on price, a deal may be possible. Other important issues, such as financial and regulatory approvals, if necessary, would have to be completed before the negotiation process could lead to a completed transaction.

Disclosure of Merger Negotiations

Before 1988 it was not clear what obligations companies involved in merger negotiations had to disclose their activities. However, in 1988, in the landmark *Basic Inc. v. Levinson* decision, the U.S. Supreme Court made it clear that a denial that negotiations were taking place when the opposite was the case is improper. Companies may not deceive the market by disseminating inaccurate or deceptive information, even when the discussions are preliminary and do not show much promise of coming to fruition.

The Court's position reversed earlier positions that had treated proposals or negotiations as being immaterial. The *Basic v. Levinson* decision does not go so far as to require companies to disclose all plans or internal proposals involving acquisitions. Negotiations between two potential merger partners, however, may not be denied.

The exact timing of the disclosure is still not clear. Given the requirement to disclose, a company's hand may be forced by the pressure of market speculation. It is often difficult to confidentially continue such negotiations and planning for any length of time. Rather than let the information slowly leak, the company has an obligation to conduct an orderly disclosure once it is clear that confidentiality may be at risk or that prior statements the company has made are no longer accurate.

In cases in which there is speculation that a takeover is being planned, significant market movements in stock prices of the companies involved—particularly the target—may occur. Such market movements may give rise to an inquiry from the exchange on which the company trades or from the National Association of Securities Dealers (NASD). Although exchanges have come under criticism for being somewhat lax about enforcing these types of rules, an insufficient response from the companies involved may give rise to disciplinary actions against the companies.

MERGER APPROVAL PROCEDURES

Each state has a statute that authorizes mergers and acquisitions of corporations. The rules may be different for domestic and foreign corporations. Once the board of directors of each company reaches an agreement, they adopt a resolution approving the deal. This resolution should include the names of the companies involved in the deal and the name of the new company. The resolution should include the financial terms of the deal and other relevant information such as the method that is to be used to convert securities of each company into securities of the surviving corporation. If there are any changes in the articles of incorporation, these should be referenced in the resolution.

At this point the deal is taken to the shareholders for approval. Once approved by the shareholders, the merger plan must be submitted to the relevant state official, usually the secretary of state. The document that contains this plan is called the *articles for merger or consolidation.* Once the state official determines that the proper documentation has been received, it issues a certificate of merger or consolidation.

Special Committees of the Board of Directors

The board of directors may choose to form a special committee of the board to evaluate the merger proposal. Directors who might personally benefit from the merger, such as when the buyout proposal contains provisions that management directors may potentially profit from the deal, should not be members of this committee. The more complex the transaction, the more likely that a committee will be appointed. This committee should seek legal counsel to guide it on legal issues such as the fairness of the transaction, the business judgment rule, and numerous other legal issues. This committee, and the board in general, needs to make sure that it carefully considers all relevant aspects of the transaction. A court may later scrutinize the decision-making process, such as what occurred in the *Smith v. Van Gorkom* case, which is discussed in Chapter 13. In that case the court found the directors personally liable because it thought that the decision-making process was inadequate, even though the decision itself was apparently a good one for shareholders.

Fairness Opinions

It is common for the board to retain an outside valuation firm, such as an investment bank or a firm that specializes in valuations, to evaluate the transaction's terms and price. This firm may then render a fairness opinion in which it may state that the offer is in a range that it determines to be accurate. These opinions may be somewhat terse and usually are devoid of a detailed financial analysis. Presumably, however, underlying the opinion itself is such a detailed financial analysis. As part of the opinion that is rendered, the evaluator should state what was investigated and verified and what was not. The fees received and any potential conflicts of interest should also be revealed.

Upon reaching agreeable terms and receiving board approval, the deal is taken before the shareholders for their approval, which is granted through a vote. The exact percentage necessary for stockholder approval depends on the articles of incorporation, which, in turn, are regulated by the prevailing state corporation laws. Following approval, each firm files the necessary documents with the state authorities in which each firm is incorporated. Once this step is completed and the compensation has changed hands, the deal is completed.

SHORT-FORM MERGER

A short-form merger may take place in situations in which the stockholder approval process is not necessary. Stockholder approval may be bypassed when the corporation's stock is concentrated in the hands of a small group, such as management, which is advocating the merger. Some state laws may allow this group to approve the transaction on its own without soliciting the approval of the other stockholders. The board of directors simply approves the merger by a resolution.

A short-form merger may occur only when the stockholdings of insiders are beyond a certain threshold stipulated in the prevailing state corporation laws. This percentage varies depending on the state in which the company is incorporated.

FREEZEOUTS AND THE TREATMENT OF MINORITY SHAREHOLDERS

A majority of shareholders must provide their approval before a merger can be completed. A 51% margin is a common majority threshold. When this majority approves the deal, minority shareholders are required to tender their shares, even though they did not vote in favor of the deal. Minority shareholders are said to be *frozen out* of their positions. This majority approval requirement is designed to prevent a *holdout problem,* which may occur when a minority attempts to hold up the completion of a transaction unless they receive compensation over and above the acquisition stock price.

This is not to say that dissenting shareholders are without rights. Those shareholders who believe that their shares are worth significantly more than what the terms of the merger are offering may go to court to pursue their *shareholder appraisal rights.* To successfully pursue these rights, dissenting shareholders must follow the proper procedures. Paramount among these procedures is the requirement that the dissenting shareholder object to the deal within the designated period of time. Then they may demand a cash settlement for the difference between the "fair value" of their shares and the compensation they actually received. Of course, corporations resist these maneuvers because the payment of cash for the value of shares will raise problems relating to the positions of other stockholders. Such suits are very difficult for dissenting shareholders to win. Dissenting shareholders may only file a suit if the corporation does not file suit to have the fair value of the shares determined, after having been notified of the dissenting shareholders' objections. If there is a suit, the court may appoint an appraiser to assist in the determination of the fair value.

PURCHASE OF ASSETS COMPARED WITH PURCHASE OF STOCK

The most common form of merger or acquisition involves purchasing the stock of the merged or acquired concern. An alternative to the stock acquisition is to purchase the target company's assets. In doing so, the acquiring company can limit its acquisitions to those parts of the firm that coincide with the acquirer's needs. When a significant part of the target remains after the asset acquisition, the transaction is only a partial acquisition of the target. When all the target's assets are purchased, the target becomes a corporate shell with only the cash or securities that it received from the acquisition as assets. In these situations, the corporation may choose to pay stockholders a liquidating dividend and dissolve the company. Alternatively, the firm may use its liquid assets to purchase other assets or another company.

ASSUMPTION OF THE SELLER'S LIABILITIES

If the acquirer buys all the target's stock, it assumes the seller's liabilities. The change in stock ownership does not free the new owners of the stock from the seller's liabilities. Most state laws provide this protection, which is sometimes referred to as *successor liability.* One way the acquirer can try to avoid assuming the seller's liabilities is to buy only the assets rather than the stock of the target. In cases in which a buyer purchases a substantial portion of the target's assets, the courts have ruled that the buyer is responsible for the seller's liabilities. This is known as the *trust funds doctrine*. The court may also rule that the transaction is a *de facto* merger—a merger that occurs when the buyer purchases the assets of the target, and, for all intents and purposes, the transaction is treated as a merger.

The issue of successor liability may also apply to other commitments of the firm, such as union contracts. The National Labor Relations Board's position on this issue is that collective bargaining agreements are still in effect after acquisitions.

ADVANTAGES OF ASSET ACQUISITIONS

One of the advantages of an asset acquisition, as opposed to a stock acquisition, is that the bidder may not have to gain the approval of its shareholders. Such approval usually is only necessary when the assets of the target are purchased using shares of the bidder and when the bidder does not already have sufficient shares authorized to complete the transaction. If there are not sufficient shares authorized, the bidder may have to take the necessary steps, which may include amending the articles of incorporation, to gain approval. This is very different from the position of the target company where their shareholders may have to approve the sale of a substantial amount of the company's assets. The necessary shareholder approval percentage is usually the same as for stock acquisitions.

ASSET SELLOFFS

When a corporation chooses to sell off all its assets to another company, it becomes a corporate shell with cash and/or securities as its sole assets. The firm may then decide to distribute the cash to its stockholders as a liquidating dividend and go out of existence. The proceeds of the assets sale may also be distributed through a *cash repurchase tender offer*. That is, the firm makes a tender offer for its own shares using the proceeds of the asset sale to pay for shares. The firm may also choose to continue to do business and use its liquid assets to purchase other assets or companies.

Firms that choose to remain in existence without assets are subject to the Investment Company Act of 1940. This law, one of a series of securities laws passed in the wake of the Great Depression and the associated stock market crash of 1929, applies when 100 or more stockholders remain after the sale of the assets. It requires that investment companies register with the SEC and adhere to its regulations applying to investment companies. The law also establishes standards that regulate investment companies. Specifically, it covers:

- Promotion of the investment company's activities
- Reporting requirements
- Pricing of securities for sale to the public
- Issuance of prospectuses for sales of securities
- Allocation of assets within the investment company's portfolio

If a company that sells off all its assets chooses to invest the proceeds of the asset sale in Treasury bills, these investments are not regulated by the act.

There are two kinds of investment companies: *open-end investment companies* and *closed-end investment companies*. Open-end investment companies, commonly referred to as mutual funds, issue shares that are equal to the value of the fund divided by the number of shares that are bought, after taking into account the costs of running the fund. The number of shares in a mutual fund increases or decreases depending on the number of new shares sold or the redemption of shares already issued.

Closed-end investment companies generally do not issue new shares after the initial issuance. The value of these shares is determined by the value of the investments that are made using the proceeds of the initial share offering.

HOLDING COMPANIES

Rather than a merger or an acquisition, the acquiring company may choose to purchase only a portion of the target's stock and act as a *holding company*, which is a company that owns sufficient stock to have a controlling interest in the target. Holding companies trace their origins back to 1889, when New Jersey became the first state to pass a law that allowed corporations to be formed for the express purpose of owning stock in other corporations.

If an acquirer buys 100% of the target, the company is known as a *wholly owned subsidiary*. However, it is not necessary to own all of a company's stock to exert control over it. In fact, even a 51% interest may not be necessary to allow a buyer to control a target. For companies with a widely distributed equity base, effective working control can be established with as little as 10% to 20% of the outstanding common stock.

Advantages

Holding companies have certain advantages that may make this form of control transaction preferable to an outright acquisition. Some of these advantages are:

- *Lower cost.* With a holding company structure, an acquirer can attain control of a target for a much smaller investment than would be necessary in a 100% stock acquisition. Obviously, a smaller number of shares to be purchased permits a lower total purchase price to be set. In addition, because fewer shares are demanded in the market, there is less upward price pressure on the firm's stock and the cost per share may be lower. The acquirer may attempt to minimize the upward price pressure by gradually buying shares over an extended period of time.

- *No control premium.* Because 51% of the shares were not purchased, the control premium that is normally associated with 51% to 100% stock acquisitions would not have to be paid.

- *Control with fractional ownership.* As noted, working control may be established with less than 51% of the target company's shares. This may allow the controlling company to exert certain influence over the target in a manner that will further the controlling company's objectives.

- *Approval not required.* To the extent that it is allowable under federal and state laws, a holding company may simply purchase shares in a target without having to solicit the approval of the target company's shareholders. As is discussed in Chapter 3, this has become more difficult to accomplish because various laws make it difficult for the holding company to achieve such control if serious shareholder opposition exists.

Disadvantages

Holding companies also have certain disadvantages that make this type of transaction attractive only under certain circumstances. Some of these disadvantages are:

- *Multiple taxation.* The holding company structure adds another layer to the corporate structure. Normally, stockholder income is subject to double taxation. Income is taxed at the corporate level, and some of the remaining income may then be distributed to stockholders in the form of dividends. Stockholders are then taxed individually on this dividend income.

  Holding companies receive dividend income from a company that has already been taxed at the corporate level. This income may then be taxed at the holding company level before it is distributed to stockholders. This amounts to *triple taxation* of corporate income. However, if the holding company owns 80% or more of a subsidiary's voting equity, the Internal Revenue Service allows filing of consolidated returns in which the dividends received from the parent company are not taxed. When the ownership interest is less than 80%, returns cannot be consolidated, but between 70 and 80% of the dividends are not subject to taxation.

- *Antitrust problems.* A holding company combination may face some of the same antitrust concerns with which an outright acquisition is faced. If the regulatory authorities do find the holding company structure anticompetitive, however, it is comparatively easy to require the holding company to divest itself of its holdings in the target. Given the ease with which this can be accomplished, the regulatory authorities may be more quick to require this compared with a more integrated corporate structure.

- *Lack of 100% ownership.* Although the fact that a holding company can be formed without a 100% share purchase may be a source of cost savings, it leaves the holding company with other outside shareholders who will have some controlling influence in the company. This may lead to disagreements over the direction of the company.

JOINT VENTURES

Another type of business combination is a *joint venture*. In a joint venture, companies can enter into an agreement to provide certain resources toward the achievement of a particular business goal. For example, one company could provide financing while another firm contributes physical assets or technological expertise. The venture would realize certain returns, and they would be shared among the venture partners according to a prearranged formula.

In recent years a number of international joint ventures have taken place in the automobile industry. United States companies have entered into agreements with Japanese manufacturers to take advantage of certain comparative advantages these firms might enjoy, such as technological advantages and quality controls. Some of the ventures provided for the establishment of manufacturing facilities in the United States to produce automobiles to be sold in the U.S. market under American manufacturers' brand names. The goal was to enable American manufacturers to produce cars that offered some of the beneficial features of Japanese cars, such as quality, durability, and fuel economy, without having to invest the significant resources to develop this technology and manufacturing know-how. The Japanese manufacturers would also be able to take advantage of the American manufacturers' brand names, distribution network, and other marketing advantages that American manufacturers enjoyed, such as good financing subsidiaries. In addition, the agreements using U.S. manufacturing facilities and U.S. workers would allow Japanese manufacturers to avoid trade restrictions that might affect them if they were to sell directly to the U.S. market. One example of such an arrangement was the joint venture between Chrysler Motors and Mitsubishi Motors, in which the companies agreed to jointly manufacture automobiles in Bloomington, Illinois.

Another example that illustrates the combination of the characteristics of a joint venture and a holding company is the 1995 relationship formed between Packard Bell and NEC, in which NEC purchased a 20% stake in the closely held Packard Bell for $170 million. In addition to providing Packard Bell with needed cash, the companies agreed to supply components to each other and to make joint purchases of computer parts and engage in joint product development. The companies also agreed to the mutual use of each firm's marketing channels.

STRATEGIC ALLIANCES

An alternative to a joint venture is a *strategic alliance*. A strategic alliance is a more flexible concept than a joint venture and refers to a myriad of arrangements between firms whereby they work together for varying periods of time to accomplish a specific goal. Through such alliances links can be readily established and easily disbanded. An organizational entity usually is not created with a strategic alliance, whereas it often is in a joint venture. This may be an advantage because the potential agency costs associated with the managers of the joint venture are not incurred. The added flexibility of strategic alliances may be of special benefit to growing firms because it allows them to quickly establish links when they are needed. These links can often accomplish goals that may require a significant investment and financial resources. This is another reason growing firms, such as high technology companies, may find this alternative of particular benefit. One example of a high-tech development alliance was NCR's 1990 agreement with Seagate Technology to jointly develop high-performance storage systems.[1] An example of a high-tech marketing agreement was the alliance between 3Com Corporation and Sync Research, in which 3Com Corporation would provide marketing assistance to Sync Research's products.

The downside of alliances is the greater potential for opportunistic behavior by the partners. Companies that share business strategy and business secrets may put these valuable

---

1. SuHan Chan, John S. Kensinger, Arthur Keown, and John Martin, "Do Strategic Alliances Create Value," *Journal of Financial Economics,* 46, no. 2, November 1997, pp.199–222.

intangible assets at greater risks than what might occur in a more integrated organizational structure.

Given the usual loose nature of alliances, there is a tendency to have posturing by the partners so that they create a need for each other. This may involve sharing only essential information when necessary. The partners will continue to cooperate only as long as there is a benefit from the association. If the partners can show each other that there are benefits from a continued association into the future, there is an incentive for greater cooperation.

REFERENCES

Chan, SuHan, John S. Kensinger, Arthur Keown, and John Martin. "Do Strategic Alliances Create Value." *Journal of Financial Economics* 46, no. 2, November 1997.

2

HISTORY OF MERGERS

Five periods of high merger activity, often called merger waves, have taken place in the history of the United States. These periods were characterized by cyclic activity, that is, high levels of mergers followed by periods of relatively fewer mergers. The first four waves occurred between 1897 and 1904, 1916 and 1929, 1965 and 1969, and 1984 and 1989. Merger activity declined at the end of the 1980s but resumed again in the early 1990s to begin the current fifth merger wave. The various merger waves provoked major changes in the structure of American business. They were instrumental in transforming American industry from a collection of small and medium-sized businesses to the current form, which includes thousands of multinational corporations.

This chapter focuses more closely on the later merger periods because they are, of course, more relevant to recent trends in the world of mergers. This is particularly the case starting with the fourth and fifth merger waves.

THE FIRST WAVE, 1897–1904

The first merger wave occurred after the Depression of 1883, peaked between 1898 and 1902, and ended in 1904 (Table 2.1 and Figure 2.1.). Although these mergers affected all major mining and manufacturing industries, certain industries clearly demonstrated a higher incidence of merger activity.[1] According to a National Bureau of Economic Research study by Professor Ralph Nelson, eight industries—primary metals, food products, petroleum products, chemicals, transportation equipment, fabricated metal products, machinery, and bituminous coal—experienced the greatest merger activity. These industries accounted for approximately two-thirds of all mergers during this period.

The mergers of the fourth wave were predominantly horizontal combinations (Table 2.2 and Figure 2.2). The many horizontal mergers and industry consolidations of this era often resulted in a near monopolistic market structure. For this reason, this merger period is known for its role in creating large monopolies. This period is also associated with the first billion dollar megamerger deal when U.S. Steel, founded by J. P. Morgan, later joined with Carnegie Steel, founded by Andrew Carnegie, and combined with its other major rivals. The resulting steel giant merged 785 separate firms. At one time U.S. Steel accounted for as much as 75% of the United States' steel-making capacity.

---

1. Ralph Nelson, *Merger Movements in American Industry: 1895–1956* (Princeton, N.J.: Princeton University Press, 1959).

Table 2.1.   Mergers, 1897–1904

Year	Number of Mergers
1897	69
1898	303
1899	1,208
1900	340
1901	423
1902	379
1903	142
1904	79

Source: Merrill Lynch Business Brokerage and Valuation, *Mergerstat Review,* 1989.

Besides USX Corporation (formerly U.S. Steel), some of today's great industrial giants originated in the first merger wave. These include DuPont Inc., Standard Oil, General Electric, Eastman Kodak, American Tobacco Inc., and Navistar International (formerly International Harvester). While these companies are major corporations today with large market shares, some were truly dominant firms by the end of the first merger wave. For example, U.S. Steel was not the only corporation to dominate its market. American Tobacco enjoyed a 90% market share, and Standard Oil, owned by J. D. Rockefeller, commanded 85% of its market.

In the first merger movement, there were 300 major combinations covering many industrial areas and controlling 40% of the nation's manufacturing capital. Nelson estimates that in excess of 3,000 companies disappeared during this period as a result of mergers.

By 1909 the 100 largest industrial corporations controlled nearly 18% of the assets of all industrial corporations. Even the enactment of the Sherman Antitrust Act (1890) did not

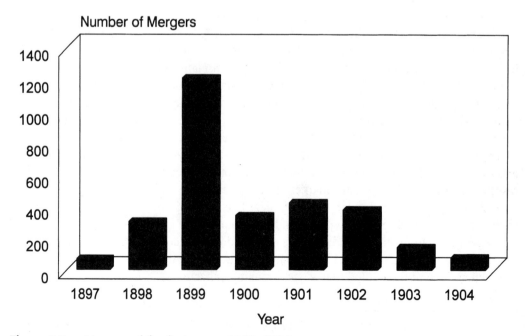

Figure 2.1.   Mergers of the first wave, 1897–1904.

Table 2.2.   Mergers by Types, 1895–1904

Type of Merger	Percentage (%)
Horizontal	78.3
Vertical	12.0
Horizontal and Vertical	9.7
Total	100.0

Source: Neil Fligstein, *The Transformation of Corporate Control* (Cambridge, Mass.: Harvard University Press, 1990), p. 72.

impede this period of intense activity. The Justice Department was largely responsible for the limited impact of the Sherman Act. During the period of major consolidation of the early 1900s, the Justice Department, charged with enforcing the act, was understaffed and unable to aggressively pursue antitrust enforcement. The agency's activities were directed more toward labor unions. Therefore, the pace of horizontal mergers and industry consolidations continued unabated without any meaningful antitrust restrictions.

By the end of the first great merger wave, a marked increase in the degree of concentration was evident in American industry. The number of firms in some industries, such as the steel industry, declined dramatically, and in some areas only one firm survived. It is ironic that monopolistic industries formed in light of the passage of the Sherman Act. However, in addition to the Justice Department's lack of resources, the courts initially were unwilling to literally interpret the antimonopoly provisions of the act. For example, in 1895 the U.S. Supreme Court ruled that the American Sugar Refining Company was not a monopoly that

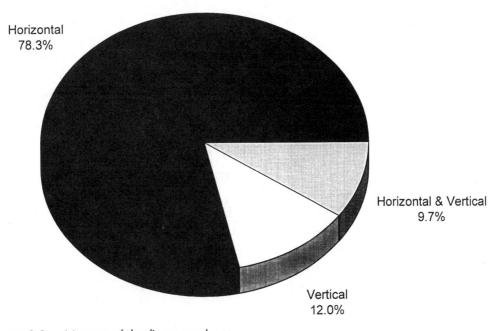

Figure 2.2.   Mergers of the first wave by type.

Source: Nelson 1959 and Neil Fligstein, *The Transformation of Corporate Control* (Cambridge, Mass.: Harvard University Press, 1990), p. 72.

restrained trade. The courts initially saw the law's focus to be on regulating stockholder trusts, in which investors would invest funds in a firm and entrust their stock certificates with directors who would ensure that they received dividends for their "trust certificates." For this reason, the law was not applied to hinder the formation of monopolies in several industries in the first merger wave.

The trusts were formed by dominant business leaders, such as J. P. Morgan of the House of Morgan and John D. Rockefeller of Standard Oil and National City Bank, as a response to the poor performance of many of the nation's businesses as they struggled with the weak economic climate. They saw the structure of many industries, which included many small and inefficient companies, as part of the reason for this poor performance. They used the voting powers entrusted to them to force multiple mergers in certain industries in an effort to reduce the level of competition and to allow the surviving companies to enjoy certain economies of scale. The end result was that certain trusts, such as the American Cottonseed Oil Trust and the National Lead Trust, dominated their respective industries. Morgan Bank, in turn, controlled First National Bank, the National Bank of Commerce, the First National Bank of Chicago, Liberty National Bank, Chase National Bank, Hanover National Bank, and the Astor National Bank.[2]

In addition to lax enforcement of federal antitrust laws, other legal reasons explain why the first merger wave thrived. For example, in some states, corporation laws were gradually relaxed. In particular, corporations became better able to secure capital, hold stock in other corporations, and expand their lines of business operations, thereby creating a fertile environment for firms to contemplate mergers. Greater access to capital made it easier for firms to raise the necessary financing to carry out an acquisition, and relaxed rules controlling the stockholdings of corporations allowed firms to acquire the stock in other firms with the purpose of acquiring them.

Not all states liberalized corporate laws. As a result, the pace of mergers and acquisitions was greater in some states than in others. New Jersey, in which the passage of the New Jersey Holding Company Act of 1888 helped liberalize state corporation laws, was the leading state in mergers and acquisitions, followed by New York and Delaware. This act pressured other states to enact similar legislation rather than see firms move to reincorporate in New Jersey. Many firms, however, did choose to incorporate in New Jersey, which explains the wide variety of New Jersey firms that participated in the first merger wave. This trend declined dramatically by 1915, when the differences in state corporation laws became less significant.

The development of the U.S. transportation system was another of the major factors that initiated the first merger wave. Following the Civil War, the establishment of a major railway system helped create national rather than regional markets that firms could potentially serve. Transcontinental railroads, such as the Union Pacific–Central Pacific, which was completed in 1869, linked the western United States with the rest of the country. Many firms, no longer viewing market potential as being limited by narrowly defined market boundaries, expanded to take advantage of a now broader based market. Companies, now facing competition from distant rivals, chose to merge with local competitors to maintain their market share. Changes in the national transportation system made supplying distant markets both easier and less expensive. The cost of rail freight transportation fell at an av-

---

2. Nell Irvin Painter, *Standing at Armageddon: The United States, 1877–1919* (New York: W.W. Norton & Company) 1987, pp. 178–179.

erage rate of 3.7% per year from 1882 to 1900.[3] In the early 1900s transportation costs increased very little despite a rising demand for transportation services.

Several other structural changes helped firms service national markets. For example, the invention of the Bonsack continuous process cigarette machine enabled the American Tobacco Company to supply the nation's cigarette market with a relatively small number of machines.[4]

As firms expanded, they exploited economies of scale in production and distribution. For example, the Standard Oil Trust controlled 40% of the world's oil production by using only three refineries. It eliminated unnecessary plants and thereby achieved greater efficiency.[5] A similar process of expansion in the pursuit of scale economies took place in many manufacturing industries in the U.S. economy during this time. Companies and their managers began to study the production process in an effort to enhance their ability to engage in ever-expanding mass production.[6] The expansion of the scale of business also required greater managerial skills and led to further specialization of management.

As mentioned, the first merger wave did not start until 1897, but the first great *takeover battle* began much earlier—in 1868. Although the term *takeover battle* is commonly used today to describe the sometimes acerbic conflicts among firms in takeovers, it can be more literally applied to the conflicts that occurred in early corporate mergers. One such takeover contest involved an attempt to take control of the Erie Railroad in 1868. The takeover attempt pitted Cornelius Vanderbilt against Daniel Drew, Jim Fisk, and Jay Gould. As one of their major takeover defenses, the defenders of the Erie Railroad issued themselves large quantities of stock, even though they lacked the authorization to do so. At that time, because bribery of judges and elected officials was common, legal remedies for violating corporate laws were particularly weak. The battle for control of the railroad took a violent turn when the target corporation hired guards, equipped with firearms and cannons, to protect their headquarters. The takeover attempt ended when Vanderbilt abandoned his assault on the Erie Railroad and turned his attention to weaker targets.

In the late nineteenth century, as a result of such takeover contests, the public became increasingly concerned about unethical business practices. Corporate laws were not particularly effective during the 1890s. Not until the passage of antitrust legislation in the late 1800s and early 1900s, and tougher securities laws after the Great Depression, did the legal system attain the necessary power to discourage unethical takeover tactics.

Lacking adequate legal restraints, the banking and business community adopted its own voluntary code of ethical behavior. This code was enforced by an unwritten agreement among investment bankers, who agreed to do business only with firms that adhered to their higher ethical standards. Today Great Britain relies on such a voluntary code. Although these informal standards did not preclude all improper activities in the pursuit of takeovers, they did set the stage for reasonable behavior during the first takeover wave.

Ethical Issues emerged

---

3. Ibid.

4. Alfred D. Chandler, *The Visible Hand: The Managerial Revolution in American Business* (Cambridge, Mass.: Belknap Press, 1977), p. 249.

5. Alfred D. Chandler, "The Coming of Oligopoly and Its Meaning for Antitrust," in *National Competition Policy: Historian's Perspective on Antitrust and Government Business Relationships in the United States,* Federal Trade Commission Publication, August 1981, p. 72.

6. Robert C. Puth, *American Economic History* (New York: Dryden Press, 1982), p. 254.

Financial factors rather than legal restrictions forced the end of the first merger wave. First, the shipbuilding trust collapse in the early 1900s brought to the fore the dangers of fraudulent financing. Second, and most important, the stock market crash of 1904, followed by the Banking Panic of 1907, closed many of the nation's banks and ultimately paved the way for the formation of the Federal Reserve system. As a result of a declining stock market and a weak banking system, the basic financial ingredients for fueling takeovers were absent. Without these, the first great takeover period came to a halt.

Some economic historians have interpreted the many horizontal combinations that took place in the first wave as an attempt to achieve economies of scale. Through mergers and acquisitions the expanding companies sought to increase their efficiency by lower per-unit costs. The fact that the majority of these mergers failed implies that these companies were not successful in their pursuit of enhanced efficiency.

Under President Theodore Roosevelt, whose tenure in the executive office lasted from 1901 to 1909, the antitrust environment steadily became more stringent. Although he did not play a significant role in bringing an end to the first wave, Roosevelt, who came to be known as the *trust buster*, continued to try to exert pressure on anticompetitive activities.The government was initially unsuccessful in its antitrust lawsuits, but toward the end of Roosevelt's term in office it began to realize more successes in the courtrooms. However, although President Roosevelt holds the reputation of being the trustbuster, it was his successor, William Howard Taft, who succeeded in breaking up some of the major trusts.

It is ironic that many of the companies formed in the breakup of the large trusts became very large businesses. For example, Standard Oil was broken up into companies such as Standard Oil of New Jersey, which later became Exxon; Standard Oil of New York, which became Mobil; Standard Oil of California, which became Chevron; and Standard Oil of Indiana, which became Amoco. The recent combination of Exxon and Mobil marks a partial reversal of this breakup.

THE SECOND WAVE, 1916–29

George Stigler, a Nobel prize–winning economist and former professor at the University of Chicago, has contrasted the first and second merger waves as "merging for monopoly" versus "merging for oligopoly." During the second merger wave, several industries were consolidated. Rather than monopolies, the result was often an oligopolistic industry structure. The consolidation pattern established in the first merger period continued into the second period. During this second period, the American economy continued to evolve and develop, primarily because of the post–World War I economic boom, which provided much investment capital for eagerly waiting securities markets. The availability of capital, which was fueled by favorable economic conditions and lax margin requirements, set the stage for the stock market crash of 1929.

The antitrust environment of the 1920s was stricter than the environment that had prevailed before the first merger wave. By 1910 Congress had become concerned about the abuses of the market and the power wielded by monopolies. It also had become clear that the Sherman Act was not an effective deterrent to monopoly. As a result, Congress passed the Clayton Act in 1914, a law that reinforced the antimonopoly provisions of the Sherman Act. (For a detailed discussion of the Clayton Act, see Chapter 3.) As the economy and the banking system rebounded in the late 1900s, this antitrust law became a somewhat more important deterrent to monopoly. With a more stringent antitrust environment, the second merger wave produced fewer monopolies but more oligopolies and many vertical mergers. In addition, many companies in unrelated industries merged. This was the first large-scale formation of conglomerates. However, although these business combinations involved firms that did not directly produce the same products, they often had similar product lines.

CASE STUDY: ALLIED CHEMICAL CORPORATION

Allied Chemical Corporation, one of the conglomerates formed in this period, con-solidated control over five different companies: General Chemical, Barrett, Solvay Process, Semet-Solvay, and National Aniline and Chemical. Although these firms clearly had different product lines, they operated in related business areas: General Chemical was a combination of 12 producers of sulfuric acid; Barrett sold by-prod-ucts of ammonia as well as coal tar products; Solvay Process was the country's largest producer of ash; Semet sold coal tar products; and National Aniline and Chemical was the nation's largest seller of dyestuffs. Consolidated under the single aegis of the Allied Chemical Corporation, these various different production processes united under a single management structure. Thus, Allied was able to ex-ploit the various economies that existed across these production processes and their related marketing activities.[a]

---

a. Jesse Markham, "Survey of the Evidence and Findings on Mergers," in *Business Concentration and Public Policy* (Princeton, N.J.: Princeton University Press, 1995). See comments by George W. Stocking, pp. 208–209.

Armed with the Clayton Act and the Sherman Act, the government was in a better posi-tion to engage in more effective antitrust enforcement than had occurred during the first merger wave. Nonetheless, its primary focus remained on cracking down on unfair busi-ness practices and preventing cartels or pools, as opposed to stopping anticompetitive mergers (Figure 2.3). At this time widespread price-fixing occurred in many industries, which was thought to be a more pressing threat to competition than mergers, which now were mainly vertical or conglomerate transactions.

Just as in the first merger wave, the second merger period witnessed the formation of many prominent corporations that still operate today. These include General Motors, IBM, John Deere, and the Union Carbide Corporation.

Between 1926 and 1930, a total of 4,600 mergers took place, and from 1919 to 1930, 12,000 manufacturing, mining, public utility, and banking firms disappeared. According to Earl Kintner, during the period from 1921 to 1933, $13 billion in assets were acquired through mergers, representing 17.5% of the nation's total manufacturing assets.[7] The con-tinued development of a nationwide rail transportation system, combined with the growth of motor vehicle transportation, continued to transform local markets into national mar-kets. Competition among firms was enhanced by the proliferation of radios in homes as a

---

7. Earl W. Kintner, *Primer on the Law of Mergers* (New York: Macmillan Publishing Co., 1973), p. 9.

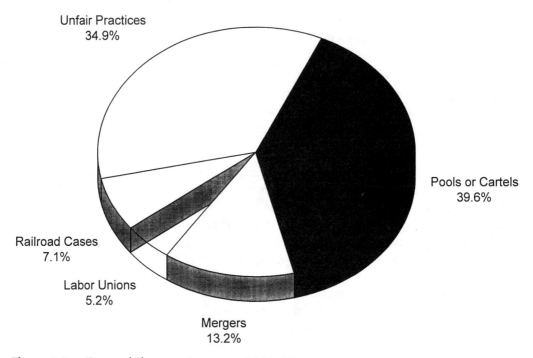

Figure 2.3.   Types of Sherman Act cases, 1901–20.

Source: The Federal Antitrust Laws (Washington, D.C.: U.S. Government Printing Office, 1938) and Neil Fligstein, *The Transformation of Corporate Control* (Cambridge, Mass.: Harvard University Press, 1990), p. 79.

Advertising

major form of entertainment. This led to the increased use of advertising as a form of product differentiation. Marketers took advantage of this new advertising medium to start national brand advertising. The era of mass merchandising had bcgun.

The public utility industry in particular experienced marked concentration. Many of these mergers involved public utility holding companies that were controlled by a relatively small number of stockholders. These utilities were often organized with a pyramidal corporate structure to provide profits for these stockholders and, according to the Federal Trade Commission (FTC), did not serve the public interest. The utility trusts were eventually regulated by the Public Utility Holding Company Act (PUHCA) of 1935. This law, which was designed to curb abuses, empowered the Securities and Exchange Commission (SEC) to regulate the corporate structure and voting rights of public utility stockholders. The act also gave the SEC the right to regulate the issuance of securities by utilities as well as their acquisition of assets or securities of other firms. Because the utilities' abuses of corporate power and fiduciary responsibilities were far more common at that time than they are today, the PUHCA essentially serves little purpose today.

Although mergers affected industries across the board, the following industries experienced a disproportionate number of mergers:

- Primary metals
- Petroleum products
- Food products

- Chemicals
- Transportation equipment

Mergers were facilitated not only by the limited enforcement of antitrust laws but also by the federal government's encouragement of the formation of business cooperatives to enhance the nation's productivity as part of the war effort. Rather than compete with each other during a time of war, the nation's firms, particularly those in manufacturing and mining, were urged to work together. Even after the war ended, however, the government maintained these policies through the 1920s.

The second merger wave bears some similarity to the fourth merger wave in that there was a significant use of debt to finance the deals that took place. Companies used a significant amount of debt in their capital structure, which provided the opportunity for investors to earn high returns but also brought downside risk if the economy slowed, as it soon did. One type of capital structure that became popular was the pyramid holding company, in which a small group of investors could control big businesses with a relatively small amount of invested capital.

The second merger wave ended with the stock market crash on October 29, 1929. "Black Thursday" would mark the largest stock market drop in history until the crash of October 1987. Although this collapse was not *per se* the cause of the Great Depression, it played a large role in it, for in contributing to a dramatic drop in business and investment confidence, business and consumer spending was further curtailed, thereby worsening the depression. After the crash, the number of corporate mergers declined dramatically. No longer focusing on expansion, firms sought merely to maintain solvency amid the rapid and widespread reduction in demand.

Investment bankers played key roles in the first two merger periods, exercising considerable influence among business leaders. They often vetoed a merger when they thought the merger was against the investment bank's policies or ethical interests by withholding funds from a firm seeking financing. The investment banks easily achieved controlling influence because a small number of them controlled the majority of the capital available for financing mergers and acquisitions. The investment banking industry was more concentrated in those years than it is today. The bulk of its capital was controlled by a small group of bankers who tended not to compete with each other. For example, one investment banker generally did not attempt to solicit business from another; each banker had his own clients, and those relationships tended not to change. This contrasts with the high degree of competition that exists in the industry today.

The number of mergers that took place during the first two waves demonstrates that investment banks generally supported merger activities. However, in the third merger period, the conglomerate era, the financial impetus for mergers would come from sources other than investment banks.

THE 1940s

Before we proceed to a discussion of the third merger period, we will briefly examine the mergers of the 1940s. During this decade, larger firms acquired smaller, privately held companies for motives of tax relief. In this period of high estate taxes, the transfer of businesses within families was very expensive; thus, the incentive to sell out to other firms arose. These mergers did not result in increased concentration because most of them did not represent a significant percentage of the total industry's assets. Most of the family business combinations involved smaller companies.

The 1940s did not feature any major technological changes or dramatic development in the nation's infrastructure. Thus, the increase in the number of mergers was relatively small. Nonetheless, their numbers were still a concern to Congress, which reacted by passing the Celler-Kefauver Act in 1950. This law strengthened Section 7 of the Clayton Act. (For further details on the Clayton Act, see the following section and Chapter 3.)

THE THIRD WAVE, 1965–69

The third merger wave featured a historically high level of merger activity. This was brought about in part by a booming economy. During these years, often known as the conglomerate merger period, it was not uncommon for relatively smaller firms to target larger companies for acquisition. In contrast, during the two earlier waves, the majority of the target firms were significantly smaller than the acquiring firms. Peter Steiner reports that the "acquisition of companies with assets over $100 million, which averaged only 1.3 per year from 1948 to 1960, and 5 per year from 1961 to 1966, rose to 24 in 1967, 31 in 1968, 20 in 1969, 12 in 1970 before falling to 5 each year in 1971 and 1972."[8]

The number of mergers and acquisitions during the 1960s is shown in Table 2.3 and Figure 2.4. These data were compiled by W. T. Grimm and Company (now provided by Houlihan Lokey Howard & Zukin), which began recording merger and acquisition announcements on January 1, 1963. As noted, a larger percentage of the mergers and acquisitions that took place in this period were conglomerate transactions. The FTC reported that 80% of the mergers that took place in the 10-year period between 1965 and 1975 were conglomerate mergers.[9]

The conglomerates formed during this period were more than merely diversified in their product lines. The term *diversified firms* is generally applied to firms that have some subsidiaries in other industries but a majority of their production within one industry category. Unlike diversified firms, conglomerates conduct a large percentage of their business activities in different industries. Good examples are Ling-Temco-Vought (LTV), Litton Industries, and ITT. In the 1960s ITT acquired such diverse businesses as Avis Rent a Car, Sheraton Hotels, Continental Baking, and other far-flung enterprises such as restaurant chains, consumer credit agencies, home building companies, and airport parking firms.

As firms with the necessary financial resources sought to expand, they faced tougher antitrust enforcement. The heightened antitrust atmosphere of the 1960s was an outgrowth of the Celler-Kefauver Act of 1950, which had strengthened the antimerger provisions of the Clayton Act of 1914. The Clayton Act made the acquisition of other firms' stock illegal when the acquisition resulted in a merger that significantly reduced the degree of competition within an industry. However, the law had an important loophole: It did not preclude the anticompetitive acquisition of a firm's assets. The Celler-Kefauver Act closed this

8. Peter O. Steiner, *Mergers: Motives, Effects and Policies* (Ann Arbor: University of Michigan Press, 1975).

9. *Statistical Report on Mergers and Acquisitions,* Federal Trade Commission, Washington D.C., 1977.

Table 2.3.   Third Merger Wave, 1963–70

Year	Mergers
1963	1,361
1964	1,950
1965	2,125
1966	2,377
1967	2,975
1968	4,462
1969	6,107
1970	5,152

loophole. Armed with tougher laws, the federal government adopted a stronger antitrust stance, coming down hard on both horizontal and vertical mergers. Expansion-minded firms found that their only available alternative was to form conglomerates.

The more intense antitrust enforcement of horizontal mergers was partially motivated by the political environment of the 1960s. During this decade, Washington policymakers, emphasizing the potential for abuses of monopoly power, worked through the FTC and the Justice Department to curb corporate expansion, which created the potential for monopolistic abuses. Prime advocates of this tougher antitrust enforcement were Attorney General John Mitchell and Assistant Attorney General Richard McLaren, the main architect of the federal government's antitrust efforts during the 1960s. In his book *Managing,* Harold Geneen, then chief executive officer of ITT, has described the difficulty his company had in

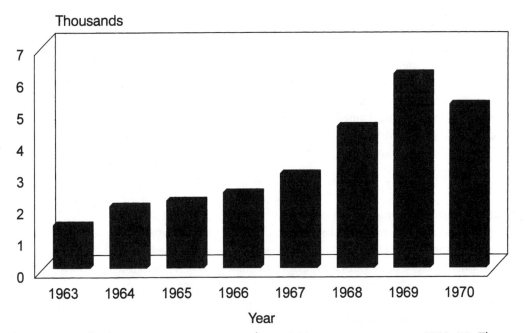

Figure 2.4.   Third merger wave, merger and acquisition announcements, 1963–70. The third merger wave peaked in 1969. The decline in the stock market, coupled with tax reforms, reduced the incentive to merge.

acquiring companies when McLaren was in office.[10] McLaren opposed conglomerate acquisitions based on his fears of "potential reciprocity." This would occur, for example, if ITT and its other subsidiaries gave Hartford Insurance, a company ITT acquired, a competitive edge over other insurance companies. ITT was forced to compromise its plans to add Hartford to its conglomerate empire. It was able to proceed with the acquisition only after agreeing to divest itself of other divisions with the same combined size of Hartford Insurance and to not acquire another large insurance company for 10 years without prior Justice Department approval.

With the election of Richard M. Nixon toward the end of the decade, Washington policymakers advocated a freer market orientation. Nixon supported this policy through his four appointees to the U.S. Supreme Court, who espoused a broader interpretation of concepts such as market share. The tough antitrust enforcement of the Justice Department came to an end in 1972 as the Supreme Court failed to accept the Justice Department's interpretation of antitrust laws. For example, the Supreme Court began to use a broad international market view as opposed to a more narrow domestic or even regional market definition. Consequently, if as a result of a merger, a firm had a large percentage of the U.S. market or a region of the nation but a small percentage of the international market, it could be judged to lack significant monopolistic characteristics. By this time, however, the third merger wave had already come to an end.

Management Science and Conglomerates

The rapid growth of management science accelerated the conglomerate movement. Schools of management began to attain widespread acceptability among prominent schools of higher education, and the master of business administration degree became a valued credential for the corporate executive. Management science developed methodologies that facilitated organizational management and theoretically could be applied to a wide variety of organizations, including corporations, government, educational institutions, and even the military. As these management principles gained wider acceptance, graduates of this movement believed they possessed the broad-based skills necessary to manage a wide variety of organizational structures. Such managers reasonably believed that they could manage a corporate organization that spanned several industry categories. The belief that the conglomerate could become a manageable and successful corporate entity started to become a reality.

Industry Concentration and the Conglomerate Wave

Because most of the mergers in the third wave involved the formation of conglomerates rather than vertical or horizontal mergers, they did not increase industrial concentration. For this reason, the degree of competition in different industries did not change appreciably despite the large number of mergers. Some 6,000 mergers, entailing the disappearance of 25,000 firms, took place; nonetheless, competition, or market concentration, in the U.S. economy was not greatly reduced. This clearly contrasts with the first merger wave, which resulted in a dramatic increase in industry concentration in many industries.

---

10. Harold Geneen, *Managing* (New York: Avon Books, 1989), pp. 228–229.

The Price-Earnings Game and the Incentive to Merge

As mentioned previously, investment bankers did not finance most of the mergers in the 1960s, as they had in the two previous merger waves. Tight credit markets and high interest rates were the concomitants of the higher credit demands of an expanding economy. As the demand for loanable funds rose, both the price of these funds and interest rates increased. In addition, the booming stock market prices provided equity financing for many of the conglomerate takeovers.

The bull market of the 1960s bid stock prices higher and higher. The Dow Jones Industrial Average, which was 618 in 1960, rose to 906 in 1968. As their stock prices skyrocketed, investors were especially interested in growth stocks. Potential bidders soon learned that acquisitions, financed by stocks, could be an excellent "pain-free" way to raise earnings per share without incurring higher tax liabilities. Mergers financed through stock transactions may not be taxable. For this reason, stock-financed acquisitions had an advantage over cash transactions, which were subject to taxation.

Companies played the price-earnings ratio game to justify their expansionist activities. The *price-earnings ratio (P/E ratio)* is the ratio of the market price of a firm's stock divided by the earnings available to common stockholders on a per share basis. The higher the P/E ratio, the more investors are willing to pay for a firm's stock given their expectations about the firm's future earnings. High P/E ratios for the majority of stocks in the market indicate widespread investor optimism; such was the case in the bull market of the 1960s. These high stock values helped finance the third merger wave. Mergers inspired by P/E ratio effects can be illustrated as follows.

Let's assume that the acquiring firm is larger than the target firm with which it is considering merging. Let's further assume that the larger firm has a P/E ratio of 25:1 and annual earnings of $1 million, with 1 million shares outstanding. Each share sells for $25. The target firm has a lower P/E ratio of 10:1 and annual earnings of $100,000, with 100,000 shares outstanding. This firm's stock sells for $10. The larger firm offers the smaller firm a premium on its stock to entice its stockholders to sell. This premium comes in the form of a stock-for-stock offer in which one share of the larger firm, worth $25, is offered for two shares of the smaller firm, worth a total of $20. The large firm issues 50,000 shares to finance the purchase.

This acquisition causes the earnings per share (EPS) of the higher P/E firm to rise. The earnings per share of the higher P/E firm has risen from $1.00 to $1.05. We can see the effect on the price of the larger firm's stock if we make the crucial assumption that its P/E ratio stays the same. This implies that the market will continue to value this firm's future earnings in a manner similar to the way it did before the acquisition. The validity of this type of assumption is examined in greater detail in Chapter 13.

Based on the assumption that the P/E ratio of the combined firm remains at 25, the stock price will rise to $26.25 (25 x $1.05). We can see that the larger firm can offer the smaller firm a significant premium while its EPS and stock price rises. This process can continue with other acquisitions, which also result in further increases in the acquiring company's stock price. This process will end if the market decides not to apply the same P/E ratio. A bull market such as occurred in the 1960s helped promote high P/E values. When the market falls, however, as it did at the end of the 1960s, this process is not feasible.

The process of acquisitions, based on P/E effects, becomes increasingly untenable as a firm seeks to apply it to successively larger firms. The crucial assumption in creating the

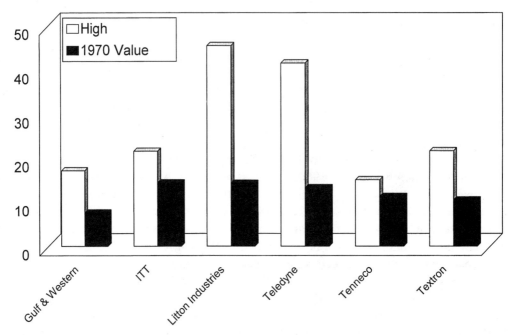

Figure 2.5. Third merger wave, conglomerate P/E ratios 1960, 1970. The end of the third merger wave was signaled by the dramatic decline in the P/E ratios of some of that era's leading conglomerates.

expectation that stock prices will rise is that the P/E ratio of the high P/E firm will apply to the combined entity. However, as the targets become larger and larger, the target becomes a more important percentage of the combined firm's earning power. After a company acquires several relatively lower P/E firms, the market becomes reluctant to apply the original higher P/E ratio. Therefore, it becomes more difficult to find target firms that will not decrease the acquirer's stock price. As the number of suitable acquisition candidates declines, the merger wave slows down. Therefore, a merger wave based on such "finance gimmickry" can last only a limited time period before it exhausts itself, as this one did.

With its bull market and the formation of huge conglomerates, the term the *go go years* was applied to the 1960s. When the stock market fell in 1969, it affected the pace of acquisitions by reducing P/E ratios. Figure 2.5 and Table 2.4 demonstrate how this decline affected some of the larger conglomerates.

Table 2.4. Conglomerate P/E Ratios in the 1960s

Corporation	High	1970 Value
Gulf & Western	17.2	7.6
ITT	21.6	14.4
Litton Industries	45.5	14.3
Teledyne	41.6	13.3
Tenneco	15.1	11.3
Textron	21.7	10.5

Source: Peter O. Steiner, *Mergers: Motives, Effects and Policies* (Ann Arbor: University of Michigan Press, 1975), p. 104.

Accounting Manipulations and the Incentive to Merge

Various accounting manipulations that allowed firms to realize "paper gains" on their financial statements also helped create an incentive for firms to merge in the 1960s. The result, in turn, was a temporary inflation in their stock prices. The two methods of accounting for mergers are *pooling of interests* and *purchase accounting.* Before changes in the accounting rules, however, each method gave the firm an opportunity to incur paper gains while consummating mergers. The pooling of interests method, which is discussed in greater detail in Chapter 15, assumes that the transaction between stockholders is just an exchange of equity securities. Therefore, the capital stock of the target firm is eliminated, and the acquirer issues new stock to replace it. The two firms' assets and liabilities are combined at their historical book values as of the acquisition date. With the purchase method, assets and liabilities are entered on the merged firm's books at their values as of the acquisition date.[11] This accounting valuation method is based on the idea that the resulting values, recorded on the firm's books, should reflect the values generated in the bargaining process. This process should result in a fairer representation of the valuation of these assets. At that time, using the pooling of interests method, the acquiring firm could generate additional paper earnings if it acquires "undervalued assets." The acquiring company may generate earnings whenever it likes by selling these assets at their actual market values. To illustrate this accounting manipulation, A.J. Briloff recounts how Gulf & Western generated earnings in 1967 by selling off the films of Paramount Pictures, which it had acquired in 1966.[12] The bulk of Paramount's assets were in the form of feature films, which it listed on its books at a value significantly less than their market value. In 1967 Gulf & Western sold 32 of the films of its Paramount subsidiary. This generated significant "income" for Gulf & Western in 1967, which succeeded in supporting Gulf & Western's stock price.

Peter O. Steiner states that these accounting manipulations made fire and casualty insurance companies popular takeover targets during this period.[13] He hypothesizes that conglomerates found their large portfolios of undervalued assets to be particularly attractive in light of the impact of a subsequent sale of these assets on the conglomerate's future earnings. Even the very large Hartford Insurance Company, which had assets of nearly $2 billion in 1968 (approximately $9.8 billion in 1999 dollars), had assets that were clearly undervalued. ITT capitalized on this undervaluation when it acquired Hartford Insurance.

Another artificial incentive that encouraged conglomerate acquisitions involved securities, which were used to finance acquisitions. Acquiring firms would issue convertible debentures in exchange for common stock of the target firm. Convertible debentures are debt securities that can be converted into a specific amount of common stock. In such a situation the target's earnings are added without an increase in common stock outstanding. If the stock price rose, however, the value of the convertible debentures would also rise because their conversion values rise. When convertible debentures are used to finance acquisitions, the earnings of the two firms are added together but the stock of the target has been replaced by

---

11. See Joseph H. Marren, *Mergers and Acquisitions* (Homewood, Ill.: Dow Jones Irwin, 1985), p. 210.

12. A. J. Briloff, "Accounting Practices and the Merger Movement," *Notre Dame Lawyer* 45, no. 4 (Summer 1970): 604–628.

13. Steiner, *Mergers: Motives, Effects and Policies,* p. 116.

debt. Earnings per share rise because the target earnings are added to the acquiring firm, but the total shares outstanding initially remain the same. This phenomenon is referred to as the *bootstrap effect.* If the same P/E ratio is applied to the merged firm, the stock price rises, thereby yielding a profit for the convertible debenture holders. Several laws enacted toward the end of the 1960s helped to end the third merger wave. In 1968 the Williams Act placed limits on the aggressiveness of tender offers and takeover attempts. Still a very influential piece of takeover regulation, the Williams Act is discussed in detail, along with tender offers, in Chapter 3. Although the act limited some abusive takeover tactics, it did not stop hostile takeovers. Ironically, it may unintentionally actually have facilitated some hostile deals.

Decline of the Third Merger Wave

The decline of the conglomerates may be first traced to the announcement by Litton Industries in 1968 that its quarterly earnings declined for the first time in 14 years.[14] Although Litton's earnings were still positive, the market turned sour on conglomerates, and the selling pressure on their stock prices increased.

In 1968 Attorney General Richard McLaren announced that he intended to crack down on the conglomerates, which he believed were an anticompetitive influence on the market. In addition, Congress held hearings, led by Congressman Emmanuel Celler, on the adverse impact of conglomerates. This added to the downward pressure on the conglomerate stock prices.

In 1969 passage of the Tax Reform Act ended some of the manipulative accounting abuses that created paper earnings that temporarily support stock prices. Specifically, it limited the use of convertible debt to finance acquisitions. Before enactment of this law, debt holders were willing to accept very low rates in exchange for the future capital gains on the sale of the convertible debentures. The low debt rates did not increase the riskiness of the corporation's capital structure because the associated fixed payments were low. The 1969 Tax Reform Act ended the use of low-rate convertible debt to finance acquisitions by stipulating that these bonds would be treated as common stock for the purpose of earnings per share computations. Consequently, earnings per share would not enjoy a paper increase because, for the purpose of its calculation, the number of common shares had, in effect, risen. This law also placed limits on the valuation of undervalued assets of targets that were to be sold at higher values to generate increased earnings.

When the stock market fell in 1969, the P/E game could no longer be played. Indeed, many analysts thought that the conglomerate mergers helped collapse this market inasmuch as when securities attain values far in excess of the underlying economic basis for their valuation, a collapse is sure to follow. This is one lesson to be learned from the stock market crash of October 1987.

Market Efficiency and Artificial Manipulations of Stock Prices

Many conglomerate mergers of this period were inspired by financial manipulations that would create the appearance that the combined firms were in better financial condition

---

14. Stanley H. Brown, *Ling: The Rise, Fall and Return of a Texas Titan* (New York: Atheneum Publishing Co., 1972), p. 166.

than their underlying economic earning power would imply. Should stock prices have risen in response to these financial manipulations? The finance literature questions the efficacy of such manipulations in an efficient market. However, many believe that these manipulations were, in part, the basis for the third merger wave.

Market efficiency refers to the ability of market prices to reflect all available information in a timely manner. An efficient market, which quickly assimilates all relevant and available information, should not be fooled by purely artificial manipulations of financial statements. Numerous research studies have tested the efficiency of markets in response to various events such as announcements of earnings, stock splits, or world events. This research is referred to as *event studies*.

Many event studies were conducted in the late 1960s and 1970s to examine the influence of accounting changes on stock prices.[15] In an efficient market, stock prices should not respond to accounting changes that do not reflect the firm's changed economic value. Altered entries on its books or variations in "reported earnings" that do not have corresponding cash flow effects do not affect the firm's true earning capacity. T. Ross Archibald has examined the reaction of stock prices to changes in the method of depreciation from accelerated depreciation to straight-line depreciation for financial statement purposes.[16] As a result of these changes, 65 of the firms that Archibald examined experienced an increase in reported profits without any change in their underlying economic earning power. Archibald notes that price changes following the announcements tended to be negative. This implies that investors saw through the reported profit changes and evaluated the stocks in terms of their true investment potential.

Other studies have supported the efficient market's view that firms should not be able to easily fool the market by making accounting changes designed to present a false picture of economic viability. As Robert Kaplan and Richard Roll show, a firm's stock price eventually fell, even though the firm engaged in accounting changes that presented a more favorable appearance while having a poor performance.[17] However, Kaplan and Roll observed that the stock prices of these firms did experience some temporary benefits. These studies on the efficiency of securities markets are consistent with the experiences of the conglomerate era in the history of mergers. In the long term, the market is relatively efficient in processing information. However, some evidence supports the existence of some short-term inefficiency.

The conglomerate firms achieved temporary gains through financial manipulations. The more exaggerated these gains, however, the more certain it is that the market will eventually respond with a more accurate evaluation. This occurred when the market turned against the conglomerates, which marked the end of the third merger wave.

---

15. E. F. Fama, L. Fisher, M. Jensen, and R. Roll, "The Adjustment of Stock Prices to New Formation," *International Economic Review* 10, no. 1 (February 1969): 1–21. Philip Brown and Ray Ball, "An Empirical Evaluation of Accounting Income Numbers," *Journal of Accounting Research* 6, no. 2 (Autumn 1963): 159–178; Frank Rielly and Eugene Drzyminski, "Tests of Stock Market Efficiency Following World Events," *Journal of Business Research* 1, no. 2 (Summer 1973): 57–72.

16. T. Ross Archibald, "Stock Market Reaction to the Depreciation Switch-Back," *Accounting Review* 47, no. 2 (Summer 1973): 22–30.

17. Robert S. Kaplan and Richard Roll, "Investor Evaluation of Accounting Information: Some Empirical Evidence," *Journal of Business* 45, no. 2 (April 1972): 225–257.

Performance of Conglomerates

Little evidence exists to support the advisability of many of the conglomerate acquisitions. Buyers often overpaid for the diverse companies they purchased. Many of the acquisitions were followed by poor financial performance. This is confirmed by the fact that 60% of the cross-industry acquisitions that occurred between 1970 and 1982 were sold or divested by 1989.[18]

There is no conclusive explanation for why conglomerates failed. Economic theory, however, points out the productivity-enhancing effects of increased specialization. Indeed, this has been the history of capitalism since the Industrial Revolution. The conglomerate era represented a movement away from specialization. Managers of diverse enterprises often had little detailed knowledge of the specific industries that were under their control. This is particularly the case when compared with the management expertise and attention that is applied by managers who concentrate on one industry or even one segment of an industry. It is not surprising, therefore, that companies like Revlon, a firm that has an established track record of success in the cosmetics industry, saw its core cosmetics business suffer when it diversified into unrelated areas such as health care.

TRENDSETTING MERGERS OF THE 1970s

The number of merger and acquisition announcements in the 1970s fell dramatically, as is shown in Table 2.5 and Figure 2.6. Even so, the decade played a major role in merger history. Several path-breaking mergers changed what was considered to be acceptable takeover behavior in the years to follow. The first of these mergers was the International Nickel Company (INCO) acquisition of ESB (formerly known as Electric Storage Battery Company).

INCO versus ESB Merger

After the third merger wave, a historic merger paved the way for a type that would be pervasive in the fourth wave: the hostile takeover by major established companies.

In 1974 the Philadelphia-based ESB was the largest battery maker in the world, specializing in automobile batteries under the Willard and Exide brand names as well as other consumer batteries under the Ray-O-Vac brand name. Its 1974 sales were more than $400 million. Although the firm's profits had been rising, its stock prices had fallen in response to a generally declining stock market. Several companies had expressed an interest in acquiring ESB, but all these efforts were rebuffed. On July 18, 1974, INCO announced a tender offer to acquire all outstanding shares of ESB for $28 per share, or a total of $157 million. The Toronto-based INCO controlled approximately 40% of the world's nickel market and was by far the largest firm in this industry. Competition in the nickel industry had increased in the previous 10 years while demand proved to be increasingly volatile. In an effort to smooth their cash flows, INCO sought an acquisition target that was less cyclical.

---

18. J. William Petty, Arthur J. Keown, David F. Scott, Jr., and John D. Martin, *Basic Financial Management,* 6th edition (Englewood Cliffs, N.J.: Prentice-Hall, 1993), p. 798.

Table 2.5. Merger and Acquisition Announcements, 1969–80

Year	Announcements
1969	6,107
1970	5,152
1971	4,608
1972	4,801
1973	4,040
1974	2,861
1975	2,297
1976	2,276
1977	2,224
1978	2,106
1979	2,128
1980	1,889

Source: Merrill Lynch Business Brokerage and Valuation, *Mergerstat Review,* 1989.

International Nickel Company ultimately selected ESB as the appropriate target for several reasons. As part of what INCO considered to be the "energy industry," ESB was attractive in light of the high oil prices that prevailed at that time. In addition, the possibility of a battery-driven car made a battery producer all the more appealing. International Nickel Company saw ESB's declining stock price as an inexpensive way to enter the booming energy field while helping smooth out the volatility of its own sales. Unfortunately, the acquisition of ESB did not prove to be a wise move for INCO. Although the battery business did have great potential, ESB was not a technological leader in the industry.

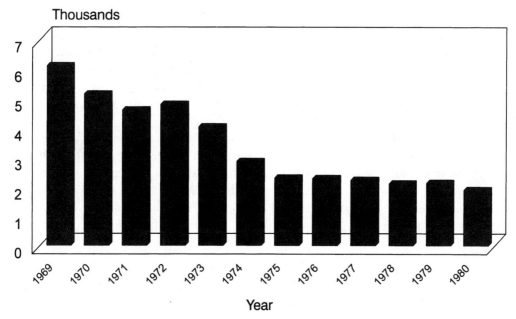

Figure 2.6. Merger and acquisition announcements, 1969–80.

Source: Merrill Lynch Business Brokerage and Valuation, *Mergerstat Review*, 1989.

It developed a low-maintenance auto battery while competitors marketed a maintenance-free product. It also lost market shares to the Duracell and Eveready long-life batteries, which it lacked. Because the takeover was an unfriendly acquisition, INCO did not have the benefit of a detailed financial analysis using internal data. Before INCO acquired ESB, major reputable corporations did not participate in unfriendly takeovers; only smaller firms and less respected speculators engaged in such activity. If a major firm's takeover overtures were rebuffed, the acquisition was discontinued. Moreover, most large investment banks refused to finance hostile takeovers.

At this time, the level of competition that existed in investment banking was putting pressure on the profits of Morgan Stanley, INCO's investment banker. Although it was seeking additional sources of profits, Morgan Stanley was also concerned that by refusing to aid INCO in its bid for ESB, it might lose a long-term client. Morgan Stanley, long known as a conservative investment bank, reluctantly began to change posture as it saw its market share erode because of the increasingly aggressive advance of its rivals in the investment banking business. Underwriting, which had constituted 95% of its business until 1965, had become less profitable as other investment banks challenged the traditional relationships of the underwriting business by making competitive bids when securities were being underwritten.[19] Many banks, seeking other areas of profitability, expanded their trading operations. By the 1980s trading would displace underwriting as the investment bank's key profit center.[20] This situation would change once again toward the end of the 1980s as fees related to mergers and acquisitions became an increasingly important part of some investment banks' revenues.

ESB found itself unprepared for a hostile takeover, given the novelty of this type of action. International Nickel Company gave it only a three-hour warning of its "take it or leave it" offer. ESB had installed some antitakeover defenses but they were ineffective. It sought help from the investment bank of Goldman Sachs, which tried to arrange a friendly takeover by United Aircraft, but by September 1974 INCO's hostile takeover of ESB was completed.[21] The takeover of ESB proved to be a poor investment primarily because INCO, as a result of legal actions associated with antitrust considerations, was not given a free hand to manage the company. Not until 39 months after INCO had completed the acquisition did it attain the right to exercise free control over the company. Moreover, as noted previously, ESB's competitors were already aggressively marketing superior products. By 1981 ESB was reporting operating losses; INCO eventually sold it in four separate parts.

Although the acquisition was not financially successful, it was precedent setting. It set the stage for hostile takeovers by respected companies in the second half of the 1970s and through the fourth merger wave of the 1980s. This previously unacceptable action—the hostile takeover by a major industrial firm with the support of a leading investment banker—now gained legitimacy. The word *hostile* now became part of the vocabulary of mergers and acquisitions. "'ESB is aware that a hostile tender offer is being made by a for-

---

19. John Brooks, *The Takeover Game* (New York: E. P. Dutton, 1987), p. 4.

20. Ken Auletta, *Greed and Glory on Wall Street: The Fall of the House of Lehman* (New York: Random House, 1986). Auletta provides a good discussion of this trend at the investment bank of Lehman Brothers.

21. For an excellent discussion of this merger, see Jeff Madrick, *Taking America* (New York: Bantam Books, 1987), pp. 1–59.

precedent of hostile takeover by a respected company

eign company for all of ESB's shares,' said F. J. Port, ESB's president. 'Hostile' thus entered the mergers and acquisitions lexicon."[22]

Morgan Stanley received a $250,000 fee for its advisory services. This fee, which did not involve the outright risk of the firm's capital and was considered attractive at the time, pales by comparison to the merger advisory fees of the 1980s. For example, in 1989 Morgan Stanley and three other investment banks received $25 million in advisory fees from Kohlberg Kravis & Roberts in the approximately $25 billion leveraged buyout (LBO) of Nabisco.

United Technologies versus Otis Elevator

As suggested previously, following INCO's hostile takeover of ESB, other major corporations began to consider unfriendly acquisitions. Firms and their chief executives who had inclined to be raiders but had been inhibited by public censure from the business community now became unrestrained. United Technologies was one such firm.

In 1975 United Technologies had recently changed its name from United Aircraft through the efforts of its chairman, Harry Gray, and president, Edward Hennessy, who were transforming the company into a growing conglomerate. They were familiar with the INCO-ESB acquisition, having participated in the bidding war for ESB as the unsuccessful white knight that Goldman Sachs had solicited on ESB's behalf. By mid-1975 Otis Elevator's common stock was selling for $32 per share, with earnings of $43.5 million on sales of $1.1 billion. Otis Elevator was an attractive target, with a book value of $38 per share and a stock price as high as $48 per share in 1973. United Technologies had never participated in a hostile takeover before its takeover of Otis Elevator.

At that time the growth of the elevator manufacturing business was slowing down and its sales patterns were cyclical inasmuch as it was heavily dependent on the construction industry. Nonetheless, this target was extremely attractive. One-third of Otis's revenues came from servicing elevators, revenues that tend to be much more stable than those from elevator construction. That Otis was a well-managed company made it all the more appealing to United Technologies. Moreover, 60% of Otis's revenues were from international customers, a detail that fit well with United Technologies' plans to increase its international presence. By buying Otis Elevator, United could diversify internationally while buying an American firm and not assuming the normal risk that would be present with the acquisition of a foreign company.

United initially attempted friendly overtures toward Otis, which were not accepted. On October 15, 1975, United Technologies bid $42 per share for a controlling interest in Otis Elevator, an offer that precipitated a heated battle between the two firms. Otis sought the aid of a white knight, the Dana Corporation, while filing several lawsuits to enjoin United from completing its takeover. A bidding war that ensued between United Technologies and the Dana Corporation ended with United winning with a bid of $44 per share. Unlike the INCO-ESB takeover, however, the takeover of Otis proved to be an excellent investment of United's excess cash. Otis went on to enjoy greater than expected success, particularly in international markets.

---

22. "Hostility Breeds Contempt in Takeovers, 1974," *Wall Street Journal,* 25 October 1989.

United's takeover of Otis was a ground-breaking acquisition; not only was it a hostile takeover by an established firm, but also it was a successful venture. Hostile takeovers were now an avenue through which established firms could profitably expand. The larger U.S. companies began considering hostile takeovers as ways to enhance future profitability. The financial community now felt the competitive pressures to provide the requisite financing needed for these unfriendly takeover bids. The takeover business was quickly changing.

Colt Industries versus Garlock Industries

Colt Industries' takeover of Garlock Industries was yet another precedent-setting acquisition, moving hostile takeovers to a sharply higher level of hostility. The other two hostile takeovers by major firms had amounted to heated bidding wars but were mild in comparison to the aggressive tactics used in this takeover.

In 1964 the Fairbanks Whitney Company changed its name to Colt Industries, which was the firearms company it had acquired in 1955. During the 1970s the company was almost totally restructured, with Chairman George Strichman and President David Margolis divesting the firm of many of its poorly performing businesses. The management wanted to use the cash from these sales to acquire higher growth industrial businesses. By 1975 Colt Industries was a successful conglomerate with sales of $1 billion. Its target, Garlock Industries, manufactured packing and sealing products and had sales of approximately $160 million, with a rising earnings per share. At the time of Colt's offer, Garlock's common stock was selling for $20 per share and its book value exceeded $21 per share.

Having abandoned the option of a friendly takeover bid, Colt planned a surprise attack on Garlock. At that time a surprise attack was feasible because the Williams Act allowed a shorter waiting period for tender offers. Garlock had already initiated antitakeover defenses, such as staggered elections of directors and acquisitions that would absorb excess cash. Garlock also filed several lawsuits designed to thwart Colt's bid. They filed suit in federal court, for example, alleging that Colt Industries had failed to abide by federal securities disclosure laws. Their legal actions also alleged that the proposed Colt Industries–Garlock merger would violate antitrust laws. One of Garlock's most acerbic defenses was its use of public relations as an antitakeover defensive strategy. Garlock had employed the public relations firm of Hill and Knowlton, which was widely regarded as one of the leading firms in its field. The firm played on the Colt Industries name by placing advertisements in the *New York Times* and the *Wall Street Journal* in which it asserted that the sudden Colt tender offer, which it called a "Saturday-night special," was not in the stockholders' interests.

In the end the public relations defense, as well as all other defenses, proved ineffectual. Garlock accepted Colt's bid, and the Saturday-night special became an effective takeover tactic. The Colt-Garlock battle brought the level of bellicosity of takeover contests to an all-time high, and in the years that followed this aggressive behavior would only increase. Potential takeover targets now realized that no existing antitakeover defense could protect them from hostile bids; all companies were now vulnerable to such moves. The gloves were off in the battles to take over targets. Companies began scrambling to erect yet stronger defenses. Playing on these fears, investment bankers offered to sell their defensive skills to worried potential targets, and many were put on retainers as specialists in antitakeover defenses. The game had changed, and the hostile takeover had become an acceptable part of the world of modern corporate finance.

THE FOURTH WAVE, 1981–89

The downward trend that characterized mergers and acquisitions in the 1970s through 1980 reversed sharply in 1981. Table 2.6 shows the number of merger and acquisition announcements for the period from 1970 to 1989, and Figure 2.7 shows the decrease from 1974 to 1994. Here we merely highlight the major trends that differentiate this wave from the other three; the characteristics unique to each wave are discussed separately and in detail in various chapters of this book. The unique characteristic of the fourth wave is the significant role of hostile mergers. As noted previously, hostile mergers had become an acceptable form of corporate expansion by 1908, and the corporate raid had gained status as a highly profitable speculative activity. Consequently, corporations and speculative partnerships played the takeover game as a means of enjoying very high profits in a short time. Whether takeovers are considered friendly or hostile generally is determined by the reaction of the target company's board of directors. If the board approves the takeover, it is considered friendly; if the board is opposed, the takeover is deemed hostile.

Although the absolute number of hostile takeovers is not high with respect to the total number of takeovers, the relative percentage of hostile takeovers in the total value of takeovers is large. Table 2.7 and Figure 2.8 reflect the absolute number of tender offers for publicly traded companies as compared with the total number of mergers and acquisitions. The data in Table 2.7 are somewhat deceptive because it appears that the total number of tender offers and contested transactions as a percentage of total transactions is very small.

Table 2.6. Merger and Acquisition Transactions, 1970–89 ($ millions)

Year	Total Dollar Value Paid	Number
1970	16,414.9	5,152
1971	12,619.3	4,608
1972	16,680.5	4,801
1973	16,664.5	4,040
1974	12,465.6	2,861
1975	11,796.4	2,297
1976	20,029.5	2,276
1977	21,937.1	2,224
1978	34,180.4	2,106
1979	43,535.1	2,128
1980	44,345.7	1,889
1981	82,617.6	2,395
1982	53,754.5	2,346
1983	73,080.5	2,533
1984	122,223.7	2,543
1985	179,767.5	3,001
1986	173,136.9	3,336
1987	173,136.9	2,032
1988	246,875.1	2,258
1989	221,085.1	2,366

Source: Mergerstat Review, 1998.

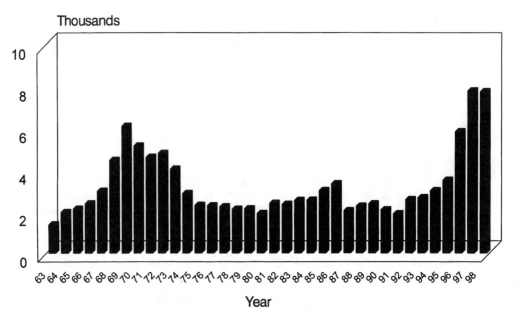

Figure 2.7. Merger and acquisition transactions, 1963–98.

Source: Mergerstat Review, 1999.

Table 2.7.   Mergers and Hostile Tender Offers, 1974–98

Year	Merger and Acquisition Announcements	Tender Offers	Contested Tender Offers
1974	2,861	76	12
1975	2,297	58	20
1976	2,276	70	18
1977	2,224	69	10
1978	2,106	90	18
1979	2,128	106	26
1980	1,889	53	12
1981	2,395	75	28
1982	2,346	68	29
1983	2,533	37	11
1984	2,543	79	18
1985	2,001	84	32
1986	3,336	150	40
1987	2,032	116	31
1988	2,258	217	46
1989	2,366	132	28
1990	2,074	56	8
1991	1,877	20	2
1992	2,574	18	2
1993	2,663	32	3
1994	2,997	70	10
1995	3,510	85	11
1996	5,848	166	8
1997	7,800	160	14
1998	7,809	179	22

Source: Mergerstat Review, 1999.

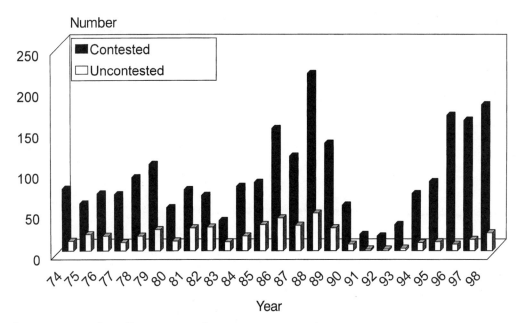

Figure 2.8. Tender offers: contested versus uncontested, 1974–98.

Source: Mergerstat Review, 1999.

However, the dollar value of these deals was sometimes quite high, resulting in a more significant percentage of the total dollar volume of mergers and acquisitions.

The fourth merger period may also be distinguished from the other three waves by the size and prominence of the merger and acquisition targets. Some of the nation's largest firms became targets of acquisition during the 1980s. The fourth wave became the wave of the megamerger. The total dollar value paid in acquisitions rose sharply during this decade. Table 2.8 and Figure 2.9 show how the average and median prices paid have risen since 1970. In addition to the rise in the dollar value of mergers, the average size of the typical transaction increased significantly. The number of $100 million transactions increased more than 23 times from 1974 to 1986. This was a major difference from the conglomerate era of the 1960s, in which the acquisition of small and medium-sized businesses predominated. The 1980s became the period of the billion dollar mergers and acquisitions.

Table 2.9 indicates the rising importance of the larger merger and acquisition announcements among the total number of such announcements. As shown in this table, the higher dollar categories were responsible for an increasingly greater percentage of the total merger and acquisition transactions between 1976 and 1986. Given the comparatively low inflation of the 1980s, inflationary influences only explain a small part of this trend. The size of merger and acquisition targets rose significantly during this period. Some of the megadeals of the 1980s are listed in Table 2.10.

Not all industries experienced a rapid growth in mergers in the 1980s. The oil industry, for example, experienced more than its share of mergers, which resulted in a greater degree of concentration within that industry. The oil and gas industry accounted for 21.6% of the total dollar value of mergers and acquisitions from 1981 to 1985. During the second half of

Table 2.8.   Average and Median Purchase Price, 1970–98 ($ millions)

Year	Average Price	Median Price
1970	9.8	NA
1971	7.4	NA
1972	8.6	2.8
1973	10.6	3.4
1974	12.5	3.6
1975	13.9	4.3
1976	20.1	5.1
1977	21.3	6.6
1978	31.9	8.1
1979	41.6	8.5
1980	49.8	9.3
1981	73.4	9.0
1982	57.8	10.5
1983	67.9	16.5
1984	112.8	20.1
1985	136.2	21.1
1986	117.9	24.9
1987	168.4	51.3
1988	215.1	56.9
1989	202.5	36.6
1990	126.4	21.0
1991	98.6	22.7
1992	101.8	22.5
1993	163.2	26.0
1994	168.2	33.0
1995	205.2	30.5
1996	186.7	25.3
1997	209.2	29.2
1998	385.6	33.5

Source: Mergerstat Review, 1999.

the 1980s, drugs and medical equipment deals were the most common (Table 2.11). One reason some industries experienced a disproportionate number of mergers and acquisitions as compared with other industries was deregulation. When the airline industry was deregulated, for example, air fares became subject to greater competition, causing the competitive position of some air carriers to deteriorate because they could no longer compete effectively. The result was numerous acquisitions and a consolidation of this industry. The banking and petroleum industries experienced a similar pattern of competitively inspired mergers and acquisitions.

deregulation → more competitive → mergers and acquisitions

Role of the Corporate Raider

In the fourth wave, the term *corporate raider* made its appearance in the vernacular of corporate finance. The corporate raider's main source of income is the proceeds from takeover attempts. The word *attempts* is the curious part of this definition because the raider frequently earned handsome profits from acquisition attempts without ever taking ownership of the targeted corporation. The corporate raider Paul Bilzerian, for example, participated in numerous raids before his acquisition of the Singer Corporation in 1988.

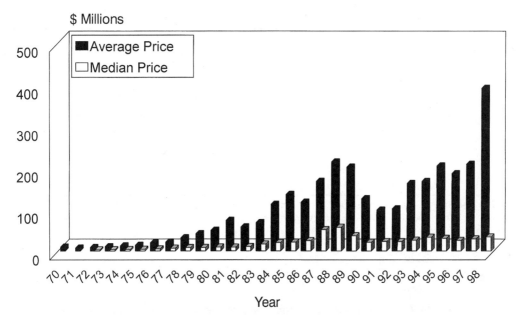

Figure 2.9.   Average and median purchase price, 1968–98.

Source: Mergerstat Review, 1999.

Table 2.9.   Number of Net Merger and Acquisition Announcements by Purchase Price Distribution, 1976–98

Year	$0.5–5.0 MM	$5.1–25.0 MM	$25.1–99.9 MM	$100.0–499.9 MM	$500.0–999.9 MM	Over 999.9 MM	Base*
1976	498 (50%)	344 (34%)	117 (12%)	35 (4%)	3	1	998
1977	451 (44%)	377 (36%)	163 (16%)	39 (4%)	2		1,032
1978	417 (39%)	404 (38%)	170 (16%)	76 (7%)	3	1	1,071
1979	387 (36%)	393 (38%)	184 (18%)	69 (7%)	11 (1%)	3	1,047
1980	306 (35%)	324 (36%)	166 (19%)	80 (9%)	10 (1%)	4	890
1981	388 (35%)	433 (36%)	192 (17%)	86 (8%)	15 (1%)	12 (1%)	1,126
1982	296 (32%)	338 (36%)	180 (20%)	96 (10%)	14 (2%)	6	930
1983	321 (30%)	380 (35%)	238 (22%)	104 (10%)	23 (2%)	11 (1%)	1,077
1984	270 (25%)	361 (33%)	253 (23%)	166 (15%)	16 (2%)	18 (2%)	1,084
1985	296 (23%)	454 (34%)	300 (23%)	204 (15%)	30 (2%)	36 (3%)	1,320
1986	219 (15%)	519 (35%)	384 (26%)	260 (18%)	59 (4%)	27 (2%)	1,468
1987	92 (10%)	294 (30%)	285 (29%)	218 (22%)	47 (5%)	36 (4%)	972
1988	101 (9%)	320 (28%)	359 (31%)	267 (23%)	57 (5%)	45 (4%)	1,149
1989	127 (12%)	321 (29%)	316 (29%)	250 (23%)	43 (4%)	35 (3%)	1,092
1990	166 (19%)	294 (34%)	215 (26%)	135 (16%)	25 (3%)	21 (2%)	856
1991	140 (19%)	234 (32%)	198 (28%)	120 (17%)	17 (2%)	13 (2%)	722
1992	197 (21%)	298 (31%)	255 (17%)	158 (17%)	24 (2%)	18 (2%)	950
1993	192 (18%)	342 (32%)	305 (18%)	198 (18%)	17 (2%)	27 (2%)	1,081
1994	185 (14%)	411 (27%)	369 (27%)	290 (22%)	42 (3%)	51 (4%)	1,348
1995	227 (13%)	554 (32%)	492 (29%)	333 (19%)	55 (3%)	74 (4%)	1,735
1996	466 (18%)	858 (32%)	694 (26%)	467 (18%)	79 (3%)	94 (2%)	2,658
1997	457 (15%)	955 (32%)	726 (24%)	625 (21%)	130 (4%)	120 (4%)	3,013
1998	447 (15%)	920 (30%)	818 (26%)	632 (20%)	116 (4%)	158 (5%)	3,091

*Base: Number of transactions disclosing a purchase price.

Source: Mergerstat Review, 1999.

Table 2.10.   Ten Largest Acquisitions, 1981–89

Year	Buyer	Target	Price ($ billions)
1988	Kohlberg Kravis	RJR Nabisco	25.1
1984	Chevron	Gulf Oil	13.3
1988	Philip Morris	Kraft	13.1
1989	Bristol Myers	Squibb	12.5
1984	Texaco	Getty Oil	10.1
1981	DuPont	Conoco	8.0
1987	British Petroleum	Standard Oil of Ohio	7.8
1981	U.S. Steel	Marathon Oil	6.6
1988	Campeau	Federated Stores	6.5
1986	Kohlberg Kravis	Beatrice	6.2

Source: Wall Street Journal, November 1988. Reprinted by permission of the *Wall Street Journal,* copyright © Dow Jones & Company, Inc. All rights reserved.

Although he earned significant profits from these raids, he did not complete a single major acquisition until Singer.

Many of the takeover attempts by raiders were ultimately designed to sell the target shares at a higher price than that which the raider originally paid. The ability of raiders to receive greenmail payments (or some of the target's valued assets) in exchange for the stock that the raider had already acquired made many hostile takeover attempts quite profitable. Even if the target refused to participate in such transactions, the raider may have succeeded in putting the company "in play." When a target goes into play, the stock tends to be concentrated in the hands of arbitragers, who readily sell to the highest bidder. This process often results in a company's eventually being taken over, although not necessarily by the original bidder.

Although arbitrage is a well-established practice, the role of arbitragers in the takeover process did not become highly refined until the fourth merger wave. Arbitrageurs, such as

Table 2.11.   Value of Mergers and Acquisitions Ranked by Industry, 1994–98

Industry Classification	Dollar Value (Rank)				
	1994	1995	1996	1997	1998
Drugs, medical supplies, and equipment	27,961.4 (1)	22,986.5 (4)	11,166.8 (17)	11,795.4 (16)	43,259.9 (8)
Banking and finance	25,423.4 (2)	74,712.2 (1)	36,962.6 (3)	112,700.0 (1)	213,980.4 (1)
Broadcasting	17,581.5 (3)	47,708.2 (2)	27,245.9 (5)	27,162.5 (7)	57,257.7 (6)
Insurance	13,852.6 (4)	17,821.2 (6)	31,763.8 (4)	30,387.7 (6)	65,105.8 (5)
Computer software, supplies and services	13,275.2 (5)	25,961.5 (3)	20,287.1 (8)	22,085.1 (9)	52,678.1 (7)
Leisure and entertainment	12,349.8 (6)	6,783.8 (13)	16,201.2 (10)	31,745.6 (5)	16,639.9 (15)
Retail	10,440.3 (7)	10,356.7 (8)	22,359.5 (7)	12,146.8 (15)	38,774.5 (9)
Electric, gas, water and sanitary services	10,422.6 (8)	22,423.6 (5)	47,491.1 (2)	48,130.8 (4)	65,469.2 (4)
Health services	9,288.2 (9)	7,332.7 (11)	15,532.5 (11)	15,046.7 (13)	12,237.1 (19)
Food processing	9,131.5 (10)	9,688.7 (10)	4,639.6 (25)	7,878.3 (23)	7,033.7 (25)
Communications	5,914.2 (13)	9,895.1 (9)	76,607.7 (1)	54,912.5 (3)	170,311.3 (2)

Source: Mergerstat Review, 1999.

the infamous Ivan Boesky, would gamble on the likelihood of a merger being consummated. They would buy the stock of the target in anticipation of a bid being made for the company. Arbitrageurs became a very important part of the takeover process during the 1980s. Their involvement changed the strategy of takeovers. Moreover, the development of this "industry" helped facilitate the rising number of hostile takeovers that occurred in those years.

raiders

arbitragers

Other Unique Characteristics of the Fourth Wave

The fourth merger wave featured several other interesting and unique characteristics. These features sharply differentiated this time from any other period in U.S. merger history.

Aggressive Role of Investment Bankers

The aggressiveness of investment bankers in pursuing mergers and acquisitions was crucial to the growth of the fourth wave. In turn, mergers were a great source of virtually risk-free advisory fees for investment bankers. The magnitude of these fees reached unprecedented proportions during this period. Merger specialists at both investment banks and law firms developed many innovative products and techniques designed to facilitate or prevent takeovers. They pressured both potential targets and acquirers into hiring them either to bring about or to prevent takeovers. Partially to help finance takeovers, the investment bank of Drexel Burnham Lambert pioneered the development and growth of the junk bond market. These previously lowly regarded securities became an important investment vehicle for financing many takeovers. Junk bond financing enabled expansionist firms and raiders to raise the requisite capital to contemplate acquisitions or raids on some of the more prominent corporations.

Increased Sophistication of Takeover Strategies

The fourth merger wave featured innovative acquisition techniques and investment vehicles. Offensive and defensive strategies became highly intricate. Potential targets set in place various preventive antitakeover measures to augment the active defenses that could deploy in the event that they received an unwanted bid. Bidders also had to respond with increasingly more creative takeover strategies to circumvent such defenses. These antitakeover strategies are discussed in detail in Chapter 5.

Increased Use of Debt

Many of the megadeals of the 1980s were financed with large amounts of debt. This was one of the reasons small companies were able to make bids for comparatively larger targets. During this period the term *leveraged buyout* became part of the vernacular of Wall Street. Through LBOs debt may be used to take public companies private. It often was the company's own management that used this technique in *management buyouts*. Although public corporations had been brought private before the fourth wave, this type of transaction became much more prominent during the 1980s.

Legal and Political Strategies

During this period new conflicts arose between the federal and the state governments. Besieged corporations increasingly looked to their state governments for protection against unwanted acquisition offers. They often were able to persuade local legislatures to pass antitakeover legislation, which brought the federal and state governments into direct conflict. Some representatives of the federal government, such as the SEC, believed that these laws were an infringement of interstate commerce. For their part, some state governments believed that such laws were based on their constitutionally granted state rights. Clearly, however, some state governments became protectors of indigenous corporations.

Foreign Takeovers

Although most of the takeovers in the 1980s involved U.S. firms taking over other domestic companies, foreign bidders effected a significant percentage of takeovers. For example, one of the megadeals of the fourth wave was the 1987 acquisition of Standard Oil by British Petroleum for $7.8 billion. Many of the deals were motivated by non-U.S. companies seeking to expand into the larger and stable U.S. market. The United States offers a more stable political climate combined with the largest economy in the world. However, this period also featured a significant number of deals in which U.S. companies used acquisitions to expand beyond their national boundaries.

In addition to the normal considerations that are involved in domestic acquisitions, foreign takeovers also introduce currency valuation issues. If the dollar falls against other currencies, as it did in the 1990s relative to many currencies, stock in American corporations declines in value and the purchasing value of foreign currencies rises. A falling dollar may make U.S. acquisitions attractive investments for Japanese or European companies. The increased globalization of markets in the 1980s and 1990s brought foreign bidders to U.S. shores in increased numbers. Although American companies may also engage in acquisitions in foreign markets, as many have, a falling dollar makes such acquisitions more expensive.

— Currency Issue in International M&A

THE FIFTH WAVE

Starting in 1992 the number of mergers and acquisitions once again began to increase (Table 2.12 and Figure 2.10). Large deals, some similar in size to those that occurred in the fourth merger wave, began to occur once again. Although the fifth merger wave featured many large megamergers, there were fewer hostile deals and more strategic mergers occurred. As the economy recovered from the 1990–91 recession, companies began to seek

Table 2.12.   Merger and Acquisition Transactions, 1990–98

Year	Number	Value ($ billions)
1990	2,074	$108.2
1991	1,877	71.2
1992	2,574	96.7
1993	2,663	176.4
1994	2,997	226.7
1995	3,510	356.0
1996	5,848	495.0
1997	7,800	657.1
1998	7,809	1,191.8

Source: Mergerstat Review, 1999.

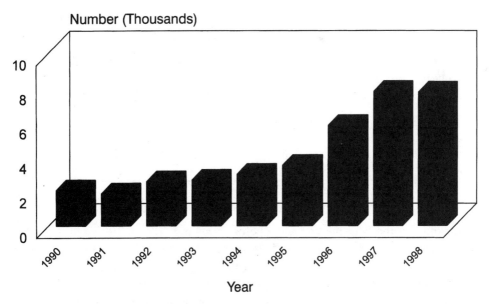

Figure 2.10.   Merger and acquisition transactions, 1990–98.

Source: Mergerstat Review, 1999.

to expand and mergers once again were seen as a quick and efficient manner in which to do that. Unlike the deals of the 1980s, however, the transactions of the 1990s emphasized strategy more than quick financial gains. These deals were not the debt-financed bustup transactions of the fourth merger wave. Rather, they were financed through the increased use of equity, which resulted in less heavily leveraged combinations. This is reflected in Figure 2.11, which shows that the number of all cash deals in the 1990s was in the 25%

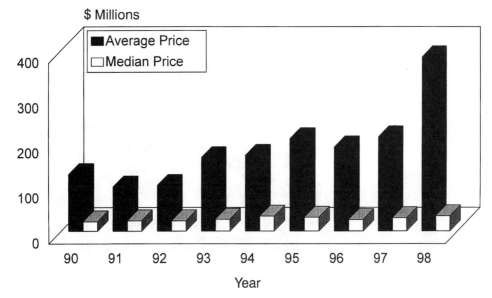

Figure 2.11.   Average and median purchase price, 1990–98.

Source: Mergerstat Review, 1999.

Table 2.13.   Average and Median Purchase Price, 1990–98 ($ millions)

Year	Average Price	Median Price
1990	126.4	21.0
1991	98.6	22.7
1992	101.8	22.5
1993	163.2	26.0
1994	168.2	33.0
1995	205.2	30.5
1996	186.7	25.3
1997	218.1	30.0
1998	385.6	33.5

Source: Mergerstat Review, 1999.

range for most of the fifth merger wave before reaching 40% in 1997 and 44% in 1998. These percentages are well below the 51% recorded in 1985. With a lower degree of financial leverage, the acquiring companies of the early 1990s were less vulnerable to economic downturns than many of the highly leveraged deals of the 1980s.

Because the deals of the early 1990s did not rely on as much debt, there was not as much pressure to quickly sell off assets to pay down the debt and reduce the pressure of debt service. The deals that occurred were motivated by a specific strategy of the acquirer that could more readily be achieved by acquisitions and mergers than through internal expansion.

As Table 2.13 and Figure 2.12 show, the price of the average deal fell dramatically after the end of the fourth merger wave. Starting in 1992 the average deal price rose significantly so that by 1997 it surpassed the peak reached in 1988. Although the average deal price started to increase quickly starting in 1992, it has yet to reach the peak it hit in 1988.

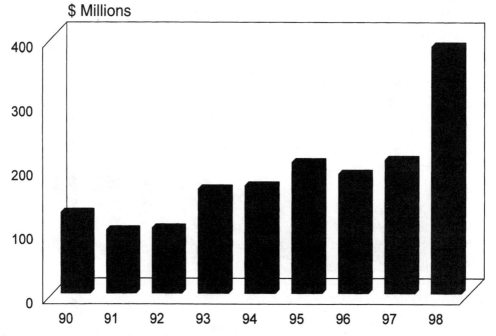

Figure 2.12.   Average deal price.

Source: Mergerstat Review, 1999.

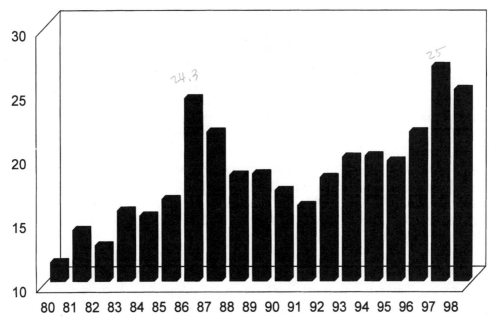

Figure 2.13.   Average P/E offered.

Source: Mergerstat Review, 1994, 1999.

Consistent with the trends in the bull market, higher and higher P/E ratios were offered for companies. The highest P/E offered in the fourth merger wave occurred in 1986, when it reached 24.3. However, the P/E offered in the fifth wave rose steadily through 1997 to reach 25 (Figure 12.13).

Industries with Significant Merger Volume and Consolidation

The fifth merger wave featured certain industries that had a high merger volume as the industries consolidated. Part of the reason for this was deregulation as well as the pace of technological change. Two of the leading consolidating industries were the banking and telecommunications industries.

deregulation , technological change
— banking , telecomm industry

CASE STUDY: LING-TEMCO-VOUGHT—
THE GROWTH OF A CONGLOMERATE

The growth of the Ling-Temco-Vought (LTV) Corporation is one of the classic stories of the growth of conglomerates during the third merger wave. The company was led by James Joseph Ling—the Ling of Ling-Temco-Vought. The story of how he parlayed a $2,000 investment and a small electronics business into the fourteenth largest industrial company in the United States is a fascinating one. Ling-Temco-Vought was a sprawling industrial corporation, which at its peak included such major enterprises as Jones & Laughlin Steel, the nation's sixth largest steel company; Wilson & Co, a major meat packing and sporting goods company; Braniff Airways, an airline that serviced many domestic and international routes; Temco and Vought Aircraft, both suppliers of aircraft for the military; and several other companies.

The company originated in a small Texas electrical contracting business that Jimmy Ling grew, through a pattern of diverse acquisitions, into one of the largest U.S. corporations. The original corporate entity, the Ling Electric Company, was started in 1947 with a modest investment of $2,000, which was used to buy war surplus electrical equipment and a used truck. By 1956 Ling Electronics had enjoyed steady growth and embarked on one of its first acquisitions by buying L. M. Electronics. Various other electronic and defense contractors were then acquired, including the American Microwave Corporation, the United Electronics Company, and the Calidyne Company. Acquisitions such as these—companies that lacked the requisite capital to expand—were financed by Ling through a combination of debt and stock in his company, which traded on the over-the-counter market.

By 1958 this master dealmaker sold an offering of convertible debentures in a private placement that was arranged by the Wall Street investment bank of White Weld & Company. This type of securities offering was particularly popular with the dealmakers of the third wave because it did not have an immediate adverse impact on earnings per share, thus leaving the company in a good position to play the "P/E game." With its stock price trading in the $40s, Ling started the process of buying targets that were much bigger than the acquiring company by the 1958 stock-for-stock acquisition of Altec Companies, Inc., a manufacturer of sound systems.

After some other small acquisitions, Ling initiated his largest acquisition when he merged his company with the Texas Engineering and Manufacturing Company, Temco. This deal enabled Ling to accomplish a long-term goal when the merged company, Ling-Temco Electronics, became part of the Fortune 500. Shortly thereafter Ling prevailed in a hostile takeover of the Vought Aircraft Company to form Ling-Temco-Vought.

Ling-Temco-Vought went through a period of lackluster financial performance, which forced Ling to restructure the company by selling off poorly performing divisions. In 1967 Ling successfully completed a tender offer for Wilson & Company, a firm twice the size of LTV. This deal vaulted LTV to number 38 on the Fortune 500 list. Wilson was composed of three subsidiaries, Wilson & Company, the meat packing business; Wilson Sporting Goods; and the Wilson Pharmaceutical and Chemical Corporation. Traders sometimes referred to these divisions as "meatball, golf ball, and goof ball." The next step Ling took in assembling this massive conglomerate was to buy the Great America Corporation, which was a holding company with investments in a variety of businesses such as Braniff Airlines and National Car Rental as well as banks and insurance companies. Although few beneficial commonalities appeared to be associated with this acquisition, Ling was able to exploit several, such as the insurance companies writing insurance for a variety of LTV units and employees.

After an unsuccessful takeover of the Youngstown Sheet and Tube Company, Ling set his sights on the fourth largest steel producer in the United States, Jones & Laughlin Steel. Ling-Temco-Vought bought Jones & Laughlin in an $85 tender offer for a company with a preannouncement price of $50. This $425 million bid was the largest cash tender offer as of that date and represented a 70% premium for a company in a low-growth industry. Unfortunately, the takeover of Jones & Laughlin drew the ire of Assistant Attorney General Richard McLaren, who saw it as another anticompetitive conglomerate acquisition. The Justice Department filed an antitrust lawsuit, which was bad news for any defendant because the government won a very high percentage of such cases. The market seemed to concur with this legal assessment because the stock price declined after the announcement. Because of the lawsuit, LTV was prevented from playing an active role in the management of Jones & Laughlin and taking steps to turn around the poorly performing steel company that had just announced its worst earnings performance in a decade. With the addition of Jones & Laughlin, LTV now had two major components of its empire—Braniff Airlines being the other one—reporting sizable losses. A settlement of the lawsuit was reached in which LTV agreed to sell off Braniff and the Okonite Company, a cable and wire manufacturer.

   Although LTV was able to achieve a favorable settlement, its stock suffered, partly as a result of the lawsuit, the poor performance of its subsidiaries, and the overall decline in the market. These factors gave rise to pressures from dissident shareholders and bondholders to remove Ling from control of LTV. Ling was not able to survive these pressures and was demoted from his position as chief executive and eventually left LTV. The story of Jimmy Ling and the huge conglomerate that he built is one of a man who was ahead of his time. He was probably the most renowned of the great conglomerate builders of the third merger wave. Whereas the 1980s featured such raiders as Carl Icahn and Boone Pickens, Ling was joined in the third wave by other "conglomerators" such as Lawrence Tisch of Loews, Charles Bluhdorn of Gulf & Western, and Ben Heineman of Northwest Industries. Long before the 1980s Ling had mastered the art of the LBO and hostile takeover. Unlike many of the raiders of the 1980s, however, Ling was opposed to trying to turn a quick profit on acquisitions by selling off assets. He bought companies with a more long-term strategy in mind, which, nonetheless, many criticized. Although it has undergone many changes since the third merger wave, including a bankruptcy, LTV still operates today.[a]

---

   a. See Stanley H. Brown, *Ling: The Rise and Fall of a Texas Titan* (New York: Atheneum Publishing Co., 1972).

Banking Industry

Deregulation helped motivate the frantic pace of mergers and acquisitions that took place in the fifth merger wave. The prior regulatory environment promoted many small banks and areas in which it was difficult to expand across state boundaries. This started to change in the 1980s and the regulatory environment relaxed. One of the first responses was the growth of the superregional banks such as Bank One and NationsBank. These superregional banks grew significantly in the 1980s. However, in the 1990s their growth became dramatic as they grew in size to rival even the larger money center banks. Banks sought to take advantage of the perceived economies of scale in this industry by expanding into new markets. Mergers and acquisitions is the fastest way this can be accomplished. Table 2.14 shows some of the large banking mergers that took place during the fifth merger wave.

Table 2.14.   The Ten Largest U.S. Commercial Bank Deals

Year	Acquirer	Target	Price ($ billions)
1998	NationsBank Corp.	BankAmerica	43.2
1998	Travelers Group Inc.	Citicorp	36.0
1998	Norwest Corp.	Wells Fargo & Co.	31.7
1997	First UnionCorp.	CoreStates	17.1
1997	NationsBank Corp.	Barnett Banks	14.8
1995	Wells Fargo & Co.	First Interstate Bankcorp.	10.9
1995	Chemical Banking Corp.	Chase Manhattan Corp.	10.4
1999	HSBC Holdings PLC	Republic New York Corp.	10.0
1996	NationsBank Corp.	Boatmen's Bancshares	9.6
1997	First Bank System	U.S. Bankcorp.	8.9

Source: Securities Data Company.

Telecommunications Industry

Another industry that featured a regularly changing market structure is telecommunications (Table 2.15). The 1984 breakup of AT&T left AT&T facing initially small rivals in the long-distance market and jettisoned the operating businesses into seven larger holding companies. Significant technological change took place in the industry with the development of new products and markets such as cellular telephones. AT&T began to lose market share to growing rivals such as MCI and Sprint. In addition, small upstarts such as LDDS, an initially insignificant long-distance reseller, used mergers and acquisitions to eventually become one of the largest telecommunications companies in the world—Worldcom.

Consolidations and Tendency Towards Oligopoly

The volume of consolidating megamergers that occurred in many industries during the fifth merger wave led to a movement towards an oligopolistic market structure. Often the number of competitors declined as companies acquired or merged with their rivals. While

Table 2.15.   The Ten Largest Telecommunications Acquisitions, 1993–99

Year	Acquirer	Target	Size ($ billions)
1998	SBC	Ameritech	61.4
1998	Bell Atlantic	GTE	52.9
1999	U.S. West	Global Crossing	37.0
1997	Worldcom	MCI	35.3
1996	Bell Atlantic	NYNEX	25.5
1996	SBC	Pacific Telesis	16.7
1996	Worldcom	MFS Communications	14.0
1998	AT&T	Teleport Communications	12.9
1993	AT&T	McCaw Cellular	12.6
1998	AT&T	British Telecom	10.0
1998	Northern Telecom	Bay Networks	7.7
1995	Time Warner	Turner Broadcasting	7.5
1998	Tellabs	Ciena	6.9
1995	Westinghouse	CBS	5.4
1993	U.S. West	Time Warner Cable	2.5
1997	Microsoft	Comcast	1.0

Source: Securities Data Company.

the resulting companies were clearly larger, they did not necessarily increase their market power. In some industries many of the surviving companies were stronger and able to better compete with each other. Moreover, as companies continue to face global markets they face a broader range of international competitors. Examples of industries where a few competitors commanded relatively high market share are shown in Figures 2.14 (a) and (b).

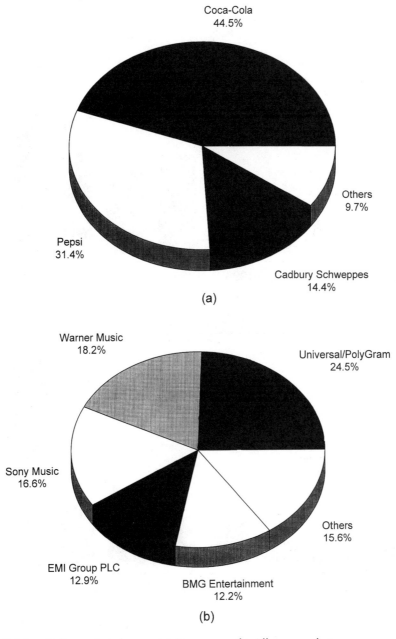

Figure 2.14.   U.S. market shares, (a) Beverages (b) Album market.

Source: Wall Street Journal, March 8, 1999.

Foreign Mergers

The growth in merger in the fifth merger wave was not confined to just U.S. companies or the United States itself. As Figures 2.15 (a) and (b) shows, U.S. companies were aggressive in the purchases of foreign firms during the 1990s. While foreign companies were initially slower to get into the U.S. acquisition market, by 1995 they were major purchasers of U.S. companies. In addition, the fifth merger wave spread to Europe by the late 1990s. Some of

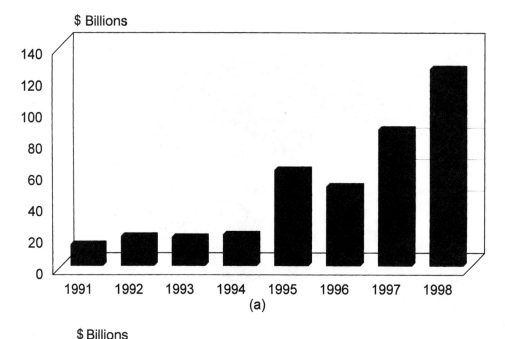

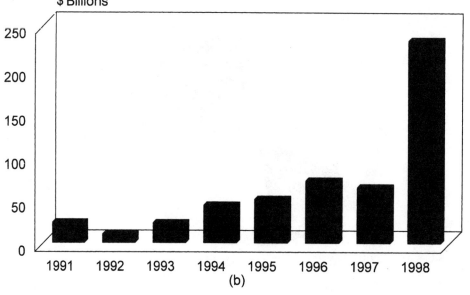

Figure 2.15. (a) Foreign acquisitions by U.S. companies, and (b) U.S. acquisitions by foreign companies.

Source: J.P. Morgan Securities, Inc.

the same industry-specific trends apparent in the United States earlier in the decade, took hold in Europe. Examples include the rash of banking deals in countries such as France.

SUMMARY

This chapter has described the ebb-and-flow development of corporate mergers and acquisitions in the United States, which was characterized by four main periods of intense merger activity called merger waves. The earlier merger waves were greatly influenced by the technological growth of the United States into a major industrial economy. The first merger wave included many horizontal combinations and the consolidations of several industries. The second wave included mainly horizontal deals but also many vertical transactions. The third wave was the conglomerate era, which refers to the acquisition of companies in different industries. The fourth merger wave was unique in that it featured the appearance of the corporate raider, who often used the junk bond market to finance highly leveraged deals. This debt financing also was used for other types of related financial transactions such as the LBO. Although corporate raiders existed before the 1980s, the fourth wave brought forth a raider armed with a larger arsenal of junk bond financing, which was used to attack some of America's largest corporations. In doing so, the raider permanently changed the outlook of corporate management, which previously had not been exposed to such formidable outside threats. When the junk bond market collapsed toward the end of the 1980s and the economy moved into a recession, it appeared that the hectic pace of merger and acquisition activity had come to an end. The lull in mergers, however, was short lived and the volume of transactions picked up in 1992. This marked the start of the fifth merger wave. This period featured even larger megamergers than the transactions of the 1980s. Deals of this period were different from many of those of the fourth merger wave. More of them were strategic mergers that involved companies seeking to expand into new markets or to take advantage of perceived synergies. The remainder of this book more fully describes the recent developments of the world of mergers and acquisitions. The different dimensions of merger activity are explored in depth so that the reader will obtain a more complete understanding of the intricacies of this continually evolving field.

REFERENCES

Allen, Julius. *Corporate Takeovers: A Survey of Recent Developments and Issues.* Congressional Research Service, Library of Congress, Washington, D.C., August 6, 1987.

Archibald, T. Ross. "Stock Market Reaction to the Depreciation Switch-Back." *Accounting Review* 47, no. 1 (January 1972).

Auletta, Ken. *Greed and Glory on Wall Street: The Fall of the House of Lehman* (New York: Random House, 1986.)

Brancato, Carolyn Kay, and Jan E. Christopher. *Merger and Acquisition Activity: The Level of Hostile Mergers.* Congressional Research Service, Library of Congress, Washington, D.C.

Briloff, A. J. "Accounting Practices and the Merger Movement." *Notre Dame Lawyer* 45, no. 4 (Summer 1970).

Brooks, John. *The Takeover Game* (New York: E. P. Dutton, 1987).

Brown, Philip, and Ray Ball. "An Empirical Evaluation of Accounting Income Numbers." *Journal of Accounting Research* 6, no. 2 (Autumn 1963).

Brown, Stanley. *Ling* (New York: Atheneum Publishing Co., 1972).

Chandler, Alfred D. *The Visible Hand: The Managerial Revolution in American Business* (Cambridge, Mass.: Belknapp Press, 1977).

Chandler, Alfred D. "The Coming of Oligopoly and Its Meaning for Antitrust." In *National Competition Policy: Historian's Perspective on Antitrust and Government Business Relationships in the United States.* Federal Trade Commission Publication, August 1981.

Fama, E. F., L. Fisher, M. Jensen, and R. Roll. "The Adjustment of Stock Prices to New Information." *International Economic Review* 10, no. 1 (February 1969).

Geneen, Harold. *Managing* (New York: Avon Publishing Co., 1984).

"Hostility Breeds Contempt in Takeovers, 1974." *Wall Street Journal,* 25 October 1989.

Kaplan, Robert S., and Richard Roll. "Investor Evaluation of Accounting Information: Some Empirical Evidence." *Journal of Business* 45, no. 2 (April 1972).

Kintner, Earl W. *Primer on the Law of Mergers* (New York: Macmillan Publishing Co., 1973).

Madrick, Jeff. *Taking America* (New York: Bantam Books, 1987).

Markham, Jesse. "Survey of the Evidence and Findings on Mergers." In *Business Concentration and Public Policy* (Princeton N.J.: Princeton University Press, 1955).

Marren, Joseph H. *Mergers and Acquisition* (Homewood Ill.: Dow Jones Irwin, 1985).

Melicher, R. W., J. Ledolter, and L. D'Antonio. "A Time Series Analysis of Aggregate Merger Activity." *Review of Economics and Statistics* 65 (August 1983).

Mergerstat Review, 1998.

Nelson, Ralph. *Merger Movements in American Industry: 1895–1956* (Princeton, N.J.: Princeton University Press, 1959).

Puth, Robert C. *American Economic History* (New York: Dryden Press, 1982).

Rielly, Frank, and Eugene Drzyminski. "Tests of Stock Market Efficiency Following World Events." *Journal of Business Research* 1, no. 1 (Summer 1973).

Steiner, Peter O. *Mergers: Motives, Effects and Policies* (Ann Arbor: University of Michigan Press, 1975).

Weston, J. Fred, and Thomas E. Copeland. *Managerial Finance* (Chicago: Dryden Press, 1986).

Winch, Kevin F. *Hostile Corporate Takeovers: Investment Advisor Fees.* Report No. 87–217E, Congressional Research Service, Library of Congress, Washington, D.C.

3

LEGAL FRAMEWORK

OVERVIEW

The legal requirements governing mergers and acquisitions differ depending on whether a transaction is a friendly merger or a hostile deal. Within each of these categories the rules vary depending on whether the transactions are cash or stock financed. The regulatory framework of each of these alternatives is described below.

- *Friendly merger—cash financed.* The bidder is required to file a proxy statement with the SEC which describes the deal. Usually the bidder has to file a preliminary statement first. If the Commission makes comments, the preliminary statement may be changed before it is finalized. The finalized proxy statement is then mailed to shareholders along with a proxy card which they fill out and return. Following this, the deal has to be approved at a shareholders meeting whereupon the deal can then be closed.
- *Friendly merger—stock financed.* This process is similar to a cash financed merger except that the securities used to purchase target shares have to be registered. The bidder does this by filing a registration statement. Once this is approved, the combined registration/proxy statement can be sent to shareholders.
- *Hostile deal—cash tender offer.* The bidder initiates the tender offer by disseminating tender offer materials to target shareholders. Such offers have to be made pursuant to the requirements of the Williams Act. This law is discussed at length in this chapter. However, unlike the friendly transactions described above, the SEC does not have an opportunity to comment on the materials that are sent to shareholders prior to their dissemination. The SEC may do so, however, during the minimum offer period which will be described later in this chapter.
- *Hostile deal—stock tender offer.* The bidder first needs to submit a registration statement and wait until it is declared effective prior to submitting tender offer materials to shareholders. The SEC may have comments on the preliminary registration statement which have to be resolved before the statement can be considered effective. Once this is done the process proceeds similar to a cash tender offer.

LAWS GOVERNING MERGERS, ACQUISITIONS, AND TENDER OFFERS

Several laws regulate the field of mergers and acquisitions. These laws set forth the rules that govern the merger and acquisition process. Because target companies use some of these laws as a defensive tactic when contemplating a takeover, an acquiring firm must take careful note of legal considerations. The three main groups of laws are securities laws, antitrust laws, and state corporation laws.

SECURITIES LAWS

There are various securities laws that are important to the field of mergers and acquisitions. The more important parts of these laws are reviewed in this chapter, beginning with the filing of an 8K and then with a detailed discussion of the Williams Act. The more important sections of this law, as they relate to the corporate finance of mergers, are discussed.

Filing of an 8K

The Securities Exchange Act of 1934 requires that an 8K filing must be made within 15 calendar days after the occurrence of certain specific events. Such events include the acquisition and disposition of a significant amount of assets including companies. The filing will include information such as:

- Description of the assets acquired or disposed of
- Nature and amount of consideration given or received
- Identity of the persons from whom the assets were acquired
- In the case of an acquisition, the source of the funds used to finance the purchase
- Financial statements of the business acquired

Acquisitions are determined to involve a significant amount of assets if the equity interest in the assets being acquired, or the amount paid or received in an acquisition or disposition, exceeds 10% of the total book assets of the registrant and its subsidiaries.

Williams Act

The Williams Act, which was passed in 1968, is one of the most important pieces of securities legislation in the field of mergers and acquisitions. It had a pronounced impact on merger activity in the 1970s and 1980s. Before its passage, tender offers were largely unregulated, a situation that was not a major concern before 1960 because few tender offers were made. In the 1960s, however, the tender offer became a more popular means of taking control of corporations and ousting an entrenched management.

In tender offers that used securities as the consideration, the disclosure requirement of the Securities Act of 1933 provided some limited regulation. In cash offers, however, there was no such regulation. As a result, the Securities and Exchange Commission (SEC) sought to fill this gap in the law, and Senator Harrison Williams, as chairman of the Senate Banking Committee, proposed legislation for that purpose in 1967. The bill won congressional approval in July 1968.

The Williams Act provided an amendment to the Securities Exchange Act of 1934, a legal cornerstone of securities regulations. This act, together with the Securities Act of 1933, was inspired by the government's concern for greater regulation of securities markets. Both acts have helped eliminate some of the abuses that many believed contributed to the stock market crash of October 1929.

Specifically, these laws provide for greater disclosure of information by firms when they issue securities. For example, the Securities Act of 1933 requires the filing of a detailed disclosure statement when a company goes public. In addition, the Securities Exchange Act of 1934 proscribed certain activities of the securities industry, including wash sales and churning of customer accounts. It also provided an enforcement agency, the SEC, which was established to enforce federal securities laws. In amending the Securities Exchange Act of 1934, the Williams Act added five new subsections to this law.

The Williams Act had four major objectives:

1. *To regulate tender offers.* Before the Williams Act was passed, stockholders of target companies often were stampeded into tendering their shares quickly to avoid receiving less advantageous terms.

2. *To provide procedures and disclosure requirements for acquisitions.* Through greater disclosure, stockholders could make more enlightened decisions regarding the value of a takeover offer. Disclosure would enable target shareholders to gain more complete knowledge of the potential acquiring company. In a stock-for-stock exchange, the target company stockholders would become stockholders in the acquiring firm. A proper valuation of the acquiring firm's shares depends on the availability of detailed financial data.

3. *To provide shareholders with time to make informed decisions regarding tender offers.* Even if the necessary information might be available to target company stockholders, they still need time to analyze the data. The Williams Act allows them to make more informed decisions.

4. *To increase confidence in securities markets.* By increasing investor confidence, securities markets can attract more capital. Investors will be less worried about being placed in a position of incurring losses when making decisions based on limited information.

In an attempt to achieve the preceding goals, the five subsections of the Williams Act were organized as follows:

- Section 13(d) regulates substantial share acquisitions.
- Section 14(d) regulates tenders offers.
- Section 14(e) prohibits material misrepresentations and other improper practices in tender offer solicitation and opposition.
- Section 14(f) requires disclosure if share ownership changes result in the replacement of the board of directors without shareholder approval.
- Section 13(e) regulates issuer purchases.

Section 13(d) of the Williams Act

Section 13(d) of the Williams Act provides an early warning system for stockholders and target management, alerting them to the possibility that a threat for control may soon occur. This section provides for disclosure of a buyer's stockholdings when these holdings reach 5% of the target firm's total common stock outstanding. When the law was first passed, this threshold level was 10%; this percentage was later considered too high and the more conservative 5% was adopted.

The disclosure of the required information, pursuant to the rules of Section 13(d), is necessary even when there is no tender offer. The buyer who intends to take control of a corporation must disclose the required information following the attainment of a 5% holding in the target. The buyer makes this disclosure by filing a Schedule 13D.

A filing may be necessary even though no one individual or firm actually owns 5% of another firm's stock. If a group of investors act in concert, under this law their combined stockholdings are considered as one group. Specifically, the law states that:

> When two or more persons act as a partnership, limited partnership, syndicate or other group for the purpose of acquiring, holding or disposing of securities of an issuer, such a syndicate or group shall be deemed a person for the purpose of this subsection.
>
> When the individual members of a group reach an agreement to attempt to take control of a company, they must make the required disclosure within the stipulated time frame. The stockholdings of each individual member of the group become the holdings of this new legal entity as far as this section of the law is concerned. The group filing requirement also applies to management, which might act in concert to defeat a tender offer. When stockholding managers and/or directors act together, they are subject to the same 13(d) filing requirements as outside investors.[1]

The definition of a group attracted much attention in the late 1980s in association with the alleged *stock parking* scandal involving Ivan Boesky. Stock parking occurs when bidders hide their purchases by having another investor buy the target company's stock for them. Brokerage firms obviously are in a good position to buy stock in this manner because they regularly purchase stock in many companies for various clients. When a brokerage firm is merely concealing the true ownership of the stock, however, the transaction may be a violation of the Williams Act. It was asserted that Boesky's brokers, Jefferies and Company, amassed holdings of stock for Boesky while they were aware of Boesky's intent to circumvent disclosure requirements. The enforcement authorities alleged that this constituted a group in the eyes of the Williams Act, and that both parties should therefore have made proper disclosure.

There may be a significant economic incentive to illegally pursue a stock parking arrangement with another party. Once disclosure is made, the marketplace becomes aware of the acquiring firm's intentions. The market is also aware that the stock of a target company tends to rise significantly in takeover attempts. Thus, other speculators, such as arbitragers, may seek to profit by buying the target firm's stock, hoping to sell their stock at higher prices to those who will eventually bid for control of the company. This type of speculating is an example of one form of *risk arbitrage.*

Schedule 13D

Section 13(d) provides for the filing of a Schedule 13D. Firms are required to file six copies of this schedule with the SEC within 10 days of acquiring 5% of another firm's outstanding

---

1. *Warner Communications, Inc. v. Murdoch,* 581 F. Supp. 1482 (D. Del., March 16, 1984).

stock. In addition, a copy must be sent by registered or certified mail to the executive offices of the issuer of the securities. Another copy must be sent in the same manner to each organized exchange on which the stock is traded. Figure 3.1 presents a copy of Schedule 13D.

Schedule 13D requires the disclosure of the following information:[2]

- The name and address of the issuing firm and the type of securities to be acquired. For example, a company may have more than one class of securities. In this instance, the

OMB APPROVAL
OMB Number: 3235-0145
Expires: September 30, 1988

SECURITIES AND EXCHANGE COMMISSION
Washington, D.C. 20549

SCHEDULE 13D

Under the Securities Exchange Act of 1934
(Amendment No. _____)*

_____
(Name of Issuer)

_____
(Title of Class of Securities)

_____
(CUSIP Number)

_____
(Name, Address and Telephone Number of Person Authorized to Receive Notices and Communications)

_____
(Date of Event which Requires Filing of this Statement)

If the filing person has previously filed a statement on Schedule 13G to report the acquisition which is the subject of this Schedule 13D, and is filing this schedule because of Rule 13d-1(b)(3) or (4), check the following box ☐.

Check the following box if a fee is being paid with the statement ☐. (A fee is not required only if the reporting person: (1) has a previous statement on file reporting beneficial ownership of more than five percent of the class of securities described in Item 1; and (2) has filed no amendment subsequent thereto reporting beneficial ownership of five percent or less of such class.) (See Rule 13d-7.)

Note: Six copies of this statement, including all exhibits, should be filed with the Commission. See Rule 13d-1(a) for other parties to whom copies are to be sent.

*The remainder of this cover page shall be filled out for a reporting person's initial filing on this form with respect to the subject class of securities, and for any subsequent amendment containing information which would alter disclosures provided in a prior cover page.

The information required on the remainder of this cover page shall not be deemed to be "filed" for the purpose of Section 18 of the Securities Exchange Act of 1934 ("Act") or otherwise subject to the liabilities of that section of the Act but shall be subject to all other provisions of the Act (however, see the Notes).

SEC 1746 (2-87)

Figure 3.1.   Sample of Schedule 13D.

_____

2. Bryon E. Fox and Eleanor M. Fox, *Corporate Acquisitions and Mergers,* Vol. 2 (New York: Matthew Bender Publishing Co., 1994), p. 27.

SCHEDULE 13D

CUSIP No. ______________ | Page _____ of _____ Pages

1	NAME OF REPORTING PERSON S.S. OR I.R.S. IDENTIFICATION NO. OF ABOVE PERSON		
2	CHECK THE APPROPRIATE BOX IF A MEMBER OF A GROUP*		(a) ☐ (b) ☐
3	SEC USE ONLY		
4	SOURCE OF FUNDS*		
5	CHECK BOX IF DISCLOSURE OF LEGAL PROCEEDINGS IS REQUIRED PURSUANT TO ITEMS 2(d) or 2(E)		☐
6	CITIZENSHIP OR PLACE OF ORGANIZATION		
NUMBER OF SHARES BENEFICIALLY OWNED BY EACH REPORTING PERSON WITH	7	SOLE VOTING POWER	
	8	SHARED VOTING POWER	
	9	SOLE DISPOSITIVE POWER	
	10	SHARED DISPOSITIVE POWER	
11	AGGREGATE AMOUNT BENEFICIALLY OWNED BY EACH REPORTING PERSON		
12	CHECK BOX IF THE AGGREGATE AMOUNT IN ROW (11) EXCLUDES CERTAIN SHARES*		☐
13	PERCENT OF CLASS REPRESENTED BY AMOUNT IN ROW (11)		
14	TYPE OF REPORTING PERSON*		

***SEE INSTRUCTIONS BEFORE FILLING OUT!**

Figure 3.1. Continued

acquiring firm must indicate the class of securities of which it has acquired at least 5%.

- Detailed information on the background of the individual filing the information, including any past criminal violations.
- The number of shares actually owned.
- The purpose of the transaction. At this point the acquiring firm must indicate whether it intends to take control of the company or is merely buying the securities for investment purposes.

- The source of the funds used to finance the acquisition of the firm's stock. The extent of the reliance on debt, for example, must be disclosed. Written statements from financial institutions documenting the bidder's ability to procure the requisite financing may be required to be appended to the schedule.

Amendments Required under Section 13(d)(2)

Section 13(d)(2) requires the prompt filing, with the SEC and the exchanges, by the issuer when there has been a material change in the facts that were set forth in Schedule 13D. As with much of the Williams Act, the wording is vague regarding what constitutes a material change or even the time period that is considered prompt. Generally, a filing within 10 days of the material change might be acceptable unless the change is so significant that a more timely filing is appropriate.[3] Such significance could be found in the market's sensitivity and reliance on the new information as well as prior information disclosed in the original filing that now may be significantly different.

Remedies for Failure to Comply with Section 13(d)

If there is a perceived violation of Section 13(d), either shareholders or the target company may sue for damages. The courts are more mindful of the target's shareholders' rights under Section 13(d) than those of the target corporation itself because this section of the statute was designed for their benefit as opposed to protecting the interests of the target corporation. Courts have been more inclined to grant equitable relief, such as in the form of an injunction, as opposed to compensatory relief in the form of damages. They are more concerned about making sure the proper disclosure is provided to shareholders as opposed to standing in the way of an acquisition. In addition to the courts, the SEC may review the alleged violation of Section 13(d) and could see fit to pursue an enforcement action. Parties that are found guilty of violating Section 13(d) may face fines and possible disgorgement.

Schedule 13G

The SEC makes special provisions for those investors who acquire 5% or more of a company's shares but who did not acquire more than 2% of those shares in the previous 12 months and who have no interest in taking control of the firm. Such investors are required to file the much less detailed Schedule 13G. Schedule 13G must be filed on February 14 of each year. These shareowners are sometimes called 5% *beneficial owners*.

---

3. John H. Matheson and Brent A. Olson, *Publicly Traded Corporations: Governance, Operation and Regulation* (New York: Clark, Boardman and Callaghan, 1994), p. 809.

Employee Stock Ownership Plans

The SEC may consider the trustee of an employee stock ownership plan to be a beneficial owner of the shares of stock in the plan. An employee stock ownership plan may have a trustee who is a bank adviser or an investment adviser. In making the determination of whether the trustee is the beneficial owner, the SEC would consider whether the trustee has discretionary authority to vote or dispose of the shares. If the trustee has such discretionary powers, there may be an obligation to file.

Section 14(d)

The Williams Act also provides for disclosure of various information in tender offers, principally through Section 14(d).

To Whom Should Disclosure Be Made
The disclosure must come in the form of a Schedule 14D-1 and must be submitted to those parties indicated under this section of the law. Ten copies of this schedule must be sent to the SEC, and another copy must be hand delivered to the executive offices of the target company. A copy also must be hand delivered to other bidders, if any. In addition, the acquiring firm must not only telephone each of the exchanges on which the target company's stock is traded to notify them of the tender offer but also mail a copy of the Schedule 14D-1 to them. If the target's stock is traded on the over-the-counter market, similar notice must be provided to the National Association of Securities Dealers. Figure 3.2 shows the front page of Campeau Corporation's Schedule 14D-1 pursuant to its tender offer for Federated Stores.

Information Requested on Schedule 14D-1
Figure 3.3 shows the first two pages of a Schedule 14D-1. A partial list of this schedule's more notable supplemental information requirements follows, according to the item number as it appears on the filing instructions of the schedule. (Based on the numbers on the actual schedules, this is only a partial listing.)

- Item 1—The name of the target company and the class of securities involved
- Item 2—The identity of the person, partnership, syndicate, or corporation that is filing. Additional background information on the corporate officers, including past criminal violations, should also be included.
- Item 3—Any past contracts between the bidder and the target company
- Item 4—The source of the funds that will be used to carry out the tender offer. This item has been a frequent source of considerable debate in hostile takeover attempts.

  The target firm frequently contends that the financing of the acquiring firm is insufficient to complete the takeover. This issue has been the focus of much litigation.
- Item 5—The purpose of the tender offer. The company must reveal any plans it may have to change the target company. For example, the company must fully disclose if it plans to sell off any assets, or change the board of directors, the dividend policy, or the target's capital structure.

SECURITIES AND EXCHANGE COMMISSION
WASHINGTON, D.C. 20549

SC 14D1

88 01 2414

SCHEDULE 14D-1

Tender Offer Statement
Pursuant to Section 14(d)(1),
of the Securities Exchange Act of 1934

Federated Department Stores, Inc.
(Name of Subject Company)

CRTF Corporation
(Bidder)

Common Stock, $1.25 par value
(Title of Class of Securities)

314099 3 10 2
(CUSIP Number of Class of Securities)

JAN 27 1988

Bechtel Information Services
Gaithersburg, Maryland

RECD S.E.C.

JAN 25 1988

FEB

Patrick H. Bowen, Esq.
CRTF Corporation
1114 Avenue of the Americas
24th Floor
New York, New York 10036
(212) 764-2538
(Name, Address and Telephone Number
of Person Authorized to Receive Notices
and Communications on Behalf of Bidder)

Copies to:

Robert A. Kindler, Esq.
Cravath, Swaine & Moore
One Chase Manhattan Plaza
New York, New York 10005
(212) 422-1640

CALCULATION OF FILING FEE

Transaction Valuation*	Amount of Filing Fee
$4,251,681,100*	$850,336.22*

* For purposes of calculating fee only. This amount assumes the purchase of 90,461,300 shares of Common Stock of Federated Department Stores, Inc. ("Federated"), including the associated Preferred Stock Purchase Rights issued pursuant to the Rights Agreement dated as of January 23, 1986, as amended, between Federated and Manufacturers Hanover Trust Company, as Rights Agent, at $47 per share net. Such number of shares represents all shares reported to be outstanding as of November 28, 1987, and assumes the exercise of all stock options appearing to be outstanding as of January 31, 1987.

☐ Check box if any part of the fee is offset as provided by Rule 0-11(a)(2) and identify the filing with which the offsetting fee was previously paid. Identify the previous filing by registration statement number, or the form or schedule and the date of its filing.

Amount Previously Paid:	N/A	Filing Party:	N/A
Form or Registration No:	N/A	Date Filed:	N/A

Figure 3.2. Sample Campeau Corporation's Schedule 14D-1.

- Item 9—The bidder's financial statements. This is another item that often is a major point of contention. Many targets of unwelcome bids contend that the bidder has not made adequate disclosure of its true financial condition. Targets in hostile bids may argue that, pursuant to Item 9, the financial data and financing terms indicate that the resulting combined firm may be significantly riskier.
- Item 10—Information material to the transaction, including information such as any antitrust conflicts or current litigation that the bidder may be involved in. Here again, acquiring firms and target firms have had varying interpretations of this item. Target firms often claim that acquiring firms have not made complete disclosure pursuant to Item 10.

OMB APPROVAL
OMB Number: 3235-0102
Expires: January 31, 1990

SECURITIES AND EXCHANGE COMMISSION
Washington, D.C. 20549

SCHEDULE 14D-1

Tender offer statement pursuant to section 14(d)(1) of the Securities Exchange Act of 1934.

(Amendment No.)*

____
(Name of Subject Company [Issuer])

____
(Bidder)

____
(Title of Class of Securities)

____
(CUSIP Number of Class of Securities)

____
(Name, Address and Telephone Numbers of Person Authorized to Receive
Notices and Communications on Behalf of Bidder)

Calculation of Filing Fee

Transaction valuation*	Amount of filing fee

*Set forth the amount on which the filing fee is calculated and state how it was determined.

☐ Check box if any part of the fee is offset as provided by Rule 0-11(a)(2) and identify the filing with which the offsetting fee was previously paid. Identify the previous filing by registration statement number, or the Form or Schedule and the date of its filing.

Amount Previously Paid: ____________________

Form or Registration No.: ____________________

Filing Party: ____________________

Date Filed: ____________________

Note: The remainder of this cover page is only to be completed if this Schedule 14D-1 (or amendment thereto) is being filed, inter alia, to satisfy the reporting requirements of section 13(d) of the Securities Exchange Act of 1934. See General Instructions D, E and F to Schedule 14D-1.

* The remainder of this cover page shall be filled out for a reporting person's initial filing on this form with respect to the subject class of securities, and for any subsequent amendment containing information which would alter the disclosure provided in a prior cover page.

The information required in the remainder of this cover page shall not be deemed to be "filed" for the purpose of Section 18 of the Securities Exchange Age of 1934 ("Act") or otherwise subject to the liabilities of that section of the Act but shall be subject to all other provisions of the Act (however, see the Notes).

Figure 3.3. Schedule 14D-1 form.

- Item 11—Any exhibits relevant to the schedule, such as copies of loan agreements for financing the acquisition, or any relevant written opinions of professionals hired by the acquiring firm. For example, opinions related to the fairness of the offer price or the tax consequences of the transaction should be appended.

Commencement of the Offer

The time period of the tender offer may be crucially important in a contested takeover battle. Therefore, the date on which the offer is initially made is important. According to Rule

1)′ Names of Reporting Persons S.S. or I.R.S. Identification Nos. of Above Person _____

2) Check the Appropriate Box if a Member of a Group (See Instructions)
   □ (a) _____
   □ (b) _____

3) SEC Use Only _____

4) Sources of Funds (See Instructions) _____

5) □ Check if Disclosure of Legal Proceedings is Required Pursuant to Items 2(e) or 2(f).

6) Citizenship or Place of Organization _____

7) Aggregate Amount Beneficially Owned by Each Reporting Person _____

8) □ Check if the Aggregate Amount in Row 7 Excludes Certain Shares (See Instructions).

9) Percent of Class Represented by Amount in Row 7 _____

10) Type of Reporting Person (See Instructions) _____

Figure 3.3. Continued

14d-2, the tender offer will begin on 12:01 A.M. on the date that any one of the following occurs:

- Publication of the tender offer
- Advertisement of the tender offer
- Submittal of the tender offer materials to the target

Following an announcement of an offer the bidder has five business days to disseminate the tender offer materials.

Press Release Announcing the Offer

Tender offers typically are accompanied by a press release by the bidder announcing the offer. A bidder may issue one release to announce its intentions to make a tender offer, followed by a later press release announcing that the offer has commenced (Figure 3.4).

Position of the Target Corporation

The Williams Act originally only required the bidder to file a disclosure statement. In 1980 the Act was amended to require the target to comply with disclosure requirements. The target company must now respond to the tender offer by filing a Schedule 14D-9 (Figure 3.5) within 10 days after the commencement date, indicating whether it recommends acceptance or rejection of the offer. If the target contends that it maintains no position on the offer, it must state its reasons.

In addition to filing with the SEC, the target must send copies of the Schedule 14D-9 to each of the organized exchanges on which the target's stock is traded. If the stock is traded

AMERICAN HOME PRODUCTS CORPORATION

FIVE GIRALDA FARMS, MADISON, NEW JERSEY 07940, (201) 660-5000

EXECUTIVE OFFICES

FOR IMMEDIATE RELEASE:

Investor Contact: Media Contact:
John R. Considine   Louis V. Cafiero
(201) 660-6429   (201) 660-5013

AMERICAN HOME PRODUCTS TO COMMENCE CASH TENDER OFFER FOR AMERICAN CYANAMID AT $95 PER SHARE

Madison, N.J., August 9, 1994 -- American Home Products Corporation (NYSE:AHP) announced today that its Board of Directors has formally approved the Company's previously announced offer to purchase American Cyanamid Company for $95 per share in cash. In furtherance of this offer, the Board authorized the commencement of a cash tender offer for all of the outstanding stock of American Cyanamid at that price, subject to customary conditions for an offer of this nature.

John R. Stafford, Chairman, President and Chief Executive Officer of American Home Products, stated that "although we are starting our tender offer, we are confident that American Cyanamid's Board of Directors will recognize the inherent value of our offer to their stockholders, and we hope they will quickly accept our invitation to begin meaningful discussions for a negotiated transaction."

American Home Products also announced that it was commencing litigation designed to eliminate the applicability to its offer of certain of American Cyanamid's anti-takeover and other defensive provisions. In addition, American Home Products stated that it intends to solicit other American Cyanamid stockholders to join it in calling for a special stockholders meeting to act on matters relating to the American Home Products offer.

#####

Figure 3.4. American Home Products press release.

on the over-the-counter market, the National Association of Securities Dealers must also be sent a copy of this schedule.

Time Periods of the Williams Act

Minimum Offer Period

According to the Williams Act, a tender offer must be kept open for a minimum of 20 business days, during which the acquiring firm must accept all shares that are tendered. However, it may not actually buy any of these shares until the end of the offer period. The min-

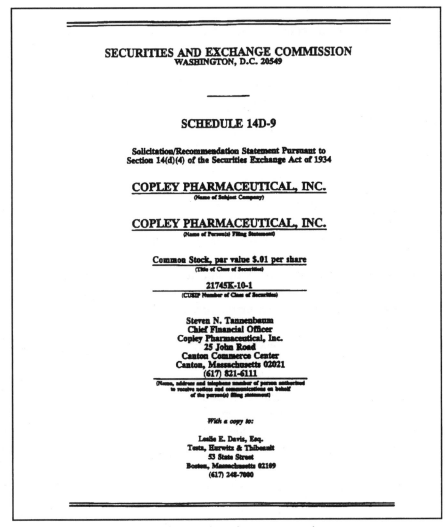

SECURITIES AND EXCHANGE COMMISSION
WASHINGTON, D.C. 20549

SCHEDULE 14D-9

Solicitation/Recommendation Statement Pursuant to
Section 14(d)(4) of the Securities Exchange Act of 1934

COPLEY PHARMACEUTICAL, INC.
(Name of Subject Company)

COPLEY PHARMACEUTICAL, INC.
(Name of Person(s) Filing Statement)

Common Stock, par value $.01 per share
(Title of Class of Securities)

21745K-10-1
(CUSIP Number of Class of Securities)

Steven N. Tannenbaum
Chief Financial Officer
Copley Pharmaceutical, Inc.
25 John Road
Canton Commerce Center
Canton, Massachusetts 02021
(617) 821-6111
(Name, address and telephone number of person authorized
to receive notices and communications on behalf
of the person(s) filing statement)

With a copy to:

Leslie E. Davis, Esq.
Testa, Hurwitz & Thibeault
53 State Street
Boston, Massachusetts 02109
(617) 248-7000

Figure 3.5. Schedule 14D-9 filed by Copley Pharmaceutical, Inc.

imum offer period was added to discourage shareholders from being pressured into tendering their shares rather than risk losing out on the offer. With a minimum time period, shareholders can take their time to consider this offer and compare the terms of the offer with that of other offers. The offering firm may get an extension on the 20-day offer period, if, for example, it believes there is a better chance of getting the shares it needs. The acquiring firm must purchase the shares tendered (at least on a pro rata basis) at the offer price unless the firm does not receive the total number of shares it requested in the terms of the tender offer. The acquirer may, however, still choose to purchase the tendered shares.

The tender offer may be worded to contain other escape clauses. For example, when antitrust considerations are an issue, the offer may be contingent on attaining the regulatory agencies' approval. Therefore, the offer might be so worded as to state that the bidder is not bound to buy if the Justice Department or the Federal Trade Commission (FTC) objects to the merger. The mere presence of an investigation by the regulatory authorities might allow a bidder to refuse to purchase the tendered shares.

Withdrawal Rights

The Williams Act has been amended several times to enhance shareholders' rights to withdraw their shares from participation in the offer. In 1986 the SEC enacted Rule 14d-7, which allows shareholders to withdraw their shares any time during the entire period the offer remains open. The goal of this rule is to allow shareholders sufficient time to evaluate the offer or offers in the case of multiple bids.

Pro Rata Acceptance

In many instances tender offers are oversubscribed. For example, an offer to purchase 51% of a target company's stock may receive 80% of the total shares outstanding. According to the earlier wording of the law, under Rule 14d-6, in a partial tender offer that is oversubscribed, the bidder must accept the securities tendered within the first 10 calendar days following the dissemination of the tender offer materials, or within 10 calendar days after a notice of an increase in the consideration of an offer has been distributed.[4] Based on this proration period, approximately five-eighths of each share submitted would be accepted if all 80% of the shares were tendered during the first 10 days of an offer to purchase 51% of the outstanding stock. If an additional 10% were submitted after the tenth calendar day of the offer, these shares would not be accepted unless the acquiring company decided to accept more shares than were stipulated in the 51% offer.

At first, the proration period frustrated the 20-day offer period. In the case of partial tender offers, stockholders had an incentive to rush to tender within the first 10 days of the offer, thus avoiding being closed out of even pro rata appearance if the offer were oversubscribed. Many stockholders would tender early to take advantage of the proration period while reserving the right to withdraw their shares until the end of the withdrawal rights periods.

The proration period rules were changed in 1982, when the SEC adopted Rule 14d-8. This rule requires a bidder in a partial tender offer to accept on a pro rata basis all shares tendered during the entire offer period. Therefore, when offers are extended, the proration period is automatically extended. The proration period is not, however, automatically extended by the extension of the withdrawal rights period. Rule 14d-8 ties the proration period to the offer period. The offer period, however, is not extended when the withdrawal rights period is extended. The SEC believed that a longer proration period was necessary to help small investors who may need more than the first 10 days of the offer period to make an informed decision. The SEC's amendment reduced the significance of the proration period.

Definition of a Tender Offer

The Williams Act is purposefully vague regarding the definition of a tender offer. Not surprisingly, this vagueness gave rise to litigation as tender offer participants chose to adopt the definition of a tender offer that was most favorable to them. In *Kennecott Copper Corporation v. Curtiss-Wright Corporation,* the court found that open market purchases with-

---

4. Ibid., p. 2.05 [3].

out a deadline and for which no premium was offered did not constitute a tender offer.[5] However, in *Wellman v. Dickinson* the court set forth the *Eight Factor Test*.[6] These factors are listed here and are revisited in Chapter 6.

1. Active and widespread solicitation of public shareholders for shares of an issuer
2. Solicitation made for a substantial percentage of an issuer's stock
3. Offer to purchase made at a premium over the prevailing market price
4. Terms of the offer are firm rather than negotiated
5. Offer contingent on the tender of a fixed number of shares and possibly specifying a maximum number of shares
6. Offer only open for a limited time period
7. Offeree subject to pressure to sell stock
8. Public announcements of a purchasing program that precede or are coincident with a rapid accumulation of shares[7]

In *Hanson Trust PLC v. SCM Corp.*, the Second Circuit has recognized that the *Wellman* factors are relevant to determining whether certain action by a bidder constitutes a tender offer.[8] However, the court stopped short of saying that these factors are a "litmus test." This court preferred to consider whether offerees would be put at an informational disadvantage if official tender offer procedures are not followed. Other courts have put forward more basic tests. In a district court opinion in *S-G Securities, Inc. v. Fuqua Investment Co.*, the court concluded that a tender offer exists if the following occurs:

- A bidder publicly announces its intention to acquire a substantial block of a target's shares for the purposes of acquiring control of the company, and
- A substantial accumulation of the target's stock by the bidder through open market or privately negotiated purchases.[9]

---

5. *Kennecott Copper Corp. v. Curtiss-Wright Corp.*, 584 F. 2d 1195 (CA2 1978).

6. *Wellman v. Dickinson*, 475 F. Supp. (SD NY 1979), *aff'd* 632 F. 2d 355 (CA2 1982), *cert. denied* 460 U.S. 1069 (1983).

7. This last factor was added after the *Wellman v. Dickinson* decision.

8. *Hanson Trust PLC v. SCM Corp.*, 744 F.2d 47 (2d Cir. 1985).

9. *S-G Securities, Inc. v. Fuqua Investment Co.*, 466 F. Supp. 1114 (D. Mass. 1978).

CASE STUDY: SUN OIL VERSUS BECTON DICKINSON

The Becton Dickinson Corporation is a medical products company that is located in Bergen County, New Jersey. The company was run by Fairleigh S. Dickinson Jr. until 1973. He was the son of the founder of the company, Fairleigh Dickinson Sr., who also founded Fairleigh Dickinson University. Fairleigh Dickinson Jr. had turned over the day-to-day control to a management team headed by Wesley Howe and Marvin Ashe. As time passed, disagreements occurred between Fairleigh Dickinson Jr. and Howe and Ashe. For example, they disagreed on certain personnel decisions and on other strategic decisions such as the acquisition of National Medical Care—a Boston-based medical care company. Fairleigh Dickinson Jr. opposed this particular acquisition because the equity offered for the purchase would dilute his shareholdings and his ownership percentage. The pattern of disagreements came to a head in a board of directors' meeting in which Ashe and Howe called for the removal of Fairleigh Dickinson Jr. as chairman of the board of directors.

While the internecine conflicts were ongoing at Becton Dickinson, Sun Oil, Inc., a Philadelphia-based corporation, was pursuing an expansion program that would help them diversify outside the petroleum industry. They were working with their investment banker, Salomon Brothers, to find suitable non-oil acquisition candidates. Given its position in its industry, they found Becton Dickinson an attractive takeover target. Salomon Brothers, the investment banker for both Sun Oil and Fairleigh Dickinson Jr., was more easily able to reach an understanding between the two parties, which provided for Fairleigh Dickinson Jr. to sell his 5% holdings in Becton Dickinson to Sun Oil at the appropriate time.

Sun Oil obtained commitments from 33 financial institutions to buy 20% of the outstanding shares of Becton Dickinson. On one day couriers were sent to these institutions to purchase these shares. Following the stock purchase, Sun Oil informed the New York Stock Exchange and Becton Dickinson of their actions. They did not file a 14D-1 but did file a 13D.

In a lawsuit that followed, the court ruled that the manner in which the shares were purchased did not constitute a tender offer. In doing so, the court set forth the basis for what has now become known as the Eight Factor Test. The court did rule that Sun Oil had violated the Williams Act by not filing a 13D when it had reached its understanding with Fairleigh Dickinson to purchase his 5%.

Materials That Shareholders Receive

Shareholders receive an "Offer to Purchase" (Figure 3.6) and a "Letter of Transmittal" (Figure 3.7). The Offer to Purchase sets forth the terms of the offer. Chief among these terms are the number of shares to be purchased, the offer price, and the length of time the offer will remain open. The Offer to Purchase may be many pages in length (e.g., 30 pages) and may contain much additional information for shareholders to consider, such as withdrawal rights, a discussion of tax considerations, and more details on the terms of the offer.

Method of Tendering Shares

Stockholders tender their shares through an intermediary, such as a commercial bank, which is referred to as the paying agent. As stockholders seek to participate in the tender offer, they submit their shares to the paying agent in exchange for cash or securities, in accordance with the terms of the offer. Attached to their shares must be a letter of transmittal. The agent accumulates the shares but does not pay the stockholders until the offer expires. In the event that the offer is extended, the paying agent holds the shares until the new offer expires, unless instructed otherwise by the individual stockholders.

CASE STUDY: CONISTON PARTNERS VERSUS T. W. SERVICES

On October 28, 1988, the New York investment group Coniston Partners initiated a $28 tender offer for the 81% of T. W. Services, Inc. that it did not already own. T. W. Services, a Delaware corporation, was a diversified food and medical services company. T. W. Services rejected the offer and asserted its desire to remain independent. The company cited anticipated growth in its food services divisions, which include the Denny's chain, Canteen Corporation, and Spartan, which was a franchisee of the Hardees' restaurant chain. T. W. Services was vulnerable because of poor performance of some of these units, most notably the Denny's chain, which it had acquired in 1987. This vulnerability was already observed in a prior unwanted bid from Ronald Perelman, which T. W. Services managed to thwart.

Undaunted by T. W. Services's opposition, Coniston's offer was repeatedly extended through the expiration dates that are listed here as T. W. Services fought to remain independent.

February 2, 1989
February 9, 1989
February 16, 1989
February 23, 1989
March 9, 1989
March 21, 1989
April 4, 1989
April 18, 1989
May 2, 1989
May 16, 1989

Throughout the nine-month battle, the two companies fought in court about various issues, including the validity of T. W. Service's defenses. However, in spite of the installation of defenses that included a supermajority provision and a shareholder rights plan, in June 1989 Coniston raised its bid to $34. The board of T. W. Services finally approved the higher offer and Coniston took over T. W. Services.

The bidder may extend an undersubscribed tender. In fact, it is not unusual for an offer to be extended several times as the bidder tries to get enough shares to ensure control. If the bidder decides to extend the offer, it must announce the extension no later than 9:00 A.M. on the business day following the day on which the offer was to have expired. At that time the bidder must disclose the number of shares that have already been purchased.

If the stockholder wishes to withdraw shares, he or she must submit a *letter of withdrawal*. Stockholders may want to withdraw to take advantage of a more attractive offer. In this case, the originator of the other competing offer may attempt to facilitate this process by sending stockholders a letter urging them to withdraw and providing them a letter of withdrawal form. This letter of withdrawal must be accompanied by a *signature guarantee*, verifying that the signature is authentic. A formal letter of withdrawal form, however, is not required to withdraw the shares. Although such a form is often used, any slip of

Offer to Purchase for Cash
All Outstanding Shares of Common Stock
(Including the Associated Preferred Stock Purchase Rights)

of

American Cyanamid Company

at

$95.00 Net Per Share

by

AC Acquisition Corp.
a wholly owned subsidiary of

American Home Products Corporation

THE OFFER AND WITHDRAWAL RIGHTS WILL EXPIRE AT 12:00 MIDNIGHT,
NEW YORK CITY TIME, ON WEDNESDAY, SEPTEMBER 7, 1994,
UNLESS THE OFFER IS EXTENDED.

THE OFFER IS CONDITIONED UPON, AMONG OTHER THINGS: (1) THERE BEING
VALIDLY TENDERED AND NOT PROPERLY WITHDRAWN PRIOR TO THE EXPIRATION OF
THE OFFER A NUMBER OF SHARES OF COMMON STOCK OF THE COMPANY WHICH
CONSTITUTES AT LEAST 80% OF THE VOTING POWER (DETERMINED ON A FULLY
DILUTED BASIS), ON THE DATE OF PURCHASE, OF ALL SECURITIES OF THE COMPANY
ENTITLED TO VOTE GENERALLY IN THE ELECTION OF DIRECTORS OR IN A MERGER;
(2) THE COMPANY'S PREFERRED STOCK PURCHASE RIGHTS HAVING BEEN REDEEMED
BY THE COMPANY'S BOARD OF DIRECTORS, OR THE PURCHASER BEING SATISFIED, IN
ITS SOLE DISCRETION, THAT SUCH PREFERRED STOCK PURCHASE RIGHTS HAVE BEEN
INVALIDATED OR ARE OTHERWISE INAPPLICABLE TO THE OFFER AND THE PROPOSED
MERGER DESCRIBED HEREIN; (3) THE PURCHASER BEING SATISFIED, IN ITS SOLE
DISCRETION, THAT THE RESTRICTIONS ON BUSINESS COMBINATIONS CONTAINED IN
SECTION 611-A OF THE MAINE BUSINESS CORPORATION ACT (OR ANY SIMILAR PROVI-
SION) ARE INVALID OR OTHERWISE INAPPLICABLE TO THE PROPOSED MERGER (AS A
RESULT OF ACTION BY THE COMPANY'S BOARD OF DIRECTORS, FINAL JUDICIAL
ACTION OR OTHERWISE); AND (4) THE PURCHASER BEING SATISFIED, IN ITS SOLE
DISCRETION, THAT THE PURCHASER HAS OBTAINED SUFFICIENT FINANCING TO
ENABLE IT TO CONSUMMATE THE OFFER AND THE PROPOSED MERGER DESCRIBED
HEREIN AND TO PAY RELATED FEES AND EXPENSES. THE OFFER IS ALSO SUBJECT TO
OTHER TERMS AND CONDITIONS. SEE THE INTRODUCTION AND SECTIONS 1, 9 AND 14.

(Continued on next page)

The Dealer Manager for the Offer is:

GLEACHER & CO. INC.

August 10, 1994

Figure 3.6. Offer to purchase.

paper is acceptable if it indicates the stockholder's intention to withdraw the shares and is accompanied by the appropriate signature guarantee.

Stockholders, as well as brokers acting on behalf of stockholders, may wait until the last minute before tendering their shares in the hope that a better offer will materialize. As the expiration date approaches, a broker may still take advantage of the offer by submitting a *notice of guaranteed delivery* (Figure 3.8). This guarantees that the broker will send the shares within five New York Stock Exchange business days. Based on this written guarantee, these shares will be included in the offer. The letter of guarantee can be offered only by brokers, not by individuals. An individual, however, can take advantage of this option by asking a broker to submit the guarantee.

LETTER OF TRANSMITTAL
To Tender Shares of Common Stock
(Including the Associated Preferred Share Purchase Rights)
of

Texas Eastern Corporation

Pursuant to the Offer to Purchase dated January 17, 1989
of

Colorado Interstate Corporation
a wholly owned subsidiary of

The Coastal Corporation

THE OFFER AND WITHDRAWAL RIGHTS WILL EXPIRE AT 12:00 MIDNIGHT, NEW YORK
CITY TIME, ON MONDAY, FEBRUARY 13, 1989, UNLESS THE OFFER IS EXTENDED.

The Depositary:
CITIBANK, N.A.

By Courier:
CITIBANK, N.A.
c/o Citicorp Data Distribution, Inc.
404 Sette Drive
Paramus, New Jersey 07653

By Mail:	*Facsimile Copy Number:*	*By Hand:*
CITIBANK, N.A.	(201) 262-7521	CITIBANK, N.A.
c/o Citicorp Data Distribution, Inc.	*Telex Number:*	111 Wall Street
P.O. Box 7072	TWX 7109904964	Mergers & Acquisitions Window
Paramus, New Jersey 07653	CDDI-PARA (answer back)	5th Floor
		New York, New York

To confirm receipt:
(201) 262-4743
(Call collect)

Delivery of this instrument to an address other than as set forth above, or transmission of instructions via a facsimile or telex number other than as set forth above, will not constitute a valid delivery.

This Letter of Transmittal is to be used either if certificates for Shares (as defined below) and/or Rights (as defined below) are to be forwarded herewith or if tender of Shares and/or Rights, if available, is to be made by book-entry transfer to the account maintained by the Depositary at The Depository Trust Company, the Midwest Securities Trust Company or the Philadelphia Depository Trust Company (each a "Book-Entry Transfer Facility") pursuant to the procedures set forth in Section 3 of the Offer to Purchase (as defined below). Stockholders who tender Shares and/or Rights, if available, by book-entry transfer are referred to herein as "Book-Entry Stockholders" and other stockholders are referred to herein as "Certificate Stockholders." Delivery of documents to a Book-Entry Transfer Facility does not constitute delivery to the Depositary. **Unless the Rights are redeemed or the Purchaser (as defined below) determines they are invalid, stockholders are required to tender one Right for each Share tendered to effect a valid tender of Shares.**

Stockholders whose certificates are not immediately available, or who cannot deliver their certificates (or who cannot comply with the book-entry transfer procedures on a timely basis) and all other documents required hereby to the Depositary on or prior to the Expiration Date (as defined in the Offer to Purchase) must tender their Shares and/or Rights according to the guaranteed delivery procedure set forth in Section 3 of the Offer to Purchase. See Instruction 2.

NOTE: SIGNATURES MUST BE PROVIDED BELOW.
PLEASE READ THE ACCOMPANYING INSTRUCTIONS CAREFULLY.

☐ CHECK HERE IF TENDERED SHARES ARE BEING DELIVERED BY BOOK-ENTRY TRANSFER MADE TO THE ACCOUNT MAINTAINED BY THE DEPOSITARY WITH A BOOK-ENTRY TRANSFER FACILITY AND COMPLETE THE FOLLOWING:
Name of Tendering Institution
Check Box of applicable Book-Entry Transfer Facility:
☐ The Depository Trust Company
☐ Midwest Securities Trust Company
☐ Philadelphia Depository Trust Company
Account Number
Transaction Code Number

☐ CHECK HERE IF TENDERED SHARES ARE BEING DELIVERED PURSUANT TO A NOTICE OF GUARANTEED DELIVERY PREVIOUSLY SENT TO THE DEPOSITARY AND COMPLETE THE FOLLOWING:
Name(s) of Registered Holder(s)
Window Ticket Number (if any)
Date of Execution of Notice of Guaranteed Delivery
Name of Institution which guaranteed delivery
If Delivered by Book-Entry Transfer, Check Box of Applicable Book-Entry Transfer Facility:
☐ The Depository Trust Company
☐ Midwest Securities Trust Company
☐ Philadelphia Depository Trust Company
Account Number
Transaction Code Number

Figure 3.7. Letter of transmittal of Texas Eastern Corporation.

Throughout the process, a stockholder can obtain up-to-date information on the offer from the paying agent or through a special information agent. An information agent is usually a proxy firm, which is hired by the bidder as a source of information on the offer.

Changes in the Tender Offer

The Williams Act allows a modification in the offer period if there is a material change in the terms of the offer. The length of the extension in the offer period depends on the significance of the change, which generally is considered a *new offer.* A new offer ensures the

☐ CHECK HERE IF TENDERED RIGHTS ARE BEING DELIVERED BY BOOK-ENTRY TRANSFER MADE TO THE
ACCOUNT MAINTAINED BY THE DEPOSITARY WITH A BOOK-ENTRY TRANSFER FACILITY AND COMPLETE
THE FOLLOWING:

Name of Tendering Institution _____
Check Box of applicable Book-Entry Transfer Facility:
☐ The Depository Trust Company
☐ Midwest Securities Trust Company
☐ Philadelphia Depository Trust Company
Account Number _____
Transaction Code Number _____

☐ CHECK HERE IF TENDERED RIGHTS ARE BEING DELIVERED PURSUANT TO A NOTICE OF GUARANTEED
DELIVERY PREVIOUSLY SENT TO THE DEPOSITARY AND COMPLETE THE FOLLOWING:

Name(s) of Registered Holder(s) _____
Window Ticket Number (if any) _____
Date of Execution of Notice of Guaranteed Delivery _____
Name of Institution which guaranteed delivery _____
If Delivery by Book-Entry Transfer, Check Box of Applicable Book-Entry Transfer Facility:
☐ The Depository Trust Company
☐ Midwest Securities Trust Company
☐ Philadelphia Depository Trust Company
Account Number _____
Transaction Code Number _____

DESCRIPTION OF SHARES TENDERED

Name(s) and Address(es) of Registered Holder(s) (Please fill in, if blank)	Certificate(s) Tendered (Attach additional signed list if necessary)		
	Certificate Number(s)*	Total Number of Shares Evidenced by Certificate(s)*	Number of Shares Tendered**
	Total Shares		

*Need not be completed by Book-Entry Stockholders.
**Unless otherwise indicated, it will be assumed that all Shares evidenced by any certificate(s) delivered to the Depositary are being tendered. See Instruction 4.

DESCRIPTION OF RIGHTS TENDERED*

Name(s) and Address(es) of Registered Holder(s) (Please fill in, if blank)	Certificate(s) Tendered (Attach additional signed list if necessary)		
	Certificate Number(s)**	Total Number of Rights Evidenced by Certificate(s)**	Number of Rights Tendered***
	Total Rights		

*If the tendered Rights are represented by separate certificates, complete using the certificate numbers of such Rights certificates. If the tendered Rights are not represented by separate certificates, or if such certificates have not been distributed, complete using the certificate numbers of the Shares with respect to which the Rights were issued. Stockholders tendering Rights which are not represented by separate certificates should retain a copy of this description in order to accurately complete a supplementing Letter of Transmittal if certificates for Rights are received.
**Need not be completed by Book-Entry Stockholders.
***Unless otherwise indicated, it will be assumed that all Rights evidenced by any certificate(s) delivered to the Depositary are being tendered. See Instruction 4.

The name and address of the registered holders should be printed, if not already printed above, exactly as they appear on the certificates representing Shares and/or Rights tendered hereby. The certificates and the number of Shares and/or Rights that the undersigned wishes to tender should be indicated in the appropriate boxes.

Figure 3.7. Continued

stockholders a 20-day period to consider the offer. A higher price might be considered such a significant change. A less significant change results in an *amended offer,* which provides for a 10-day minimum offer period. An increase in the number of shares to be purchased might be considered an amended offer.

Best Price Rule and Other Related Rules

Under Section 14(d)(7), if the bidder increases the consideration offered, the bidder must pay this increased consideration to all those who have already tendered their shares at the lower price. The goal of this section is to ensure that all tender shareholders are treated equally, regardless of the date within the offer period that they tender their shares. Under SEC Rule 14d-10, a bidder may offer more than one type of consideration. In such cases, however, selling stockholders have the right to select the type of consideration they want.

NOTICE OF GUARANTEED DELIVERY
to
Tender Shares of Common Stock
(Including the Associated Preferred Stock Purchase Rights)
of

American Cyanamid Company

As set forth in Section 3 of the Offer to Purchase described below, this instrument or one substantially equivalent hereto must be used to accept the Offer (as defined below) if certificates for Shares (as defined below) and the associated Preferred Stock Purchase Rights (the "Rights") are not immediately available or the certificates for Shares or Rights and all other required documents cannot be delivered to the Depositary prior to the Expiration Date (as defined in Section 1 of the Offer to Purchase) or if the procedure for delivery by book-entry transfer cannot be completed on a timely basis. This instrument may be delivered by hand or transmitted by facsimile transmission or mail to the Depositary.

The Depositary for the Offer is:
CHEMICAL BANK

By Mail:	*By Facsimile:*	*By Hand or Overnight Delivery:*
Chemical Bank	(for Eligible Institutions only)	Chemical Bank
Reorganization Department	(212) 629-8015	55 Water Street
P.O. Box 3085	(212) 629-8016	Second Floor—Room 234
G.P.O. Station		New York, New York 10041
New York, New York	Confirm by Telephone:	Attention:
10116-3085	(212) 613-7137	Reorganization Department

**DELIVERY OF THIS INSTRUMENT TO AN ADDRESS OTHER THAN AS SET FORTH
ABOVE OR TRANSMISSION OF INSTRUCTIONS VIA FACSIMILE TRANSMISSION
OTHER THAN AS SET FORTH ABOVE WILL NOT CONSTITUTE A VALID DELIVERY.**

This form is not to be used to guarantee signatures. If a signature on a Letter of Transmittal is required to be guaranteed by an Eligible Institution under the instructions thereto, such signature guarantee must appear in the applicable space provided in the signature box in the Letter of Transmittal.

Ladies and Gentlemen:

The undersigned hereby tenders to AC Acquisition Corp., a Delaware corporation and a wholly owned subsidiary of American Home Products Corporation, a Delaware corporation, upon the terms and subject to the conditions set forth in the Offer to Purchase dated August 10, 1994 (the "Offer to Purchase"), and in the related Letter of Transmittal (which together constitute the "Offer"), receipt of which is hereby acknowledged, the number of shares of Common Stock, $5.00 par value per share (the "Shares"), and the number of Rights, indicated below of American Cyanamid Company, a Maine corporation, pursuant to the guaranteed delivery procedure set forth in Section 3 of the Offer to Purchase.

Figure 3.8. Notice of guaranteed delivery to tender shares of the American Cyanamid Company.

Bidder Purchases Outside of Tender Offer

Under Rule 10b-13, a bidder may not purchase shares outside the tender offer on terms that are different from those of the tender offer. There may be exceptions to this rule if the SEC agrees to exempt the transactions based on its belief that the purchases are not manipulative, fraudulent, or deceptive. Such purchases, however, are permitted in the event that the tender offer concludes or is withdrawn.

Exemptions from Tender Offer Rules

Section 14(d)(8) exempts certain tender offers from Section 14(d) of the Williams Act. Among those that are exempt from the tender offer filing requirements are stock purchasers

Signature(s) ....   Address(es) ....

Name(s) of Record Holders   ....
                                                                          Zip Code
....
Please Type or Print   Area Code and Tel. No(s)....................

Number of Shares and Rights ....   (Check one box if Shares and Rights will be ten-
                                      dered by book-entry transfer)
Certificate Nos. (If Available)
                                      ☐ The Depository Trust Company
....
                                      ☐ Midwest Securities Trust Company
....
Dated 1994   ☐ Philadelphia Depository Trust Company

                                      Account Number ....

                                      ....

GUARANTEE
(Not to be used for signature guarantee)

The undersigned, a firm that is a member of a registered national securities exchange or of the National Association of Securities Dealers, Inc. or a commercial bank or trust company having an office, branch or agency in the United States, (a) represents that the above named person(s) "own(s)" the Shares and/or Rights tendered hereby within the meaning of Rule 14e-4 under the Securities Exchange Act of 1934, as amended ("Rule14e-4"), (b) represents that such tender of Shares complies with Rule 14e-4, (c) guarantees to deliver to the Depositary either the certificates evidencing all tendered Shares, in proper form for transfer, or to deliver Shares pursuant to the procedure for book-entry transfer into the Depositary's account at The Depository Trust Company, the Midwest Securities Trust Company or the Philadelphia Depository Trust Company (each a "Book-Entry Transfer Facility"), in either case together with the Letter of Transmittal (or a facsimile thereof), properly completed and duly executed, with any required signature guarantees or an Agent's Message (as defined in the Offer to Purchase) in the case of a book-entry delivery, and any other required documents, all within five New York Stock Exchange, Inc. ("NYSE") trading days after the date hereof and (d) guarantees, if applicable, to deliver certificates representing the Rights ("Rights Certificates") in proper form for transfer, or to deliver such Rights pursuant to the procedure for book-entry transfer into the Depositary's account at a Book-Entry Transfer Facility together with, if Rights are forwarded separately, the Letter of Transmittal (or a facsimile thereof), properly completed and duly executed with any required signature guarantees or an Agent's Message (as defined in the Offer to Purchase) in the case of a book-entry delivery, and any other required documents, all within five NYSE trading days after the date hereof or, if later, five business days after Rights Certificates are distributed to holders of Shares.

....
Name of Firm   Authorized Signature
....   Name ....
Address   Please Type or Print
....   Title ....
                        Zip Code
Area Code and Tel. No. ....   Dated 1994

NOTE: DO NOT SEND CERTIFICATES FOR SHARES OR RIGHTS WITH THIS NOTICE. CERTIFICATES SHOULD BE SENT WITH YOUR LETTER OF TRANSMITTAL.

Figure 3.8.   Continued

who have bought less than 2% of a company's equity within the previous 12 months. Companies that make a tender offer to purchase their own stock are exempt from Section 14(d) but are governed by Section 13(e).

Payment Following Completion of the Offer

The law provides that the tendered shares must be either paid for promptly after the offer is terminated or returned to the shareholders. This prompt payment may be frustrated by other regulatory requirements, such as the Hart-Scott-Rodino Act. The bidder may postpone payment if other regulatory approvals must still be obtained after the Williams Act offer period expires.

Taking Control after a Successful Tender Offer

It is common that after a successful tender offer the target and the bidder agree that the bidder may elect a majority of the board of directors. This would allow the bidder to take control of the board of directors without calling a meeting of the shareholders. However, when antitakeover defenses that limit the ability of an offeror to appoint members to the board are in place, this process may be more difficult. If this is not the case, the board change may go smoothly. If the target agrees to the change in control of the board, it must communicate to the SEC and its shareholders information about the new directors similar to that which would normally be disclosed if they were nominees in an election of directors.

Competing Tender Offers

An initial tender offer often attracts rival tender offers in takeover battles. Because the law was designed to give stockholders time to carefully consider all relevant alternatives, an extension of the offer period is possible when there is a competing offer. The Williams Act states that, in the event of a new tender offer, stockholders in the target company must have at least 10 business days to consider the new offer. In effect, this 10-day consideration period can extend the original offer period. Consider, for example, that we are 16 days into the first offer when a new bidder makes a tender offer for the target firm; then target shareholders have at least 10 days to decide on the original offer. As a result, the original offer period is extended 6 more days, or a total of 26 days. If, on the other hand, the new offer occurred on the fourth day of the first offer period, there would not be an extension of the original offer period.

Williams Act Merger Tactics

Although most securities laws offer protection to stockholders, they often give the participants in a takeover battle opportunities for tactical maneuvering. The *two-tiered tender offer* is a tactical tool sometimes used by the acquiring firm to offset the influence of the Williams Act. In a two-tiered offer, the bidder offers a higher price or better terms for an initial percentage of the target, which might give the bidder control. The second tier tends to receive less advantageous terms.

The two-tiered offer tries to give stockholders an incentive to rush to tender, even though the Williams Act allows them a 20-day waiting period. Recognizing that two-tiered offers would counteract the effectiveness of the Williams Act waiting period, in 1982 the SEC ruled that the proration period for two-tiered tender offers would be 20 days. Therefore, stockholders would be guaranteed participation in the first tier and would not have an incentive to rush their decision. This ruling reduced the popularity of two-tiered tender offers among hostile bidders.

Comparison with Foreign Takeover Rules: Case of Great Britain

The takeover laws of the United States differ considerably from those of other nations. British takeover regulation, for example, is a form of self-regulation by the corporate sector and the securities industry. This regulation is based on the Code of Takeovers and Mergers, a collection of standards and regulations on takeovers and mergers, and is enforced by the Panel on Takeovers and Mergers. This panel is composed of members of the Bank of England, London Stock Exchange members, and various other financial leaders. Its chief responsibility is to make sure that a "level playing field" exists, that is, that all investors have equal access to information on takeover offers. The panel also attempts to prevent target firms from adopting antitakeover measures without prior shareholder approval. Some of the more important provisions of the British code are:

- Investors acquiring 30% or more of a company's shares must bid for the remaining shares at the highest price paid for the shares already acquired.
- Substantial partial offers for a target must gain the approval of the target and the panel.
- Antitakeover measures, such as supermajority provisions or the issuance of options to be given to friendly parties, must be approved by the target's shareholders.

The unique aspect of the British system is that compliance is voluntary; the panel's rulings are not binding by law. Its rulings are considered most influential, however, and are commonly adopted.

Regulation of Proxy Solicitation

State corporation laws require annual shareholder meetings. In order to achieve a quorum, the company solicits proxies from shareholders. Bidders attempting to take over a company may also solicit proxies from shareholders. Section 14(a) of the Securities Exchange Act regulates these solicitations. As part of these regulations, a solicitor must file a proxy statement and a Schedule 14A, which must also be given to security holders. According to Rule 14a-6, proxy materials must be filed with the Securities Exchange Commission 10 days before they are used. An exception exists for more noncontroversial events such as annual meetings. However, in no case must the materials be submitted prior to their being used.

In light of the substantial mailing costs that security holders who have their own proposals may incur, the law requires the issuer to include a supporting statement (up to 500 words) which is included with management proxy proposals. Only a very small percentage of such security holder solicitations are successful.

BUSINESS JUDGMENT RULE

The *business judgment rule* is the standard by which directors of corporations are judged when they exercise their fiduciary duties in the course of an attempted takeover. Under this standard it is presumed that directors acted in a manner that is consistent with their fiduciary obligations to shareholders. Thus, any party contesting this presumption must conclusively demonstrate that their fiduciary duties were violated. Specific court decisions have highlighted certain relevant issues regarding how directors must act when employing antitakeover defenses. Through these decisions, standards such as the *Revlon duties* and the *Unocal standard* have been developed.

Unocal Standard

In *Unocal v. Mesa Petroleum,* the Delaware Supreme Court reviewed the actions of the Unocal board of directors as they implemented an antitakeover strategy to thwart the unwanted tender offer by Mesa Petroleum, led by its colorful chief executive officer, T. Boone Pickens.[10] This strategy included a self-tender offer in which the target made a tender offer for itself in competition with the offer initiated by the bidder. In reaching its decision, the court noted its concern that directors may act in their own self-interest, such as in this case, in which they were allegedly favoring the self-tender as opposed to simply objectively searching for the best deal for shareholders. In such instances directors must demonstrate that they had reason to believe that there was a danger to the pursuit of a corporate policy that was in the best interest of shareholders. In addition, they must show that their actions were in the best interest of shareholders. Subsequent courts have refined the Unocal Standard to feature a two-part responsibility that includes the following:

- *Reasonableness test.* The board must be able to clearly demonstrate that their actions were reasonable in relation to their perceived beliefs about the danger to their corporate policies.
- *Proportionality test.* The board must also be able to demonstrate that their defensive actions were in proportion to the magnitude of the perceived danger to their policies.[11]

Once these Unocal standards are satisfied, the normal presumptions about director behavior under the business judgment rule apply.

Revlon Duties

In *Revlon, Inc. v. MacAndrews and Forbes Holdings,* the Delaware Supreme Court ruled on what obligations a target board of directors has when faced with an offer for control of their company.[12] In this transaction, which is discussed further in Chapter 5 in the context of lockup options, the court ruled that certain antitakeover defenses that favored one bidder over another were invalid. The court determined that rather than promoting the auction process, which should result in maximizing shareholder wealth, these antitakeover defenses, a lockup option and a no-shop provision, inhibited rather than promoted the auction process.

---

10. *Unocal Corp. v. Mesa Petroleum Co.,* 493 A.2d 946 (Del. 1985).
11. *Moore Corp. v. Wallace Computer Services,* 907 F. Supp. 1545, 1556 (D. Del. 1995).
12. *Revlon, Inc. v. MacAndrews & Forbes Holdings, Inc.,* 506 A.2d 173, CCH Fed. Sec. L. Rep. ¶ 92,348 (Del. 1986).

Revlon duties come into play when it is clear that the sale or breakup of the company is inevitable. At that time, directors have a responsibility to maximize the gains for their shareholders. That is, they have a responsibility to shift their focus away from actions that they normally would take to preserve the corporation and its strategy to actions that will result in the greatest gains for shareholders, such as making sure they get the highest bid possible for shareholders.

In reaching its decision rendering the lockup options and no-shop provisions invalid, the court did not go so far as to say that the use of the defenses was invalid *per se*. The use of defenses that might favor one bidder over another could be consistent with the board's Revlon duties if they promoted the auction process by enabling one bidder to be more competitive with another bidder, thereby causing offer prices to rise. On the other hand, defenses that hinder the auction process are not valid.

Time-Warner–Paramount

In March 1989 Time, Inc. entered into a merger agreement with Warner Communications, Inc. The deal was a planned stock-for-stock exchange that would be put before the shareholders of both companies for their approval. Paramount Communications, Inc. then entered the fray with a hostile tender offer for Time. This offer was structured by Paramount to be higher than the valuation that was inherent to the original Time-Warner agreement. Time then responded with a tender offer for Warner that featured a cash offer for 51% of Warner followed by a second-step transaction using securities as consideration.

Paramount sued and contended that the original merger agreement between Time and Warner meant that there was an impending change in control, thereby bringing the Revlon duties of the directors into play. In *Paramount Communications, Inc. v. Time, Inc.,* the court rejected Paramount's argument that there would be a change in control.[13] The court was impressed by the fact that both companies were public and their shares were widely held. Based on such reasoning, the court concluded that this was not an acquisition in which one company was acquiring another but rather a strategic merger. Therefore, Revlon duties were not triggered, and the normal business judgment rule standard applied.

The significance of this decision is that the announcement of a strategic merger between two companies is not a signal that either of the companies is for sale. Therefore, the directors do not have to consider other offers as if there were an auction process. This implies that if there is an unwanted bid, the directors may consider the use of antitakeover measures to avoid the hostile bid while they go ahead with the strategic merger.

ANTITRUST LAWS

The ability to merge with or acquire other firms is limited by antitrust legislation. Various antitrust laws are designed to prevent firms from reducing competition through mergers. Many mergers are never attempted, simply because of the likelihood of governmental intervention on antitrust grounds. Other mergers are halted when it becomes apparent that the government will likely oppose the merger.

13. *Paramount Communications, Inc. v. Time, Inc.,* 571 A.2d 1140 (Del. 1989).

The government has changed its stance on the antitrust ramifications of mergers several times since 1890. As noted previously, in recent years the government's attitude has been evolving toward a freer market view, which favors a more limited government role in the marketplace. Although many horizontal mergers were opposed during the 1980s, many others proceeded unopposed. This is in sharp contrast to the government's earlier position in the 1960s. During that period, mergers and acquisitions involving businesses only remotely similar to the acquiring firm's business were often opposed on antitrust grounds. This situation encouraged large numbers of conglomerate mergers, which generally were not opposed.

Sherman Antitrust Act

The Sherman Antitrust Act, which was originally passed in 1890, is the cornerstone of all U.S. antitrust laws. The first two sections of the law contain its most important provisions:

Section 1: This section prohibits all contracts, combinations, and conspiracies in restraint of trade.

Section 2: This section prohibits any attempts or conspiracies to monopolize a particular industry.

The Sherman Act made the formation of monopolies and other attempts to restrain trade unlawful and criminal offenses punishable under federal law. The government or the injured party can file suit under this law, and the court can then decide the appropriate punishment, which may range from an injunction to more severe penalties, including triple damages and imprisonment.

The first two sections of the Sherman Act make it immediately clear that it is written broadly enough to cover almost all types of anticompetitive activities. Surprisingly, however, the first great merger wave took place following the passage of the law. This first merger wave, which took place between 1897 and 1904, was characterized by the formation of monopolies. The resulting increased concentration in many industries, combined with the formation of many powerful monopolies, revealed that the act was not performing the functions its first two sections implied.

The apparent ineffectiveness of the Sherman Act was partly due to the law's wording. Specifically, it stated that all contracts that restrained trade were illegal. In its early interpretations, however, the court reasonably refused to enforce this part of the law on the basis that this implies that almost all contracts could be considered illegal. The court had difficulty finding an effective substitute. Court rulings such as the 1895 Supreme Court ruling that the American Sugar Refining Company was not a monopoly in restraint of trade made the law a dead letter for more than a decade after its passage. The lack of government resources also made it difficult for the government to enforce the law. The law started to have more impact on the business community under the pressure of trustbusting President Theodore Roosevelt and his successor, William Howard Taft. In an effort to correct the deficiencies associated with the wording of the law and the lack of an enforcement agency, the government decided to make a more explicit statement of its antitrust position. This effort came with the passage of the Clayton Act.

Clayton Act

The goal of the Clayton Act was to strengthen the Sherman Act while also specifically proscribing certain business practices. Some of its more prominent provisions are:

Section 2: Price discrimination among customers was prohibited except when it could be justified by cost economies.

Section 3: Tying contracts were prohibited. An example of a tying contract would be if a firm refused to sell certain essential products to a customer unless that customer bought other products from the seller.

Section 7: The acquisition of stock in competing corporations was prohibited if the effect was to lessen competition.

Section 8: Interlocking directorates were prohibited when the directors were on the boards of competing firms.

The Clayton Act did not prohibit any activities that were not already illegal under a broad interpretation of the Sherman Act. The Clayton Act, however, clarified which business practices unfairly restrain trade and reduce competition. The bill did not address the problem of the lack of an enforcement agency charged with the specific responsibility for enforcing the antitrust laws. With the passage of the Federal Trade Commission Act in 1914, the FTC was established to address this problem. The FTC was charged specifically with enforcing antitrust laws, such as the Clayton Act and the Federal Trade Commission Act. The FTC was also given the power to issue cease and desist orders to firms engaging in unfair trade practices.

Section 7 is particularly relevant to mergers and acquisitions: "No corporation shall *acquire* the whole or any part of the stock, or the whole or any part of the assets, of another corporation where in any *line of commerce* in any *section of the country* the effect of such an acquisition may be to substantially lessen competition or tend to create a *monopoly.*" This section reflects four main aspects of the Clayton Act.

1. *Acquisition.* Originally the Clayton Act prohibited only the acquisition of stock in a corporation if the effect was to lessen competition. However, the marketplace quickly exposed a loophole in the wording of the section. The loophole involved the acquisition of the assets of a target company. This was later amended, with the law covering both stock and asset acquisitions.

2. *Line of commerce.* Through the use of the term *line of commerce,* the act adopted a broader focus than just a particular industry. This broader focus allows antitrust agencies to consider the competitive effects of a full range of a firm's business activities.

3. *Section of the country.* The act can be applied on a regional rather than a national basis. Through this provision, the antitrust authorities can look at regional market shares rather than national market shares. Therefore, a firm that dominated a regional market and enjoyed a monopoly in that section of the country could be found in violation of this law. The antitrust authorities often require the violating firm to divest the operations in the affected region in order to diminish their market power in that area.

4. *Tendency to lessen competition.* The wording of this part of Section 7 is quite vague. It states that a firm may lessen competition or tend to create a monopoly. This vague

wording is intentionally designed to take into account the possibility that the effect on competition may not be immediate. This wording gives the antitrust authorities the power to act if there is only a reasonable probability that competition will be lessened. This almost assumes that if a firm has the power to limit competition, it will do so. Therefore, the law seeks to prevent these activities before they occur. This view of business behavior changed considerably over the past two decades.

Federal Trade Commission Act of 1914

One weakness of the Sherman Act was that it did not give the government an effective enforcement agency to investigate and pursue antitrust violations. At that time the Justice Department did not possess the resources to be an effective antitrust deterrent. In an effort to address this problem, the Federal Trade Commission Act, which was passed in 1914, established the FTC. The FTC was charged with enforcing both the Federal Trade Commission Act and the Clayton Act. In particular, it was passed with the intention of creating an enforcement arm for the Clayton Act. The main antitrust provision of the Act is Section 5, which prohibits unfair methods of competition. Although the FTC was given the power to initiate antitrust lawsuits, it was not given a role in the criminal enforcement of antitrust violations. The act also broadened the range of illegal business activities beyond those mentioned in the Clayton Act.

Celler-Kefauver Act of 1950

Section 7 of the Clayton Act was written broadly enough to give the antitrust authorities wide latitude in defining an antitrust violation. However, through a loophole in the Clayton Act, corporations were engaging in acquisitions even when these acquisitions represented a clear lessening of competition.

As noted, the Clayton Act was originally worded to prohibit the acquisition of another corporation's stock when the effect was to lessen competition. Historically, corporations and raiders have continually found loopholes in the law. Many firms were able to complete acquisitions by purchasing a target firm's assets rather than its stock. Under the original wording of the Clayton Act, this would not be a violation of the law. This loophole was eliminated by the passage of the Celler-Kefauver Act of 1950, which prohibited the acquisition of assets of a target firm when the effect was to lessen competition. The Celler-Kefauver Act also prohibited vertical mergers and conglomerate mergers when they were shown to reduce competition. The previous antitrust laws were aimed at horizontal mergers, which are combinations of firms producing the same product. The Celler-Kefauver Act set the stage for the aggressive antitrust enforcement of the 1960s.

Hart-Scott-Rodino Antitrust Improvements Act of 1976

The Hart-Scott-Rodino Act requires that the FTC and the Justice Department be given the opportunity to review proposed mergers and acquisitions in advance. According to the act, an acquisition or merger may not be consummated until these authorities have reviewed the transaction. These two agencies must decide which of the two will investigate the particular transaction.

The law prevents consumption of a merger until the end of the specified waiting periods. Therefore, failure to file in a timely manner may delay completion of the transaction.

The Hart-Scott-Rodino Act was passed to prevent the consummation of transactions that would ultimately be judged to be anticompetitive. Thus, the Justice Department would be able to avoid disassembling a company that had been formed in part through an anticompetitive merger or acquisition. The law became necessary because of the government's inability to halt transactions through the granting of injunctive relief while it attempted to rule on the competitive effects of the business combination. When injunctive relief was not obtainable, mandated divestiture, designed to restore competition, might not take place for many years after the original acquisition or merger. The Hart-Scott-Rodino Act was written to prevent these problems before they occurred.

Filing Requirements

Both companies are required to file if both of the following tests are met:

1. One company has $100 million or more in total assets or annual net sales and the other company has $10 million or more in assets or annual sales; and
2. The transaction is an offer for $15 million of stock or assets or when it is an offer for more than 50% of a company that has sales or total assets equal to or greater than $15 million. The $15 million filing threshold effectively makes it very difficult to secretly accumulate shares in advance of a bid. In addition, a series of share purchases, such as in *creeping stock acquisitions,* are considered one transaction under this law.

Who Must File

The original wording of the Hart-Scott-Rodino Act is somewhat vague, leading some people to believe that it did not apply to certain business entities, such as partnerships. The act requires that persons or corporations file if they meet the firm and purchase size criteria previously described.

Type of Information to Be Filed

The law requires the filing of a 16–page form. (See Figure 3.9, which shows page 1 of that form.) Business data describing the business activities and revenues of the acquiring and the target firms' operations must be provided according to Standard Industrial Classification (SIC) codes. Most firms already have this information because it must be submitted to the U.S. Bureau of the Census. In addition, when filing, the acquiring firm must attach certain reports it may have compiled to analyze the competitive effects of this transaction. This presents an interesting conflict. When a transaction is first being proposed within the acquiring firm, its proponents may tend to exaggerate its benefits. If this exaggeration comes in the form of presenting a higher market share than what might be more realistic, the firm's ability to attain antitrust approval may be hindered. For this reason, when the firm is preparing its premerger reports, it must keep the antitrust approval in mind.

The Antitrust Premerger Review Time Periods

The time periods for review vary, depending on whether the offer is an all-cash offer or includes securities in the compensation package.

16 C.F.R. Part 803 · Appendix	Approved by OMB 3084-0005 Expires 9-30-88

NOTIFICATION AND REPORT FORM FOR CERTAIN MERGERS AND ACQUISITIONS

THE INFORMATION REQUIRED TO BE SUPPLIED ON THESE ANSWER SHEETS IS SPECIFIED IN THE INSTRUCTIONS

FOR OFFICE USE ONLY
TRANSACTION NUMBER

➡ Attach the Affidavit required by § 803.5 to this page.

Is this Acquisition a CASH TENDER OFFER?   ☐ YES   ☐ NO   ☐ CTO   ☐ ETR

Do you request Early Termination of the Waiting Period?   ☐ YES   ☐ NO
(Grants of early termination are published in the Federal Register.)

ITEM 1

(a) NAME AND HEADQUARTERS ADDRESS OF PERSON FILING NOTIFICATION *(ultimate parent entity)*

(b) PERSON FILING NOTIFICATION IS

☐ an acquiring person   ☐ an acquired person   ☐ both

(c) LIST NAMES OF ULTIMATE PARENT ENTITIES OF ALL ACQUIRING PERSONS	LIST NAMES OF ULTIMATE PARENT ENTITIES OF ALL ACQUIRED PERSONS

(d) THIS ACQUISITION IS *(put an X in all the boxes that apply)*

☐ an acquisition of assets
☐ a merger (see § 801.2)
☐ an acquisition subject to § 801.2(e)
☐ formation of a joint venture or other corporation (see § 801.40)
☐ an acquisition subject to § 801.30 *(specify type)*: _____
☐ other *(specify)* _____

☐ a consolidation (see § 801.2)
☐ an acquisition of voting securities
☐ a secondary acquisition
☐ an acquisition subject to § 801.31

(e) INDICATE HIGHEST NOTIFICATION THRESHOLD IN § 801.1(h) FOR WHICH THIS FORM IS BEING FILED *(acquiring person only)*

☐ $15 million   ☐ 15%   ☐ 25%   ☐ 50%

(f) VALUE OF VOTING SECURITIES	VALUE OF ASSETS

(g) PUT AN X IN THE APPROPRIATE BOX TO DESCRIBE ENTITY FILING NOTIFICATION

☐ corporation   ☐ partnership   ☐ other *(specify)* _____

(h) DATA FURNISHED BY

☐ calendar year   ☐ fiscal year *(specify period)*: _____ *(mon/day)* to _____ *(mon/day)*

(i) PUT AN X IN THE APPROPRIATE BOX AND GIVE THE NAME AND ADDRESS OF THE ENTITY FILING NOTIFICATION *(if other than ultimate parent entity)*

☐ NA   ☐ This report is being filed on behalf of a foreign person pursuant to § 803.4.   ☐ This report is being filed on behalf of the ultimate parent entity by another entity within the same person authorized by it to file pursuant to § 803.2(a).

NAME OF ENTITY FILING NOTIFICATION	ADDRESS

THIS FORM IS REQUIRED BY LAW and must be filed separately by each person which, by reason of a merger, consolidation or acquisition, is subject to § 7A of the Clayton Act, 15 U.S.C. § 18a, as added by Section 201 of the Hart-Scott-Rodino Antitrust Improvements Act of 1976, Pub. L. No. 94-435, 90 Stat. 1390, and rules promulgated thereunder (hereinafter referred to as "the rules" or by section number). The statute and rules are set forth in the Federal Register at 43 FR 33450; the rules may also be found at 16 CFR Parts 801-03. Failure to file this Notification and Report Form, and to observe the required waiting period before consummating the acquisition, in accordance with the applicable provisions of 15 U.S.C. § 18a and the rules, subjects any "person," as defined in the rules, or any individuals responsible for noncompliance, to liability for a penalty of not more than $10,000 for each day during which such person is in violation of 15 U.S.C. § 18a.

All information and documentary material filed in or with this Form is confidential. It is exempt from disclosure under the Freedom of Information Act, and may be made public only in an administrative or judicial proceeding, or disclosed to Congress or to a duly authorized committee or subcommittee of Congress.

Complete and return two notarized copies (with one set of documentary attachments) of this Notification and Report Form to Premerger Notification Office, Bureau of Competition, Room 303, Federal Trade Commission, Washington, D.C. 20580, and three notarized copies (with one set of documentary attachments) to Director of Operations, Antitrust Division, Room 3218, Department of Justice, Washington, D.C. 20530. The central office for information and assistance with respect to matters in connection with this Notification and Report Form is Room 303, Federal Trade Commission, Washington, D.C. 20580, phone (202) 326-3100.

FTC Form C 4 (rev 3/87)   1

Figure 3.9. Page one of the Hart-Scott-Rodino Antitrust Improvements Act form.

All-Cash Offers

In an all-cash offer, the regulatory authorities have 15 days in which to review the filing. However, the agency may decide that it needs additional information before it can make a judgment on the antitrust ramifications of the merger or acquisition. It may therefore take another 10 days before it decides whether to challenge a transaction. The request for additional information usually indicates that the deal will not receive antitrust approval. In all-cash offers, the waiting period begins when the acquirer files the required forms.

Securities Offers

In offers that include securities in the compensation package, the initial review period is 30 days. If the regulatory authorities request additional information, they may take an additional 20 days to complete the review. For offers that are not all-cash offers, the waiting period starts when both firms have filed the necessary forms. A bidding firm may request an early termination of the waiting period if it believes that the transaction does not create any antitrust conflicts. Early terminations have been much more common in recent years. An early termination, however, is totally up to the discretion of the regulatory agencies.

The waiting period is designed to provide the antitrust agency with an opportunity to identify those transactions that might reduce competition. The reasoning is that it is far easier to prevent a deal from occurring than to disassemble a combined firm after the merger has been completed. If the antitrust agencies determine that there is an antitrust problem, they normally file suit to prevent the merger. Target firms may use the waiting period as a defensive tactic. Targets of hostile bids may be purposefully slow to report the required information. Firms that receive favorable friendly bids, however, may choose to expedite the selling process by responding quickly.

Impact of Notice of Government Opposition

If the Justice Department files suit to block a proposed acquisition, that usually is the end of the deal. Even if the bidder and the target believe that they might ultimately prevail in the lawsuit, it may not be in either company's interest to become embroiled in a protracted legal battle with the government that may last years. Such was the case in 1995 when Microsoft dropped its bid for financial software maker Intuit. This deal would have been the largest software acquisition in history, with Intuit's equity being valued in the range of $2.3 billion. A bidder may perceive that a strategic acquisition may provide synergistic benefits within a certain window of opportunity. However, if an indefinite delay is imposed before the companies can take action to realize these benefits, they typically will terminate the deal rather than risk incurring the significant acquisition costs with a more uncertain prospect of ever reaping these benefits. In the time it would take for the lawsuit to run its course, the competitive environment could change significantly, closing the window of opportunity. Sometimes the bidder may be able to convince the Justice Department to agree to take steps to speed up the trial, but even a more "speedy" trial may take many months to complete. In the case of the computer industry, for example, even six months can erase competitive opportunities.

Deadlines for Filing
A bidder must file under the Hart-Scott-Rodino Act as soon as it announces a tender offer or any other offer. The target is then required to respond. This response comes in the form of the target's filing, which must take place 15 days after the bidder has filed.

Federal Trade Commission Rules
The Federal Trade Commission has set forth various rules that refine the Hart-Scott-Rodino Act. These rules address the aforementioned creeping acquisition case. They also eliminate the need for repeated filings for each share acquisition beyond the original one that may have required a filing. These rules indicate that a purchaser does not have to file for additional purchases if during a five year period after the expiration of the original filing requirement period the total share purchases did not reach 25% of the outstanding

shares of the issuer. If there are continued purchases after the 25% level which had required an additional filing, the purchaser does not have to file again until the 50% threshold is reached.

Exemptions to the Hart-Scott-Rodino Act

Certain acquisitions supervised by governmental agencies, as well as certain foreign acquisitions, are exempt from the requirements of the Hart-Scott-Rodino Act. The *investment exception* is one that tends to attract much attention in tender offers because it is in many ways a gray area.

The investment exception. The investment exception applies to the filing requirement associated with the purchase of $15 million worth of voting securities. It permits an individual to acquire up to 10% of an issuer's voting securities as long as the acquisition is "solely for the purposes of investment."[14] The investment exception is designed to exempt those buyers of securities who are passive investors and have no interest in control. It allows investors to buy a large dollar amount of voting securities in a particular company without having to adhere to the Hart-Scott-Rodino filing requirement.

Tender offers have been a source of problems for the enforcement authorities. Clearly, certain tender offers are designed to take control of a target corporation. However, the investment exception may cover the initial purchases of stock. If the purchasing company does not file, relying on the applicability of the investment exception, its motives may subsequently be questioned if it later initiates a tender offer for a controlling share holding. In cases in which the stock has been accumulated over an extended time period, the regulatory authorities may find it difficult to prove that the initial purchases were part of an overall plan to take control of the target.

The classic challenge to the investment exception was the unsuccessful takeover attempt of Houston Natural Gas by the Coastal Corporation. Before its takeover attempt, Coastal held $15 million worth of shares in Houston Natural Gas. On January 19, 1984, Coastal bought 75,500 shares of Houston Natural Gas but did not file under the Hart-Scott-Rodino Act. Coastal relied on the applicability investment exception. On January 27, 1984, Coastal announced a tender offer for Houston Natural Gas. The Department of Justice sued Coastal, contending that it had purposefully evaded the requirements of the Hart-Scott-Rodino Act, which it believed were binding in this case. Coastal agreed to a settlement and paid a fine equal to $230,000, which was based on a maximum fine of $10,000 per day for each day between January 19 and February 11, when it eventually did file.

The convertible securities exception. Securities that are convertible into voting securities are exempt from the filing requirements of the Hart-Scott-Rodino Act, as are options and warrants. Before these securities are converted, or before these options and warrants are exercised, the holders must file under the Hart-Scott-Rodino Act.

Raiders may try to evade the filing requirements of the Hart-Scott-Rodino Act by purchasing *call options.* A call option gives the holder the right to purchase a particular security at a particular price during a certain period of time. For this right the purchaser pays the issuer, who usually is a securities firm, a fee called the *option's premium.* Under the

---

14. Ralph Ferrara, Meredith Brown, and John Hall, *Takeovers: Attack and Survival* (Stoneham, Mass.: Butterworth Legal Publishers, 1987), p. 151.

convertible securities exemption of the Hart-Scott-Rodino Act, a raider could postpone announcing his or her intentions by purchasing options. The raider could then exercise the option at an advantageous time. Although the wording of the law may seem to allow this loophole, such purchases of options have been challenged. These challenges have come as a surprise to those raiders who believed they were relying on the explicit wording of the law.

The government's position on this issue was evident in the government lawsuit against Donald Trump. Donald Trump purchased call options for the stock of the Holiday Corporation and the Bally Manufacturing Corporation in August 1986. The government later filed a civil suit charging that Trump was in violation of the Hart-Scott-Rodino Act. The government contended that, before purchasing the call options, Trump should have filed a notification with the FTC. Trump settled the suit in April 1988 without admitting any wrongdoing. He agreed to pay a $750,000 fine in return for the FTC dropping the legal action.

Purchases by brokerage firms. The takeover market provides great financial rewards for its participants who are able to buy the stock of targets before the market is aware that the firm is a takeover target. This provides a strong incentive to find ways around the laws and regulations that govern mergers and acquisitions. One approach that acquiring firms and raiders have taken to avoid compliance with the Hart-Scott-Rodino Act is through stock purchases by brokerage firms. Ostensibly, these purchases will not be in the name of the acquiring firm, which has not openly declared its intentions to acquire the target. At a predetermined time, the acquiring firm will announce its intentions, and shares in the target will be transferred from the name of the brokerage firm to that of the acquiring firm.

This type of evasive maneuver occurred in March 1986 when the First City Financial Corporation had its broker, Bear Stearns and Company, acquire stock in Ashland Oil. The Justice Department and the FTC alleged that First City had Bear Stearns buy the stock while providing First City with the option of subsequently transferring the stock to First City's account. Ultimately, First City agreed to pay a fine of $400,000 without admitting any wrongdoing. Through this action, the Justice Department and the FTC put all potential bidders on notice that the use of brokerage firms to avoid the disclosure requirements of the Hart-Scott-Rodino Act would not be tolerated.

Tender Offers and the Hart-Scott-Rodino Act

It is important to note that the Hart-Scott-Rodino Act adds another layer of regulation to tender offer rules. That is, in addition to the limitations imposed on bidders by the Williams Act, tender offers may not be completed until the antitrust regulatory authorities have provided their approval.

Antitrust Approval of International Mergers

For mergers of companies that do a substantial business outside the United States, the merger partners must address international antitrust guidelines as well as domestic ones. This was underscored when Ernst & Young and KPMG announced in February 1998 to abandon their plans to merge because of the fact that the European antitrust authorities had begun an investigation of the anticompetitive ramifications of the deal. The announcement of this investigation followed the European commission's efforts in 1997 to block the Boeing and McDonnell Douglas merger until they obtained certain concessions from Boeing. Both Ernst & Young and KPMG are global companies with offices in most major countries. The European commission's investigation was followed by notices from the antitrust authorities of Australia and Canada that they also were starting investigations of the antitrust ramifications of the proposed merger. Such investigations may be time-consuming, with the final result and date of the decision uncertain. This may to some extent leave the merger partners suspended in an "antitrust limbo," unable to pursue their planned merger strategy but also unable to follow an alternative one. Such delays and uncertainties may cause companies to abandon their merger plans.

Enforcement of Antitrust Laws: Justice Department and the Federal Trade Commission Interaction

Both the Justice Department and the FTC share the responsibility for enforcing U.S. antitrust laws. When the Justice Department brings a suit, it is heard in federal court, whereas when the FTC initiates an action, it is heard before an administrative law judge at the FTC and the decision is reviewed by the commissioners of the FTC. If a defendant wants to appeal an FTC decision, it may bring an action in federal court. Both the Justice Department and the FTC may take steps to halt objectionable behavior by firms. The Justice Department may try to get an injunction, whereas the FTC may issue a cease and desist order. Criminal actions are reserved for the Justice Department, which may seek fines or even imprisonment for the violators as well as the costs of bringing the action. Readers should not infer that the government are the sole parties who may bring an antitrust action. Individuals and companies may also initiate such actions. Indeed, it is ironic that such private actions constitute a significant percentage of the total antitrust proceedings in the United States.[15]

Companies often fear the long delays associated with the FTC antitrust merger challenges. For example, in October 1990 the FTC challenged the $537 million acquisition of Meredith/Burda Co. by R. R. Donnelly but an administrative law judge did not issue a decision until January 1994. However, it was not until August 1995 that R. R. Donnelly was able to have the antitrust charges dismissed through an appeal. In an effort to rectify the delays associated with its actions, the FTC recently announced new rules that offer companies a "fast track" process they could opt for in which they could have a decision within 13 months. It is important to note that although we have devoted much attention to antitrust enforcement actions, the majority of deals do not incite enforcement actions. For example, during the period from 1993 to 1996 period, enforcement actions occurred in only 0.4% of all the transactions filed under the Hart-Scott-Rodino Act.[16]

---

15. Lawrence White, *Private Antitrust Litigation: New Evidence, New Learning* (Cambridge, Mass: MIT Press), 1989.

16. Malcolm B. Coate, "Merger Enforcement at the Federal Trade Commission," unpublished working paper, January, 1998, p.4.

CHANGING PATTERNS OF ANTITRUST ENFORCEMENT
IN THE UNITED STATES

The courts have adopted varying positions on antitrust enforcement throughout the twentieth century. These positions are reflected in the various court decisions that have established legal precedents on which the courts subsequently have relied. In 1911 two major decisions, one against Standard Oil of New Jersey[17] and the other against the American Tobacco Company,[18] found that these two companies had monopolized their respective markets. In both cases the court concluded that each company had engaged in certain improper activities to attain a monopoly position in their respective markets. The court then ruled that each of these giant companies must be split into smaller components in an effort to institute competition in these markets.

In 1920, however, the Court reversed direction by applying the *Rule of Reason* in the *U.S. v. Steel Corporation et al.* decision.[19] Here, even though the Court found that U.S. Steel's chairman, Judge E. H. Gary, had colluded with rival steel producers to establish prices and limit competition, these actions were not anticompetitive. In applying the Rule of Reason, however, the Court found that U.S. Steel did not use its dominant position, which featured a market share that was once as high as 65%, to unduly restrain competition. Surprisingly, the Court even seemed to find benefits in the price-fixing because it saw this otherwise anticompetitive behavior as leading to a more orderly market. In reaching its decision, the Court concluded that size alone was not anticompetitive and that U.S. Steel did not use its sizable market share to limit competition.

The posture of the Court again shifted in the opposite direction in 1945, when the Court ruled against the Aluminum Company of America.[20] In his now-famous ruling, Judge Learned Hand found that Alcoa had built up its bauxite reserves with the intent of monopolizing the aluminum industry. The Court's solution required that Alcoa sell some of its facilities to Reynolds Metals and Kaiser Aluminum and not build any new plants for a period of time.

The decision in the Alcoa case contrasts with the Supreme Court's position in the U.S. Steel case. The Alcoa decision implied that an industry could be judged by its structure. Given the fact that Alcoa had amassed such large bauxite reserves, it had achieved a monopoly position. Under the *structure argument,* such a firm is guilty of monopolization based on the implication that a monopolistic structure will cause a firm to behave like a monopolist. The *behavior argument* is consistent with the U.S. Steel decision. Under this view, an industry may have a monopolistic structure without exhibiting the negative characteristics normally associated with monopoly. For example, a firm may have a large market share but does not use its size and the benefits that derive from size, such as the ability to buy on favorable terms, to drive out smaller competitors.

The Alcoa lawsuit was followed by another major case, the 1946 *U.S. v. New York Great Atlantic and Pacific Tea et al.* decision.[21] In this decision the Court found A&P manage-

---

17. *U.S. v. Standard Oil of New Jersey et al.,* 221 U.S. 1, 76 (1911).

18. *U.S. v. American Tobacco Company,* 221 U.S. 106 (1911).

19. *U.S. v. U.S. Steel Corporation et al.,* 223 F. 55 (1915), 251 U.S. 417 (1920).

20. *U.S. v. Aluminum Company of America et al.,* 148 F. 2d 416, 424 (1945).

21. *U.S. v. New York Great Atlantic and Pacific Tea Company et al.,* 67 F. Supp. 626 (1946), 173 F. 2d (1949).

ment guilty of anticompetitive behavior. Based on these two strict antitrust decisions, along with the passage of the Celler-Kefauver Act of 1950, many companies were reluctant to fight the Justice Department to a decision. Several companies entered into consent decrees in which they basically capitulated to the pressure of an aggressive Justice Department. The 1950s and 1960s featured the most intense antitrust enforcement of any similar period in U.S. history (Figure 3.10).

Significant cases of this period include the 1955 challenge to the acquisition of G. R. Kinney, the eighth largest shoe company in the United States, by Brown Shoe, which was the third largest company. The Court was concerned about the vertical aspects of this merger between a shoe manufacturer, Brown Shoe, and a company that had numerous retail outlets—G. R. Kinney. The fact that the combined companies would only account for 2% of the total national retail capacity was not enough to offset the Court's concerns about the combined firm's retail outlets selling its own shoes at lower prices than those of competitors.

As extreme as this ruling might seem by today's standards, it was easily topped by the government's challenge to the 1966 proposed merger between two Los Angeles supermarket chains. Even though Vons Grocery Co. and Shopping Bag Food's proposed deal would result in a combined city market share of 7.5%, the court was more concerned about the

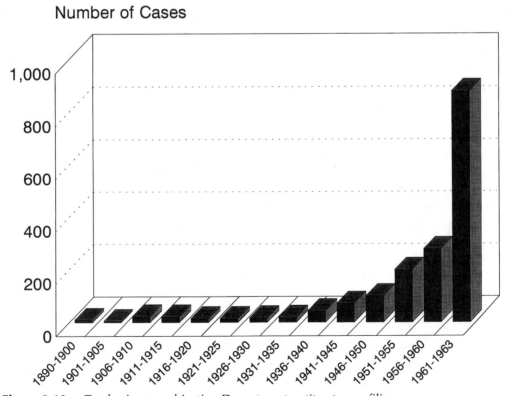

Figure 3.10.   Total private and Justice Department antitrust case filings.

Source: Richard A. Posner, "A Statistical Study of the Antitrust Enforcement," in *The Causes and Contingencies of Antitrust,* edited by Fred S. McChesney and William F. Shugart II (Chicago and London: The University of Chicago Press, 1970).

potential adverse impact on the thousands of small grocery stores in that market. It is ironic that even the man who argued the case for the government, Richard Posner, concedes that "today it looks like a ridiculous case." He goes on to say, "That was the view that monopoly problems were pervasive—a kind of general hostility or skepticism about business."[22]

With the personnel changes that took place in the Justice Department in the 1970s, along with the changing composition of the Supreme Court, a more pro-business atmosphere took hold in the world of antitrust enforcement. This resulted in a more lenient stance toward mergers and their antitrust ramifications. The enforcers also came to recognize that markets may be better able to deal with competitors than the government. This was underscored when the government dropped its decade-long case against IBM when competitors were making their own inroads against the once-dominant computer giant. This posture seemed to hold until the 1990s, when signs of a stiffer antitrust stance began to materialize. The government's challenges to the Microsoft acquisition of Intuit and its subsequent challenge to Microsoft underscored a somewhat activist antitrust enforcement process. This became quite clear in 1997, when the Staples, Inc. acquisition of Office Depot was stopped. In 1998 there were several other major challenges to mergers, including the proposed $1.72 billion acquisition of Amerisource Corporation by McKesson Corporation and the $2.41 billion proposed acquisition of Bergen Brunsweig Corporation by Cardinal Health, Inc. These companies were four of the largest wholesalers in the industry.

Probably the most notable deal to be opposed in the late 1990s was the $8.3 billion takeover of Northrop Grumman Corp. by Lockheed Martin Corp. Each of the two deal partners was the product of a prior major merger, with Northrop and Grumman merging in 1994 in a $2.17 billion deal and Lockheed and Martin Marietta merging in 1995 in a $10 billion deal. The defense industry was undergoing a general consolidation as competitors sought to gain efficiencies to cope with the post–Cold War defense environment. In December 1996 Boeing Co. bought McDonnell Douglas Corp. for $14 billion, and in 1997 Raytheon acquired the defense business of Hughes Electric Corp. for $12.5 billion. There were several other acquisitions in the industry involving whole companies or defense-related divisions of companies, such as Loral's 1993 acquisition of IBM's defense business and the 1994 merger between FMC and Harsco-BMY. In the face of the contracting competitive environment the Lockheed Martin–Northrop Grumman deal was vigorously opposed by Raytheon. The Justice Department also began to be concerned and initiated an extensive investigation, which led to a suit to block the deal. This action signaled that the consolidations that were symptomatic of the fifth merger wave, particularly in industries such as the defense industry, but also possibly in telecommunications and banking, could not continue indefinitely before reaching a point of being objectionable. One of the lessons from the failure of this deal to gain antitrust approval is that when an industry is consolidating, it is important not to be one of the later deals that cause the quantitative measures of concentration to reach objectionable levels. The shrewder competitors may anticipate the eventual consolidation of the industry and merge or acquire early, whereas later would-be dealmakers may find themselves the target of an antitrust enforcement action.

---

22. Roger Lowenstein, "Antitrust Enforcers Drop the Ideology, Focus on Economics, *Wall Street Journal,* 27 February 1997, p. A1.

MEASURING CONCENTRATION AND DEFINING MARKET SHARE

MEASURING CONCENTRATION AND DEFINING MARKET SHARE

A key factor that the Court has relied on in deciding antitrust cases has been the market share of the alleged violator of antitrust laws and the degree of concentration in the industry. The Justice Department's method of measuring market share and concentration has varied over the years. The varying standards have been set forth in various merger guidelines.

1968 Justice Department Merger Guidelines

In 1968 the Justice Department issued merger guidelines that set forth the types of mergers that the government would oppose. Through these guidelines, which were used to help interpret the Sherman Act and the Clayton Act, the Justice Department presented its definitions, in terms of specific market share percentages, of highly concentrated and less highly concentrated industries. The guidelines used concentration ratios, which are the market shares of the top four or top eight firms in the industry.

Under the 1968 guidelines, an industry was considered to be highly concentrated if the four largest firms held at least 75% of the total market. The guidelines for horizontal acquisitions that could give rise to a challenge are set forth in Table 3.1 in terms of market shares of the merger partners.

The issuance of these guidelines made antitrust enforcement more mechanistic. Companies considering a merger with another firm could be better able to ascertain in advance the position of the Justice Department on the merger. Moreover, the Justice Department used these guidelines to determine its enforcement policies.

1982 Justice Department Guidelines

The limitations of such a rigid antitrust policy began to be felt in the 1970s; a policy that allowed more flexibility was clearly needed. Such a policy was instituted in 1982 through the work of William Baxter, head of the antitrust division of the Justice Department. Baxter was both a lawyer and an economist. Using his economics training, he introduced certain quantitative measures into the antitrust enforcement process, making it more mechanistic, predictable, and consistent with prevailing economic theory. Chief among these

Table 3.1. 1968 Justice Department Merger Guidelines

Market	Acquiring Company	Acquired Company
Highly Concentrated	4%	4% or more
	10%	2% or more
	15%	1% or more
Less Highly Concentrated	5%	5% or more
	10%	4% or more
	15%	3% or more
	20%	2% or more
	25%	1% or more

measures was the *Herfindahl-Hirschman (HH) Index* to American antitrust policy. The Herfindahl-Hirschman Index is the sum of the squares of the market shares of each firm in the industry.

$$HH = \sum_{i=1}^{n} s_i^2$$

where
s_i = the market share of the ith firm.

Using this index rather than simple market shares of the top four or top eight firms in the industry provides a more precise measure of the impact of increased concentration that would be brought on by a merger of two competitors. It is important to note, however, that when using the Herfindahl-Hirschman Index (or even concentration ratios), the assumption that each of the merged firms would maintain their market shares needs to be carefully examined. The post-merger combined market share needs to be considered even when this may be difficult.

Properties of the Herfindahl-Hirschman Index

The Herfindahl-Hirschman Index possesses certain properties that make it a better measure of merger-related market concentration than simple concentration ratios.

- The index increases with the number of firms in the industry.
- The index sums the squares of the firms in the industry. In doing so, it weights larger firms more heavily than smaller firms. Squaring a larger number will have a disproportionately larger impact on the index than squaring a smaller number. Moreover, a merger that increases the size differences between firms will result in a larger increase in the index than would have been reflected using simple concentration ratios.
- Because larger firms have greater impact on the index, the index can provide useful results even if there is incomplete information on the size of the smaller firms in the industry.

In evaluating market concentration, the antitrust enforcement authorities sets forth the following numerical ranges:

Post-merger HH less than 1000	Unconcentrated market. This is unlikely to cause an antitrust challenge unless there are other anticompetitive effects.
Post-merger HH between 1000 and 1800	Moderately concentrated. If a merger increases the HH index by less than 100 points, this is unlikely to be a problem, but if it raises the index by more than 100 points, there may be concentration-related antitrust concerns.

Post-merger HH above 1800   Highly concentrated market. If a merger only raises the index by less then 50 points, this is unlikely to be objectionable. Increases of greater than 50 points "raise significant antitrust concerns."

Example of the Herfindahl-Hirschman Index

Consider an industry composed of eight firms, each of which has a 12.5% market share. The Herfindahl-Hirschman Index then is equal to:

$$HH = \sum_{i=1}^{8} = (12.5)^2$$

$$= 1,250$$

If two of these equal-sized firms merge, the index is computed to be:

$$HH = \sum_{i=1}^{6} = (12.5)^2 + 625$$

$$= 1,562.5$$

Just as it did in the 1968 merger guidelines, the Justice Department established a threshold level for concentration in the industry. Instead of the concentration ratios used in the 1968 guidelines, the 1982 guidelines were set in terms of HH Index values.

HH > 1,800 Highly concentrated
HH > 1,000 Moderately concentrated
HH < 1,000 Unconcentrated

1984 Justice Department Guidelines

On June 14, 1984, the Justice Department again revised its merger guidelines in an attempt to further refine its antitrust enforcement policies. The department recognized that its prior guidelines, including the more accurate Herfindahl-Hirschman Index, were too mechanistic and inflexible. In an attempt to enhance the flexibility of its policies, the department allowed the consideration of *qualitative* information in addition to the quantitative measures it had been employing. This qualitative information would include factors such as the efficiency of firms in the industry, the financial viability of potential merger candidates, and the ability of U.S. firms to compete in foreign markets.

The 1984 merger guidelines also introduced the 5% test. This test requires the Justice Department to make a judgment on the effects of a potential 5% increase in the price of each product of each merging firm. This test is based on the assumption that there may be an increase in market power resulting from the merger. If so, the merged firms may have the ability to increase prices. The test attempts to examine the potential effects of this increase on competitors and consumers.

One macroeconomic measure that provides an indication of the responsiveness of consumers and competitors is the concept of *elasticity*. The price elasticity of demand provides an indication of the consumers' responsiveness to a change in the price of a product. It is measured as follows:

$e > 1$ Demand is elastic. The percentage change in quantity is more than the percentage change in price.

$e = 1$ Unitary elasticity. The percentage change in quantity is equal to the percentage change in price.

$e < 1$ Inelastic demand. The percentage change in quality is less than the percentage change in price.

If demand is inelastic over the 5% price change range, this implies greater market power for the merged firms; if, however, demand is elastic, consumers are not as adversely affected by the merger.

The 1982 and 1984 merger guidelines recognized the possibility of efficiency-enhancing benefits from mergers. Although they do not have the force of law, the 1968 merger guidelines were found to warrant some legal consideration.

1992 Merger Guidelines

The current position of the Justice Department and the FTC is set forth in the jointly issued 1992 merger guidelines, which were revised in 1997. They are similar to the 1984 guidelines in that they also recognize potential efficiency-enhancing benefits of mergers. However, these guidelines indicate that a merger will be challenged if there are anticompetitive effects, such as through price increases, even when there are demonstrable efficiency benefits. Clearly, mergers that lead to an anticompetitive increase in market powers will be challenged.

The 1992 guidelines provide a clarification of the definition of the relevant market, which often is a crucial issue of an antitrust lawsuit. They state that a market is the smallest group of products or geographic area where a monopoly could raise prices by a certain amount, such as by 5%. Like the 1984 guidelines, they also use the Herfindahl-Hirschman Index to measure the competitive effects of a merger.

The 1992 guidelines set forth a five-step process that the enforcement authorities follow:

1. Assess whether the merger significantly increases concentration. This involves a definition of the relevant market, which may be an issue of dispute.
2. Assess any potential anticompetitive effects of the deal.
3. Assess whether the potential anticompetitive could be mitigated by entry into the market by competitors. The existence of barriers to entry needs to be determined.

4. Determine if there could be certain offsetting efficiency gains that may result from the deal and which could offset the negative impact of the anticompetitive effects.
5. Determine whether either party would fail or exit the market but for the merger. These possible negative effects are then weighed against the potential anticompetitive effects.

The 1997 revisions highlight the antitrust authorities' willingness to consider the net antitrust effects of a merger. Adverse anticompetitive effects may be offset by positive efficiency benefits. The merger participants need to be able to demonstrate that the benefits are directly related to the merger. It is recognized that such benefits may be difficult to quantify in advance of the deal, but their demonstration may not be vague or speculative. Practically, the merger-specific efficiencies offset only minor anticompetitive effects, not major ones.

STATE ANTITAKEOVER LAWS

Many non-Americans are confused and dismayed by the sometimes conflicting combination of federal laws and state laws that characterizes the U.S. legal system. Indeed, under current federal and state takeover laws, it is possible that conforming to some aspects of the federal laws means violating certain state laws. The line of demarcation between federal takeover laws and their state counterparts has to do with the focus of each. Federal laws tend to be directed at securities regulation, tender offers, and antitrust considerations, whereas state laws govern corporate charters and their bylaws.

Currently, a broad array of inconsistent state laws exists across the United States. Many of these laws were passed in response to pressure by particular corporations who found themselves the object of interest by potential acquirers. The usual scenario is that a local firm petitions the state legislature to pass an antitakeover law or amend the current one to make it more difficult for a local corporation to be taken over. The political pressure that is brought to bear on the state legislatures comes in the form of allegations that a takeover by a "foreign raider" will mean a significant loss of jobs as well as other forms of community support, such as charitable donations by the local corporation.

Genesis of State Antitakeover Laws

State antitakeover laws were first developed in the late 1960s and early 1970s. These statutes typically required that disclosure materials be filed following the initiation of the bid. The problem with these "first-generation" state antitakeover laws was that they applied to firms that did only a small amount of business in that state. This seemed unfair to bidding corporations. Thus, the stage was set for a legal challenge.

Edgar v. MITE
The constitutionality of these first-generation antitakeover laws was successfully challenged in 1982 in the famous *Edgar v. MITE* decision.[23] In this decision the U.S. Supreme

---

23. *Edgar v. MITE Corporation,* 102 S. Ct. 2629 (1982).

Court ruled that the Illinois Business Takeover Act was unconstitutional. The Illinois law permitted the state to block a nationwide tender offer for a state-affiliated target corporation if the bidder failed to comply with the disclosure laws of Illinois. The challenge to the Illinois law caused states with similar laws to question their constitutionality and redevelop their provisions. The states still wanted to inhibit takeovers, which they thought were not in the best interest of their states, but now they had to adopt a different approach, which came in the form of the "second-generation" laws.

The second-generation state antitakeover laws had a narrower focus than the first-generation laws. They tended to apply only to those firms that were incorporated within the state or that conducted a substantial part of their business activities within state boundaries. They were not directed at regulating disclosure in tender offers, as the first-generation laws were. Rather, they focused on issues of corporate governance, which traditionally are the domain of state corporation laws.

Components of Second-Generation Laws

Most second-generation laws incorporate some or all of the following provisions:[24]

- Fair price provision
- Business combination provision
- Control share provision
- Cash-out statute

Fair Price Provision
A fair price provision requires that in a successful tender offer all shareholders who do not decide to sell will receive the same price as shareholders who do accept the offer. These provisions are designed to prevent the abuses that may occur in two-tiered tender offers. With two-tiered bids, a high price is offered to the first-tier tenders, whereas a lower price or less advantageous terms (such as securities of uncertain value instead of cash) are offered to the members of the second tier. The following states have fair price statutes: Connecticut, Florida, Georgia, Illinois, Louisiana, Mississippi, Pennsylvania, Washington, and Wisconsin.[25]

Business Combination Provision
This provision prevents business agreements between the target company and the bidding company for a certain time period. For example, the wording of a business combination provision may rule out the sales of the target's assets by the bidding company. These provisions are designed to prevent leveraged acquisitions. When an acquiring company assumes a large amount of debt to finance a takeover, it may be relying on the sales of assets by the target to pay the high interest payments required by the debt. The law is designed to

---

24. For an excellent and more detailed discussion of these and other provisions of second-generation laws, see Robert Winter, Robert Rosenbaum, Mark Stumpf, and L. Stevenson Parker, *State Takeover Statutes and Poison Pills* (Englewood Cliffs, N.J.: Prentice-Hall, 1988).

25. Ibid.

prevent the transformation of local firms, with a low-risk capital structure, into riskier leveraged companies. The following states have business combination statutes: Arizona, Connecticut, Delaware, Georgia, Idaho, Indiana, Kansas, Kentucky, Maine, Maryland, Massachusetts, Michigan, Minnesota, Missouri, Nebraska, New Jersey, New York, Pennsylvania, South Carolina, Tennessee, Virginia, Washington, and Wisconsin.[26]

Control Share Provision

A control share provision requires that acquiring firms obtain prior approval of current target stockholders before the purchases are allowed. These provisions typically apply to stock purchases beyond a certain percentage of the outstanding stock. They are particularly effective if the current share ownership includes large blocks of stock that are held by groups of people who are generally supportive of management, such as employee stockholders. The following states have control share provisions: Arizona, Florida, Hawaii, Idaho, Indiana, Kansas, Louisiana, Maryland, Massachusetts, Michigan, Minnesota, Missouri, Nebraska, Nevada, North Carolina, Ohio, Oklahoma, Oregon, South Carolina, Tennessee, Utah, and Virginia.[27]

Cash-out Statute

This provision, like the fair price requirement, is designed to limit tender offers. It typically requires that if a bidder buys a certain percentage of stock in a target firm, the bidder is then required to purchase all the remaining outstanding shares at the same terms given to the initial purchase. This provision limits acquiring firms that lack the financial resources for a 100% stock acquisition. It also limits leveraged acquisitions because it may require the bidder to assume an even greater amount of debt with the associated high debt service. Bidders might therefore be discouraged because of their inability to obtain financing for a 100% purchase or simply because they do not believe their cash flow will service the increased debt. The following states have cash-out statutes: Maine, Pennsylvania, and Utah.[28]

Dynamics v. CTS

The *Edgar v. MITE* decision delivered a severe blow to the first-generation laws. Many opponents of antitakeover legislation attacked the second-generation laws, which they believed were also unconstitutional. These legal actions resulted in the *Dynamics v. CTS* decision of April 1987.[29] In this case, the CTS Corporation used the Indiana law to fight off a takeover by the Dynamics Corporation. Dynamics challenged the law, contending that it was unconstitutional. In *Dynamics v. CTS,* the U.S. Supreme Court ruled that the Indiana antitakeover law was constitutional. This law allows stockholders to vote on whether a buyer of controlling interest can exercise his or her voting rights. The CTS decision gave the Supreme Court's approval to the second-generation state takeover laws. Since the April 1987 CTS decision, many states have adopted antitakeover laws. Today most states have some kind of law regulating takeovers.

---

26. Ibid.
27. Ibid.
28. Ibid.
29. *Dynamics Corporation of America v. CTS Corporation,* 637 F. Supp. 406 (N.D. Ill. 1986).

Amanda Acquisition Corporation v. Universal Foods Corporation

In November 1989 the Supreme Court refused to hear a challenge to the Wisconsin anti-takeover law. The Court's unwillingness to hear this challenge further buttressed the legal viability of state antitakeover laws. The Wisconsin law requires a bidder who acquires 10% or more of a target company's stock to receive the approval of the other target share-holders or wait three years to complete the merger. The three-year waiting period makes heavily leveraged buyouts, which were typical of the fourth merger wave, prohibitively expensive.

The Supreme Court decision arose out of a legal challenge by the Amanda Acquisition Corporation, which is a subsidiary of the Boston-based High Voltage Engineering Corporation. Amanda challenged the Wisconsin law that prevented it from proceeding with a ten-der offer for the Milwaukee-based Universal Foods Corporation. The directors of Universal Foods opposed the takeover. Amanda Acquisition Corporation charged that the Wisconsin law was an interference with interstate commerce and was harmful to share-holders. The Supreme Court failed to agree and refused to hear the challenge to the law. The Court's position in this case reaffirms the *Dynamics v. CTS* decision that upheld the constitutionality of the Indiana antitakeover law in 1987. Based on the *Dynamics v. CTS* decision, as well as the Court's position in the *Amanda Acquisition Corporation v. Universal Foods Corporation* case, state antitakeover laws appear to be safe from challenge and may well be a permanent fixture in the laws of mergers.

Delaware Antitakeover Law

The Delaware antitakeover law is probably the most important of all the state antitakeover laws because more corporations are incorporated in Delaware than in any other state. The popularity of Delaware as the preferred state of incorporation is due to its advantageous corporation laws and highly specialized court system. The state's Fortune 500 companies, such as General Motors, Mobil, Rockwell International, and Dow Chemical, are among the 180,000 companies that have incorporated in Delaware. One-half of all New York Stock Exchange companies are incorporated there, along with 56% of the Fortune 500 companies.

The Delaware antitakeover law was passed in 1988 but was made retroactive to December 23, 1987, the date before corporate raider Carl Icahn acquired 15% of Texaco Corporation. The law was passed in response to an intense lobbying effort by companies seeking to adopt a protective statute. They threatened that if such a protective statute was not passed, they would reincorporate in states that did have antitakeover laws. The fact that incorporation fees account for nearly 20% of the Delaware state budget underscored the importance of this threat.[30] The choice of the effective date testifies to the power of this lobbying effort.

The law stipulates that an unwanted bidder who buys more than 15% of a target company's stock may not complete the takeover for three years except under the following conditions:[31]

---

30. Robert A. G. Monks and Well Morow, *Corporate Governance* (Cambridge, Mass.: Blackwell Business), 1995, p. 35.

31. Section 203 of the Delaware General Corporation Law.

- If the buyer buys 85% or more of the target company's stock. This 85% figure may not include the stock held by directors or the stock held in employee stock ownership plans.
- If two-thirds of the stockholders approve the acquisition.
- If the board of directors and the stockholders decide to waive the antitakeover provisions of this law.

Being primarily a business combination statute, the law is designed to limit takeovers financed by debt. Raiders who have financed their takeovers by large amounts of debt often need to sell off company assets and divisions to pay off the debt. The need to pay off the debt quickly becomes significant in the case of the billion dollar takeover, as in the 1980s when interest payments were as much as half a million dollars per day.

Although the Delaware law might discourage some debt-financed takeovers, it is not very effective against cash offers. Moreover, even debt-financed offers at a very attractive price may be sufficiently appealing for stockholders to waive the antitakeover provisions of the law.

Pennsylvania Antitakeover Law

In April 1990 the Pennsylvania state legislature approved the strongest antitakeover law in the United States. This law, sometimes referred to as the *disgorgement statute,* was designed to deal with the changes that took place in the hostile takeover market during the late 1980s. These changes included the increased use of proxy fights as an alternative to a hostile tender offer. As the junk bond market declined, many raiders lacked the requisite financing to make credible tender offers. Some then resorted to proxy fights to initiate hostile bids. In addition, those who were able to finance hostile tender offers or to extract greenmail under the threats of a takeover enjoyed great financial gains at the expense of the target. The Pennsylvania statute is directed at reducing the incentive to engage in these activities.

The law restricts the voting rights of any investor or group that purchases 20% or more of a target's stock.[32] In addition, the statute allows Pennsylvania corporations to sue a "controlling person or group," which is defined as a 20% voting interest, to seek disgorgement of all profits of short-term investors who disposed of their shares within 18 months of the acquisition of the controlling position.[33] The law, which does not distinguish between friendly and unfriendly takeovers, applies not only to those who actually acquire a controlling interest but also to those who declare an intent or otherwise seek to acquire such an interest. The statute may also be applied to those who solicit proxies unless they satisfy certain restrictive conditions, such as if the proxy votes are not given in exchange for consideration. The statute may be deactivated by the board of directors.

Protection was given to labor contracts, and severance pay was guaranteed for cases of successful hostile bids. Labor contracts may be enforced, and severance pay may be guaranteed in the case of a successful hostile bid.

---

32. Diane B. Henriques, "A Paradoxical Antitakeover Bill," *New York Times,* 8 April 1990, p. 15.

33. Robert D. Rosenbaum and L. Stevenson Parker, *The Pennsylvania Takeover Act of 1990* (Englewood Cliffs, N.J.: Prentice-Hall, 1990).

The latest disgorgement statute is added to the other statutes, which together make up the strictest antitakeover laws of any state. The prior antitakeover statutes in Pennsylvania had already included a cash-out provision, a business combination rule, and a control share provision. Combined with the disgorgement statute, this law is the strongest state antitakeover statute. Many of the largest Pennsylvania firms, such as Westinghouse Electric Corp., H. J. Heinz Co., and Sun Oil Co., decided that they did not want to be covered by some of the strong provisions of the new Pennsylvania law. Other firms, such as Mellon Bank Corp. and PNC Financial, decided to completely exempt themselves from the law.[34]

Sunil Wahal, Kenneth Wiles, and Marc Zenner analyzed the characteristics of firms that decided to opt out of the Pennsylvania antitakeover law.[35] They found that firms that declined to be covered by the protective provisions of this law were larger, had lower insider control of voting rights, and were less likely to have a poison pill in place. They conclude that firms that are more insulated from outside market forces will be more likely to retain the protective benefits of the law.

Why Do State Antitakeover Laws Get Passed

Most state antitakeover laws get passed as a result of lobbying efforts of companies that are concerned about being taken over. For example, the Pennsylvania antitakeover law was passed partly as a result of the efforts of Armstrong World Industries of Lancaster, Pennsylvania, which was concerned about being taken over by the Belzberg family of Canada. Harcourt Brace Jovanovich and Gillette promoted the respective Florida and Massachusetts control share statutes. Burlington Industries promoted North Carolina's antitakeover law, whereas Dayton-Hudson and Boeing promoted antitakeover laws in Minnesota and Washington, respectively. Ironically, some indigenous companies are so aggressive in promoting such laws that they even draft the statute for lawmakers. The result is a patchwork of many different state laws across America.

Wealth Effects of State Antitakeover Laws

In a study of 40 state antitakeover bills introduced between 1982 and 1987, Karpoff and Malatesta found a small but statistically significant decrease in stock prices of companies incorporated in the various states contemplating passage of such laws.[36] They even found that companies doing significant business in these states also suffered a decline in stock prices. Szewczyk and Tsetsekos found that Pennsylvania firms lost $4 billion during the time this state's antitakeover law was being considered and adopted.[37] It should be kept in

---

34. Vindu Goel, "Many Pennsylvania Firms Opt Out of Provisions in State Antitakeover Law," *Wall Street Journal,* 27 July 1990, p. A5B.

35. Sunil Wahal, Kenneth W. Wiles, and Marc Zenner, "Who Opts Out of State Antitakeover Protection? The Case of Pennsylvania's SB 1310," *Financial Management* 24 (3) Autumn 1995, 22–39.

36. Johnathan M. Karpoff and Paul Malatesta, "The Wealth Effects of Second Generation State Takeover Legislation," *Journal of Financial Economics,* 25(2), December 1989, 291–322.

37. S.H. Szewczyk and G.P. Tsetsekos, " State Intervention in the Market for Corporate Control: The Case of Pennsylvania Senate Bill 1310," *Journal of Financial Economics,* February 1992, 3–23.

mind, however, that these effects are short-term effects based on the reactions of traders in the market during that time period. Nonetheless, it does indicate that in the short term investors do not have a positive evaluation of such laws.

State Antitrust Actions

Many states have their own antitrust laws. The wording of these laws is often similar to that of the federal laws. In addition, the states have the power, under federal law, to take action in federal court and to block mergers they believe are anticompetitive, even when the Justice Department or the FTC fails to challenge the merger. The states' ability to do so was greatly enhanced by a 9 to 0 U.S. Supreme Court ruling in April 1990. The ruling came as a result of California officials' challenge to the $2.5 billion takeover of Lucky Stores, Inc. by American Stores Company in June 1988. The ruling, written by Justice John Paul Stevens, overturned a 1989 U.S. Court of Appeals Ninth Circuit ruling in 1989, which held that the Clayton Act did not permit California to block the Lucky Stores and American Stores merger. California obtained a stay of the ruling from Chief Justice Sandra Day O'Connor in August 1989. This prevented combining the operations of Lucky Stores, the state's largest supermarket chain, with Alpha Beta, owned by American Stores and the state's fourth largest supermarket chain, until the matter was finally adjudicated. California's argument that the merger would cost the California consumers $440 million per year in grocery bills was found to be compelling by the U.S. Supreme Court.[38] This ruling opens the door for states to be active in opposing mergers on antitrust grounds when the federal government decides to adopt a pro-business stance and to limit its antitrust enforcement. This also makes antitrust enforcement less sensitive to the political makeup of the executive branch of the federal government.

REGULATION OF INSIDER TRADING

The SEC rules specify remedies for shareholders who incur losses resulting from insider trading. Insiders are bound by SEC Rule 10b-5, which states that insiders must "disclose or abstain" from trading the firm's securities. Insider trading regulation was buttressed by the passage of the Insider Trading and Securities Fraud Enforcement Act of 1988. This law imposed maximum penalties of up to $1 million and up to 10 years in prison while also setting up a bounty program whereby informants could collect up to 10% of the insider's profits. It also established the possibility of top management's being liable for the insider trading of subordinates. The 1988 law followed the passage of the Insider Trading Sanctions Act of 1984, which gave the SEC the power to seek treble damages for trading on inside information. This law provided a dual-pronged approach for regulators, who now could seek civil remedies in addition to the criminal alternatives that were available before the passage of the 1984 act.

Illegal insider trading may occur, for example, if insiders, acting on information that is unavailable to other investors, sell the firm's securities before an announcement of poor performance. Other investors, unaware of the upcoming bad news, may pay a higher price for the

---

38. *California v. American Stores Co.,* 697 F. Supp. 1125 (C.D. Cal. 1988).

firm's securities. The opposite might be the case if insiders bought the firm's stock or call options before the announcement of a bid from another firm. Stockholders might not have sold the shares to the insiders if they knew of the upcoming bid and its associated premium.

Who Are Insiders?

Insiders may be defined more broadly than the management of a company. They may include outsiders such as attorneys, investment bankers, financial printers, or consultants who can be considered "temporary insiders." Under Rule 10b-5, however, the U.S. Supreme Court held that outside parties who trade profitably based on their acquired information did not have to disclose their inside information. This was the case in the 1980 *Chiarella v. United States,* in which a financial printer acquired information on an upcoming tender offer by reviewing documents in his print shop.[39] If an individual misappropriates confidential information on a merger or acquisition and uses it as the basis for trade, however, Rule 10b-5 will apply. The rule is applicable only to SEC enforcement proceedings or criminal actions, but not to civil actions, under the Insider Trading Sanctions Act of 1984, which permits the recovery of treble damages on the profits earned or the loss avoided.

A classic example of illegal insider trading was the famous Texas Gulf Sulphur case. In 1963 Texas Gulf Sulphur discovered certain valuable mineral deposits, which it did not disclose for several months; actually, the firm publicly denied the discovery in a false press release. Meanwhile, officers and directors bought undervalued shares based on their inside information. The SEC successfully brought a suit against the insiders.

The short swing profit rule prohibits any officer, director, or owner of 10% of a company's stock from a purchase and sale, or a sale and purchase, within a six-month period. Profits derived from these transactions must be paid to the issuer even if the transactions were not made on the basis of insider information.

Insider Trading Scandals of the 1980s

The world of mergers and acquisitions has been plagued with several notorious insider trading scandals in which some of the field's leading participants were convicted of insider trading violations. Each of the major cases provided information that led to the subsequent conviction of other violators.

In June 1986 Dennis Levine, an investment banker at Drexel Burnham Lambert, pleaded guilty to securities fraud, tax evasion, and perjury. He had acquired information on upcoming merger deals through payments to other investment bankers. Levine was an important link in the conviction of Ivan Boesky, a leading risk arbitrager on Wall Street. Boesky would, for example, purchase the securities of firms that he anticipated would be taken over. If he bought these securities before any increase in the target's price, he could realize significant profits. Boesky had illegally acquired insider information from investment bankers on deals before a public announcement of a merger or acquisition.

Information provided, in turn, by Boesky and others, such as Boyd Jefferies, a broker at Jefferies and Company (who had already pleaded guilty in April 1987 to breaking securi-

---

39. *Chiarella v. United States,* 445 U.S. 222, 100 S. Ct. 1108, 63 L. Ed. 2d, 348 (1980).

ties laws), led to Michael Milken's guilty plea to six felony counts in 1990. Milken was later fined and sentenced to a 10-year prison term. Milken, the leading figure in the junk bond market, was the government's most significant conviction in its campaign to stamp out insider trading. His legal problems were one of the major factors that led to the collapse of Drexel Burnham Lambert and the junk bond market.

Changing Theory of Insider Trading

Fiduciary vs. Misappropriation Theory
In the early 1980s it was more difficult for the enforcement authorities to bring a successful action because the fiduciary theory was the prevailing law on insider trading. This law was applied in the *Chiarella v. United States* case, wherein the court overturned a conviction of an employee of a financial printer who derived insider information on a takeover. The Court held that no fiduciary duty existed between the employee of the printer and the shareholders.

Later in the 1980s proving insider trading became easier when the courts adopted the misappropriation theory. Under this theory a trader may be convicted of insider trading if he improperly gains access to inside information. Under the misappropriation theory, the trader does not have to be a fiduciary for shareholders. One of the prominent cases here was the *U.S. v. Carpenter* decision, in which a writer for the *Wall Street Journal,* Foster Winans, was convicted of violating insider trading laws even though he was not an insider or even had what would normally be defined as insider information. He was convicted of selling in advance the content of the stories he would write in the "Heard on the Street" column. Many people had questioned whether the Supreme Court would ever endorse the misappropriation theory. However, in 1997 the Supreme Court did endorse it in the *U.S. v. O'Hagan* case, which involved a Minneapolis attorney, James O'Hagan, who gained a $4.3 million profit in 1988 after buying shares of Pillsbury, which was bought by Grand Metropolitan.[40] O'Hagan was an attorney at the law firm that represented Grand Metropolitan but he was not involved in the deal. The defense contended that they were not fiduciaries for Pillsbury, but the Supreme Court rejected this argument, thereby solidifying the misappropriation theory.

Just when the pendulum appeared to swing strongly in favor of the enforcement authorities, their job became more difficult with the *SEC v. Pegram* decision. In this case, a federal appeals court introduced the use test. In doing so, the court accepted the defense's argument that the trades by Mr. Pegram, founder of Comtronix Corp, were part of a preexisting plan to diversify his holdings. In reaching its decision, the court stated that the SEC must demonstrate that the insider information was used to initiate the trades.

Do Insider Trading Laws Effectively Deter Insider Trading?

One research study by Nejat Seyhun has questioned the effectiveness of laws in curbing insider trading.[41] In addition, Lisa Muelbroek empirically confirmed that stock price run-ups before takeover announcements do reflect insider trading.[42] More recent research, which

---

40. *U.S. v. O'Hagan,* 117 S. Ct. 2199, 1997.

41. Nejat H. Seyhun, "The Effectiveness of Insider Trading Regulations," *Journal of Law and Economics,* 35 1992, 149–182.

42. Lisa Muelbroek, "An Empirical Analysis of Insider Trading," *Journal of Finance,* 47, 1661–1700.

may more fully reflect the impact of the 1998 law, given the long lag that is associated with litigation, seem to indicate that such laws may have a significant deterrent effect. Jon Garfinkel examined insider trading around earnings announcements and found that after the passage of the Insider Trading and Securities Fraud Enforcement Act, insiders appeared to adjust the timing of their transactions so that the trades occurred after the release of the relevant information.[43] The fact that the laws and the enforcement activity do seem to have a positive effect does not negate the fact that insider trading seems to remain a part of merger and acquisition activity of public companies.

A COMPANY'S OBLIGATION TO DISCLOSE MERGER NEGOTIATIONS

Firms are not obligated to disclose merger negotiations until a final agreement has been reached, which is acknowledged as the point when both parties agree on price and financial structure. If both elements are not in place, a firm may not be bound to make any disclosures. The courts have even found that a press release issued by Heublein executives denying that they knew of any factors that would explain the increased trading volume in Heublein stock on the New York Stock Exchange was not misleading.[44] The Supreme Court, however, later disagreed with that court's position on this matter.

---

43. Jon A. Garfinkel, "New Evidence on the Effects of Federal Regulations on Insider Trading: The Insider Trading and Securities Fraud Enforcement Act," *Journal of Corporate Finance* 3, April 1997, 89–111.

44. *Greenfield v. Heublein, Inc.*, 742 F. 2d, 751 (CA3 1984).

CASE STUDY: VIACOM–PARAMOUNT–QVC

On September 12, 1993, the Paramount board of directors approved a merger with Viacom that was valued at $69.14 per share. The friendly merger between these two companies was interrupted on September 20 by an unwanted bid from QVC valued at $80 per share. QVC announced that two of its largest shareholders, Liberty Media and the Comcast Corporation, each agreed to put up $500 million to help finance the QVC offer. One of the unique characteristics of this takeover battle was that each side enlisted merger partners to provide financing in exchange for certain considerations. Viacom responded with a $600 million investment from Blockbuster Entertainment and a $1.2 investment from NYNEX. QVC then received some financial support from the acquisition of Tele-Communication, Inc. by Bell Atlantic. Tele-Communications was in the process of acquiring Liberty Media. On October 17 Advance Publications and Cox Enterprises agreed to provide $500 million each to help finance QVC's bid.

Armed with the financial support of its various merger partners, QVC announced a two-stage tender offer for Paramount valued at $80 per share. The first step was a cash offer for 51%, to be followed by a closeout transaction using stock. The Paramount board authorized its management to meet with QVC on October 5, but it was not until November 1 that they met with QVC.

Viacom responded to the QVC tender offer with a $85 cash offer, which Paramount accepted. Concerns about potential antitrust conflicts were allayed by QVC when it announced on November 11 that it would sever its association with Liberty Media, which would be sold to Bell South for $1 billion. Bell South would then provide the $500 that Liberty Media was contributing to the QVC bid. On November 12 QVC then announced that it was topping the Viacom bid with its own $90 per share offer.

The takeover battle then moved to the courts, where QVC came out the victor, with the Delaware Chancery Court ruling that the Paramount board acted improperly in not exercising its Revlon duties and allowing defensive measures, such as lockup options, termination fees, and lucrative stock options, to give Viacom an advantage. This decision was upheld on December 9 by the Delaware Supreme Court. Paramount was then forced to withdraw its support for the Viacom bid, and the auction process began. QVC upped its bid to $88.50 and Paramount's board recommended acceptance, but Viacom came back with an even higher $10 billion offer that ultimately won the takeover contest.

In 1988 the Supreme Court, in a 6 to 0 ruling, took the position that the issuance of misleading information on the status of merger negotiations was illegal. This was the case in the 1978 acquisition of Basic, Inc. by Combustion Engineering, Inc. Basic's stockholders sued because Basic's management made misleading statements in denying that merger talks were under way. Although management denied the existence of merger negotiations, the two firms had been working on a deal for more than a year. In reaching its decision, the Supreme Court endorsed the efficient market view of securities pricing, which implies that securities markets reflect all available information. Shareholders, relying on management's misleading statements, sold shares at a lower price than the market would have paid had the information on the merger negotiations been available. The Supreme Court ruled that shareholders could sue even if they did not explicitly rely on management's statements when making their trades.

SUMMARY

To more fully understand the world of mergers and acquisitions, it is necessary to understand the laws that regulate the process. These laws are divided into three categories: securities law, antitrust laws, and state corporation laws. The leading securities law for mergers and acquisitions is the Securities Exchange Act of 1934, of which the Williams Act is an amendment. The Williams Act regulates tender offers, which are important to takeovers—particularly hostile deals. The law is designed to provide shareholders with more information about bidders as well as the time to analyze this information. Section 13D of the law regulates the disclosure required of purchase of more than 5% of the outstanding stock of a company. Section 14D regulates the disclosure necessary to tender offers. The Sherman Antitrust Act and the Clayton Act were two of the early antitrust laws. These laws were augmented by the Federal Trade Commission Act and the Celler-Kefauver Act. However, the interpretation of these laws has varied over the course of modern U.S. history. It has varied from being very intense during the 1950s and 1960s to being relatively relaxed in the 1980s. The 1990s, however, have exhibited signs of a movement back toward somewhat more aggressive antitrust enforcement. In addition to the aforementioned antitrust laws, the Hart-Scott-Rodino Act is a law that is directed toward mergers and acquisitions. It is designed to provide a clear sign of opposition to a takeover if such a transaction would possibly be anticompetitive.

State corporation laws play an important role in mergers and acquisitions. In particular, many state antitakeover laws provide protection against hostile takeover for corporations located within states. These laws sometimes even cover corporations that are incorporated in a state other than the one that has passed a particular law. State antitakeover laws are divided into four categories: fair price laws, business combination statutes, control share statutes, and cash out laws.

REFERENCES

Bebchuk, Lucian A. "The Case for Facilitating Competing Tender Offers: A Reply and an Extension." *Stanford Law Review* 35 (1982).

Boesky, Ivan. *Merger Mania* (New York: Holt, Rinehart & Winston, 1985).

Breit, William, and Kenneth G. Elzinga. *The Antitrust Book,* 2nd ed. (Chicago: Dryden Press, 1989).

Carlton, Dennis W., and Jeffrey M. Perloff. *Modern Industrial Organization,* 2nd ed. (New York: HarperCollins, 1994).

Chiarella v. United States, 445 U.S. 222, 100 S. Ct. 1108, 63 L. Ed. 2d, 348 (1980).

Coffee, John C. Jr. "Regulating the Market for Corporate Control: A Critical Assessment for the Tender Offer's Role in Corporate Governance." *Columbia Law Review* 84 (1984).

DeBondt, Werner F. M., and Harold E. Thompson. "The Williams Act: Bane or Boon to the Market for Corporate Control?" Working Paper, University of Wisconsin–Madison, October 1989.

Delaware General Corporation Law, Section 203.

Dynamics Corp. of America v. CTS Corp., 637 F. Supp. 406 (N.D. Ill. 1986).

Edgar v. MITE Corporation, 102 S. Ct. 2629 (1982).

Ferrara, Ralph, Meredith Brown, and John Hall. *Takeovers: Attack and Survival* (Stoneham, Mass.: Butterworth Legal Publishers, 1987).

Fox, Bryon E., and Eleanor M. Fox. *Corporate Acquisitions and Mergers,* Vol. 2 (New York: Matthew Bender Publishing Co., 1987).

Gilson, Ronald J. *The Law and Finance of Corporate Acquisitions* (Mineola, N.Y.: Foundation Press, 1986).

Goel, Vindu. "Many Pennsylvania Firms Opt Out of Provisions in State Antitakeover Law." *Wall Street Journal,* 27 July 1990.

Greer, Douglas. *Industrial Organization and Public Policy,* 3rd ed. (New York: Macmillan Publishing Co., 1992).

Greenfield v. Heublein, Inc., 742 F. 2d 751 (3rd Cir. 1974), *cert. denied* 105 S. Ct. 1189 (1985).

Kennecott Copper Corp. v. Curtiss Wright Corp., 584 F. 2d 1195 (CA2 1978).

Levinson v. Basic, Inc., CCH Fed. Sec. L. Rep. 91, 801 (N.D. Ohio 1984).

Lipton, Martin, and Erica H. Steinberger. *Takeovers and Freezeouts* (New York: Law Journal Seminars Press, 1987).

Loss, Louis, and Joel Seligman. *Fundamentals of Securities Regulation,* 3rd ed. (Boston: Little, Brown, 1995).

Pollack, Ellen Joan, and Ann Hagedorn. "Milken Faces Myriad Civil Suits." *Wall Street Journal,* 26 April 1990.

Rosenbaum, Robert D., and L. Stevenson Parker. *The Pennsylvania Takeover Pact of 1990* (Englewood Cliffs, N.J.: Prentice-Hall, 1990).

Scharf, Charles A., Edward E. Shea, and George C. Beck. *Acquisitions, Mergers, Sales, Buyouts and Takeovers,* 3rd ed. (Englewood Cliffs, N.J.: Prentice-Hall, 1985).

Scherer, Frederick M. *Industrial Market Structure and Economic Performance,* 3rd ed. (Boston: Houghton Mifflin, 1990).

SEC v. Materia, CCH Fed. Sec. L. Rep., 99, 526 (S.D.N.Y. 1983), *aff'd* 745 F. 2d 197, *cert. denied.*

SEC v. Texas Gulf Sulphur Company, 401 F. 2d 833, 852 (2nd Cir. 1968), *cert. denied* 394 U.S. 976 (1969).

Smiley, Robert. "The Effect of the Williams Amendment and Other Factors on Transaction Costs in Tender Offers." *Industrial Organization Review* 3 (1975).

Smiley, Robert. "The Effect of State Securities Statutes on Tender Offer Activity." *Economic Inquiry* 19 (1985).

Soderquist, Larry D. *Understanding Security Laws,* 3rd ed. (New York: Practicing Law Institute, 1994).

U.S. v. Aluminum Company of America et al., 148 F. 2d 416, 424 (1945).

U.S. v. American Tobacco Company, 221 U.S. 106 (1911).

U.S. v. International Harvester Company, U.S. 693 (1927).

U.S. v. New York Great Atlantic and Pacific Tea Company et al., 67 F. Supp. 626 (1946), 173 F. 2d (1949).

U.S. v. Standard Oil of New Jersey et al., 221 U.S. 1, 76 (1911).

U.S. v. U.S. Steel Corporation et al., 223 Fed. 55 (1915), 251 U.S. 417 (1920).

Warner Communications Inc. v. Murdoch, 581 F. Supp. 1482 (D. Del. March 16, 1984).

Wellman v. Dickinson, 475 F. Supp. (SD NY 1979), *aff'd* 632 F. 2d 355 (CA2 1982), *cert. denied* 460 U.S. 1069 (1983).

Winter, Robert, Robert Rosenbaum, Mark Stumpf, and L. Stevenson Parker. *State Takeover Statutes and Poison Pills* (Englewood Cliffs, NJ: Prentice-Hall, 1988).

4

MERGER STRATEGY

This chapter focuses on the strategic motives and determinants of mergers and acquisitions. It begins with a discussion of one of the most often cited motives for mergers and acquisitions—synergy. Proponents of a deal will often point to anticipated synergy as the justification for a specific purchase price. The different types of synergy, operating and financial synergy, are explored in this chapter. It will be seen that operating synergy, including both economies of scale and economies of scope, has the most economically sound basis. Financial synergy is a more questionable motive for a merger or an acquisition.

Companies often merge in an attempt to diversify into another line of business. The history of mergers is replete with diversification transactions. The track record of these diversifications, with notable exceptions, is not very impressive. However, certain types of diversifying transactions, those that do not involve a movement to a very different business category, have a better track record. Companies experience greater success with horizontal combinations, which result in an increase in market share, and even with some vertical transactions, which may provide other economic benefits. Unfortunately, a less noble motive such as hubris, or pride of the management of the bidder, also may be a motive for an acquisition. This determinant, along with others, such as improved management and tax benefits, may serve as the motivation for a deal. These motives, with their respective shareholder wealth effects, are analyzed.

GROWTH

One of the most fundamental motives for mergers and acquisitions is growth. Companies seeking to expand are faced with a choice between internal growth and growth through mergers and acquisitions. Internal growth may be a slow and uncertain process. Growth through mergers and acquisitions may be a much more rapid process, although it brings with it its own uncertainties. Companies may grow within their own industry or they may expand outside their business category. Expansion outside one's industry means diversification. Because diversification has been a controversial topic in finance, it is discussed separately later in this chapter. In this section we focus on growth within a company's own industry.

If a company seeks to expand within its own industry, there are two alternatives: internal growth versus external growth. Sometimes internal growth is not an acceptable alternative. For example, if a company has a window of opportunity that will remain open for only a limited period of time, slow internal growth may not suffice. As the company grows slowly through internal expansion, competitors may respond quickly and take market share. Advantages that a company may have can dissipate over time or be whittled away by the actions of competitors. The only solution may be to acquire another company that has the resources, such as offices, management, and other resources, in place.

There are many examples of opportunities that must be acted on immediately lest they disappear. It could be that a company has developed a new product or process and has a time advantage over competitors. Even if it is possible to patent the product or process, this does not prevent competitors from possibly developing a competing product or process that does not violate the patent. Another example would be if a company developed a new merchandising concept. Being first to develop the concept provides a certain limited time advantage. If not properly taken advantage of, the opportunity may slip by and become an opportunity for larger competitors with greater resources.

Another example of using mergers and acquisitions to facilitate growth is when a company wants to expand to another geographic region. It could be that the company's market is in one part of the country but it would want to move into other markets within the country such as an East Coast U.S. company wanting to expand to the Midwest or the West. It also could be that the company wants to expand to other national markets, such as a U.S. firm wanting to expand to Europe. In many instances, it may be quicker and less risky to expand geographically through acquisitions than through internal development. This may be particularly true of international expansion, where many characteristics are needed to be successful in a new geographic market. The company needs to know all of the nuances of the new market and to recruit new personnel and circumvent many other hurdles such as language and custom barriers. Internal expansion may be much slower and difficult. Mergers, acquisitions, joint ventures, and strategic alliance may be the fastest and lower risk alternative.

SYNERGY

The term *synergy* is often associated with the physical sciences rather than with economics or finance. It refers to the type of reactions that occur when two substances or factors combine to produce a greater effect together than that which the sum of the two operating independently could account for. For example, a synergistic reaction occurs in chemistry when two chemicals combine to produce a more potent total reaction than the sum of their separate effects. Simply stated, synergy refers to the phenomenon of $2 + 2 = 5$. In mergers this translates into the ability of a corporate combination to be more profitable than the individual parts of the firms that were combined.

CASE STUDY: ALLEGIS—SYNERGY THAT NEVER MATERIALIZED

The case of the Allegis Corporation is a classic example of synergistic benefits that had every reason to occur but failed to materialize. The concept of Allegis was the brainchild of Richard Ferris, CEO of the Allegis Corporation. Ferris had risen through the ranks of the firm's precursor, United Airlines (UAL), which had been the world's largest investor-owned airline.

Ferris's dream was to form a diversified travel services company that would be able to provide customers with a complete package of air travel, hotel, and car rental services. Accordingly, United Airlines bought Hertz Rent a Car from RCA in June 1986. United paid $587 million—a price that was considered to be a premium. In addition to buying Pan American Airways Pacific routes, Ferris bought the Hilton International hotel chain from the Transworld Corporation for $980 million. The Hilton International purchase on March 31, 1987, was also considered to be expensive. United Airlines had already acquired the Westin International hotel chain in 1970 for only $52 million.

On February 18, 1987, United Airlines changed its name to Allegis Corporation. The change of name underscored the management's efforts to have the company perceived as a diversified travel services company. The concept was intended to allow customers the ability to do "one-stop" travel shopping. With one telephone call they could book their air travel, hotel reservations, and car rental within the same corporate umbrella. Allegis hoped to weave the network together through a combination of cross-discounts, bonus miles, and other promotional savings and the introduction of a new computer system called Easy Saver. Through Easy Saver, customers could check prices and book reservations through the Allegis network. All travel services could be charged on an Allegis credit card. Travel agents using United Airlines' Apollo computer reservation system, the largest in the airline industry, would pull up Allegis's air, hotel, and car services before any other competitor's products.

Despite the concept's appeal, the market failed to respond. Whatever the long-term outlook of Allegis's much vaunted effort to package air travel, hotel, and car rental services might have been, consumers just have not seen much benefit. And the system has posed some early snarls for travel agents. "Consumers just don't believe in the value of synergies that Allegis says exist between airlines, rental cars and hotels," says Daniel T. Smith, director of consumer affairs at the International Airline Passengers Association, a consumer group with approximately 10,000 members.[a]

Investors joined the public in failing to respond to the full-service travel service concept. At a time when the stock market was providing handsome returns to investors, the Allegis stock price fell; in February 1987 its stock price was in the low- to mid-$50 range. The market did respond, however, when Coniston Partners, a New York investment firm, accumulated a 13% stake in the travel company. Coniston planned to sell off the various parts of the Allegis travel network and distribute the proceeds to the stockholders. Allegis responded on April 1, 1987, with a large recapitalization plan proposal that would have resulted in the company's assuming $3 billion worth of additional debt to finance a $60 special dividend. The recapitalization plan was intended to support the stock price while instilling stockholder support for Allegis and away from the Coniston proposal. The United Airlines Pilots Union followed up Allegis's recapitalization plan proposal with its own offer to buy the airline and sell off the nonairline parts. Their offer would have paid $70 to stockholders.

The pressure on CEO Ferris continued to mount, leading to a pivotal board of directors meeting. According to Chairman of the Board Charles Luce, the board, watching the company's stock rise, "thought the market was saying that Allegis was

---

a. Robert Johnson, "Full Service Didn't Fly with Public, Travel Agents," *Wall Street Journal,* 11 June 1987, p. 22.

worth more broken up and that the current strategy should be abandoned." Although the outside directors had supported Ferris during the company's acquisition program, they now decided that Ferris was an obstacle to restructuring the company "There comes a point," said Luce, "when no board can impose its own beliefs over the opposition of the people who elected it." Ferris was replaced by Frank A. Olsen, chairman of Allegis's Hertz subsidiary.[b]

See Table 1 for a listing of events leading to Ferris's downfall. Following Ferris's resignation, Allegis sold off Hertz and Hilton International.

Table 1.   CEO Richard Ferris and the Allegis Corporation

	Ferris's Bumpy Ride at Allegis
1962	Bachelor's degree from Cornell University in hotel management. Later that year joins Western International Hotels, Westin's predecessor, as staff planner.
1971	Joins UAL as president of its food services division.
1979	Named chief executive officer of UAL and quickly faces industry-wide crisis of confidence in the DC-10 following a disastrous American Airlines crash in Chicago; Mr. Ferris grounds United's entire fleet of DC-10s.
1982	Becomes UAL's chairman and president. Air traffic controller's strike, fare wars, and recession thrust UALs results deep into the red.
May 1985	Mr. Ferris's demand that United pilots accept a two-tier wage system triggers a 29–day walkout by 5,000 United pilots. UAL blames the strike for a $91–million second-quarter loss.
June 1985	In the biggest step so far toward implementing Mr. Ferris's broad travel services strategy, UAL agrees to acquire RCA Corp.'s Hertz unit, prompting speculation that other airlines will follow its expansion into travel services.
October 1985	UAL acquires Pan American World Airways' Pacific operations for $750 million.
August 1986	Labor strife wrecks United's plan to acquire Frontier Airlines.
December 1986	UAL agrees to buy Transworld Corp.'s Hilton International Co. unit in a transaction valued at $980 million.
April 1987	The union representing United pilots launches a $4.5 billion takeover bid for the airline; Allegis's management rejects the offer as "grossly inadequate" and grants golden parachutes to Mr. Ferris and seven other top officials.
May 12, 1987	Boeing Co. enters an unusual antitakeover aircraft-financing arrangement with Allegis.
May 26, 1987	Coniston Partners, a New York investment firm that holds a 13% Allegis stake, announces it will seek to gain control of the Allegis board.
May 28, 1987	Allegis directors proposes a plan to distribute $60 a share to stockholders and keep the company intact in a last-ditch effort to forestall a takeover.
June 4, 1987	United pilots propose a restructuring plan that would break up the company and pay holders $70 a share. Allegis stock soars as a result, heightening pressure on management to sweeten its offer.

Source: Wall Street Journal, 11 June 1987, p. 22.

b. Arthur Fleisher Jr., Geoffrey C. Hazard Jr., and Miriam Z. Klipper, *Board Games: The Changing Shape of Corporate America* (Boston: Little, Brown, 1988), p. 192.

The anticipated existence of synergistic benefits allows firms to incur the expenses of the acquisition process and still be able to afford to give target shareholders a premium for their shares. Synergy may allow the combined firm to appear to have a positive *net acquisition value* (NAV).

$$NAV = V_{AB} - [V_A + V_B] - P - E \qquad (4.1)$$

where

V_{AB} = the combined value of the two firms
V_B = the market value of the shares of B
P = premium paid for B
E = expenses of the acquisition process
V_A = A's measure of its own value.

Reorganizing equation 4.1, we get:

$$NAV = [V_{AB} - (V_A + V_B)] - (P+E) \qquad (4.2)$$

The term in the brackets is the synergistic effect. This effect must be greater than the sum of P + E to justify going forward with the merger. If the bracketed term is not greater than the sum of P + E, the bidding firm will have overpaid for the target.

What is to be included in the area of synergistic effects? Some researchers view synergy broadly and include the elimination of inefficient management by installing the more capable management of the acquiring firm.[1] Although it is reasonable to define synergy in this manner, this chapter defines the term more narrowly and treats management-induced gains separately. This approach is consistent with the more common uses of the term *synergy.*[2]

The two main types of synergy are operating synergy and financial synergy. *Operating synergy* comes in two forms: revenue enhancements and cost reductions. These revenue enhancements and efficiency gains or operating economies may be derived in horizontal or vertical mergers. *Financial synergy* refers to the possibility that the cost of capital may be lowered by combining one or more companies.

Operating Synergy

Revenue-Enhancing Operating Synergy

Revenue-enhancing operating synergy may be more difficult to achieve than cost reduction synergies. Clemente and Greenspan refer to this as revenue-enhancing opportunity (REO). They define it as "a newly created or strengthened product or service that is for-

---

1. Paul Asquith, "Merger Bids, Uncertainty and Stockholder Returns," *Journal of Financial Economics* 11, no. 1–4 (April 1983), pp. 51–83; Michael Bradley, Anand Desai, and E. Han Kim, "The Rationale Behind Interfirm Tender Offers: Information or Synergy," *Journal of Financial Economics* 11, no. 1–4 (April 1983), pp. 183–206.

2. Michael Jensen and Richard Ruback, "The Market for Corporate Control: The Scientific Evidence," *Journal of Financial Economics* 11, no. 1–4 (April 1983), pp. 5–50.

mulated by the fusion of two distinct attributes of the merger partners and which generates immediate and/or long-term revenue growth."[3] There are many potential sources of revenue enhancements, and they may vary greatly from deal to deal. They may come from a sharing of marketing opportunities by cross-marketing each merger partner's products. With a broader product line, each company could sell more products and services to their product base. Cross-marketing has the potential to enhance the revenues of each merger partner, thereby enabling each company to expand its revenues quickly.

The multitude of ways in which revenue-enhancing synergies may be achieved defies brief descriptions. It may come from one company with a major brand name lending its reputation to an upcoming product line of a merger partner. Alternatively, it may arise from a company with a strong distribution network merging with a firm that has products of great potential but questionable ability to get them to the market before rivals can react and seize the period of opportunity. Although the sources may be great, revenue-enhancing synergies are sometimes difficult to achieve. Such enhancements are more difficult to quantify and build into valuation models. This is why cost-related synergies are often highlighted in merger planning, whereas the potential revenue enhancements may be discussed but not clearly defined. It is easier to say we have certain specific facilities that are duplicative and can be eliminated than to specifically show how revenues can be increased through a combination of two companies. Potential revenue enhancements often are vaguely referred to as merger benefits but are not clearly quantified. This is one reason some deals fail to manifest the anticipated benefits. The reason can be found in poor premerger planning caused by failing to specifically quantify revenue enhancements.

Cost-Reducing Operating Synergies

Merger planners tend to look for cost-reducing synergies as the main source of operating synergies. These cost reductions may come as a result of *economies of scale*—decreases in per-unit costs that result from an increase in the size or scale of a company's operations.

Manufacturing firms typically operate at high per-unit costs for low levels of output. This is because the fixed costs of operating their manufacturing facilities are spread out over relatively low levels of output. As the output levels rise, the per-unit costs decline. This is sometimes referred to as *spreading overhead.* Some of the other sources of these gains arise from increased specialization of labor and management and the more efficient use of capital equipment, which might not be possible at low output levels. This phenomenon continues for a certain range of output, after which per-unit costs may rise as the firm experiences diseconomies of scale. Diseconomies of scale may arise as the firm experiences higher costs and other problems associated with coordinating a larger scale operation. The extent to which diseconomies of scale exist is a topic of dispute for many economists. Some economists cite as evidence the continued growth of large multinational companies, such as Exxon and General Motors. These firms have exhibited extended periods of growth while still paying stockholders an acceptable return on equity. Others contend that such firms would be able to provide stockholders a higher rate of return if they were smaller, more efficient companies.

Figure 4.1, which depicts scale economies and diseconomies, shows that an optimal output level occurs when per-unit costs are at a minimum. This implies that an expansion

3. Mark N. Clemente and David S. Greenspan, *Winning at Mergers and Acquisitions: The Guide to Market-Focused Planning and Integration* (New York: John Wiley & Sons), 1998, p. 46.

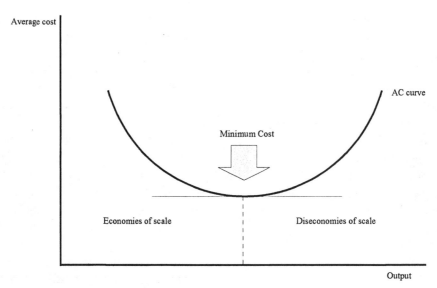

Figure 4.1. Economies and diseconomies of scale.

through the horizontal acquisition of a competitor may increase the size of the acquiring firm's operation and lower per-unit costs.

Several examples of mergers and acquisitions motivated by the pursuit of scale economies have occurred in the cruise industry, which has undergone a series of consolidating mergers and acquisitions. The 1989 acquisition of Sitmar Cruises by Princess Cruises and the 1994 merger between Radisson Diamond Cruises and Seven Seas Cruises enabled the combined cruise lines to offer an expanded product line in the form of more ships, beds, and itineraries while lowering per-bed costs. The cruise industry has learned that a sales force of a given size can service a greater number of ships and itineraries. As cruise lines combine, they find that they do not need to maintain the same size administrative facilities and sales forces. For example, each cruise line has its own network of district sales managers who call on travel agencies within an area. When one cruise line buys another, one company's sales force may be able to service the combined itineraries of both groups of ships. This enables the acquiring company to purchase the target's projected revenues with less than the target's historical cost structure.

Another example of scale economies related to these cruise mergers is the use of marketing expenditures. Partly because of the size of its fleet, Princess Cruises is able to maintain a national television advertising campaign. A cruise line needs to be of a certain minimum size for a national television advertising campaign to be feasible. By buying Sitmar, which offered similar cruises and was of similar size, Princess was better able to market its "Love Boat" theme nationally. They were also able to expand capacity quickly through this acquisition while at the same time ordering new ships to be built. When the new ships arrived, they sold off some of the older Sitmar ships. The Sitmar acquisition served its purpose of providing an avenue for quick expansion to take advantage of a window of opportunity.

In the cruise industry, the smaller cruise lines have difficulty competing with the bigger lines because they are not large enough to be able to spread out the costs of a national television campaign across a large enough number of ships to make such marketing costs effective. They then are relegated to other forms of marketing that do not have the same effectiveness as television in generating consumer awareness. Therefore, acquisitions are one way to develop a larger enough revenue base to support the use of the more expensive marketing media used by larger competitors.

Another example of scale economies that may be achieved through mergers and acquisitions is found in the brewing industry. Through mergers, Heilmans, Strohs, and Pabst put together a national distribution network with production at regional centers. Scale economies were achieved in production, distribution, and advertising. Further economic advantages were achieved when Strohs merged with Schaeffer and later with Schlitz.

Some empirical research supports the assertion that mergers and acquisitions are used to achieve operating economies. For example, Lictenberg and Siegel detected improvements in the efficiency of plants that had undergone ownership changes.[4] In fact, they found that those plants that had performed the worst were the ones that were most likely to experience an ownership change. It should not, however, be concluded that simply because some evidence exists that mergers are associated with operating economies, mergers are the best way to achieve such economies. That proposition is not supported by economic research.

Another concept that is closely related to and sometimes confused with economies of scale is *economies of scope,* which is the ability of a firm to utilize one set of inputs to provide a broader range of products and services. A good example of scope economies arises in the banking industry. In the banking industry, for example, scope economies may be as important as economies of scale in explaining mergers and acquisitions.[5] The pursuit of these economies is one of the factors behind the consolidation within the banking industry that occurred in the fifth merger wave.

When financial institutions merge, they can share inputs to offer a broader range of services, such as a trust department, consumer investment products unit, or economic analysis group. Smaller banks might not be able to afford the costs of these departments. Inputs such as a computer system may be shared to process a wide variety of loans and deposit accounts. Whether these benefits are either the true reason or a sufficient reason for the increased number of banking mergers that have taken place in the recent period of deregulation is a very different issue.[6] The many bank mergers that occurred during the fourth merger resulted in a a new breed of bank in the industry—the superregional bank. The acquisition of other regional banks largely accounts for the growth of the superregional banks of the 1980s. These superregional banks, such as the Bank One Corporation, Barnett Bank, and NationsBank, grew to the point where they were competitive with the larger money center banks in the provision of many services. Others banks, such as the Bank of New England, expanded too rapidly through acquisitions and encountered financial difficulties. In the 1990s certain of the superregionals, such as NationsBank and First Union, continued to expand and became two of the largest banks in the United States.

---

4. Frank Lictenberg and Donald Siegel, "Productivity and Changes in Ownership of Manufacturing Plants," *Brookings Papers on Economic Activity* 3 (1987), pp. 643–683.

5. Loretta J. Mester, "Efficient Product of Financial Services: Scale and Scope Economies," Review, Federal Reserve Bank of Philadelphia, January/February 1987, pp. 15–25.

6. Patrick A. Gaughan, "Financial Deregulation, Banking Mergers and the Impact on Regional Business," Proceedings of the Pacific Northwest Regional Economic Conference, University of Washington, Spring 1988.

It often is the case that synergistic benefits are touted as the reason for expensive mergers. However, these benefits often fail to materialize. An example of anticipated synergistic benefits that were expected to derive from expected economies of scale and economies of scope but never materialized is described in this chapter's case study of the Allegis Corporation.

Synergy and Acquisition Premiums

In Chapter 13 we discuss the concept of acquisition premiums, which typically are paid in control share acquisitions. This premium is a value in excess of the market value of a company that is paid for the right to control and proportionately enjoy the profits of the business. Bidders often cite anticipated synergy as the reason for the payment of a premium. Given the track record of some acquisitions that have not turned out as anticipated, the market sometimes questions the reasonableness of this synergy, especially when it is used as the justification for an unusually high premium. Synergy requires that the bidder receive gains, such as in the form of performance improvements, that offset the premium.[7] It is hoped that these gains will be realized in the years following the transaction. In order for the premium payment (P) to make sense, the present value of these gains must exceed the premium payment (P). This relationship is expressed as follows:

$$P = SG_1/(1 + r) + SG_2/(1 + r)^2 + ... + SG_n/(1 + r)^n$$

One of the complicating factors in rationalizing the payment of a significant premium is that the premium is usually paid up-front, with the gains coming over the course of time. The further into the future these gains are realized, the lower their present value. In addition, the higher the discount rate that is used to convert the synergistic gains to present value, the more difficult it is to justify a high premium. If the bidder also anticipates that there will be a significant initial period before the gains begin manifesting themselves, such as when the bidder is trying to merge the two corporate cultures, this pushes the start of the gains further into the future. If a bidder is using a high discount rate and/or does not expect gains to materialize for an extended period of time, it is hard to justify a high premium. Moreover, the higher the premium, the more pressure the combined company is under to realize a high rate of growth in future synergistic gains.

Process of Realizing Synergistic Gains

The process of realizing synergistic gains is summarized in Figure 4.2.

The successful pursuit of synergistic gains begins with careful strategic planning. Such planning needs to be well-researched, thorough, and firmly grounded in realism. The more well thought out the merger planning, the better the chance that the deal will be successful. Sometimes the pressure to complete the deal quickly is one cause of insufficient premerger planning.[8] This may be a particular problem in cases in which the bidder is dealing with a

---

7. See Mark L. Sirower, *The Synergy Trap* (New York: The Free Press, 1997), pp. 44–81.

8. D.B. Jemison and S.B. Sitkin, "Acquisitions: The Process Can Be a Problem," *Harvard Business Review* 64 (March/April 1986), pp. 107–116.

Competitors Responses

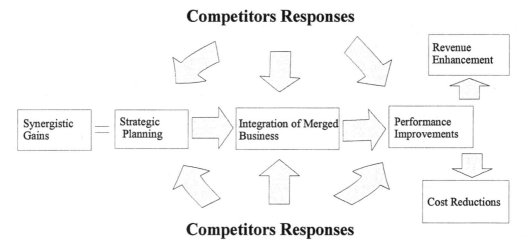

Competitors Responses

Figure 4.2. The process of realizing synergistic gains.

target's resistance or when there are other bidders. It helps if the planners are personally familiar with the industry. When one knows more about the industry, one is better able to realistically assess assumptions about future performance. This is one reason deals that are more within or close to a bidder's industry tend to perform better than those outside the bidder's industry.

Following the acquisition or merger, the next major step is to integrate the two separate businesses. The more diverse the two corporate cultures, the more difficult this task is. Sound advance planning may enable the bidder to be aware of any significant cultural differences that could impede the integration process. Although these factors are very important to the success of an acquisition or a merger, they often are difficult to quantify and build into a financial model. Nonetheless, the financial effects of a failed integration process will be clear in the financial results in the years after the deal. Sometimes the potential merger partners can learn a lot about the other firm's corporate culture in the negotiation process. Cultural differences and "significant operational and strategic differences" were cited as the reason for PhyCor and MedPartners, two large physician management companies, calling off their planned $6.25 billion 1998 merger.[9] These two companies were fortunate that they were able to assess the potential problems before the merger and were able to call off the deal in advance. Many other merger partners are not as fortunate and end up trying to force a corporate match that should never have been.

As noted previously, the final realization of synergistic gains may be broken down into two areas: revenue enhancement and cost reduction. The potential revenue enhancements, which may come in several ways, such as through the cross-selling that may take place when a company has a broader product line, may make it worthwhile for a bidder to pay a significant premium. Cost reductions, such as those that often come from the elimination of duplicate costs in the merged companies, may enable the buyer to pay a higher premium because the target may be more profitable to the buyer than it is to itself. An example of successful cost reduction was the 1991 acquisition of Manufacturers Hanover

---

9. Anita Sharpe, "PhyCor, MedPartners Call Off Merger Because of Cultural Differences," *Wall Street Journal,* January 8, 1998, A2.

Trust by Chemical Bank in 1991. When the deal was announced, the companies declared that they anticipated savings of approximately $650 million. However, the actual savings derived from closing unnecessary branches and eliminating redundant overhead proved to be $750 million.[10] The success of this deal was one factor that led Chemical Bank to merge with Chase Manhattan in a $13 billion deal in 1995. The best situation is when the business is able to realize both revenue enhancement and cost reduction. When a bidder has paid a significant premium, it implicitly assumes more pressure to realize greater revenue enhancement and more cost reductions. The higher the premium, the more of both are needed.

Throughout the process the bidder needs to be aware of the actual and anticipated responses of competitors. Enhanced revenues may come at the expense of competitors' revenues. It may not be realistic to assume that they will stand still and watch a competitor improve its position at their expense through acquisitions. When a company can demonstrate such performance improvements through mergers and acquisitions, competitors may respond with their own acquisition programs. Once again, the myriad of different responses may be somewhat difficult to model, but they, nonetheless, need to be carefully considered. Although it has already been mentioned, it is so important that it is worth mentioning again how easy it is to build a financial model that shows whatever result one wants to see. Assumptions can be built into the valuation models that are developed in Chapters 13 and 14 to show both revenue enhancement and cost reductions. As the merged business takes steps to realize the theorized financial gains, it may discover that the financial model building process was the easiest part, whereas working through all the other steps necessary to realize the actual gains proves to be the most difficult task.

Financial Synergy

Financial synergy refers to the impact of a corporate merger or acquisition on the costs of capital to the acquiring firm or the merging partners. The extent to which financial synergy exists in corporate combinations, the costs of capital should be lowered. Whether financial synergy actually exists, however, is a matter of dispute within corporate finance.

As noted, the combination of two firms may reduce risk if the firms' cash flow streams are not perfectly correlated. If the acquisition or merger lowers the volatility of the cash flows, suppliers of capital may consider the firm less risky. The risk of bankruptcy would presumably be less, given the fact that wide swings up and down in the combined firm's cash flows would be less likely. This implies that it is less likely that cash flows would fall so low that the firm could become technically insolvent. Technical insolvency occurs when a firm cannot meet its current obligations as they come due.

Technical insolvency may occur even when total assets exceed total liabilities. Another more serious form of business failure occurs when total liabilities exceed total assets and the net worth of the firm is negative. Even though technical insolvency may be less serious than this form of bankruptcy, it may be sufficient to result in a fall in the firm's credit rating, which may cause the cost of capital to rise.

---

10. Bruce Wasserstein, *Big Deal* (New York: Warner Books, 1998), pp. 140–141.

Higgins and Schall explain this effect in terms of *debt coinsurance.*[11] If the correlation of the income streams of two firms is less than perfectly positively correlated, the bankruptcy risk associated with the combination of the two firms may be reduced. Under certain circumstances one of the firms could experience conditions that force it into bankruptcy. It is difficult to know in advance which one of two possible firms would succumb to this fate. In the event that one of the firms fails, creditors may suffer a loss. If the two firms were combined in advance of these financial problems, however, the cash flows of the solvent firm that are in excess of its debt service needs would cushion the decline in the other firm's cash flows. The offsetting earnings of the firm in good condition might be sufficient to prevent the combined firm from falling into bankruptcy and causing creditors to suffer losses.

The problem with the debt-coinsurance effect is that the benefits accrue to debt holders at the expense of equity holders. Debt holders gain by holding debt in a less risky firm. Higgins and Schall observe that these gains come at the expense of stockholders, who lose in the acquisition. These researchers assume that total returns that can be provided by the combined firm are constant (R_T). If more of these returns are provided to bondholders (R_B), they must come at the expense of stockholders (R_S).

$$R_T = R_S + R_B$$

In other words, Higgins and Schall maintain that the debt-coinsurance effect does not create any new value but merely redistributes gains among the providers of capital to the firm. There is no general agreement on this result. Lewellen, for example, has concluded that stockholders gain from these types of combinations.[12] Other studies, however, fail to indicate that the debt-related motives are more relevant for conglomerate acquisitions than for nonconglomerate acquisitions.[13]

Higgins and Schall show that the stockholders' losses may be offset by issuing new debt after the merger. The stockholders will then gain through the tax savings on the debt interest payments. Galais and Masulis have demonstrated this result.[14] The additional debt would increase the debt-equity ratio of the postmerger firm to a level that stockholders must have found desirable, or at least acceptable, before the merger. With the higher debt-equity ratio, the firm becomes a higher risk–higher return investment.

As noted previously, a company may experience economies of scale through acquisitions. These economies are usually thought to come from production cost decreases, attained by operating at higher capacity levels or through a reduced sales force or a shared distribution system. As a result of acquisitions, financial economies of scale are also possible in the form of lower flotation and transaction costs.[15]

---

11. Robert C. Higgins and Lawrence C. Schall, "Corporate Bankruptcy and Conglomerate Mergers," *Journal of Finance* 30 (March 1975), pp. 93–113.

12. Wilbur G. Lewellen, "A Pure Rationale for the Conglomerate Merger," *Journal of Finance,* vol. 26, no. 2 (May 1971), pp. 521–545.

13. Pieter T. Elgers and John J. Clark, "Merger Types and Shareholder Returns: Additional Evidence," *Financial Management,* vol. 9, issue 2 (Summer 1980), pp. 66–72.

14. Dan Galais and Ronald W. Masulis, "The Option Pricing Model and the Risk Factor of Stock," *Journal of Financial Economics,* vol. 3(1/2) (January/March 1976), pp. 53–81.

15. Haim Levy and Marshall Sarnat, "Diversification, Portfolio Analysis and the Uneasy Case for Conglomerate Mergers," *Journal of Finance,* vol. 25, no. 4 (September 1970), pp. 795–802.

In financial markets, a larger company has certain advantages that may lower the cost of capital to the firm. It enjoys better access to financial markets, and it tends to experience lower costs of raising capital, presumably because it is considered to be less risky than a smaller firm. Therefore, the costs of borrowing by issuing bonds are lower because a larger firm would probably be able to issue bonds offering a lower interest rate than a smaller company. In addition, there are certain fixed costs in the issuance of securities, such as Securities and Exchange Commission (SEC) registration costs, legal fees, and printing costs. These costs would be spread out over a greater dollar volume of securities because the larger company would probably borrow more capital with each issue of bonds.

The analysis is similar in the case of equity securities. Flotation costs per dollar raised would be lower for larger issues than for smaller issues. In addition, the selling effort required may be greater for riskier issues than for less risky larger firms. It is assumed in this discussion that larger firms are less risky and bear a lower probability of bankruptcy and financial failure. If a larger firm, which might result from a combination of several other firms, is so inefficient, however, that profits start to fall, the larger combination of companies could have a greater risk of financial failure. Levy and Sarnat have developed a model to show the diversification effect that occurs when two or more imperfectly correlated income streams combine to lower the probability of default. This lower risk level induces capital holders to provide capital to the combined firm or conglomerate at lower costs than they would have provided to the individual, premerger components. Their analysis presents the financial synergistic benefits as an economic gain that results from mergers.

DIVERSIFICATION

Diversification means growing outside a company's current industry category. This motive played a major role in the acquisitions and mergers that took place in the third merger wave—the conglomerate era. During the late 1960s firms often sought to expand by buying other companies rather than through internal expansion. This outward expansion was often facilitated by some creative financial techniques that temporarily caused the acquiring firm's stock price to rise while adding little real value through the exchange. The legacy of the conglomerates has drawn poor, or at least mixed, reviews. Indeed, many of the firms that grew into conglomerates in the 1960s were disassembled through various spinoffs and divestitures in the 1970s and 1980s. This process of *deconglomerization* raises serious doubts as to the value of diversification based on expansion.

Although many companies have regretted their attempts at diversification, others can claim to have gained significantly. One such firm is General Electric (GE). Contrary to what its name implies, GE is no longer merely an electronics company. Through a pattern of acquisitions and divestitures, the firm has become a diversified conglomerate with operations in insurance, television stations, plastics, medical equipment, and so on. Table 4.1 chronicles some of GE's acquisitions and divestitures. Figure 4.3 shows the major components of the firm's business.

During the 1980s and 1990s, at a time when the firm was acquiring and divesting various companies, earnings rose significantly (Table 4.2 and Figure 4.4). The market responded favorably to these diversified acquisitions by following the rising pattern of earnings.

Table 4.1. General Electric's Acquisitions and Divestitures, 1984–97

Acquisitions and Divestitures of $100 Million or More

Acquisitions

1984	Buys Employers Reinsurance for $1.1 billion
1986	Buys RCA for $6.3 billion
	Buys 80% of Kidder Peabody for approximately $600 million
1987	Buys Miami Television Station for approximately $270 million
	Buys D&K Financial for $100 million
	Buys the medical equipment business of Thomson S.A. of France in exchange for GE consumer electronics business
	Buys Gelco Corp. for $250 million
1988	Buys Montgomery Ward's credit card operation for $1 billion and assumption of $1.8 billion in debt
	Buys Roper Corp. for $510 million
	Agrees to buy Borg-Warner's plastics business for $2.3 billion
1989	Buys minority interest in Tungsram Co. in Hungary; established joint ventures in appliances, power generation, and electrical equipment in U.K.
1990	Buys majority interest in Tungsram Co.
	Buys leasing operations of MNC Financial, Inc.
	Buys all leasing operations of the Burton Group
	Buys Travelers Mortgage Services, Inc.
1991	Buys engine overhaul and maintenance facility from British Airways
	Buys NBC Financial News Network
	Buys certain leasing operations from Chase Manhattan Bank
1992	Buys both Lemag and Agut S.A. of Spain
1993	Buys Japanese X-ray manufacturer
	Buys INS, a leading European supplier of electronic data interchange
1994	Buys Northern Telecom Finance Corporation
	Buys Minebea Credit
	Buys Linder Licht in Germany
1995	Buys Pallas Group in U.K.
	Buys French finance company SOVAC
	Buys Frankona Re and Aachen Re in Germany
	Buys AEG Low-Voltage business in Germany
	Buys Multilin of Canada
1996	Buys 73% of DAKO S.A. in Brazil
	Buys Groenendijk Yellowcabin in Europe
	Buys Smith Self Drive in U.K.
	Buys the fleet management and leasing operations of the JMJ Group in Australia
	Buys 80% of Marubeni Car System Co. in Japan
	Buys AmeriData in U.S. and CompuNet in Germany
	Buys PT Sinar Baru Electric (SiBalec) in Indonesia
	Buys National M.D.
	Buys Procond Elettronica in Italy
1997	Buys Greenwich Air Services and UNC Incorporated
	Buys Woodchester in Ireland
	Buys selected assets of Flame Electrical Ltd. in South Africa
	Buys Lockheed Martin Medical Systems and Innomed of Germany as well as a 20% stake in ALI
	Buys Resinmec in Italy and Polimeros Argentinos S.A. in Argentina
	Buys the gas turbine division of Stewart & Stevenson Services

Divestitures

1983	Sells housewares division to Black & Decker for about $300 million
1984	Sells Utah International for $2.4 billion
	Sells GE Credit's second-mortgage unit for $600 million
	Sells housewares business to Black & Decker
1985	Sells interest in Australian coal fields for $390 million

Table 4.1.   Continued

1987	Sells North American Co. for Life & Health for $200 million
	Sells consumer electronics business to Thomson S.A. in exchange for Thomson's medical equipment business and cash
1988	Sells RCA Global Communications for $160 million
	Sells five radio stations for $122 million
1990	Sells Ladd Petroleum Corporation
1991	Sells NBC's interest in RCA Columbia Home Video
	Sells most of its auto auction business
1992	Transfers GE's aerospace business, GE Government Services, and other businesses to new company controlled by Martin Marietta shareholders
1994	Sells assets of the terminated Kidder, Peabody to Paine Webber

Sources: Wall Street Journal, August 4, 1988, p, 1. Reprinted by permission of the Wall Street Journal, copyright © 1988 Dow Jones & Company, Inc. All rights reserved worldwide. General Electric *Annual Reports,* 1983–1997.

Diversification and the Acquisition of Leading Industry Positions

Part of the reasoning behind GE's successful diversification strategy has been the types of companies they have acquired. General Electric sought to acquire leading positions in the various industries in which it owned businesses. Leading is usually interpreted as the first or second rank according to market shares. It is believed by acquirers like GE that the number one or number two position provides a more dominant position, which affords advantages over the smaller competitors. These advantages can manifest themselves in a

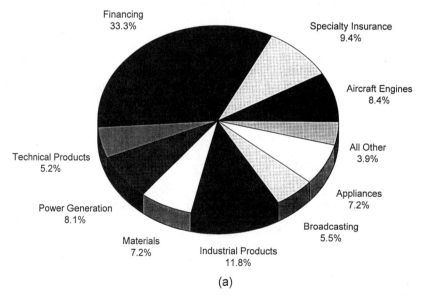

Figure 4.3.   General Electric's revenue percentages by business segment (a) 1997; (b) 1980.

Source: General Electric Company, *Annual Reports.*

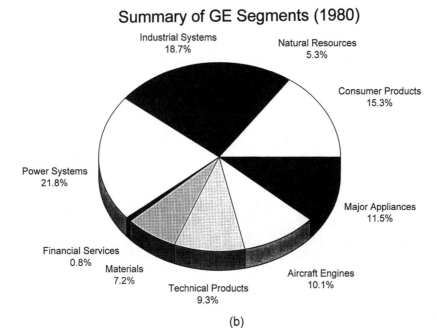

Summary of GE Segments (1980)

Industrial Systems 18.7%
Natural Resources 5.3%
Consumer Products 15.3%
Power Systems 21.8%
Major Appliances 11.5%
Financial Services 0.8%
Materials 7.2%
Technical Products 9.3%
Aircraft Engines 10.1%

(b)

Figure 4.3. Continued

number of ways, including broader consumer awareness in the marketplace as leading positions in distribution. Corporations in the secondary ranks, such as numbers 4 or 5, may sometimes be at such a disadvantage that it is difficult for them to generate rewarding returns. Companies within the overall company framework that do not hold a leading position, and do not have reasonable prospects of cost-effectively acquiring such a position,

Table 4.2.   General Electric, Net Income and Stock Prices

Year	Earnings per Share	Stock Prices
1983	2.02	6.50
1984	2.28	6.75
1985	2.28	8.10
1986	2.49	9.75
1987	2.92	13.15
1988	3.75	10.75
1989	4.36	13.55
1990	4.85	15.70
1991	2.64	16.40
1992	4.73	20.05
1993	4.32	23.50
1994	4.73	23.50
1995	6.57	30.75
1996	7.28	43.90
1997	8.20	62.25[*]
1998	9.30	85.83

* 2–for-1 stock split (4/28/97)

Source: GE Company, *Annual Reports* (1983–98).

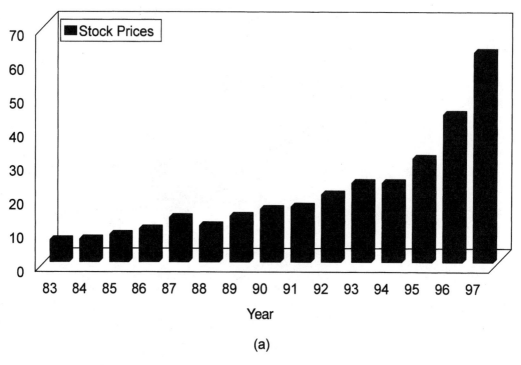

(a)

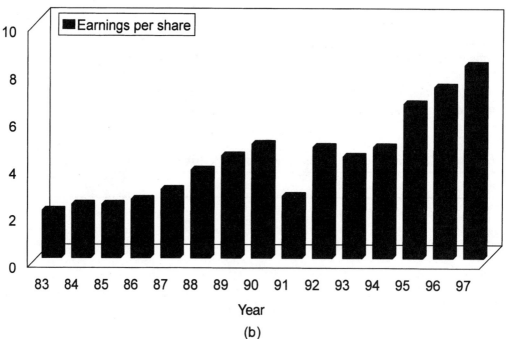

(b)

Figure 4.4. General Electric (a) stock prices; (b) earnings per share.

Source: General Electric Company, *Annual Reports.*

become candidates for divestiture. The released resources derived from such a divestiture can then be reinvested in other companies to exploit the benefits of their dominant position or used to acquire leading companies in other industries.

There are several other examples of very diversified companies that have enjoyed significant success by pursuing the strategy of trying to acquire a leading position in each business category they are in. Allied Signal, which is based in Morris Township, New Jersey, is a good example of a diversified manufacturer that has enjoyed impressive earnings growth and a high market valuation. For companies like Allied Signal, being diversified does not mean that they are not regularly involved in mergers and acquisitions. In fact, during the tenure of its current chief executive officer (CEO), Lawrence Bossidy, who took over the company when it had a price-earnings ratio (P/E) of only 8, he carefully analyzed the performance of the many business units within Allied Signal and sold off units that did not fit or did not exhibit at least the potential for a profit margin in excess of 15%. The result was a company with fewer but more profitable business units that could be more closely monitored.

By expanding through the acquisition of other firms, the acquiring corporation may attempt to achieve some of the benefits that investors receive by diversifying their portfolio of assets. The portfolio theory research literature in finance has attempted to quantify some of the risk-reduction benefits that an investor may enjoy through diversification. This research clearly supports the intuitive belief of investors that "putting all one's eggs in one basket" is not a wise decision. However, when this strategy is applied to capital assets and whole corporations, it loses some of its appeal. A company often will pursue diversification outside its own industry when management is displeased by the current volatile level of earnings. A volatile income stream makes it more difficult to pay regular dividends and creates an unstable environment for long-term planning. Financial markets may interpret a falloff in earnings that results in a reduction or cancellation of a quarterly dividend as a negative sign.

CASE STUDY: SEARS ROEBUCK—A FAILED DIVERSIFICATION STRATEGY

Sears Roebuck has long been one of the leading retailers in the United States. However, the company was dissatisfied with what it perceived as insufficiently rapid growth. It also wanted to take advantage of the company's good name and established customer base, which brought a steady flow of traffic into its nationwide network of stores. Pursuit of this goal led the company to engage in a series of acquisitions that included Allstate Insurance, which, in turn, made other diversifying acquisitions involving banks and mortgage companies. The parent company's diversification program extended to acquisitions of Dean Witter Reynolds, a securities brokerage firm, and Coldwell Banker, a real estate company. While the company expanded aggressively into financial services, its core merchandising business suffered. In addition, it was unable to find offsetting gains from the new Sears Financial Services Center, which it had established in an attempt to tie together the different components of the financial services network it had put together.

In retrospect, Sears Roebuck did not understand how the various components of its new financial services network were marketed. It thought it could sell securities, houses, and insurance through the same distributions channels through which it was selling air conditioners, lawnmowers, and dishwashers. Although it may not have been happy with the growth in its core businesses, Sears had a good reputation for quality products and standing behind the goods it sold. However, the company somehow believed that customers who came to buy a dishwasher or school clothing for their children would stop by the Sears Financial Services Center and buy stock or maybe a house while they are at the mall. As silly as this sounds, it served as the basis for a very expensive acquisition strategy. Finally, after intense pressure from institutional investors who clearly saw that the strategy was not working, Sears decided to spin off Dean Witter and Coldwell Banker in 1992 and refocused its efforts on its core business, which had continued to decline over the prior decade. Sure enough, once its focus returned to what the company was good at, it was able to capitalize on its strengths and started to grow. The lesson from the Sears failed diversification strategy is twofold. First, just because you are good at one business does not mean that you can extend the assets and managerial resources of your organization to another very different business. The second lesson is that forays into more exciting business categories in which you have not demonstrated any expertise may be expensive and losing propositions. It often is better to simply stay with the boring business that you are good at and learn ways to improve your performance. It is much easier to make small but meaningful improvements in a business in which you have established success than to move to a totally different business area.

Diversification to Enter More Profitable Industries

One reason management may opt for diversified expansion is its desire to enter industries that are more profitable than the acquiring firm's current industry. It could be that the parent company's industry has reached the mature stage or that the competitive pressures within that industry preclude the possibility of raising prices to a level where extranormal profits can be enjoyed.

One problem that some firms may encounter when they seek to expand by entering industries that offer better profit opportunities is the lack of an assurance that those profit opportunities will persist for an extended time in the future. Industries that are profitable now may not be as profitable in the future.[16] Competitive pressures serve to bring about a movement toward a long-term equalization of rates of return across industries. Clearly, this does not mean that the rates of return in all industries at any moment in time are equal. The forces of competition that move industries to have equal returns are offset by opposing forces, such as industrial development, that cause industries to have varying rates of return. Those above average return industries that do not have imposing barriers to entry will experience declining returns until they reach the cross-industry average.

Economic theory implies that in the long run only industries that are difficult to enter will have above-average returns. This implies that a diversification program to enter more

---

16. Michael Gort, "Diversification, Mergers and Profits," in *The Corporate Merger,* edited by William W. Alberts (Chicago: University of Chicago Press, 1974), p. 38.

profitable industries will not be successful in the long run. The expanding firm may not be able to enter those industries that exhibit persistently above-average returns because of barriers that prevent entry and may only be able to enter the industries with low barriers. When entering the low-barrier industry, the expanding company will probably be forced to compete against other entrants who were attracted by temporarily above-average returns and low barriers. The increased number of competitors will drive down returns and cause the expansion strategy to fail.

Financial Benefits of Diversification

One possible area of benefits of diversification that has been cited is the coinsurance effect. This occurs when firms with imperfectly correlated earnings combine and derive a combined earnings stream that is less volatile than either of the individual firm's earnings stream. The covariance is a statistical measure of the linear association between two variables. In this case the variables in question are the earnings of two merger candidates, companies A and B. If, for example, the covariance between E_A and E_B is negative, there would appear to be an opportunity to derive coinsurance benefits from a merger between firm A and firm B.

$$\text{Cov } (E_A, E_B) = \mu E_A E_B = E[(E_A - \mu_{EA})(E_B - \mu_{EB})] < 0 \qquad (4.3)$$

CASE STUDY: ITT—DIVIDEND POLICY
AND THE VULNERABILITY TO A TAKEOVER

During the early 1980s ITT was a conglomerate undergoing a major restructuring. The successful and highly diversified conglomerate that Harold Geneen had built had begun to show signs of wear. The 1980s were a period of deconglomerization in which large, diversified companies were selling off divisions in an attempt to increase earnings and lift stock prices as conglomerates fell into disfavor.

ITT had been increasing its common stock dividend every year until the Fall of 1983. The company was paying out approximately $450 million per year in dividends. Between 1979 and 1983 much of the dividends paid out were financed by asset sales. The proceeds of asset sales in the company's restructuring program could not be used to revitalize the company because earnings were not sufficient to meet the expected dividend payments.

In the summer of 1983 ITT announced that it would cut its $2.76 quarterly dividend to $1.00. Investors reacted to the dividend cut, and the stock price fell. ITT common stock was priced at approximately $35 before the dividend cut and fell to a low of $20 after the announcement.

The full impact of the dividend cut was partially offset by the Pritzger group's stock purchases. The Pritzger group, led by financier Jay Pritzger, had been purchasing ITT common stock as a prelude to an eventual bid to take control of ITT in a leveraged buyout. The dividend cut enabled them to acquire a toehold interest in the company at a less expensive price. The fall in the stock price made the takeover bid all the more feasible.

The Pritzger bid was partially dependent on management support. The deal contained various financial incentives, which CEO Rand Araskog termed a *bribe* for management to support the bid.[a] Management strongly opposed the takeover. After a protracted struggle, the bid was withdrawn and ITT remained independent.

The problems associated with ITT's conglomerate structure persisted, however, until 1995, when the company announced a major restructuring in which it was split into three separate divisions.

---

a. Rand Araskog, *ITT Wars* (New York: Henry Holt Publishers, 1989).

An example of the acquisition of a company whose earnings have a negative correlation with the acquiring company would be that of a cyclical and a countercyclical company. If the acquiring company has a cyclical earnings stream, its earnings may be highly responsive to cyclical fluctuations in the economy. The term *business cycles* actually is a misnomer. Cycles implies a regular and repetitive pattern that is not indicative of the actual fluctuations in the economy. The ups and downs of the U.S. and world economies occur unpredictably and nonrepetitively.

Figure 4.5 depicts the sales of two companies: one that is procyclical and another that is countercyclical.

An example of a cyclical business would be a steel or automobile company. A business that has procyclical sales and earnings may want to attenuate the amplitude of its "cycles" by acquiring a noncyclical or even a countercyclical firm. A countercyclical firm is one whose revenues vary opposite to the movements of the economy.

It is difficult to find a purely countercyclical firm; it is easier to find targets whose revenues and earnings are less responsive to fluctuations in the economy. Typically, manufacturers of capital goods and consumer durables tend to be hit the hardest by economic downturns. The construction industry is particularly vulnerable to recessions. Nondurable industries, however, tend to be less volatile relative to the economy as a whole. The downside risk of such cyclical firms tends to be offset by the fact that capital goods manufacturers and construction industry firms tend to expand more in good times than do most other businesses. A firm that already has a cyclical sales and earnings pattern, however, may not be sufficiently attracted by a target's positive performance in good times, which comes at the cost of sharp downturns in poorer times. Therefore, the cyclical firm, interested in lowering its level of risk, may choose to acquire a noncyclical target.

Corporate Finance Theory and Diversification

Many firms have pursued diversification as a means of becoming less volatile. The acquisition of Electric Storage Battery (ESB) by the International Nickel Company (INCO) is a clear example of a volatile, commodity-based firm seeking to acquire a firm with a more stable pattern of earnings. The large conglomerates that rose up in the 1960s, such as Tenneco, Gulf & Western, ITT, Teledyne, and Ling-Temco-Vought (LTV), were all highly diversified corporations.

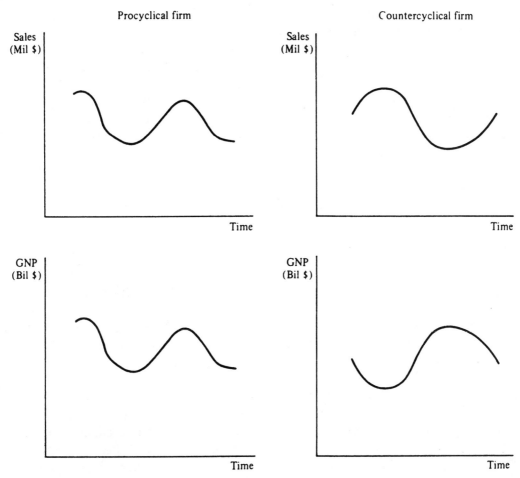

Figure 4.5.   In a procyclical sales pattern, a firm's sales may rise as the economy rises. In a countercyclical sales pattern, which is a less common occurrence, a firm's sales may move opposite the market.

Corporate finance theory takes a dim view of acquisitions in which diversification is the main motive.[17] The main reason is because the acquiring company is providing a service to stockholders that they can accomplish better themselves. Let us consider, for example, a steel company that has a typical pattern of cyclical sales and is considering acquiring a pharmaceutical company that exhibits a recession-resistant sales pattern. Presumably, these stockholders already have a portfolio that is diversified in accordance with their own risk and return preferences.

Financial theory states that the managers of the steel company are doing their stockholders a disservice through the acquisition of companies outside their industry. If stockholders in the steel company wanted to be stockholders in the pharmaceutical firm, they could easily adjust their portfolio to add shares of the pharmaceutical firm or another company with

17. Haim Levy and Marshall Sarnat, "Diversification, Portfolio Analysis and the Uneasy Case for Conglomerate Mergers," *Journal of Finance* 25 (September 1970), pp. 795–802.

a noncyclical earnings pattern. Stockholders can accomplish such transactions in a far less costly manner than through a corporate acquisition. Moreover, the fact that stockholders in the steel company allocated that part of their portfolio to a company that clearly had a pattern of cyclical earnings indicates that they were willing to accept the downturns in earnings—presumably because of the upside potential.

Another disadvantage of mergers that are motivated by diversification is the tendency to stretch the acquiring company's management skills. The ability to successfully manage a firm in one industry does not necessarily extend to other businesses. The history of U.S. business is replete with instances of companies that have diversified into areas beyond their managerial expertise. A classic example would be the acquisition by a regulated company, such as a public utility, of a firm in an unrelated industry that depends on intensive marketing and quick reactions. The managers of a power utility may desire to be in the hotel or restaurant industry but may lack the necessary expertise to manage such a business.

Empirical Evidence on Acquisition Programs of the 1960s

The conglomerate wave of the 1960s provided abundant evidence of the effects of large-scale diversifications into unrelated fields. These types of diversifications have attracted much criticism. Some evidence, however, indicates that, at least initially, the market responded favorably to the announcements of such acquisition programs. Katherine Schipper and Rex Thompson have analyzed the wealth effects of firms that announced acquisition programs.[18] Specifically, they considered what impact an announcement of an acquisitions program had on the value of the acquiring firm. They examined announcements of such programs before 1967 to 1970 because regulatory changes such as the Williams Act and the Tax Reform Act of 1969 took place in these years. These regulatory changes created certain impediments to the types of acquisitions that occurred in the 1960s. The study found that during this period acquisition programs were capitalized as positive net present value programs. Figure 4.6 shows that cumulative abnormal returns for the acquiring firm's stock responded positively to the acquisition program announcement. These results indicate that, at least before the regulatory changes of the late 1960s, the market had a positive view of acquisition programs, many of which involved substantial diversification. The favorable response of the market to the diversifying acquisitions of that time helps explain why the third takeover wave was as significant as it was.

Although Schipper and Thompson have shown that the market had a positive reaction to the announcement of the diverse acquisition programs of the 1960s, the poor performance of many of these acquisitions during the years that followed has shown that the market may have been overly optimistic in its initial assessment of the likelihood of conglomerate acquisitions to be successful. The undoing of many of these deals, sometimes through bustup takeovers, has confirmed the questionable nature of this expansion strategy.

---

18. Katherine Schipper and Rex Thompson, "The Value of Merger Activity," *Journal of Financial Economics* 11, no. 1–4 (April 1983), pp. 85–119.

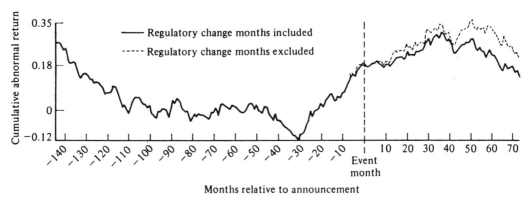

Figure 4.6.   Cumulative abnormal returns relative to acquisition programs of acquiring firms.

Source: Katherine Schipper and Rex Thompson, "Evidence on the Capitalized Value of Merger Activity for Acquiring Firms," *Journal of Financial Economics* (April 1983): 100.

Stock Market Performance of Diversified Companies: More Evidence from the Third Merger Wave

One way to test the implications of corporate finance theory for diversified companies is to compare the performance of the highly diversified conglomerates that expanded through widespread acquisitions in the 1960s with that of nondiversified firms. Frederick Scherer and David Ravenscraft compared the performance of the stocks of the 13 leading conglomerates in the 1960s with that of the market as a whole.[19] They assumed that a hypothetical investor would make a $1,000 investment in the common stock of each conglomerate in 1965, before the conglomerate stock market boom, or in 1968, at the peak of the conglomerate stock market boom (Table 4.3). They accounted for such factors as stock splits and assumed that all dividends would be reinvested. The study showed that if investors were sufficiently prescient to invest in the conglomerate before the conglomerate boom, they would have performed 3.6 times better than the Standard & Poor's (S&P) 500 by 1968. By 1983 this portfolio would have been 2.7 times the value of the S&P 500. However, those investors whose timing was not so fortuitous, who bought the conglomerate stocks at the peak and thereby paid a premium for their investment, did not fare nearly as well. This portfolio failed to keep pace with the S&P 500.

Scherer and Ravenscraft's results confirm the belief of corporate finance theory that implies that diversified firms are not providing investors a benefit when they diversify. This result is reflected in the market performance of diversified firms (Table 4.3). It can be seen that the distribution of stock value growth for diversified firms was highly skewed. Six of the conglomerates fall below the S&P 425, whereas three are slightly better and three others are significantly better. The study showed that one conglomerate, Teledyne, performed 16

19. David Ravenscraft and Frederick Scherer, "Mergers and Managerial Performance," in John Coffee, Louis Lowenstein, and Susan Rose Ackerman, eds. *Knights, Raiders and Targets* (New York: Oxford University Press, 1988), pp. 194–210.

Table 4.3.   1983 Value of a $1,000 1965 Investment in Each of 13 Leading Conglomerates or the S&P Industrials

Rank	Company	1983 Value
1	Teledyne	$65,463
2	Whittaker	24,025
3	Gulf & Western	16,287
4	U.S. Industries	7,152
5	Textron	4,947
6	Walter Kidde	4,813
7	Chromalloy-American	6,672
	S&P 425 Industrials	4,106
8	Beatrice	3,992
9	Consolidated Foods	3,820
10	ITT	3,625
11	Litton Industries	2,691
12	W. R. Grace	2,587
13	Genesco	408

Source: John C. Coffee Jr., Louis Lowenstein, and Susan Rose Ackerman, ed., *Knights, Raiders and Targets* (New York: Oxford University Press, Inc., 1988).

times better than the S&P 425. The authors of the study point out that this type of distribution would have been what one would have expected if the investments were made in individual high-tech firms as opposed to diversified, and supposedly less risky, conglomerates.

Market timing determines whether conglomerates provide positive returns just like any other investment. The fact that a firm is a conglomerate does not improve its probability of yielding higher than normal returns. Although this notion does not conclusively refute corporate finance theory's view of the drawbacks of diversified corporations, it clearly fails to provide support.

Perhaps the strongest indictment of large-scale diversification, as practiced by the sizable conglomerates of the 1960s, is the dismantling of many of them through sell-offs. Many of the leveraged buyouts that occurred in the late 1970s and 1980s were the result of divestiture efforts by diversified firms. These firms made a decision that the company could be better managed and could achieve greater profits if its operations were concentrated in fewer areas.

Positive Evidence of Benefits of Conglomerates

The Scherer and Ravenscraft study downplays the risk-reduction benefits of conglomerates. Other research studies, however, cast the wealth effects of conglomerates in a better light. For example, one research study has shown that returns to stockholders in conglomerate acquisitions are greater than in nonconglomerate acquisitions.[20]

The study, which examined 337 mergers between 1957 and 1975, found that conglomerate mergers provided superior gains relative to nonconglomerate mergers. The researchers reported these gains for both buyer and seller firms, with substantial gains registered by stockholders of seller firms and moderate gains for buying company stockholders.

20. Peter T. Elgers and John J. Clark, "Merger Types and Shareholder Returns: Additional Evidence," *Financial Management,* vol. 9, issue 2 (Summer 1980), pp. 66–72.

This finding was confirmed by later research that focused on 52 nonconglomerate and 151 conglomerate mergers. It was also found, however, that returns to shareholders were larger in horizontal and vertical acquisitions than in conglomerate acquisitions.[21]

Recent Evidence on the Effects of Diversification in Firm Value

Using a large sample of firms over the 1986–91 sample period, a study found that diversification resulted in a loss of firm value that averaged between 13% and 15%.[22] This study estimated the imputed value of a diversified firm's segments as if they were separate firms. The results found that the loss of firm value was not affected by firm size but was less when the diversification occurred within related industries. The loss of firm value results were buttressed by the fact that the diversified segments showed lower operating profitability than single-line businesses. The results also showed that diversified firms overinvested in the diversified segments more than single-line businesses. This implies that overinvestment may be a partial cause of the losses of value associated with diversification.

These findings are supported by another recent study of a sample of exchange-listed firms from 1978 to 1989, which found that increased corporate focus or specialization was consistent with shareholder wealth maximization.[23] It concluded that the commonly cited benefits of diversification, economies of scope, go unrealized and that the access to greater internal capital does not appear to affect the diversified firm's propensity to pursue external capital. One "benefit" of diversification that was found was that diversified firms tend to be targets of hostile takeovers less frequently than their less diversified counterparts. Nonetheless, diversified firms were more active participants, as both buyers and sellers, in the market for corporate control.

These more recent studies imply that if the evidence of benefits from conglomerates and diversification drawn from earlier years is to be accepted, it is not well supported in evidence drawn from the more recent financial performance of such firms.

---

21. James Wansley, William Lane, and Ho Yang, "Abnormal Returns to Acquired Firms by Type of Acquisition and Method of Payment," *Financial Management,* vol. 12, no. 3 (Autumn 1983), pp. 16–22.

22. P. G. Berger and E. Ofek, "Diversification's Effect on Firm Value," *Journal of Financial Economics* 37, no. 1 (January 1995), pp. 39–65.

23. R. Comment and G. Jarrell, "Corporate Focus and Stock Returns," *Journal of Financial Economics* 37, no. 1 (January 1995), pp. 67–87.

CASE STUDY: NATIONAL INTERGROUP— A STUDY OF DIVERSIFICATION GONE SOUR

In 1980 National Steel was the sixth largest steel company in the United States. Howard Love had just become president, and one of his goals was to make the firm a diversified corporation that would be somewhat insulated from the cyclical nature of the steel industry. His program of diversification involved the sale of some steel assets and the use of the proceeds to acquire other nonsteel businesses. National Steel sold one steel mill to employees of the company and a 50% share in three other mills to NKK Corporation of Tokyo.

As part of the firm's efforts to deemphasize the role of steel in the firm's future, National Steel changed its name to National Intergroup in 1983. This name change coincided with the firm's effort to diversify its operations by acquiring thrift institutions. The firm had previously purchased one of the nation's largest and best managed thrift institutions, First Nationwide Financial Corporation. This business was eventually sold for $426 million, even though it was doing well.

It is ironic that Love had commissioned a study by the management consulting firm of Bain and Company. He requested the firm to find other fields for National Intergroup's expansion. *Business Week* reported that the Bain report indicated that the management consulting firm recommended to Love that National Intergroup build closely on its expertise in wholesale steel distribution. Nonetheless, National Intergroup continued to expand outside the steel industry.

In 1985 National Steel acquired the Permian Corporation, a supplier of crude oil. The acquisition cost three million shares of National Steel common stock, $88 million in cash, and the assumption of $234 million worth of debt. In 1986 National Steel acquired Fox Meyer, Inc. Based in Dallas, Fox Meyer was the third largest wholesaler in the drug industry. The cost of $343 million was approximately double the market value of the company. The acquisition was completely financed by debt. Although National paid a high price for the company, Fox Meyer did have several appealing attributes. The drug industry is generally noncyclical. It is not capital intensive and does not tend to need large infusions of cash. Labor is relatively cheap compared with that for the steel industry. Given the overall growth of the health care industry, the move into the pharmaceutical wholesaling industry could be considered a move into a growth area. In 1986 Fox Meyer, through its subsidiary, bought Ben Franklin Stores, a large five-and-dime chain, and Lawrence Pharmaceuticals, a regional drug distributor. Both firms were purchased at a premium: The combined cost of the two was $62 million in cash and the assumption of $57 million in debt.

In retrospect, National Steel's diversification efforts have not been successful. Following the acquisition of Permian Oil, oil prices declined and Permian went into the red. Moving from a cyclical industry, such as the steel industry, into an inherently volatile commodity-based industry, such as the oil industry, provided few anticyclical benefits. The Fox Meyer acquisition initially also looked attractive, but it never fulfilled its expectations. The division experienced higher than anticipated costs in a project to sell supplies to hospitals. It also was forced to abandon an ambitious program to sell computer services to pharmacists. In addition, not long after Fox Meyer was acquired, an industry price war developed and cut sharply into Fox Meyer's profit margins.

National Intergroup thought the Ben Franklin Stores chain would blend well with the Fox Meyer operation. Moreover, National Intergroup's management believed that Fox Meyer's computer inventory system could be applied to Ben Franklin's operations. The continued efforts to implement the computerization of Ben Franklin Stores drained Fox Meyer's cash reserves and management resources. The computer-based problems at Ben Franklin caused the company to be unable to fill orders and sales fell. The five-and-dime chain was forced to close 43 stores by mid-1988. Part of the problem was that National Intergroup did not understand the trends in that part of the retail industry. Five-and-dime stores were having a difficult time remaining competitive with the more attractive, innovative chains such as K-Mart and Wal-

Mart. On the surface it appeared that Ben Franklin Stores would have certain synergies with Fox Meyer, but those gains never materialized.

The acquisition spree left National Intergroup with more than $440 million worth of long-term debt. In 1988 debt and long-term liabilities were double the value of equity. The acquisitions were purchased at a premium, and most performed poorly. Although the steel industry, beset with all the problems that the domestic steel industry faced along with its overall cyclical nature, was an unglamorous business, the acquisitions that National Intergroup added proved to be worse. National Intergroup expanded out of areas in which it had expertise into areas in which it had little to offer. In addition, the high prices paid for many of the targets put pressure on management to show even greater gains than the previous management had. Because the firm was out of its element, these additional gains failed to materialize. In June 1990 the firm announced that it planned to sell all units except Fox Meyer. Its embattled chairman, Howard Love, agreed to step down. Following the sales, the company would be renamed Fox Meyer.

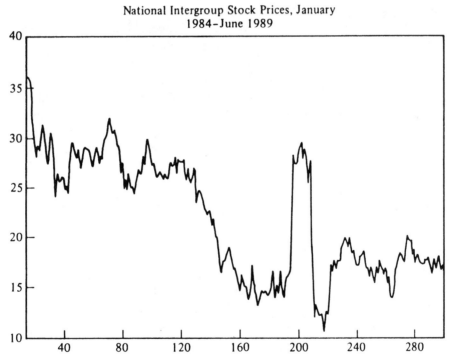

Figure 1. The failure of National Intergroup's diversification strategy was reflected in a decline in the firm's stock price.

Sources: Company reports: Ernest Beazley, "Steelmaker Suffers from a Case of Diversification Blues, *Wall Street Journal;* "National Intergroup: How Pete Went Wrong," *Business Week,* March 6, 1989, pp. 56–57; "Last Chance for Love?" *Business Week,* April 24, 1989, p. 31; "National Intergroup Chairman to Resign After Firm Sheds All Units But Fox Meyer," *Wall Street Journal,* 6 June 1990, p. A3; and "Intergroup Sees Profits in Drugs," *New York Times,* 11 June 1990, p. D8.

Related versus Unrelated Diversification

Diversification does not mean conglomerization. That is, it is possible to diversify into fields that are related to the buyer's business. An example of a related diversification occurred in 1994 when Merck purchased Medco. Merck is one of the largest pharmaceutical companies in the world and Medco is the largest marketer of pharmaceuticals in the United States. The two businesses are different in that one company is a manufacturer and the other company is a distributor. Nonetheless, the two companies are both in the pharmaceutical industry, and each has a greater knowledge of the other's business than an outside firm would have. In addition, there may be a more reliable expectation of economies of scale and scope in related diversifications because a buyer may be better able to leverage its current resources and expertise if it stays closer to its current business activities.

Related versus Unrelated Diversification Research

The track record of related acquisitions is significantly better than that of unrelated acquisitions. Morck, Shleifer, and Vishny found that the market punished shareholders in companies that engaged in unrelated acquisitions, whereas shareholders in companies that made related acquisitions did significantly better.[24] Their study of 326 acquisitions between 1975 and 1987 presented a more favorable picture of this type of diversification. Rather, a particular form of diversification, unrelated diversification, showed poor results. They measured relatedness by determining if the two firms had at least one of their top three lines of business in the same Standard Industrial Classification (SIC) code.

   Not all the research on related diversification shows the same results. For example, the result found by Agrawal, Jaffe, and Mandelker was the opposite of the result of Morck, Shleifer, and Vishny. Their result showed that unrelated acquisitions outperformed related acquisitions.[25] The market performance of diversified firms is discussed further later in this chapter.

ECONOMIC MOTIVES

In addition to economies of scale and diversification benefits, there are two other economic motives for mergers and acquisitions: horizontal integration and vertical integration. *Horizontal integration* refers to the increase in market share and market power that results from acquisitions and mergers of rivals. *Vertical integration* refers to the merger or acquisition of companies that have a buyer-seller relationship.

Horizontal Integration

Combinations that result in an increase in market share may have a significant impact on the combined firm's market power. Whether market power actually increases depends on

---

24. Randall Morck, Andrei Shleifer, and Robert Vishny, "Do Managerial Objectives Drive Bad Acquisitions?" *Journal of Finance* 45, no. 1 (March 1990), pp. 31–48.

25. A. Agrawal, J.F. Jaffe, and G.N. Mandelker, "The Post-Merger Performance of Acquiring Firms: A Reexamination of an Anomaly," *Journal of Finance* 47, no. 4, September 1992, pp. 1605–1671.

the size of the merging firms and the level of competition in the industry. Economic theory categorizes industries within two extreme forms of market structure. On one side of this spectrum is pure competition, which is a market that is characterized by numerous buyers and sellers, perfect information, and homogeneous, undifferentiated products. Given these conditions, each seller is a price taker with no ability to influence market price. On the other end of the industry spectrum is monopoly, which is an industry with one seller. The monopolist has the ability to select the price-output combination that maximizes profits. Of course, the monopolist is not guaranteed a profit simply because it is insulated from direct competitive pressures. The monopolist may or make not earn a profit, depending on the magnitude of its costs relative to revenues at the optimal "profit-maximizing" price-output combination. Within these two ends of the industry structure spectrum is monopolistic competition, which features many sellers of a somewhat differentiated product. Closer to monopoly, however, is oligopoly, in which there are a few (i.e., 3 to 12) sellers of a differentiated product. Horizontal integration involves a movement from the competitive end of the spectrum toward the monopoly end.

Market Power

Market power, which is sometimes also referred to as monopoly power, is defined as the ability to set and maintain price above competitive levels. Because in the long run sellers in a competitive industry only earn a normal return and do not earn "economic rent," competitive firms set price equal to marginal cost. Market power refers to the ability to set price in excess of marginal cost. Abba Lerner developed what has been known as the *Lerner Index,* which measures the magnitude of the difference between price and marginal cost relative to price. Simply having a positive difference between price and marginal cost, however, does not guarantee profits because fixed costs could be sufficiently high that the firm generates losses.

$$Lerner\ Index = (P - MC)/P$$

where:
   P = price
   MC = marginal cost

There are three sources of market power: product differentiation, barriers to entry, and market share. Through horizontal integration, a company is able to increase its market share. It could be the case that even with a substantial increase in market share, the lack of significant product differentiation or barriers to entry could prevent a firm from being able to raise its price significantly above marginal cost. If an industry does not possess imposing barriers to entry, raising price above marginal cost may only attract new competitors who will drive price down toward marginal costs.

Even in industries that have become more concentrated, there may be a substantial amount of competition. For example, the domestic automobile industry has become more concentrated, with only three U.S. automobile companies remaining after decades of horizontal mergers and acquisitions. Globalization, however, brought many international competitors to the U.S. market, which has intensified the level of competition in this industry.

Social Cost of Increased Concentration

The costs to society that result from increased concentration are a function of the state of competition that exists after the horizontal mergers. If the industry structure formed approximates monopoly, the social costs may be significant. This can be seen by the fact that in pure competition each firm is a price taker, and competitive firms produce an output where price equals marginal costs. In a monopoly, a firm maximizes profits by setting marginal revenue equal to marginal costs. The rule is the same for the competitive firm, but in the instance of monopoly, marginal revenue is less than price. The end result is that a competitive industry has lower prices and higher output levels than a monopolized version of the same industry. This is seen in Figure 4.7. If a competitive pricing rule is used (P = MC), an output level equal to X_c results, with price equal to P_c. If such an industry were to become so concentrated that a monopoly resulted, a lower output level equal to X_m, and a higher price equal to P_m, would result. The end result is that consumers would pay higher prices in the monopolized industry and would have a lower total output available. One way to see the effect on society is to consider a concept that economists call deadweight loss or welfare loss—that is, the loss of *consumer surplus* and *producer surplus*. Consumer surplus is the difference between the price paid and the height up to the demand curve for all units bought by consumers. The height up to the demand curve reflects the maximum that

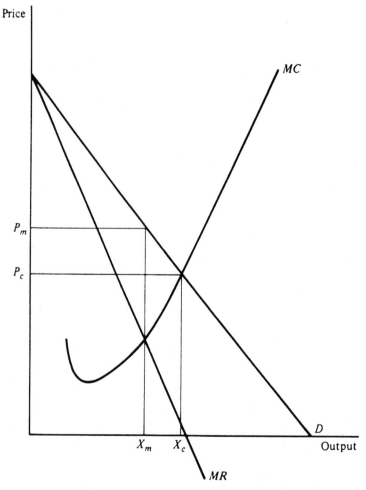

Figure 4.7. Consumers benefit more from a competitive market. They buy more output (X_c) than in a monopolized market (X_m) and pay less ($P_c < P_m$).

consumers would be willing to pay for each unit. This maximum declines as consumers purchase more units. Producer surplus is the difference between the height up to the supply curve and the price that producers receive for each unit. The supply curve reflects the producers' cost conditions. In a competitive market, the supply curve is the horizontal summation of the individual marginal cost curves of each producer above the average cost curve. In such a market, the height up to the supply curve reflects the costs of producing additional units. Producers should not accept less than the marginal costs of producing each additional unit. The upward-sloping shape of the supply curve reflects diminishing returns in production.

Gains from trade occur for both parties: Consumers pay less than the maximum they would have been willing to pay for all units up to X_e, and producers receive a price greater than the additional costs of producing each unit for all units up to X_e. The total gains from trade are depicted in Figure 4.8, and the combined total of the two triangular areas depict consumer surplus (CS) and producer surplus (PS).

The welfare loss in monopoly occurs because fewer units are sold, and each is sold for a higher price than in competition. Given that trading ends at an output level of X_m instead of X_c, a loss of consumer and producer surplus results. The combined loss of consumer and producer surplus is the deadweight or welfare loss. The upper triangle in Figure 4.9 refers to the loss of consumer surplus, and the lower shaded triangle shows the loss of producer surplus.

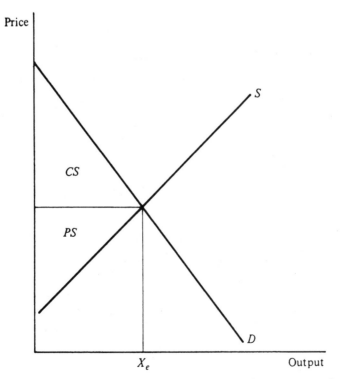

Figure 4.8.   A free market system brings about an exchange between suppliers and demanders in which the gains from trade are maximized. Consumer gains are denoted by consumer surplus (CS) and supplier gains are denoted by producer surplus (PS).

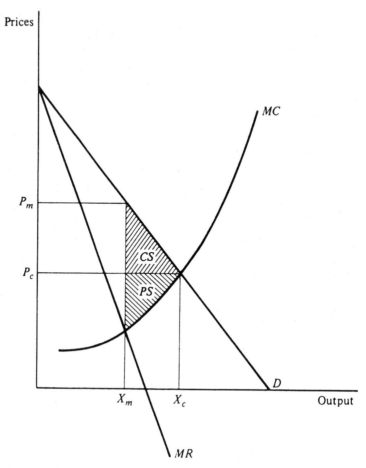

Figure 4.9. The deadweight loss or welfare loss of monopoly derives from the loss of the gains from trade. The loss of the consumer and producer surplus is shown in the shaded region. X_m units are traded instead of X_c. The marketplace loses the gains from trade (CS and PS) on the units that are not traded.

The obvious practical question that arises is whether horizontal mergers result in a welfare loss to society. Economists have written many theoretical papers that purport to measure the welfare loss.[26] In reality, these are interesting exercises, but they have failed to provide a convincing quantitative measure of the deadweight loss in the extreme case of monopoly. Neither do they provide guidance for the intermediate cases of oligopoly, which are more relevant to the horizontal mergers that have occurred throughout the world.

It is important to note, however, that there is no real basis for assuming that a deadweight loss occurs when firms combine horizontally but the industry structure falls short of being monopolized. The mere fact that a more concentrated industry structure results does not imply that competition has declined. The final outcome might be a number of strong competitors who engage in a heightened state of competition characterized by competitively determined prices and differentiated products. If so, the argument for a dead-

26. See Arnold C. Harberger, "Three Basic Postulates for Applied Welfare Economics," *Journal of Economic Literature* 9, no. 3 (September 1971), pp. 785–797.

weight loss resulting from increased concentration is weakened. The existence of a welfare loss resulting from the formation of oligopolies should be considered on an individual, industry-by-industry basis.

Empirical Evidence on the Monopoly Hypothesis

There is little empirical evidence that firms combine to increase their monopoly power. Much of the evidence that elucidates this question is indirect. A doctoral dissertation by Robert S. Stillman in 1983 showed that competitors failed to react when other firms in the same industry announced a combination.[27] The analysis considered the value of the stock of firms in the affected industry when events took place that increased the probability of mergers in that industry. It also considered the fact that product prices might rise after horizontal mergers, benefiting other firms in the industry. With higher product prices, resulting from a more concentrated industry, the equity values of the firms in the industry should also rise.

The study examined a small sample of 11 mergers that were challenged on antitrust grounds under Section 7 of the Clayton Act. No statistically significant abnormal returns for 9 of the 11 mergers were found. Of the other two, one showed positive abnormal returns and the other showed ambiguous results. These results fail to support the view that firms merge in an effort to seek monopoly power.

A similar study, also based on a doctoral thesis, was conducted by B. Epsen Eckbo on a larger sample of 126 horizontal and vertical mergers in the manufacturing and mining industries.[28] Approximately half of Eckbo's sample were horizontal mergers. An average of 15 rival firms existed in each industry category. If the market power hypothesis delineated previously was valid, negative abnormal returns would be observed for firms in industries that had announced mergers that were challenged on antitrust grounds. The reasoning is that the merger is less likely when there is an antitrust challenge. When challenges take place, negative abnormal returns should be associated with the announcement of the challenge. Eckbo found statistically insignificant abnormal returns. The study also showed that firms initially showed positive and statistically significant abnormal returns when the mergers were first announced but failed to show a negative response after the complaint was filed.

Like Stillman's results, Eckbo's research does not support the belief that firms merge to enjoy increases in market power. Curiously, Eckbo's results reveal that "stockholders of bidder and target firms in challenged (horizontal) mergers earn larger abnormal returns than do the corresponding firms in unchallenged mergers."[29] Eckbo concludes that the gains found in mergers are not related to increases in market power but rather are motivated by factors such as efficiency gains.

Although the Stillman and Eckbo studies of the early 1980s provide little support for the pursuit of market power as a motive for mergers and acquisitions, more recent research

---

27. Robert S. Stillman, "Examining Antitrust Policy Towards Mergers," Ph.D. dissertation, University of California at Los Angeles, 1983. This dissertation was later published in the *Journal of Financial Economics* 11, no. 1 (April 1983), pp. 225–240.

28. B. Epsen Eckbo, "Horizontal Mergers, Collusion and Stockholder Wealth," *Journal of Financial Economics* 11, no. 1 (April 1983), pp. 241–273.

29. Ibid.

implies that market power may be a motive for some deals. Specifically, Kim and Singal found that mergers in the airline industry during the late 1980s resulted in higher prices on routes served by merging firms compared with a control group of routes that were not involved in control transactions.[30] Indeed, some critics of deregulation have cited the unfettered ability of previously regulated competitors to merge and the subsequent increase in airfares as an example of failure of deregulation. Their study took into account many factors such as the existence of financially distressed firms as well as possible premerger excess supply and any postmerger quality improvements. Even after all these factors were taken into account, they showed that market power and its associated price increases dominated any postmerger efficiency effects to result in a welfare loss.

Additional evidence is found in research by Judith Chevalier on the supermarkets industry, which underwent a series of major control changes that featured several high-profile leveraged buyouts (LBOs), including LBOs of Safeway ($5.3 billion), Kroger ($4.1 billion leveraged recapitalization), Supermarkets General ($1.8 billion), and Stop & Shop ($1.2 billion).

Chevalier found that as of the date of her study, 19 of the 50 largest supermarket chains underwent an LBO. She found that these leveraged control deals were associated with price increases in their respective markets. Firms that underwent such LBOs were the high-priced firms in their markets.

Based on some of the more recent research, it appears that the pursuit of market power through horizontal mergers and acquisitions may be one reason firms merge. This result is intuitive in the sense that it helps explain why companies may pay a premium over market value to rivals. If they can achieve market power, the present value of the posttransaction gains may offset the initial deal costs. Whether such achieved market power is long-lasting depends on other economic factors such as the presence of barriers to entry.

Horizontal Integration, Consolidation and Roll-Up Acquisition Programs

The 1990s featured a consolidation within certain industries. Many of these deals involved larger companies buying smaller rivals in a series of acquisitions. The acquired companies are then combined into an ever-growing larger company. Such deals are sometimes referred to as *roll-up acquisitions*. In the following sections we highlight three such roll-up acquisition programs: those conducted by Worldcom and Westinghouse and the consolidation that is taking place in the funeral home industry.

---

30. E. Han Kim and Vijay Singal, "Mergers and Market Power: Evidence from the Airline Industry," *American Economic Review* 83, no. 3 (June 1993), pp. 549–569.

CASE STUDY: FIRST UNION CORPORATION'S ACQUISITION OF FIRST FIDELITY

The June 1995 acquisition of First Fidelity and its $1.4 billion in revenues by First Union with its $6.26 billion of revenues formed the sixth largest bank in the United States in the largest banking merger in U.S. history to that date (Table 1). First Union commanded a major presence in the Southeast with its 1,287 branches, while First Fidelity operated 685 branches primarily in the Northeast, including New Jersey, Con-

Table 1. Top Ten Banks, Ranked by Assets as of March 31, 1995 ($ Billions)

Rank	Bank's Name	Assets 6/30/96	Assets 3/31/95
1.	Chemical Banking/	297.0	185.3
	Chase Manhattan		121.7
2.	Citicorp	257.0	269.0
3.	BankAmerica	226.0	223.2
4.	NationsBank	184.1	184.9
5.	J.P. Morgan	166.0	167.1
6.	First Union/First Fidelity	123.7	123.7
7.	First Chicago	120.1	72.4
8.	Bankers Trust N.Y.	102.9	107.4
9.	Banc One	86.7	87.8
10.	KeyCorp	67.4	67.4

Source: Wall Street Journal, 20 June 1995, p. B4, and August, 28, 1995, A6.

necticut, and Pennsylvania markets. The merger gave the combined bank almost 2,000 branches in a 13–state market that stretched from Florida to Connecticut (Table 2).

One of the advantages for First Union was that the addition of First Fidelity provided a new market where through the 685 added branches First Union could offer its new commercial financial products, such as asset securitizations eliminate as well as sell mutual funds and annuities to First Fidelity's upscale customers. In addition to geographic market expansion, First Union also saw synergies in the form of economies of scale that might be realized by eliminating redundant processing facilities and corporate staff. First Union estimated that it could eliminate $64 million in First Fidelity's costs by 1996.[a] The benefits were so impressive to First Union that it was willing to tolerate a $0.24 initial dilution in earnings per share to complete the

Table 2. A Look at the First Union/First Fidelity Merger

	Company Fundamentals Based on 1994 Results		Regions Covered	
Headquarters	First Union Charlotte, NC	First Fidelity Newark, NJ/ Philadelphia	First Union	First Fidelity
Revenues (billions)	$6.26	$1.40	Maryland Virginia	Maryland Pennsylvania
Net Income (millions)	$925.4	$451.1	Tennessee North Carolina	New Jersey New York
Assets (billions)	$88.3	$35.4	South Carolina Georgia	Connecticut Rhode Island
Branches	1,287	685	Florida	
Employees	32,000	12,000		

Source: Wall Street Journal, June 20, 1995, p. B4.

$5.4 billion stock-for-stock buyout. The market, however, registered its concern about the magnitude of the $64.29 offer price, and First Union's stock fell on the announcement. To appease its shareholders, First Union then announced a stock buyback and stock dividend program to support its share price.

---

a. Martha Brannigan and Timothy O'Brien, "First Union Is Viewed as Paying Dearly for First Fidelity," *Wall Street Journal*, 20 June 1995, p. B4.

Worldcom

One classic example of such a consolidation acquisition program was the acquisitions of Worldcom, formerly LDDS, over the second half of the 1980s and 1990s. Worldcom, based in Jackson, Mississippi, was formed through a series of more than 40 acquisitions, culminating in the $37 billion acquisition of MCI in 1998. Many of these deals were acquisitions of regional long-distance telecommunication resellers who added more minutes to Worldcom's market clout while bringing a regionally based sales force to service the acquired market. It is ironic that Worldcom was a telecommunication business owned by ITT that was later acquired by LDDS. ITT was a conglomerate that underwent a series of downsizing transactions, which are discussed in Chapter 10, whereas LDDS went on to grow horizontally to become the second leading long-distance company in the U.S. market. In paying a high price for MCI, which enabled it to outbid British Telecom, Worldcom asserted that it would realize significant cost savings from combining these two long-distance companies. Although only time will tell whether such gains ever manifest themselves, Worldcom certainly can draw on significant experience with making such consolidating mergers and realizing gains. One could make an argument that repeat acquirers within their own industry should be able to realistically appraise the magnitude of potentially realizable gains.

Westinghouse

There are numerous other examples of consolidating, roll-up acquisition programs that became popular in the 1990s. Westinghouse's sales and acquisitions are a good example of a company's deciding to unload businesses that it thought had few growth prospects and acquire a greater market share in a growth business. Specifically, Westinghouse sold off its defense business and, in the face of better financed rivals, decided in November 1997 to sell its power generation business to Siemans AG for $1.53 billion. Westinghouse realized that becoming a leading player in the international power generation market was a costly proposition. To achieve such a position, it would have to invest a large amount of capital without the prospect of high growth to offset the costs. Instead it sold off such capital-demanding businesses and used the proceeds to continually expand its presence in broadcasting. Siemans, on the other hand, decided to focus on power generation, and the acquisition of Westinghouse's power generation business helped enhance its already strong position in the world market.

Although television may be the glamourous side of broadcasting, Westinghouse used roll-up acquisitions to steadily expand its radio station network, which already had a presence in this business through Westinghouse's Group W stations. The $5.4 billion acquisition of CBS in August 1995 was a costly major acquisition. Following that, Michael Jordan, Westinghouse's CEO, added two large chains of radio stations. The first was Infinity Broadcasting, which owned 83 radio stations. This was followed by the $2.6 billion acquisition of American Radio Systems Corp., which owned 98 radio stations. The company continued to sharpen its focus on broadcasting with the sale of its Thermo-King, which marketed refrigerated transport equipment, to Ingersoll Rand for $2.56 billion.

Funeral Home Industry

Still another example of the roll-up acquisitions of the 1990s was the consolidation with the funeral home industry. This industry has changed from being one of many small independent homes run by individuals who were known in the community to chains of homes run by larger corporations. It still includes many small independent businesses, but the share owned by the chains has risen significantly. Ironically, the large-scale acquisitions that took place in this industry went on without most consumers even being aware of it because the local names were often kept and the acquirers also retained many of the former employees. This is a reversal of many such deals where the acquirer wants the market to be aware of the benefits of its brand name. The consolidating acquisitions in the industry were associated with significant increases in market prices. The ability of consumers to take advantage of competition in the industry is somewhat mitigated by the fact that they are purchasing the service at a time of distress, coupled with the fact that even if they approach a competitor with a very different name, it may be owned by the same company and offer similar prices. The industry almost took a giant step toward increased concentration in 1996, when Service Corp., the largest funeral home company in the world, made a $2.8 billion offer for the Loewen Group, the second largest company. The hostile bid was eventually withdrawn as a result of the intervention of antitrust regulators.

Vertical Integration

Vertical integration involves the acquisition of firms that are closer to the source of supply or to the ultimate consumer. An example of a movement toward the source of supply was Chevron's acquisition of Gulf Oil in 1984. Chevron bought Gulf primarily to augment its reserves, a motive termed *backward integration*. In the same year Mobil bought Superior Oil for similar reasons. Mobil was strong in refining and marketing but low on reserves, whereas Superior had large oil and gas reserves but lacked refining and marketing operations. An example of *forward integration* would be if a firm with large reserves bought another company that had a strong marketing and retailing capability.

CASE STUDY: ATOMIZATION OF BIG OIL[a]

It is interesting to note that some have questioned the benefits of vertical integration of larger petroleum companies. During the 1990s returns of the large vertically integrated petroleum companies lagged behind the market while smaller and more fo-

---

a. This case study is based upon the article by Timothy Bleakley, David S. Gee, and Ron Hulme, "The Atomization of Big Oil," *The McKinsey Quarterly,* vol. 2, 1997, pp. 123–142.

cused petropreneurs are better able to compete within their market niches. Some of these companies have enjoyed annual growth rates as high as 20% and have become major players in the industry. For example, Enron's revenues have risen to $20.3 billion in 1997 while Tosco has reached $13.3 billion. These petropreneurs have been able to grow rapidly through acquisitions—often from the major oil companies. However, they have proved to be more aggressive and have found more innovative ways to compete. Although still a relative small segment of this large industry, their growth compared to the slow growth of their large vertically integrated rivals, is a reason for the oil giants to be concerned.

Another example of forward integration took place in the securities industry when Shearson Lehman Brothers bought E. F. Hutton. Shearson was attracted by E. F. Hutton's strong network of retail brokers. This vertical combination was motivated by a movement toward the consumer. It is also an example of a previously vertically integrated firm that wanted to expand its access to the consumer. Before the merger, Shearson Lehman had a large network of retail brokers. After the merger, however, it acquired a retail capacity to rival all competitors, including Merrill Lynch. Although this strategy of combining seemingly complementary and closely related businesses appeared to make sense, it also was later undone and the firms were sold off.

Still another example of a vertical combination was the 1989 merger between Time and Warner. This deal was designed to form a vertically integrated media company, with Time's strength being its avenues of distribution of print publishing as well as through HBO and cable systems. Although Warner also had some presence in distribution through its own cable assets, its strengths were its film studios and record label. Warner primarily provided content while Time provided avenues through which this content could reach the consumer. Although the merger strategy had intuitive appeal, many shareholders questioned the companies' rejection of the generous $200 per share offer from Paramount to pursue this strategy, which has yet to yield similar returns.

Motives for Vertical Integration

A firm might consider vertically integrating for several reasons. As seen in the case of the Mobil–Superior Oil combination, companies may vertically integrate to be assured of a *dependable source of supply*. Dependability may be determined not just in terms of supply availability but also through quality maintenance and timely delivery considerations. Having timely access to supplies helps companies to provide their own products on a reliable basis. In addition, as companies pursue *just-in-time* inventory management, they may take advantage of a vertically integrated corporate structure to lower inventory costs.

It is popularly believed that when a company acquires a supplier it is obtaining a cost advantage over its rivals. The thinking is that it will not have to pay the profit to suppliers that it was previously paying when it was buying the inputs from independent suppliers. This raises the question: What is the appropriate *internal transfer price*? It is the price carried on the company's books when it acquires its supplies or inputs from a supplier that it now controls and may be a subsidiary. If the price for these inputs is less than the prevailing market price, the parent company will appear to be more profitable than it really is. The reason is that the lower costs and higher profits for the parent company come at the cost of lower profitability for the subsidiary. This is a paper transfer, however, and does not result in increased value to the combined firm.

Consider the case of an automobile manufacturer that purchases tires from a tire manufacturing company at a unit price of $40, which we will assume is a competitive price for this type of tire. The cost to the automobile manufacturer may contain a $5 profit to the tire maker. If the car company then buys a tire manufacturing company, which it operates as a subsidiary, it should still record the tire cost at $40. The management of the automobile manufacturing company would be fooling itself if it thought it was saving $5 per tire by buying the tire maker. To purchase the tire company, the car company is investing capital for which it would be earning a zero return but that allows the parent company to earn a higher return. However, if the subsidiary is allowed to earn a $5 profit by charging the parent the full $40 market price, the investment in the tire manufacturing company will show a positive return, whereas the automobile manufacturer's return should remain at the preacquisition level. The transaction as described is merely a paper transfer and does not result in increased value.

Although the establishment of an accurate transfer price helps dismiss the illusion that supplies derived from a newly acquired supplier come at a lower cost, there may be other cost savings from acquiring a supplier. These savings may come in the form of lower *transactions costs*.[31] By acquiring a supplier and establishing a long-term source of supply at prearranged costs, the acquiring firm may avoid potential disruptions that might occur when agreements with independent suppliers end. When the buyer owns the supplier, it may be better able to predict future supply costs and avoid the uncertainty that normally is associated with renegotiation of supply agreements.

Still another reason for vertical integration could arise from the need to have *specialized inputs*. These may be custom-designed materials or machinery that might have little or no market other than the buyer. The buyer may then be at the mercy of these companies if they choose not to provide the products. It may be difficult to switch to other suppliers if there are fixed costs associated with the initial manufacture of the materials. Other suppliers may be unwilling to produce the specialized products unless the buyer compensates for the initial costs or enters a long-term supply agreement that allows the supplier to amortize the up-front costs. One way to eliminate this problem is to acquire the supplier. The buyer can then have access to these specialized inputs and be in an even better position to oversee the maintenance of the company's own standards of manufacturing.

Another interesting example of vertical integration occurs in the marketing of automobiles. Automobile manufacturers have long realized that they may need to provide potential buyers with financial assistance, in the form of less expensive and more readily available credit, to sell more cars. For this reason, General Motors formed General Motors Acceptance Corporation (GMAC). General Motors Acceptance Corporation provides low-cost credit to many car buyers who might not be able to get the financing necessary to buy a new car. Financing incentives have become a regular part of the competition among automakers. Firms may lower the financing costs well below the cost of capital to sell certain car models that are experiencing slow sales. General Motors Acceptance Corporation will sell commercial paper at money market rates that at times may be above the financing costs it charges customers. These costs have sometimes gone as low as 0%.

---

31. Dennis Carlton and Jeffrey Perloff, *Modern Industrial Organization,* 2nd ed. (New York: HarperCollins, 1994), p. 502.

One advantage of keeping GMAC as an independent subsidiary is that the high debt levels generated by the aggressive procurement of capital by GMAC do not directly affect the debt-equity ratio of the parent company. General Motors does not suffer a lower debt and credit rating that would increase its cost of capital.

Vertical Integration and the Competitive Advantage

Vertical integration may be used to reinforce a supplier's competitive position. The following excerpt relates how metal producers used forward integration to create a pull-through demand for substitute products. In the 1970s and early 1980s steel and aluminum manufacturers actively competed for the can market. Each group of manufacturers tried to enhance any competitive advantage.

A strategy practiced successfully by the aluminum industry, among others, is to forward integrate selectively into downstream products to create pull-through demand for a substitute. A related strategy is to induce end-users to backward integrate into the intermediate industry to get around intermediate producers who are unwilling to substitute. By integrating forward and creating demand with end-users, a firm can sometimes force recalcitrant intermediate buyers to bear the switching costs of substitution. Forward integration can also demonstrate the performance of the substitute and be a means for developing procedures for its use and for lowering switching costs.[32]

Vertical integration was a successful tool in the can industry. The end-users, beverage companies, incurred few costs in switching to aluminum cans. The problem for the aluminum manufacturers was that, to reach the end-users, the aluminum companies had to go through the can makers. Can makers, however, face considerable costs related to the investment in capital equipment to switch. The aluminum manufacturers' strategy was very successful; by the late 1980s they completely dominated the can market. By 1989, 99.9% of all beer cans and 96% of all beverage cans were made of aluminum.[33]

Forward integration may help overcome the reluctance to incur the increased switching costs because the aluminum manufacturers ultimately make that decision. The outcome of this process is that vertical integration may enable firms to be better able to compete. To the extent that this occurs, consumers are better off. Vertical integration may also result in lower prices to consumers, which can be demonstrated by making more extensive use of economic analysis.[34]

Vertical Integration as a Threat to Competition

Having pointed out that vertical integration may facilitate competition, it must be noted that a vertically integrated company may move to foreclose competition in ways that would not be available to a nonvertically integrated company. A classic example of this effect occurred in the airline industry.[35]

---

32. Michael Porter, *Competitive Advantage* (New York: Free Press, 1985), pp. 308–309.

33. "BevPak Brings Back the Shine to Steel Cans," *Wall Street Journal,* 8 June 1989.

34. This example draws on an example developed by Charles Baird in *Intermediate Microeconomics* (Minneapolis, Minn.: West Publishing Co., 1975), pp. 250–253.

35. This example is based on material in Margaret E. Guerin-Calvert, "Airline Computer Reservation Systems" in *The Antitrust Revolution* (Glenview, Ill.: Scott, Foresman, 1989), pp. 338–363.

An extended battle took place in the early 1980s, resulting from actions brought by the Civil Aeronautics Board (CAB) and the Department of Justice regarding airline computer reservation systems (CRS) and competition among airlines. Certain airlines complained that the hold the leading airlines had on the industry through their CRS outlets established at travel agencies restrained their ability to compete. Certain airlines had engaged in forward integration by expanding their operations to include the provision of airline reservation systems in travel agencies.

Table 4.4 shows that the computer reservation systems of American, United, and TWA accounted for 80% of the total travel agency revenues in the industry. American and United accounted for 70% by themselves. This is important because travel agencies are responsible for approximately 70% of all airline tickets sold.

Airlines that did not have major CRS systems contended that they were unable to compete with those airlines that had these systems. The non-CRS airlines pointed out that the CRS displays were biased in that they first showed the CRS provider's own airline's flights even if they were less convenient for the traveler.

Airlines such as Air Florida, New York Air, and Midway contended that, in addition to bias in providing information to travel agencies, they were charged higher booking fees than other airlines. These higher fees, which were unrelated to the actual costs of adding an airline to the system, were held to be discriminatory pricing and a means whereby established airlines created barriers to entry, making it more expensive for new airlines to enter the industry and be competitive.

The non-CRS airlines maintained that the goal of this form of forward integration by certain airlines was to foreclose competition. The Justice Department agreed with this position and urged the CAB to enact changes that would correct the problems of bias in the computer reservation systems and the pricing of the system itself. The CAB was particularly concerned that these practices would undermine the gains that had been made in enhancing industry competition through deregulation.

In July 1984 the CAB instituted new rules that sought to correct the problems. Specifically, these rules disallowed the bias and discriminatory pricing policies. Some air carriers believe that although these new rules went a long way toward correcting the problem, they did not totally eliminate what they believed were the anticompetitive practices made possible by forward integration.

Table 4.4.   CRS Market Shares

Airline	CRS	Domestic Travel Agency Revenues ($ millions)	Percentage of Total (%)
American	Sabre	6,376.3	43
United	Apollo	4,040.9	27
TWA	PARS	1,561.1	10
Eastern	SODA	605.3	4
Delta	Datas II	259.8	2
—	Mars Plus	281.9	2
—	Unautomated	1,822.5	12
Total		14,947.8	100

Source: Margaret E. Guerin-Calvert, "Airline Computer Reservation Systems," in *The Antitrust Revolution* (Glenview, Ill.: Scott, Foresman, 1989), pp. 338–363.

HUBRIS HYPOTHESIS OF TAKEOVERS

An interesting hypothesis regarding takeover motives has been proposed by Richard Roll.[36] He considers the role that hubris, or the pride of the managers in the acquiring firm, may play in explaining takeovers. The hubris hypothesis implies that managers seek to acquire firms for their own personal motives and that the pure economic gains to the acquiring firm are not the sole motivation or even the primary motivation in the acquisition.

Roll uses this hypothesis to explain why managers might pay a premium for a firm that the market has already correctly valued. Managers, he claims, have superimposed their own valuation over that of an objectively determined market valuation. Roll's position is that the pride of management allows them to believe that their valuation is superior to that of the market. Implicit in this theory is an underlying conviction that the market is efficient and can provide the best indicator of the value of a firm. Many would dispute this point. As evidence, Roll draws on a wide body of research studies. This evidence is described in the following section.

Empirical Evidence

Roll states that if the hubris hypothesis explains takeovers, the following should occur for those takeovers motivated by hubris:

- The stock price of the acquiring firm should fall after the market becomes aware of the takeover bid. This should occur because the takeover is not in the best interests of the acquiring firm's stockholders and does not represent an efficient allocation of their wealth.
- The stock price of the target firm should increase with the bid for control. This should occur because the acquiring firm is not only going to pay a premium but also may pay a premium in excess of the value of the target.
- The combined effect of the rising value of the target and the falling value of the acquiring firm should be negative. This takes into account the costs of completing the takeover process.

A number of studies show that the acquiring firm's announcement of the takeover results in a decline in the value of the acquirer's stock. Dodd found statistically significant negative returns to the acquirer following the announcement of the planned takeover.[37] Other studies have demonstrated similar findings.[38] Not all studies support this conclusion, however. Paul Asquith failed to find a consistent pattern of declining stock prices following the announcement of a takeover.[39]

36. Richard Roll, "The Hubris Hypothesis of Corporate Takeovers," *Journal of Business* 59, no. 2 (April 1986): 197–216.

37. P. Dodd, "Merger Proposals, Managerial Discretion and Stockholder Wealth," *Journal of Financial Economics* 8 (June 1980): 105, 138.

38. C. E. Eger, "An Empirical Test of the Redistribution Effect of Mergers," *Journal of Financial and Quantitative Analysis* 18 (December 1983): 547–572.

39. Paul Asquith, "Merger Bids, Uncertainty and Stockholder Returns," *Journal of Financial Economics* 11 (April 1983): 51–83.

There is more widespread agreement on the positive price effects for target stockholders who have been found to experience wealth gains following takeovers. Bradley, Desai, and Kim show that tender offers result in gains for target firm stockholders.[40] Admittedly, the hostile nature of tender offers should produce greater changes in the stock price than in friendly takeover offers. Most studies, however, show that target stockholders gain following both friendly and hostile takeover bids. Varaiya showed that bidders do overpay.[41] In a study that examined the relationship between the bid premium and the combined market values of the bidder and the target, it was found that the premium paid by bidders was too high relative to the value of the target to the acquirer.

The research on the combined effect of the upward movement of the target's stock and the downward movement of the acquirer's stock does not seem to provide strong support for the hubris hypothesis. Malatesta examined the combined effects and found that "the evidence indicates that the long-run sequence of events culminating in merger has no net impact on combined shareholder wealth."[42] It could be countered, however, that Malatesta's failure to find positive combined returns does support the hubris hypothesis.

More recent research seems to support the hubris hypothesis.[43] Using a sample of 106 large acquisitions, Hayward and Hambrick found CEO hubris positively associated with the size of premiums paid. Hubris was measured by the variables such as the company's recent performance and CEO self-importance (as reflected by media praise and compensation relative to the second highest paid executive). The study also considered independent variables such as CEO inexperience, as measured by years in that position, along with board vigilance, as measured by the number of insider directors versus outside directors (Figure 4.10).

Roll did not intend the hubris hypothesis to explain all takeovers. He merely proposed that an important human element enters takeovers when individuals are interacting and negotiating the purchase of a company. Management's acquisition of a target may be motivated purely by a desire to maximize stockholder wealth. However, other motives may include a desire to enter a target's industry or to become "the largest firm in the business." The extent to which these motives may play a role will vary from takeover to takeover. It is therefore of some interest that much evidence does support the hubris hypothesis. Surely the questionably high premiums paid for some firms, such as Federated Stores and RJR Nabisco, imply some element of hubris. The fact that Campeau Corporation was forced to declare bankruptcy not long after the acquisition of Federated Stores lends support to the view that it overpaid in the highly leveraged deal.

The Winner's Curse Hypothesis of Takeovers

The winner's curse of takeovers is the ironic hypothesis that states that bidders who overestimate the value of a target will most likely win a contest. This is due to the fact that they

40. Michael Bradley, Anand Desai, and E. Han Kim, "The Rationale Behind Interfirm Tender Offers: Information or Synergy," *Journal of Financial Economics* 11, no. 1 (April 1983), pp. 183–206.

41. Nikhil P. Varaiya, "Winners Curse Hypothesis and Corporate Takeovers," *Managerial and Decision Economics* 9 (1989), p. 209.

42. Paul Malatesta, "Wealth Effects of Merger Activity," *Journal of Financial Economics* 11, no. 1 (April 1983), pp. 178–179.

43. Mathew L. A. Hayward and Donald C. Hambrick, "Explaining Premiums Paid for Large Acquisitions: Evidence of CEO Hubris," unpublished manuscript, July 1995.

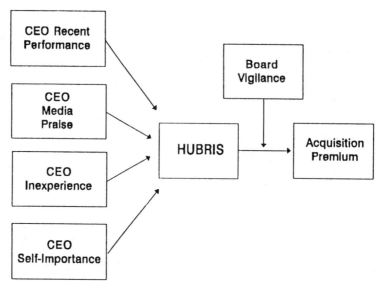

Figure 4.10.   Model of CEO hubris and acquisition premiums.

Source: Hayward, Mathew L. A. and Donald C. Hambrick, *Explaining Premiums Paid for Large Acquisitions: Evidence of CEO Hubris,* unpublished manuscript, July, 1995.

will be more inclined to overpay and outbid rivals who more accurately value the target. This result is not specific to takeovers but is the natural result of any bidding contest.[44] One of the more public forums where this regularly occurs is the free agent markets of sports such as baseball and basketball.[45] In a study of 800 acquisitions from 1974 to 1983, Nikhil Varaiya showed that on average the winning bid in takeover contests significantly overstated the capital market's estimate of any takeover gains by as much as 67%.[46] He measured overpayment as the difference between the winning bid premium and the highest bid possible before the market responded negatively to the bid. This study provides support for the existence of the winner's curse, which, in turn, also supports the hubris hypothesis.

Do Bad Bidders Become Good Targets

Given that many acquisitions have failed to live up to expectations, the questions arises: Does the market punish companies that make bad acquisitions? Using a sample of 1,158 companies, Mark Mitchell and Kenneth Lehn examined their control transactions from 1980 to 1988.[47] They determined that companies that make acquisitions that cause their

---

44. M. Baserman and W. Samuelson, "I Won the Auction but I Don't Win the Prize," *Journal of Conflict Resolution* 27, 1983. 618–634.

45. J. Cassing and R. Douglas, "Implication of the Auction Mechanism in Baseball's Free Agent Draft," *Southern Economic Journal* 47, July, 1980, 110–121.

46. Nikhil Varaiya, "The Winner's Curse Hypothesis and Corporate Takeovers," *Managerial and Decision Economics* 9 (1988), pp. 209–219.

47. Mark L. Mitchell and Kenneth Lehn, "Do Bad Bidders Become Good Targets?" *Journal of Political Economy* 98, no. 2 (1990), pp. 372–398.

equity to lose value are increasingly likely to become takeover targets. That is, they found that "the likelihood of becoming a takeover target is significantly and inversely related to the abnormal stock price performance with the firm's acquisitions."[48] Their analysis shows that takeovers may be both a problem and a solution. Takeovers that reduce market value may be bad deals, assuming the market correctly assesses them, and this is a problem. The deals market, however, may take care of the problem through another takeover of the "bad bidder." The Mitchell and Lehn analysis also implies that just looking at the returns to acquirers, which research has shown may be zero or slightly negative, obscures the picture because it aggregates good deals and bad deals. When the negative market impact of bad deals is taken into account, it becomes clear that good acquisitions should have a positive impact on share values, whereas bad deals should cause the stock price of these acquirers to lag behind the market.

Executive Compensation and Corporate Acquisition Decisions

One theory of acquisitions that is closely related to the hubris hypothesis is the theory that managers of companies acquire other companies to increase their size, which, in turn, allows them to enjoy higher compensation and benefits.[49] Ajay Khorana and Marc Zenner analyzed the role that executive compensation played in the corporate acquisition decisions of 51 firms that made 84 acquisitions between 1982 and 1986.[50] For companies that engaged in acquisitions, they found a positive relationship between firm size and executive compensation but not for those that did not. However, when they separated good acquisitions from bad acquisitions, they found that good acquisitions increased compensation whereas bad deals did not have a positive effect on compensation. When the fact that bad deals may result in departures from the firm is taken into account, there is even a negative relationship between bad acquisitions and executive compensation.

IMPROVED MANAGEMENT HYPOTHESIS

Some takeovers are motivated by a belief that the acquiring firm's management can better manage the target's resources. The bidder may believe that its management skills are such that the value of the target would rise under its control. This leads the acquirer to pay a value for the target in excess of the target's current stock price.

The improved management argument may have particular validity in cases of large companies making offers for smaller, growing companies. The smaller companies, often led by entrepreneurs, may offer a unique product or service that has sold well and facilitated the rapid growth of the target.

The growing enterprise may find that it needs to oversee a much larger distribution network and may have to adopt a very different marketing philosophy. Many of the decisions

---

48. Ibid., p. 393.

49. William Baumol, *Business Behavior, Value and Growth,* 2nd ed. (New York: Macmillan Publishing Co.), 1959.

50. Ajay Khorana and Marc Zenner, "Executive Compensation of Large Acquirers in the 1980s," *Journal of Corporate Finance* 4 (1988), pp. 209–240.

that a larger firm has to make require a different set of managerial skills than those that resulted in the dramatic growth of the smaller company. The lack of managerial expertise may be a stumbling block in the growing company and may limit its ability to compete in the broader marketplace. These managerial resources are an asset that the larger firm can offer the target.

Little significant empirical research has been conducted on the importance of improved management motive. The difficulty is determining which takeovers are motivated solely by this factor because improved management usually is just one of several factors in the acquirer's decision to make a bid. It is difficult to isolate improved management and to explain its role in the bidding process. The argument that takeover offers by large companies for smaller, growing companies are motivated in part by managerial gains may be reasonable. For large public firms, a takeover may be the most cost-efficient way to bring about a management change. Proxy contests may enable dissident stockholders to oust the incumbent management, whom they may consider incompetent. One problem with this process is that corporate democracy is not very egalitarian. It is costly to use a proxy fight to replace an incumbent management team. The process is biased in favor of management, who may also occupy seats on the board of directors. It is therefore difficult to win a proxy battle. The proxy process is explained in detail in Chapter 6.

CASE STUDY: AMES DEPARTMENT STORES—IMPROVED MANAGEMENT THAT FAILED TO IMPROVE ITS TARGET

In October 1988 Ames Department Stores acquired the Zayre discount chain of nearly 400 stores for $778 million. Ames, whose operations were concentrated mainly in the New England area, was the nation's fourth largest discount retailer behind K-Mart, Wal-Mart, and Target. Ames's management thought it possessed the expertise necessary to turn around the Zayre chain, which had been experiencing sagging sales before the acquisition. This optimistic belief was based in part on Ames's continued growth in sales and profits before 1989. Given the seeming similarity of the two chains, it was believed that much of the managerial expertise at Ames would readily transfer to Zayre.

On completing the takeover, Ames instituted a number of major changes, which included changing the name of all the Zayre stores to Ames and changing the Zayre pricing and advertising policies. For example, Ames reduced the number of weekly circulars that Zayre had previously used for its direct mail marketing. Fashionable clothing, a staple at the Zayre stores, was replaced by more basic apparel. The strategy failed miserably. What had worked for Ames failed to apply to the Zayre stores. The sales at the acquired stores declined 16% after the takeover. The poor performance was also reflected in a reported $228 million loss for the combined firm for the fiscal year ending January 27, 1990 (Figure 1). The board of directors suspended the firm's $02.5 per share dividend, which, in turn, was followed by a decline in the stock price. Industry analysts reported that, in addition to the managerial errors cited here, Ames tried to merge the Ames and Zayre computer systems too rapidly. This error resulted in technical problems that caused suppliers to be paid late. Alienated

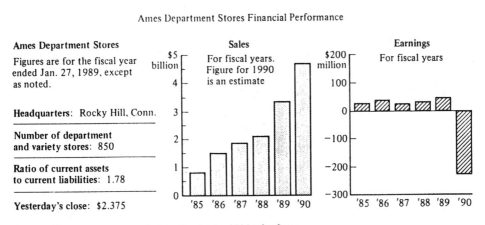

Figure 1. Steady sales and sudden losses.

Source: Company reports; analysts' estimates for 1990 sales figure. The *New York Times,* 11 April 1990, p. DI. Copyright © 1990 by The New York Times Company. Reprinted by permission.

suppliers then refused to sell on credit and demanded cash in advance. This created a liquidity crisis at Ames. The liquidity crisis came at a time when Ames was reporting large losses. Firms with large losses are not generally considered to be ideal credit risks by lenders. As of the middle of 1990 Ames was forced to file for bankruptcy protection.

Source: Eric Berg, "Ames' Rocky Retailing Marriage," *Wall Street Journal,* 11 April 1990, p. D1.

Given that the proxy process is a costly method of replacing management, in certain circumstances the hostile tender offer becomes a more reasonable tool to effect a management change. In other words, if displeased stockholders cannot accomplish a change in management that will increase the value of their investment from within the firm, it may be more efficient to attempt such a change from outside the company. Failed proxy fights by Coniston Partners seeking to replace the management of Gillette and the proxy battle by Carl Icahn to take over Texaco are examples of the weaknesses of the proxy tool as a way of changing management. If the current management is causing the reduction in stockholder wealth, a takeover, rather than an internal change, may be the only way to implement a management change. One problem, however, particularly in the examples cited, is the existence of antitakeover laws that make changes in control more difficult. Another problem occurs when the capital necessary to implement a successful tender offer is not available. In these instances, the proxy fight becomes a more effective alternative.

TAX MOTIVES

Whether tax motives are an important determinant of mergers and acquisitions has been a much debated topic in finance. Certain studies have concluded that acquisitions may be an effective means to secure tax benefits. Gilson, Scholes, and Wolfson have set forth the theoretical framework demonstrating the relationship between such gains and mergers and acquisitions.[51] They assert that for a certain small fraction of mergers, tax motives could have played a significant role. Carla Hayn, on the other hand, has empirically analyzed this relationship and has found that "potential tax benefits stemming from net operating loss carry forwards and unused tax credits positively effect announcement-period returns of firms involving tax-free acquisitions, and capital gains and the step-up in the acquired assets' basis affect returns of firms involved in taxable acquisitions."[52] Moreover, whether the transaction can be structured as a tax-free exchange may be a prime determining factor in whether to go

---

51. Ronald Gilson, Myron S. Scholes, and Mark A. Wolfson, "Taxation and the Dynamics of Corporate Control: The Uncertain Case for Tax-Motivated Acquisitions," in John Coffee, Louis Lowenstein, and Susan Rose Ackerman, eds. *Knights, Raiders and Targets* (New York: Oxford University Press, 1988), pp. 273–299.

52. Carla Hayn, "Tax Attributes as Determinants of Shareholder Gains in Corporate Acquisitions," *Journal of Financial Economics* 23, no. 1 (June 1989), pp. 121–153.

CASE STUDY: SHAW INDUSTRIES

The carpet industry underwent a dramatic transformation from 1977 to 1994. In the 1950s carpeting was expensive and was found in only a small percentage of American homes. Industry shipments grew dramatically, however, in the 1960s and 1970s so that by the mid-1980s, wall-to-wall carpet accounted for 70% of the floor covering market (Table 1 and Figure 1).

As the industry grew, it underwent numerous structural changes. Technological innovations, primarily the introduction of DuPont's StainMaster (a stain-resistant nylon fiber) in 1986, added brand identification and increased demand by adding to the durability and long-term appearance of the product. Other major changes in technology included cut-to-order distribution in which the manufacturers shipped directly to retailers, bypassing traditional wholesale channels such as distributors. In the past distributors would serve as the intermediary between the manufacturer and the retailer. The distributor would maintain an inventory, which it would ship directly to the retailer. Most carpet manufacturers are located in Dalton, Georgia, and the distributor was the regional local source of supply for retailers. This changed when the manufacturers started to ship direct to retailers. At the start of the 1980s distributors accounted for more than 60% of shipments. By the end of the 1980s they accounted for less than 20%, with many of the leading wholesalers going out of business.[a]

In the 1950s the industry was composed of many small inefficient mills. As technology improved the production process, demand increased in response to improved

---

a. *Infinity Carpets,* Harvard Business School Case Study, 9–293–077, May 27, 1993, p. 6.

Table 1.   Carpet Shipments and Sales (1977–96)

Year	Shipments (Square Yards)	Sales ($ millions)
1977	1,024.9	4,119.0
1978	1,146.2	4,729.3
1979	1,175.3	5,028.4
1980	1,025.4	4,835.5
1981	968.0	5,191.3
1982	864.0	4,904.2
1983	1,069.0	5,985.8
1984	1,094.6	6,406.2
1985	1,134.6	6,547.0
1986	1,235.2	7,261.3
1987	1,276.3	7,877.1
1988	1,304.1	8,366.8
1989	1,300.0	8,385.2
1990	1,360.0	8,527.2
1991	1,278.0	7,980.4
1992	1,419.2	8,749.3
1993	1,482.0	9,282.5
1994	1,574.7	9,530.6
1995	1,589.2	9,769.7
1996	1,640.6	10,117.5

Source: U.S. Department of Commerce; Carpet & Rug Institute, 1997 Industry Review.

quality. Some manufacturers grew and engaged in heightened competition. Many of the inefficient mills went out of business or were bought out by larger rivals. One of the most aggressive manufacturers was Shaw Industries. This company's dramatic growth featured aggressive horizontal and vertical integration.

Shaw Industries traces its origins to Clarence Shaw, who in 1946 started the Star Dye Company, which dyed tufted scatter rugs. Robert Shaw took over after the death

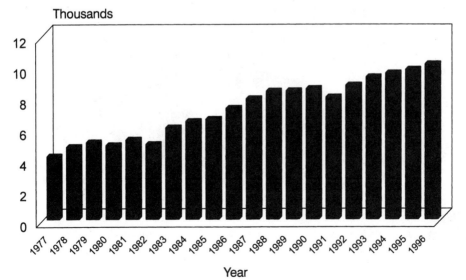

Figure 1.   U.S. carpets' sales, 1977–96.

Source: U.S. Department of Commerce, *Carpet and Rug Institute Industry Review,* 1997.

of his father in 1958. The Star Finishing Company was founded as a business that applied backing and finishing to tufted carpets. In 1967 the Philadelphia Holding Company was formed as a result of the merger of five companies: Star Dye, Philadelphia Carpet Company, Star Finishing, Sabre Carpet, and Rocky Creek Mills.[b] The company went public in 1971 and changed its name to Shaw Industries.

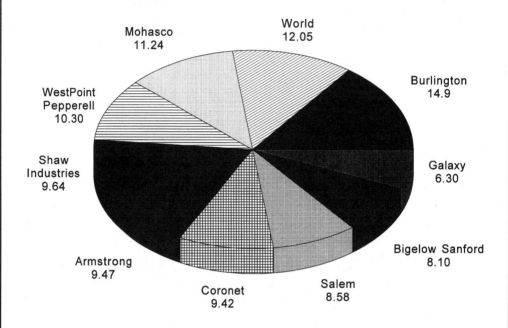

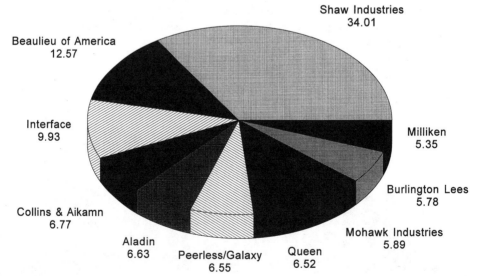

Figure 2. Top ten carpet mills' market shares: (a) 1982; (b) 1992.

---

b. J. Esquivel, *Shaw Industries Company Report,* Shearson Lehman Brothers, supplied by The Investext Group, August 22, 1990.

By the 1980s the growth in the $8.7 billion carpet industry slowed to a meager 1.5% annual compound rate of growth. Only the most efficient manufacturers survived. (Figure 2) Shaw's revenues, however, grew at an impressive 20.8% rate of growth while its net income grew at an even higher 25.4% rate. This impressive revenue and net income growth demonstrated by Shaw Industries reflects the successful implementation of the company's strategy to increase its capacity and lower its average costs through acquisitions. The carpet industry is a capital-intensive and cyclical industry that derives the demand for its products from such cyclical sectors as the residential and commercial construction and home remodeling industries. Shaw believed that it could be more competitive and better able to handle the inherent volatility of this industry by being the lowest cost producer. Its motto, which hangs high in its boardroom, is to "maintain sufficient market share to allow full utilization of our production facilities."[c] With a growing market share created by regular larger scale acquisitions, the company could run its plants at high capacity even when demand was sluggish.

Shaw purchased West Point Pepperell's carpet operations in November 1987, and that was followed by the acquisition of Armstrong World Industries' carpet division in December 1989. In 1992 it initiated another major acquisition by buying the fourth largest carpet manufacturer, Salem Carpet Mills. The company also vertically integrated backward by acquiring a yarn-making facility, thus controlling its sources of supply. This allowed the company to manufacturer 96% of its nylon, polyester, and polypropylene yarn.[d] It integrated forward, setting up its own distribution centers and thereby bypassing distributors. Shaw's strategy in circumventing distributors or wholesalers was underscored by the fact that by 1994, 96% of the company's revenues were shipped directly to major retailers and independent dealers.

By the 1990s Shaw Industries was the dominant company in the industry. Shaw Industries is a case study in aggressive growth through the use of large acquisitions to achieve economies of scale. Consumers were clearly not hurt by Shaw's increasing dominance in the carpet industry. This is clear from the fact that carpet prices have lagged the consumer price index.

---

c. J. Esquivel, *Shaw Industries Company Report,* Shearson Lehman Brothers, supplied by The Investext Group, August 22, 1990.

d. Esquivel, *Shaw Industries Company Report.*

---

forward with a deal. Sellers sometimes require tax-free status as a prerequisite of approving the sale of the company. Failing to structure a deal so that it is tax-free to the sellers may sometimes prevent its completion. The tax status may be a bargaining chip used by the seller when negotiating with multiple bidders. The area of taxation is so important and detailed that Chapter 15 is devoted to the tax issues that play a role in takeovers. Chapter 15 also discusses the various ways in which transactions may be structured so that they are tax-free.

SUMMARY

We have seen that there are a wide variety of motives and determinants of mergers and acquisitions. One of the most basic motives for mergers and acquisitions is growth. Mergers and acquisitions provide a means whereby a company can grow quickly. Often the only alternative is to grow more slowly through internal expansion. Competitive factors, however, may make such internal growth ineffective.

Firms may acquire another firm with hope of experiencing economic gains. These economic gains may come as a result of economies of scale or economies of scope. *Economies of scale* are the reductions in per-unit costs that come as the size of a company's operations, in terms of revenues or units production, increases. *Economies of scope* occur when a business can offer a broader range of services to its customer base.

Some of these gains are reported as motives for horizontal and vertical acquisitions. Horizontal deals involve mergers between competitors, whereas vertical transactions involve companies that have a buyer-seller relationship. Although the pursuit of monopolistic power is sometimes believed to be a cause of horizontal mergers, the research in this area fails to support that assertion. Vertical transactions may sometimes provide valuable benefits, but they sometimes generate unforeseen adverse effects.

Other gains may come in the form of financial benefits when a larger firm that resulted from the combination of two or more smaller firms has better access to capital markets. This improved access could come in the form of a lower cost of capital. However, this latter motive has been the subject of considerable debate in finance. Its importance and validity is still disputed.

Another motivation for mergers and acquisitions may take the form of improved management. A bidding firm may be able to pay a premium for a target because of the anticipated gains it will experience when it applies its superior management skills to the target's business. The bidder, on the other hand, may falsely believe that it can extract higher returns than what the market believes are possible from the target. Hubris, rather than objective analysis, may motivate a takeover. These last two motives are examples of the ever-present human element that permeates takeovers. Ideally, sound analysis should not be replaced by the individual motivations of managers. The human element, however, cannot be discounted as an important part of the world of mergers and acquisitions.

The role of taxes as a determinant of mergers and acquisitions has been much debated. Some studies indicate it is only important in a relatively small number of deals, whereas other studies indicate that its role is much more important.

REFERENCES

Agrawal, A., J. F. Jaffe, and G. N. Mandelker. "The Post-Merger Performance of Acquiring Firms: A Reexamination of an Anomaly." *Journal of Finance* 47, no. 4, September 1992.

Asquith, Paul. "Merger Bids, Uncertainty and Stockholder Returns." *Journal of Financial Economics* 11 (April 1983).

Baird, Charles. *Intermediate Microeconomics* (Minneapolis, MN: West Publishing Co., 1975).

Baserman, M., and W. Samuelson. "I Won the Auction but I Don't Win the Prize." *Journal of Conflict Resolution* 27, 1983.

Baumol, William. *Business Behavior, Value and Growth,* 2nd ed. (New York: Macmillan, 1959).

Berger, P. G., and E. Ofek. "Diversification's Effect on Firm Value." *Journal of Financial Economics* 37, no. 1 (January 1995).

"BevPak Brings Back the Shine to Steel Cans." *Wall Street Journal,* 8 June 1989.

Bradley, Michael, Anand Desai, and E. Han Kim. "The Rationale Behind Interfirm Tender Offers: Information or Synergy." *Journal of Financial Economics* 11, no. 1 (April 1983).

Brannigan, Martha, and Timothy O'Brien. "First Union Is Viewed as Paying Dearly for First Fidelity." *Wall Street Journal,* 20 June 1995.

Carlton, Dennis, and Jeffrey Perloff. *Modern Industrial Organization,* 2nd ed. (New York: HarperCollins, 1994).

Cassing, J., and R. Douglas. "Implication of the Auction Mechanism in Baseball's Free Agent Draft." *Southern Economic Journal* 47, July, 1980.

Comment, R., and G. Jarrell. "Corporate Focus and Stock Returns." *Journal of Financial Economics* 37, no. 1 (January 1995).

Dodd, P. "Merger Proposals, Managerial Discretion and Stockholder Wealth." *Journal of Financial Economics* 8 (June 1980).

Eckbo, Epsen B. "Horizontal Mergers, Collusion and Stockholder Wealth." *Journal of Financial Economics* 11, no. 1 (April 1983).

Eger, C. E. "An Empirical Test of the Redistribution Effect of Mergers." *Journal of Financial and Quantitative Analysis* 18 (December 1983).

Elger, P., and J. Clark. "Merger Types and Shareholder Returns." *Financial Management* (Summer 1980).

Esquivel, J. *Shaw Industries Company Report.* Shearson Lehman Brothers, August 22, 1990, supplied by The Investext Group, New York.

Fleisher, Arthur Jr., Geoffrey C. Hazard Jr., and Miriam Z. Klipper. *Board Games: The Changing Shape of Corporate America* (Boston: Little, Brown, 1988).

Galas, Dan, and Ronald W. Masulis. "The Option Pricing Model and the Risk Factor of Stock." *Journal of Financial Economics,* vol. 3(1/2) (January/March 1976).

Gaughan, Patrick A. "Financial Deregulation, Banking Mergers and the Impact on Regional Businesses." Proceedings of the Pacific Northwest Regional Economic Conference, University of Washington, Spring, 1988.

Gilson, Ronald, Myron S. Scholes, and Mark A. Wolfson. "Taxation and the Dynamics of Corporate Control: The Uncertain Case for Tax-Motivated Acquisitions." In John Coffee, Louis Lowenstein, and Susan Rose Ackerman, eds. *Knights, Raiders and Targets* (New York: Oxford University Press, 1988).

Gort, Michael. "Diversification, Mergers and Profits." In *The Corporate Merger* (Chicago: University of Chicago Press, 1974).

Guerin-Calvert, Margaret E. "Airline Computer Reservation Systems." In *The Antitrust Revolution* (Glenview, Ill.: Scott, Foresman, 1989).

Harberger, Arnold C. "Three Basic Postulates for Applied Welfare Economics." *Journal of Economic Literature* 9, no. 3 (September 1971).

Hayn, Carla. "Tax Attributes as Determinants of Shareholder Gains in Corporate Acquisitions." *Journal of Financial Economics* 23, no. 1 (June, 1989).

Hayward, Mathew L. A., and Donald C. Hambrick. "Explaining Premiums Paid for Large Acquisitions: Evidence of CEO Hubris" Unpublished manuscript, July 1995.

Higgins, Robert C., and Lawrence C. Schall. "Corporate Bankruptcy and Conglomerate Mergers." *Journal of Finance* 30 (March 1975).

Jemison, D. B., and S. B. Sitkin. "Acquisitions: The Process Can Be a Problem." *Harvard Business Review* 64 (March/April 1986).

Jensen, Michael, and Richard Ruback. "The Market for Corporate Control: The Scientific Evidence." *Journal of Financial Economics* 11, no. 1–4 (April 1983).

Khorana, Ajay and Marc Zenner. "Executive Compensation of Large Acquirers in the 1980s." *Journal of Corporate Finance* 4, 1988.

Kim, E. Han and Vijay Singal. "Mergers and Market Power: Evidence from the Airline Industry." *American Economic Review* 83, no. 3 (June 1993).

Kolb, Robert. *Principles of Finance* (Glenview, Ill.: Scott, Foresman, 1988).

Koutsoyianis, A. *Modern Microeconomics* (New York: John Wiley & Sons, 1975).

Levy, Haim, and Marshall Sarnat. "Diversification, Portfolio Analysis and the Uneasy Case for Conglomerate Mergers." *Journal of Finance* 25 (September 1970).

Lewellen, G. Wilbur. "A Pure Rationale for the Conglomerate Merger." *Journal of Finance,* vol. 26, no. 2 (May 1971).

Lictenberg, Frank, and Donald Siegel. "Productivity and Changes in Ownership of Manufacturing Plants." *Brookings Papers on Economic Activity* 3 (1987).

McClosky, Donald M. *The Applied Theory of Price* (New York: Macmillan Publishing Co., 1982).

Malatesta, Paul. "Wealth Effects of Merger Activity." *Journal of Financial Economics* 11, no. 1 (April 1983).

Mester, Loretta J. "Efficient Product of Financial Services: Scale and Scope Economies." Federal Reserve Bank of Philadelphia, January/February 1987.

Miller, Morton, and Franco Modigliani. "Dividend Policy, Growth and the Valuation of Shares." *Journal of Business* 34 (October 1961).

Mitchell, Mark L., and Kenneth Lehn. "Do Bad Bidders Become Good Targets?" *Journal of Political Economy* 98, no. 2 (1990).

Morck, Randall, Andrei Shleifer, and Robert W. Vishny. "Do Managerial Objectives Drive Bad Acquisitions?" *Journal of Finance* 45, no. 1 (March 1990).

"National Intergroup Chairman to Resign After Firm Sheds All Units But Fox Meyer." *Wall Street Journal,* 6 June 1990, p. A3.

O'Rourke, Tracy. "Postmerger Integration." In Richard S. Bibler, ed. *The Arthur Young Management Guide to Mergers and Acquisitions* (New York: John Wiley & Sons, 1989).

Porter, Michael. *Competitive Advantage* (New York: Free Press, 1985).

Ravenscraft, David J., and Frederick M. Scherer. "Mergers and Managerial Performance." In John Coffee, Louis Lowenstein, and Susan Rose Ackerman, eds. *Knights, Raiders and Targets* (New York: Oxford University Press, 1988).

Ravenscraft, David J., and Frederick M. Scherer. *Mergers, Sell-Offs and Economic Efficiency.* Washington, DC: Brookings Institution, 1987, p. 151.

Roll, Richard. "The Hubris Hypothesis of Corporate Takeovers." *Journal of Business* 59, no. 2 (April 1986).

Ross, Stephen. "The Determination of Financial Structure: The Incentive Signaling Approach." *Bell Journal of Economics,* vol. 8, (Spring 1977).

Schipper, Katherine, and Rex Thompson. "The Value of Merger Activity." *Journal of Financial Economics* 11, no. 1–4 (April 1983).

Sharpe, Anita. "PhyCor, MedPartners Call Off Merger Because of Cultural Differences." *Wall Street Journal,* January 8, 1998, A2.

Sirower, Mark L. *The Synergy Trap* (New York: The Free Press, 1997).

Stillman, B. S. "Examining Antitrust Policy Towards Mergers." *Journal of Financial Economics* 11, no. 1 (April 1983).

Van Horne, James C. *Financial Management and Policy* (Englewood Cliffs, N.J.: Prentice-Hall, 1989).

Varaiya, Nikhil P. "The Winner's Curse Hypothesis and Corporate Takeovers." *Managerial and Decision Economics* 9 (1989).

Wansley, James, William Lane, and Ho Yang. "Abnormal Returns to Acquired Firms by Type of Acquisition and Method of Payment." *Financial Management,* vol. 12, no. 3 (Autumn 1983).

Wasserstein, Bruce. *Big Deal* (New York: Warner Books 1998).

Williamson, Oliver E. "Economics as an Antitrust Defense: The Welfare Trade-offs." *American Economic Review* 58 (March 1968).

Williamson, Oliver E. *Antitrust Economics* (Oxford: Basil Blackwell, 1987).

Part Two

HOSTILE TAKEOVERS

5

ANTITAKEOVER MEASURES

Corporate takeovers reached new levels of hostility during the 1980s. This heightened bellicosity was accompanied by many innovations in the art of corporate takeovers. Although hostile takeover tactics advanced, the methods of corporate defense were initially slower to develop. As a result of the increased application of financial resources by threatened corporations, however, antitakeover defenses became quite elaborate and more difficult to penetrate. By the end of the 1980s, the art of antitakeover defenses became very sophisticated. Major investment banks organized teams of defense specialists who worked with managements of larger corporations to erect formidable defenses that might counter the increasingly aggressive raiders of the fourth merger wave. After installing the various defenses, teams of investment bankers, along with their law firm counterparts, stood ready to be dispatched in the heat of battle to advise the target's management on the proper actions to take to thwart the bidder. By the 1990s approximately 85% of large U.S. corporations had in place some form of antitakeover defense.[1]

The array of antitakeover defenses can be divided into two categories: preventative and active measures. Preventative measures are designed to reduce the likelihood of a financially successful hostile takeover, whereas active measures are employed after a hostile bid has been attempted.

This chapter describes the more frequently used antitakeover defenses. The impact of these measures on shareholder wealth, a highly controversial topic, is explored in detail. Opponents of these measures contend that they entrench management and reduce the value of stockholders' investment. They see the activities of raiders as an element that seeks to keep management "honest." They contend that managers who feel threatened by raiders will manage the firm more effectively, which will, in turn, result in higher stock values. Proponents of the use of antitakeover defenses argue, however, that these measures prevent the actions of the hostile raiders who have no long-term interest in the value of the corporation but merely are speculators seeking to extract a short-term gain while sacrificing the future of the company that may have taken decades to build. Thus, proponents are not reluctant to take actions that will reduce the rights of such short-term shareholders because they believe that they are not equal, in their eyes, to long-term shareholders and other *stakeholders,* such as employees and local communities. The evidence on shareholder wealth effects does not, however, provide a consensus, leaving the issue somewhat unresolved. Some studies purport clear adverse shareholder wealth effects, whereas others

---

1. Marcia Parker, "Companies Not Ringed With Defensive Armor," *Pensions and Investments,* vol. 18, no. 20 (September 1990), p. 21.

fail to detect an adverse impact on the shareholders' position. This chapter includes the results of most of the major studies in this field so that readers can make an independent judgment.

MANAGEMENT ENTRENCHMENT HYPOTHESIS VERSUS STOCKHOLDER INTERESTS HYPOTHESIS

The *management entrenchment hypothesis* proposes that nonparticipating stockholders experience reduced wealth when management takes actions to deter attempts to take control of the corporation. This theory asserts that managers of a corporation seek to maintain their positions through the use of active and preventative corporate defenses. According to this view, stockholder wealth declines in response to a reevaluation of this firm's stock by the market.

The shareholder interests hypothesis, sometimes also referred to as the convergence of interests hypothesis, implies that stockholder wealth rises when management takes actions to prevent changes in control. The fact that management does not need to devote resources to preventing takeover attempts is considered a cost savings. Such cost savings might come in the form of management time efficiencies savings, reduced expenditures in proxy fights, and a smaller investor relations department. The shareholder interests hypothesis can also be extended to show that antitakeover defenses can be used to maximize shareholder value through the bidding process. Management can assert that it will not withdraw the defenses unless its receives an offer that is in the shareholder's interests.

The shareholder wealth effects of various antitakeover measures, both preventative and active, are examined with an eye on the implications of the validity of these two competing hypotheses. If the installation of a given antitakeover defense results in a decline in shareholder wealth, this event lends some support to the management entrenchment hypothesis. If, however, shareholder wealth rises after the implementation of such a defense, the shareholder interests hypothesis gains credence.

Given that the evidence from the various shareholder wealth effects studies of antitakeover measures is somewhat conflicting, the reader is presented with the evidence from several studies and can make his or her own determination of which theory is valid. However, other research studies on these hypotheses, which do not involve antitakeover defenses, have also been conducted. Some of this additional evidence is initially presented so that the reader may also consider it along with the antitakeover defenses evidence.

Morck, Shleifer, and Vishny examined the validity of these two competing hypotheses separate from a consideration of antitakeover defenses.[2] They considered the entrenchment of managers along with several other relevant factors, such as management's tenure with the company, personality, and status as a founder, and other factors such as the presence of a large outside shareholder or an active group of outside directors. The study examined the relationship between Tobin's q—the market value of all of a company's securities divided by the replacement costs of all assets—as the dependent variable, and the

2. R. Morck, A. Shleifer, and R. W. Vishny, "Management Ownership and Market Valuation: An Empirical Analysis," *Journal of Financial Economics,* vol. 20, no. 1/2 (Jan/March 1988), pp. 293–315.

shareholdings of the board of directors in a sample of 371 of the Fortune 500 firms in 1980. They found that Tobin's q rises as ownership stakes rise. The positive relationship was not uniform in that it applied to ownership percentages between 0% and 5% as well as to those above 25%, whereas a negative relationship applied for those between 5% and 25%. The positive relationship for all ownership percentages, except the 5% to 25% range, provides some support for the shareholder interests hypothesis because higher ownership percentages imply greater entrenchment, which, in turn, was shown to be associated with higher values of securities except the intermediate range of 5% to 25%.

The conflicting results for the intermediate 5% to 25% range notwithstanding, Morck, Shleifer, and Vishny have provided some weak support for the shareholder interest hypothesis which the reader can consider while evaluating the numerous antitakeover defenses studies that are discussed throughout this chapter.

PREVENTATIVE ANTITAKEOVER MEASURES

Preventative antitakeover measures are becoming an increasingly important part of corporate America. Most Fortune 500 companies have considered and developed a plan of defense in the event that the company becomes the target of a hostile bid. Some of these plans are directed at reducing the value that a bidder can find in the firm. The value-enhancing characteristics of a target are outlined in Chapter 14. These include characteristics such as high and steady cash flows, low debt levels, and low stock price relative to the value of the firm's assets. The presence of these factors may make a firm vulnerable to a takeover. Therefore, some preventative measures are designed to alter these characteristics of the firm in advance, or upon completion of a hostile takeover, so that the financial incentive a raider might have to acquire the target is significantly reduced.

Early Warnings Systems: Monitoring Shareholding and Trading Patterns

One of the first steps in developing a preventative antitakeover defense is to analyze the distribution of share ownership of the company. Certain groups of shareholders, such as employees, tend to be loyal to the company and probably will vote against a hostile bidder. Institutional investors usually invest in the security to earn a target return and may eagerly take advantage of favorable pricing and terms of a hostile offer. If a company is concerned about being a target of a hostile bid, it may closely monitor the trading of its shares. A sudden and unexpected increase in trading volume may signal the presence of a bidder who is trying to accumulate shares before having to announce its intentions. Such an announcement will usually cause the stock price to rise, so it's in a bidder's interest to accumulate as many shares as possible before an announcement.

Types of Preventative Antitakeover Measures

In effect, the installation of preventative measures is an exercise in wall building. Higher and more resistant walls need to be continually designed and installed because the raiders, and their investment banking and legal advisers, devote their energies to designing ways of scaling these defenses.

Among the preventative measures that are discussed in this chapter are:

Poison pills: These are securities issued by a potential target to make the firm less valuable in the eyes of a hostile bidder. There are two general types of poison pills: flip-over and flip-in. They can be an effective defense that has to be taken seriously by any hostile bidder.

Corporate charter amendments: The target corporation may enact various amendments in its corporate charter that will make it more difficult for a hostile acquirer to bring about a change in managerial control of the target. These corporate charter changes are sometimes referred to as shark repellents. Some of the amendments that are discussed are supermajority provisions, staggered boards, fair price provisions, and dual capitalizations.

Golden parachutes: The attractive severance agreements sometimes offered to top management may be used as a preventative antitakeover measure. Alone, they will not prevent a takeover. However, they may help enhance the effect of some of the preceding measures and create a disincentive to acquire the target. These defenses, however, are far less powerful than poison pills and corporate charter amendments.

First-Generation Poison Pills—Preferred Stock Plans

Poison pills were invented by the famous takeover lawyer Martin Lipton, who used them in 1982 to defend El Paso Electric against General American Oil and again in 1983 during the Brown Foreman versus Lenox takeover contest. Brown Foreman was the fourth largest distiller in the United States, marketing such name brands as Jack Daniels whiskey, Martel cognac, and Korbel champagne, and generating annual sales of $900 million. Lenox was a major producer of china. Lenox's shares were trading at approximately $60 per share on the New York Stock Exchange. Brown Foreman believed that Lenox's stock was undervalued and offered $87 a share for each share of Lenox. This price was more than 20 times the previous year's per share earnings of $4.13. Such an attractive offer is very difficult to defeat.

Martin Lipton suggested that Lenox offer each common stockholder a dividend of preferred shares that would be convertible into 40 shares of Brown Foreman stock if Brown Foreman took over Lenox. These convertible shares would be an effective antitakeover device because, if converted, they would seriously dilute the Brown family's 60% share ownership position.

The type of poison pill Lenox used to fend off Brown Foreman is referred to as a *preferred stock plan*. Although they may keep a hostile bidder at bay, these first-generation poison pills had certain disadvantages. First, the issuer could only redeem them after an extended period of time, which might be in excess of 10 years. Another major disadvantage is that they had an immediate adverse impact on the balance sheet. This is because when an analyst computes the leverage of a company, the preferred stock may be added to the long-term debt, thus making the company more heavily leveraged and therefore more risky in the eyes of investors after the implementation of the preferred stock plan.

Second-Generation Poison Pills—Flip-Over Rights

Poison pills did not become popular until late 1985 when their developer, Martin Lipton, perfected them. The new pills did not involve the issuance of preferred stock so that, by being easier to use, the pills would be more effective. They would also eliminate any adverse impact that an issue of preferred stock might have on the balance sheet. Preferred stock is considered to be fixed-income security by financial analysts. An increase in the amount of preferred stock would generally be interpreted as increased financial leverage and risk.

The perfected pills came in the form of rights offerings that allowed the holders to buy stock in the acquiring firm at a low price. Rights are a form of call option issued by the corporation, entitling the holders to purchase a certain amount of stock for a particular price during a specified time period. The rights certificates used in modern poison pills are distributed to shareholders as a dividend and become activated after a triggering event. A typical triggering event would be one of the following:

- An acquisition of 20% of the outstanding stock by any individual, partnership, or corporation
- A tender offer for 30% or more of the target corporation's outstanding stock

Flip-over poison pills seemed to be a most potent defense until they were effectively overcome in the takeover of the Crown Zellerbach Corporation by the Anglo-French financier Sir James Goldsmith (see the case study that follows).

CASE STUDY: GOLDSMITH versus CROWN ZELLERBACH CORPORATION

Crown Zellerbach was a San Francisco–based forest products company with substantial holdings of forest-related assets. Sir James Goldsmith saw great value in Crown Zellerbach's assets at a time when the market failed to reflect its worth. "I do believe in forests. I do believe in forest lands. Everybody says they are a disaster. But they're still making profits. And forest lands will one day be as valuable as they were."[a]

Crown Zellerbach's chairman, William T. Creason, who was concerned about the company's vulnerability to a takeover from a raider such as Goldsmith, adopted an elaborate set of antitakeover defenses designed to maintain the company's independence. These measures were as follows (use of the antitakeover measures, other than poison pills, are described later in this chapter):

1. *Formation of a defensive team.* Crown Zellerbach formed a well-rounded defensive team that included the prestigious investment bank Salomon Brothers and attorney Martin Lipton. Crown Zellerbach also included the publicist

---

a. Moira Johnson, *Takeover* (New York: Penguin Books, 1986), p. 55.

Gershon Kekst, whose involvement highlights the important role public relations may play in takeover contests.

2. *Updating of the stockholders list.* The corporation updated its stockholders list so that if a takeover battle ensued, it would be in a position to quickly contact important institutional and individual investors.

3. *Staggering the board of directors.* The board of directors' elections were staggered to make it more difficult to take control of the board.

4. *Enactment of the antigreenmail amendment.* An antigreenmail amendment was enacted in Crown Zellerbach's corporate charter to preempt the possibility that a raider would make a bid in the hope of attracting greenmail compensation.

5. *Addition of a supermajority provision.* This alteration of the corporate charter required a two-thirds majority vote on future bylaw changes.

6. *Issuance of a poison pill.* Crown Zellerbach's poison pill allowed stockholders to buy $200 worth of stock in the merged concern for $100. This significant discount for current Crown Zellerbach stockholders would make the company less valuable. As noted previously, the pill was issued in the form of rights that were activated when either an acquirer bought 20% of Crown Zellerbach's stock or an acquirer made a tender offer for 30% of Crown Zellerbach stock. The rights became exercisable after a bidder bought 100% of the company's stock.

The rights were thought to be such a formidable obstacle to a raider that no bidder would trigger them. Because of the large financial incentives involved, however, the market developed a means of evading the effects of the defenses. This innovative tactic was first developed by the team representing Sir James Goldsmith.

Designed to enable Crown to still make a deal with a favored suitor, the rights, trading independently of the shares, could be redeemed or canceled by the board by buying them back from shareholders for 50 cents each. But once a raider had acquired 20% of Crown's stock, the rights could no longer be redeemed and would not expire for 10 years.

The pill's consequences were so devastating, it was hoped Goldsmith would hold short of the 20% threshold. But what if he kept buying? Would the pill be any defense against his gaining control on the open market? Martin Lipton warned: "The plan wouldn't prevent takeovers; it would have no effect on a raider who was willing to acquire control and not obtain 100% ownership until after the rights expired."[b]

Goldsmith's tactic entailed buying just over 50% of Crown Zellerbach stock. He bought this stock gradually but stopped purchasing once he had a controlling interest in the company. The rights were issued when Goldsmith bought more than 20%, but they never became exercisable because he didn't buy 100 percent.

The ironic part of this takeover was that Goldsmith used Crown Zellerbach's poison pill against Crown Zellerbach. After the rights were issued, the company found

---

b. Ibid., p. 121.

it more difficult to pursue other options such as a friendly bidder, sometimes referred to as a white knight. The fact that these wealth-reducing rights were outstanding lowered the interest of potential white knights. Ironically, this made Crown Zellerbach more vulnerable. Crown Zellerbach's management, after a protracted but futile struggle, was forced to agree to a takeover by Goldsmith.

Household International and the Legality of Poison Pills

Various legal challenges have been made to the modern versions of poison pills. One such challenge involved the poison pills issued by Household International Corporation (see the related case study). In a November 1985 ruling in the Delaware Supreme Court, the court upheld the legality of Household's use of a poison pill. The court's position was that the pills did not necessarily keep bidders away; rather, they gave target corporations the opportunity to seek higher bids.

CASE STUDY: DYSON-KISSNER-MORAN versus HOUSEHOLD INTERNATIONAL

Household International Inc. was a large financial services company located in Prospect Heights, Illinois. Although its main operations were in the financial services industry, it possessed diversified holdings, which included Household Finance, National Car Rental, and a retail food business. John Moran, one of the largest shareholders and the director of Household, planned to make a bid to take over Household through his New York–based investment company, Dyson-Kissner-Moran.

Dyson-Kissner-Moran was estimated to be 1% the size of the larger Household International. It never made a hostile bid for Household, but it did engage in negotiations to buy the company. The other directors, unwilling to allow Household International to be acquired by Moran's investment company, decided to try to prevent the acquisition by adopting a poison pill that would be activated when a bidder bought more than 20% of Household. Moran believed that management and the directors adopted the pill to preserve their own positions. Therefore, represented by the famous takeover lawyer Joseph Flom, Moran sued Household on August 17, 1984, in Delaware, where Household was incorporated. He lost at the Chancery Court level but appealed to the Delaware Supreme Court. In November 1985, however, the Delaware Supreme Court upheld the legality of Household's poison pill.

The Household decision was extremely important because it helped establish the legality of poison pills as an antitakeover defense. This decision has had great impact because so many corporations are incorporated in Delaware.[a]

---

a. Moira Johnson, *Takeover* (New York: Penguin Books, 1986), p. 55.

After the use of poison pills was upheld in the courts, large corporations rushed to adopt their own poison pill defenses. In the 1990s poison pill defenses are commonplace (Figure 5.1).

Third Generation Poison Pills: Flip-In Poison Pills

Flip-over poison pills have the drawback that they are only effective if the bidder acquires 100% of the target; they are not effective in preventing the acquisition of a controlling but less than 100% interest in the target. Given that most acquirers want to obtain 100% of the target's stock so as to have unrestricted access to the target's resources, flip-over provisions may prevent many, but not all, control transactions.

Flip-in poison pills were an innovation designed to deal with the problem of a bidder who was not trying to purchase 100% of the target. With the flip-over provisions, a bidder could avoid the impact of the pill simply by not buying all of the target's outstanding stock. *Flip-in* provisions allow holders of rights to acquire stock in the target, as opposed to *flip-over* rights, which allow holders to acquire stock in the acquirer. The flip-in rights were designed to dilute the target company regardless of whether the bidder merged the target into his company. They can be effective in dealing with raiders who seek to acquire a controlling influence in a target while not even acquiring majority control. Controlling ownership can often be achieved with stockholdings less than 51%. This is particularly true of widely held corporations in which most stockholders have a small percentage of the outstanding stock. The presence of flip-in rights makes such controlling acquisitions very expensive.

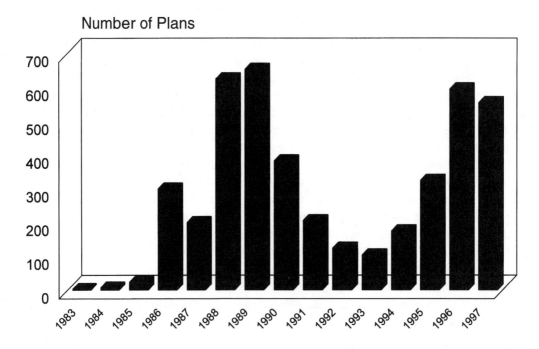

Figure 5.1. Poison pill adopted.

Source: Securities Data Company.

A flip-over plan may also contain flip-in provisions, thus combining the advantages of a flip-over plan, which is used against a 100% hostile acquisition, with a flip-in plan, which is used against a control share acquisition that is not a 100% share acquisition.

Back-End Plans

Another variant on the poison pill theme are *back-end plans,* also known as *note purchase rights plans.* The first back-end plan was developed in 1984. Under a back-end plan shareholders receive a rights dividend, which gives shareholders the ability to exchange this right along with a share of stock for cash or senior securities that are equal in value to a specific "back-end" price stipulated by the issuer's board of directors. These rights may be exercised after the acquirer purchases shares in excess of a specific percentage of the target's outstanding shares. The back-end price is set above the market price, so back-end plans establish a minimum price for a takeover. The board of directors, however, must in good faith set a reasonable price.

Back-end plans are used to try to limit the effectiveness of two-tiered tender offers. In fact, the name *back-end* refers to the back end of a two-tiered offer. These plans may, however, place the board of directors in a seemingly conflicting position of establishing a price for the company when the board may also be taking the position that the company is not for sale.

Voting Plans

Voting plans were first developed in 1985. They are designed to prevent any outside entity from obtaining voting control of the company. Under these plans the company issues a dividend of preferred stock. If any outside entity acquires a substantial percentage of the company's stock, holders of preferred stock become entitled to supervoting rights. This prevents the larger block holder, presumably the hostile bidder, from obtaining voting control of the target. The legality of these plans has been successfully challenged in court. Therefore, they are not very commonly used.

Mechanics of Issuing Poison Pills

Poison pills are issued by distributing to common stockholders a dividend of one right for each share of stock they own. Rights holders receive the right to purchase one share of stock during the exercise period, which is typically 10 years in length. Rights plans are usually authorized by the board of directors without shareholder approval. Until the occurrence of a triggering event, such as the purchase of 20% of the issuer stock or an offer for 30% of its shares, the rights trade with the common shares and no separate rights certificates are issued. Once the triggering event occurs, however, the rights detach and become exercisable. At that time rights certificates are mailed to shareholders.

As noted previously, the issuer may redeem the rights for a nominal amount, such as $0.02 per right, if it decides that it is advantageous. For example, if the issuer receives a bid that it finds desirable, the existence of the rights may be an impediment to an advantageous deal and the issuer may want to remove them.

Blank Check Preferred Stock

Although a board of directors may have authority to issue rights, its ability to issue shares is dictated by the corporate charter. For this reason, it is standard practice for boards to create and reserve a certain amount of preferred stock that can be issued in the event that the rights become exercisable.[3] This prevents the board from having to solicit shareholder approval to amend the charter to allow for the issuance of shares to satisfy the rights. Such a request for shareholder approval would be tantamount to a referendum on the poison pill itself. It would also mean additional delay and uncertainty and would effectively weaken the poison pill defense.

Dead Hand Provisions

Poison pills can be deactivated by the target's board of directors. Bidders can try to use this feature to offset the poison pill by initiating a tender offer that is contingent on the removal of the pill. The higher the premium offered, the more pressure on the board to remove the pill defense. Dead hand provisions give the power to redeem the poison pill to the directors who were on the target's board of directors before the takeover attempt. Even if these directors are ousted, they retain the voting power to control the pill's redemption.

Dead hand provisions have been ruled invalid under New York law in the *Bank of New York v. Irving Bank* case. More recently a Delaware court has also ruled that this version of a poison pill is coercive and disenfranchises shareholders of their proper rights. This case did not involve a takeover battle. Rather, it involved a suit brought by shareholders who sued Toll Brothers, Inc., a Pennsylvania company incorporated in Delaware that had installed this type of poison pill.[4] Although Delaware is the most important state, there are some states that have held that dead hand provisions are legitimate. In the lawsuit involving the hostile bid by Invacare for Healthdyne Technologies, Inc., a Georgia court ruled that such provisions were valid because they were implemented into the corporate charter. In his ruling in Toll Brothers, Judge Jack Jacobs implied that if such provisions were implemented in the corporate charter, it might make them legitimate.

Recent Court Rulings Limiting the Use of Poison Pills

Recent court rulings have limited to some extent the indiscriminate use of poison pills as an antitakeover defense. These rulings are described as follows.

---

3. Arthur Fleischer, Jr. and Alexander Sussman, *Takeover Defense,* 5th ed. (New York: Aspen Law & Business, 1995), pp. 5–105.

4. As of the date of this publication, it is not known if Toll Brothers will appeal.

Maxwell v. Macmillan, 1988. British publisher Robert Maxwell successfully challenged Macmillan's poison pill defense. A Delaware court ruled that Macmillan's
poison pill defense unfairly discriminated against Maxwell's offer for the New York
publishing firm. The court ruled that the poison pill should be used to promote an
auction. Macmillan's pill, the court ruled, prevented an effective auction.

Rales v. Interco, 1988. A Delaware court reached a similar decision when it ruled that Interco's poison pill unfairly favored Interco's own recapitalization plan while discrimi-
nating against the Rales' tender offer. (This case is discussed later in this chapter.)

Bank of New York v. Irving Bank, 1988. A New York State court ruled that Irving
Bank's poison pill unfairly discriminated against the Bank of New York's bid for
Irving. The ruling did not totally strike down Irving's pill, but only those provisions
that did not allow the Bank of New York, which held 4.9% of Irving at the time of
ruling, also to buy Irving shares at a discounted price in the event that an acquirer
bought a 20% stake. The court ruled that if other shareholders could buy shares at
half price, so could the Bank of New York.

Impact of Poison Pills on Stock Prices

Several studies have examined the impact of poison pill provisions on stock prices.

Malatesta and Walking (1988)

A study by Paul Malatesta and Ralph Walking considered what effect the announcement of
the adoption of a poison pill had on 132 firms between 1982 and 1986.[5] They found that
poison pill defenses appeared to reduce stockholder wealth and that, on average, the firms
that announced poison pill defenses generated small but statistically significant, abnormal
negative stock returns (−0.915%) during a two-day window around the announcement
date. When these firms abandoned their poison pill plans, they showed abnormal positive
returns.

Malatesta and Walking's results provide some support for the managerial entrenchment
hypothesis in that the firms adopting the pills tended to have below-average financial performance. They also found that, on average, the managerial ownership percentage was significantly less for firms that adopted poison pills compared with industry averages. This
implies that management of firms that adopted pills did a poorer job managing their companies and enacted defenses that would result in a decrease in shareholder wealth, which
they were less affected by because they held less of the company's stock themselves.

Ryngaert (1988)

The findings of Malatesta and Walking were confirmed by Michael Ryngaert in his study
of 380 firms that had adopted poison pill defenses between 1982 and 1986.[6] Ryngaert

---

5. Paul H. Malatesta and Ralph A. Walking, "Poison Pills Securities: Stockholder Wealth, Profitability and Ownership Structure," *Journal of Financial Economics* 20, no. 1/2 (January/March
1988), pp. 347–376.

6. Michael Ryngaert, "The Effects of Poison Pill Securities on Stockholder Wealth," *Journal of
Financial Economics* 20 (January/March 1988), pp. 377–417.

found statistically significant stock price declines from firms that adopted pill defenses and that were perceived as takeover targets. Ryngaert also analyzed the impact on the target firm's stock of legal challenges to the pill defense. He noted negative excess stock returns in 15 of 18 pro-management court decisions (upholding the legality of the pill) and positive excess returns in 6 of 11 pro-acquirer decisions (invalidating the pill).

Ryngaert's research also touched on the effectiveness of poison pills as an antitakeover defense. He found that hostile bids are more likely to be defeated by firms that have a poison pill in place. Thirty-one percent of the pill-protected firms remained independent after receiving unsolicited bids, compared with 15.78% for a control group of non–pill-protected firms that also received unsolicited bids. Moreover, in 51.8% of the unsolicited bids, pill-protected firms received increased bids, which Ryngaert attributes to the presence of the pill defense. This finding is consistent with other research such as the Georgeson study that is discussed next.

Impact of Poison Pills on Takeover Premiums

Two often cited studies concerning the impact of poison pills on takeover premiums were conducted by Georgeson and Company, a large proxy solicitation firm. In a study released in March 1988, the firm showed that companies protected by poison pills received 69% higher premiums in takeover contests than unprotected companies. The study compared the premiums paid to pill-protected companies with those paid to companies without pill protection. Protected corporations in the Georgeson sample received premiums that were 78.5% above where the company's stock was trading six months before the contest. Nonprotected corporations received 56.7% premiums. The firm did a later study in November 1997 analyzing transactions from 1992 to 1996. The results were similar, although the difference between premiums was less. Premiums paid to pill-protected companies averaged eight percentage points, or 26% higher than those without pill protection. As Figure 5.2 shows, the difference was greater for small capitalization companies than for large capitalization companies.

The positive impact of poison pills on takeover premiums that was found in both Georgeson studies has also been confirmed by academic research. Robert Comment and G. William Schwert also found that poison pills are associated with higher takeover premiums.[7] More generally, Nikhil Varaiya found that antitakeover measures were one of the determinants of takeover premiums.[8]

The Georgeson studies contradicted the previously widely held belief that poison pills are bad for stockholders. Some of this research has demonstrated that poison pills cause stock prices to decline, presumably because pill-protected companies are more difficult takeover targets. Therefore, there is a lower likelihood that this type of company will be the object of a takeover bid. However, the Georgeson studies show that, in the event of a bid, the premium will be higher.

7. Robert Comment and G. William Schwert, "Poison or Placebo: Evidence on the Deterrence and Wealth Effects of Modern Antitakeover Measures," *Journal of Financial Economics* 39 (1995), pp. 3–43.

8. Nikhil P. Varaiya, "Determinants of Premiums in Acquisition Transàctions," *Managerial and Decision Economics* 8 (1987), pp. 175–184.

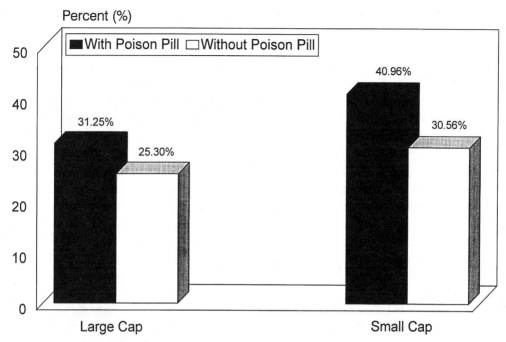

Figure 5.2.   Takeover premium and poison pills, by target market cap (large cap ≥ $1b.; small cap < $1b.).

Source: Poison Pills and Shareholder Value: 1992–96, Georgeson & Company, November 1997.

Poison Pills and the Auction Process

The fact that poison pills result in high takeover premiums has been supported by more recent research on the relationship between poison pills and the auction process.[9] One of the reasons poison pills result in higher premiums is that they facilitate the auction process. Bradley, Desai, and Kim have shown that auctions result in an added takeover premium of 11.4%,[10] whereas Comment and Schwert found added premiums equal to 13%. Poison pill defenses are often circumvented when the bidder increases its bid or makes an attractive all-cash offer. All-cash offers have been associated with 12.9% higher premiums.[11] In the face of increased prices brought about by an auction that may have been combined with more attractive compensation, such as an all-cash offer, target boards are often pressured to deactivate the poison pill.

---

9. Robert Comment and G. William Schwert, "Poison or Placebo? Evidence on the Deterrence and Wealth Effects of Modern Antitakeover Measures," *Journal of Financial Economics* 39 (September 1995), pp. 3–43.

10. Michael Bradley, Anand Desai, and E. Han Kim, "Synergistic Gains From Corporate Acquisitions and Their Division Between the Shareholders of the Target and Acquiring Firms," *Journal of Financial Economics* 21 (May 1988), pp. 3–40.

11. Yen-Sheng Huang and Ralph A. Walking, "Target Abnormal Returns Associated With Acquisition Announcements: Payment, Acquisition Form, and Managerial Resistance," *Journal of Financial Economics* 19 (December 1987), pp. 329–349.

Conclusion of Research on Shareholder Wealth Effects of Poison Pills

The consensus of the research is that the implementation of poison pill defenses tends to be associated with negative, although not large, excess returns to the target's stock. We must remember, however, that these studies focus on a narrow time period around the date when the adoption of the pill plan was announced. Pill-protected firms that ultimately are acquired may exhibit higher returns as a result of the pill defense. These higher premiums were not reflected in this body of research.

Poison Puts

Poison puts are a unique variation on the poison pill theme. They involve an issuance of bonds that contain a *put option* exercisable only in the event that an unfriendly takeover occurs. A put option allows the holder to sell a particular security to another individual or firm during a certain time period and for a specific price.

The issuing firm hopes that the holders' cashing of the bonds, which creates large cash demands for the merged firm, will make the takeover prospect most unattractive. If the acquiring firm can convince bondholders, however, not to redeem their bonds, these bond sales may be avoided. In addition, if the bonds are offered at higher than prevailing interest rates, the likelihood of redemption will not be as high. The existence of poison puts does not ensure that a firm will not be a target of an unwanted bid. The July 1990 offer of $410 million by Ratners Group P. L. C., the world's largest jewelry chain, for Kay Jewelers, Inc. is an example. Under the terms of the offer, Ratners would pay Kay $17 per share, which was a $6 per share premium. The bid, however, was made contingent on Kay's bondholders accepting 75 cents on the dollar for their bonds. This is ironic because Kay's bondholders had the right to put their bonds back to the company at 100 cents on the dollar. Ratners rationalized the bond component of their offer by pointing out that at the time of the bid the bonds were trading at 70 cents on the dollar, and they had earlier traded as low as 45 cents on the dollar. Therefore, Ratners believed that bondholders were receiving a "premium." Bondholders, however, were dissatisfied and believed they were only being offered 75% of the amount they had lent the firm.

Corporate Charter Amendments

Changes in the corporate charter are common antitakeover devices. The extent to which they may be implemented depends on state laws, which vary among states. Corporate charter changes generally require shareholder approval. The majority of antitakeover charter amendments are approved. Only in extreme cases of poor management performance do stockholders actively resist antitakeover amendments. This is partly because management is generally much more organized in its lobbying efforts than those shareholders who may oppose the proposed charter changes. Another important reason that shareholders tend to approve these amendments is that the majority of shareholders in large U.S. corporations are institutions, which have in the past been known to side with management. Some evidence suggests that this tendency is starting to change. Moreover, institutions as a whole are not unified in their support of management.

Brickley, Lease, and Smith point out that certain types of institutional investors, such as banks, insurance companies, and trusts, are more likely to vote in favor of management's proposals than other institutions, such as mutual funds, public pension funds, endowments, and foundations.[12] They believe that the latter category of investors is more independent of management in that they do not generally derive income from the lines of business controlled by management. When the charter amendment proposal clearly reduces shareholder wealth, institutions in general are more clearly found to be in opposition to the amendment. The process of proxy approval of shareholder amendments is discussed in Chapter 6.

A later study by Brickley, Lease, and Smith explored the circumstances under which managers are more constrained by the voting process.[13] They found that although there is a high rate of passage of proposals put forward by management, managers tend to only make such proposals when they are highly likely to pass. In addition, in a study of 670 antitakeover corporate charter amendments involving 414 firms, they showed that managers are more constrained by voting when the following conditions apply: (1) in small companies with more concentrated ownership, (2) in companies that have large outside blockholders, (3) when information about possible adverse shareholder wealth effects has attracted media attention, and (4) in companies that have stringent voting rules.

Some of the more common antitakeover corporate charter changes are:

- Staggered terms of the board of directors
- Supermajority provisions
- Fair price provisions
- Dual capitalizations

Staggered Terms of the Board of Directors

To understand how staggering the terms of directors helps inhibit hostile takeovers, the reader needs to have a general idea of how boards function.

Operations of Boards of Directors

The board of directors is a body of individuals who have been elected by the stockholders to oversee the actions of management and to recommend actions to stockholders. The position is a part-time one that provides compensation in the form of either an annual stipend or a fee for each meeting attended. These fees are highly variable. One study by Graef S. Crystal found average compensation equal to $56,200, with the range equal to as low as $3,600 and the high equal to $181,000.[14]

Most large corporations have boards composed of notable figures who may be chief executive officers (CEOs) of other large corporations. For many directors, the position is

---

12. James Brickley, Ronald Lease, and Clifford Smith, "Ownership Structure and Voting on Antitakeover Amendments," *Journal of Financial Economics* 20, no. 1/2 (January/March 1988), pp. 267–292.

13. James A. Brickley, Ronald C. Lease, and Clifford W. Smith, "Corporate Voting: Evidence from Corporate Charter Amendment Proposals," *Journal of Corporate Finance* 1 (1994), pp. 5–31.

14. Judith Dobrzynski, "Are Directors Overpaid? The Answer Varies Widely," *New York Times,* 27 June 1995, p. D4.

considered prestigious and is not accepted merely for its monetary compensation. Many directors of Fortune 500 companies have annual incomes far greater than the income they receive from their directorships.

The board of directors appoints management who, in turn, manage the day-to-day operations of the corporation. The directors are generally not aware of the minutiae of the company's daily workings and tend to rely on management for this information. They often provide an overall direction to the corporation and decide on major issues and proposed changes.

Many boards are composed of the *inside board* and the *outside board.* The inside board is made up of members of management, whereas the outside board members are those directors who do not have direct managerial responsibilities for the corporation's day-to-day operations. One study showed that, on average, boards of public companies contain 13 directors, 9 of whom are outside directors.[15]

Issues, such as a bid to buy the corporation, may be required to be brought before the board of directors. The board sets forth requirements and may recommend that the particular issue be taken to the stockholders for voting approval. In some instances stockholders have sued the corporation to require the board of directors to bring all bids before stockholders for their consideration. This occurred, for example, when several Gillette stockholders sued Gillette in 1987.

If stockholders want to change the management of a corporation, they may have to change the board of directors. For example, a hostile bidder who takes control of a company may want to replace management with others who would run the company in the manner he or she sees fit. The bidder may want to become CEO of the target corporation. If the bidder has the requisite number of votes and is not impeded by any antitakeover defenses that limit the bidder's ability to hold elections and vote in new directors, he or she may elect new directors. These new directors will appoint new management according to the bidder's preferences. Normally, the managers are selected by means of a majority vote of the board of directors.

Some common stock have cumulative voting rights associated with ownership. That is, a share of stock comes with one vote for each director position available. Cumulative voting allows stockholders the right to pool their votes so that all the votes that could have been used to vote for each director in the election can be applied to one or a few of the director seats. This provides significant stockholders with the power to place their representatives on the board to advocate their positions. Most sizable, publicly held companies that are traded on the large organized exchanges, however, do not have cumulative voting. Bhagat and Brickley reported in their 1984 study that 24% of the 383 New York Stock Exchange firms in their sample had cumulative voting.[16]

It is also not considered unusual to have a corporation give membership on the board of directors to a union or bank in return for wage concessions or an easement of the provisions of a loan agreement. The policy of conceding seats on the board took an unusual turn in 1988 when, in return for voting in favor of management in their proxy fight with Carl Icahn, the Texaco Corporation was reported to have reserved a seat on Texaco's board for a representative of institutional investors. The votes of institutional investors played a crit-

---

15. Jay W. Lorsch, *Pawns or Potentates* (Boston: Harvard Business School Press, 1989), p. 19.

16. S. Bhagat and J. A. Brickley, "Cumulative Voting: The Value of Minority Shareholder Rights," *Journal of Law and Economics* 27 (October 1984), pp. 339–366.

ical role in deciding the proxy fight, defeating Icahn in the proxy contest. The more active role of institutional investors in this proxy battle is one of many instances in which institutional investors have become somewhat more active over the past 10 years.[17]

Staggered Board Amendments

The staggered board defense varies the terms of the board of directors so that only a few of the directors may be elected during any given year. This may be important in a takeover battle because the incumbent board may be made up of members who are sympathetic to current management. Indeed, boards may also contain members of management. Director approval is desirable because directors may recommend the merger to stockholders, or they may decide that the offer is not worthy of a stockholder vote. When a bidder has already bought majority control, the staggered board may prevent him or her from electing managers who will pursue the bidder's goals for the corporation, such as the sale of assets to pay down the debt incurred in the acquisition process.

Typical staggered board provision. A staggered board provision comes in the form of an amendment of the corporate charter. The ability to amend the corporate charter is dictated by the prevailing state laws. Shareholder approval is usually required to install a staggered board. A typical staggered board provision provides for one-third of the board to be elected each year for a three-year term. This type of board is sometimes referred to as a *classified board*. In contrast, every member of the nonclassified board comes up for election at each annual meeting.

Staggered elections extend the amount of time a bidder will have to wait before he or she can attain majority representation on the board. This reduces the bidder's ability to enact important changes in the direction of the corporation. Given the time cost of money, an acquirer may not want to wait two years to get control of a target.

Delaware Law and the Removal of Directors

As discussed in Chapter 3, the laws of the state of Delaware are probably the most important of all state laws, given the large number of corporations that have incorporated in this state. The Delaware law stipulates the necessary conditions for removing directors. These conditions vary depending on whether the board is a classified or nonclassified board. According to the Delaware law, classified board members may not be removed before their term expires. Nonclassified board members, however, may be removed at any time by a majority stockholder vote.

Effectiveness of Staggered Boards as an Antitakeover Defense

Staggered boards are not a sufficiently powerful antitakeover defense that they can be expected to prevent a well-financed hostile takeover attempt. Raiders typically assume that if they acquire a majority of the outstanding shares, they can deal with the incumbent board through litigation. In addition, they may assume that the prior directors will abide by the wishes of the new majority shareholder, given that boards, in principle, are fiduciaries of shareholders. The new majority shareholder may also more actively voice its position to the directors in the form of a nonbinding shareholder referendum using the proxy solicitation

---

17. Carolyn Kay Brancato, *Institutional Investors and Corporate Governance* (New York: Richard D. Irwin) 1997, pp. 81–129.

process. These options notwithstanding, the real benefit of staggered boards to the defending corporation is that they may provide one more implement for the raider to deal with. The combined obstacles that the target may put in the way of the bidder may improve the target's negotiating position and lead to higher bids.

Staggered Board Research

In DeAngelo and Rice's study of the impact of antitakeover amendments on stockholder wealth, the sample chosen consisted of 100 different firms, of which 53 had a staggered board.[18] This study demonstrated that the passage of antitakeover charter amendments yielded negative returns. Although their analysis also included other forms of antitakeover amendments, staggered boards made up a significant percentage of the amendments considered.

One drawback of the DeAngelo and Rice study is that their results showed relatively low t-statistics. The t-statistic allows the researcher using regression analysis to test whether certain explanatory variables truly influence the dependent variable within a certain degree of confidence. Low t-statistics imply that we may not be very confident of the strength of the functional relationship analyzed. When we obtain such results, it is said that we fail to find a statistically significant relationship.

Richard Ruback also failed to find a statistically significant relationship between a negative stock price effect and staggered board provisions.[19] Although his research showed a negative 1% decline in stock prices resulting from passage of staggered board provisions, these results were not statistically significant. The conclusion we must draw from this research is that there *may* be a negative impact on stock prices and stockholder wealth from the passage of staggered board provisions. Insofar as this relationship might exist, however, it seems to be relatively weak.

Supermajority Provisions

A corporation's charter dictates the number of voting shares needed to amend the corporate charter or to approve important issues such as mergers. Other transactions that may require stockholder approval are corporate liquidation, lease of important assets, sale of the company, or transactions with interested parties or substantial shareholders. The definition of a substantial shareholder may vary but it most often means a stockholder with more than 5% to 10% of the company's outstanding shares.

A supermajority provision provides for a higher than majority vote to approve a merger—typically 80% or two-thirds approval. The more extreme versions of these provisions require a 95% majority. Supermajority provisions may be drafted to require a higher percentage if the size of the bidder's shareholding is larger. They are more effective when management, or other groups that tend to be very supportive of management on issues such as mergers, hold a sufficient amount of stock to make approval of a merger more difficult. For example, if management and an employee stock ownership plan (ESOP) hold 22% of the outstanding stock and the corporation's charter requires 80% approval for mergers, it will be very difficult to complete a merger if the 22% do not approve.

18. Harry DeAngelo and Eugene Rice, "Antitakeover Charter Amendments and Stockholder Wealth," *Journal of Financial Economics* 11 (1983), pp. 329–360.

19. Richard Ruback, "An Overview of Takeover Defenses," in Alan J. Auerbach, ed., *Mergers and Acquisitions* (Chicago: National Bureau of Economic Research, University of Chicago Press, 1987), pp. 49–67.

Supermajority provisions generally contain escape clauses, sometimes called *board out clauses,* which allow the corporation to waive or cancel the supermajority provision. The most common escape clause provides that the supermajority provisions do not affect mergers that are approved by the board of directors or mergers with a subsidiary. Most of these escape clauses are carefully worded so that the members of the board of directors who are interested parties may not vote with the rest of the board on related issues. An example of the interested party qualification would be the raider who holds 12% of a target company's stock, which has allowed the raider to command one or more seats on the board of directors. The escape clause would prevent this raider from exercising his or her votes on issues of approving a merger offer.

Supermajority provisions are most frequently used in conjunction with other antitakeover corporate charter changes. Corporations commonly enact supermajority provisions after they have put other antitakeover charter amendments into place. If the supermajority provisions require a supermajority to amend the corporate charter, it is more difficult for a raider to erase the other antitakeover provisions once the supermajority provision is in place. Supermajority provisions are more effective against partial offers. Offers for 100% of the target tend to negate the effects of most supermajority provisions. Exceptions may occur when certain groups loyal to the target hold a percentage greater than the difference between 100% and the supermajority threshold.

Legality of Supermajority Provisions
The courts have upheld the legality of supermajority provisions when these provisions have been adopted *pursuant to shareholder approval.* For example, in *Seibert v. Gulton Industries, Inc.,* the court upheld a supermajority provision requiring 80% voting approval to approve a takeover by a 5% shareholder.[20] The provision required the supermajority approval before the bidder reached the 5% threshold. The courts have pointed out the obvious fact that shareholders themselves adopted the supermajority provisions and clearly possess the ability to "unadopt" them if they so choose.

Supermajority Provision Research
Several studies of antitakeover amendments have included supermajority provisions. DeAngelo and Rice[21] and Linn and McConnell[22] both conducted studies in 1983 and failed to find significant negative price effects for the various antitakeover amendments considered. These results are somewhat contradicted, however, by Gregg Jarrell and Annette Poulsen (1986), who point out that these other studies considered only the earlier versions of supermajority provisions, which do not include an escape clause.[23] They found that the later supermajority provisions, which included such escape clauses, were associated with a

---

20. *Seibert v. Gulton Industries, Inc.,* No. 5631.5 Del. J. Corp. L. 514 (Del Ch. June 21, 1974), aff'd without opinion 414 A. 2d 822 (Del 1980).

21. Harry DeAngelo and Eugene Rice, "Antitakeover Charter Amendments and Stockholder Wealth," *Journal of Financial Economics* 11 (April 1983), pp. 275–300.

22. Scott C. Linn and John J. McConnell, "An Empirical Investigation of the Impact of Antitakeover Amendments on Common Stock Prices," *Journal of Financial Economics* 11, no. 1–4 (April 1983), pp. 361–399.

23. Gregg A. Jarrell and Annette B. Poulsen, "Shark Repellents and Stock Prices: The Effects of Antitakeover Amendments Since 1980," *Journal of Financial Economics* 19, no. 1 (September 1987), pp. 127–168.

statistically significant negative 5% return. However, those supermajority provisions without escape clauses did not show significant negative returns.

In 1987 a study shed light on the effectiveness of classified boards and supermajority provisions. John Pound examined two samples of 100 firms each; one group had supermajority provisions and classified boards, whereas the control group had neither. His results showed that the frequency of takeovers was 28% for the group with the antitakeover amendments in place but 38% for the nonprotected control group.[24]

Fair Price Provisions

A fair price provision is a modification of a corporation's charter that requires the acquirer to pay minority shareholders at least a fair market price for the company's stock. This may be stated in the form of a certain price or in terms of the company's price-earnings (P/E) ratio. That is, it may be expressed as a multiple of the company's earnings per share. The P/E multiple chosen is usually derived from the firm's historical P/E ratio or is based on a combination of the firm's and the industry's P/E ratio. Fair price provisions are usually activated when a bidder makes an offer. When the fair price provision is expressed in terms of a specific price, it usually states that stockholders must receive at least the maximum price paid by the acquirer when he or she bought the holdings.

Many state corporation laws already include fair price provisions. Fair price amendments to a corporation's charter augment the fair price provisions of the state's laws. In states in which fair price provisions exist, corporate fair price provisions usually provide for higher prices for stockholders in merger offers. The target corporation may waive most fair price provisions. For the fair price provision to be rendered not applicable, it is usually necessary that there be a 95% majority and approval of the board of directors. Fair price provisions are not as common as some of the other antitakeover charter amendments, such as supermajority provisions and staggered boards. Approximately 35% of the firms that have implemented antitakeover charter amendments have fair price provisions.

Fair Price Provisions and Two-Tiered Tender Offers

Fair price provisions are most useful when the target firm is the object of a two-tiered tender offer. In such an offer, a bidder has made an offer for 51% of the target at one price and with one set of conditions, such as all cash. (Although establishing clear control through a 51% purchase offer may make most sense, not all two-tiered bids include a 51% first-step purchase offer.) The purchase of 51% of the first tier establishes control. The second tier is less valuable to the bidder. Therefore, an acquirer may want to offer a lower price for these shares as well as less attractive terms, such as compensation in the form of securities whose value may be open to interpretation.

The two-tiered offer is designed to give the target company stockholders an incentive to tender early so as to be part of the first tier. As a result of changes in the law, however, stockholders may tender their shares and have them accepted on a pro rata basis. This means they would receive a blended combination of the first- and second-tier prices and terms. A fair price provision could force the bidder to provide those in the second tier with

---

24. John Pound, "The Effectiveness of Antitakeover Amendments on Takeover Activity," *Journal of Law and Economics* 30 (October 1987), pp. 353–367.

the same prices and terms as those in the first tier. The existence of a fair price provision is a disincentive for a bidder to initiate a two-tiered offer. These provisions, along with changes in tender offer regulations, render the two-tiered offer a less popular takeover tool.

Although the fair price provision is an impediment to a raider, it is not considered a potent defense. It primarily causes a bidder to pay a blended price, which is usually higher. In periods of tense merger and acquisition activity, such as in the fourth merger wave when debt financing was abundant, these high prices alone did not slow down the pace of acquisition.

Fair Price Research

Research on the impact of fair price provisions on stockholder wealth has thus far failed to show a significant relationship between fair price amendments and stock prices. Jarrell and Poulsen reported a statistically insignificant 20.65% change in stock prices in response to the implementation of fair price amendments.[25] This means that although they found the expected sign (negative), their results were not sufficiently robust to state confidently that there is any relationship between the fair price provisions and stock prices. The main effort seems to be a restructuring of the offer with a blended price as opposed to a two-tiered structure.

Some evidence appears to contradict the Jarrell and Poulsen's mild negative stock price effect. For example, Victoria McWilliams found a positive stock price effect associated with the adoption of fair price provisions.[26]

Dual Capitalization

Dual capitalization is a restructuring of equity into two classes of stock with different voting rights. There are various reasons to have more than one class of stock other than to prevent a hostile takeover. For example, General Motors uses its Class E shares to segregate the performance and compensation of shareholders of its EDS division.

From an antitakeover perspective, however, the purpose of dual capitalization is to give greater voting power to a group of stockholders who might be sympathetic to management's view. Management often increases its voting power directly in a dual capitalization by acquiring stock with greater voting rights. A typical dual capitalization involves the issuance of another class of stock that has superior voting rights to the current outstanding stock. The stock with the superior voting rights might have 10 or 100 votes for each share of stock. This stock is usually distributed by the issuance of superior voting rights stock to all stockholders. Stockholders are then given the right to exchange this stock for ordinary stock. Most stockholders choose to exchange the supervoting rights stock for ordinary stock because the super stock usually lacks marketability or pays low dividends. However, management, who may also be shareholders, may not exchange their supervoting rights stock for ordinary stock. This results in management increasing its voting control of the corporation.

25. Gregg A. Jarrell and Annette B. Poulsen, "Shark Repellents and Stock Prices: The Effects of Antitakeover Amendments Since 1980," *Journal of Financial Economics* 19, no. 1, September 1987, pp. 127–168.

26. Victoria B. McWilliams, "Managerial Share Ownership and the Stock Price Effects of Antitakeover Amendment Provisions," *Journal of Finance* 45, no. 5, pp. 1627–1640.

CASE STUDY: TRUMP versus GRIFFIN

A classic battle for control involving superior voting rights stock was waged in 1988 between real estate tycoon Donald Trump and television personality Merv Griffin. Griffin, fresh with cash from the sale of the "Wheel of Fortune" and "Jeopardy" television shows to Coca-Cola for $250 million, set his sights on Donald Trump's Resorts casino. The Resorts Corporation was originally the Mary Carter Paint Company, but changed its name to Resorts in 1968. It is a diversified business that includes a helicopter and plane airline, a hotel in the Bahamas, and the 700–room Resorts International hotel and casino. Resorts was Atlantic City's first casino hotel.

Donald Trump, in addition to owning a significant stake in Resorts, also owned the Trump Plaza and the Trump's Castle casinos. In 1990 he constructed the 1,260–room Taj Mahal casino, which cost an estimated $1 billion. Because casino licensing regulations provide that an individual may hold only three casino licenses, Trump decided that Resorts was the most likely candidate for sale.

Resorts had two classes of stock: Class A and Class B. Class A shares only had 1/100 votes per share, whereas each Class B share had one vote for each share. Class A shares sold for as much as $75 in 1986, while Class B shares were not traded on an organized exchange. Trump had 88% of the voting shares in Resorts. Although he did have effective voting control of Resorts, he was under pressure to divest himself of one casino. Griffin, aware of Trump's position, made a bid for Resorts at $35 per share. Given his superior voting rights stock, Trump remained in control of Resorts. He could not have been compelled to sell, although he had to face the choice of selling one casino to take ownership of the Taj Mahal. Trump eventually sold his interest in Resorts and tendered his superior voting rights stock to Merv Griffin.

The Resorts deal was played out vividly in the media, given the notoriety of the two protagonists. The acquisition proved to be a disaster for Merv Griffin, who discovered that Resorts needed a greater than anticipated level of capital investment. Resorts was forced to file Chapter 11 not long after the acquisition.[a]

---

a. Pauline Yoshihashi and Neil Barsky, "Merv Griffin's Plunge into Casino Gambling Could Prove a Loser," *Wall Street Journal,* 10 February 1989, p. A1.

The effectiveness of dual capitalization was dealt a blow in July 1988 when the Securities and Exchange Commission (SEC) adopted Rule 19c-4, which prohibited public corporations from issuing new classes of stock that would diminish the voting power of existing stockholders.[27] Following this vote, the organized exchanges and the National Association of Securities Dealers adopted various restrictions on the use of stock with enhanced voting rights. In particular, the New York Stock Exchange limited the trading of new dual-class shares. In addition, the ruling contained a grandfather clause that allowed companies with existing unequal voting rights to continue trading. However, in June, 1990 a federal appeals court overturned the SEC's ruling on the grounds that the agency had overstepped its

---

27. "Share Vote Proposal Approved," *New York Times,* 8 July 1988, pp. D1, D5.

mandate. The SEC then responded with its Voting Rights Policy, which allows supervoting provisions that were permitted under its older policies. Through grandfather clauses it also allow supervoting arrangements that were already in place before its new policy. The net result of these SEC voting policies is that companies that had supervoting rights plans in place may continue them but companies are not permitted to adopt new ones.

Dual Capitalization Research

In 1987 Megan Partch, in a study of 44 companies that had instituted dual capitalization between 1962 and 1984, did not observe a significant relationship between stock prices and dual capitalization.[28] Partch reported a positive excess return of 1.2% on the announcement of the dual capitalization. On the other hand, she found as many increases as decreases in stock prices. When the longer period that started with the initial announcement of the dual capitalization and the date of the shareholders' meeting is considered, the results fail to show statistical significance. In addition, many of the firms in her study had a high degree of managerial ownership—on average, 49%. Thus, these firms are atypical of the larger New York Stock Exchange firms, which are the more active users of antitakeover devices. Given the large proportion of managerial ownership, these firms would not be likely hostile takeover targets.

In another study of dual capitalization, Gregg Jarrell and Annette Poulsen examined 94 firms that recapitalized with dual classes of stock that had different voting rights between 1976 and 1987.[29] Forty of the firms were listed on the New York Stock Exchange, with 26 on the American Stock Exchange and 31 traded over-the-counter. The study found significant abnormal negative returns equal to 0.82% for a narrow time period around the announcement of the dual capitalization. Jarrell and Poulsen also reported that the greatest negative effects were observed for firms that had high concentrations of stock held by insiders (30% to 50% insider holdings). Dual capitalization will be more effective in consolidating control in the hands of management when management already owns a significant percentage of the firm's stock. The fact that negative returns were higher when management already held more shares implies that when management entrenchment was more likely (which, in turn, implies that the potential for a successful bid was lower), the market responded by devaluing the shares.

The dual capitalization plan is subject to shareholder approval, and, following its approval, shareholders voluntarily exchange their low voting rights shares they have been given for dividend-paying stock. They may do this even though the approval and exchange may mean that the subsequent value of their holdings may be lower because of the reduced likelihood of a takeover premium when insiders attain veto power over mergers and acquisitions. Some researchers believe that shareholders willingly accept these offers because the managers in these firms are already able to block takeovers.[30] This may not be a satisfactory explanation, however, because it does not tell us why managers would go to the expense and trouble to acquire control they supposedly already possess. Because they seek to

---

28. Megan Partch, "The Creation of a Class of Limited Voting Common Stock and Shareholder Wealth," *Journal of Financial Economics* 18, no. 2 (June 1987), p. 313.

29. Gregg Jarrell and Annette Poulsen, "Dual Class Recapitalizations As Antitakeover Mechanisms," *Journal of Financial Economics* 20 (January/March 1988), pp. 129–152.

30. Richard Ruback, "Coercive Dual-Class Exchange Offers," *Journal of Financial Economics* 20 (January/March 1988), pp. 153–173.

enhance their control, we may conclude that they are in a position to block takeovers without dual classes of stock.

Antigreenmail Provisions

Antigreenmail charter amendments restrict the ability of a target corporation to pay greenmail to a potential hostile bidder. Some amendments allow the payment if shareholders extend their approval. Other variations allow for the payment of some ceiling amount such as the market price. In the case of a takeover battle, which generally causes stock prices to rise, this may still provide a hostile shareholder a profit from his activities. Greenmail is discussed later in this chapter with active antitakeover defenses.

Restrictions on Ability to Call an Election

Unless there are specific restrictions in the corporate charter, most states require corporations to call a special shareholder meeting if a certain percentage of the shareholders request it. Such meetings may be used as a forum whereby insurgents try to gain control of the company. At shareholder meetings, takeover defenses such as poison pills may be dismantled. These meetings may also be used to promote proxy fights. Given the opportunities for bidders that shareholder meetings present, companies may try to amend the charter to limit the ability to call meetings. Some of the more extreme restrictions limit the ability to call a meeting to the board of directors or only if a certain high percentage of the shareholders request it. In addition, there may be limitations imposed on the type of issues that may be raised at the shareholder meeting.

Antitakeover Amendments and Managerial Ownership Research

Victoria McWilliams conducted a study on the impact of managerial share ownership and the shareholder wealth effects of antitakeover amendments.[31] She examined 763 amendments that were adopted by 325 New York Stock Exchange and American Stock Exchange firms. McWilliams's research was partially motivated by a desire to explain why several earlier research studies fail to find a statistically significant share price response with the adoption of antitrust amendments. These earlier studies did not consider managerial share ownership, which varies by firm.

McWilliams's results show a negative relationship between managerial share ownership and the adoption of antitakeover amendment proposals (with the exception of fair price provisions). The stock price reaction to amendment proposals was positive when managerial share ownership was near zero and became negative as these ownership percentages rose. She concludes that the market is interpreting these proposals as lowering the likelihood of a takeover when proposed by companies that have high managerial share ownership.

---

31. Victoria McWilliams, "Managerial Share Ownership and the Stock Price Effects of Antitakeover Amendment Proposals," *Journal of Finance* 45 (5) (December 1990), pp. 1627–1640.

Number of Companies Having Antitakeover Measures

The Investor Responsibility Research Center (IRRC) tracks 1,500 companies and maintains a database of antitakeover provisions enacted by these companies. Table 5.1 shows the number of companies in this database that enacted specific antitakeover measures. A majority of the companies the IRRC tracked had poison pills, classified boards, and golden parachutes, whereas a relatively small percentage had antigreenmail provisions.

Golden Parachutes

Golden parachutes are special compensation agreements that the company provides to upper management. The word *golden* is used because of the lucrative compensation that executives covered by these agreements receive. Although companies typically maintain that they adopt such agreements for reasons other than the prevention of takeovers, they may have some antitakeover effects. These effects may occur whether the parachutes are used in a preventative or an active manner. They may be used in advance of a hostile bid to make the target less desirable, but they may also be used in the midst of a takeover battle. It should be kept in mind, particularly for large takeovers, that the golden parachute payments are a small percentage of the total purchase price. This implies that the antitakeover effects of these benefits may be relatively small.

Many CEOs of corporations believe that golden parachutes are a vital course of action in a takeover contest. One problem corporations face during a takeover battle is that of retaining management employees. When a takeover has been made, a corporation's management is often besieged by calls from recruiters. Managers who are insecure about their positions are quick to consider other attractive offers. Without a golden parachute agreement,

Table 5.1.   Summary of Corporate Governance Provisions for 1,500 Companies Tracked by the Investor Responsibility Research Center

Provision	1990	1993	1995
Advance notice requirement	N/A	N/A	657
Antigreenmail	84	93	90
Blank check preferred stock	N/A	N/A	1275
Classified board	850	862	895
Confidential voting	48	139	176
Consider nonfinancial effects of merger	96	111	108
Cumulative voting	263	233	216
Dual-class stock	112	122	124
Eliminate cumulative voting	131	150	156
Fair price	475	492	487
Golden parachutes	N/A	N/A	799
Limit right to call special meeting	355	424	466
Limit action by written consent	352	416	467
Poison pill	759	795	799
Supermajority vote to approve merger	252	269	267
Unequal voting rights	34	31	30

Source: Ann Yerger, "Changes in Takeover Tactics Outline in Profile," *Corporate Governance Bulletin,* Investor Responsibility Research Center, July–September 1995, XII, no. 3, p. 22.

the managers might be forced to litigate to realize certain compensation in the event that they were terminated following a change in control. Therefore, some corporations adopt golden parachutes to alleviate their employees' concerns about job security. For example, Dorman Commons, former chairman of Natomas Inc., a San Francisco–based oil company that implemented golden parachutes, believes that golden parachutes protect shareholders because they "permit key officers to respond objectively to a threat and negotiate without fear for their personal futures."[32] This view by management also finds some supporters within the academic community. Michael Jensen of Harvard University contends that properly constructed golden parachutes should result in management possessing sufficient incentives to negotiate higher takeover premiums for shareholders.[33] He states, "These control related contracts are beneficial when correctly implemented, because they help reduce the conflict of interest between shareholders and managers at times of takeover and therefore make it more likely that the productive gains stemming from changes in control will be realized."[34]

An interesting golden parachute agreement that was adopted in response to a takeover threat was the plan implemented by the Chrysler Corporation in 1995 following the aborted takeover attempt by investor Kirk Kerkorian and the Tracinda Corporation. The Chrysler plan covered 30 members of upper management. This plan is slightly unusual in that it is activated not only when there is a change in control but also if a potential acquirer tries to get upper management fired even before a takeover is completed.[35]

A study by Richard Lambert and David Larker provides some support for Jensen's view. They found that stock prices rose 3% when companies announced the adoption of golden parachutes.[36] Other studies have provided a basis for the market's positive stock price response. In a sample of 146 firms that adopted golden parachutes between 1975 and 1988, Machlin, Choe, and Miles found that the number of multiple takeover offers was significantly greater for firms that possessed golden parachute agreements than for those firms without such agreements.[37] They also found a positive relationship between the size of the golden parachute agreement and the magnitude of the takeover premium.

Mechanics of Golden Parachutes

A typical golden parachute agreement provides for lump-sum payments to certain senior management on either voluntary or involuntary termination of their employment. This agreement is usually effective if termination occurs within one year after the change in control. The agreements between the employee and the corporation may have a fixed term or may be an *evergreen* agreement, in which the term is one year but is automatically ex-

32. Dorman L. Commons, *Tender Offer* (New York: Penguin Books, 1985), p. 112.

33. Michael Jensen, "Takeovers: Causes and Consequences," in Patrick A. Gaughan, ed., *Readings in Mergers and Acquisitions* (Oxford: Basil Blackwell, 1994), pp. 15–43.

34. Jensen, "Takeovers," p. 32.

35. Gabriella Stern and Joann Lublin, "Chrysler Has Bold New Idea—In Parachutes, *Wall Street Journal,* 12 July 1995, p. B1.

36. Richard A. Lambert and David F. Larker, "Golden Parachutes, Executive Decision Making and Shareholder Wealth," *Journal of Accounting Economics* 7 (1985), pp. 179–203.

37. Judith Machlin, Hyuk Choe, and James Miles, "The Effects of Golden Parachutes on Takeover Activity," *Journal of Law and Economics* 36, no. 2 (1993), pp. 861–876.

tended for an additional year if there is not a change in control during a given year. Monies to fund golden parachutes are sometimes put aside in separate accounts referred to as *rabbi trusts*. Rabbi trusts provide assurance to the employee that the monies will be there for the payment of the parachutes.

The amount of compensation is usually determined by the employee's annual compensation and years of service. For example, the agreement could provide for the terminated employee to receive some multiple of a recent year's annual salary, possibly also including incentive and bonuses, for a certain number of years.

Golden parachutes are usually triggered by some predetermined ownership of stock by an outside entity. Lambert and Larker found that the trigger control percentage of stocks acquired by a bidder was an average 26.6% for the firms they studied.[38] They also showed that the participants in golden parachutes plans are narrowly defined. In their sample, golden parachute agreements covered only 9.7% of the executives. These agreements are extended to executives who do not have employment contracts. They are effective even if the managers leave the corporations voluntarily after a change in control.

Some golden parachutes are triggered by control share thresholds well below the 26.6% average found by Lambert and Larker. For example, Inland Steel has a clause specifying that a change in control is deemed to have occurred if the board of directors simply comes to that conclusion or an outside entity acquires 9.5% of the company's voting power.

Golden parachutes are not usually applied broadly. One unusual exception is what are known as *silver parachutes,* compensation agreements given to most employees in the firm, including lower level employees. The most common type of silver parachute is a one-year severance pay agreement.

Legality of Golden Parachutes

Golden parachutes have been challenged in court by stockholders who contend that these agreements violate directors' and management's fiduciary responsibilities. The problem arises because golden parachutes generally do not have to be approved by a stockholder vote before implementation. The courts have held that the actions of directors in enacting golden parachute agreements were within their purview under the Business Judgment Rule.[39] As discussed in Chapter 3, this rule holds that management's actions are valid as long as they are enacted while management is acting in the stockholder's best interests. The fact that management's actions may not maximize stockholder wealth, in retrospect, is irrelevant according to this rule.

Courts have generally refused to distinguish between golden parachute agreements and other types of executive compensation arrangements.[40] Part of the reason courts have not been persuaded by the self-dealing argument of golden parachute critics is because the agreements are typically approved by a compensation committee of the board of directors, which should be dominated by disinterested directors and not those who would expect to

---

38. Richard A. Lambert and David F. Larker, "Golden Parachutes, Executive Decision Making and Shareholder Wealth," *Journal of Accounting Economics* 7 (1985), pp. 179–203.

39. *Buckhorn Inc.v. Ropak Corp.,* 656 F. Supp. 209 (S.D. Ohio) *aff'd by summary order* 815 F.2d 76 (6th Cir. 1987).

40. *Royal Crown Cos. v. McMahon,* 359 S.E. 2d 379 (Ga. Ct. App. 1987), *cert. denied* (Ga. Sept. 8, 1987).

profit from the parachutes.[41] When the golden parachute agreements are triggered by the manager's own actions, however, courts have invalidated them or at least granted a preliminary injunction against their use.[42]

Criticism of Golden Parachutes

Some shareholder rights activists believe that golden parachutes are a burden on both the corporation and the stockholders. Some critics cite moral hazard concerns, and golden parachutes could be considered a form of self-dealing on the part of management and one of the more flagrant abuses of the modern takeover era. The magnitude of these compensation packages, they state, is clearly excessive. Critics contend that managers of companies that were poorly managed and have experienced a declining stock price end up being rewarded for that mismanagement. The golden parachute that was given to Michael Bergerac, former chairman of Revlon Corporation, after his resignation at the end of the unsuccessful defense against corporate raider Ronald Perelman was estimated to have provided Bergerac with a compensation package in excess of $35 million. This package included stock options worth $15 million.

The excessiveness of golden parachute agreements has given rise to the term *golden handcuffs,* which reflects the belief that golden parachutes serve only to entrench management at the expense of stockholders. This belies their role as an antitakeover device. If the compensation package is very large, some raiders might be put off from making a bid for the company. As noted previously, although a large golden parachute agreement may be a mild deterrent, it is not considered an effective antitakeover tool. In conjunction with other, stronger devices, however, these agreements may have some role as a deterrent.

The tax treatment of golden parachutes can be complex. However, Congress, in the tax reform acts of 1984 and 1986, imposed penalties on golden parachute payments. These penalties feature the payment of a nondeductible 20% tax, to be paid by the employee, for "excessive" golden parachute payments. Generally, the excess is defined as the amount greater than a typical annual compensation. In addition, the employer corporations are denied tax deductions for excessive golden parachutes. Excessive is defined as being three times the average salary of the employee in the previous five-year period.

Relevance of Golden Parachutes in the Fifth Merger Wave

While golden parachutes attracted a lot of attention in the fourth merger wave, they were less relevant in the fifth merger wave. This is mainly due to the fact that stock options were well distributed to members of management of many companies. Given that target companies often receive a significant premium in takeovers when a target company is acquired, the managers of a target company who hold a significant amount of stock may gain more through the premiums they receive for their share holdings than what they would have gained from any golden parachute.

---

41. *E. Tate & Lyle PLC v. Staley Continental, Inc.,* Fed. Sec. L. Rep. 93, 764 (Del. Ch. CCH 93, 764) (Del. Ch. May 9, 1988); *Nomad Acquisition Corp. v. Damon Corp.,* CCH Fed. Sec. L. Rep. 94, 040 (Del. Ch. Sept. 16, 1988).

42. John C. Coffee, "Shareholders Versus Managers: The Strain in the Corporate Web," in John Coffee, Louis Lowenstein, and Susan Rose Ackerman, eds., *Knights, Raiders and Targets* (New York: Oxford University Press, 1988), pp. 71–134.

CASE STUDY: BORDEN'S PEOPLE PILL

The Borden Corporation developed an innovative antitakeover defense when it instituted the so-called people pill. In January 1989 Borden revealed that its top 25 executives had signed a contract to quit the company if the firm were to be taken over by a raider who did not give stockholders a "fair" value for their investment and if a single member of the management team was demoted or fired. Both conditions must be met for the people pill to be activated.

Borden's board of directors approved the people pill out of concern that the firm might become a takeover target. The board believed that the plan would help ensure that, in the event of an unwanted bid, the stockholders of the food company would receive a fair return on their investment. The fair stock price was determined to be a cash offer for 100% of the stock's value, as determined by an opinion by the firm's investment bankers (a friendly opinion), plus a premium of at least 50% of the firm's profits that an acquirer would reasonably be expected to make from asset sales or other synergies. The pill would be activated by an offer for 85% of the firm's shares that were not already in the acquirer's hands.

This innovative antitakeover defense contributed to keeping the firm independent in the late 1980s when it appeared vulnerable to a takeover. However, it is difficult to say how effective this defense really is. At that time, when asset sales and the breakup value of the firm were of paramount importance, from a heavily leveraged raider's viewpoint, the loss of management was not as important. With the downsizing and workforce restructuring that took place in the 1990s, many think that there is a surplus of management talent, so the loss of some executives might not be very troublesome. Some raiders, with an eye on enacting a change in management, might consider a mass resignation a benefit. However, there are clear costs in assembling a competent managerial structure that is knowledgeable in the operations of any particular business. The more capable the management, the greater the effectiveness of the people pill.

CHANGING THE STATE OF INCORPORATION

Because states have antitakeover laws that vary in degrees of protection, a company may choose to relocate its legal corporate home so it is protected by another state's laws that have stronger antitakeover provisions. This is usually accomplished by a company's creating a subsidiary in the new state and then merging the parent into the subsidiary. Reincorporating in another state that has stronger antitakeover laws, however, will not ensure a firm's independence. For example, Singer moved its state of incorporation from Connecticut to New Jersey, a state that has a strong antitakeover law. The move did not prevent Singer from ultimately being taken over by raider Paul Bilzerian. Nonetheless, reincorporating may make a takeover more difficult for the raider. This stronger bargaining position may help the target get a better price for the shareholders.

Reincorporation Research

Jeffrey Netter and Annette Poulsen examined the shareholder wealth effects of reincorporation announcements for 36 firms in 1986 and 1987.[43] They divided their sample into two groups: 19 firms that reincorporated from California and the remaining 17 firms. They point out that California is a shareholder rights state whose corporation laws protect shareholder interests. Among the rights provided are mandatory cumulative voting, a prohibition against classified boards, and other shareholder rights such as the ability to remove directors without cause or to call special meetings. Netter and Poulsen reason that if there were stock price effects, they would be greater in reincorporations from California to Delaware. Their results failed to reveal any shareholder wealth effects either from the 36 reincorporations in their sample or from the California subsample. On the basis of their study, we may conclude that the greater flexibility provided to management by incorporating in Delaware will not reduce shareholder wealth.

ACTIVE ANTITAKEOVER DEFENSES

Installing the various preventative antitakeover defenses will not guarantee a company's independence. It may, however, make the takeover more difficult and costly. Some bidders may decide to bypass a well-defended target in favor of other firms that have not installed formidable defenses. Nonetheless, even those firms that have deployed a wide array of preventative antitakeover defenses may still need to actively resist raiders when they become targets of a hostile bid. The second half of this chapter describes some of the various actions a target may take after it receives an unwanted bid or learns that it is about to be the target of such a bid. The target may become aware of this in several ways, such as through the results of its stock watch or market surveillance programs or through required public filings such as a Hart-Scott-Rodino filing.

The following actions are discussed in the second half of this chapter:

Greenmail: Share repurchases of the bidder's stock at a premium.

Standstill agreements: These agreements usually accompany a greenmail payment. Here the bidder agrees not to buy additional shares in exchange for a fee.

White knight: The target may seek a friendly bidder, or white knight, as an alternative to the hostile acquirer.

White squire: The target may place shares or assets in the hands of a friendly firm or investor. These entities are referred to as white squires.

Capital structure changes: Targets may take various actions that will alter the company's capital structure. Through a *recapitalization,* the firm can assume more debt while it pays shareholders a larger dividend. The target can also simply assume more debt without using the proceeds to pay shareholders a dividend. Both alternatives make the firm more heavily leveraged and less valuable to the bidder. Targets may also alter the capital structure by changing the total number of shares outstanding. This may be done through a new offering of stock, placement of shares in the

43. Jeffrey Netter and Annette Poulsen, "State Corporation Laws and Shareholders: The Recent Experience," *Financial Management* 18, no. 3 (Autumn 1989), pp. 29–40.

hands of a white squire, or an ESOP. Instead of issuing more shares, some targets buy back shares to ensure they are not purchased by the hostile bidder.

Litigation: Targets commonly sue the bidder, and the bidder often responds with a countersuit. It is unusual to see a takeover battle that does not feature litigation as one of the tools used by either side.

Pac-Man defense: One of the more extreme defenses occurs when the target makes a counteroffer for the bidder. This is one of the more colorful takeover defenses, although it is seldom used.

The coverage of these active antitakeover defenses is similar to the coverage of the preventative measures. The use of each action is described, along with the research on its shareholder wealth effects. Bear in mind that a target may choose to use several of these defenses together as opposed to selecting merely one. It is difficult, therefore, for research studies to isolate the shareholder wealth effects of any specific defense. In addition, some of the research, using different data sets drawn from different time periods with varying market conditions, reach conflicting conclusions. As the market changes and adapts to the various defenses, their effectiveness—and therefore their impact on stock prices—also varies. These problems were also apparent in the research studies on the preventative measures. Once again, readers will have to draw their own conclusions about the impact of these defenses on stockholders and other stakeholders.

Greenmail

The term *greenmail* refers to the payment of a substantial premium for a significant shareholder's stock in return for the stockholder's agreement that he or she will not initiate a bid for control of the company. Greenmail is a form of *targeted share repurchases,* which is a general term that is more broadly applied to also include other purchases of stock from specific groups of stockholders who may not ever contemplate a raid on the company.

One of the earlier reported instances of greenmail occurred in July 1979 when Carl Icahn bought 9.9% of Saxon Industries stock for approximately $7.21 per share. Saxon repurchased Icahn's shares for $10.50 per share on February 13, 1980.[44] This stock buyback helped launch Icahn on a career as a successful corporate raider. Icahn was not the first greenmailer, however. That distinction may belong to Charles Bluhdorn, chairman of Gulf & Western Industries, "who was an early practitioner when Cannon Mills in 1976 bought back a Gulf & Western holding."[45]

Greenmail brought significant profits to those who were able to successfully pursue the practice. The Bass Brothers were said to have earned $400 million on the Texaco-Getty deal, whereas Carl Icahn reportedly received $6.6 million for his stake in American Can, $9.7 million on Owens Illinois, $8.5 million on Dan River Mills, and $19 million on Gulf & Western.[46] Saul Steinberg's 1984 attempted takeover of Disney earned him not only an impressive payout of $325 for his share holdings but also another $28 million for his expenses.

---

44. "Icahn Gets Green As Others Envy Him," *Wall Street Journal,* 13 November 1989, p. B1.
45. Ibid.
46. John Brooks, *Takeover* (New York: E. F. Dutton, 1987), p.186.

CASE STUDY: ICAHN VERSUS HAMMERMILL PAPER CORPORATION

One classic example of greenmail occurred following Carl Icahn's announcement that he owned more than 10% of Hammermill Paper Corporation's common stock. Hammermill was a high-quality manufacturer of paper products for more than 80 years.[a] During late 1979 Hammermill stock was valued at approximately $25 per share, a low valuation because the stock's book value was approximately $37 per share. Analysts thought that even this valuation was too low inasmuch as many of Hammermill's assets, such as its timberlands, were carried on the firm's books below their actual value. Icahn suggested that Hammermill be liquidated because its per share liquidation value would exceed the cost of a share of stock. Hammermill's management, busily engaged in rejuvenating the company, vehemently opposed liquidation. Both parties ultimately filed suit against each other while they pursued a proxy contest. Icahn lost the proxy battle and Hammermill eventually paid Icahn $36 per share for each of his 865,000 shares. Icahn was reported to have made a $9 million profit on an investment of $20 million.[b]

The payment of greenmail raises certain ethical issues regarding the fiduciary responsibilities of management and directors, both of whom are charged with maximizing the value of stockholder wealth. Management critics, however, state that managers use tools such as greenmail to pursue their own goals, which may conflict with the goal of maximizing stockholder wealth.

---

a. Jeff Madrick, *Taking America* (New York: Bantam Books, 1987), pp. 242–243.
b. Ibid.

Legality of Differential Payments to Large-Block Shareholders

The courts have ruled that differential payments to large-block shareholders are legal as long as they are made for valid business reasons.[47] However, the term *valid business reasons* is so broad that it gives management considerable latitude to take actions that may favor management more than stockholders. Managers may claim that to fulfill their plans for the corporation's future growth, they need to prevent a takeover of the corporation by any entity that would possibly change the company's direction.

The interpretation of legitimate business purposes may involve a difference in business philosophies between the incumbent management and a bidder. It may also simply be that managers are seeking to preserve the continuity of their business strategies. Although some managers think that the court's broad views on this matter may serve to entrench management, others see the court's position as one that helps preserve management's ability to conduct long-term strategic planning. Many corporate managers believe that the court's position allows them to enact the necessary defenses to fend off takeovers by hostile bidders who might acquire the corporation simply to sell off assets and achieve short-term returns. Considerable debate surrounds the issue of short-term versus long-term motives of corporate bidders.

---

47. C. M. Nathan and M. Sobel, "Corporate Stock Repurchases in the Context of Unsolicited Takeover Bids," *Business Lawyer* (July 1980), pp. 1545–1566.

The legality of greenmail itself was upheld in a legal challenge in the Texaco greenmail payment to the Bass Brothers. The Delaware Chancery Court found that the 1984 payment of $1.3 billion, which was a 3% premium, to the Bass Brothers was a reasonable price to pay for eliminating the potentially disruptive effects that the Bass Group might have posed for Texaco in the future.[48] The Delaware Chancery Court's approval of the greenmail payment and dismissal of a shareholder class action were upheld by the Delaware Supreme Court. The important decision clearly established a precedent for the legality of greenmail in the all-important Delaware court system. However, other states, such as California, have not been as supportive of the practice of greenmail. The board of Disney was sued by shareholders who objected to the company's alleged greenmail payments to Steinberg. The court issued an injunction and when the case was finally settled in 1989, both Steinberg's Reliance Corp. and Disney itself had to pay damages.

Greenmail Research

Much of the research on the impact of antitakeover measures on shareholder wealth uses the market model. The market model allows the calculation of the abnormal returns to common stockholders, or what are sometimes referred to as *prediction errors*, attributable to the particular antitakeover measure being studied. One of the leading studies on the effects of greenmail payments on stockholder wealth was conducted by Bradley and Wakeman. Their study considered 86 repurchases from insiders or individuals who were unaffiliated with the firms from 1974 to 1980. They looked at the impact of repurchases on abnormal returns based on the following market model:

$$R_{jt} = \alpha_j + \beta_j R_{mt} + \varepsilon_{jt}$$

where:
R_{jt} = the dividend inclusive return of security on day t
R_{mt} = the dividend inclusive return of the market on day t
α_j = the alpha of security j
β_j = the beta of security j
ε_{jt} = error term of security j at time t

Abnormal returns were defined as

$$AR_{jt} = R_{jt} - (\alpha_j + \beta_j R_{jt})$$

The Bradley and Wakeman study showed that privately negotiated purchases of a single block of stock from stockholders who were unaffiliated with the company reduced the wealth of nonparticipating stockholders.[49] Repurchases from insiders, however, were associated with increases in shareholder wealth. Bradley and Wakeman's research therefore supports the management entrenchment hypothesis. In revealing that stockholders lose money as a result of targeted share repurchases from outsiders, the study implies that these targeted share repurchases are not in the stockholder's best interest. It further implies that, by engaging in these repurchases, management is doing stockholders a disservice.

---

48. *Good v. Texaco, Inc.,* No 7501 (Del. Ch. Feb. 19, 1985), *aff'd sub nom.* Polk v. Good, 507 A. 2d 531 (Del 1986).

49. Michael Bradley and L. MacDonald Wakeman, "The Wealth Effects of Targeted Share Repurchases," *Journal of Financial Economics* 11 (April 1983), pp. 301–328.

Other research, such as a study by Dann and DeAngelo that is discussed further in the context of standstill agreements, also found negative shareholder wealth effects for non-participating shareholders when the company announced target share repurchases.[50]

In 1986 Wayne Mikkelson and Richard Ruback[51] analyzed 111 repurchases and found that only 5% occurred after the announcement of a takeover attempt. One-third of the repurchases took place after less overt attempts to change control such as formulation of preliminary plans for acquisitions or proxy fights. Almost two-thirds of the repurchases occurred without any overt indication of an impending takeover. It is interesting that the Mikkelson and Ruback study showed that the downward impact of the targeted share repurchases was more than offset by the stock price *increases* caused by purchasing the stock. Mikkelson and Ruback found a combined overall impact on stock prices of 17%! Their study supports the stockholder interests hypothesis in that it finds that the target share repurchases actually benefit incumbent stockholders. It therefore conflicts with the Bradley and Wakeman results and so has added more fuel to this debate. Mikkelson and Ruback's analysis also showed that the payment of greenmail was not associated with a lower probability of a change in control. They showed that the frequency of control changes following targeted share repurchases was three times higher than a control sample of firms that did not engage in such repurchases.

More recent research, using data derived from targeted share repurchases from 1974 to 1983, failed to provide support for the management entrenchment hypothesis.[52] Bhagat and Jefferis found that the performance of firms that pay greenmail was no worse than the performance of firms in a control group that did not engage in greenmail payments. This does not support the view that firms that engage in greenmail are poor performers who are seeking shelter from the normal market processes that might bring about a change in management.

Decline of Greenmail

For a variety of reasons, greenmail has become uncommon. For one, the pace of hostile takeover activity has declined dramatically in the 1990s, thus reducing the need to engage in greenmail payments. In addition, federal tax laws imposed a 50% tax penalty on gains derived from greenmail payments. Under this law, greenmail is defined as consideration paid to anyone who makes or threatens to make a tender offer for a public corporation. In order for the payment to be considered greenmail, the offer must not be available to all shareholders. Furthermore, although various legal decisions have upheld the legality of greenmail, defendants in greenmail-inspired lawsuits have been sufficiently uncertain of the outcome to be willing to pay large settlements. For example, in 1989 Disney and Saul Steinberg were reported to have paid $45 million to settle a lawsuit with shareholders, prompted by an alleged

50. Larry Dann and Harry DeAngelo, "Standstill Agreements, Privately Negotiated Stock Repurchases, and the Market for Corporate Control, *Journal of Financial Economics* 11, no. 1–4 (April 1983), pp. 275–300.

51. Wayne Mikkelson and Richard Ruback, "Targeted Share Repurchases and Common Stock Returns," Working Paper No. 1707–86, Massachusetts Institute of Technology, Sloan School of Management, June 1986.

52. Sanjai Bhagat and Richard H. Jefferis, "The Causes and Consequences of Takeover Defense: Evidence from Greenmail," *Journal of Corporate Finance* 1 (1994), pp. 201–231.

greenmail payment in 1984 that included a $59.7 premium.[53] Donald Trump was reported to have paid $6.5 million to settle a lawsuit involving an alleged greenmail payment that included an $18 million premium. The combined effects of the declining volume of hostile takeovers, tax penalties, antigreenmail charter amendments, and fear of litigation costs have caused greenmail to virtually disappear from the 1990s takeover scene

Standstill Agreements

A standstill agreement occurs when the target corporation reaches a contractual agreement with a potential acquirer whereby the would-be acquirer agrees not to increase its holdings in the target during a particular time period. Such an agreement takes place when the acquiring firm has established sufficient stockholdings to be able to pose a threat to mount a takeover battle for the target. Many standstill agreements are accompanied by the target's agreement to give the acquirer the right of first refusal in the event that the acquirer decides to sell the shares it currently owns. This agreement is designed to prevent these shares from falling into the hands of another bidder who would force the target to pay them standstill compensation or, even worse, to attempt to take over the target. Another version of a standstill agreement occurs when the acquirer agrees not to increase its holdings beyond a certain percentage. In other words, the target establishes a ceiling above which the acquirer may not increase its holdings. The acquiring firm agrees to these various restrictions for a fee. Like greenmail, standstill agreements provide compensation for an acquirer not to threaten to take control of the target. In fact, standstill agreements often accompany greenmail.

---

53. Ibid., p. 229.

CASE STUDY: TYPICAL STANDSTILL AGREEMENT

In August 1980 the NVF Company reached an agreement with City Investing in which NVF agreed not to acquire any more than 21% of City Investing stock for a period of five years. The agreement required that NVF not take any steps to take control of City Investing. Thus, in return for financial compensation, NVF gave up its right to pursue a proxy fight or a tender offer for City Investing stock.

City Investing was given the right of first refusal in the event that NVF decided to liquidate its holdings in City Investing. City Investing was thereby protected against the shares falling into the hands of another firm that might seek to take control of the company. NVF was given similar protection in the event that another firm sought to take control of City Investing. The agreement with the two firms stipulated that if another company made a bid for more than 21% of City Investing, NVF would also be able to bid for more than 21%.[a]

---

a. This account is based on Dunn and DeAngelo, "Standstill Agreements and Privately Negotiated Stock Repurchases," *Journal of Financial Economics* 11 (1983): 275–300; and "Posner Can Buy Up to 21% Stake in City Investing," *Wall Street Journal,* 6 August 1980, p. 3.

Standstill Research

Larry Dann and Harry DeAngelo examined 81 standstill agreements between 1977 and 1980.[54] They found that standstill agreements and negotiated stock purchases at a premium were associated with negative average returns to nonparticipating stockholders. On average, stock prices fell 4%. The Dann and DeAngelo study supports the management entrenchment hypothesis and, as such, is inconsistent with the stockholder interests hypothesis with respect to nonparticipating stockholders.

The Mikkelson and Ruback study considered the impact of greenmail payments that were accompanied by standstill agreements.[55] They found that when negative returns were associated with targeted share repurchases, they were much greater when these purchases were accompanied by standstill agreements. We may therefore conclude that these two antitakeover devices tend to have a complementary negative impact on stock prices that is greater than the negative effect we would expect if just one of them were implemented.

---

54. Larry Y. Dann and Harry DeAngelo, "Standstill Agreements and Privately Negotiated Stock Repurchases and the Market for Corporate Control," *Journal of Financial Economics* 11, April 1983, pp. 275–300.

55. Wayne Mikkelson and Richard Ruback, "Targeted Share Repurchases and Common Stock Returns," Working Paper No. 1707–86, Massachusetts Institute of Technology, Sloan School of Management, June 1986.

CASE STUDY: GILLETTE—STANDSTILL AGREEMENTS AND GREENMAIL

In 1986 Gillette was being pursued by Ronald Perelman, who had previously taken over the Revlon Corporation. When it appeared that he was about to make a tender offer for Gillette, Gillette responded by paying Revlon $558 million in return for Revlon agreeing not to make a $65 tender offer to stockholders. One unique aspect of this deal was that Gillette even paid greenmail to the investment bank that represented Revlon. Gillette paid Drexel Burnham Lambert $1.75 million in return for an agreement not to be involved in an acquisition or attempted acquisition of Gillette for a period of three years. This is testimony to the activist role that investment banks played in the takeovers of the 1980s. Gillette was worried that, having seen Gillette's vulnerability, Drexel Burnham Lambert would approach another potential suitor.

The payment of greenmail usually is only a temporary fix, as is confirmed by the fact that another bidder, Coniston Partners, initiated an attempt to take control of Gillette by means of a proxy fight. During the legal proceedings that followed the acerbic proxy fight between Gillette and Coniston, it was revealed that Gillette had entered into standstill agreements with 10 different companies: Colgate Palmolive, Ralston Purina, Anheuser-Busch, Pepsico, Metromedia, Citicorp Industrial Corporation, Salomon Brothers (acting on its own behalf), Kidder, Peabody, Kohlberg Kravis & Roberts, and Forstmann Little.[a]

---

a. "Trial Discusses Identity of 10 Firms Gillette Company Contacted as White Knights," *Wall Street Journal,* 27 June 1988, p. 16.

Gillette eventually reached a settlement with Coniston in which Coniston conceded to a standstill agreement in return for Gillette's agreement to buy back shares from Coniston and other shareholders. A total of 16 million shares were purchased at a price that was above the market price at that time of $45.[b] The Gillette case study is an example of some of the benefits of raiders that Holderness and Sheehan reported.[c] Gillette had been the target of several raiders, including Revlon's CEO, Ronald Perelman. He had agreed to a standstill agreement with Gillette after an aborted takeover attempt in November 1986. Although Perelman had a standstill agreement with Gillette, he renewed his interest in acquiring the firm in late 1987 when it appeared that other bidders were showing interest in the razor manufacturer. The constant pressure that Gillette was under appeared to have beneficial effects. Gillette responded to the various takeover threats by cutting costs and thinning out its workforce. Gillette also enacted various restructuring measures, which included reducing and eliminating weak operations within the firm.[d] By 1990 the firm had laid off a total of 2,400 workers and had sold several weak businesses. Gillette's common stock responded to the increased efficiencies by showing a 50% total return in 1989, up from the 24% average annual return the firm's stock yielded during the prior 10 years.[e] At least in the case of Gillette, the Holderness and Sheehan hypothesis on the beneficial effects of raiders seems to be borne out.

b. Alison Leigh Cowan, "Gillette and Coniston Drop Suit," *New York Times,* 2 August 1988, p. D1.
c. Clifford Holderness and Dennis Sheehan, "Raiders or Saviors? The Evidence of Six Controversial Raiders," *Journal of Financial Economics* 14, no. 4 (December 1985): 555–581.
d. "How Ron Perelman Scared Gillette into Shape," *Business Week,* 12 October 1987, p. 40.
e. Anthony Ramirez, "A Radical New Style for Stodgy Old Gillette," *New York Times,* 25 February 1990, p. 5.

White Knights

When a corporation is the target of an unwanted bid or the threat of a bid from a potential acquirer, it may seek the aid of a *white knight*—that is, another company that would be a more acceptable suitor for the target. The white knight will then make an offer to buy all or part of the target company on more favorable terms than those of the original bidder. These favorable terms may be a higher price, but management may also look for a white knight that will promise not to disassemble the target or lay off management or other employees. It is sometimes difficult to find a willing bidder who will agree to such restrictive terms. The target often has to bargain for the best deal possible to stay out of the first bidder's hands.

The incumbent managers of the target maintain control by reaching an agreement with the white knight to allow them to retain their current positions. They may also do so by selling the white knight certain assets and keeping control of the remainder of the target.

A target company may find a white knight through its own industry contacts or through the assistance of an investment banker who will survey potential suitors. The potential white knight might request favorable terms or other consideration as an inducement to enter the fray. However, if this consideration is given only to the white knight and not to the hostile bidder, and if it is so significant an advantage that it could cause the hostile bidder to withdraw, the deal with the white knight may be a violation of the target's Revlon duties.

Shareholder Wealth Effects of White Knight Bids

Research results show that white knight bids are often not in the best interests of bidding firm shareholders. One study of 100 white knights over a 10–year period between 1978 and 1987 showed that white knight shareholders incurred losses in shareholder wealth.[56] These results were confirmed in another study of 50 white knights covering the period from 1974 to 1984. The explanation for these negative shareholder wealth effects is that such bids are not part of a planned strategic acquisition and do not yield net benefits for the acquiring firm's shareholders. In addition, the white knights are bidders in a contested auction environment where prices tend to be higher than non-auction acquisitions. Research has shown that competition has a negative effect on shareholder wealth of bidding firms.[57] This negative effect is even greater for subsequent bidders.

---

56. Ajeyo Banerjee and James E. Owers, "Wealth Reduction in White Knight Bids," *Financial Management* 21, no. 3 (Autumn 1992), pp. 48–57.

57. Michael Bradley and L. MacDonald Wakeman, "The Wealth Effects of Targeted Share Repurchases," *Journal of Financial Economics* 11 (April 1983), pp. 301–328.

CASE STUDY: T. BOONE PICKENS AND MESA PETROLEUM versus CITIES SERVICE

In June 1982 T. Boone Pickens, the CEO of Mesa Petroleum, made a bid for the Cities Service Oil Company. Although not part of the Seven Sisters, the seven largest oil companies in the United States, Cities Service was approximately 20 times as large as Mesa Petroleum. Mesa had been carrying an investment in Cities Service since 1979 and had chosen this time to make a bid for the larger oil company. Pickens thought that Cities Service possessed valuable assets but was badly managed.

"Cities Service is a case study of what was wrong with Big Oil's management. Based in Tulsa, Oklahoma, Cities Service was a large company. By 1982 it ranked thirty-eighth in the Fortune 500 companies and was the nineteenth largest oil company in the country. It was unusually sluggish, even by the less-demanding standards of the oil industry, and had been for 50 years. Its refineries and chemical plants were losers, and although it had 307 million barrels of oil and 3.1 trillion cubic feet of gas reserves, it had been depleting its gas reserves for at least 10 years. Although it had leases on 10 million acres, it was finding practically no new oil and gas. Cities Service's problems were hidden by its cash flow, which continued in tandem with OPEC price increases. The stock, however, reflecting management's record, sold at approximately a third of the value of its underlying assets. The management did not understand the problem or didn't care; either condition is terminal.[a]

Mesa Petroleum made a $50 per share bid for Cities Service. Cities Service responded with a Pac-Man defense in which it made a $17 per share bid for the smaller Mesa Petroleum. The Cities Service offer was not a serious one because Mesa's stock had been trading at $16.75 before the Cities offer, which therefore did not contain a premium. Cities Service asked Gulf Oil to be its white knight. Pickens, a critic of the major oil companies, was equally critical of Gulf Oil. Gulf made a $63 per share bid for Cities Service. Cities saw Gulf as a similar type of oil company and one that would be much friendlier to Cities management than Mesa. At that time Gulf was the third largest oil company in the United States. Cities accepted Gulf's bid. Mesa ended up selling its shares back to Cities for $55 per share, which resulted in an $11 per share profit for Mesa, or a total of $40 million. However, Gulf had second thoughts about the Cities acquisition: Gulf would have taken on a significant amount of debt if it had gone through with the merger. In addition, Gulf was concerned that the FTC might challenge the merger on antitrust grounds. Much to Cities Service's surprise and chagrin, Gulf dropped its offer for Cities. Cities Service stock dropped to $30 a share following the announcement of Gulf's pullout. Cities Service management was highly critical of Gulf and stated that its action was reprehensible.

Cities Service then had to look for another white knight. Occidental Petroleum, led by the well-known Armand Hammer, made an initial offer of $50 per share in cash for the first 49% of Cities stock and securities of somewhat uncertain value for the remaining shares. Cities rejected this bid as inadequate, and Occidental upped its offer to $55 in cash for the front end and better quality securities for the back end. Cities Service then agreed to sell out to its second white knight.

---

a. T. Boone Pickens, *Boone* (Boston: Houghton Mifflin Co., 1987), p. 150.

White Squire Defense

The white squire defense is similar to the white knight defense. In the white squire defense, however, the target company seeks to implement a strategy that will preserve the target company's independence. A *white squire* is a firm that consents to purchase a large block of the target company's stock. The stock selected often is convertible preferred stock. The convertible preferred shares may be already approved through a blank check preferred stock amendment of the company's charter. The target may need to receive the approval of shareholders even if the shares are blank check preferred stock. The New York Stock Exchange, for example, requires that shareholder approval be received if such shares are issued to officers or directors or if the number issued equals 20% of the company's shares outstanding. The white squire is typically not interested in acquiring control of the target. From the target's viewpoint, the appeal is that a large amount of the voting stock in the target will be placed in the hands of a company or investor who will not sell out to a hostile bidder. The deal may be structured so that the shares given to the white squire may not be tendered to the hostile bidder.

A good example of a white squire defense was Carter Hawley Hale's sale of convertible preferred stock to the General Cinema Corporation in 1984. The stock sold to General Cinema had voting power equal to 22% of Carter Hawley Hale's outstanding votes. Carter Hawley Hale believed this was necessary to prevent a takeover by the Limited Corporation in 1984. Carter Hawley Hale accompanied this white squire defense with a stock repurchase program that increased the voting power of General Cinema's stock to 33% of Carter Hawley Hale's voting shares.

Another version of the white squire defense combines it with the white knight defense. Here the target places a block of stock or options to buy voting shares in the hands of a white knight. This strategy is designed to give the white knight an advantage over the original bidder. Such was the result in Ampco-Pittsburg's hostile bid for the Buffalo Forge Company in 1983. Buffalo Forge entered into an agreement to sell to a white knight, the Ogden Corporation. As part of this agreement, it sold Ogden 425,000 shares of treasury stock and gave Ogden the option to purchase an additional 143,000 shares at the same $32.75 price.[58] These so-called *leg-up stock options* were held to be legal in court.[59] (They are called leg-up stock options because they give one party a leg-up advantage over the other in the bidding process.)

Warren Buffett is a legendary white squire. Through his company, Berkshire Hathaway, he reportedly had invested $2 billion in white squire stock positions in companies such as Gillette, Coca-Cola, U.S. Air, and Champion International Corporation. In 1989, for example, he bought $600 million in Gillette preferred stock, which are convertible into 11% of Gillette's common stock.

Merger Agreement Provisions

Targets may seek to enter into agreements with friendly parties, such as white knights, which provide these parties with certain benefits that give them an incentive to participate in the merger process. These incentives, which may come in the form of lockup options, topping fees, or bustup fees, may work to the target's benefit by making a takeover by a hostile bidder more difficult and expensive.

Lockup Transactions

A lockup transaction is similar to a white squire defense. In the case of lockups, the target is selling assets to another party instead of stock. Sometimes the term *lockup transaction* is also used more generally to refer to the sale of assets as well as the sale of stock to a friendly third party. In a lockup transaction, the target company sells assets to a third party and thus tries to make the target less attractive to the bidder. The target often sells those assets it judges the acquirer wants most. This may also come in the form of *lockup options,* which are options to buy certain assets in the event of a change in control. These options may be written so that they become effective even if a bidder acquires less than 51% of the target.

In some instances, lockup options have been held to be invalid. The court's position has been that, in limiting the desirability of the target to the original bidder, lockup options may effectively preempt the bargaining process that might result during the 20–day wait-

---

58. Dennis Block, Nancy E. Barton, and Stephen A. Radin, *Business Judgment Rule,* 4th ed. (Englewood Cliffs, N.J.: Prentice-Hall, 1988), pp. 404–405.

59. *Buffalo Forge Co. v. Ogden Corp.,* 717 F. 2d (2nd Cir.) att'd 555 F. Supp. 892 (W.D.N.Y.).

ing period for tender offers required by the Williams Act. An example of such an invalid option was Marathon Oil's option that it gave to U.S. Steel in 1981 to buy its Yates Oil Field at a fixed price in an attempt to avoid a takeover by Mobil Oil Corporation. This option would be exercisable in the event that Marathon was taken over. It would have an important impact on future bidding contests because it was one of Marathon's most valued assets. The court invalidated this option on the grounds that it violated the spirit of the Williams Act. An appeals court later affirmed this ruling. U.S. Steel ended up acquiring Marathon Oil when Mobil's bid was stopped on antitrust grounds.

An example of the legal viability of lockup options came in subsequent takeover battles involving lockup options that were partially fought in the same Delaware Chancery Court. In the 1988 takeover contest between J. P. Stevens and West Point–Pepperell, both textile manufacturers, the court ruled that the financial enticements that J. P. Stevens offered another bidder, Odyssey Partners, were legal. The enticements included $17 million toward Odyssey's expenses and an additional $8 million if the bidding prices rose significantly. These enticements may be considered small compared with the $1.2 billion offer for J. P. Stevens. The key to the court's thinking is whether the lockup option or the financial incentives given to one bidder but not the other help facilitate the bidding process or limit it. The belief is that the bidding process will bring about higher bids and thereby maximize stockholder wealth. Chancellor William T. Allen of the Delaware Chancery Court wrote in his opinion, "The Board may tilt the playing field if, but only if, it is in the stockholders' interest to do so."[60]

---

60. "When Targets Tilt Playing Fields," *New York Times,* 21 April 1988, p. D2.

CASE STUDY: REVLON versus PANTRY PRIDE

In 1985 Ronald Perelman, CEO of Pantry Pride, made an offer for Revlon, Inc. MacAndrews and Forbes Holdings, the parent company of Pantry Pride, had built a diversified company with acquisitions between 1978 and 1984 that included a jewelry company, a cigar company, a candy manufacturer, and Pantry Pride—the supermarket chain. Charles Revson had built Revlon into one of the nation's largest cosmetics companies. Revson's successor, Michael Bergerac, a former head of the conglomerate ITT and protégé of Harold Geneen, expanded Revlon considerably through large acquisitions in the health care field. In terms of its revenues, Bergerac's Revlon was more of a health care company than a cosmetics company. In terms of assets, Revlon was approximately five times the size of Pantry Pride.

Revlon's acquisition strategy had not fared well for Bergerac, and Revlon's earnings had been declining. Perelman decided to make a bid for Revlon, his goal being to sell off the health care components and keep the well-known cosmetics business. Pantry Pride made a cash tender of $53 a share. It financed its offer for the significantly larger Revlon by borrowing $2.1 billion. Revlon's board of directors had approved an LBO plan by Forstmann Little at $56 cash per share. When Pantry Pride increased its offer to $56.25, Revlon was able to get Forstmann Little to increase its offer to $57.25 by giving Forstmann Little a lockup option to purchase two Revlon divisions for $525 million. This was reported by Revlon's investment banker to be

$75 million below these divisions' actual value.[a] This option would be activated if a bidder acquired 40% of Revlon's shares.

Delaware's Chancery Court ruled that in agreeing to this lockup agreement, the board of directors had breached its fiduciary responsibility. The court believed that this option effectively ended the bidding process and gave an unfair advantage to Forstmann Little's LBO. However, in its ruling, the court did not declare lockup options illegal. It stated that the options may play a constructive role in the bargaining process and thus increase bids and shareholder wealth.

---

a. Dennis Block, Nancy Barton, and Stephen Radin, *Business Judgment Rule* (Englewood Cliffs, N.J.: Prentice-Hall, 1988), p. 101.

Although the J. P. Stevens and West Point–Pepperell decision outlined the legally legitimate uses of lockup agreements, a subsequent decision in the Delaware Supreme Court further underscored the illegitimate uses of these agreements. The court ruled that a lockup agreement between Macmillan Inc. and Kohlberg Kravis & Roberts (KKR), which allowed KKR to buy certain valuable Macmillan assets even if the agreement between KKR and Macmillan fell through, was merely designed to end the auction process and to preempt bidding, which would maximize the value of stockholder wealth. The court stated that a lockup could be used only if it maximized stockholder wealth. In this case, the lockup was used to drive away an unwanted suitor, Maxwell Communications Corporation. The court's position remains that a lockup may be used only to promote, not inhibit, the auction process.[61]

Stock Options for Bidders

Similar to lockup options, a target may give a friendly bidder options to purchase the stock of the target at a favorable exercise price. There may be a ceiling set by the target on the gains that the bidder may enjoy from the exercise of the options. One of the benefits of the options is that it may ensure a gain for the friendly bidder and thus encourages that bidder to continue the bidding process. In addition, it may serve to discourage the hostile bidder who would have to assume these costs when it honors the option agreements following a successful takeover. Hostile bidders who believed that these stock options unfairly discriminated against their bid may file suit to invalidate them.

Topping Fees or Bustup Fees

Topping fees occur when a target agrees to compensate a bidder if the bidder loses to another bidder. These fees may come in the form of compensation for some of the bidder's costs incurred in the bidding process. It is sometimes used to encourage a bidder who may be reluctant to engage in a costly bidding process with an uncertain outcome. These fees are somewhat of a disincentive for a raider because they are liabilities of the target and, therefore, are a cost that will have to be assumed if its takeover is successful.

---

61. "Delaware High Court Rules a Company Can't Use 'Lockup' Just to Stop a Suitor," *Wall Street Journal,* 8 May 1989.

Although the two terms are sometimes used interchangeably, bustup fees usually refer to payments the target agrees to make if the target decides to cancel the transaction. Both types of fees may be subject to legal challenge if they are found to inhibit an auction process. On the other hand, if they are used by the target to assist a bidder to gain a resulting higher bid for shareholders, they would probably be found to be legal.

No-Shop Provisions
No-shop provisions are agreements that may be part of an overall acquisition agreement or letter of intent in which the seller agrees not to solicit or enter into negotiations to sell to other buyers. Targets may try to reach such an agreement with a white knight and use the existence of the no-shop provision as the reason they cannot negotiate with a hostile bidder. This was done by Paramount Communications when it was trying to avoid a hostile takeover by QVC. As in this case, the courts tend to not look kindly on these provisions because they often have the effect of inhibiting the auction process.

Capital Structure Changes

A target corporation may initiate various changes in its capital structure in an attempt to ward off a hostile bidder. These defensive capital structure changes are used in four main ways.

1. Recapitalize
2. Assume more debt
   a. More bonds
   b. Bank loan
3. Issue more shares
   a. General issue
   b. White squire
   c. ESOP
4. Buy back shares
   a. Self-tender
   b. Open market purchases
   c. Targeted share repurchases

Recapitalize
In the late 1980s recapitalization became a more popular, albeit drastic, antitakeover defense. After a recapitalization, the corporation is in dramatically different financial condition than it was before it. A recapitalization plan often involves paying a superdividend to stockholders, which is usually financed through assumption of considerable debt. For this reason, these plans are sometimes known as *leveraged recapitalizations.* When a company is recapitalized, it substitutes most of its equity for debt while paying stockholders a large dividend. In addition to the stock dividend, stockholders may receive a stock certificate called a *stub,* which represents their new share of ownership in the company.

Recapitalization as an antitakeover defense was pioneered in 1985 by the Multimedia Corporation with the assistance of the investment bank of Goldman Sachs. Multimedia, a

Greenville, South Carolina, broadcasting company, initiated a recapitalization plan after the original founding family members received unsolicited bids for the company in response to their leveraged buyout (LBO) offer. In addition to a cash payout, Multimedia stockholders saw the value of their stub increase from an original value of $8.31 to $52.25 within two years.[62] The success of the Multimedia deal led to several other recapitalizations, several of which were completed in the following two years (Table 5.2).[63]

One attraction of a recapitalization plan is that it allows a corporation to act as its own white knight. Many companies in similar situations would either seek an outside entity to serve as a white knight or attempt an LBO. The recapitalization plan is an alternative to both. In addition, the large increase in the company's debt, as reflected in the examples shown in Table 5.3, makes the firm less attractive to subsequent bidders. A recapitalization may defeat a hostile bid because stockholders receive a value for their shares that usually is significantly in excess of historical stock prices. This amount is designed to be superior to the offer from the hostile bidder.

Another feature of recapitalization that is most attractive to the target company's management is that it may give management a greater voting control in the target following the recapitalization. The target company may issue several shares of common stock to an ESOP.[64] It may also create other security options that may give management enhanced voting power. Other stockholders, however, will receive only one share in the recapitalized company (the stub) as well as whatever combination of debt and cash has been offered. The company is required to make sure that all nonmanagement stockholders receive at least a comparable monetary value for their common stockholdings as did management. The increase in concentration of shares in the hands of insiders that has occurred in some of the largest recapitalizations is shown in Table 5.4.

Many recapitalizations may require stockholder approval before they may be implemented, depending on the prevailing state laws and the corporation's own charter. When presenting a recapitalization plan to stockholders, corporations often seek approval for a variety of other antitakeover measures that are proposed as part of a joint antitakeover plan. Some of the other measures discussed previously, such as fair price provisions or staggered boards, might be included here.

Table 5.2.   Leading Recapitalization Plans

Company	Date
Metromedia	May 2, 1985
FMC Corporation	April 28, 1986
Colt Industries	July 21, 1986
Owens-Corning	August 28, 1986
Caesar's World	May 18, 1987
Harcourt Brace Jovanovich	May 26, 1987
Allegis Corporation	May 28, 1987

62. "The New Way to Halt Raiders," *New York Times,* 29 May 1988, p. D4.

63. Ibid.

64. Ralph C. Ferrara, Meredith M. Brown, and John Hall, *Takeovers: Attack and Survival* (Salem, N.C.: Butterworth Legal Publishers, 1987), p. 425.

Table 5.3. Comparative Effects of Recapitalization

Company		Before Recapitalization	After Recapitalization
Multimedia	Long-term debt	73.2	877.7
	Net worth	248.7	d576.4
	Book value/share	14.9	d52.4
FMC Corporation	Long-term debt	303.2	1787.3
	Net worth	1123.1	d506.6
	Book value/share	7.54	d11.25
Colt Industries	Long-term debt	342.4	1643.1
	Net worth	414.3	d1078.0
	Book value/share	2.55	d36.91
Owens-Corning	Long-term debt	543.0	1645.2
	Net worth	944.7	d1025.0
	Book value/share	31.7	d25.94
Holiday Corporation	Long-term debt	992.5	2500.0
	Net worth	638.7	d850.0
	Book value/share	27.1	d31.2
Harcourt Brace Jovanovich	Long-term debt	790.3	2550.0
	Net worth	531.5	d1050.0
	Book value/share	13.5	d21.0

Notes: This table includes only those six companies that actually completed the leveraged recapitalization. d denotes deficit.

Source: Robert Kleinman, "The Shareholder Gain from Leveraged Cash Outs: Preliminary Evidence," *Journal of Applied Corporate Finance* 1, no. 1 (Spring 1988): 50.

In addition to possible restrictions in the company charter and state laws, companies may be limited from using the recapitalization defense by restrictive covenants in prior debt agreements. The corporation enters into these legal agreements when it borrows from a bank or from investors through the issuance of corporate bonds. Such agreements place limitations on the firm's future options so as to provide greater assurance for the lenders

Table 5.4. Changes in Share Ownership of Insiders

Firm	Before Recapitalization (%)	After Recapitalization (%)
1. Multimedia	13.0	43.0
2. FMC Corporation	19.0	40.0
3. Colt Industries	7.0	38.0
4. Owens-Corning	1.0	16.2
5. Holiday Corporation	1.5	10.0
6. Harcourt Brace Jovanovich	7.0	30.0
7. Caesar's World	1.5	1.5*
8. Allegis	1.0	1.0*
Means*	6.4	29.5

*Note that the percentage ownership of insiders for Caesar's and Allegis does not change. In the Caesar's World case, the New Jersey Casino Control Commission rejected the leveraged recapitalization after it had been approved by stockholders. In the case of Allegis, the leveraged recapitalization was subsequently canceled in favor of restructuring. Hence, the mean value for the "after recapitalization" column excludes these two companies.

Sources: Proxy statements and the Value Line Investment Survey; Robert Kleinman, 'The Shareholder Gains from Leveraged Cash Outs: Some Preliminary Evidence," *Journal of Corporate Finance* 1, no. 1 (Spring 1988): 50.

that the debt will be repaid. The language of these restrictive covenants might prevent the company from taking on additional debt, which might increase the probability that the company could be forced into receivership.

Comparison between recapitalization plans and LBOs.   There are a number of similarities between LBOs and recapitalization plans. Some are:

> *Tax advantages of debt.* In a recapitalization plan, the firm assumes a considerable amount of debt and thereby substitutes tax-deductible interest payments for taxable dividend payments. Dividend payments are often suspended following the payout of a larger initial dividend. The effect of an LBO is similar. Firms going private in a leveraged buyout assume considerable debt to finance the LBO. This has the effect of sheltering operating income for the time period in which the debt is being paid.
>
> *Concentration of ownership in management's hands.* In an LBO, management usually receives a percentage of ownership as part of the LBO process. When the debt is repaid, this ownership position may become quite valuable, even after warrants held by debt holders are exercised. In a recapitalization plan, management often receives new shares instead of the cash payout that stockholders receive. Managers of firms involved in defensive recapitalization prefer this arrangement because the concentration of ownership in their hands helps prevent a takeover.

Robert Kleinman points out that in view of the similarities between LBOs and recapitalizations, it is not surprising that good LBO and recapitalization candidates have much in common, such as:

- A stable earnings stream that can be used to service debt.
- Low pre-LBO or pre-recapitalization plan debt levels. A low level of debt on the balance sheet gives the firm greater ability to assume more debt.
- A strong market position.
- A product line that is not vulnerable to a high risk of obsolescence.
- A business that does not need high levels of research and development or capital expenditures. The high debt service may not allow for such investments.
- A high borrowing capacity as reflected by the collateral value of the firm's assets.
- Assets and/or divisions that can be readily sold to help pay the debt.
- Experienced management with a proven track record, an important characteristic because the added pressure of the high debt service does not leave a high margin for error.[65]

Use of recapitalization plans protected by poison pills.   The recapitalization plan is the company's own offer, which is presented to stockholders as an alternative to a hostile raider's offer. Before 1988 companies used poison pills to try to counteract the bidder's tender offer while presenting their own unencumbered recapitalization plan. In November 1988 a Delaware Chancery Court struck down the combined use of these defenses.[66]

---

65. Robert Kleinman, "The Shareholder Gains from Leveraged Cash Outs," pp. 47–48.
66. "Interco Defense Against Rales Is Struck Down," *Wall Street Journal,* 2 November 1988, p. 83.

CASE STUDY: SANTA FE versus HENLEY

In 1989 the Santa Fe Corporation used the largest recapitalization plan ever implemented as a defensive tactic to prevent a takeover by the Henley Group. Henley was a conglomeration of assorted companies spun off from the Allied Signal merger. They were managed by Michael Dingman, who prides himself in bringing poorly performing companies to profitability. The term *Dingman's dogs* was sometimes used to describe these poor performers.[a] In February 1988, following the Henley Group's extended attempt to take over Santa Fe, as well as overtures from other would-be bidders such as Olympia and York, Santa Fe announced a major recapitalization plan. The plan featured the payout of a $4.7 billion dividend to stockholders, which was to be financed through the selloff of assets and the assumption of considerable debt. Santa Fe agreed to pay a $25 dividend to stockholders combined with a $5 subordinated debenture for each of its 156.5 million shares. The cash portion of this payout came to $4 billion. The debentures had a face value of $783 million and a 16% coupon rate. The repayment of the debentures was structured so that no payments would be made for five years. This requirement was designed to reduce the demands on Santa Fe's already stretched cash flows.

Santa Fe raised approximately $2.25 billion from assets sales. These included the Southern Pacific Railroad, pipelines, timberlands, and other real estate, as well as other subsidiaries. In addition, Santa Fe borrowed $1.9 billion. Santa Fe's financial leverage increased dramatically. The debt-total capital ratio rose from 26% to 87% following the recapitalization plan. This higher financial leverage represents a greater degree of risk for the corporation.

a. Kathleen Deveney, Stewart Toy, Edith Terry, and Tom Ichniowski, "Santa Fe Keeps Throwing the Raiders Off Track," *Business Week,* 15 February 1988, p. 28.

Interco, a St. Louis–based retailer, had been the object of a tender offer from the Rales Brothers in 1988. Interco was a diversified manufacturer of such well-known products as London Fog rainwear, Florsheim shoes, and Converse athletic shoes, as well as furniture under the names of Broyhill and Ethan Allen. The Rales Brothers, relatively little known investors from Washington, D.C., had made a $2.73 billion tender offer for Interco. When Interco responded with a recapitalization plan combined with its poison pill defense, the Rales Brothers sued. They contended, and the Delaware court agreed, that Interco's recapitalization offer was unfair to stockholders because the poison pill was directed against the Rales's tender offer, whereas Interco's recapitalization plan was not affected by the poison pill. The court agreed that the combined use of these two defenses was an abuse of the business judgment rule. Given the presence of the poison pill, stockholders could not consider both offers on an equal footing.

By taking away the poison pill shield, the recapitalization plan loses some of its original advantage as an antitakeover defense. In the wake of the Interco decision, a recapitalization plan, to be effective, must be financially better for stockholders. This may be difficult because tender offers may be all cash; some recapitalization plans may be more difficult to evaluate because they involve a combination of cash and securities.

Assume More Debt

Although the assumption of more debt occurs in a recapitalization plan, the firm can also directly add debt without resorting to the implementation of recapitalization to prevent a takeover. A low level of debt relative to equity can make a company vulnerable to a takeover. A hostile bidder can utilize the target's borrowing capacity to help finance the acquisition of the target. Although some may interpret a low level of debt to be beneficial to the corporation, by lowering its risk, this can also increase the company's vulnerability to a takeover. On the other hand, additional debt can make the target riskier because of the higher debt service relative to the target's cash flow. This is something of a *scorched earth defense* because preventing the acquisition by assuming additional debt may result in the target's future bankruptcy (see the Interco case study).

CASE STUDY: INTERCO—THE PROBLEMS WITH RECAPITALIZATION

In the Fall of 1988 St. Louis–based Interco found itself the object of a hostile bid from the Rales Brothers. Steven and Michael Rales had offered $74 per share in a $2.73 billion all-cash tender offer. Interco responded with a recapitalization plan defense. This defense was coupled with a poison pill, however. As is explained elsewhere in this chapter, the use of a poison pill to shield a recapitalization plan was found to be illegal by a Delaware Chancery Court. Nonetheless, the recapitalization plan proved sufficient to counter the Rales Brothers's offer. Although the recapitalization plan ensured Interco's independence, it did so at a drastic price. The plan, in part developed by merger strategists Bruce Wasserstein and Joseph Perella, increased Interco's debt service obligations beyond the firm's ability to pay. The result was a cash flow crisis that culminated in the firm's eventual default on June 15, 1990. Holders of junk bonds issued in the recapitalization process eventually had to accept equity in exchange for their bonds to avoid further losses that would result from bankruptcy.[a]

The expected success of the Interco recapitalization plan was contingent on the accuracy of the forecasts developed for assets sales and revenues from the company's operations. This plan, labeled Project Imperial, was reported by the *Wall Street Journal* to have been developed by "a few number crunching financial people with very little oversight from top officials at either Interco or Wasserstein-Perella."[b] The *Journal* reported that 10–year projections of cash flows and earnings were made by a team of financial analysts, one of whom was only one and a half years out of college, without the benefit of much basic research. Several scenarios were considered, but the worst case showed a 20% annual return following the recapitalization.

The firm of Wasserstein-Perella earned $5.5 million for its work in the antitakeover defense of Interco. The plan it developed called for the sale of divisions, such as the Ethan Allen furniture chain for approximately $500 million. However, the eventual sale price proved to be only $388 million. The Central Hardware divi-

---

a. Michael Quint, "Interco Pact Includes Conversion of Bonds to Stock," *New York Times,* 1 August 1990, p. D22.

b. George Anders and Francine Schwadel, "Wall Streeters Helped Interco Defeat Raiders–But at a Heavy Price," *Wall Street Journal,* 11 July 1990, p. 1.

sion was valued at $312 million in the recapitalization plan but brought only $245 million when it was sold. Record annual profits of $70 million were forecasted for divisions such as Converse shoes, whereas fiscal 1990 profits proved to be only $11 million. Given the volatile and competitive nature of the athletic shoe industry, the continual generation of increasing profit levels would be a most difficult task for any company in this industry. (Figure 1.)

The fate of the Interco recapitalization plan is symbolic of much of what went wrong in the world of leveraged mergers during the late 1980s. Seemingly sophisticated financial analysis could be developed to make risky leveraged deals appear attractive. The art of financial valuation, as practiced by some, has therefore fallen into much criticism.[c]

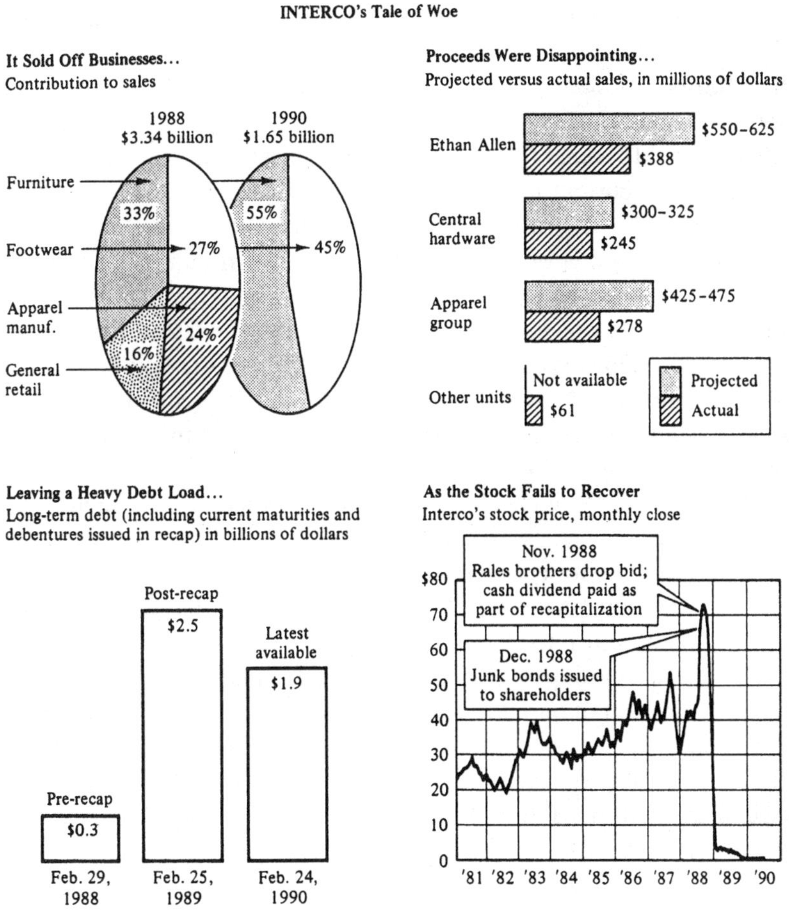

Figure 1. Interco's recapitalization problems.

Source: George Anders and Francine Schwadel, "Wall Streeters Helped Interco Defeat Raiders— But at a Heavy Price," *Wall Street Journal,* 11 July 1990, p. A7. Reprinted by permission of the *Wall Street Journal,* copyright © 1990 Dow Jones & Company Inc. All rights reserved worldwide.

---

c. Data for this case were drawn from research by George Anders and Francine Schwadel of the *Wall Street Journal.*

The target can acquire the additional debt in two ways: (1) It can borrow directly from a bank or other lender, or (2) it can issue bonds. If the target has to wait for SEC approval for the bonds to be issued, it might be taken over before the debt issuance is completed. Companies with this defense in mind can prepare for it by obtaining prior SEC approval to issue bonds and taking advantage of SEC Rule 415, which is called the *shelf registration rule.* This rule allows the corporation to register with the SEC all those securities offerings it intends to make within the upcoming two years.

Liability restructuring research.   The assumption of additional debt is a way the corporation alters its balance sheet by increasing its liabilities. Dann and DeAngelo analyzed the impact that an increase in a company's liabilities would have on its stock prices.[67] They reported an average stock price decline following liability restructurings of 22%. This implies that a measurable reduction in stockholder wealth follows these restructurings.

Issue More Shares

Another antitakeover option available to the target company is to issue more shares. Issuing more shares would change the company's capital structure because it increases equity while maintaining the current level of debt. By issuing more shares, the target company makes it more difficult and costly to acquire a majority of the stock in the target. The notion of increasing the number of shares to make it more difficult for a raider to obtain control has been around for some time. Matthew Josephson, in his book The *Robber Barons,* points out how this tactic was used to prevent Cornelius Vanderbilt from obtaining control of the Erie Railroad: "This explains how the 'Erie Gang' or the Erie Lackawanna Railroad successfully prevented the New York Central Railroad, a precursor to today's Conrails, and Cornelius Vanderbilt from taking control of Erie. Every time Vanderbilt came close to getting a majority, Erie would issue more shares."[68] On the negative side, issuing more shares dilutes stockholder equity. It is reasonable to expect the company's stock price to decline in the face of this stock issuance. This downward movement in the company's stock price is the market's reflection of the costs of this issuance. In the presence of these clear costs to stockholders, many states specifically require that corporations receive adequate compensation in return for the newly issued shares. When the shares are issued and not given to a particular group or company, they are called a *general issue.* However, because these shares might fall into hostile bidders' hands, the target often issues these shares directly into friendly hands. Such is the case in a white squire defense where the target both increases the number of shares necessary to obtain control and makes sure that these newly issued shares will not fall into the hostile bidder's hands. The white squire is presumably interested in the stock only for investment purposes and not to take control of the company.

Share issuance and ESOPs.   Another option that the target may consider is to issue the stock to the ESOP. To make it easy for the ESOP to purchase these shares, the ESOP may borrow using the corporation's guarantee. The company may also make tax-deductible con-

---

67. Larry Y. Dann and Harry DeAngelo, "Corporate Financial Policy and Corporate Control: A Study in Defensive Adjustments in Asset and Ownership Structure," *Journal of Financial Economics* 20, no. 1/2 (1988), pp. 87–128.

68. Josephson, Matthew, *The Robber Barons* (New York: Harcourt Brace & Co., 1931).

tributions into the ESOP that may then be used to repay the loan. In using ESOPs as a defensive tactic the target must make sure that the price paid by the ESOP for the target's securities is "fair." If the company pays too high a price, the transaction could be judged improper according to the federal employee benefit laws. If the ESOP is allowed to buy the shares at too low a price, directors could be charged with violating their fiduciary duties to non-ESOP shareholders. Employee stock ownership plans are discussed in greater detail in Chapter 9.

In light of the passage of the Delaware antitakeover law, leveraged "bustup" acquisitions can be impeded by placing 15% of a firm's outstanding shares in an ESOP. In December 1989 Chevron Corporation, to prevent a takeover by cash-rich Penzoil Corporation, issued 14.1 million shares to create an ESOP. Chevron borrowed $1 billion to repurchase the newly issued shares.[69] Before the issuance of these shares, employees had held 11% of Chevron's outstanding shares through a profit-sharing program. In an effort to offset the dilution effects of the share issuance, having perceived that the takeover threat had passed, Chevron announced a program of stock repurchases in 1990.

Impact of ESOPs on share prices.   Following Polaroid's successful use of the ESOP defense, more companies began to adopt ESOPs. A study by Analysis Group, Inc. showed that the formation of defensive ESOPs had a depressing effect on stock prices. Defensive ESOPs are those plans that are formed as a takeover defense.The Analysis Group study also showed that in a group of 21 firms forming ESOPs after the Polaroid ESOP was upheld in a Delaware court, the stock prices of 11 of these firms declined significantly following the announcement of the formation of the ESOP. For those firms that showed a decline, the average change was 25.1% percent (Table 5.5).[70]

69. "Chevron Purchasing Shares to Replace Stock Used for ESOP," *Wall Street Journal,* 13 February 1990, p. A.5.
70. "Use of ESOPs Against Bids Lowers Stock," *Wall Street Journal,* 6 June 1989, p. C1.

CASE STUDY: SHAMROCK HOLDINGS INC.
versus POLAROID CORPORATION

In 1988 when Polaroid was the target of a unwanted takeover offer from Shamrock Holdings Inc., it used the ESOP stock issuance defense. Shamrock Holdings Inc. was a Burbank, California, television and radio company owned by the Roy Disney family. It bought 6.9% percent of Polaroid and expressed interest in acquiring control of the company. Polaroid created an ESOP for the purpose of avoiding this takeover. It then placed 10 million newly issued shares, which constituted 14% of the outstanding stock of Polaroid, into the ESOP.

Polaroid considered this an effective defense because the ESOP would likely exercise its voting power to oppose an acquisition by Shamrock and to maintain current management. Polaroid, a Delaware-based corporation, had its defense bolstered by the ESOP stock issuance inasmuch as a bidder must buy 85% of a Delaware-incorporated target to be able to take control and sell off assets. (See Chapter 3.) With the ESOP stock issuance only 86% of the outstanding stock remained in public hands.

Table 5.5.   ESOPs and Stock Prices

Company	Takeover Rumors	Price Change (%)
Boise Cascade	No	1.1
Dunkin' Donuts	Yes	−4.9
Fairchild Industries	Yes	−1.7
ITT Corporation	No	−2.1
Lockheed Corporation	Yes	−6.2
Tribune Corporation	Yes	−9.8
Horn & Hardart	Yes	−12.1
Average		5.1

Source: Analysis Group, Inc., *Wall Street Journal,* 6 June 1989, p. C1. Reprinted by permission of the *Wall Street Journal,* copyright © 1989 Dow Jones & Company, Inc. All rights reserved worldwide.

Buy Back Shares

Another way to prevent a takeover is for the target to buy back its own shares. Such share repurchases can have several advantages for a target corporation, namely:

- Share repurchases can divert shares away from a hostile bidder. Once the target has acquired certain shares, these shares are no longer available for the bidder to purchase.

- Share repurchases can also divert shares away from the hands of arbitrageurs. Arbitrageurs can be of great assistance to a hostile bidder because they acquire shares with the explicit purpose of earning high returns by selling them to the highest bidder. This is often the hostile acquiring corporation. By preventing some of the target's shares from falling into the hostile bidder's hands, the target can make the acquisition process more difficult.

- The acquisition of the target's own shares can allow the corporation to use up its own resources. The bidder can use these resources to finance the target's own acquisition. For example, if the target uses some of its excess cash reserves to acquire its own shares, the acquirer cannot use this cash to pay off some of the debt incurred in the acquisition.

- Similar reasoning can be applied to share repurchases by the target, which are financed through debt. By borrowing, the target is using up its own borrowing capacity, which could have been used to finance some of the acquisition. This can be effective in deterring bids by raiders who are relying on the heavy use of leverage.

- The acquisition of shares can be a necessary first step in implementing a white squire defense. If the target has enough SEC-authorized shares available, it must first acquire them through share repurchases.

Federal securities laws limit the ability of a target to repurchase its own shares after it has become the recipient of a target offer. These laws require the target to file with the SEC and to provide certain disclosures, including the number of shares to be repurchased, the purpose of the transaction, and the source of funding.

Although share repurchases have several clear advantages for a target corporation, they are not without drawbacks. Share repurchases may be an instinctive first reaction by an embattled target CEO who is striving to maintain the company's independence. By repurchasing the company's shares, however, the CEO is withdrawing outstanding shares from the market. With fewer shares outstanding, it may be easier for the acquirer to obtain control because the bidder has to buy a smaller number of shares to acquire 51% of the target. One solution to this dilemma is to use targeted share repurchases. This strategy takes shares out of the hands of those who would most likely sell them to the hostile bidder. If, at the same time, these shares are placed in friendly hands, the strategy can be successful. When Carter Hawley Hale combined a buyback of 17.5 million shares in 1984 with a sale of stock to General Cinema Corporation, it was implementing a similar strategy to prevent The Limited from obtaining control of Carter Hawley Hale.

A target can implement a share repurchase plan in three ways:

1. General nontargeted purchases
2. Targeted share repurchases
3. Self-tender offer

General nontargeted purchases simply buy back a certain number of shares without regard to their ownership. Targeted share repurchases, on the other hand, are designed to take shares out of the hands of stockholders who may sell their shares to the hostile bidder. A self-tender occurs when the target makes a tender offer for its own securities. Regulations governing self-tenders are different from those that apply to tender offers by an outside party. Self-tenders are regulated by Section 13e of the Securities and Exchange Act of 1934. A company engaging in a self-tender has two main sets of filing requirements. According to Rule 13e-1, the target may not buy its own securities following a tender offer by a hostile bidder unless it first files with the SEC and announces its intentions. The target firm must disclose the following:

- Name and class of securities
- Identity of purchaser
- Markets and exchanges that will be used for the purchases
- Purpose of the repurchase
- Intended disposition of the repurchased shares[71]

The target corporation is also bound by Rule 14d-9, which requires that the company file a Schedule 14D-9 with the SEC within 10 days of the commencement of the tender offer. The 14D-9 filing, which is also required in the case of a hostile bid, requires management to indicate its position on the self-tender.

Discriminatory self-tenders: Unocal versus Mesa.   In February 1985 T. Boone Pickens announced a bid from his investor group, Mesa Partners II, for Unocal Corporation.[72] Mesa had just purchased 8% of the larger Los Angeles–based oil company. Pickens's company, Mesa Petroleum, was flush with cash from successful prior offers for Gulf and Phillips Petroleum. Pickens made $800 million on his bid for Gulf and $90 million on the offer for Phillips.[73] Pickens has stated that these gains were not greenmail, based on his

71. Brown, Ferrara, and Hall, *Takeovers,* p. 78.
72. *Unocal v. Mesa,* 493 A.2d 949, (Del 1985).
73. Madrick, Jeff, *Taking America* (New York: Bantam Books, 1987), p. 282.

long-held position of refusing to accept a higher payment for his shares unless other shareholders could participate in the buyout by the target.

Pickens increased the pressure on Phillips by increasing his holdings to 13% of Unocal's outstanding shares. He found Unocal an attractive target because of its low debt level and significant size (revenues of $11.5 billion). Mesa increased its credibility by amassing a war chest of $4 billion in financing through the help of its investment banker, Drexel Burnham Lambert. In April 1985 Pickens bid for just over 50% of Unocal at $54 per share. Unocal, led by Chairman Fred Hartley, responded with a discriminatory self-tender offer for 29% of Unocal's outstanding shares. Hartley wanted to defeat the Pickens bid but did not want to give his foe greenmail. His self-tender offer therefore contained a provision that Mesa Partners II could not participate in Unocal's offer. Pickens appealed to the Delaware Chancery Court to rule on what he believed was a clearly unfair offer by Unocal.

The Delaware Chancery Court agreed that Unocal's offer was illegal, a ruling that was later reversed by the Delaware Supreme Court. The Delaware Supreme Court concluded on May 17, 1985, that Unocal's offer was within the board of directors' rights according to the business judgment rule. The court found that Mesa's offer was a "grossly inadequate two-tiered coercive tender offer coupled with the threat of greenmail." The higher court held that Unocal's response to this type of offer was within its rights as provided by the business judgment rule. The Delaware Supreme Court ruling forced Pickens to capitulate; he agreed to a standstill agreement. Ironically, this ruling led to the SEC's review of discriminatory self-tenders, which eventually resulted in a change in tender offer rules making such discriminatory self-tenders illegal.

Market reaction to the Unocal decision.   Kamma, Weintrop, and Weir analyzed the market reaction to the Delaware Supreme Court decision expanding the board of directors' authority to take a broad range of actions to keep a company independent.[74] The market responded by lowering the probability of a potential target receiving a takeover premium in a successful hostile bid. Kamma, Weintrop, and Weir examined a sample of 124 firms that were targets of stock purchases that warranted Schedule 13D filings on May 10 and May 24, 1985. They divided these firms into two groups: 24 firms that were clearly targets of hostile bids and the remaining 100 firms that were not. These subsamples were further subdivided into Delaware and non-Delaware firms. The study results revealed that the 14 "hostile Delaware firms" earned abnormal negative returns of 1.51%. The other group of firms failed to show a statistically significant abnormal performance. Kamma, Weintrop, and Weir's results support the subsequent SEC action that made discriminatory repurchases illegal and show that such discriminatory repurchases result in a decline in stockholder wealth.

Corporate Restructuring as a Takeover Defense

Corporate restructuring is another of the more drastic antitakeover defenses. It may involve selling off major parts of the target or even engaging in major acquisitions. Defensive restructuring has been criticized as a case of "Do unto yourself as others would do unto you." Given the anticipated criticism, management usually only employs this defense as a last resort.

---

74. Sreenivas Kamma, Joseph Weintrop, and Peggy Weir, "Investors Perceptions of the Delaware Supreme Court Decision in Unocal v. Mesa," *Journal of Financial Economics* 20 (January/March 1988), pp. 419–430.

CASE STUDY: POLAROID'S $1.1 BILLION STOCK BUYOUT

As noted previously, in 1988 the Polaroid Corporation found itself the object of an unwanted bid from Roy E. Disney and his company, Shamrock Holdings, Inc. Polaroid had rejected Disney's overtures and instituted various defenses, including the placement of stock into an ESOP. However, Disney did not give up his bid to take over the camera manufacturer.

In January 1989 Polaroid announced a plan to buy back $1.1 billion worth of stock. Ironically, the stock repurchase would be financed by the sale of a large block of stock to a private investor group. The private investor group's ownership in Polaroid would rise from 8.5% to 13% due to the combined effect of both the increased number of shares and the fact that fewer shares would be outstanding as a result of the buyback. The group would pay $300 million for Polaroid preferred stock, which would be convertible into common stock at $50 per share. This would give the group, which included institutional investors, such as the California State Teachers Retirement System, 8 million new shares. "If Polaroid bought back stock at its current level, it could buy 27 million shares, reducing the 71.6 million shares outstanding to 44.6 million."[a]

Polaroid used the combination of a stock sale and a stock repurchase to take shares off the market, where they might fall into a raider's hands, and to place more shares into friendly hands. The combined effect was to make a takeover by Disney or any other raider more difficult.

———————————————

a. "$1.1 Billion Polaroid Buyback," *New York Times,* 31 January 1989, p. D1.

Defensive corporate restructuring can be both a preventative defense and an active antitakeover defense. If a firm believes it may become a takeover target, it may restructure to prevent this occurrence. Takeovers also occur in the midst of a takeover battle when the target feels that only drastic actions will prevent a takeover.

An example of a successful use of corporate restructuring as a defense against an unwanted bid occurred in 1986 when Lucky Stores sold three units and spun off a fourth to shareholders to prevent a takeover by raider Asher Edelman. The proceeds of the assets sales were used to finance a self-tender for 27% of its own shares.

It is often difficult for an incumbent management to justify restructuring to prevent an acquisition because management must take considerable liberty with stockholders' resources. Management should be able to convince stockholders, however, that such drastic changes in the nature of the target's business as well as the rejection of the bidder's proposed premium are both in their best interests.

Defensive restructuring may take the following forms:

- Take the corporation private in a LBO
- Sell off valued assets

- Acquire other companies
- Liquidate the company

Going private is often the reaction of a management that does not want to give up control of the corporation. Going private and LBOs are discussed in detail in Chapter 7. They can be justified from the stockholder's point of view when they result in higher premiums than rival bids. However, if the buyers in the going-private transaction are managing directors, the offer price must be one that is clearly fair. Fairness may be judged as a significant premium which is higher than the premium offered by other bidders.

The sale of valued assets to prevent a takeover is a highly controversial defensive action. The idea is that the target will sell off the assets the acquirer wants, and so the target will become less desirable in the eyes of the hostile bidder. As a result, the bidder may withdraw its offer. This is essentially a lockup transaction. Stockholders have often strongly opposed these actions and have sometimes successfully sued to prevent their completion. If, on the other hand, the target can establish that it received fair and reasonable value for the assets and that their loss did not lower the overall value of the firm after taking into account the receipt of the proceeds from the sale, the target may be on firmer legal ground.

A target may acquire another company to prevent its own takeover for several reasons. First, it may seek to create an antitrust conflict for the acquirer. This will then involve the acquisition of a company in one of the bidder's main lines of business. This tactic was somewhat more effective when the Justice Department exercised stricter antitrust enforcement. However, even if there is a reasonable likelihood that the takeover will be opposed on antitrust grounds, this defense can be deactivated by the sale of the acquired business following the acquirer's acquisition of the target. In its filings with the Justice Department and the Federal Trade Commission (FTC), the acquirer can clearly state its intentions to sell the target's new acquisitions. This may result in an approval of the acquisition pending the acquirer's ability to sell off the necessary parts of the target. A classic case of acquisitions designed to ward off bidders by creating antitrust conflicts occurred when Marshall Field and Company made a series of acquisitions in 1980 in areas where potential bidders were present. These acquisitions were motivated not by any economic factor but only to keep Marshall Field independent. The result was a financially weaker Marshall Field and Company.

The target might want to acquire another concern to reduce its appeal in the eyes of the acquirer. If the target is a highly profitable, streamlined company, this state of financial well-being may be quickly changed by acquiring less profitable businesses in areas in which the acquirer does not want to be. If these acquisitions involve the assumption of greater debt, this increased leverage may also make the target less appealing.

One final restructuring option available for the target company is liquidation. In liquidation the target sells all of its assets and uses the proceeds to pay a liquidating dividend to stockholders. The payment of the dividend is restricted by a variety of legal constraints that protect the rights of the firm's creditors. Therefore, the liquidating dividend needs to be calculated after financial adjustments have been made to take into account outstanding obligations that have to be satisfied. In the best interests of stockholders, this dividend payment must exceed the offer of the hostile bidder. This may be possible, however, in instances in which the target believes that, perhaps because of inordinately low securities market prices, the premium above market price offered by the bidder is below that of the liquidation value of the company.

CASE STUDY: WALT DISNEY COMPANY'S DEFENSIVE ACQUISITION OF ARVIDA

In 1984 the Walt Disney Company became the target of a hostile bid by Saul Steinberg and Reliance Group Holdings. Financed by Drexel Burnham Lambert, Steinberg made a credible offer to take over the venerable motion picture company. In an effort to ward off this hostile bid, Walt Disney sought to acquire other firms by offering Disney stock in exchange for the target's stock. In May 1984 Disney began negotiations to purchase the Arvida Corporation from the Bass Brothers. The Bass Brothers had bought this real estate concern in an LBO from the bankrupt Penn Central Corporation in 1978. Disney thought that Arvida was a natural fit because it was a real estate development firm; Disney owned extensive real estate in Florida, much of which was undeveloped. Disney, lacking the expertise to develop its real estate assets, sought this expertise in Arvida. Moreover, the acquisition of Arvida, financed by Disney stock, reduced Steinberg's holdings from 12.1% to 11.1%.[a]

One of the problems with defensive acquisitions financed by the issuance of stock is that the acquiring company may be concentrating shares in the hands of other substantial shareholders. As a result of this stock purchase, the Bass Brothers owned 5.9% of Disney stock. This problem may be alleviated if the new stockholders sign a standstill agreement and promise to support management's position in future stockholder votes. In this particular case, the Basses refused to sign such an agreement.

---

a. John Taylor, *Storming the Magic Kingdom* (New York: Ballantine Books, 1987), p. 89.

Litigation as an Antitakeover Defense

Litigation is one of the more common antitakeover defenses. In the early stages of the hostile takeover era (the mid-1970s), it was an effective means of preventing a takeover. However, its power in this area has somewhat diminished. Today litigation is only one of an array of defensive actions a target will take in hopes of preventing a takeover. Lipton and Steinberger cite four goals on antitakeover-related litigation:

1. To choose a more favorable forum
2. To preclude the raider from taking the initiative and suing first
3. To delay the bidder while the target pursues a white knight
4. To provide a psychological lift to the target's management[75]

One of the first legal maneuvers the target might try is to request that a court grant an injunction that will prevent the takeover process from continuing. Such an injunction coupled with a restraining order might bar the hostile bidder from purchasing additional stock until the bidder can satisfy the court that the target's charges are without merit.

---

75. Lipton and Steinberger, op. cit., pp. 6–144.

The temporary halting of a takeover can delay the acquisition, giving the target time to mount more effective defenses. The additional time can also allow the target to seek a white knight. Litigation and the grant of injunctive relief may provide the necessary time to allow a bidding process to develop. Other bidders will now have time to properly consider the benefits of making an offer for the target. The bidding process should result in higher offers for the target. Another major benefit of litigation is to give the bidder time to raise the offer price. The target might indirectly give the bidder the impression that if the offer price and terms were improved, it would drop the litigation.

The more common forms of defensive litigation are:

Antitrust. This type of litigation was more effective during the 1960s and 1970s when the Justice Department practiced stricter enforcement of the antitrust laws. However, given the Department's pro-business stance in the 1980s and 1990s, it has become much more difficult to establish an antitrust violation.

Inadequate disclosure. This type of lawsuit often contends that the bidder has not provided complete and full disclosure as required under the Williams Act. The target might argue that, in not providing full and complete disclosure, the acquirer has either not given stockholders adequate information or has provided information that presents an inaccurate picture of the acquirer or the acquirer's intention. The target in these types of lawsuits commonly maintains that the bidder did not convincingly state how it would raise the requisite capital to complete the purchase of all the stock bid for. The bidder usually contends that the disclosure is more than adequate or agrees to supplement his or her filings.

Fraud. This is a more serious charge and is more difficult to prove. Except in more extreme circumstances, it cannot be relied on to play a major role in the target's defense.

Litigation Research

In a 1985 study of attempted and completed takeovers that involved litigation between 1962 and 1980, Gregg Jarrell found that litigation occurred in one-third of all tender offers.[76] As noted previously, litigation may be beneficial for target shareholders even when it does not result in the acquirer's retraction of the bid. Litigation may result in a bid being delayed or forcing the bidder to raise his offer.

Jarrell found that 62% of the offers that had litigation had competing bids, whereas only 11% of those that did not have litigation had competing offers. He also found that, although it seems reasonable that litigation would cause bidders to raise their offer price to encourage the target to drop the litigation and avoid the legal expenses (as well as the possibility that the bid might be permanently halted), there was no evidence of a significant price effect. On average, a stock price decline took place when litigation was initiated. This decline occurred both for firms that were eventually acquired and for those that remained independent. However, unacquired stock returns fell 23.4%, whereas acquired returns declined slightly more than 21%.

Jarrell also found that when an auction for the firm resulted following the initiation of litigation, there was an additional 17% premium above the first offer relative to nonauc-

---

76. Gregg Jarrell, "Wealth Effects of Litigating by Targets: Do Interests Diverge in a Merge?" *Journal of Law and Economics* 28 (April 1985), pp.151–177 .

tioned firms. When litigation results in the bidder's withdrawing its offer, however, target company stockholders suffer major losses. They incur both the loss of a premium, which averaged 32% for Jarrell's sample of firms, as well as the costs of litigation. We can conclude that litigation may bring benefits for targets, but if the bid is withdrawn, it may also result in significant losses for target stockholders.

CASE STUDY: ANDERSON CLAYTON versus GERBER PRODUCTS— LITIGATION AS AN EFFECTIVE DEFENSE

In 1977 Anderson Clayton, a Houston-based food company, sought to expand by acquiring other companies. It had diversified operations including soybean processing, a coffee business, and a life insurance company. Anderson Clayton made a friendly offer for Stokley Van Camp, a major food processor. When Stokley Van Camp rejected Anderson Clayton's offer, Anderson Clayton set its eyes on other game.

Its gaze finally settled on Gerber Products, a company in Fremont, Michigan, that was famous for its line of baby foods. Anderson Clayton made friendly overtures toward Gerber Products but was immediately rebuffed. The management of Anderson Clayton decided it would go ahead with an offer for Gerber, even if this meant making an unfriendly tender offer. Anderson Clayton made a $40 bid, which amounted to a P/E multiple of 14. Gerber reacted by mounting an all-out, no-holds-barred defense. A central component of Gerber's defense was its use of litigation.

Gerber Products filed suit against Anderson Clayton in federal court in Grand Rapids, Michigan. Its suit charged that Anderson Clayton's acquisition offer would constitute an antitrust conflict. This charge would seem surprising by today's antitrust enforcement standards because Anderson Clayton and Gerber Products did not market any of the same products. However, Gerber's antitrust charges were based on the antitrust view that persisted in the 1960s and part of the 1970s, which stated that not just actual antitrust conflicts were relevant, but potential conflicts also had to be prevented. Gerber contended that Anderson Clayton could develop a baby products business in the future; therefore, it should be prevented from acquiring a potential competitor. In its suit, Gerber also stated that it had been contemplating entering the salad oil market, in which Anderson Clayton had already established its presence.

Gerber's lawsuit also charged that Anderson Clayton did not make full and sufficient disclosure in its tender offer filings of $2.1 million in questionable payments that it had made overseas. This part of the lawsuit was designed not only to put another legal roadblock in front of Anderson Clayton but also to embarrass the bidder by generating additional adverse publicity on an issue about which Anderson Clayton wanted to adopt a low profile.

Gerber believed that it had additional protection under Michigan's antitakeover law that would delay the tender offer for 60 days. This additional time allowed Gerber Products to seek an acceptable white knight. Gerber took this opportunity to begin discussions with Europe's Unilever. Gerber also contended in its suit that Anderson Clayton did not make sufficient disclosures of its financing arrangements in its tender offer filing materials. This is also required under Michigan's antitakeover law. Anderson Clayton's response was to try the friendly approach once again. It attempted to convince Gerber's board of directors that the offer should be presented to shareholders. These overtures were also rebuffed. Next Anderson Clayton filed suit contending that Gerber had made insufficient disclosures. In addition, to ensure compliance with Michigan's antitakeover law, Anderson Clayton secured a financing agreement from several New York banks.

In July 1977 at its annual meeting, Gerber disclosed that second quarter earnings had fallen 33%. This was the third quarter in a row that Gerber had declared fallen earnings. Anderson Clayton felt that Gerber was deliberately understating its earnings merely to dissuade potential bidders from making an offer for the company. Anderson Clayton's response to the earnings announcement was to lower its offer from $40 to $37. This action immediately put pressure on Gerber's board of directors because stockholders could now state that the rejection of the first $40 offer cost them $3 per share.

Anderson Clayton believed that Gerber had an advantage because Gerber's lawsuits were filed in Michigan. Indeed, a series of rulings by Judge Fox were all favorable to Gerber. Anderson Clayton faced the prospect of a trial on the securities charges in September 1977, followed by another trial in which the antitrust claims would be decided. Anderson Clayton believed that the series of legal issues that needed to be decided would not be settled until as late as 1979. Even if Anderson Clayton won, Unilever or some other bidder might materialize and escalate Gerber's price.

In light of the uncertainties of the extended legal battle, Anderson Clayton decided to withdraw its offer. The Gerber Products legal defense was credited with warding off Anderson Clayton's offer. Gerber Products' stock prices fell from $34.375 to $28.25 in one day in response to this announcement. Arbitragers, who had gambled that Gerber would be bought by some company, experienced large losses. Litigation was now recognized as a potent defense that must be carefully considered when evaluating a takeover contest.

Pac-Man Defense

The *Pac-Man defense,* so-named after the popular video game in which characters try to eat each other before they are eaten themselves, is one of the more colorful defenses employed by target companies. It occurs when the target makes an offer to buy the raider in response to the raider's bid for the target. Because of its extreme nature, this defense is considered a "doomsday machine." One of the more famous uses of this defense came when the Martin Marietta Corporation made an offer to buy Bendix following Bendix's unwanted $43 tender offer for Martin Marietta in the summer of 1982.

The Pac-Man defense is often threatened but it is seldom used. Before the Bendix-Martin Marietta takeover battle, two companies had used it in a vain effort to maintain their independence. In 1982 NLT Corporation ended up merging with its bidder—American General Corporation. As stated earlier, Cities Service tried the Pac-Man defense in response to Boone Pickens's bid from Mesa Petroleum. Although the defense halted Mesa's bid and helped to convince Mesa to accept greenmail, Cities Service was nonetheless put in play and ended up selling out to Occidental Petroleum.

In another early use of the Pac-Man defense, Houston Natural Gas Corporation (now Enron Corporation) used a 1984 bid for the raider to try to fend off the Coastal Corporation. It was not successful because Houston Natural Gas sold off nearly half its assets to maintain its independence. The Heublein Corporation, however, threatened to use the Pac-Man defense when it was confronted by General Cinema Corporation and was able to scare away General Cinema.

CASE STUDY: E-II HOLDINGS versus AMERICAN BRANDS— THE SUCCESSFUL USE OF THE PAC-MAN DEFENSE

Another of the few successful uses of the Pac-Man defense occurred in January 1988 when E-II Holdings made an offer for American Brands Corporation.[a] In January 1988 Donald Kelly, chairman of E-II Holdings, announced a $6 billion bid for American Brands, a firm in Old Greenwich, Connecticut. By 1988 megamerger offers in the billions of dollars were not unusual. Kelly took this occasion as an opportunity to announce a 4.6% stake in American Brands while revealing his plans to dismantle American Brands following a takeover. Kelly had previously taken E-II Holdings private through an LBO in which he was aided by Kohlberg Kravis & Roberts.

E-II Holdings was a diverse consumer products group of companies formed from the spin-off of 15 companies following the acquisition of Beatrice. It had lost $1.2 billion for nine months before the offer for American Brands. A total of $132 million of this loss came from interest costs, and $147.5 million was a result of the October 1987 stock market crash. E-II Holdings was heavily leveraged and would have to incur significant debt to buy American Brands.

American Brands' main businesses were tobacco, spirits, office products, and financial services. Among its popular brand names are Master Locks, Jim Beam bourbon, Titleist golf equipment, and Pall Mall cigarettes. Its financial condition was in sharp contrast to that of E-II Holdings. It had strong credit lines compared with the debt-laden E-II Holdings. Its chairman, William J. Alley, had been fine-tuning the company into good financial condition by selling off businesses that were not in the categories outlined. American Brands had recently showed record sales of $9.2 billion, which provided an income of $1.1 billion. This represented increases of 26% and 33%, respectively.

Many people speculated that Kelly was gambling and that Alley would respond with a Pac-Man defense. Kelly was rumored to have been looking for a buyer to purchase E-II Holdings. One way to get such a buyer would be to force an unwilling buyer's hand. Alley responded with an offer for E-II Holdings of $2.7 billion. The acquisition was completed, and American Brands took ownership. In the months that followed, American Brands began to disassemble E-II by selling off product lines such as Samsonite luggage and Culligan water-treatment operations. American Brands indicated that it only planned to keep five or six of the companies it acquired.

---

a. "Takeovers Are Back But Now the Frenzy Is Gone," *Business Week,* 9 February 1988, p. 24; Pamela Sebastian, "American Brands Offer to Buy Debt at E-II Holdings Gets Tepid Response," *Wall Street Journal,* 24 February 1988, p. 8; Stephen Labaton, "American Brands Set to Buy E-II," *New York Times,* 1 February 1988, p. 1.

"Just Say No"

In the most basic form of antitakeover defense, the target refuses to be taken over, simply hiding behind its poison pills and other defenses and stating that it will not deactivate them and will not bring the offer before the shareholders. In the *just say no* defense, the target may refuse to take any measures, even providing more cash to shareholders, by stating that it has more optimistic plans for the future of the company.

The Universal Foods Corporation, a manufacturer of products such as french fries and cheese, used the "just say no" defense in 1989 when it turned down an offer from the High Voltage Engineering Corporation. When High Voltage Engineering offered $38 per share, Universal responded that its investment banker, Goldman Sachs, had determined that this offer was inadequate. Universal's board of directors decided that profits were rising and that this was not the time to sell the company. Martin Lipton, the originator of the "just say no" defense, advised his client, Universal Foods, to reject the offer and not take any other action. Universal compromised by raising its dividend from 18 cents per share to 22 cents. The company's defense, especially its poison pill, was challenged in court. In March 1989 a federal court judge in Wisconsin ruled that if the company's executives believed that the offer was inadequate, they were in a position to determine an accurate value for the company.

The "just say no" defense, however, may be challenged by higher offers that will counter the board of directors' position that the future value of the company is worth more to stockholders than the offer price. There will always be some price that will leave the board of directors with no choice but to approve the offer.

INFORMATION CONTENT OF TAKEOVER RESISTANCE

Throughout this chapter we have reviewed a variety of antitakeover defenses and have analyzed the shareholder wealth effects of several of these defenses. Looking at defenses more globally, John Pound of Harvard University has studied the information content of takeover bids and the resistance of the target to the takeover.[77] Pound used consensus earnings forecasts as a proxy for the market's expected value of the targets as stand-alone entities. The effect of different types of takeover contests and defenses on the market's value of the target was assessed by considering whether the consensus changed. These tests were conducted for three samples: targets of friendly bids, targets of hostile bids that were ultimately acquired, and targets of hostile bids that remained independent. Pound observed that the consensus forecasts were unchanged after the initial takeover bid. He therefore concluded that the bids themselves do not convey important information. The unchanged forecasts also imply that the bid did not reveal to the marketplace a previously undiscovered case of undervaluation.

Pound found the resistance to a takeover to be associated with a downward revision of the average earnings forecasts of approximately 10%. This was the case both for firms that were acquired and for those that remained independent. Pound concluded that the market interprets the resistance as a negative signal about future performance.

---

77. John Pound, "The Information Effects of Takeover Bids and Resistance," *Journal of Financial Economics* 22 no. 2 (December 1988), pp. 207–227.

CASE STUDY: BENDIX versus MARTIN MARIETTA

One of the most colorful takeover battles in U.S. economic history was the contest between the Bendix Corporation and the Martin Marietta Corporation. Bendix was led by its chairman, William Agee, who got his training in acquisitions while chief financial officer of Boise Cascade Corporation. Boise Cascade was a forest products company that transformed itself into a conglomerate through diverse acquisitions in the 1960s. Agee joined Bendix in 1972 as executive vice president, reporting to Michael Blumenthal, who left to become secretary of the treasury in the Carter Administration. At the age of 38 years, Agee was named chairman of the company, which had two main lines of business, auto products, such as ignition systems and brakes, and aviation products for the defense industry.

In August 1982, after an aborted takeover attempt of RCA, Agee began his bid for Martin Marietta, a company that was an established presence in the defense industry, particularly in aerospace products such as missile systems. Bendix made a $43 tender offer for 45% of Martin Marietta (Bendix already had just under 5% of Martin Marietta), which was previously selling for $33 per share. Martin Marietta rejected the offer and initiated its own $75 per share tender offer for Bendix, which had been previously selling for $50 per share.

Although Bendix, a Delaware corporation, bid for Martin Marietta first, Martin Marietta was incorporated in Maryland and that state's corporation laws required any bidder to give the target 10 days notice before calling an election of the board of directors. This gave Martin Marietta an apparent advantage over Bendix because Martin Marietta could complete its tender offer for Bendix, following the necessary 20–day Williams Act waiting period that affected both offers, change Bendix's board of directors, and call off Bendix's tender offer before Bendix could do the same at Martin Marietta. Arthur Fleisher, of the firm Fried, Frank, Harris, Shriver and Jacobson, had advised Agee that Bendix's corporate charter's election rules should be amended to remove this advantage but that was never done.

Each firm engaged in various defenses, including litigation. Bendix adopted golden parachutes; Martin Marietta searched for a white knight. They found a gray knight, Harry Grey, chairman of United Technologies Corporation, who agreed to make a backup tender offer for Martin Marietta if its offer for Bendix failed.

Agee counted on the 23% of the company's stock that was held in an ESOP that was managed by Citibank's trustee. Martin Marietta's tender offer was two-tiered, with better consideration being offered for the first tier. Citibank concluded that its fiduciary's responsibilities were with the financial well-being of the ESOP shareholders and not based on any other loyalty to Bendix. Many of the employees, however, did not agree with this assessment.

Although Agee may have believed that he could have reached agreement with Martin Marietta to drop its offer, Martin Marietta could not count on United Technologies to simply walk away, so it went ahead with its bid for Bendix and raised the offer price. The absurdity of the deal was that it looked as if both companies would end up buying each other, with each company being debt-laden after the transaction.

Bendix contacted Edward Hennessy, then chairman of Allied Signal, to be its white knight. Hennessy bid for Bendix and won control of the company. He then reached agreement with Thomas Pownall, CEO of Martin Marietta, to exchange shares. Martin Marietta remained independent but highly leveraged. Hennessy ended up with valuable Bendix assets at a reasonable price. Agee remained president of Bendix until 1983.

SUMMARY

The art of takeover defense has evolved over the past two decades to become a sophisticated process. It may be classified into two broad groupings: preventative and active takeover defenses. Preventative defenses are those that a potential target puts in place in advance of a possible hostile bid. One of the most commonly used of these preventative defenses is the poison pill. Two versions of poison pills are found. Flip-over poison pills allow target shareholders to purchase shares in the bidder's company at a significant discount, typically 50%, if the bidder purchases 100% of the target. Flip-in poison pills allow target shareholders to purchase shares in the target at a discount if the bidder acquires a certain number of the target's shares or makes an offer for a minimum number of shares. Poison pills are one of the more effective defenses but even this defense can often be circumvented by a sufficiently attractive offer. Such an offer puts pressure on the board of directors to withdraw the pill lest they become targets of a lawsuit from shareholder alleging breach of their fiduciary duties.

Other preventative takeover defenses include a variety of corporate charter amendments, antigreenmail such as supermajority provisions, fair price provisions, dual capitalizations, blank check preferred stock, and staggering the election of the board of directors. Much research has been conducted to determine what impact the implementation of these and other antitakeover defenses has on shareholder wealth.

If the preventative antitakeover defenses are not successful in fending off an unwanted bid, the target may still implement active defenses. These defenses include greenmail and standstill agreements. Greenmail, which is the payment of a premium for the bidder's shares, has become less popular as a result of tax law changes. Greenmail is typically accompanied by a standstill agreement, wherein the bidder agrees, in exchange for a fee, not to purchase target shares beyond some agreed upon threshold.

The target may also engage in more drastic active antitakeover defenses, including capital structure changes, physical restructuring, or changing the state of incorporation. One popular form of capital structure changes, recapitalization, increases the target's leverage, and therefore its risk level, while using the proceeds to pay a superdividend to shareholders as an alternative to the hostile bid. Courts have ruled that the combination of recapitalization plans with poison pills, which use the pill to prevent the successful hostile bid while the recapitalization plan remains unaffected by the pill, is illegal. An even more drastic defense is the Pac-Man defense, in which the target makes an offer for the bidder. Although very colorful, this defense has only been implemented a few times. At the opposite end of the spectrum of severity is litigation which is very commonly used. Its effectiveness varies, but research has showed that when it does not result in the withdrawal of an offer, it tends to be associated with higher premiums.

The business judgment rule allows the use of various takeover defenses when they work to promote the bidding process and promote shareholder wealth. When such defenses are used to inhibit the auction process, they are generally found to be illegal.

The development of takeover defenses will continue to evolve as bidders refine their aggressive tactics to circumvent defenses. With the resurgence of takeovers in the 1990s, this should continue to be an importance area of corporate finance.

REFERENCES

Banerjee, Ajeyo and James E. Owers. "Wealth Reduction in White Knight Bids." *Financial Management* 21, no. 3 (Autumn 1992).

Bhagat, S., and J. A. Brickley. "Cumulative Voting: The Value of Minority Shareholder Rights." *Journal of Law and Economics* 27 (October 1984).

Bhagat, Sanjai, and Richard H. Jefferis. "The Causes and Consequences of Takeover Defense: Evidence from Greenmail." *Journal of Corporate Finance* 1 (1994).

Block, Dennis, Nancy E. Barton, and Stephen A. Radin. *Business Judgment Rule* (Englewood Cliffs, N.J.: Prentice-Hall, 1988).

Bradley, Michael, Anand Desai, and E. Han Kim. "The Rationale Behind Interfirm Tender Offers."*Journal of Financial Economics* 11 (April 1983).

Bradley, Michael, and L. MacDonald Wakeman. "The Wealth Effects of Targeted Share Repurchases." *Journal of Financial Economics* 11 (April 1983).

Brancato, Caroyln Kay. "Institutional Investors and Corporate Governance" (New York: Richard D. Irwin, 1997).

Brickley, James A., Ronald C. Lease, and Clifford W. Smith. "Corporate Voting: Evidence from Corporate Charter Amendment Proposals." *Journal of Corporate Finance* 1 (1994).

Brickley, James A., Ronald Lease, and Clifford Smith. "Ownership Structure and Voting on Antitakeover Amendments." *Journal of Financial Economics* 20, no. 1/2 (January/March 1988).

Brooks, John. *Takeover* (New York: E. F. Dutton, 1987).

Buckhorn Inc. v. Ropak Corp., 656 F. Supp. 209 (S.D. Ohio) *aff'd by summary order* 815 F. 2d 76 (6th Cir. 1987).

Buffalo Forge Co. v. Ogden Corp., 717 F. 2d (2nd Cir.) *att'd* 555 F. Supp. 892 (W.D.N.Y.).

"Chevron Purchasing Shares to Replace Stock Used for ESOP." *Wall Street Journal,* 13 February 1990, p. A5.

Coffee, John C. "Shareholders v. Managers: The Strain in the Corporate Web." In John C. Coffee, Louis Lowenstein, and Susan Rose Ackerman, eds. *Knights, Raiders and Targets* (New York: Oxford University Press, 1988), pp. 71–134.

Coll, Steve. *The Taking of Getty Oil* (New York: Atheneum Publishers, 1987).

Comment, Robert, and G. William Schwert. "Poison or Placebo: Evidence on the Deterrence and Wealth Effects of Modern Antitakeover Measures." *Journal of Financial Economics* 39 (1995).

Commons, Dorman L. *Tender Offer* (New York: Penguin Books, 1985).

Dann, Larry Y., and Harry DeAngelo. "Corporate Financial Policy and Corporate Control: A Study in Defensive Adjustments in Asset and Ownership Structure." *Journal of Financial Economics* 20, no. 1/2 (1988).

Dann, Larry Y., and Harry DeAngelo. "Standstill Agreements and Privately Negotiated Stock Repurchases and the Market for Corporate Control." *Journal of Financial Economics* 11 (April 1983).

DeAngelo, Harry, and Eugene Rice. "Antitakeover Charter Amendments and Stockholder Wealth." *Journal of Financial Economics* 11 (April 1983).

Dobrzynski, Judith. "Are Directors Overpaid? The Answer Varies Widely." *New York Times,* 27 June 1995.

E.Tate & Lyle PLC v. Staley Continental, Inc., Fed. Sec. L. Rep. 93, 764, (Del. Ch. CCH 93, 764) (Del. Ch. May 9, 1988); *Nomad Acquisition Corp. v. Damon Corp.,* CCH Fed. Sec. L. Rep. 94, 040.

Ferrara, Ralph C., Meredith M. Brown, and John Hall. *Takeovers: Attack and Survival* (Austin, TX: Butterworth Legal Publishers, 1987).

Fleischer, Arthur, Jr. and Alexander Sussman, *Takeover Defense,* 5th ed. (New York: Aspen Law & Business, 1995).

Good v. Texaco, Inc., 507 A. 2d, Delaware Supreme Court.

Herzel, Leo, and Richard Shepio. *Bidders and Targets* (Cambridge: Basil Blackwell, 1990).

Ho, Michael J. "Share Rights Plans: Poison Pill, Placebo or Suicide Table?" Master's thesis, Massachusetts Institute of Technology, Sloan School of Management.

Huang, Yen-Sheng, and Ralph A. Walking. "Target Abnormal Returns Associated With Acquisition Announcements: Payment, Acquisition Form, and Managerial Resistance." *Journal of Financial Economics* 19 (December 1987).

"Icahn Gets Green As Others Envy Him." *Wall Street Journal,* 13 November 1989.

"Interco Defense Against Rales Is Struck Down." *Wall Street Journal,* 2 November 1988.

Jarrell, Gregg. "Wealth Effects of Litigating by Targets: Do Interests Diverge in a Merge?" *Journal of Law and Economics* 28 (April 1985).

Jarrell, Gregg, and Annette Poulsen. "Dual Class Recapitalizations As Antitakeover Mechanisms." *Journal of Financial Economics* 20 (January/March 1988)

Jarrell, Gregg A. I., and Annette B. Poulsen. "Shark Repellents and Stock Prices: The Effects of Antitakeover Amendments Since 1980." *Journal of Financial Economics* 19, no. 1 (September 1987).

Jensen, Michael. "Takeover: Causes and Consequence." In Patrick A. Gaughan, ed. *Readings in Mergers and Acquisitions* (Oxford: Basil Blackwell, 1994), pp. 15–43.

Johnston, Moira, *Takeover* (New York: Arbor House Publishers, 1986).

Josephson, Matthew, *The Robber Barons* (New York: Harcourt Brace & Co., 1931).

Kamma, Sreenivas, Joseph Weintrop, and Peggy Weir. "Investors Perceptions of the Delaware Supreme Court Decision in Unocal v. Mesa." *Journal of Financial Economics* 20 (January/March 1988).

Kleinman, Robert, "The Shareholder Gains from Leveraged Cash Outs: Preliminary Evidence," *Journal of Applied Corporate Finance 1,* no. 1 (Spring 1998), p. 50.

Lambert, Richard A., and David F. Larker. "Golden Parachutes, Executive Decision Making and Stockholder Wealth." *Journal of Accounting Economics* 7 (1985).

Lebaton, Stephen. "American Brands Set to Buy E-II." *New York Times,* 1 February 1988.

Linn, Scott C., and John J. McConnell. "An Empirical Investigation of the Impact of Antitakeover Amendments on Common Stock Prices." *Journal of Financial Economics* 11 (April 1983).

Lorsch, Jay W. *Pawns or Potentates* (Boston: Harvard Business School Press, 1989).

Machlin, Judith, Hyuk Choe, and James Miles. "The Effects of Golden Parachutes on Takeover Activity." *Journal of Law and Economics* 36, no. 2 (October 1993).

Madrick, Jeff. *Taking America* (New York: Bantam Books, 1987).

Malatesta, Paul H., and Ralph A. Walking. "Poison Pill Securities: Stockholder Wealth, Profitability and Ownership Structure." *Journal of Financial Economics* 20, no. 112 (January/March 1988).

McWilliams, Victoria B. "Managerial Share Ownership and the Stock Price Effects of Antitakeover Amendment Provisions." *Journal of Finance* 45, vol. XLV, no. 5 (December 1990).

McWilliams, Victoria B. "The Stock Prices Effects of Antitakeover Amendment Proposals." Unpublished manuscript, #88–29, 1988, Northeastern University.

Mikkelson, Wayne, and Richard Ruback. "Targeted Share Repurchases and Common Stock Returns." Working Paper No. 1707–86, Massachusetts Institute of Technology, Sloan School of Management, June 1986.

Morck, R., A. Shliefer, and R. W. Vishny. "Management Ownership and Market Valuation: An Empirical Analysis." *Journal of Financial Economics,* vol. XLV, no. 5 (December 1990), pp. 293–315.

Nathan, C. M., and M. Sobel. "Corporate Stock Repurchases in the Contest of Unsolicited Takeover Bids." *Business Lawyer* (July 1980).

Netter, Jeffrey, and Annette Poulsen. "State Corporation Laws and Shareholders: The Recent Experience." *Financial Management* 18, no. 3 (Autumn 1989).

"$1.1 Billion Polaroid Buyback." *New York Times,* 31 January 1989.

Parker, Marcia. "Companies Not Ringed with Defensive Armor." *Pensions and Investments,* vol. 18, no. 20, (September 1990).

Partch, Megan. "The Creation of a Class of Limited Voting Common Stock and Shareholder Wealth." *Journal of Financial Economics* 18, no. 2 (June 1987).

Pickens, T. Boone, Jr. *Boone* (Boston: Houghton Mifflin Co., 1987).

"The Poison Pill Takes a Beating." *Wall Street Journal,* 14 November 1988.

Pound, John. "The Effectiveness of Antitakeover Amendments on Takeover Activity." *Journal of Law and Economics* 30 (October 1987).

Pound, John. "The Information Effects of Takeover Bids and Resistance." *Journal of Financial Economics* 22, no. 2 (December 1988).

Royal Crown Cos. v. McMahon, 359 S.E. 2d 379 (Ga. Ct. App. 1987), *cert. denied* (Ga. Sept. 8, 1987).

Ruback, Richard. "An Overview of Takeover Defenses." In Alan J. Auerbach, ed. *Mergers and Acquisitions* (Chicago: National Bureau of Economic Research, University of Chicago Press, 1987).

Ruback, Richard. "Coercive Dual-Class Exchange Offers." *Journal of Financial Economics* 20, (January/March 1988).

Ryngaert, Michael. "The Effects of Poison Pill Securities on Stockholder Wealth." *Journal of Financial Economics* 20 (January/March 1988).

Sah, Raaj, and Navendu Vasavada. "Unbundled Stock Units: What Went Wrong?" *Financial Management Collection* 5, no. 2 (Summer 1990).

Sebastian, Pamela. "American Brands Offer to Buy Debt at E-11 Holdings Gets Tepid Response." *Wall Street Journal,* 24 February 1988.

Seibert v. Gulton Industries, Inc. No. 5631.5 Del. J. Corp. L. 514 (Del Ch. June 21, 1974), *aff'd without opinion* 414 A. 2d 822 (Del 1980).

"Share Vote Proposal Approved." *New York Times,* 8 July 1988.

Stern, Gabriella, and Joann Lublin. "Chrysler Has Bold New Idea—In Parachutes." *Wall Street Journal,* 12 July 1995.

"Takeovers Are Back But Now the Frenzy Is Gone." *Business Week,* 8 February 1988.

Taylor, John. *Storming the Magic Kingdom* (New York: Ballantine Books, 1987).

"Trial Discusses Identity of 10 Firms Gillette Company Contacted as White Knights." *Wall Street Journal,* 27 June 1988.

"Use of ESOPs Against Bids Lowers Stock." *Wall Street Journal,* 6 June 1989.

Wallace, Anise. "Bid for Kay Stirs Bondholders Ire." *New York Times,* 12 July 1990.

"When Targets Tilt Playing Fields." *New York Times,* 21 April 1988.

White, James. "White Squires Step into Breach As Debt-Driven Investing Falters." *Wall Street Journal,* 21 February 1990.

6

TAKEOVER TACTICS

During the fourth merger wave of the 1980s, increasingly powerful takeover tactics were required to complete hostile acquisitions because potential targets erected ever-stronger antitakeover defenses. Before this period, comparatively simple tactics had been sufficient to force a usually surprised and bewildered target into submission. As hostile takeovers reached new heights of intensity, targets became more wary, and bidders were required to advance the sophistication of their takeover tactics. When the pace of takeovers slowed at the end of the fourth merger wave, hostile takeovers also became less frequent. Nonetheless, after a lull that lasted a few years, hostile takeovers started to increase in frequency. In the fifth merger wave, hostile takeovers are once again commonplace. However, because of the presence of a broad array of enhanced defenses, takeover tactics need to be correspondingly sophisticated to be successful.

This chapter analyzes the evolution of takeover tactics employed in the 1980s and 1990s and discusses the effectiveness and use of these tactics. It will become clear that the options for the hostile bidder are fewer in number compared with the broad variety of defenses that targets implement in advance of and during a hostile bid. The bidder is typically left with the choice of three main tactics: a bear hug, a tender offer, and a proxy fight. Each tactic has its strengths and weaknesses. In addition, each may be implemented in varying manners to increase the likelihood of success. The options and their shareholder wealth effects are the focus of this chapter.

Of the main takeover tactics, bear hugs are the least aggressive and often occur at the beginning of a hostile takeover. When the target is not strongly opposed to a takeover, a bear hug may be sufficient. However, for a determined and firmly entrenched bidder, it is unlikely that a bear hug will be sufficient to complete the takeover.

The most frequently used hostile takeover tactic is the tender offer. The laws regulating tender offers, which are fully discussed in Chapter 3, are approached here from the viewpoint of the impact of takeover rules on the hostile bidder's tactics. For example, we describe under what circumstances a bidder has actually made a legal tender offer and thereby become bound by the filing requirements of the Williams Act. It is shown that such factors may determine the success of the bid. The legal environment determines the rules within which a bidder must structure a tender offer. How these rules affect tender offer tactics is discussed from a strategic viewpoint.

The tender offer process, along with different variations such as two-tiered tender offers and partial tenders, are also described in this chapter. We also consider the shareholder wealth effects of the different types of tender offers and other takeover tactics, just as in

Chapter 5, where the impact of the various antitakeover measures on shareholder wealth was discussed.

Another broad category of takeover tactics covered in this chapter is proxy fights. This tactic is discussed in a manner similar to the discussion of tender offers. The corporate election process through which proxy fights are waged is considered in detail. The different types of proxy fights, such as battles for seats on the board of directors and contests that seek to produce a managerial change in the corporation, are described. Although this chapter focuses mainly on the tactics a hostile bidder may employ, an effort is also made to show the proxy fight process from the target's point of view, with a discussion of management's options. Once again, the shareholder wealth effects of this takeover tactic are analyzed through a review of the research literature in this field.

The start of the 1990s witnessed the increasing use of proxy fights as a way to enhance the effectiveness of tender offers. This tactic became necessary when the availability of junk bond financing, on which many tender offers relied in the fourth merger wave, dramatically declined. In the 1990s hostile bidders found it more difficult to circumvent the increasingly effective target defenses by aggressively raising the offer price of their all-cash tender offers. They rediscovered the proxy fight as another tool that would increase the effectiveness of their budget-constrained tender offer. However, after a period of increased popularity in the early 1990s, proxy fights again took second place after tender offers as the pace of hostile deals, now financed more with stock than they were in the 1980s, increased in the mid-1990s (Figure 6.1). For the fifth merger wave, the proxy fight resumed its position as an important takeover tactic that is appropriate in certain specialized situations when other means, such as a tender offer, are not used.

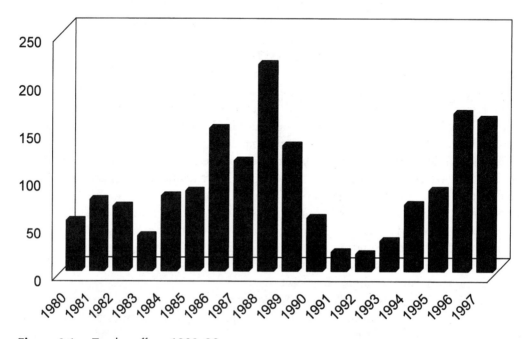

Figure 6.1. Tender offers, 1980–98.

Source: Mergerstat Review, 1998.

PRELIMINARY TAKEOVER STEPS

Establishing a Toe Hold

An initial step that is often pursued before using the various takeover tactics that are at the disposal of a hostile bidder is to begin an initial accumulation of the target's shares. In doing so, the bidder seeks to establish a toe hold from which to launch its hostile bid. One of the advantages of such share purchases is that if the market is unaware of its actions, the bidder may be able to avoid the payment of a premium. This lowers the average cost of the acquisition. In addition, it may provide the bidder with some of the same rights that other shareholders have, thus establishing a fiduciary duty, which the board would now have to the bidder in its dual role as the hostile bidder and as the target shareholder. This is why target defenses that relate to share acquisitions are exclusionary and usually leave out the accumulator/hostile bidder. This is often a subject of litigation between the company and the bidder.

It is interesting to note that there is some evidence that, despite the theoretical benefits of establishing a toe hold prior to initiating a tender offer, most bidders do not utilize toe hold share accumulations. Arturo Bris of Yale University found that only about 15% of the firms in his sample of 327 hostile deals in the United States and Britain (70% in the United States) acquired a toe hold.[1] This result is lower but similar to other research in this area.[2]

The Casual Pass

Before initiating hostile actions, the bidder may attempt some informal overture to the management of the target. This is sometimes referred to as a casual pass. It may come from a member of the bidder's management or from one of its representatives, such as its investment banker. A casual pass may be used if the bidder is unsure of the target's response. If the target has been the subject of other hostile bids that it has spurned, or if the target has publicly stated its desire to remain independent, this step may provide few benefits. In fact, it can work against the bidder because it provides the target with advance warning of the bidder's interest. In most takeover battles, the target tries to buy more time while the bidder seeks to force the battle to a quick conclusion. Managers of potential target companies are often advised by their attorneys to not engage in loose discussions that could be misconstrued as an expression of interest. They are often told to unequivocally state that the target wants to remain independent.

Bear Hugs

A bidder will sometimes try to pressure the management of the target before initiating a tender offer. This may be done by contacting the board of directors with an expression of interest in acquiring the target and the implied intent to go directly to stockholders with a tender offer if these overtures are not favorably received. This strategy—known as the

---

1. Arture Bris, "When Do Bidders Purchase a Toe Hold? Theory and Tests," Yale University Working Paper, October 1998.

2. Sandra Betton and B. Espen Eckbo, "State Contingent Payoffs in Takeovers: New Structural Payoffs," Working Paper.

bear hug—may also be accompanied by a public announcement of the bidder's intent to make a tender offer. The bear hug forces the target's board to take a public position on the possible takeover by this bidder. Such offers carry with them the implication that if it is not favorably received, it will be immediately followed by a tender offer directly to shareholders. A bear hug also puts pressure on the board of directors because it must be considered lest the board be regarded as having violated its fiduciary duties.

CASE STUDY: RAIDERS OR SAVIORS?

Raiders have been much maligned in the media. As noted previously, critics have contended that they are short-term speculators who have no long-term interest in the future of the company. They believe that the payment of greenmail to such short-term speculators can only injure the firm's future viability. This view, however, has been challenged by the results of a study by Holderness and Sheehan. They analyzed the activities of six popular raiders, Carl Icahn, Irwin Jacobs, Carl Lintner, David Murdock, Victor Posner, and Charles Bluhdorn, between 1977 and 1982.[a] Their analysis showed that stock prices rose significantly after the announcement that they had first purchased shares in a target firm. They learned that the traditional view of "raiding" was not supported by the activities of these investors over a two-year period that had followed each purchase. Holderness and Sheehan define raiders as those who would use their position as significant shareholders to try to expropriate assets from the firm. They contend that if this were the case, share prices would have declined after the initial share repurchase. Instead, the market responded with an increase in its valuation of the firm. This suggests that the market does not view these investors as expropriating raiders. Their analysis of instances in which these raiders were the recipients of repurchase offers by the target shows that the announcement of the repurchases yielded negative returns. Similar to findings of Mikkelson and Ruback, however, when the aggregate effects of the initial stock purchase, intermediate events, and the eventual share repurchase are combined, the overall effects are positive and statistically significant.

Holderness and Sheehan see part of the reason for the positive stock price effect on the announcement of share repurchases as the result of an improved management effect. They believe that the market may anticipate that these raiders either will play a direct role in the management of the firm or will seek to change management. Indeed, in 10 of the 73 target firms studied, they found that the raiders played a direct role in the management of the firm.

One final conclusion that Holderness and Sheehan draw from their analysis is that these six investors managed to purchase undervalued stocks. They attribute this "superior security analyst's acumen" either to the possession of nonpublic information or to a greater ability to analyze public information. They see the positive stock price effects around the initial announcement of the purchases as support for this view of raiders.

a. Clifford G. Holderness and Dennis P. Sheehan, "Raiders or Saviors? The Evidence of Six Controversial Raiders," *Journal of Finance and Economics* 14, no. 4 (December 1985): 555–581.

Once a bear hug becomes public, arbitragers typically accumulate the target's stock. Depending on the companies involved, they may even want to sell the bidder's shares short based on the fact that when bidders make takeover offers, the bidder's shares may decline after the announcement. The accumulation of shares by arbitragers may make large share block purchases easier for the initiator of the bear hug or any other bidder. This often puts the company "in play," which makes continued independence more difficult. Investors who have been accused of greenmail in the past, such as Carl Icahn and Boone Pickens, were active users of the bear hug. Its effectiveness in the 1990s has been reduced by the increased potency of poison pills. Nonetheless, it still is used. For example, in 1997 partnerships related to the Bass Brothers made a leveraged offer for Fisher Scientific. This caused the stock price of Fisher Scientific to rise. Fisher was put in play and eventually was acquired by Thomas H. Lee & Co.

A stronger version of the standard bear hug occurs when one bidder offers a specific price in order to, among other reasons, establish a range for damages in possible stockholder lawsuits that might follow the target management's rejection of the bid. This tactic increases the pressure on the target's board, which might be the object of the lawsuits. The typical response of an unreceptive target board is to acquire a fairness opinion from an investment bank that will say that the offer is inadequate. This gives the board of directors a "legitimate" reason to reject the offer. If the bidder makes a public announcement while engaging in a bear hug, the bidder is bound to file pursuant to Rule 14d-2 of the Williams Act and is required to disseminate tender offer materials or abandon the offer within five days. If the target discloses the offer, the bidder is not required to file.

From a strategic point of view, if the bidder sees a realistic possibility of a negotiated transaction, the bear hug may be an attractive alternative to a tender offer. It is a less expensive and less time-consuming way to conduct a "hostile" acquisition. It may also reduce the adverse consequences that sometimes are associated with hostile deals, such as the loss of key target employees and a deterioration of employee morale following the acquisition. If the bidder strongly opposes the acquisition, the bear hug may have little value because a tender offer may eventually be necessary.

Bidders who are reluctant to engage in a costly tender offer begin to use the bear hug as an initial, less expensive takeover tool. The advantage is that the pressure placed on the target's board of directors may be sufficient to complete the takeover.

TENDER OFFERS

Because the Williams Act is the key piece of federal legislation that regulates tender offers, it is ironic that the law does not even define the term. Instead, it has been left to the courts to formulate an exact definition. This ambiguity has naturally led to some confusion regarding what constitutes a tender offer. In some instances, bidders, believing that their actions were not a tender offer, have failed to follow the rules and procedures of the Williams Act. This occurred in the landmark case, discussed in Chapter 3, involving the bid by Sun Oil, Inc. for the Becton Dickinson Company. In late 1977 Sun Oil structured a deal with Fairleigh S. Dickinson, founder of the New Jersey private college of the same name, to purchase shares that Fairleigh Dickinson, his family, and other related parties held. Because the company did not file the proper disclosure statements at the time this agreement was reached, the court ruled that it had violated the Williams Act under the definition of a group as offered by the law. In deciding the case, the federal district court ruled that the establishment of an agreement between Dickinson and the Sun Oil to sell shares to Sun and to have Dickinson become chairman of Becton Dickinson following its acquisition by Sun Oil warranted a disclosure filing. In arriving at its decision, the court established a definition of a tender offer, naming eight factors that are characteristic of a tender offer.[3] These factors, which were covered in Chapter 3, are listed in Table 6.1.

The eighth point was not relevant to the *Wellman v. Dickinson* case and was not discussed in this ruling. It is derived from an earlier ruling. Not all eight factors must be present for an offer to be judged a tender offer. The court did not want the eight factors to constitute an automatic litmus test for tender offers. Rather, in deciding whether the circumstances of a given stock purchase constitute a tender offer, the eight factors are considered together, along with any other relevant factors.

Open Market Purchases

The courts have generally found that open market purchases do not by themselves represent a tender offer. They do require that the purchaser file according to Section 13(d) of the Williams Act, but they do not mandate the additional extensive filings associated with a tender offer. One version of open market purchases is a *creeping tender offer,* which is the process of gradually acquiring shares in the market or through private transactions. Although these purchases may require a Schedule 13D filing, the courts generally do not regard such purchases as a legal tender offer. The courts have repeatedly found that the purchase of stock from sophisticated institutional investors is not under the domain of the Williams Act.[4] However, the courts have maintained that a publicly announced intention to acquire control of a company followed by a rapid accumulation of that firm's stock is a tender offer.[5]

Table 6.1.   Tender Offer Eight-Factor Test

1. Active and widespread solicitation of public shareholders for the shares of an issuer
2. Solicitation made for the substantial percentage of an issuer's stock
3. Offer to purchase made a premium over the prevailing market price
4. Terms of the offer firm rather than negotiated
5. Offer contingent on the tender of a fixed number of shares, often subject to a fixed maximum number to be purchased
6. Offer open only a limited period of time
7. Offeree subject to pressure to sell his stock
8. Public announcements of a purchasing program concerning the target company precede or accompany rapid accumulation of larger amounts of the target company's securities

Source: Larry D. Soderquist, *Understanding Securities Laws* (New York: Practicing Law Institute, July 1987), p. 236.

---

3. *Wellman v. Dickinson,* 475 F. Supp. 783 (S.D.N.Y. 1979).

4. *Stromfeld v. Great Atlantic & Pacific Tea Company,* 484 F. Supp. 1264 (S.D.N.Y. 1980), *aff'd* 6464 F. 2d 563 (2nd Cir. 1980). *Kennecott Cooper Corp. v. Curtiss Wright Corp.,* 584 F. 2d 1195 (2nd Cir. 1978).

5. *S-G Securities, Inc. v. Fuqua Investment Company,* 466 F. Supp. 1114 (D. Mass. 1978).

History of the Tender Offer

The tender offer was the most frequently used tool of hostile takeovers in the 1980s, whereas the proxy fight was the weapon of choice in earlier years. Early on, tender offers were first recognized as a powerful means of taking control of large corporations in the acquisition by International Nickel Company (INCO) of the Electric Storage Battery (ESB) Corporation in 1973 (see Chapter 2). International Nickel Company employed its tender offer strategy with the help of its investment banker, Morgan Stanley & Company. As noted in Chapter 2, this takeover was the first hostile takeover by a major, reputable corporation, and the fact that a major corporation and the leading investment bank chose to launch a hostile takeover helped give legitimacy and acceptability to hostile takeovers.

Tender offers had been used even before the ESB acquisition. As early as the 1960s, there was much concern that less reputable business people would use tender offers to wrest control of companies from their legitimate owners. Tender offers were not considered acceptable practice within the corporate community. Moreover, banking institutions, including both investment banks and commercial banks, generally did not provide financing for tender offers. Nonetheless, the effectiveness of tender offers was increasingly being recognized, and in the late 1960s their use began to increase. Tender offers also proliferated outside the United States and represented an important hostile takeover method in Great Britain. In response to the fear of the corporate and financial community that the use of tender offers was growing out of control, the New York Stock Exchange and the American Stock Exchange imposed certain limitations on them. Even so, their numbers continued to rise—from 8 in 1960 to 45 in 1965.

As their use proliferated, a swell of opposition developed on Capitol Hill. Spearheaded by Senator Harrison Williams, the Williams Act was passed in 1968 (see Chapter 3). This law initially had a dampening effect on the number of tender offers, which declined from 115 in 1968 to 34 in 1970. Eventually the market adjusted to the regulations of the new law, and the number rose to 205 in 1981. One reason for the strong rebound following the passage of the Williams Act may have been that, although the law made abusive tender offer practices illegal, it gave a certain legitimacy to the method by providing rules to regulate their use. The clear implication was that if tender offers were made in accordance with federal laws, they were a reasonable business practice. The Williams Act also helped increase the premium associated with tender offers. The average cash takeover premium paid to target stockholders had increased from 32% before the passage of the law to 53% after its enactment.

Overall, the Williams Act facilitated the development of the art of takeover defenses. Before this legislation was passed, tender offers could be so structured that stockholders could be forced to make a quick decision on them. The Williams Act provided management with an extended offer period before the bidder could purchase the shares, giving the targets time to mount increasingly effective takeover defenses.

Reason for Using a Tender Offer

A company usually resorts to a tender offer when a friendly negotiated transaction does not appear to be a viable alternative. The costs associated with a tender offer, such as legal filing fees and publication costs, make the tender offer a more expensive alternative than a negotiated deal. The initiation of a tender offer usually means that the company will be taken over, although not necessarily by the firm that initiated the tender offer. The tender offer may put the company in play, which may cause it to be taken over by another firm that may seek to enter the bidding contest for the target. The auction process may significantly increase the cost of using a tender offer. It also tends to increase the returns enjoyed by target shareholders.

Success Rate of Tender Offers

Based on experience in the years from 1980 to 1997, the success rate of total attempted tender offers for publicly traded companies was 83.4%.[6] This high rate of success is attributable to the fact that the success rate of uncontested tender offers was 91.6%, whereas the success rate for contested tender offers over this period was 52.4% (Figure 6.2).

White knights play an important role in unsuccessful, contested tender offers. For example, in 1988 there were 19 unsuccessful tender offers, of which 6 remained independent and 13 were acquired by a white knight.[7] The historical experience between 1976 and 1989 shows that more companies that are targets of unsuccessful tender offers are taken over by white knights than those that remain independent. From 1990 to 1997 a higher percentage remained independent. For example, for the unsuccessful tender offers that were followed by *Mergerstat Review* from 1993 to 1997, 75% remained independent.

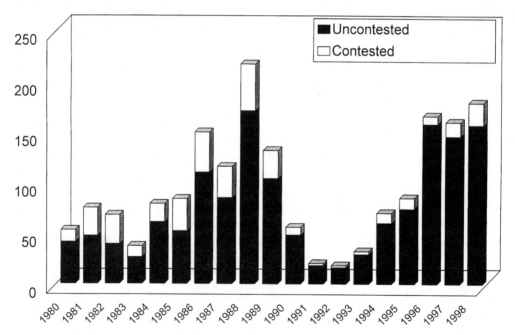

Figure 6.2.   Tender offers, 1980–98: contested vs. uncontested.

Source: Mergerstat Review, 1998, 1999.

---

6. *Mergerstat Review:* 1988, p. 85, and 1998, p. 38.

7. Ibid., p. 86.

Cash versus Securities Tender Offers

The firm that is initiating a tender offer may go with an all-cash tender offer or may use securities as part or all of the consideration used for the offer. Securities may be more attractive to some of the target stockholders because under certain circumstances the transaction may be considered tax-free. (The tax aspects of mergers are discussed in Chapter 15.) The bidding firm may create a more flexible structure for target shareholders by using a double-barreled offer, which is an offer in which the target shareholders are given the option of receiving cash or securities in exchange for their shares. If securities are used in the transaction, they must be registered with the Securities and Exchange Commission (SEC) under the Securities Act of 1933. The securities must also be issued in compliance with the relevant state's Blue Sky Laws, which regulate the issuance and transfer of securities.

The SEC review process may also slow down the tender offer. The acquiring firm is encumbered by the waiting periods of the Williams Act and the Hart-Scott-Rodino Act (see Chapter 3). The use of securities may add another waiting period while the firm awaits the SEC review. The SEC's Division of Corporate Finance has designed a system of selective review whereby it responds to repeat issuers more expeditiously.[8] This system permits only brief review of firms that may have already gone through a thorough review process for prior issues of securities. In these cases, the securities registration and review process may present little or no additional delays beyond the Williams Act and Hart-Scott-Rodino waiting periods.

10-Day Window of the Williams Act

As noted in Chapter 3, the Williams Act requires that purchasers of 5% of the outstanding shares of a company's stock register with the SEC within 10 days by filing a Schedule 13D. The filing of this schedule notifies the market of the purchaser's intentions and alerts stockholders to an impending tender offer. It is in the bidder's interest to purchase shares as quickly as possible during the 10-day period after the acquirer reaches the 5% threshold. If the bidder is able to purchase securities during this period, the stock price may be lower than it would be following the notification to the market of the bidder's intentions. The filing gives the stockholders notice that a bidder may be about to make a bid. This implies a dramatic increase in the demand for the securities and makes them more valuable. Stockholders will demand a higher price to part with their stock, knowing that an upcoming bid and its associated premium may be forthcoming. The 10-day window gives the bidder an opportunity to purchase a larger amount of stock without having to pay the postfiling premium—assuming, however, that rumors have not already anticipated the content of the filing. It is difficult to purchase large amounts of stock and keep the identity of the purchaser secret.

The 10-day window may be turned into a 12-day window if the initial purchases are made on a Wednesday. This would require the purchaser to file on a Saturday. The SEC usually allows the purchaser to file on the next business day, which would be two days later, on Monday.

---

8. Martin Lipton and Erica H. Steinberger, *Takeovers and Freezeouts* (New York: Law Journal Seminar Press, 1987, updated 1994), pp. 1–12.

Response of the Target Management

How should the target company respond to a tender offer? Target company stockholders often view tender offers as a favorable development because they tend to bring high offer premiums. The appropriate response of the target company's management, which will maximize the stock offer premium, is not always clear. The debate centers around whether an active resistance to a tender offer will increase the offer premium. Martin Lipton argues that hostile tender offers may not be in the target stockholders' best interests because they may not maximize stockholder value. Lipton cites evidence that the premium should not be a strong inducement to sell. In the cases he considered, the stock price most often rose above the premium-inclusive offer price.[9] According to Lipton, stockholders were better off in more than 50% of certain tender offers he considered between 1974 and 1979. His analysis did not, however, adjust for the present value of the offer prices that occurred in different years. Lipton's view is that the market price of stocks is usually undervalued and does not reflect the value of a controlling interest in a company. This explanation is reasonable because the price quoted in the marketplace reflects the purchase of a small quantity and does not include a control premium. Lipton presents evidence that the market prices are between 50% and 66.6% of the value to someone acquiring control.

Given the lack of a sufficient control premium, Lipton concludes that the board of directors should not be bound to accept a tender offer. Indeed, the board's ability to reject an offer it considers undervalued is protected by the business judgment rule. Lipton's view is underscored in the case of *Panter v. Marshall Field & Co.*, in which the court upheld the legality of the board of directors of Marshall Field & Co. using defensive measures to thwart a tender offer from Carter Hawley Hale that they considered undervalued. Stockholders sued Marshall Field & Co. when the firm used corporate resources to make defensive acquisitions that would create an antitrust conflict for potential bidders and make the company less attractive. Marshall Field & Co. had become a target because its performance lagged behind that of similar department store chains. Carter Hawley Hale offered more than a 100% premium to Marshall Field & Co. in its tender offer, but the board of directors resisted the bid. These measures were successful, and Carter Hawley Hale was forced to abandon its tender offer. The court reasoned as follows:

> Directors of publicly owned corporations do not act outside the law when they, in good faith, decide that it is in the best interest of the company, and its shareholders, that it remain an independent business entity. Having so determined, they can authorize management to oppose offers which, in their best judgment, are detrimental to the company and its shareholders.[10]

Lipton goes further in citing the evils of tender offers. He believes that tender offers are not in the long-term best interests of corporate America and the competitive position of the U.S. economy. The interests of speculators, who use tender offers to reap bountiful profits, he states, should not be held above the "nation's corporate system."

---

9. Martin Lipton, "Takeover Bids in the Target's Boardroom," *Business Lawyer* 35 (November 1979), pp. 101–133.

10. *Panter v. Marshall Field & Co.*, 486 F. Supp. 1168, N.D. Ill. 1980, as cited in Martin Lipton, "Takeover Bids in the Target's Boardroom: An Update After One Year," *Business Lawyer* 36 (April 1981), pp. 1017–1028.

Two of the most vocal critics of Lipton's position on this issue are Frank Easterbrook and Daniel Fischel.[11] Neither sees much stockholder wealth-maximizing benefits from defensive antitakeover measures. They contend that opposition to a takeover decreases stockholder welfare and that stockholders are better off when the target does not offer resistance to hostile bids. They base their argument on an efficient markets view of securities prices. That is, they see securities markets as being efficient and, therefore, as allowing little deviation between the stock price and its intrinsic value. Their reliance on the accuracy of stock prices is based on the belief that if there were a deviation between price and value, investors would "reap windfall gains." Investors would buy underpriced securities and sell overpriced ones, a process that, in their perspective, would result in accurately valued securities.

If the notion that the market accurately values stock prices is accepted, a significant premium above the market price represents a potential increase in wealth for stockholders. Easterbrook and Fischel believe that takeover defenses deprive stockholders of this increased value. They therefore oppose the court's deference to the business judgment rule in allowing boards of directors to use takeover defenses to defeat tender offers. Easterbrook and Fischel took issue with the application of the business judgment rule in the *Panter v. Marshall Field* decision.

The Marshall Field case is an ideal vehicle for comparing our approach with Lipton's approach. Lipton argues, using the Marshall Field case as an example, that shareholder wealth is maximized if managers are allowed to pursue a policy of independence. But how are stockholders benefited by a legal rule that allows the managers of a target corporation to spend huge sums of stockholders' money (in lawsuits, defensive actions, hiring professionals, and so forth) for the purpose of preventing them from more than doubling the value of their investment? And why should the business judgment rule, a doctrine designed to prevent second-guessing of business decisions by directors, shield this type of conduct from judicial review?[12]

Some theorists argue that takeover defenses may be used to maximize stockholder wealth if they force the bidder to increase the premium but do not defeat the tender offer. Defensive measures may lead to an auction process whereby the premium is bid up to a higher level than the original offer. Easterbrook and Fischel, however, contend that stockholders do not necessarily benefit from this use of defensive measures. They consider the potential for an even higher premium being offered in the future. The defensive measures, they state, may prevent such a bid from being initiated. The target may then be settling for a lower premium than that which might ultimately be offered in the absence of any defensive measures. They believe that merely looking at the premium that resulted from an auction process does not fully capture all the wealth effects of defensive measures. Defensive measures may depress preoffer stock prices, which makes the premium that results from an auction process less attractive.

Looking back to Chapter 5, the reader may recall that research showed that pill-protected companies received higher premiums compared with non–pill-protected firms. Easterbrook and Fischel's view would not accept these positive shareholder wealth effects;

---

11. Frank H. Easterbrook and Daniel R. Fischel, "The Proper Role of a Target's Management in Responding to a Tender Offer," *Harvard Law Review* 94, no. 6 (April 1981), pp. 1161–1202.

12. Frank H. Easterbrook and Daniel R. Fischel, "Takeover Bids, Defensive Tactics and Shareholders Welfare," *Business Lawyer* 36 (July 1981), pp. 1733–1750.

however, they would be concerned about the companies that never received bids because of the presence of the poison pill defense.

Tender Offers and Keeping Management Honest

Supporters of hostile tender offers view them as a monitoring mechanism that keeps management honest and limits agency costs.[13] Without the possibility of a hostile tender offer, managers might be free to take actions that would maximize their own welfare but would fail to produce stock prices that maximize the wealth of equity holders. Knowledge that tender offers can be an effective means of taking control may keep management wary and conscious of the value of the firm's stock. The effectiveness of tender offers makes the possibility of a successful hostile bid most real. In this way, tender offers help to deal with the agency problem of corporations (see Chapter 7).

Individual stockholders have neither the incentive nor the resources to launch a tender offer. A hostile bidder, on the other hand, may have both resources and incentive. The bidder may compare the value of the company under its management and may decide that it exceeds the company's current market value by a sufficient margin to be able to offer stockholders a significant premium and still profit from the takeover. When presented with a takeover bid, shareholders have the opportunity to consider the bidder's valuation, compare it with the value that has been realized by management, and select the one that maximizes their return.

Creation of a Tender Offer Team

The bidding firm assembles its team of essential players and coordinates its actions throughout the tender offer process. The team may be composed of the following members outside the corporation's own management and in-house counsel:

Investment bank. The investment bank will play a key role in providing the requisite financing and advisory services through the tender offer. The investment bank may provide bridge financing, which allows the bidder to "buy now and pay later." It also may ultimately finance the bid by issuing securities such as junk bonds or through securing loan agreements. The investment bank's merger expertise is most important in cases of actively fought hostile acquisitions in which the target employs more sophisticated defensive maneuvers.

Legal advisers. Attorneys who are knowledgeable in the tactics and defenses employed to evade tender offers may be an invaluable source of advice for the bidder. During the 1990s a larger number of law firms began to play prominent roles in merger and acquisition advising. This differed from the 1980s, when two law firms dominated this market.

Information agent. The information agent is typically one of the major proxy soliciting firms, such as Georgeson and Company and D. F. King and Company. The informa-

---

13. Frank H. Easterbrook and Daniel R. Fischel, *The Economic Structure of Corporate Law* (Boston: Harvard University Press, 1991), pp. 171–172

tion agent is responsible for forwarding tender offer materials to stockholders. Proxy firms may also actively solicit the participation of stockholders in tender offers by means of a telephone and mail campaign.

Depository bank. The depository bank handles the receipt of the tender offers and the payment for the shares tendered. The bank makes sure that shares have been properly tendered. An ongoing tabulation is kept for the bidder, allowing the probability of success to be determined throughout the tender offer.

Forwarding agent. The bidder may decide to retain a forwarding agent in addition to the depository bank. The forwarding agent enhances the resources of the depository bank and transmits tenders received to the depository bank. A forwarding agent is particularly useful when there is a concentration of shares in a given area that is not well serviced by the depository bank.

Two-Tiered Tender Offers

A two-tiered tender offer is sometimes referred to as a *front end–loaded* tender offer. It provides for superior compensation for a first-step purchase, followed by inferior compensation for the second tier or the *back end* of the transaction. The technique is designed to exert pressure on stockholders who are concerned that they may become part of a second tier and that they may receive inferior compensation if they do not tender early enough to become part of the first tier. If sufficient shares are tendered in the first tier and if the merger or acquisition is approved, the remaining shareholders can be "frozen out" of their positions and may have to tender their shares for the inferior compensation. The compensation for the two tiers may be broken down into a first-tier, all-cash offer at a higher price for 51% of the target and a second-tier offer at a lower price that may provide noncash compensation such as debentures. The noncash compensation in the form of debentures is often considered inferior when its value is less clear and less exact relative to cash consideration. The two-tiered pricing strategy is often considered coercive to stockholders because it attempts to stampede them into becoming part of the first tier.

The aggressive bidder must choose between two strong alternatives: an all-cash bid for "any-and-all" shares tendered and a two-tiered offer. During the early 1980s the two-tiered offer was a popular weapon of the hostile bidder. As the fourth merger wave progressed, however, hostile bidders, having gained access to large amounts of capital through the junk bond market, found that the all-cash, any-and-all offer was a more effective offensive strategy. The target's board of directors finds it difficult to resist the appeal of the all-cash offer; that is, directors find it hard to justify turning down such an offer at a fixed price that includes a significant premium. When bidders had easy access to junk bond funds, they could more readily finance the higher all-cash premiums. This situation changed toward the end of the 1980s when the junk bond market declined. All-cash offers became far fewer and were often replaced by offers that were financed by more equity and less high-risk debt. This made it more difficult for smaller bidders to participate in major megadeals. However, when the fifth merger wave began to gain momentum in 1997, there was once again a rise in the cash component of transactions.

Bidders who do not have access to large amounts of capital sometimes use the two-tiered offer. They then choose to use their relatively limited capital where it will have the greatest effect. They may concentrate the cash reserves on the first tier of a two-tiered offer while offering securities for the second tier. Mesa Petroleum used such a financing technique in 1982 when it acquired the Great American Oil Company. Mesa borrowed $500 million to make a $40 per share offer for one-half of Great American. This gave Mesa control of Great American and facilitated the merger of the two companies. Mesa's offer provided for the issuance of securities, equity, and subordinated debentures issued by the combined firm. The value of the securities amounted to less than $40 per share.[14]

Regulation of Two-Tiered Tender Offers

When more than the requested number of shares are tendered into the first tier, prorationing is required. For example, in the case of a 100% two-tiered offer, with superior compensation being offered for the first tier, shareholders receive a blended price as follows:

$$P_B = \alpha P_f + (1 - \alpha)P_b \qquad (6.1)$$

where

P_B = blended price of the offer,
P_f = tender offer price for first tier,
P_b = tender offer price for second tier,
P_p = preoffer market price, and
α = percent of shares purchased in the first tier.

The premium is computed as follows:

$$[(P_B/P_p) - 1] \times 100$$

Those who oppose the two-tiered bid maintain that it is too coercive and unfair to shareholders in the second tier, who are entitled to equal treatment under the Williams Act. Two-tiered offers may be coercive in that shareholders in the front end receive better compensation than back-end shareholders. Although courts have ruled that two-tiered tender offers are not illegal *per se,* calls for horizontal equity, equal treatment for all shareholders, gave rise to changes in state corporation laws. In many states these statutes have been amended to try to bring about equitable treatment for all tendering shareholders. These amendments included fair price provisions and redemption rights.

Fair price provisions may require that all shareholders, even those in the second tier, receive a fair price. This price may be equal to the prices paid to the first-tier shareholders. Redemption rights may allow shareholders to redeem their shares at a price similar to the price paid to the first tier.

Corporations also reacted to the use of two-tiered offers in the 1980s. Many have amended their corporate charters to include fair price provisions. Jarrell and Poulsen have reported a dramatic rise in the adoption of fair price provisions in corporate charters in response to the increased use of front end-loaded offers.[15] They found that 354 adoptions of

---

14. Martin Lipton and Erica H. Steinberger, *Takeovers and Freezeouts* (Washington, DC: Law Journal Seminar Press, 1987), pp. 1–85.

15. Greg Jarrell and Annette Poulsen, "Shark Repellents and Stock Prices: The Effects of Anti-takeover Amendments Since 1980," *Journal of Financial Economics* 19, no. 1 (September 1987), pp. 127–168.

fair price amendments took place between 1983 and 1984, which is in sharp contrast to the total of 38 amendments passed between 1979 and 1982. Jarrell and Poulsen attribute this increase to the greater incidence of two-tiered bids in the early 1980s. These corporate charter amendments, however, combined with the passage of specific state laws, have limited the effectiveness of two-tiered bids.

Effect of Two-Tiered Tender Offers on Stockholder Wealth

The charge that two-tiered tender offers are coercive and cause decreases in stockholder wealth remains an open issue. A study by Robert Comment and Greg Jarrell failed to detect such a decline in stockholder wealth resulting from two-tiered bids.[16] They examined 210 cash tender offers between 1981 and 1984 and found far fewer two-tiered offers than any-and-all offers. Their results also showed that stockholders do as well when confronted with a front end-loaded bid than when they have an any-and-all offer. Comment and Jarrell attribute this finding to management's ability to enter into a negotiated transaction with the bidder and achieve equal gains in stockholder wealth when offered two-tiered bids as compared with receiving any-and-all offers. They found that the average premium for the 144 any-and-all offers was 56.6%, whereas the average premium for the 39 two-tiered offers in their sample was 55.9%. It is interesting that the Comment and Jarrell results were not caused by fair price provisions because only 14 of the 210 tender offers in their sample were for firms that had fair price amendments in place. Their sample period predates the passage of many of the fair price amendments. They conclude that there is no need for regulatory changes that prohibit two-tiered bids because they do not appear to have had an adverse impact on shareholder wealth.

Any-and-All versus Partial Tender Offers

Before initiating a tender offer, the bidder must decide whether to make an offer for any-and-all shares tendered or to structure the offer so that only a certain percentage of the outstanding shares are bid for. Generally, the any-and-all offer is considered a more effective takeover tactic and is therefore more difficult to defend against. Partial offers are not considered as valuable because of the risk of oversubscription. In an oversubscribed offer, shares are accepted on a pro rata basis unless the buyer agrees to accept all shares tendered. Stockholders incur the risk that they will not receive the full premium for all the shares they would like to tender. This is not the case in an any-and-all offer.

A partial offer that is designed to take control of the target without a second-step close-out transaction is less attractive to stockholders because they may be left holding shares that have a reduced value after the partial buyout is completed. If some or all of their shares are not included in the shares purchased by the bidder, their price may decline as the market assesses the likelihood of an eventual second-step transaction. If a second-step transaction eventually does occur, it may not contain the same premium as the first-step transaction because the first-step transaction contained a control premium. After the first-step transaction is completed, control is usually established, and the remaining shares may be less valuable to the bidder. First-step transactions are often for cash, which has a clear,

16. Robert Comment and Greg Jarrell, "Two-Tiered and Negotiated Tender Offers," *Journal of Financial Economics* 19, no. 2 (December 1987), pp. 283–310.

fixed value, whereas second-step transactions often use debt or equity securities as consideration. The debt securities may be considered more risky inasmuch as the bidder may have incurred considerable debt to finance the all-cash first-step transaction. As noted previously, stockholders may differ with the bidder on the value of the debt securities in the second-step offer. The bidder sometimes tries to ameliorate these concerns by structuring the all-securities second-step transaction so that it constitutes a tax-free exchange. This advantage for the second-step shareholders may partially offset the higher premium that the first-step shareholders received.

Second-step shareholders also have to be concerned about the bidder's ability to purchase the remaining shares in the second tier. The bidder may be straining its financial resources to take control through the first-step transaction and may later be unable to complete the purchase of the remaining shares. For example, William Farley ran out of money after purchasing 95% of West Point–Pepperell. He had expected to complete the $2.5 billion takeover of West Point–Pepperell through the issuance of junk bonds by his investment banker, Drexel Burnham Lambert, but Drexel Burnham Lambert's financial difficulties, coupled with the decline of the junk bond market, prevented it. Farley was unable to service the debt he held as a result of the 95% share purchase. He realized a lower than expected price for a division of West Point–Pepperell, Cluett, Peabody & Co. ($350 million plus a $60 million note from the buyer).[17] The combined effect of these developments was his eventual default in March 1990.

Transactions are sometimes structured in three steps. A bidder using a three-step transaction is sometimes referred to as a *three-piece suitor.* The general process for such transactions involves the bidder making an initial stock purchase followed by a second-step tender offer. Once control is established and a majority of the shareholders have tendered their shares in the tender offer, a third-step freezeout purchase of the minority shareholders who have not tendered their shares is conducted.

Empirical Evidence on the Effects of Tender Offers

The debate between Lipton and Easterbrook and Fischel has helped define and crystallize the issues. Neither side, however, presents substantive quantitative evidence that measures the purported gains and losses. One study that addresses this issue in a quantitative manner was conducted by Harvard University Professor Paul Asquith as an outgrowth of his doctoral dissertation at the University of Chicago.[18] Asquith examined successful and unsuccessful merger bids between 1962 and 1976 and considered the impact of the bids on daily excess returns to stockholders in the affected companies. Daily excess returns are measures developed by Professor Myron Scholes of Stanford University and are calculated as follows:

$$E_x R_{it} = R_{it} - E(R_{it}) \tag{6.2}$$

---

17. Robert Johnson, "William Farley's Quest for Status Threatens to Topple His Empire." *Wall Street Journal,* 30 April 1990, p. Al.

18. Paul Asquith, "Merger Bids and Stock Returns." *Journal of Financial Economics* 11, no. 1–4 (April 1983), pp. 51–83.

where

E_xR_{it} = excess return for asset i for day t,

t = the day under consideration,

R_{it} = return on asset i on day t, and

$E(R_{it})$ = the expected return to asset i on day t.

The expected return is estimated by adjusting for the risk level of the firm's stock through application of the beta for that security. Beta is a measure of systematic or undiversifiable risk. This concept is discussed further in Chapter 13 and is covered in most corporate finance textbooks.

Asquith's results indicate a strong positive cumulative excess return for targets of successful bids when considering a 60–day window before and after the offer. In is interesting that the market was efficient in anticipating the offer, as reflected by the fact that most of the nearly 20% cumulative excess return was reached before the announcement date (press day). Unsuccessful targets lose most of their almost 10% gains by the end of the 60–day period after the announcement.

According to Asquith, acquiring firms in successful bids experience relatively small gains that persist 60 days after the takeover. Those potential acquirers in unsuccessful takeovers display a 25% cumulative excess return 60 days after the attempted takeover (Figures 6.3 and 6.4).

Wealth Effects of Unsuccessful Tender Offers

Although the premium associated with a successful bid may increase the target shareholder's wealth, the question exists whether the increase in the target's shares caused by the announcement of a bid persists when the bid fails. Michael Bradley, Anand Desai, and E. Han Kim analyzed the returns to stockholders by firms that either received or made *unsuccessful* control-oriented tender offers between 1963 and 1980.[19] They defined a control-oriented tender offer as one in which the bidding firm holds less than 70% of the target's shares and is attempting to increase its holdings by at least 15%. They considered a total of 697 tender offers. The Bradley study measured the impact of the tender offers by examining the cumulative abnormal returns to both the target and the bidding firm. *Abnormal returns* are those that cannot be fully explained by market movements. Cumulative abnormal returns are defined as follows:

$$R_{it} = \alpha_i + \beta_{mt}R_{mit} + \epsilon_{it} \tag{6.3}$$

where:

R_{it} = the cumulative dividend monthly stock return for the ith firm in month t,

R_{mit} = the return on an equally weighted market portfolio month t relative to the announcement of offer,

α, β = the regression parameters, and

e_{it} = a stochastic error term with a mean of zero.

---

19. Michael Bradley, Anand Desai, and E. Han Kim, "The Rationale Behind Interfirm Tender Offers: Information or Synergy," *Journal of Financial Economics* 11 (April 1983), pp. 183–206.

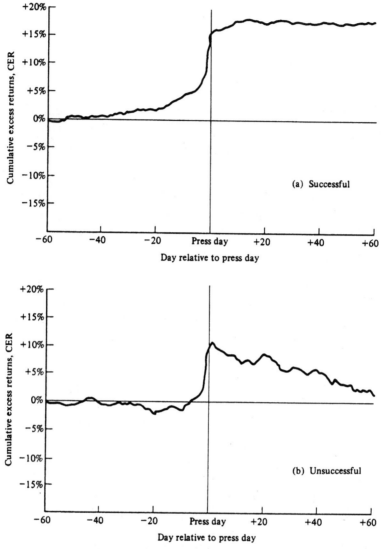

Figure 6.3. Average cumulative excess returns for 211 successful and 91 unsuccessful target firms from 60 days before until 60 days after the merger day in the period 1962–76.

Source: Paul Asquith, "Merger Bids and Stock Returns," *Journal of Financial Economics* 11, nos. 1–4 (April 1983): 70.

One goal of the study was to ascertain whether there were permanent wealth effects from tender offers on the target firm and the acquiring firm. These effects are discussed separately in the following sections.

Target

The results show that target shareholders realize positive abnormal returns surrounding the month of the announcement of the tender offer. The cumulative abnormal returns "show a positive revaluation of the target shares which does not dissipate subsequent to the rejection of the offer."[20] In their total sample of unsuccessful tender offers, 76.8% of the firms

---

20. Ibid., p.192.

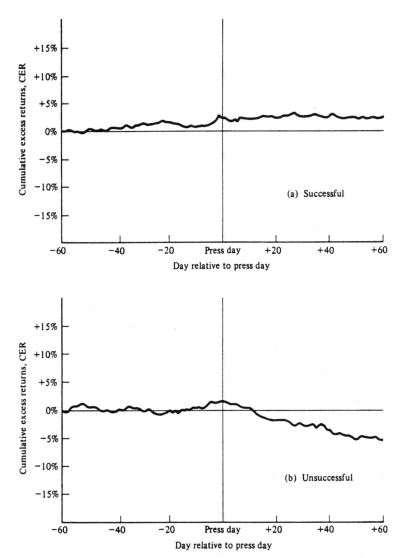

Figure 6.4. Average cumulative excess returns for 196 successful and 89 unsuccessful bidding firms from 60 days before until 60 days after the merger day in the period 1962–76.

Source: Paul Asquith, "Merger Bids and Stock Returns," *Journal of Financial Economics* 11, nos. 1–4 (April 1983): 71.

were taken over and 23.2% were not. A review of Figure 6.5 shows that this positive effect is the case for those that are eventually taken over, whereas it is very different for those that are not taken over.

Bidder

The Bradley study reveals interesting results regarding the impact of tender offers on acquiring firms. As Figure 6.6 shows, the cumulative abnormal returns for bidding firms remain nonnegative when the target is independent and there is no change in control. When the target is acquired by another bidder and the bidder in question loses the tender offer, the value of the bidding firm falls significantly. Bradley and colleagues interpret this effect

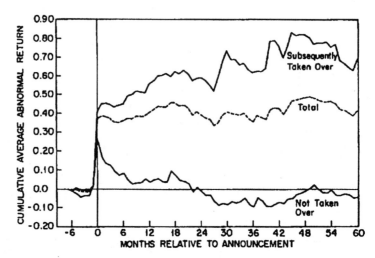

Figure 6.5. Cumulative abnormal returns to unsuccessful target firms—total sample, and "subsequently taken over" and "not taken over" subsamples, in the period 1963–80.

Source: Michael Bradley, Anand Desai, and E. Han Kim, "The Rationale Behind Interfirm Tender Offers: Information or Synergy," *Journal of Financial Economics* 11 (April 1983): 192.

as the market's perception that the bidding firm has lost an opportunity to acquire a valuable resource. This effect is sometimes caused by competitors acquiring resources that will provide a competitive advantage over the firm that lost the bid.

The Bradley study traced the time frame for the wealth effects on unsuccessful bidders and found that, for their sample of tender offers between 1963 and 1980, the average gap between the announcement of the unsuccessful bid and the subsequent successful tender

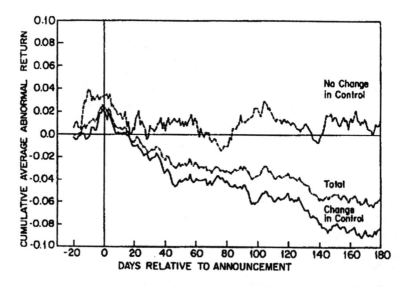

Figure 6.6. Cumulative abnormal returns to unsuccessful bidding firms—total sample, and "no change in control" and "change in control" subsamples, in the period 1963–80.

Source: Michael Bradley, Anand Desai, and E. Han Kim, "The Rationale Behind Interfirm Tender Offers: Information or Synergy," *Journal of Financial Economics* 11 (April 1983): 200.

offer was 60.6 days. Almost all the decline in the value of a portfolio of unsuccessful bidding firms had occurred by day 21. The value of the portfolio declined 2.84% by day 21.

Tender Offer Premiums and Director Independence

Independent directors are those who are not employees and who do not have any other relationship with the corporation. Finance theorists have long contended that the more independent a board is, the greater the return to shareholders.[21] Cotter, Shivdasani, and Zenner studied 169 tender offers between 1989 and 1992.[22] Their results supported Fama and Jensen's hypothesis. They found that targets of tender offers experience shareholder gains that are 20% higher when the board is independent compared with less independent tender offer targets. They also found that bid premium revisions were also higher when the board was more independent. These findings suggest that independent directors are more active supporters of shareholder value than nonindependent directors. Cotter and colleagues extended their research to determine the source of the increased shareholder gains. Their results suggest that the higher target gains come at the expense of returns to bidder shareholders.

Are "Bad Bidders" More Likely to Become Targets?

The impact of poor acquisitions was discussed in Chapter 4 in the context of conglomerate or diversification mergers that performed poorly. It was also discussed in Chapter 2 in the context of the acquisitions that occurred in the third merger wave. The issue of how a firm is affected by a poor acquisition is of interest to stockholders in the bidding firm as they consider whether they should favor a certain acquisition.

In 1988 Mark L. Mitchell and Kenneth Lehn analyzed the effects of poor acquisitions on acquiring firms.[23] They found that the probability of becoming a takeover target was inversely related to the cumulative average returns associated with the firm's acquisitions. They used a logistic regression, which is an econometric technique in which the dependent variable may vary between 0 and 1. In this case, the 0 or 1 represents the probability of whether a firm became a target. Some studies of the impact of acquisitions on acquiring firms show a zero or negative impact while providing clear benefits for the target firm. Mitchell and Lehn contend that the market differentiates between good and bad acquiring firms. Although they found returns to acquirers to be approximately zero, they observed that subsamples of good acquirers outperformed acquiring firms that pursued failed acquisition strategies, or what Mitchell and Lehn refer to as bad bidders. For example, as shown in Figure 6.7, acquiring firms that did not subsequently become targets themselves showed clearly positive returns over a 60–day window around the acquisition announcement. Acquiring firms that became targets of either friendly or hostile acquisitions showed clearly negative returns. In other words, acquisitions by companies that become targets, especially

21. Eugene Fama and Michael Jensen, "Separation of Ownership and Control," *Journal of Law and Economics* 26, 1983, pp. 301–325.

22. James Cotter, Anil Shivdasani, and Marc Zenner, "Do Independent Directors Enhance Target Shareholder Wealth During Tender Offers?" *Journal of Financial Economics*, vol. 43 (2), February 1997, pp. 195–218.

23. Mark L. Mitchell and Kenneth Lehn, "Do Bad Bidders Become Good Targets?" *Journal of Applied Corporate Finance* 3, no. 2 (Summer 1990), pp. 60–69.

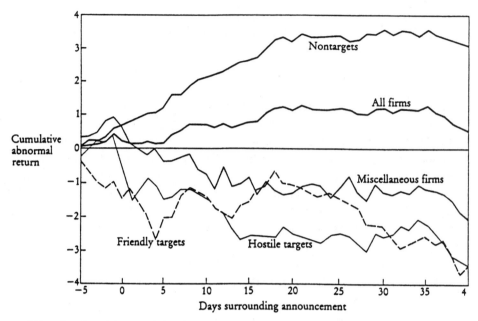

Figure 6.7. Stock price reactions to acquisition announcements, 1982–86.

Source: Mark L. Mitchell and Kenneth Lehn, "Do Bad Bidders Become Good Targets?" *Journal of Applied Corporate Finance* 3, no. 2 (Summer 1990): 60–69.

hostile targets, cause the acquiring company's stock price to fall, whereas acquisition by companies that do not become targets results in an increase in the acquiring firm's stock price.

Mitchell and Lehn's explanation for the returns depicted in Figure 6.7 is twofold. Acquiring companies that become targets make acquisitions that the market expects will reduce the combined profitability of these companies. That is, the market is saying that this is a bad acquisition. The second possible explanation for this phenomenon is that the acquiring company is overpaying for the target. It could be that at some lower price the acquisition would be a better one.

The authors of this study went on to trace the relationship between the acquisitions and subsequent divestitures. They found a statistically significantly negative stock price response (average of 24%) to acquisitions that were subsequently divested. For acquisitions that were not divested, they found a small, not statistically significant, positive stock price response (average of 1.9%). The import of this result is that it seems that at the time of the acquisition announcement, the market is making a prediction regarding which acquisitions are good and which are bad. Mitchell and Lehn's analysis suggests that the market is an efficient predictor of the success of acquisitions.

OPEN MARKET PURCHASES AND STREET SWEEPS

A hostile bidder may accumulate stock in the target before making a tender offer. As noted previously, the purchaser usually tries to keep these initial purchases secret to put as little upward pressure as possible on the target's stock price. To do so, the acquisitions are often made through various shell corporations and partnerships whose names do not convey the true identity of the ultimate purchaser.

Upon reaching the 5% threshold, the purchaser has 10 days before it is necessary to make a public disclosure. This time may be used to augment the bidder's stockholdings. If a bidder engages in an aggressive purchasing program, it is not unusual for the bidder to acquire up to 20% of a target. The larger the purchaser's position in the target, the more leverage the firm has over the target. This leverage may enable the bidder to launch a tender offer that has a high probability of success, given the stockholdings the bidder already possesses. The bidder is also in a better position, as a result of the number of votes he or she already controls, to make a credible threat of a proxy fight. Even if the bidder fails to take control of the board of directors, it may be able to place representatives on the board. This could make operations more difficult for management and enable the bidder to force the company to take actions that favor the bidder, such as paying additional dividends.

Significant stockholdings accumulated through open market purchases may be sufficient to offset defenses such as supermajority voting provisions. They may also be used as a negotiating tool to convince the target to agree to a "friendly tender offer" and to discourage potential white knights from making a bid for the target. The would-be white knight knows that it will have to deal with an unwanted substantial stockholder even if it succeeds in obtaining majority control of the target. The hostile bidder may not want to relinquish its stockholding without receiving a high premium, which may be tantamount to greenmail. The white knight is then faced with the unappealing prospect of paying a premium to the other target shareholders and greenmail to the hostile bidder.

The open market purchase of stock may be a precursor to a tender offer, but it may also be an effective alternative to a tender offer. When a hostile bidder concludes that the tender offer may not be successful, it may decide not to initiate one. The result may be large-scale open market purchases of stock. The goal of these purchases may be to try to acquire enough stock to take control of the target. The hostile bidder's investment bank assists the bidder by providing the necessary financing for these purchases and by locating large blocks of stock to be bought. These share purchases may be made through secret accumulations by the bidder's investment bank through various corporations or partnerships. Once the 5% threshold is crossed, the bidder still has 10 days to file a Schedule 13D. The purchases, however, are sometimes difficult to keep secret because they may also be subject to the filing requirements of the Hart-Scott-Rodino Act. As covered in Chapter 3, a filing under this law is necessary if a bidder purchases more than $15 million of a target's voting stock or acquires control (51%).

The use of street sweeps as an effective takeover tactic was pioneered in 1985 by Hanson Trust PLC. In that year Hanson Trust terminated its tender offer for SCM Corporation and immediately bought 25% of SCM's outstanding stock from arbitragers. The 25% holding was accumulated in just six transactions. This block of stock, which brought Hanson Trust's holdings up to 34.1%, was purchased in response to SCM's defensive leveraged buyout (LBO) proposal. The buyout was prevented by Hanson Trust's stock acquisition because under New York law (where SCM was incorporated), major transactions such as LBOs must be approved by a two-thirds majority. Hanson's 34.1% position prevented SCM from obtaining the requisite two-thirds approval level.

Hanson Trust PLC took advantage of the fact that in a takeover contest larger blocks of stock begin to be concentrated in the hands of arbitragers. This creates an attractive alternative to a tender offer. An astute investment bank advising a bidder knows that a larger holding can be amassed through a small number of transactions.

The Hanson Trust street sweep was challenged in court.[24] The court of appeals ruled that Hanson Trust's open market purchase of stock after its cancellation of its tender offer was not bound by the requirements of the Williams Act. This ruling established a precedent that made street sweeps legal and not in violation of the Williams Act (see the case study, Campeau Corp. v. Allied Stores). The ruling also highlights a loophole in the Williams Act that renders targets vulnerable to street sweeps following an attempted tender offer because of the concentration of shares in the hands of arbitragers, which increases the probability of success for a street sweep.

CASE STUDY: CAMPEAU CORPORATION versus ALLIED STORES— A LOOK AT THE EFFECTIVENESS OF STREET SWEEPS

One notable example of the effectiveness of street sweeps occurred in 1986 when Campeau Corporation, a real estate concern in Toronto, abandoned its tender offer for Allied Stores and immediately purchased 48% of Allied's stock on the open market. Robert Campeau, chairman of the Campeau Corporation, had become involved into a bidding war with Edward J. DeBartolo, who runs a closely held corporation with real estate interests in more than 50 shopping malls, hotels, condominiums, and office buildings. DeBartolo had entered into a partnership with raider Paul Bilzerian, and together they made a $3.56 billion tender offer at $67 per share for Allied. This offer topped Campeau's $66 per share offer. Realizing that his tender offer would not be successful, Campeau canceled the offer and, within 30 minutes of the cancellation, bought 25.8 million shares of Allied, or 48% of the outstanding stock. The stock acquisition was made possible by the work of Jeffries Group, Inc., the brokerage firm that assembled the block of stock. Lipton and Steinberger report that the Jefferies Group had offered the block to the competing bidders before selling it to Campeau.[a]

The street sweep was challenged by the SEC, which argued that the 48% stock purchase was a continuation of Campeau's tender offer. A settlement was reached, and the legal challenge to the street sweep was abandoned.

---

a. Lipton and Steinberger, *Takeovers and Freezeouts*, pp. 1–43.

ADVANTAGES OF TENDER OFFERS OVER OPEN MARKET PURCHASES

Open market purchases may at first seem to provide many advantages over tender offers. For example, they do not involve the complicated legal requirements and costs associated with tender offers. (The bidder must be concerned that the open market purchases will be legally interpreted as a tender offer.) The costs of a tender offer may be far higher than the brokerage fees incurred in attempting to take control through open market purchases of the

---

24. *Hanson Trust PLC v. SCM Corp.*, 774 F. 2d 47 (2d Cir. 1985).

target's stock. As noted previously, Robert Smiley estimated that the total cost of tender offers averaged approximately 13% of the post–tender offer market price of the target's shares.[25]

Open market purchases also have clear drawbacks that are not associated with tender offers. A bidder who purchases shares in the open market is not guaranteed that he or she will be able to accumulate sufficient shares to acquire clear control. If 51% clear control is not achieved, the bidder may become stuck in an undesirable minority position. One advantage of a tender offer is that the bidder is not bound to purchase the tendered shares unless the desired number of shares has been tendered. The bidder who becomes mired in a minority position faces the following alternatives:

- *Do a tender offer.* In this case, the bidder incurs the tender offer expenses in addition to the costs of the open market purchasing program.
- *Begin a proxy fight.* This is another costly means of acquiring control, but the bidder, after having already acquired a large voting position, is now in a stronger position to launch a proxy fight.
- *Sell the minority stock position.* These sales would place significant downward pressure on the stock price and may result in significant losses.

Large-scale open market purchases are also difficult to keep secret. Market participants regard the stock purchases as a signal that a bidder may be attempting to make a raid on the target. This may then change the shape of the target's supply curve for its stock by making it more vertical above some price.[26] This can make a street sweep effective but expensive. Other shareholders may also have the idea that a higher price may be forthcoming and may be reluctant to sell unless a very attractive offer is made. This threshold price may be quickly reached as the available supply of shares on the market, which may be relatively small compared with the total shares outstanding, becomes exhausted. As stockholders come to believe that a bid may be forthcoming, they have an incentive to *hold out* for a higher premium. The holdout problem does not exist in tender offers because the bidder is not obligated to purchase any shares unless the amount requested has been tendered. If the requested amount has not been tendered at the end of the expiration date of the offer, the bidder may cancel the offer or extend it.

A street sweep may be more effective when a bidder is able to locate large blocks of stock in the hands of a small group of investors. In cases in which there have been offers for the company or speculation about impending offers, stock often becomes concentrated in the hands of arbitragers. Although these investors are often eager to sell, they will often only do so at a high price. The existence of large blocks of stock in the hands of *arbitragers* may enable a bidder to amass a significant percentage of the target's stock, perhaps enough to gain effective control of the company, but only if the bidder is willing to pay a possibly painful price. Often the cost will make this method of acquisition prohibitively expensive.

---

25. Robert Smiley, "Tender Offers, Transactions Costs and the Theory of the Firm," *Review of Economics and Statistics* 58 (1976), pp. 22–32.

26. Lloyd R. Cohen, "Why Tender Offers? The Efficient Markets Hypothesis, the Supply of Stock and Signaling," *Journal of Legal Studies* 19, no. 1 (January 1990), pp. 113–143.

PROXY FIGHTS

A *proxy fight* is an attempt by a single shareholder or a group of shareholders to take control or bring about other changes in a company through the use of the proxy mechanism of corporate voting. In a proxy fight, a bidder may attempt to use his or her voting rights and garner support from other shareholders to oust the incumbent board and/or management.

Proxy Fight Data

The number of proxy fights increased significantly toward the end of the fourth merger wave. For example, they rose from 21 in 1987 to 36 in 1988 and to a peak of 41 in 1989, followed by 35 in 1990 (Figure 6.8). The rise in proxy contests at the end of the fourth merger wave coincided with the collapse of the junk bond market, which made tender offer financing more difficult to find. Just as the number of mergers and acquisitions fell dramatically in the early 1990s, so did proxy fights, which declined steadily through 1993 but rebounded starting in 1994. Since then proxy fights have maintained an important role in control contests.

To know how the proxy device may be used to take control of a target company, we need a basic understanding of the workings of the corporate election process.

Corporate Elections

Corporate elections for seats on the board of directors are typically held once a year at the annual stockholders' meeting. The board of directors is particularly important to the cor-

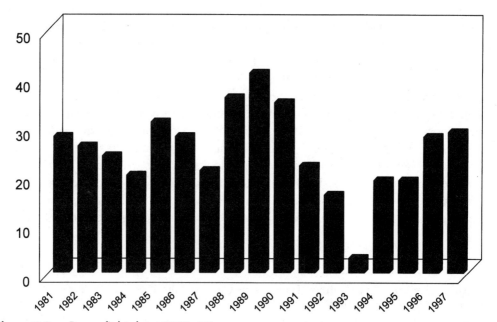

Figure 6.8.   Proxy fight data, 1981–97.

Source: Georgeson & Company, Inc.

poration because the board selects the management who, in turn, run the corporation on a day-to-day basis. The date and time of the stockholders' meeting is stipulated in the company's articles of incorporation. The date is usually chosen to coincide with the end of the company's fiscal year, when the annual report and the summary of the firm's financial results are available for the stockholders' review. Securities and Exchange Commission rules require that the annual report be sent to stockholders before the annual meeting. Because it takes time to produce the annual report, the annual meeting is usually held four to five months after the close of the firm's fiscal year.[27]

Regulation of Proxy Contests

The proxy solicitation process was originally governed by state laws. The process fell within the oversight of federal law through the Securities and Exchange Act of 1934. This law provided for the SEC to enforce and administer the proxy rules that are set forth in this law. At that time, in the wake of the stock market crash of 1929, the primary perceived need was for more complete disclosure in the proxy solicitation process. The Securities and Exchange Act provided for more detailed and complete disclosure in communications with shareholders through the solicitation process. This disclosure is required pursuant to Section 14 of the Securities Exchange Act.

Shareholder Apathy

Shareholder elections tend to be characterized by considerable voter apathy. Some theorists contend that shareholders who supply capital to corporations should not necessarily have an interest in managing the company's affairs.[28] They assert that shareholders may adopt the easier route of voting with their feet; that is, by selling their shares when the firm and its management do not perform up to expectations. In their view, the sale of the shares is a far less expensive option than a collective action to alter the course of the company or to take control away from management. Moreover, they believe that the federal proxy laws, which require extensive disclosure, add further burdensome costs to dissenting groups, which creates a disincentive to engage in a proxy fight.

Smaller individual shareholders are naturally apathetic, given their share of ownership in the company, but, surprisingly, larger institutional shareholders often display similar apathy. Institutional shareholders are increasingly dominating equity markets and now account for more than 42.7% of the total equity holdings in the United States.[29] Although they are an important factor in equity markets, they have historically been passive investors and do not tend to take an active role in the control of the companies in which they invest.[30]

---

27. Herbert A. Einhorn and J. William Robinson, *Shareholder Meetings* (New York: Practicing Law Institute, 1984), p. 27.

28. Frank Easterbrook and Daniel Fischel, "Voting in Corporate Law," *Journal of Law and Economics* 23 (1983), pp. 395–427.

29. Carolyn K. Brancato and Patrick A. Gaughan, Institutional Investors and Their Role in Capital Markets, Columbia University Center for Law and Economics Monograph, 1988.

30. Robert Monks and Nell Minow, "Article on the Employee Benefit Research Institute Report on Proxy Voting," Institutional Shareholders Services, Washington, D.C.

The traditionally passive role of institutionalized shareholders is starting to change, as in celebrated instances such as the public battle in 1985 between Ross Perot and Roger Smith, chief executive officer (CEO) of General Motors.[31] Additional evidence of institutional shareholders' activism came in the 1989 proxy fight between Carl Icahn and Texaco. One of the largest pension funds in the United States, the California Public Employees Retirement System (CALPERS), sided with management and against Icahn. In return, the $56 billion pension fund was rewarded with a director being named from their list of candidates. The CALPERS' position in the Texaco proxy fight notwithstanding, the late 1980s and early 1990s were periods of rising institutional shareholder activism.[32] This somewhat higher level of shareholder activism maintained itself into the fifth merger wave.[33]

One impediment to such activism is the fear that the corporations will pressure institutions such as pension funds to vote with management.[34] That pressure may come from a CEO who gives the company's pension fund managers explicit instructions to vote with management in proxy contests.

Take the case of Avon Products, whose CEO, Hicks Waldron, is an outstanding hawk on proxy voting. In a speech to institutional investors last year, Waldron said that when his company's managers intend to vote against management, "they must have my approval. Then we instruct the investment managers how to vote." And in an interview with this magazine last Spring for an article on shareholder activism (May 1987), Waldron said that during the previous proxy season he had ordered his managers to reverse all their antimanagement votes.[35]

Although institutions may be becoming more active, the evidence still indicates that, despite their ability to collectively wield considerable power and control proxy contests, they do not often choose to use this power. Considering that the institutional money managers' primary goal is to maximize the value of their portfolios, it is not surprising that they show little interest in the day-to-day running of the companies in which they invest. Not until the firm's performance flags do they look to divest their holdings.

The sale of an institution's large holdings may depress the stock price. In such an event, the institution may be locked into its position and thereby create an incentive for great activism by institutions. The active monitoring of individual companies by institutions, however, is hampered by the fact that it may hold equity in hundreds of companies. The large number of firms held in an institution's portfolio precludes micromanagement of their holdings. The fact that institutions may be temporarily locked into some of their positions, and the difficulties in micromanagement of their portfolios, helps explain why institutions are not active investors.

---

31. Doron P. Levin, *Irreconcilable Differences* (Boston: Little, Brown, 1989).

32. Robert Monks and Nell Minow, *Power and Accountability* (New York: Harper Business, 1991), pp. 230–237.

33. Carolyn Kay Brancato, *Institutional Investors and Corporate Governance* (New York: Richard D. Irwin, 1997), pp. 81–131.

34. Speech at the United Shareholders' Meeting by Nell Minow, Institutional Shareholders Services, Washington, D.C.

35. Hilary Rosenberg, "The Proxy Voting Crackdown," *Pensions* (April 1988), pp.105–110.

CASE STUDY: ICAHN versus TEXACO— THE ROLE OF INSTITUTIONAL INVESTORS

Institutional investors account for almost 43% of total equity markets.[a] The percentage has been steadily rising for the past few decades. Given the significant holdings they account for, combined with the fact that a small number of institutions may control larger percentages of a company's stock, these investors may be the key to the success of a proxy contest. Historically, however, they have been loyal supporters of management. One example of this loyalty was the 1988 unsuccessful proxy contest that Carl Icahn waged to gain five seats on Texaco's 14-member board of directors. At that time Texaco was in bankruptcy after its disastrous lawsuit with Penzoil. Icahn favored various strategic changes, including asset sales, such as the sale of Texaco Canada and Caltex Petroleum. He even interposed himself as a possible buyer by initiating his own $60–per-share tender offer for the large oil company, which would be partially financed through the sale of $5.3 billion of Texaco assets.[b]

In spite of his intensive lobbying, including the able assistance of the leading proxy solicitation firm D. F. King, Icahn failed to win the crucial support of the institutional investors. He lost the battle by a 41.3% to 58.7% margin in Texaco's favor. The key to Texaco's win was Icahn's failure to receive support from the institutions holding large blocks of Texaco stock. Icahn's abortive attempt to take control of the company was not without benefits for the bidder. Texaco acquiesced to his pressure by announcing two special dividends of $8 per share. Texaco was also forced to redeploy $7 billion in assets, including the sale of Deutsche Texaco and Texaco Canada.

This proxy contest is instructive for several reasons. First, it highlights the crucial role that institutions may play; Icahn failed to garner sufficient institutional support and thereby lost the contest. Second, it highlights the problematic nature of proxy contests, in which a well-financed insurgent, aided by the best proxy advisors and a substantial share position of 14.9% of Texaco's equity, may fail to be successful. On the other hand, even in failure, Icahn remained a credible threat and was able to accomplish several of the structural changes he sought.

---

a. Carolyn Brancato and Patrick A. Gaughan, "The Growth of Institutional Investors in U.S. Capital Markets," The Institutional Investor Projects: Columbia University School of Law, November 1988.
b. Mark Stevens, *King Icahn* (New York: Dutton Publishing Co.,1993), p. 254.

Voting by Proxy

Approximately 80% of annual shareholder meetings are held in the Spring at a site selected by management. Not all interested stockholders find it possible to attend the stockholders' meeting to execute their votes, simply because they have other commitments or because they are scattered throughout the world. The voting process has been made easier through the use of proxies. Under the proxy system, shareholders may authorize another person to vote for them and to act as their "proxy." Most corporate voting is done by proxies.

Calling a Stockholders' Meeting

The ability to call a stockholders' meeting is very important to a bidder who is also a stockholder in the target firm. Upon establishing an equity position in the target, the hostile bidder may want to attempt to remove the board of directors and put in place a board that is favorable to the bidder. Such a board may then approve a business combination or other relationship with the bidding firm. The meeting may also be used to have the stockholders approve certain corporate actions, such as the deactivation of antitakeover defenses or the sale of certain assets and the payment of a dividend from the proceeds of this sale. If the next annual meeting is not scheduled for several months, the bidder may want to call a meeting sooner. The ability to call a special meeting, at which the issue of a merger or a new election may be considered, is determined by the articles of incorporation, which are governed by the prevailing state corporation laws. Most state laws allow meetings to be called if a certain percentage of shareholders request it. As an antitakeover defense, companies sometimes try to amend the corporate charter so that there are limitations on the ability of certain types of shareholders to call a special meeting.

Record Date

The corporation must notify all *stockholders of record* of an election. Only those stockholders recorded on the stock transfer books as owners of the firm's stock on the record date may vote at the election. The record date is used for other purposes as well, such as to decide who will receive dividends or notice of a particular meeting. The record date is important because the firm's stock may trade actively, with the owners changing continually. The record date is usually no more than 60 days, but no less than 10 days, from the meeting date. As the owners of stock change, the record date specifies which stockholders will be able to vote. Stockholders who buy the stock before the meeting but after the meeting date do not receive notice of the meeting. If the stock is held under a *street name,* such as a brokerage firm, the stockholder relinquishes the right to receive notice of events such as meetings.

A stock price will often fall after the record date in a proxy contest.[36] This reflects that the market considers a stock less valuable when it does not carry the right to participate in an upcoming proxy contest. Presumably, this reflects some of the value of the right of voting participation in proxy fights.

Shares Held in Street Names

Stock may be held in street names for a variety of reasons. Stockholders who turn over their portfolios often may keep their stocks in their brokerage firm's name to expedite the registration of their securities. Many stockholders decide they do not want to be bothered with keeping their share certificates and simply leave their shares with the broker, who keeps them in the firm's name. A stockholder may be required to leave the purchased shares with the stockbroker if they were used as collateral in a margin purchase. The shareholdings are left with the broker in case the value of the collateral, the shares, falls. The stockholder will then get a margin call, and the shares might be sold if the shareholder cannot provide more collateral.

---

36. Ronald C. Lease, John J. McConnell, and Wayne E. Mikkelson, "The Market Value of Control in Publicly Held Corporations," *Journal of Financial Economics* 11 (1983), pp. 439–472.

Bidders who are considering taking control of a company may want to keep the shares in the name of their brokerage firm to conceal the true identity of the owner of the shares. If the market anticipates an upcoming bid, the share price may rise. Keep in mind that under the Williams Act, bidders must make sure that they register their cumulative holdings, should they rise to the 5% level, with the SEC.

Approximately 70% of all corporate stock is held in street names, 30% in the name of brokerage firms and the remaining 40% in bank nominee names.[37]

The physical exchange of shares is not the *modus operandi* of stock sales and purchases. Most brokerage firms do not hold the shares entrusted to them at the brokerage firm; rather, they keep them at a *depository.* One of the largest depositories in the United States is the Depository Trust Company located in New York City. When the shares are held in a depository, they are usually in the depository's name. Although the issuing corporation may obtain the names of the owners of the shares from the depository, this list may not be very helpful. The depository will show the street names for those shares held by brokerage firms. This may not indicate, however, who the real beneficial owners are. Efforts have been made in recent years to require that the depository list reflect the true owners of the firm's stock.

Two Forms of Proxy Contests

Typically, there are two main forms of proxy contests.

1. *Contests for seats on the board of directors.* An insurgent group of stockholders may use this means to replace management. If the opposing slate of directors is elected, it may then use its authority to remove management and replace them with a new management team.

2. *Contests about management proposals.* These proposals concern the approval of a merger or acquisition. Management may oppose the merger, and the insurgent group of stockholders may be in favor. Other relevant proposals might be the passage of antitakeover amendments in the company's charter. Management might be in favor, whereas the insurgent group might be opposed, believing that its opposition will cause the stock price to fall and/or reduce the likelihood of a takeover.

Regulation of Proxy Contests

The SEC regulates proxy contests, and its staff monitors the process to ensure that the participants comply with proxy regulations. All materials that are used to influence the outcome of the contest must be submitted to the SEC examiners in advance. This includes newspaper announcements, materials being mailed to shareholders, and press releases. If the examiners find some of these materials objectionable, they may require that the information be reworded or include additional disclosure.

---

37. James Heard and Howard Sherman. *Conflicts of Interest in the Proxy System* (Washington, DC: Investor Responsibility Research Center, 1987), p. 74.

In an effort to strike back against the use of proxy fights by insurgents, companies sometimes petition the SEC to have it issue a "no action" letter. A no action letter disallows a shareholder proposal. The SEC is empowered to do this under Section 14 (a) 8 of the Securities and Exchange Act. Such a letter may be issued if it can be demonstrated that the proposal is clearly not in the interests of other shareholders, serves only the personal interests of its proponent, or if it is designed to redress a personal claim of grievance of the shareholder.

Proxy Contests: From the Insurgents' Viewpoint

In a proxy contest, an insurgent group attempts to wrest control of the target by gathering enough supporting votes to replace the current board with board members of the group's choosing. The following characteristics increase the likelihood that a proxy fight will be successful.

Insufficient voting support for management. Management normally can count on a certain percentage of votes to support its position. Some of these votes might be through management's own stockholdings. Without a strong block of clear support for management among the voting shareholders, management and the incumbent board may be vulnerable to a proxy fight.

Poor operating performance. The worse the firm's recent track record, the more likely other stockholders will vote for a change in control. Stockholders in a firm that has a track record of declining earnings and a poor dividend record are more likely to support an insurgent group advocating changes in the way the firm is managed.

Sound alternative operating plan. The insurgents must be able to propose changes that other stockholders believe will reverse the downward direction of the firm. These changes might come in the form of asset sales with the proceeds paid to stockholders by means of higher dividends. Another possibility could be a plan that provides for the removal of antitakeover barriers and a receptive approach to outside offers for the sale of the firm.

Effectiveness of Shareholder Activism

In 1989 John Pound conducted a study of the effectiveness of shareholder activism by examining various countersolicitations by shareholders who opposed management's antitakeover proposals. Pound analyzed a sample of 16 countersolicitation proxy fights by shareholder groups that occurred in the 1980s. He reported the following results:[38]

- Countersolicitations were unsuccessful more often than they were successful. Dissidents in Pound's sample were successful only 25% of the time.
- When shareholders approved the contested provisions, the net-of-market share values of the company dropped an average of 6%. The range of stock price reactions was be-

38. John Pound, "Shareholder Activism and Share Values," *Journal of Law and Economics* (October 1989), pp. 357–379; also in Patrick A. Gaughan, ed., *Readings in Mergers and Acquisitions* (Boston: Basil Blackwell, 1994), pp. 235–254.

tween 23% and 230%. Pound found that when the amendments were defeated, stock prices rose.

- The majority of the countersolicitations that Pound examined were preceded by a direct attempt to take control. In 8 of 16 countersolicitations in his sample, the dissidents had made an outright offer to take control of the company. In another 7 cases, the dissidents had purchased a large stake in the firm. In only 1 of the 16 cases was there no attempt to take control.

CASE STUDY: TORCHMARK VERSUS AMERICAN GENERAL

Insurgents may lose a proxy fight and still achieve some of their objectives. A hotly contested battle for control may set in motion a process that may bring about major changes in the way a firm is managed or even the sale of the firm. The 1990 proxy battle for American General is a case in point. Torchmark Corporation had attempted to place 5 new members on American General's 15–member board of directors. Torchmark, a small insurance company located in Birmingham, Alabama, was approximately one-sixth the size of the larger insurance company. Torchmark criticized what it thought was the poor performance of American General compared with the performance of Torchmark. As is typical of proxy fights, Torchmark conducted this critical campaign through full-page advertisements in the major financial media. The advertisement placed in the *New York Times* cited the relatively higher growth in dividends, stock prices, earnings per share, and return on equity of Torchmark. American General won its proxy battle with Torchmark, which had sought to take over American General. Its success may be partially attributed to support from institutional investors who controlled approximately 70% of American General's shares.[a]

Institutions, however, were disappointed with American General's relatively poor performance. In response to criticism, American General's management announced an increase in its quarterly dividend from $0.39 to $0.80 per share. In addition, at their victorious annual meeting in May 1990, CEO Harold Hook announced that the company, which was vulnerable to a hostile takeover because of its lagging stock price (approximately $40 per share before the meeting), would be put up for sale.[b]

---

a. Michael Allen and Randall Smith, "Sale of American General Sought in Spite of Vote," *Wall Street Journal,* 3 May 1990, p. A3.

b. Ibid.

The Proxy Fight Process

It is easier to understand the proxy fight process if it is broken down into discrete steps such as the following:

Step 1. *Starting the Proxy Fight.* A proxy fight for control of a company may begin when a bidder, who is also stockholder, decides to attempt to change control at the upcoming stockholders' meeting. An insurgent group of stockholders may have the right to call a special meeting at which the replacement of management may be formally considered. A proxy fight might also come as a result of a management proposal for a major change, such as the sale of the firm or the installation of certain antitakeover defenses.

Step 2. *The Solicitation Process.* In advance of the stockholders' meeting, the insurgent stockholder group attempts to contact other stockholders to convince them to vote against management's candidates for the board of directors or to vote for an acquisition or against certain antitakeover amendments. The process of contacting stockholders is usually handled by the proxy solicitor hired by the insurgent group. Management may have a proxy firm on retainer and, if the proxy battle is particularly contentious, may choose to hire other proxy firms. These proxy firms, which may have their own lists of stockholders compiled from various sources, may use a staff of workers to repeatedly call stockholders to convince them of the merits of their client's position. Materials are then distributed to the beneficial owners of the stock. The depositories will submit a list of shareholders and their holdings to the issuing corporation.

The issuing corporation will try to deal directly with the beneficial owners of the shares. An insurgent group may sue to have the issuing corporation share this information with the insurgent stockholders so as to have the interested parties on a more equal footing. When the shares are registered in the names of banks and trust companies, these institutions may or may not have voting authority for these shares. The banks may have voting authority to vote on all, some, or no issues. This voting authority may be such that the bank may vote on minor issues but must consult the beneficial owners on major issues such as a merger.

When the shares are held in a brokerage firm's name, the broker may or may not have the authority to vote the shares. Stock exchange rules and SEC regulations determine whether the broker may do so. If the broker is not a trustee, the broker must contact the shareholder for voting instructions. Normally, if the broker does not hear from the stockholder at least 15 days before the meeting, he or she may vote the shares (assuming the broker has attempted to contact the shareholder at least 25 days before the meeting). In a contest for control, or when there is a rival insurgent group with counterproposals or candidates, however, the broker may not vote even if he or she has not received instructions from the beneficial owner. A beneficial owner is a broad definition of the legal owners of a security. The beneficial owner has the ultimate power to dispose of the holding. This is generally the party listed on the stock transfer sheets as the owner on the record date.

To expedite the process, the brokerage firm will tabulate the votes from its various proxies and submit its own summary master proxies reflecting the combined votes of its various clients.

Step 3. *The Voting Process.* Upon receiving the proxies, stockholders may then forward their votes to the designated collector, such as a brokerage firm. The votes are sent to the proxy clerks at the brokerage firms to tabulate them.

The brokerage firm or bank usually keeps a running total of the votes as they are received and submits the vote results shortly before the corporation meeting. When the votes are submitted to the issuing corporation, tabulators appointed by the company count them. Voting inspectors are often used to oversee the tabulation process and help ensure its accuracy. The process takes place in an area that is sometimes referred to as the "snake pit." In a proxy fight, both the issuing corporation and the dissident group frequently have their own proxy solicitors present throughout the voting tabulation process to help ensure that their client's interests are dealt with fairly. Proxy solicitors are alert to any questionable proxies, which they then will challenge.

A proxy might be challenged if the same shares are voted more than once or if it was not signed by the party with voting authority. In cases in which more than one vote has been submitted, the vote with the latest date is usually selected. Major discrepancies in the voting process are usually followed by legal actions in which the losing party sues to invalidate the election.

ROLE OF THE INDEPENDENT ELECTION CORPORATION OF AMERICA

The Independent Election Corporation of America (IECA) may be hired to carry out most of its proxy-related functions. The IECA helps ensure that stockholders who are interested in exercising their votes receive their proxy materials in time to participate in the election. The IECA receives the list of the beneficial owners of the shares from the brokerage firms in advance of the election. The IECA then notifies the issuing company that it will be contacting the shareholders and asks the issuing company to forward a specific number of proxy materials to the IECA.

Upon receipt of the proxy materials, the IECA forwards them to the beneficial owners in a timely manner. The IECA sends a shareholder vote authorization form with the proxy materials.[39] The shareholder provides the voting instructions on the form. Votes are totaled by the IECA, and the issuing company is informed of the results.

Voting Analysis

The votes of stockholders are grouped into the following categories.[40]

Shares controlled by insurgents and shareholder groups unfriendly to management. This is the core of the insurgents' support. The greater the number of shares that this group commands, the more likely it is that the proxy fight will be successful.

Shares controlled by directors, officers, and employment stock ownership plans (ESOPs). This category tends to represent the core of management's support. Directors and officers will surely vote with management. Shares held in ESOPs also tend to vote with management because workers may be concerned that a change in control may mean layoffs. In the 1990 proxy battle between Harold Simmons of NL

39. James E. Heard and Howard Sherman, *Conflicts of Interest in the Proxy Voting System* (Washington, D.C.: Investor Responsibility Research Center, 1987), p. 83.

40. This section is adapted from a presentation by Morris J. Kramer, "Corporate Control Techniques: Insurgent Considerations." In James W. Robinson, ed., *Shareholders Meetings and Shareholder Control in Today's Securities Market* (New York: Practicing Law Institute, 1985).

Industries and the Lockheed Corporation, Simmons attributed his defeat in part to the 18.91% of the outstanding shares of Lockheed that were held in the firm's ESOP, which was formed in 1989.[41]

CASE STUDY: HAROLD SIMMONS versus LOCKHEED

An example of one of the proxy contests that took place following the end of the fourth merger wave was the battle between investor Harold Simmons and the Lockheed Corporation. Simmons attempted to take control of Lockheed through the proxy process. Through his company NL Industries, Simmons launched a proxy battle for control of Lockheed Corporation. Using Houston-based NL industries, which owned 19% of Lockheed, he nominated its own slate of directors and submitted a proposal to shareholders to eliminate some antitakeover defenses such as Lockheed's poison pill. This poison pill becomes effective when a shareholder acquires more than 20%.[a] In this instance, however, Simmons failed to convince enough institutional owners of the firm's stock that they should vote for his directors and proposal. As a conciliatory gesture to the insurgents on shareholder rights issues, however, management agreed to take steps to have Lockheed elect to be exempt from the antitakeover provisions of the Delaware antitakeover law. In addition, management, in response to pressure from institutional investors, agreed to allow confidential shareholder voting.[b]

---

a. Randall Smith and David Hilder, "Raiders Shorn of Junk Gird for Proxy Fights," *Wall Street Journal,* 7 March 1990, p. C1.

b. Wartzman and Blumenthal, "Lockheed Wins Proxy Battle with Simmons," *Wall Street Journal,* 11 April 1990, p. A3.

Shares controlled by institutions. As noted previously, large institutions control equity markets; they are by far the largest category of stockholders. Institutions have historically tended to be passive shareholders and have usually voted with management. This situation is starting to change as institutions are becoming more outspoken and are putting more pressure on management to maximize the value of their shareholdings. If the institutions can be convinced that a change in control may greatly increase value, they may vote in favor of the insurgent's position.

Shares controlled by brokerage firm. Certain stock exchange rules, such as those instituted by the New York Stock Exchange and the American Stock Exchange, do not allow brokerage firms to vote the shares held in their name on behalf of clients without receiving voting instructions from the owners of the shares. Voting instructions tend to be required for issues such as mergers or antitakeover amendments. Large amounts of shares tend to be held in street names. Brokerage firms, however, are generally not active voters in proxy fights. The reason for this may be traced to the

---

41. Rick Wartzman and Karen Blumenthal, "Lockheed Wins Proxy Battle with Simmons," *Wall Street Journal,* 11 April 1990, p. A3.

problems of securing voting instructions, coupled with the fact that one of the brokerage firm's goals is to maximize its commissions and the value of its portfolios. Voting in proxy fights may not pay a return in the foreseeable future. The corporation sends voting materials to the brokerage firms, which, in turn, are supposed to forward these materials to the "beneficial owners" of the shares. As of 1986 the issuing corporation has been able to send the materials directly to the beneficial owners by asking the brokerage firm for the names and addresses of the owners. These names and addresses are supplied unless the shareholders have asked that they not be given out.

Shares controlled by individuals. Given the larger equity base of many public corporations, this group of stockholders may not constitute a large percentage of the votes. In some cases, however, they may be important. Individual stockholders tend to vote with management. In some instances, major individual shareholders may be the focal point of the tender offer. For example, Kamal Adham, a major stockholder in Financial General Bankshares, Inc., solicited shareholder support for a proxy fight in favor of the approval of an acquisition of Financial General by a company owned by Adham and others.[42] Adham lost the proxy fight, but a plan for the serious consideration of a merger was later adopted.

The Costs of a Proxy Fight

A proxy fight may be a less expensive alternative to a tender offer. Tender offers are costly because they are offers to buy up to 100% of the outstanding stock at a premium that may be as high as 50%. In a tender offer, the bidder usually has certain stockholdings that may be sold off in the event the tender offer is unsuccessful. The bidder may take a loss unless there is an available buyer, such as a rival bidder or the target corporation. The stock sales, however, may be a way for the bidder to recapture some of the costs of the tender offer. Although a proxy fight does not involve the large capital outlays that tender offers require, they are not without significant costs. The losers in a proxy fight do not have a way to recapture their losses. If the proxy fight is unsuccessful, the costs of the proxy battle are usually not recoverable. In a minority of circumstances, however, the insurgents may recover their costs from the corporation.

The major cost categories of a proxy fight are as follows:

Professional fees. A team of professionals is necessary to carry out a successful proxy fight. This team usually includes proxy solicitors, investment banks, and attorneys. The larger the company and the more contentious the issues, the more professionals involved and the greater the fees.

Printing, mailing costs, and "communications costs." The proxy materials must be printed and distributed to stockholders. A staff may be assembled by the proxy solicitation firm to contact stockholders directly by telephone. This may be supplemented through full-page advertisements in the *Wall Street Journal,* such as the

42. "NLT Holders Reject by 5–3 Margin a Plan to Create Group to Study Acquisition Bids," *Wall Street Journal,* 13 May 1982, p. 6.

advertisement placed by Lockheed's CEO citing the board of directors' opposition to Harold Simmons's proxy fight (Figure 6.9). Brokerage firms must be compensated for the costs of forwarding the proxy materials to stockholders. Major proxy battles, such as the 1990 Lockheed–NL Industries contest, may bring firms like D. F. King and Company, which represented NL Industries, or Georgeson and Company, which represented Lockheed, in excess of $1 million.[43]

Litigation costs. Proxy fights, like tender offers, tend to be actively litigated. Both parties incur significant legal fees. For example, the insurgent group may have to sue for access to the stockholder list. The corporation pays management's legal fees, whereas the insurgent group must pay its own legal expenses. Management also has the advantage in this area.

Other fees. Various other expenses, such as tabulation fees, are associated with the voting process. The tabulation may be done by the issuing company, the company's transfer agent, or a firm that specializes in tabulation work for corporate elections.

Shareholder Wealth Effects of Proxy Contests

Peter Dodd and Jerrold Warner conducted a study of 96 proxy contests for seats on the boards of directors of companies on the New York Stock Exchange and the American Stock Exchange.[44] Their research revealed a number of interesting findings on the impact of proxy contests to the value of stockholders' investments in these firms. They showed that a positive stock price effect is associated with proxy contests. In a 40–day period before and including the announcement of the proxy contest, a positive, abnormal stock price performance of 0.105 was registered. Based on these results, Dodd and Warner concluded that proxy contests result in an increase in value inasmuch as they help facilitate the transfer of resources to more valuable uses.

The positive wealth effects of the Dodd and Warner study were confirmed in later research by DeAngelo and DeAngelo.[45] In a study of 60 proxy contests for board seats, they found an average abnormal shareholder wealth increase equal to 4.85% in a two-day window around the announcement of the dissident activity, whereas an 18.76% increase was associated with a 40–day window, which is the same time period as that of the Dodd and Warner study. DeAngelo and DeAngelo traced the source of the shareholder gains cases in which the dissident activity led to the sale or liquidation of the company.

More recent research further confirmed the positive shareholder wealth effect of prior studies. In a large study of 270 proxy contests that occurred between 1979 and 1994, J. Harold Mulherin and Annette B. Poulsen found that proxy contests help create shareholder value.[46] They traced most of the gains to the acquisition of the firms that occurred around

43. Richard Hylton, "Advisers in Forefront of New Proxy Wars," *New York Times,* 30 March 1990, p. DI.

44. Peter Dodd and Jerrold Warner, "On Corporate Government: A Study of Proxy Contests," *Journal of Financial Economics* 11, no. 1–4 (April 1983), pp. 401–438.

45. Hamj DeAngelo and Linda DeAngelo, "The Role of Proxy Contests in the Governance of Publicly Held Companies," *Journal of Financial Economics* (June 1989), pp. 29–60.

46. J. Harold Mulherin and Annette B. Poulsen, "Proxy Contests and Corporate Change: Implications for Shareholder Wealth," *Journal of Financial Economics* 47, 1998, pp. 279–313.

✈️Lockheed Shareholders:

IMPORTANT INFORMATION ABOUT YOUR INVESTMENT
(Part One)

Harold Simmons is a Texas investor who to our knowledge has no experience in the management of an aerospace company. NL Industries, Inc., a company he controls, has launched a proxy fight to replace your Board of Directors with its nominees, including Mr. Simmons. NL Industries is seeking to take control of your company without making an offer to acquire it or announcing any specific plans. Your Board of Directors opposes the election of Harold Simmons and his slate to Lockheed's Board because we believe it would be contrary to the interests of Lockheed shareholders.

Your Board of Directors is committed to taking any and all steps necessary to protect and enhance the value of all shareholders' investment in Lockheed.

We will be communicating with you shortly with additional information about Mr. Simmons and his associates as well as about your company's plans and progress, and we will be providing you with a revised **BLUE Proxy Card.** We urge you not to sign any proxy card you may receive from Mr. Simmons and his associates. Please sign, date, and return your new **BLUE Proxy Card** when you receive it!

We think it important, however, for you to be immediately aware of a few facts about Mr. Simmons and his associates:

- Many of those NL Industries has named to its slate have been promised $20,000 each if they are not elected and they are, we believe, personal friends or business associates of Mr. Simmons. None of these nominees has any direct personal investment in Lockheed.

- According to his 13D filings with the Securities and Exchange Commission, Mr. Simmons, who was found by a court to have violated his fiduciary duties under Federal Retirement Law (ERISA) and has been enjoined from further violations until 1992, is currently under investigation by the Securities and Exchange Commission regarding trading in the securities of Lockheed and another company.

- NL Industries has indicated that it intends to propose a shareholder resolution recommending that the Board terminate the company's Shareholder Rights Plan. According to Simmons' public filings, NL's indicated interest in making this proposal is so that it can continue buying Lockheed stock in excess of 20%. The Rights Plan, while restricting certain changes in control without Board approval, is designed in part to protect against the acquisition of control in the marketplace by any shareholder without paying a full and fair price for that right. We oppose NL's proposal because we believe that control of the company rests with ALL the shareholders and that you should reap an economic benefit from any transfer of control through stock acquisitions by anyone. Accordingly, your Board of Directors strongly recommends that you vote AGAINST any proposal NL Industries may make to recommend termination of the Rights Plan.

You, our shareholders, are the owners of Lockheed. We are keenly aware of our fiduciary obligations to you.

1989 was a transition year for Lockheed and your Board of Directors and management are moving aggressively to maximize shareholder value. We will continue to keep you informed of significant developments concerning your investment in Lockheed.

On behalf of your Board of Directors,

Daniel M. Tellep

Daniel M. Tellep
*Chairman of the Board
and Chief Executive Officer*

IMPORTANT

If your shares are held in "Street-Name," only your broker or banker can vote your shares and only upon receipt of your specific instructions. Please contact the person responsible for your account and instruct that individual to vote the new **BLUE Proxy Card** on your behalf in accordance with your Board's recommendations.

If you have any questions or need further assistance, please call our proxy solicitor, *GEORGESON & COMPANY INC.*, at 1-800-223-2064.

Reprinted by permission of the Lockheed Corporation.

Figure 6.9. *Wall Street Journal* announcement by Lockheed Corporation to its shareholders.

the contest period. Gains were even found, however, when the company was not acquired if that firm experienced management turnover. They found that the new management tended to engage in restructuring, which also created shareholder value. Either way, the proxy contest helped remove poorly performing managers, thus raising shareholder value.

Value of Shareholders' Votes

The value of shareholders' votes was also examined in the Dodd and Warner study. They attempted to test the hypothesis originally proposed by Henry Manne, which stated that a positive stock price effect in proxy fights is associated with the increased value of the votes held by shareholders.[47] This value is perceived by participants in the contest who lobby for the support of shareholders. If their efforts are responsible for some of the increased value of shares, the value should decline after the record date. Shares purchased after the record date may only be voted under restricted and limited circumstances. For the 42 contests in which they had the specific record date, Dodd and Warner found negative results, which seems to support the Manne vote-value hypothesis.

Nature of the Dissidents and Dissident Campaigns

Research shows that the dissidents are often former managers of the target or those who have prior experience in the target's line of business. The Dodd and Warner study found that only a minority of the proxy contests involved a battle between an outside entity and the target corporation. Almost half of the contests were waged between former insiders who left the company following a policy dispute or other disagreement. DeAngelo and DeAngelo found that in almost 50% of the contests in their sample, the dissident leader had prior experience in the target's line of business. In almost one-third of the cases, the dissident leader was at one time employed by the target company.

Long-Term Effects of Proxy Contests

The DeAngelo and DeAngelo study found that dissidents prevailed in one-third of the contest in their sample, whereas another one-third of the companies had changes in top management within three years of the contest, with most of these changes occurring in the first year. In addition, they found that only 20% of the sample firms remained independent publicly held companies run by the same management team that was in place before the proxy fight. In fact, one-quarter of the companies were either sold or liquidated shortly after the contest.

One of the conclusions of the DeAngelo and DeAngelo study is that once a proxy contest starts, it is more than likely that the company will not remain the same but will undergo some significant changes. It is common that proxy contests result in changes in the managerial structure of the company.

---

47. Henry Manne, "The Higher Criticism of the Corporation," *Columbia Law Review* 62 (1962), pp. 399–432.

COMBINATION OF A PROXY FIGHT AND A TENDER OFFER

A proxy fight is sometimes used in conjunction with an offer to buy the target. For example, on May 1, 1986, Asher Edelman made an offer to buy Fruehauf. Edelman had bought 5% of Fruehauf and wanted to acquire the entire corporation. He proposed the acquisition to the Fruehauf board of directors, which rejected the offer. Edelman responded by increasing his shareholdings to 9.5% and the bid price to $42 per share.[48] At the annual meeting, Edelman also engaged in a proxy fight. He proposed his own slate of directors, who would, of course, be in favor of approving the bid. Edelman lost the proxy fight but followed with a formal tender offer at $44 per share.

A proxy fight may be an effective ancillary tool when coupled with a tender offer. The hostile bidder may use the proxy fight to effect the approval of a shareholder proposal that would dismantle the target's antitakeover defenses. For example, a bidder could use a proxy fight to have the target dismantle its poison pill or other antitakeover defenses. This would then be followed by a more effective tender offer. Another option available to the bidder and/or insurgent is to have the target agree to elect not to be bound by the prevailing state antitakeover laws.

PROXY FIGHTS AND TAKEOVERS IN THE 1990s

The collapse of the junk bond market and the associated fall of the leading junk bond investment bank, Drexel Burnham Lambert, reduced the effectiveness of debt-financed cash tender offers. With a shrunken junk bond market, the large amounts of cash that had made tender offers such an effective hostile takeover tool were not available. This limited the options of less well financed bidders, who had traditionally relied on the junk bond market for the financing necessary to pressure a board of directors or to entice shareholders to accept the bid. These bidders then began to look to proxy fights as an alternative. This helps explain the increase in the number of proxy fights at the end of the 1980s. Unfortunately, proxy battles have a lower probability of achieving success than the junk bond–financed tender offers that were typical of the mid-1980s.

---

48. John Bussey, "Edelman Plans $44-a-Share Bid for Fruehauf," *Wall Street Journal,* 12 June 1986, p. 12.

CASE STUDY: IBM versus LOTUS

The IBM successful tender offer for Lotus Development Corporation is an example of the type of tender offers that took place in the middle of the 1990s. They were hostile offers that were financed primarily by equity rather than cash offers that used debt financing, such as those that were more common in the fourth merger wave. On June 6, 1995, the traditionally conservative IBM launched a $3.3 billion, $60 per share cash tender offer. The aggressive offer of IBM resulted in a quick win, unlike some of the drawn-out takeover battles of the fourth merger wave. The speed of the successful bid was particularly important to this deal because much of Lotus's assets were its skilled personnel rather than physical assets. A rancorous contest could

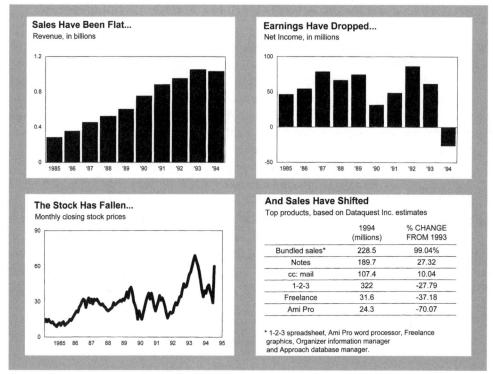

Figure 1. A Look at Lotus Development

Software Landscape

IBM's $3.52 billion purchase of Lotus would make IBM's personal computer software business look more like Microsoft Corp. IBM would still have an uphill battle against Microsoft in the two main product areas.

	Microsoft	IBM	Lotus
Operating System	MS-DOS and Windows	IBM-DOS and OS/2	————
Application Suite	Microsoft Office	————	Lotus SmartSuite
Communications	Microsoft Network Microsoft Exchange (in development)	Internet acces in OS/2 and 50 percent ownership in Prodigy	Lotus Notes (stand-alone and on AT&T network)

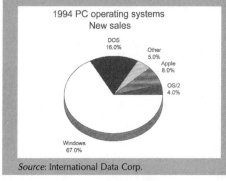

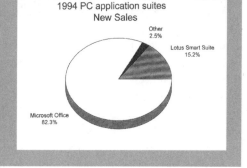

Source: International Data Corp.

Figure 2. IBM & Lotus' Industry Position

mean the loss of key employees. Concern about defections of programmers and other human assets was one of the reasons no more software acquisitions occurred in the 1980s.

After months of discussions with Lotus failed to bear fruit, IBM moved with speed and skill, using acumen derived from the lessons of the 1980s along with new tricks developed in the early 1990s. IBM considered a friendly deal and was going to start with a bear hug but rejected this plan out of concern that Lotus's chairman, James Manzi, would seek a white knight. Consequently, IBM went with a rich $60 per offer, which was a 100% premium above the preannouncement price of $30 per share. IBM's concern about personnel defections prompted the company to start with a high preemptive bid rather than risk other bidders coming on the scene. The high bid also made serious resistance by management more difficult to justify. The all-cash offer avoided the delays that assembling the financing may cause.

Being concerned about the loss of key personnel but constrained by legal restrictions that limit the bidder's ability to contact target employees, IBM applied some new techniques specific to this industry. IBM placed information about the bid, including a copy of the letter that IBM chairman, Louis Gerstner, sent to Manzi, on the Internet. IBM also had other former members of Lotus's management contact current Lotus managers to "take their temperature."

IBM's legal team prepared a lawsuit designed to get Lotus to rescind its poison pill defense. It also took advantage of a clause in Lotus's bylaws that allowed an appeal directly to shareholders if other means were not successful. The public relations campaign and legal maneuvering were all secondary to the high all-cash offer, which they increased to $64 per share before Lotus accepted the $3.53 billion bid, which was the largest computer software deal in history.

The buyout of Lotus places IBM in direct competition with Microsoft. The acquisition of Lotus's Notes product enables IBM to directly compete with Microsoft in the growing area of groupware, which links computers and facilitates communication across networks. This is one area in which IBM will now have an advantage over Microsoft, which is developing a product called Exchange to compete with Notes. Having lost the operating system battle to Microsoft, such gains are of particular importance to IBM.

With the increase in takeovers that occurred in the fifth merger wave, the importance of proxy fights declined somewhat compared with the increased use of tender offers. They still maintain their traditional role as a tool that may be used under certain circumstances to achieve specific goals.

SUMMARY

This chapter discusses the main alternatives available to a hostile bidder: a bear hug, a tender offer, and a proxy fight. A bear hug is an offer made directly to the directors of the target corporation. A bear hug puts pressure of the directors because it carries with it the implication that if the offer is not favorably received, a tender offer will follow. There are several variations of a tender offer, such as the all-cash tender offer and the two-tiered tender offer. The effectiveness of tender offers has varied over time as firms developed better defenses and the availability of financing changed. The regulatory environment has also greatly affected the use of this takeover tool. Laws regulating tender offers not only set forth the rules within which an offer must be structured but also provide strategic opportunities for both the bidder and the target. The use of tender offers grew significantly in both size and number during the 1980s. Large corporations that once considered themselves invulnerable to takeover succumbed to the junk bond–financed tender offers. When the junk bond market declined in the late 1980s, hostile bidders were forced to look elsewhere. Proxy fights, which work through the corporate election proxy, once again became a viable tool. Proxy contests may bring about a change in control or seek more modest goals, such as the enactment of shareholder provisions in the company's corporate charter.

The process of conducting a proxy fight was also described. Bidders have discovered that a successful proxy battle may be a less expensive alternative to a tender offer, although unsuccessful insurgents have little to show at the end of the contest. Bidders have also found that the use of a proxy fight in conjunction with a tender offer presents additional opportunities. Proxy fights, for example, may be used to dismantle the target's defenses, making it more vulnerable to a less well financed tender offer.

Research on the shareholder wealth effects of proxy fights has consistently shown that they tend to be associated with increased shareholder wealth. The gains seem to be related to the acquisition of the target company or to management turnover.

The playing field of hostile deals again reversed itself by the middle of the 1990s, with the tender offer once again becoming a more effective tool for implementing hostile takeovers. With the rebound of the tender offer, now financed more with equity and less with debt, proxy fights again played a less important role. Just as with antitakeover defenses, takeover tactics are continually evolving. Bidders are forced to adapt to the increasingly effective defenses that targets have erected. This process will continue to evolve in the future.

REFERENCES

Asquith, Paul. "Merger Bids and Stock Returns." *Journal of Financial Economics* 11, no. 1–4 (April 1983).

Bradley, Michael, Anand Desai, and E. Han Kim. "The Rationale Behind Interfirm Tender Offers: Information or Synergy." *Journal of Financial Economics* 11 (April 1983).

Brancato, Carolyn Kay. *Institutional Investors and Corporate Governance* (New York: Richard D. Irwin, 1997).

Brancato, Carolyn K. and Patrick A. Gaughan. *Institutional Investors and Their Role in Capital Markets.* Columbia University Center for Law and Economics Monograph, 1988.

Bussey, John. "Edelman Plans $44–a-Share Bid for Fruehauf." *Wall Street Journal,* 12 June 1986.

Cohen, Lloyd R. "Why Tender Offers? The Efficient Markets Hypothesis, the Supply of Stock and Signaling." *Journal of Legal Studies* 19, no. 1 (January 1990).

Comment, Robert, and Greg Jarrell. "Two-Tiered and Negotiated Tender Offers." *Journal of Financial Economics* 19, no. 2 (December 1987).

Cotter, James, Anil Shivdasani, and Marc Zenner. "Do Independent Directors Enhance Target Shareholder Wealth During Tender Offers?" *Journal of Financial Economics*, vol. 43 (2), February 1997.

DeAngelo, Hamj, and Linda DeAngelo. "The Role of Proxy Contests in the Governance of Publicly Held Companies." *Journal of Financial Economics,* vol. 23, no. 1 (June 1989).

Dodd, Peter, and Jerrold Warner. "On Corporate Government: A Study of Proxy Contests." *Journal of Financial Economics* 11, no. 1–4 (April 1983).

Easterbrook, Frank H., and Daniel R. Fischel. "The Proper Role of a Target's Management in Responding to a Tender Offer." *Harvard Law Review* 94, no. 6 (April 1981).

Easterbrook, Frank H., and Daniel R. Fischel. "Takeover Bids, Defensive Tactics and Shareholders Welfare." *The Business Lawyer* 36 (July 1981).

Easterbrook, Frank H., and Daniel R. Fischel. "Voting in Corporate Law." *Journal of Law and Economics* 23 (1983).

Easterbrook, Frank H., and Daniel R. Fischel. *The Economic Structure of Corporate Law* (Boston: Harvard University Press, 1991).

Einhorn, Herbert A., and J. William Robinson. *Shareholder Meetings* (New York: Practicing Law Institute, 1984).

Fama, Eugene, and Michael Jensen. "Separation of Ownership and Control." *Journal of Law and Economics* 26, 1983.

Hanson Trust PLC v. SCM Corp., 774 F. 2d 47 (2d Cir. 1985).

Heard, James, and Howard Sherman. *Conflicts of Interest in the Proxy System* (Washington, D.C.: Investor Responsibility Research Center, 1987).

Holderness, Clifford G., and Dennis P. Sheehan. "Raiders or Saviors? The Evidence of Six Controversial Raiders." *Journal of Financial Economics* 14, no. 4 (December 1985).

Hylton, Richard. "Advisers in Forefront of New Proxy Wars." *New York Times,* 30 March 1990.

Ingersoll, Bruce. "Campeau's Purchase of 48% of Allied Was Illegal, SEC Will Argue in Court." *Wall Street Journal,* 30 October 1986.

Jarrell, Greg, and Annette Poulsen, "Shark Repellents and Stock Prices: The Effects of Antitakeover Amendments Since 1980." *Journal of Financial Economics* 19, no. 1 (September 1987).

Johnson, Robert. "William Farley's Quest for Status Threatens to Topple His Empire." *Wall Street Journal,* 30 April 1990.

Kennecott Cooper Corp. v. Curtiss Wright Corp., 584 F. 2d 1195 (2nd Cir. 1978).

Kramer, Morris J. "Corporate Control Techniques: Insurgent Considerations." In James W. Robinson, ed. *Shareholders Meetings and Shareholder Control in Today's Securities Markets* (New York: Practicing Law Institute, 1985).

Lease, Ronald C., John J. McConnell, and Wayne E. Mikkelson. "The Market Value of Control in Publicly Held Corporations." *Journal of Financial Economics* 11 (1983).

Levin, Doron P. *Irreconcilable Differences* (Boston: Little, Brown, 1989).

Lipton, Martin. "Takeover Bids in the Target's Boardroom." *Business Lawyer* 35 (November 1979).

Lipton, Martin, and Erica H. Steinberger. *Takeovers and Freezeouts* (Washington, D.C.: Law Journal Seminar Press, 1987).

Madrick, Jeffrey. *Taking America: How We Got From the First Hostile Takeover to Megamergers, Corporate Raiding, and Scandal* (New York: Bantam Books, 1987).

Manne, Henry. "The Higher Criticism of the Corporation." *Columbia Law Review* 62 (1962).

Mergerstat Review: 1988. Merrill Lynch.

Mitchell, Mark L., and Kenneth Lehn. "Do Bad Bidders Become Good Targets?" *Journal of Applied Corporate Finance* 3, no. 2 (Summer 1990).

Monks, Robert, and Nell Minow. "Article on the Employee Benefit Research Institute Report on Proxy Voting." Institutional Shareholders Services, Washington, D.C.

Monks, Robert, and Nell Minow. *Power and Accountability* (New York: Harper Business, 1991).

Mulherin, J. Harold, and Annette B. Poulsen. "Proxy Contests and Corporate Change: Implications for Shareholder Wealth." *Journal of Financial Economics* 47 (1998).

"NLT Holders Reject by 5–3 Margin a Plan to Create Group to Study Acquisition Bids." *Wall Street Journal,* 13 May 1982.

Oesterle, Dale. "The Rise and Fall of Street Sweep Takeovers." *Duke Law Journal* (1989).

Panter v. Marshall Field & Company, 486 F. Supp. 1168, N.D. III.

Phalon, Richard. *The Takeover Barons of Wall Street* (New York: Putnam Publishing Co., 1981).

Pound, John. "Shareholder Activism and Share Values." *Journal of Law and Economics* (October 1989).

Rosenberg, Hilary. "The Proxy Voting Crackdown." *Pensions* (April 1988).

S-G Securities, Inc. v. Fuqua Investment Company, 466 F. Supp. 1114 (D. Mass., 1978).

Smiley, Robert. "Tender Offers, Transactions Costs and the Theory of the Firm." *Review of Economics and Statistics* 58 (1976).

Smith, Randall, and David Hilder. "Raiders Shorn of Junk Gird for Proxy Fights." *Wall Street Journal,* 7 March 1990.

Soderquist, Larry D. *Understanding Securities Laws* (New York: Practicing Law Institute, July 1987).

Stromfeld v. Great Atlantic & Pacific Tea Company, 484 F. Supp. 1264 (S.D. N. Y. 1980), *aff'd* 6464 F. 2d 563 (2nd Cir. 1980).

Stevens, Mark. *King Icahn* (New York: Dutton Publishing Co., 1993).

Wartzman, Rick, and Karen Blumenthal. "Lockheed Wins Proxy Battle with Simmons." *Wall Street Journal,* 11 April 1990.

Weinberger v. U.O.P., 457 A. 2d 701 (Del. 1983).

Wellman v. Dickinson, 475 F. Supp. 783 (S.D.N.Y. 1979).

Part Three

LEVERAGED TRANSACTIONS

7

LEVERAGED BUYOUTS

A leveraged buyout (LBO) is a financing technique used by a variety of entities, including the management of a corporation, or outside groups, such as other corporations, partnerships, individuals, or investment groups. Specifically, it is the use of debt to purchase the stock of a corporation, and it frequently involves taking a public company private.

The number of large LBOs increased dramatically in the 1980s, but they first began to occur with some frequency in the 1970s as an outgrowth of the 1960s bull market. Many private corporations took advantage of the high stock prices and chose this time to go public, thereby allowing many entrepreneurs to enjoy windfall gains. Even though some of these firms were not high quality, their stock was quickly absorbed by the growing bull market. When the stock market turned down in the 1970s, the prices of some lower quality companies fell dramatically. The bulk of this falloff in prices occurred between 1972 and 1974, when the Dow Jones Industrial Average fell from 1036 in 1972 to 578 in 1974. In 1974 the average price-earnings (P/E) ratio was six, which is considered quite low.

When the opportunity presented itself, managers of some of the companies that went public in the 1960s chose to take their companies private in the 1970s and 1980s. In addition, many conglomerates that had been built up in the 1960s through large-scale acquisitions began to become partially disassembled through selloffs, a process that is called *de-conglomeration.* Part of this process took place through the sale of divisions of conglomerates through LBOs. This process was ongoing through the 1980s and is partially responsible for the rising trend in divestitures that occurred during that period.

LBO DATA

The value and number of LBOs increased dramatically starting in the early 1980s and peaking by the end of the decade (Figures 7.1 and 7.2). By the mid-1980s larger companies were starting to become the target of LBOs; the average LBO transaction increased from $39.42 million in 1981 to $137.45 million in 1987. Although LBOs attracted much attention in the 1980s, they were still small in both number and dollar value compared with mergers. For example, in 1987 there were 3,701 mergers but only 259 LBOs. Leveraged buyouts accounted for only 7% of the total number of transactions. In terms of total value, LBOs accounted for a higher percentage of the total value of transactions. In 1987 LBOs made up 21.3% of the total value of transactions, which shows that the typical LBO tends to have a larger dollar value than the typical merger. Figure 7.1 shows that the dollar value of LBOs fell dramatically in 1990 and 1991. This decrease coincided with the decline in

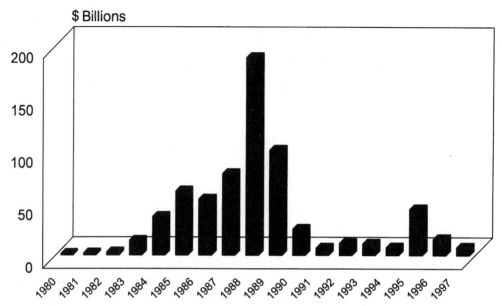

Figure 7.1.   Leveraged buyouts, 1980–97.

Source: Securities Data Company.

the junk bond market that started in late 1988. The number of LBOs began to increase as we entered the fifth merger wave, but they were not the megadeals that characterized the 1980s. Leveraged buyouts remain a smaller but still important part of the mergers and acquisitions business.

By far the largest LBO was the 1988 $24.6 billion RJR Nabisco deal. This food and tobacco company was taken private in a much-acclaimed takeover battle that was won by the

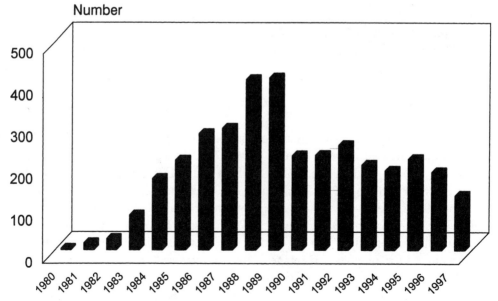

Figure 7.2.   Number of LBOs, 1980–97.

Source: Securities Data Company.

buyout firm of Kohlberg Kravis & Roberts (KKR) (Table 7.1). Kohlberg Kravis & Roberts won a bidding war against a rival group that was led by the former chief executive officer (CEO) of the company, Ross Johnson. Johnson was attempting to implement a management buyout but lost when his initial offer put the company in play and he was outbid. Like many other LBOs, however, the deal failed to generate gains for the contest winners, and KKR eventually sold off their interest in the company after experiencing disappointing returns.

COSTS OF BEING A PUBLIC COMPANY

Being a public company carries with it certain costs—both monetary and nonmonetary. First, federal securities laws mandate periodic filings with the Securities and Exchange Commission (SEC); for small firms these filings may be a burden both in money and in management time. They may help explain why small and medium-sized firms may want to go private, but not why large firms go private.[1]

The costs of maintaining public ownership vary significantly according to the size of the company. Therefore, it is difficult to put forward meaningful averages. These costs include all of the costs associated with doing the necessary filings with the SEC and communicating with shareholders. For smaller companies, the costs are considerably lower

Table 7.1.   Top Ten LBO Deals

Year Announced	Company Name (Business/Product Line)	Purchase Price ($ millions)	Average P/E Offered	Premium Offered (%)
1988	RJR Nabisco (tobacco and food giant)	24,561.6	19.5	92.1
1985	Beatrice Cos. (diversified food and consumer products)	5,361.6	10.7	14.9
1986	Safeway Stores Inc. (supermarket chain)	4,198.4	18.4	43.8
1987	Borg-Warner Corp. (diversified manufacturing)	3,798.6	20.4	30.7
1987	Southland Corp. (convenience food stores)	3,723.3	13.8	14.1
1986	Owens-Illinois Inc. (packaging, financial services, nursing homes)	3,631.9	19.6	36.0
1988	Hospital Corp. Of America (hospitals)	3,602.1	N/A	44.7
1988	Fort Howard Paper Corp. (paper products)	3,574.2	22.6	35.5
1989	NWA Inc. (airline)	3,524.5	18.5	12.6
1985	R. H. Macy (department store chain)	3,484.7	18.4	54.5

Source: Mergerstat Review, 1998.

---

1. Victor Brudney and Marvin A. Chirelstein, "A Restatement of Corporate Freezeouts," *Yale Law Journal* 87 (June 1978), pp. 1136–1137.

than the costs of larger companies. However, on a percentage basis, the costs may be more significant for smaller companies than they are for large firms. In addition, public companies have all of the other costs of dealing with shareholders, which some former owners and/or managers who have taken their company public find difficult to accept. These latter costs are more difficult to quantify but they may be even more significant than the direct monetary costs. Owners of public companies may want to receive a large payout for part of their shares when they take their company public but they may find it difficult to accept that the company they may have created is only partially owned by them.

The average cost of an LBO has been measured by Robert Kieschnick to equal approximately \$102 million.[2] This value is somewhat skewed by the large dollar value LBOs that occurred in the 1980s. It is clearly less representative of the costs of many of the smaller LBOs that occurred in the fifth merger wave.

When stock prices fall significantly (as they did in the 1970s), managers of the recently public companies may seize the opportunity to take their firm private. When stockholders are offered a premium for their stock at a time when the market is declining, they often jump at the opportunity. These going-private transactions are frequently financed with debt. Hence, the LBO started to become increasingly commonplace as the number of LBOs grew in the 1970s.

MANAGEMENT BUYOUTS

A *management buyouts* (MBO), a special type of LBO, occurs when the management of a company decides it wants to take its publicly held company, or a division of the company, private. Because of large sums necessary to complete the purchase, management usually has to rely on borrowing to accomplish this objective. To convince stockholders to sell, managers must be able to offer them a premium above the current market price. Thus, management may have to make the firm even more profitable as a private company than it was as a publicly held concern. The theoretical basis for this type of reasoning is found in the area of financial research known as *agency theory*—the belief that a public corporation is characterized by certain agency costs.[3] These costs are incurred by stockholders, the true owners of the corporation, who rely on agents, the managers of the company, to manage the company in a way that will maximize their returns. Managers, however, have their own set of objectives, which may not coincide with those of the stockholders. For example, managers may want to devote more resources to the perks of office, such as more luxuriously decorated and spacious offices and company jets, than are necessary.

An extreme version of the agency problem occurs when management fraudulently takes corporate resources for their own without the stockholders' approval. A classic example is the Equity Funding Scandal of 1973, in which management committed fraud and hid it from stockholders for nine years, reporting nonexistent profits and assets during those years. As a result, stockholders lost several hundred million dollars. The fraud was eventu-

2. Robert L. Kieschnick, "Management Buyouts of Public Corporations: An Analysis of Prior Characteristics," in Yakov Amihud, ed. *Leveraged Management Buyouts* (Homewood, Ill.: Dow Jones Irwin, 1989), pp. 35–38.

3. Michael Jensen and William Mackling, "Theory of the Firm: Managerial Behavior, Agency Costs and Ownership Structure," *Journal of Financial Economics* 3 (October 1976), pp. 305–360.

ally detected, and the president of the corporation and 18 managers and employees were arrested and sentenced to imprisonment. Not all agency costs that a firm experiences are as dramatic as these, but they may still be significant to the firm's owners.

One of the more common ways such costs are thought to manifest themselves is by having larger companies than would be economically efficient. Assuming that the stockholders' goal is to maximize profits, the optimal output level may be determined by microeconomic marginal analysis. The profit-maximizing output level is shown in Figure 7.3 as X^*—the point at which marginal revenue and marginal costs are equal. At this point, profit reaches its maximum level of π_{max}. Beyond X^* further sales will generate more additional costs than additional revenues. A profit-maximizing firm would not produce output beyond this level.

The managers of the firm may decide that they could more easily justify higher salaries and other perks if the company were larger. Additional compensation might also come in the form of psychic gratification associated with being the CEO of one of the larger companies in that industry. The increased size may be achieved through acquisitions of other companies. Managers, however, are somewhat constrained by the fact that they must provide stockholders with a certain level of profitability and dividends. The range between the profit-maximizing level of profitability π_{max} and π_1, for example, may be significant (Figure 7.3). Mueller, for example, hypothesized that the compensation that managers of larger firms derived is a motive for conglomerate acquisitions. In Mueller's view, managers will even accept a lower rate of return or hurdle rate to be able to complete acquisitions that will lead to greater compensation.[4] If profits fall too low (such as to π_2), stockholders

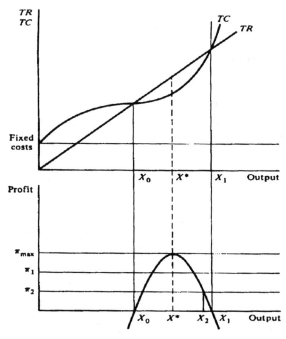

Figure 7.3.   Total cost, total revenues, and profit functions.

---

4. Dennis Mueller, "A Theory of Conglomerate Mergers," *Quarterly Journal of Economics* 83 (1969), pp. 643–659.

might have an incentive to incur the costs involved in forcing a change in management through a proxy fight. The process of removing directors and management, however, sometimes requires a proxy fight that may be very costly with uncertain results. In an effort to deal with the managers' potentially conflicting goals, owners may take various actions to ensure that management's actions are more consistent with their own objectives. One such set of actions involves establishing a set of monitoring systems that will keep track of management's performance.[5] The board of directors helps fulfill this control mission for stockholders. However, when the board is composed of several members of management, this process may not work as efficiently. One way to ensure that the board will fulfill its policing mission is to have a greater percentage of outside directors—those who do not have management positions within the firm. (Inside directors are managers of the company.) Given the fact that many outside directors are often suggested and recommended by the chairman and other inside board members, there are serious concerns that today's corporate boards really perform this function.

Owners may also help ensure that the agents will pursue owners' goals by creating profit incentives for managers through profit-sharing plans or stock options.[6] Although this approach may reduce agency costs, it is an imperfect solution to the problem. Seldom does a manager gain more by sacrificing direct gains, in the form of bonuses, perks, and a higher expense account, in return for a share of the higher profits that may result from all managers making similar sacrifices. The *free rider problem* may occur when one manager attempts to keep his or her perks and expenses high while hoping that other managers will lower theirs.

It is difficult to determine the optimal level of profitability for each company. One important guide is the profitability of similar sized firms in the same industry. Several measures may be utilized, such as average industry profits or the industry average rate of return on equity. The company may come under increased scrutiny and pressure if it falls too far below the industry average. If management can demonstrate that its profitability is consistent with industry norms, then it may be able to avoid pressure from stockholders.

Going private may yield gains by making the agents and the owners one. This clearly makes sense in theory, but there may be a big difference between theoretical gains and the actual gains derived from attempting to eliminate agency costs (see Figure 7.4).

LEVERAGED BUYOUT PROCESS

As stated previously, LBOs are acquisitions that are financed primarily with debt. They are usually cash transactions in which the cash is borrowed by the acquiring firm. Much of the debt may be secured by the assets of the corporation being taken private. This section provides an overview of the LBO process. The financing of these deals is discussed in greater detail later in this chapter.

The target company's assets are often used to provide collateral for the debt that is going to be incurred to finance the acquisition. Thus, the collateral value of these assets needs to

---

5. Eugene Fama and Michael Jensen, "Separation of Ownership and Control," *Journal of Law and Economics* 26 (1983), pp. 323–329.

6. Eugene Fama, "Agency Problems and the Theory of the Firm," *Journal of Political Economy* vol. 7, no. 2 (April 1980), pp. 288–307.

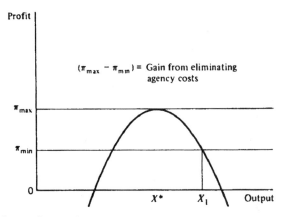

Figure 7.4. Gains from eliminating agency costs.

be assessed. This type of lending is often called *asset-based lending*. Firms with assets that have a high collateral value can more easily obtain such loans; thus, LBOs are often easier to conduct in capital-intensive industries—firms that usually have more assets that may be used as collateral than non–capital-intensive firms. It is not surprising, therefore, that Waite and Fridson found that LBO activity was more predominant in manufacturing than in nonmanufacturing industries.[7] Still, LBOs are possible for firms that do not have an abundance of assets that may be used as collateral. Service industries are one example. They tend not to have high-asset values, but they may still be good LBO candidates if their cash flows are high enough to service the interest payments on the debt that will arise when the buyout is completed.

The following is a step-by-step process of a hypothetical LBO in which a division of a firm is taken private through an MBO. Although the process is presented in steps to make it easier to understand, the exact order of the steps may vary somewhat, depending on the particular circumstances of the buyout.

Step 1. *The Decision to Divest Is Made.* The management of Diversified Industries (DI) has observed that the chemicals division is performing poorly and has become a drain on the company. It is decided at a board of directors meeting that DI will divest itself of the chemicals division. The company does not want to be in the chemicals industry and would rather focus its resources on areas that show more promise. The managers of DI are concerned about the welfare of the division's employees. They inform the management of the chemicals division of their plans and express their interest in remaining with the division after divestiture.

Step 2. *Management of the Division Makes the Decision to Purchase the Division.* After much deliberation, the managers of the chemicals division decide to attempt a buyout. The reasons may vary from a belief that the parent company never realized the true potential of the division to basic concerns about job security. They then determine the financial resources they can devote toward its purchase. The

---

7. S. Waite and M. Fridson, "The Credit Quality of Leveraged Buyouts," in *High Performance* (New York: Morgan Stanley, January 1989).

management of the overall company, as well as the management of the division, approach DI's investment bank to assess the availability of LBO financing.

Step 3. *A Financial Analysis of the Division Is Conducted.* A financial analysis of the chemicals division is conducted. The main focus of this analysis is to determine whether the division, on its own, is sufficiently creditworthy to support the assumption of the debt levels needed to finance the buyout. Several financial measures are often used to facilitate this assessment. Many of them are discussed in Chapters 12 through 14. Three of the more frequently used measures for LBOs are highlighted here.

Division's book value of assets. This measure indicates the value of the division's assets carried on the firm's books. It may or may not accurately reflect the value of the division's assets.

Replacement value of assets. This is the cost to a purchaser of replacing the assets. It is a more accurate reflection of the true value of the division's assets because it provides a better indication of the value the market places on these assets.

Liquidation value of assets. This measure indicates what a lender might receive if the assets were liquidated, such as in the case of a bankruptcy. It is one measure of the lender's protection in the event the division fails as an independent company. It is an imperfect measure, however, because assets sometimes sell at fire sale prices in liquidation proceedings.

Step 4. *The Purchase Price Is Determined.* Diversified Industries agrees on a sale price that is in excess of the value of the division's liquidation value of assets. This value should be considered a floor value because DI presumably could sell off the division's assets for at least this amount. How much above the liquidation value depends on the relative bargaining abilities of the groups involved in the transaction as well as the intensity of DI's desire to rid itself of the chemicals division. A firm may sometimes feel an obligation to the employees of the division and will allow them to buy the division at a price that is not far above what would be considered a giveaway of company assets. However, in the 1980s the LBO sector sometimes featured intense bidding contests for LBO targets. Such an atmosphere puts pressure on the management of the parent company to seek the maximum value attainable.

Step 5. *Investment By the Division's Management is Determined.* Once the purchase price has been determined, the managers of the division must decide the extent of their own capital investment in the transaction. This is often required as a condition of the lenders because managers who have a personal financial stake in the future of the company will presumably help ensure the company's financial well-being and thereby protect the lenders' interests. Although the amount of this investment may be small compared with the total capital raised, it may constitute a significant part of the total wealth of the managers.

Step 6. *The Lending Group Is Assembled.* At this point in the process, the investment banker puts together the lending group—the group of lenders who will supply the capital that is borrowed to finance the LBO. Small transactions sometimes involve only one lender. In larger transactions, however, one lender may not want to commit to the full amount. Lenders seek protection against the risks of default by diversifying their assets. The effort to spread out the exposure to this particular LBO among several lenders is part of that process. In contributing to LBO funds, investors are able to partake in the high returns available by investing in LBOs while retaining the protection provided by diversification. These investors pool their resources to invest in a diversified group of LBOs. (Leveraged buyout funds are discussed later in this chapter.) The process of assembling the debt capital may become more complicated for larger transactions. Commitments for different types of secured or unsecured debt may have to be obtained in advance.

Step 7. *External Equity Investment Is Acquired.* The investment banker, in conjunction with the parties to the transaction, determines whether an additional outside equity investment is necessary. This may be necessary if sufficient debt is not available in the market for this type of transaction. It may also be a requirement of the lenders, who may think that the risk level of the transaction does not warrant the high percentage of debt relative to equity that would be necessary without outside equity investors. Step 7 is performed in conjunction with steps 5, 6, and 8 because the results of this analysis will affect the investors' willingness to support the transaction.

Step 8. *Cash Flow Analysis Is Conducted.* Once the relative components of debt and equity have been tentatively assessed, a cash flow analysis is conducted to determine whether the division's cash flow will be sufficient to service the interest payments on the debt. This is usually done by assuming restrictive budgets for the time necessary to pay off the debt. These restrictions may come in the form of lower research and development and capital outlays. Often the cash flow analysis will be redone under different assumptions that will alter the financial structure of the deal, thereby requiring steps 5 through 7 to be repeated. Several repetitions of this iterative process may occur before the financial structure is agreed to.

Step 9. *Financing Is Agreed To.* If the cash flows are sufficient to service the debt, within a reasonable range for error, the financing is agreed to and the deal is consummated.

The preceding scenario was explained within the framework of an MBO. The process is similar, however, when the LBO is conducted by an outside entity such as a corporation. The key is the target's ability to raise and service the requisite debt financing.

FINANCING FOR LEVERAGED BUYOUTS

Two general categories of debt are used in LBOs—secured and unsecured debt—and they are often used together.[8] Secured debt, which is sometimes called *asset-based lending,* may contain two subcategories of debt: senior debt and intermediate-term debt. In some

---

8. For an excellent discussion of the use of secured and unsecured debt in leveraged buyouts, see Stephen C. Diamond, ed. *Leveraged Buyouts* (Homewood, Ill.: Dow Jones Irwin, 1985), pp. 41–57.

smaller buyouts these two categories are considered one. In larger deals there may be several layers of secured debt, which vary according to the term of the debt and the types of assets used as security. Unsecured debt, which is sometimes known as *subordinated debt* and *junior subordinated debt,* lacks the protection of secured debt but generally carries a higher return to offset this additional risk.

Secured LBO Financing

Within the category of secured financing, there are two subcategories—senior debt and intermediate-term debt.

Senior Debt

Senior debt consists of loans secured by liens on particular assets of the company. The collateral, which provides the downside risk protection required by lenders, includes physical assets such as land, plant and equipment, accounts receivable, and inventories. The lender projects the level of accounts receivable that the firm would average during the period of the loan. This projection is usually based on the amount of accounts receivable the firm has on its books at the time the loan is closed, as well as the historical level of these assets.

Lenders will commonly advance 85% of the value of the accounts receivable and 50% of the value of the target's inventories, excluding the work in progress.[9] Accounts receivable, which are normally collected in short periods such as 30 days, are more valuable than those of longer periods. The lender must make a judgment on the value of the accounts receivable; similar judgments have to be made as to the marketability of inventories. The process of determining the collateral value of the LBO candidate's assets is sometimes called *qualifying* the assets. Assets that do not have collateral value, such as accounts receivable that are unlikely to be collected, are called *unqualified assets.*

Intermediate-Term Debt

Intermediate-term debt is usually subordinate to senior debt. It is often backed up by fixed assets such as land and plant and equipment. The collateral value of these assets is usually based on their liquidation value. Debt backed up by equipment typically has a term of six months to one year.[10] Loans backed up by real estate tend to have a one- to two-year term. The relationship between the loan amounts and the appraised value of the assets varies depending on the circumstances of the buyout. Generally, debt can equal 80% of the appraised value of equipment and 50% of the value of real estate. As the real estate market rebounded in the 1990s, lenders became willing to advance higher percentages using real estate as collateral. These percentages will vary depending on the area of the country and the conditions of the real estate market. The collateral value of assets, such as equipment and real estate, is based on the auction value of these assets, not the value they carry on the firm's books. When the auction value is greater than the book value of the assets, the firm's borrowing capacity is greater than what its balance sheet would reflect. Lenders look for

---

9. Michael R. Dabney, "Asset Based Financing," in Milton Rock, ed. *Mergers and Acquisitions* (New York: McGraw-Hill, 1987), pp. 393–399.

10. Ibid.

certain desirable characteristics in borrowers, even when the borrower has valuable collateral. Some of these factors are discussed in the following sections.

Desirable Characteristics of Secured Leveraged Buyout Candidates

There are certain characteristics that lenders look for in a prospective LBO candidate. Some of the more commonly cited features are discussed here.

- *Stable cash flows.* One of the most important characteristic of LBO candidates is the existence of regular cash flows as determined by examining the pattern of historical cash flows for the company. Statistical measures such as the standard deviation may be used to measure this variability. The more erratic the historical cash flows, the greater the perceived risk in the deal. Even in cases in which the average cash flows exceed the loan payments by a comfortable margin, the existence of high variability may worry a lender. Dependable cash flows alone are not sufficient to guarantee the success of an LBO.

   The financial difficulties of the Southland Corporation after its $4.9 billion buyout in 1987 is a case in point. The company's main business was the "cash cow" 7–Eleven convenience chain. Southland's problems emerged when some of the 7–Eleven cash flows were directed to noncore real estate ventures instead of paying off the buyout debt. This misadventure left the post-buyout Southland on the verge of bankruptcy in spite of the firm's sizable cash flows.

   Although historical cash flows are used to project future cash flows, the past may be an imperfect guide to the future. Market conditions change and the future business environment may be less favorable than what the company's historical data reflect. The lender must make a judgment as to whether the past will be a reliable indicator of what the future will hold. Lenders and borrowers usually construct cash flow projections based on restrictive budgets and new cost structures. Such budget planning takes place for both secured and unsecured LBOs, but it is even more critical for cash flow LBOs. These budgets may include lower research and development expenditures and labor costs. The target attempts to find areas where costs may be cut—at least temporarily. These cost savings may be used to meet the loan payments on the LBO debt. The importance of cash flows to LBOs was underscored by a study by Kenneth Lehn and Annette Poulsen.[11] They showed that buyout premiums were positively related to the firm's free cash flow. That is, the market is willing to pay higher premiums for greater cash flow protection.

- *Stable and experienced management.* Stability is often judged by the length of time management is in place. Lenders feel more secure when management is experienced; that is, if management has been with the firm for a reasonable period of time, it may imply that there is a greater likelihood that management will stay on after the deal is completed. Creditors often judge the ability of management to handle an LBO by the cash flows that were generated by the firms they managed in the past. If their prior management experience was with firms that had significant liquidity problems, lenders will be much more cautious about participating in the buyout.

---

11. K. Lehn and A. Poulsen, "Free Cash Flow and Stockholder Gains in Going Private Transactions," University of Washington Working Paper, February 1987.

- *Room for significant cost reductions.* Assuming additional debt to finance an LBO usually imposes additional financial pressures on the target. These pressures may be alleviated somewhat if the target can significantly cut costs in some areas, such as fewer employees, reduced capital expenditures, elimination of redundant facilities, and tighter controls on operating expenses. Frank Lichtenberg and Donald Siegel showed that LBO employee cutbacks were concentrated at the administrative levels of employment, with an average administrative workforce reduction of 16%, while there tended to be minimal cutbacks at the manufacturing level.[12]

- *Equity interest of owners.* The collateral value of assets provides downside risk protection to lenders. The equity investment of the managers or buyers and outside parties also acts as a cushion to protect lenders. The greater the equity cushion, the more likely secured lenders will not have to liquidate the assets. The greater the managers' equity investment, the more likely they will stay with the firm if the going gets tough. Leveraged buyout lenders in the 1990s demand a much greater equity cushion than they did for the heavy debt deals they financed in the mid-1980s.

- *Ability to cut costs.* Many LBO candidates are inefficient and need cost restructuring. Leveraged buyout dealmakers work on finding areas where cost can be cut without damaging the business. When these cost cuts are focused on areas of waste or unnecessary expenditures, they may be of great benefit to the LBO candidate. The target may suffer, however, when the cuts are made in areas that will hurt the company in the future. Cuts in research and development, for example, may cause the company to fall behind its competitors and eventually lose market share. Industry factors may determine the extent to which research and product development expenditures may be cut. Reductions are often difficult to implement in rapidly evolving, high-tech industries such as the computer industry. The company may survive the LBO and pay off the debt only to be left behind by its competitors. A good example of a high-tech LBO that should not have been conducted was the 1987 $866 million buyout of defense contractor Tracor, Inc. The company found itself with an unpredictable cash flow after defense industry cutbacks. This, coupled with the capital demands of this high-tech industry, left the firm struggling to meet the LBO debt payments.

- *Limited debt on the firm's balance sheet.* The lower the amount of debt on the firm's balance sheet relative to the collateral value of the firm's assets, the greater the borrowing capacity of the firm. If the firm's balance sheet is already encumbered by significant financial leverage, it may be more difficult to finance the LBO. The prior debt limits the company's borrowing capacity. Even companies with low pre-LBO debt levels end up exhausting their borrowing capacity after the LBO.

- *Separable, noncore businesses.* If the LBO candidate owns noncore businesses that can be sold off to quickly "pay down" a significant part of the firm's post-LBO debt, the deal may be easier to finance. This may be important for both secured and unsecured LBOs. Problems may occur when debt is incurred based on an unrealistic sales price for noncore divisions. The inability to sell components of the firm on a timely basis, at prices similar to those expected by investment bankers, was one of the main factors that caused the bankruptcy of the Campeau Corporation in 1989. Deals that

---

12. Frank Lichtenberg and Donald Siegel, "The Effects of Takeovers on Employment and Wages of Central Office and Other Personnel," Columbia Graduate School Working Paper #FB-89-05, 1989.

are dependent on the large-scale selloff of most of the firm's businesses are referred to as *breakup LBOs*.

- *Other factors.* Each LBO candidate has a different product or service and a different history. The existence of unique or intangible factors may provide the impetus for a lender to provide financing when some ambivalence exists. A dynamic, growing, and innovative company may provide lenders with sufficient incentives to overlook some shortcomings. However, these factors, which are sometimes referred to as "the story," only go so far in making up for deficiencies.

Costs of Secured Debt

The costs of senior debt vary depending on market conditions. Senior debt rates are often quoted in relation to other interest rates such as the prime rate. They often range between two and five points above the prime rate for a quality borrower with quality assets. The *prime rate* is the rate that banks charge their best customers. Less creditworthy borrowers have to pay more. Interest rates, in turn, are determined by many economy-wide factors, such as the Federal Reserve's monetary policy or the demand for loanable funds. Therefore, rates on secured LBO financing will be as volatile as other interest rates in the marketplace. However, these rates will also be influenced by the lenders' demand for participation in this type of financing. Inasmuch as this varies, secured LBO rates may fluctuate even more than other rates in the economy.

Sources of Secured Financing

Secured LBO financing is often obtained through the asset-based lending subsidiary of a major New York bank or other money center bank. The number and types of lenders participating in this type of lending grew significantly during the mid-1980s as the rates of return rose. The size of this group contracted sharply by 1990.

Financing Gap

Leveraged buyout lenders are partial to buyouts in which the target company has significant assets that may be used as collateral. However, even then their value may not be sufficient to cover the total purchase cost of the target. In this case, a financing gap exists; that is, the financing needs of the LBO exceed the collateral coverage. At this point the investment bank must seek other sources of financing. These sources may be covered by equity, subordinated debt, or a loan that exceeds the collateral value of the assets.

Equity capital may be raised by exchanging an ownership interest in the target to outside investors in exchange for financing. *Subordinated debt* is debt that has a secondary claim on the assets used for collateral. As a result of this inferior claim on assets, this debt usually has higher interest costs. Loans beyond the collateral value of the target's assets are often motivated by less tangible forms of security for the lender, such as the existence of dependable cash flows, which make it more likely that the debt payments will be met.

Unsecured LBO Financing

Leveraged buyouts are typically financed by a combination of secured and unsecured debt. The unsecured debt, sometimes referred to as subordinated and junior subordinated debt, is debt that has a secondary claim of the assets of the LBO target—hence the term *subordi-*

nated. The term *mezzanine layer financing* is often applied to this financing because it has both debt and equity characteristics; although it is clearly debt, it is equity-like in that lenders typically receive warrants that may be converted into equity in the target. Warrants are a derivative security offered by the corporation itself. They allow the warrant holder to buy stock in the corporation at a certain price for a defined time period. Unlike call options, which are offered by brokerage firms, when warrants are exercised, the corporation either issues new stock or satisfies the warrant holder's demands by offering treasury stock.

When the warrants are exercised, the share of ownership of the previous equity holders is diluted. This dilution often occurs just at the time the target is becoming profitable. It is then that the warrants become valuable. In an MBO, for example, managers may have held a very high percentage of ownership in the company. If the target becomes profitable in the future, management might have its share of ownership dramatically diluted by exercising the warrants by the junior subordinated lenders. Although such forms of debt may have undesirable characteristics for management, they may be necessary to convince lenders to participate in the LBO without the security of collateral.

It is important to be aware of the role of the warrants in computing the return to the providers of mezzanine layer financing. Their return is more than simply the interest payments they receive. The value of the equity derived from the exercise of the warrants, adjusted for the probability that the firm will be sufficiently profitable to justify exercising of the warrants, needs to be added to the interest payments to compute the return. This analytical process is demonstrated later in this chapter.

In the preceding discussion, mezzanine layer financing was used in conjunction with senior debt to cover the financing gap. However, some LBOs may be financed solely through unsecured financing. This type of LBO lending is not as desirable to some lenders because it lacks the downside risk protection that marketable collateral provides. Most deals include both secured and unsecured lending.

Cash Flow LBOs

The risk a lender incurs when a loan is made is that the interest and principal payments may not be met. Collateral may be a source of protection in the event these payments are not made. Dependable cash flows, however, may also be an invaluable source of protection. The more regular the cash flows, the more assurance the lender has that the loan payments will be made.

Unsecured LBOs are sometimes called *cash flow LBOs*. These deals tend to have a more long-term focus, with a maturity of 10 to 15 years. In contrast, secured LBOs might have a financing maturity of only up to 5 years. Cash flow LBOs allow firms that are not in capital-intensive industries to be LBO candidates. This is most important in the U.S. economy because the United States has become a more service-oriented economy. Many service industries, such as advertising, lack significant physical assets relative to their total revenue but have large cash flows. Cash flow LBOs are generally considered riskier for lenders. In return for the burden of assuming additional risk, lenders of unsecured financing typically require a higher interest rate as well as an *equity kicker.* This equity interest often comes in the form of warrants or direct shares in the target. The percentage of ownership may be as little as 10% or as high as 80% of the companies' shares. The percentage is higher when the lender perceives greater risk.

Because the loan is not collateralized does not mean that the lenders are not protected by the firm's assets. Unsecured lenders are entitled to receive the proceeds of the sale of the secured assets after full payment has been made to the secured lenders. Unsecured LBOs started to become more common in the mid-1980s, when the demand for mergers, acquisitions, and LBOs drove up the premiums paid for targets. As premiums rose above the value of the target's assets, lenders were increasingly being requested to lend beyond the limits of the target's collateral. Many deals then became structured using both secured and unsecured debt. The unsecured component received a higher return to compensate for assuming the greater risk. Most of the larger LBOs that attract so much media attention are largely unsecured deals.

The main advantage of mezzanine layer financing is the profit potential that is provided by either a direct equity interest or warrants convertible into equity to go along with the debt position of the lender. This added return potential offsets the lack of security that secured debt has. There are often several types of mezzanine layer financing in an LBO. The debt is structured in several layers, with each layer subordinate to another layer. Each layer that is subordinate to the layer before it in order of liquidation priority generally contains additional compensation for the lender to offset the lower degree of security. This source of LBO financing, which was often funded through the issuance of junk bonds, declined dramatically when the high-yield bond market collapsed toward the end of the 1980s. Leveraged buyouts continued in the 1990s at a much slower pace and often without the aid of this type of financing.

CAPITAL STRUCTURE OF UNSECURED LBO FIRMS

After the completion of the deal, the capital structure of a company taken private in an LBO is usually different from its structure before the buyout. A capital structure for a typical unsecured LBO is outlined in Table 7.2 (see also Figure 7.5). Some of the sources of LBO financing listed in this table, however, such as many banks, are generally no longer active participants in LBO financing.

The capital structure does not remain constant after the buyout. The goal of both the company and the lender is to reduce the total debt through debt retirements. After the buyout, the firm is very heavily leveraged. As time passes, the firm's goal should be to retire the debt and return to a more normal capital structure. Companies usually try to retire most of the LBO debt within five to seven years.

The costs of different components of the firm's capital structure vary. Generally, short-term debt costs are lower than long-term debt because of the additional risk imposed by

Table 7.2. LBO Capital Structure

Securities	Percent of Capitalization (%)	Source
Short-term or intermediate senior debt	5–20	Commercial banks
Long-term senior or subordinated debt	40–80	Life insurance companies, some banks, LBO funds
Preferred stock	10–20	Life insurance companies and venture capital firms
Common Stock	1–20	Life insurance companies, venture capital firms, and managers

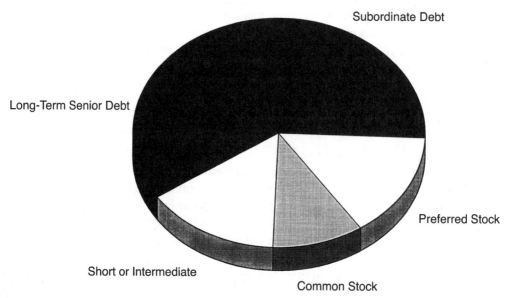

Figure 7.5.   Capital structure of an LBO.

longer-term lending commitments. The longer the term, the greater the opportunity for something to go wrong. Long-term debt is generally less costly than preferred stock, which, in turn, is less expensive to the issuer than common stock. These cost differences are in direct relation to the high degree of risk associated with equity versus debt.

SOURCES OF LBO FINANCING

Table 7.2 points out the participation of the nonbank sources of financing. These sources grew dramatically during the fourth merger wave. They participated in both secured and unsecured financing, and they included different categories of institutional investors such as life insurance companies and pension funds. Institutional investors actively took part in direct LBO funding or indirectly through an LBO fund. These pools of funds were developed to invest in LBOs. By investing in LBOs, institutional investors anticipated realizing higher returns than those available from other forms of lending. Also, by pooling the funds, they could achieve broad diversification and the resulting risk reduction. Diversification is designed to limit the exposure to default by any one borrower.

Although some institutional investors, such as insurance companies, tended to be unsecured investors, they participated in more than one type of LBO financing. This type of financing is sometimes referred to as *vertical strips*. In a vertical strip, investors may participate in several layers of financing within the same deal. For example, they may hold some secured debt and more than one form of unsecured debt as well as some equity.

With the collapse of many leveraged deals of the 1980s, institutions in the 1990s tend to shy away from these transactions. With dramatically reduced availability of institutional nonbank financing, it is now more difficult to complete a large-scale LBO.

LBO FUNDS

One of the financial innovations of the 1980s was the appearance of LBO funds. As mentioned, these investment funds were established to invest in LBO transactions. They contain the invested capital of a variety of investors who seek to enjoy the high returns that may be achieved through LBOs. Like most funds, such as common stock mutual funds, LBO funds provide the investor with broad diversification that lowers the risk level of the investment. Leveraged buyouts offer great opportunities for investors to earn significant gains. However, because of the high debt levels generally associated with these types of transactions, the risk of default may be high. Through the diversification that LBO funds provide, investors may anticipate the possibility of achieving high gains while having a lower degree of risk.

During the 1980s a broad range of investors allocated capital to LBO funds. These often included conservative institutional investors such as pension funds and insurance companies. In addition, because these investment opportunities were more of a U.S. phenomenon, LBO funds attracted significant foreign investors. For example, in 1988 the Nippon Life Insurance Company committed several hundred million dollars to Shearson's LBO fund, and Yamaichi Securities committed $100 million to the Lodestar Corporation Company, which is a boutique LBO fund.[13] Like pension funds, the pace of foreign investment in LBOs slowed dramatically as the 1980s came to an end. Without the investment capital of these investors, LBO funds declined significantly in 1990 but rose steadily through the mid-1990s as institutional investors such as pension funds began to reconsider buyout funds as a way of realizing sufficient returns to meet the needs of retirees who were living longer. Pension funds account for approximately one-third of the capital being invested in LBO funds in the 1990s.[14] It is interesting that the capital raised by LBO funds in 1994 and 1995 exceeded the levels of 1988 and 1989 (Figure 7.6). It is ironic that one of the problems the funds have encountered in the 1990s is not the access to capital but rather the paucity of deals.[15] Gone are the mega-LBOs of the fourth merger wave, and LBO funders now have to search harder to find deals that will afford them returns their investors are seeking.

LBO FIRMS

Several investment firms specialize in LBOs. These LBO specialists raise capital by offering investors an opportunity to enjoy the high returns attainable through investing in LBOs. Many of them assemble an LBO fund that they manage and use to invest in LBOs of their choosing. Investors are usually promised a certain percentage of the return that the fund will earn. One of the first LBO firms was Gibbons Green & van Amerongen, which was formed in 1969 to handle leveraged acquisitions. They were joined in the mid-1970s by Forstmann Little & Clayton Dubilier. They were later joined by the Blackstone Group

13. *New York Times,* 7 August 1988.

14. Greg Steinmetz, "LBO Funds Lure Investors But Returns Worry Some," *Wall Street Journal,* 29 June 1994, p. C1.

15. Laura Jereski, "Buyout Funds Have Lots of Money, but Few Deals," *Wall Street Journal,* 26 April 1995, p. C1.

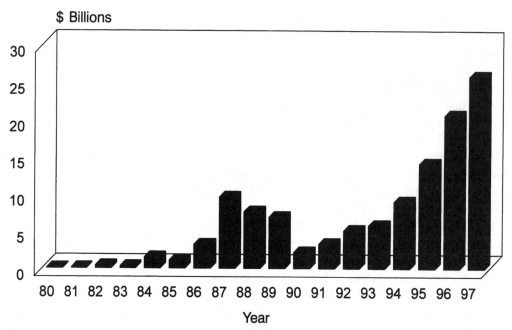

Figure 7.6.   Capital investment in buyout funds.

Source: Asset Alternatives, Inc.

and Kohlberg Kravis & Roberts—the largest LBO firm. Although Kohlberg Kravis & Roberts has been involved in many transactions, it is most famous for taking RJR Nabisco private in 1988 and putting together the 1984 buyout of Beatrice. As the LBO boom died at the end of the 1980s, several of these firms altered their focus and directed their activities to nonleveraged transactions. Some firms even focused on bankruptcy transactions, which ironically involved the unraveling of some of the LBOs that LBO firms helped put together.

The typical LBO firms are not interested in becoming day-to-day managers of the target company. Firms such as Kohlberg Kravis & Roberts usually select a management team to run the daily operations. The expertise of the LBO firm is in selecting the right target, raising capital, and overseeing cost reductions that will ensure the repayment of debt and a sufficient return for investors. It may be possible to accomplish this by keeping the management that was in place at the time of the LBO. On the other hand, this management may not look kindly on the sale of complete divisions to repay the debt. When the current managers are not agreeable to the changes the LBO firm has in mind, they are usually replaced.

Risk Analysis for LBOs

The financial analysis that is done for an LBO is not very different from that which is done for nonleveraged buyouts. Therefore, much of the financial analysis that is discussed in the valuation chapters of this book also applies to LBOs. One of the differences, however, is that additional emphasis is focused on the ability of the LBO candidate to service the newly acquired debt and to generate sufficient performance to eventually retire the debt and allow the LBO sponsors to realize a return that sufficiently rewards them for participating in this risky transaction. As part of this process, cash flows are projected into the future and compared with the projected cost structure of the post-LBO. This cost structure would then include a new component that represents the debt service and principal retirement payments. To analyze the impact of this on the firm, an analyst may employ some of the same financial tools that are used in capital budgeting.[16]

As part of the financial analysis, the deal evaluators may want to do some statistical analysis of the projected post-LBO cash flows. Given that these cash flows are not known with certainty, a probability distribution of projected annual cash flows may be constructed where each possible projected cash flow is assigned a specific probability of occurrence. From this probability distribution, an *expected value* (EV) can be computed. This value represents the weighted average annual cash flows that are expected to occur given the assigned probabilities (P_i)

$$EVCF = \sum_{i=1}^{n} p_i(CF_i - EV)^2 \tag{7.1}$$

Just as in capital budgeting analysis, the riskiness of the transaction can be assessed by computing the variance (VAR) and the standard deviation (SD) of the projected annual cash flows. The higher the standard deviation, the greater the perceived risk. The *coefficient of variation* (CV), which is the ratio of the standard deviation to the expected value, is another statistical risk evaluation tool but one that eliminates the bias that can be caused by size alone. The CV can be employed to compare the riskiness of more than one proposed transaction.

$$VAR = \sum_{i=1}^{n} p_i(CF_i - EV)^2 \tag{7.2}$$

$$SD = \sqrt{VAR} \tag{7.3}$$

$$CV = SD/EV \tag{7.4}$$

In addition to the basic statistical tools just described, the analysis of a proposed LBO can further draw on the standard capital budgeting tools to examine the anticipated effects of different assumptions about the future financial environment. For example, the capital structure of the LBO might feature adjustable interest rates, which may have a significant impact of the projected net cash flows, depending on how interest rates vary. An LBO company that might be profitable with one set of assumed interest rates could be unable to service its debt if interest rates rise.

To assess the potential impact of different interest rate assumptions, as well as other important assumptions that went into the projection of future net cash flows, *sensitivity analysis* is employed. Sensitivity analysis is a technique that measures the change in a dependent variable in response to a change in an independent variable. It allows the analyst to ask "what if" questions. For example, net cash flows might be projected using a "most

---

16. Robert W. Kolb and Ricardo J. Rodriguez, *Principles of Finance* (Denver, Colorado: Kolb Publishing Co., 1995).

likely" estimate of various factors such as sales, interest costs, labor costs, and so on. Sensitivity analysis may then be used to see what the firm's financial performance would be for a given change in sales or interest rates or any other factor that is believed to be crucial. If the assumed levels of specific factors are varied, it is possible to determine how sensitive the performance of the LBO is to changes in specific factors. For example, the result of such an analysis might be that a hypothetical LBO could still be profitable even when labor costs rise 10% but would experience losses if interest rates rose 200 basis points or if sales were to decline 10%. In such a case, the LBO would be found to be sensitive to sales and interest rate assumptions but not very sensitive to labor costs assumptions.

Once the sensitivity analysis has been conducted, it should be more clear which factors are the most crucial to the viability of the post-LBO firm. The variations that caused the projections to yield losses, such as the 200–basis point increase in interest rates, need to be more closely examined. If, after such an examination, it is determined that such an occurrence is unlikely over the projection horizon, the LBO may still be considered to be not inordinately risky. If, on the other hand, the interest rates entered into the original projection were rates that approach historical lows, the possibility of a 200–basis point interest rate increase would be quite real. This might change the risk assessment of the LBO.

Types of LBO Risk

The riskiness of an LBO may be broken down into two main categories: business risk and interest rate risk.

Business risk refers to the risk that the firm going private will not generate sufficient earnings to meet the interest payments and other current obligations of the firm. This risk category takes into account factors such as cyclical downturns in the economy and competitive factors within the industry, such as greater price and nonprice competition. Firms that have very cyclical sales or companies that are in very competitive industries tend not to be good LBO candidates.

Interest rate risk is the risk that interest rates will rise, thus increasing the firm's current obligations. This is quite important to firms that have more variable rate debt. Interest rate increases could force a firm into bankruptcy even when it experienced greater than anticipated demand and held nonfinancial costs within reasonable bounds. The level of interest rates at the time of the LBO may be a guide to the probability that rates will rise in the future. For example, if interest rates are low at the time of the buyout, interest rate increases may be more likely than if interest rates were at peak levels.

FINANCIAL ANALYSIS OF LBO CANDIDATES

A careful financial analysis of an LBO candidate is critically important. The most basic question the participants in an LBO must consider is whether the company will be able to service the debt following the LBO. The second, but equally important, consideration is whether the changes necessary to enable the firm to service the debt will cause it to lose market share and not be viable after the debt has been retired. The heated pace of LBOs in the late 1980s focused increasing criticism on LBO dealmakers for forsaking this second objective while focusing solely on debt service. However, some LBO dealmakers, such as Ted Forstmann of Forstmann Little & Co., contend that they never go forward with a deal unless it fulfills both criteria. This firm has been known to turn down many deals that do not make economic sense.

The financial analysis of an LBO candidate is similar to that of a merger or an acquisition. It begins with financial statement analysis. This often starts with the construction of pro forma financial statements that project the firm's financial condition and income for several years into the future. A rule of thumb is to construct the pro forma statements to depict the firm five years or more into the future. During this period LBO debt pressures are usually highest because most of the debt is still outstanding. Financial statement analysis is covered in most corporate finance textbooks. This book presents a review of the basic concepts as they apply to mergers and LBOs in Chapter 12.[17]

A commonly used tool of financial statement analysis is financial ratio analysis. Ratios such as those presented in Chapter 12 are used to assess the overall financial condition of a company and to identify potential problem areas. Leveraged buyout candidates are expected to be sufficiently liquid, as reflected by current and quick ratios that meet or exceed industry norms, and to have debt levels, as reflected by ratios such as the debt ratio and the debt-equity ratio, that indicate unused debt capacity. A cash flow projection, based on reasonable assumptions, that shows sufficient cash flows to support the post-LBO debt services is a fundamental component of the LBO financial analysis.

RETURNS TO STOCKHOLDERS FROM LBOs

DeAngelo, DeAngelo, and Rice analyzed the gains to both stockholders and management from management buyouts of 72 companies that proposed to go private between 1973 and 1980.[18] These researchers found average premiums above the market value of the LBO target's stock price equal to 56%. They concluded that managers are willing to offer a premium to public stockholders because they may achieve other productivity gains following the buyout. The fact that they are willing to offer a 56% average premium indicates that managers anticipate gains in excess of this premium. Their results are interesting in that they show a comparatively high rate of return, relative to nonleveraged transactions, that is derived from the time period that precedes the takeover mania of the fourth merger wave.

The DeAngelo, DeAngelo, and Rice results have been confirmed by other research studies. In a study of 28 MBO proposals between 1979 and 1984, the average premium above the market value of the firm 30 days before the announcement of the offer was 48%.[19] This premium was as high as 79% when there were three or more offers. (This commonsense result also supports the arguments for mandated auctions in LBOs.)

---

17. See Charles Moyer, James R. McGuigan, and William Kretlow, *Contemporary Financial Management,* 5th ed. (St. Paul, Minn.: West Publishing Co., 1992), pp. 156–204; J. Fred Weston and Thomas E. Copeland, *Managerial Finance,* 9th ed. (Orlando, Fla., Dryden Press, 1992), pp. 173–205; and Eugene F. Brigham and Louis C. Gapinski, *Intermediate Financial Management,* 3rd ed. (Chicago: Dryden Press, 1990), pp. 650–682.

18. Harry DeAngelo, Linda DeAngelo, and Eugene Rice, "Going Private: Minority Freezeouts and Stockholder Wealth," *Journal of Law and Economics* vol. 27, no. 2 (October 1984), pp. 367–402. Similar results are found in L. Marais, K. Schipper, and A. Smith, "Wealth Effects of Going Private on Senior Securities," *Journal of Financial Economics* 23, no. 1 (June 1989), p. 155.

19. Louis Lowenstein, *What's Wrong with Wall Street?* (Reading, Mass.: Addison-Wesley, 1988), pp. 183–184.

A study by Travlos and Cornett shows a statistically significant negative correlation between abnormal returns to shareholders and the P/E ratio of the firm relative to the industry.[20] This implies that the lower the P/E ratio, compared with similar firms, the greater probability that the firm is poorly managed. Travlos and Cornett interpret the low P/E ratios as reflecting greater room for improvement through changes such as the reduction of agency costs. Some of these efficiency gains may then be realized by going private. These gains become the source of the buyout premium.

The mere fact that public stockholders receive high premiums does not necessarily mitigate the need for regulation. Auctions generally increase shareholder premiums. Therefore, a high premium offer by management may be surpassed when it is placed in an auction environment. Moreover, the true market potential of a buyout candidate may never be realized unless an auction takes place.

RETURNS TO STOCKHOLDERS FROM DIVISIONAL BUYOUTS

Many MBOs result from a management group buying a division from the parent company. Many of these transactions have been criticized for not being "arm's-length" deals. Managers of the parent company are often accused of giving preferential treatment to a management bid. The parent company may forsake the auction process and accept management's offer without soliciting other higher offers.

In 1989 Gailen Hite and Michael Vetsuypens conducted a study designed to show whether divisional buyouts had adverse effects on the wealth of parent stockholders.[21] Many researchers believe that divisional buyouts may present opportunities for efficiency-related gains as the division becomes removed from the parent company's layers of bureaucracy.[22] This may be a source of value to the managers of the buying group but does not negate the often-cited possibility that a fair price, such as that which might be derived from an auction, was not paid for the division.

Hite and Vetsuypens failed to find any evidence of a reduction in shareholder wealth following divisional buyouts by management. Their results show small, but statistically significant, wealth gains for a two-day period surrounding the buyout announcement. They interpret these results as indicating that division buyouts result in a more efficient allocation of assets. The existence of small wealth gains indicates that shareholders in the parent company shared in some of these gains.

EFFICIENCY GAINS FROM LBOs

Some supporters of LBOs see these transactions as a source of efficiency gains. One proponent of this view, Professor Michael Jensen of Harvard University, has contended that

---

20. Nicholas G. Travlos and M. M. Cornett, "Going Private Buyouts and Determinants of Shareholder Returns," *Journal of Accounting, Auditing and Finance,* no. 8 (Winter 1993), pp. 1–25.

21. Gailen L. Hite and Michael R. Vetsuypens, "Management Buyouts of Divisions and Shareholder Wealth," *Journal of Finance* 44, no. 4 (September 1989), pp. 953–970.

22. Eugene Fama and Michael Jensen, "Separation of Ownership Control," *Journal of Law and Economics* 26 (1983), pp. 323–329.

the post-LBO corporation, with its highly leveraged capital structure, high percentage of ownership of managers, and close monitoring by the sponsors of the buyout, has an incentive structure that is superior to the pre-LBO corporation.[23] Jensen states that there is reason to believe that the post-LBO corporation is in a better position to outperform the pre-LBO version of the same company.

Critics of LBOs do not share Jensen's optimistic view. They argue that sponsors of successful LBOs typically cash out of their investment within five to seven years after the LBO.[24] Indeed, much of the LBO financial analysis incorporates such cash-out assumptions. Steven Kaplan of the University of Chicago showed that approximately 45% of larger LBOs completed between 1979 and 1986 returned to public ownership before August 1990.[25] He found that the median time period of private ownership was 6.8 years. These findings provide some support for the view held by some critics that financial dealmakers facilitate the buyout process for their personal enrichment with little thought for the long-term welfare of the company. They contend that the end product is a heavily leveraged firm that has a much higher probability of falling into bankruptcy, with few offsetting gains in profitability or efficiency. They further argue that even if there are efficiency gains, pre-buyout shareholders who have already sold their shares cannot share in any post-buyout successes.

Another study by Steven Kaplan, however, contradicts some of the critics' arguments.[26] His research finds additional value in post-LBO firms. This result seems to justify the high premiums associated with the buyout. Kaplan cites two main sources of value of LBOs: efficiency gains and tax benefits. He shows that, compared with industry median values, post-buyout companies experienced positive increases in operating income and margins for the first two years after the buyout. These same companies were shown to reduce inventories and capital expenditures relative to industry medians. All of these are clearly positive except capital expenditures, which could also be considered a sacrifice of the company's future.

In another study, Kaplan quantified the tax benefits that post-buyout firms enjoy.[27] "A comparison of the excess returns earned by pre-buyout and post-buyout investors to several measures of tax benefits is consistent with pre-buyout shareholders receiving most of the potential tax benefits. The returns to post-buyout investors are not related to the tax benefits created by the buyout. This is consistent with a market for corporate control that forces the buyout companies to pay public stockholders tax benefits that are ex-post predictable and obtainable by other bidders."[28]

Kaplan showed that the tax benefits of LBOs are largely predictable and are incorporated in the premium that pre-LBO stockholders receive. This implies that the post-LBO

---

23. Michael Jensen, "The Eclipse of the Public Corporation," *Harvard Business Review.*

24. Albert Rappaport, "The Staying Power of the Public Corporation," *Harvard Business Review* 1 (1990), pp. 953–970.

25. Steven Kaplan, "The Staying Power of Leveraged Buyouts," *Journal of Financial Economics* 29 (October 1991), pp. 287–314.

26. Steven Kaplan, "Management Buyouts: Efficiency Gains or Value Transfers," University of Chicago Working Paper No. 244, October 1988, Chicago.

27. Steven Kaplan, "Management Buyouts: Evidence on Taxes As a Source of Value," *Journal of Finance* 3 (July 1989), pp. 611–632.

28. Steven Kaplan, "Management Buyouts," University of Chicago Working Paper No. 245, p. 44.

investors need to find other sources of value. Both Kaplan studies imply that any sweeping criticism of LBOs may be unwarranted. That is, the buyout process may create value. Therefore, an evaluation must be made on a case-by-case basis.

REVERSE LBOs

A reverse LBO occurs when a company goes private in an LBO only to be taken public again at a later date. This may be done if the buyers who take the company private believe that it is undervalued, perhaps because of poor management. They may buy the firm and institute various changes, such as replacing senior management and other forms of restructuring. If the new management converts the company into a more profitable private enterprise, it may be able to go through the initial public offer process again.

The opportunity to conduct a successful reverse LBO is greater when the going-private transaction takes place when the stock market is down and the public offering occurs in a bull market.[29] This may make the assets of the LBO candidate undervalued in a poor market and possibly overvalued in the bull market. This reasoning, however, implies that the seller is somewhat naive and does not realize the impact of the short-term market fluctuation.

Reverse LBO Research

Muscarella and Vetsuypens reviewed 72 reverse LBOs that went public since 1983 and had undergone a buyout.[30] Their study presents a favorable picture of the post-buyout performance of these firms. They found that the ownership structure tended to be quite concentrated, with management retaining a substantial fraction of the equity. Using traditional accounting measures of performance and financial condition, they found improvements in profitability that were the result of cost reductions as opposed to increased revenues. These results were more dramatic for divisional LBOs than for full firm buyouts. Reductions in capital expenditures were one of the more significant sources of efficiency gains but reduction in staffing was not. Even though the firms increased their leverage to finance the buyout, management took steps to reduce debt after the buyout. These results imply that the post-buyout firms are in better condition than their pre-buyout predecessors. It is not surprising, therefore, that shareholders pay more when the firms go public for the second time compared with the price the company sold for in the LBO. One question arises, however: If the management group is essentially the same before and after the buyout, why did management not enact these increased efficiencies as part of the fiduciary responsibilities for shareholders when they were running the pre-buyout company? This criticism may be less relevant for divisional buyouts, in which management may be able to take broader actions because they are not part of a larger bureaucratic structure of a parent company.

Holthausen and Larker analyzed the post-buyout accounting and stock price performance of 90 companies that engaged in reverse LBOs from 1983 to 1988.[31] They found

---

29. Leslie Wayne, "Reverse LBOs Bring Riches," *New York Times,* 23 April 1987, p. D1.

30. Chris J. Muscarella and Michael R. Vetsuypens, "Efficiency and Organizational Structure: A Study of Reverse LBOs," *Journal of Finance* 45, no. 5 (December 1990), pp. 1389–1414.

31. Robert W. Holthausen and David F. Larker, "The Financial Performance of Reverse Leveraged Buyouts," *Journal of Financial Economics* 42, no. 3 (November 1996), pp. 293–332.

that these companies outperformed their industries over the four years following the initial public offering. In addition, they noted that reverse LBOs also increased capital expenditures and working capital levels following the offering. They also noted that when the ownership structure became less concentrated in the hand of managers, firm performance declined.

LBO Performance Record: Research Results

One nonacademic study of the performance of companies that went private in LBOs was conducted by the buyout firm Kohlberg Kravis & Roberts.[32] Not surprisingly, this study found increases in employment, capital spending, and research and development expenditures after the buyouts. The study's sample contained 13 companies that KKR had taken private. Shortly after the study was released, however, some of the companies in their sample defaulted on the LBO debt.

Other research shows that the returns from reverse LBOs are mixed. In a study of 70 reverse LBOs, Hirt and Block found an average return of only 4.2%.[33] Table 7.3 reveals that the range was quite variable, with some big winners and losers.

CASE STUDY: THE REVERSE LBO OF GIBSON GREETING CARDS

One of the classic reverse LBOs was the buyout of Gibson Greeting Cards by the Wesray Corporation. This buyout firm, led by former Treasury Secretary William Simon and his partner, Raymond Chambers, bought Gibson Greeting Cards from RCA in 1982. They paid $58 million in cash and assumed $22.6 million in liabilities. In May 1983 Wesray took Gibson public in a stock offering valued at $330 million.

Ironically, Gibson Greeting Cards has had a troubled financial history since its famous reverse LBO in 1983. As of 1995 it holds a 10% share of the greeting card market after American Greetings and Hallmark. In 1994 it lost $28.6 million on revenues of $548.8 million.[a] It continued to make financial history in the 1990s when it disclosed in 1994 that it lost $23 million on derivative investments (interest rate swaps). This bad news followed the 1992 bankruptcy of its largest customer, Phar-Mor, Inc. Later in 1994 another of Gibson's large customers, F&M Distributors, Inc., also filed for Chapter 11 bankruptcy.

---

a. Raju Narisetti and Wendy Bounds, "Sale of Gibson Greetings Inc. Is Considered," *Wall Street Journal,* July 7, 1995, p.A4.

Other research studies have failed to find such widespread benefits from LBOs. William Long and David Ravenscraft compared the results of the KKR study with other research in the field and concluded that the KKR results were not consistent with those of other major

---

32. Kohlberg Kravis & Roberts, "Presentation on Leveraged Buyouts," January, 1989.

33. Stanley B. Block and Geoffrey A. Hirt, *Foundations of Financial Management,* 7th ed. (Blue Ridge, Ill: Irwin Publishing Co., 1994) p. 576.

Table 7.3.   Winners and Losers in Reverse LBOs, 8/31/91–8/31/92

Biggest Winners among Reverse LBOs	Percent (%)	Biggest Losers among Reverse LBOs	Percent (%)
Perrigo	98.4	Health-O-Meter Products	−58.0
Comp USA	79.2	Buttrey Food &Drug	−57.1
R.P. Scherer	70.1	Alliance Imaging	−55.9
Tetra Tech	66.7	Menley & James	−54.8
Lincare Hldg	58.9	AGCO	−48.2

Source: Block and Hirt, *Foundations of Financial Management,* 7th ed. (Blue Ridge, Ill.: Irwin Publishing Co., 1994), p. 576.

research studies.[34] These studies are reviewed next and are broken down by topic categories.

Employment Effects
The KKR study found that the average annual employment of the companies in their sample was 13% higher than the pre-LBO employment levels. In their critique of the KKR findings, Long and Ravenscraft point out that the Kaplan and Muscarella and Vetsuypens studies found either negative or no employment effects. Another study by James Kitching showed neutral employment effects.

Research and Development
The impact of LBOs on research and development is less clear. A National Science Foundation study found that "R&D declined between 1986 and 1987 by 12.8% for 8 out of the 200 leading U.S. R&D performing companies which had undergone LBO, buybacks, or other restructuring."[35] A total of 176 firms that were not involved in mergers, LBOs, or other restructurings increased R&D by an average of 5.4%. This observation provides some evidence, albeit weak, that LBOs may be associated with lower R&D expenditures.

Capital Spending
Steven Kaplan's research shows small declines in capital expenditures, whereas Ivan Bull found a 24.7% industry adjusted decline (21.9% unadjusted) between one year before the LBO and two years afterward. One must be careful about drawing conclusions from these

34. Long and Ravenscraft compare the major conclusions of the KKR research with the following studies: William F. Long and David J. Ravenscraft, "The Record of LBO Performance," Paper presented at the New York University Conference on Corporate Governance, May 17, 1989; Steven Kaplan, "A Summary of Sources of Value in Management Buyouts," paper presented at the New York University Conference on Management Buyouts, May 20, 1988; Ivan Bull, "Management Performance in Leveraged Buyouts," paper presented at the New York University Conference on Management Buyouts, May 20, 1988; Chris J. Muscarella and Michael R. Vetsuypens, "Efficiency and Organizational Structure: A Study of Reverse LBOs," *Journal of Finance* 45, no. 5 (December 1990), pp. 1389–1414; National Science Foundation, "An Assessment of the Impact of Recent Leveraged Buyouts and Other Restructurings on Industrial Research and Development Expenditures," prepared for the House of Representatives Committee on Energy and Commerce, 1989; James Kitching, "Early Returns on LBOs," *Harvard Business Review* (November/December 1989), pp. 74–81. (The Kitching study was not included in the Long and Ravenscraft review.)

35. Long and Ravenscraft, "The Record of LBO Performance," p. 2.

results because they refer to different time periods. The longer the time after the buyout, the lower the debt pressures should be. If the LBO requires that capital expenditures or R&D be curtailed, this policy should be abandoned as the interest payment pressures subside. The longer the time period, the lower the capital expected spending effects.

CONFLICTS OF INTEREST IN MANAGEMENT BUYOUTS

A clear conflict of interest may exist in MBOs. Managers are responsible for managing the corporation to maximize the value of stockholders' investment and provide them with the highest return possible. These same managers take on a very different role when they are required to present an offer to stockholders to buy the company. This was the case when the management of RJR Nabisco presented an offer to stockholders to take Nabisco private in an MBO. This offer was quickly superseded by a competing offer from Kohlberg Kravis & Roberts as well as other responding offers from management.[36] If management truly attempts to maximize the value of stockholders' investments, why does it choose to advocate an offer that it knows is clearly not in the stockholders' best interests? Many researchers believe that managers cannot serve this dual, and sometimes conflicting, role as agent for both the buyer and the seller.

One proposed solution to this conflict is *neutralized voting,* whereby the proponents of a deal do not participate in the approval process. If the proponents are stockholders, their votes are not included in the approval process. They may have to participate in the voting process because under some state laws a quorum may not be possible without their participation if they hold a certain number of shares.[37] The appointment of an independent financial adviser to render a fairness opinion is a common second step in this process, which is meant to help reduce the conflicts of interest.

Even if these precautionary measures are adopted, certain practical considerations may limit their effectiveness. Although those members of the board of directors who may profit from the LBO may not vote for its approval, other members of the board may have a close relationship to them and consider themselves obliged to support the deal. Lawsuits by stockholders suing directors for breach of fiduciary duty have placed limits on this tendency. Fairness opinions put forward by investment bankers who have done much business with management or who may have a financial interest in the deal may be of questionable value.

Although these steps are an important attempt to try to reduce some of the conflicts inherent in the MBO process, they do not address the issue of the manager being both the buyer's and the seller's agent. One solution that has been proposed is to have mandated auctions of corporations presented with an MBO.[38]

According to current case law, directors are not allowed to favor their own bid over another bid once the bidding process has begun. The prohibition on an unfair bidding process was set forth by a number of important court decisions. In *Revlon, Inc. v. MacAndrews &*

---

36. See Bryan Burrough and John Helyar, *Barbarians at the Gate: The Fall of RJR Nabisco* (New York: Harper & Row, 1990).

37. Arthur M. Borden, *Going Private* (New York: Law Journal Seminar Press, 1987), pp. 1–6.

38. Louis Lowenstein, *What's Wrong with Wall Street?* (Reading, Mass.: Addison-Wesley, 1987), p. 184.

Forbes Holdings, Inc., the Delaware Supreme Court ruled that Revlon's directors breached their fiduciary duty in granting a lockup option to "white knight" Forstmann Little & Co.[39] The court ruled that this constituted an unfair bidding process that favored Forstmann Little & Co. over hostile bidder, Pantry Pride.

In *Hanson Trust PLC v. SCM Corporation,* the Second Circuit Court took a similar position on the use of lockup options to favor an LBO by Merrill Lynch instead of a hostile bid by Hanson Trust PLC.[40] Hanson Trust had initially made a tender offer for SCM at $60 per share. In response to Merrill Lynch's LBO offer at $70 per share, Hanson Trust upped its bid to $72. The court ruled that SCM gave preferential treatment to Merrill Lynch by granting lockup options on two SCM divisions to Merrill Lynch.

In *Edelman v. Fruehauf,* the circuit court concluded that the board of directors had decided to make a deal with management and did not properly consider other bids such as the all-cash tender offer by Asher Edelman.[41] The court held that the Fruehauf board of directors did not conduct a fair auction for the company.[42]

Although the preceding decisions establish a precedent that an auction for a firm must be conducted fairly, the courts stop short of spelling out the rules for conducting or ending the bidding process. These decisions fall within the purview of the business judgment rule. The law is also unclear regarding when or even if an auction is required.

The formation of an independent directors committee may facilitate the auction process.[43] This process is often used when management has proposed a buyout. When faced with a management proposal to take the firm private, the board of directors will usually respond by creating a special committee of independent, nonmanagement directors to ensure that shareholders receive fair, if not maximal, value for their investment. The committee may then decide to have its own valuation formulated, hire independent counsel, and conduct an auction.

SEC Rule 13e-3

SEC Rule 13e-3, which attempted to regulate some of the problems of management self-dealing associated with going private, is an amendment to the Securities Exchange Act of 1934. The rule governs repurchases in going-private transactions, and it applies to share repurchases that result in fewer than 300 shareholders or when the previously public company would no longer be listed on public stock exchanges or would no longer be quoted in an interdealer quotation system. The rule requires that the firm going private file a Schedule 13E-3, on which it discloses information similar to that disclosed on a Schedule 13D or 14D-1. This information must be disseminated to stockholders and includes the following:

39. *Revlon, Inc. v. MacAndrews & Forbes Holdings, Inc.,* 506 A. 2d. 173 (Del. Sup. 1986).

40. *Hanson Trust PLC v. SCM Corporation,* 781 F. 2d 264 (2d Cir. 1986).

41. *Edelman v. Fruehauf,* 798 F. 2d 882, 886–87 (6th Cir. 1986).

42. Lawrence Lederman and Barry A. Bryer, "Representing a Public Company in a Leveraged Transaction," in Yakov Amihud, ed. *Leveraged Management Buyouts* (Homewood, Ill.: Dow Jones Irwin, 1989), pp. 111–174.

43. Joseph Grunfest, "Management Buyouts and Leveraged Buyouts: Are the Critics Right?" in Yakov Amihud, ed. *Leveraged Management Buyouts* (Homewood, Ill.: Dow Jones Irwin, 1989), pp. 241–261.

- Disclosure of offers by unaffiliated parties within the previous 18 months
- Detailed discussion of the fairness of the transaction
- Inclusion of any fairness opinions
- Alternatives to the MBO that were considered
- Disclosure of the position of the outside directors

Rule 13e-1 provides valuable information that stockholders may consider when evaluating a going-private proposal. Even though the disclosure has benefits for shareholders, it does not eliminate an opportunity for management self-dealing.

Leveraged Buyouts as White Knights

Managers in target firms have used LBOs as part of an antitakeover strategy, providing stockholders an offer they may accept instead of the hostile bid. This phenomenon became more commonplace in the fourth merger wave and declined with the overall slowdown in LBO activity in the 1990s.

In a study of 11 MBOs between 1980 and 1984, Andrei Shleifer and Robert Vishny found that 6 of the 11 buyouts were responses to hostile threats. These threats came in the form of an outright hostile tender offer or the acquisition of shares with the intention to make a bid for control of the firm.[44]

Leveraged Buyouts and the Position of Other Debt Holders

One area of interest to many critics in recent years has been the potential impact of the assumption of high amounts of LBO debt, and the associated issuance of junk bonds, on the value of the investment of current bondholders. The fact that bondholders are not part of the approval process has attracted much attention. The additional debt increases the fixed payments that the firm has to make after the buyout. In doing so, it increases the likelihood that the firm will be unable to meet these payments and be forced into receivership.

This problem came to the fore in the RJR Nabisco buyout of November 1988. The value of current bonds dropped sharply after the announcement of the LBO. Some bonds fell as much as 15 points, or $150 for each $1,000 face value amount, in the week the buyout was announced. Although the losses incurred by bondholders drew widespread attention in the RJR Nabisco buyout, bondholders have recognized it as a problem for some time. When the R. H. Macy and Company $3.6 billion buyout proposal was announced in 1985, the stock price rose $16 per share, whereas the price of Macy notes fell more than three points.

Investors who are holding bonds in a corporation that is involved in an LBO see the value and rating of their bonds deteriorate rapidly following the LBO announcement. This has alienated bondholders, particularly institutional investors who are becoming increasingly vocal. "'High credit bonds are converted into junk bonds overnight,' fumed John J.

44. Andrei Shleifer and Robert W. Vishny, "Management's Buyouts as a Response to Market Pressure," in Alan Auerbach, ed. *Mergers and Acquisitions* (Chicago: University of Chicago Press, 1988), pp. 87–103.

Creedon, chief executive officer of Metropolitan Life Insurance Company. 'We think management has a duty to all constituents of the company, including bondholders'."[45] Metropolitan Life saw its $340 million worth of A-rated RJR bonds downgraded to a junk-bond rating for a $40 million loss.

The impact of takeover and LBO activity on bonds became so pronounced in the 1980s that the rating agencies often lowered the rating of a firm if it became a takeover or LBO candidate. During the fourth merger wave, the probability of a future LBO became an additional factor that rating agencies took into consideration along with traditional business fundamentals and economic factors.

The state of acrimony between bondholders and RJR Nabisco following the announcement of the LBO led Metropolitan Life Insurance Company to sue Nabisco in a New York State court. Metropolitan's suit alleged that a small group of Nabisco's management sought to enrich themselves at the expense of bondholders who had invested capital in Nabisco in good faith. Opponents of the bondholders contended that the bondholders were seeking to control the operations and decisions of the corporation in a manner that should only be reserved for stockholders. They thought that if bondholders wanted such control, they should have taken the risk of buying stock, not the relatively lower risk bonds.

The conflict between bondholders and stockholders is illustrated in Figure 7.7. As the takeover battle for RJR Nabisco heated up during October and November 1988, the value of Nabisco stock rose, as is typical during a takeover contest. However, the value of Nabisco's outstanding bonds declined in response to the market's perception of the added risk and the increased probability of default that the post-buyout Nabisco would have. Figure 7.8 shows that the fallout in the bond market went beyond Nabisco bonds. The value of new issues of corporate bonds declined following the erosion of the values of bonds related to LBO debt sales.

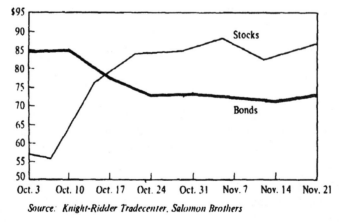

Source: Knight-Ridder Tradecenter, Salomon Brothers

Figure 7.7. RJR Nabisco bonds slip as stock soars: price of the $8^{3/8}$ bond due in 2017 and the closing price of RJR Nabisco stock.

Source: "Battle Erupts Over Bonds," *New York Times,* 27 November 1988, p. 21. Copyright © 1988 by the New York Times Company. Reprinted by permission.

---

45. "Bondholders Are As Mad As Hell—And No Wonder," *Business Week,* 5 December 1988, p. 28.

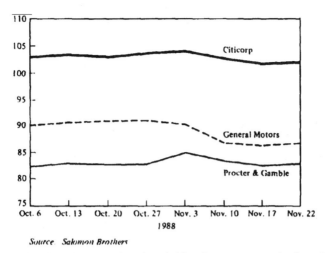

Figure 7.8. How other bonds have fared: weekly closing prices for bonds of three leading companies: Proctor & Gamble, $8^{5/8}$ due 2016; General Motors, $8^{1/8}$ due 2016; Citicorp, $10^{3/4}$ due 2015.

Source: "Battle Erupts Over Bonds," *New York Times,* 27 November 1988, p. 21. Copyright © 1988 by the New York Times Company. Reprinted by permission.

Bondholders contend that buyouts involve a transferal or misappropriation of wealth from bondholders to stockholders; they believe that the board of directors has a fiduciary obligation to bondholders and to stockholders. Others contend that bondholders have to bear "event risk" just like stockholders. They believe that the occurrence of an LBO is another form of event risk that a bondholder must assume when purchasing corporate debt.

On May 31, 1989, a federal judge ruled that an "implied covenant" *did not* exist between the corporation and the RJR Nabisco bondholders, which would prevent the corporation from engaging in actions, such as an LBO, that would dramatically lower the value of the bonds. The court ruled that, to be binding, such agreements had to be in writing.

EMPIRICAL RESEARCH ON WEALTH TRANSFER EFFECTS

There has been much public outcry in the media regarding the losses that bondholders have incurred after going-private transactions. Such media coverage implies that there is a general wealth transfer effect from bondholders to equity holders in these transactions. A study by Kenneth Lehn and Annette Poulsen failed to confirm the existence of such an effect.[46] They found no decrease in value of preferred stock and bonds associated with LBOs. This result, however, was to some extent contradicted by Travlos and Cornett.[47]

---

46. Ken Lehn and Annette Poulsen, "Leveraged Buyouts: Wealth Created or Wealth Distributed," in M. Weidenbaum and K. Chilton, eds. *Public Policy Towards Corporate Takeovers* (New Brunswick, N.J.: Transaction Publishers, 1988).

47. Travlos Nicholas and M.M. Cornett, "Going Private Buyouts and Determinants of Shareholder Returns," *Journal of Accounting, Auditing and Finance* 8, no. 8 (Winter 1993).

Although their analysis did reveal a decline in the value of bonds and preferred stock following the announcement of going-private proposals, the decline they reported was relatively small.

The limited research in this area fails to provide support for a large wealth transfer effect. The empirical research indicates that if such an effect exists, it is not very significant. The reality of the Nabisco transaction, however, contradicts this conclusion. This seems to imply that these results may not be relevant to very large transactions, such as the Nabisco buyout, in which there is a dramatic change in the bond rating and the financial leverage of the firm. Given the decline in the junk bond market, the supply of such large transactions has been limited. This will reduce the supply of data for additional research on this issue.

PROTECTION FOR BONDHOLDERS

After the unfavorable federal court decision in the Metropolitan Life Insurance case, bond purchasers began to demand greater protection against the financial losses resulting from "event risk." In response, they received from bond issuers agreements that would allow them to get back their full principal in the event of a buyout that would lower the value of their debt holdings. The covenants are usually triggered by actions such as the purchase of a block of stock by a hostile bidder or other actions such as a management-led buyout. In return for the added protection, bond buyers pay a somewhat higher interest rate, which is dependent on the issuer's financial condition. The rate may be structured to the magnitude of the rating change.

CASE STUDY: REVCO LEVERAGED BUYOUT

On March 11, 1986, Revco received a buyout bid from a management group led by Sidney Dworkin who was the group's CEO at the time. The bid offered $1.16 billion for the drugstore chain, which at that time was the second largest LBO in this industry. Following the LBO, however, the firm performed below expectations and became one of the first major LBOs to fail. For this reason, the Revco LBO merits further study.

Industry Background

Drugstore sales had been growing rapidly during the 10 years before the buyout, increasing at an average annual rate of 11.6% between 1976 and 1986.[a] Sales for the 1987–88 period ran close to the 7.5% to 8.0% range that was projected during the buyout negotiations. In response to growing consumer demand, many drugstore chains opened new outlets. Others expanded by buying other chains. One example was the Rite Aid Corporation's acquisition of the Grey Drug Fair chain, which was owned by the Sherwin-Williams Paint Company.

The pharmaceutical industry instituted many other innovations designed to improve productivity, including the increased use of computers to track and enhance inventory control. However, competitive forces require that the industry be even more efficient. Competition comes from a combination of food and drugstore chains as well as from discount drug chains. Pharmaceuticals is considered one of the two recession-resistant industries in the U.S. economy. (The other is the food industry.) All other factors being constant, a noncyclical firm is a better candidate for an LBO because there is a lower probability that the cash flows will suffer a sudden, unpredictable falloff as a result of a cyclical reduction in demand.

The drugstore industry continued to do well in the two years after the buyout. Sales continued to rise without a significant reduction in profit margins. The increased use of private labels provided firms with higher margin products that could be sold to consumers at competitive prices. The Revco buyout may have been inspired by the October 1985 LBO of Eckerd Drug Stores, which went private for $1.184 billion. The rise in the number of large LBO offers in the drugstore industry may be attributed to the general well-being of the industry, combined with the decline in interest rates and the cash-flow–generating ability of these firms.

Revco's Position in the Industry

As of August 23, 1986, Revco was the largest drugstore chain in the United States, with 2,049 stores in 30 states. Most of the company's stores were concentrated in Michigan, Ohio, Pennsylvania, North Carolina, South Carolina, Georgia, Virginia, Tennessee, Arizona, and Texas. Although Revco had diversified into other areas, most of its income came from traditional drugstore products. Revco's Odd Lot and Tangible Industries subsidiaries accounted for approximately 5% of its 1986 sales. These subsidiaries are wholesalers of closeout merchandise. Another 5% of its 1986 sales came from generic and private label drugs and vitamins.

Background of the Revco LBO

Revco was formerly Regal D. S., Inc., a Detroit-based drugstore chain. In 1966 the company went public under the name Revco and moved its headquarters to Cleveland, Ohio. It expanded and purchased Carter-Glogau Laboratories, a vitamin manufacturer. Revco also bought the Stanton Corporation, which administered lie detector tests. Revco's CEO, Sidney Dworkin, had been with the firm since 1956, when he joined the company as an accountant. He oversaw Revco's development into one of the largest drugstore chains in the country. By 1983 the company had 1,700 stores in 28 states. Its sales were almost $2 billion, with profits increasing at an impressive 37% per year.

In 1983 vitamins made by Carter-Glogau were blamed for the tragic deaths of 38 infants. As a result, the price of Revco stock fell, and Dworkin feared that the now undervalued Revco would be taken over. His defense was to place a large block of stock in what he believed would be friendly hands. In May 1984 Revco bought Odd Lot Trading Company, which had a chain of 70 discount stores, for $113 million in stock. This amounted to 12% of Revco's outstanding shares.

There have been numerous reports of personal conflicts between Dworkin and his new larger stockholders, the previous owners of Odd Lot Trading—Bernard Marden and Isaac Perlmutter.[b] According to these reports, Dworkin favored the close in-volvement of his two sons in Revco's business operations, a move opposed by Mar-den and Perlmutter. It is further reported that Marden and Perlmutter threatened to take over Revco. Revco eventually bought back their shares for $98.2 million. The conflict between Dworkin and Marden and Perlmutter, together with the resulting stock buyback, marked the decline of Dworkin's role in Revco. When the board of directors opposed the involvement of Dworkin's sons, he was forced to hire a new president from the outside—William Edwards.

The stock buyback put financial pressure on Revco because it was financed by debt. The increased fixed charges associated with the interest payments came at a time when Revco was having trouble keeping the Odd Lot Trading business prof-itable. By 1985 Revco experienced a loss of $35 million, mainly as a result of a large supply of unsold video cartridges.

Revco's LBO

Dworkin's solution to Revco's financial problems and his declining role in the com-pany was to retain Salomon Brothers and Transcontinental Services Group, which was a European investment group, to arrange an LBO. Dworkin offered the stock-holders $36 per share, which was $6 per share higher than the price the stock was trading for four months earlier when the news of the LBO was first announced. However, the LBO offer attracted the interest of the Haft family who, through their company, the Dart Group, made a higher offer. Dworkin responded by raising his offer to $38.50 per share, or $1.25 billion. The bidding process took seven months to complete before Dworkin's bid was accepted.

The LBO increased Revco's debt four times to $1.3 billion. Revco had planned to pay down the debt by selling off the nondrug businesses. Curiously, Revco also planned to expand at the same time, its goal being to open 100 new stores. This was an unusual move because most LBOs require downsizing and asset sales to "pay down" the debt. Increasingly concerned about Revco's financial condition, the board of directors favored a new marketing approach, which William Edwards, Revco's president, implemented. This marketing strategy abandoned the everyday low prices that Revco had been known for in favor of weekend specials and promotions. A major thrust of this marketing strategy was to expand Revco's product line to include televisions, furniture, and VCRs. Customers became confused when they saw furni-ture for sale in stores they had previously known as pharmacies. Revco's profits fell, reflecting the public's negative reaction.

In March 1987 Dworkin was removed as CEO. Edwards made various other at-tempts to turn the failing company around. For example, he cut prices to clear out in-ventories, and he rearranged the stores to promote better store traffic. The result was yet more customer confusion, and the company continued to decline. In October 1987 Boake Sells, a former Dayton Hudson president, was appointed CEO and charged with turning Revco around. But this was too little, too late. The 1987 Christmas sea-son was a disaster, with Revco in short supply of many essential and basic products, such as toothpaste, but with stockpiles of televisions and furniture. Cash flow problems became acute as revenues declined while fixed charges remained high.

Revco's Financial Condition

Sixteen months after going private through an LBO, Revco became the first of the big LBOs to fail when it missed a $46 million interest payment. In the 1980s, before the LBO, it had shown consistent profitability. Net income remained positive until 1987, when the firm was unable to generate sufficient revenues to meet its higher fixed expenses. To say that sales were not sufficient would be misleading, however. Sales rose in each year before 1987, when they declined to their 1985 levels. However, Revco relied on pre-LBO forecasts, which projected a continually higher sales volume. The 1987 decline in sales should not have forced a firm that was not highly leveraged into bankruptcy, but the pressures of the LBO debt left little room for error. Indeed, the report of the examiner confirmed that the pre-LBO predictions were unrealistically optimistic. This characteristic was symptomatic of other troubled LBOs.

Even before entering the LBO, Revco was not in a very liquid position. One of Revco's problems was its large holdings of nonmarketable inventories. This problem was compounded by the fact that Revco had too high a level of pre-LBO debt. The result was a company that could not meet its overly optimistic sales projections and had to file for bankruptcy. In doing so, Revco became the first major LBO to file for bankruptcy.

Revco eventually emerged from Chapter 11 bankruptcy protection in 1992. It wasted no time, however, in getting back into the merger and acquisition business. In April 1994 it purchased the Hook-SupeRx drugstore chain for $600 million, which placed Revco back in the number three ranking in the drugstore hierarchy behind Walgreen Co. and Rite Aid Corp. In late 1995, however, Rite Aid attempted to purchase Revco for $27.50 per share, or $1.8 billion, to form the largest drugstore chain in the United States with 4,500 outlets. The deal was disallowed in April 1996 by the Federal Trade Commission because of perceived antitrust conflicts.

---

a. U.S. Industrial Outlook, U.S. Department of Commerce, Washington, D.C., 1998.
b. "Revco: The Anatomy of a Failed Buyout," *Business Week*, October 3, 1998, pp. 58–59.

Much of the protection provided by the covenant agreements is in the form of a poison put allowing the bondholders to sell the bonds back to the issuer at an agreed upon price. Before the Nabisco case, poison puts were usually confined to privately held company bonds or new issue junk bonds. After the Nabisco bond downgradings, buyers of higher quality public issues demanded some of the same protection once they saw that their bonds could quickly fall into the same categories as the other higher risk issues (Table 7.4). Poison puts had also been used as a form of "shark repellent"; that is, companies would issue poison puts as a means of creating a financial obstacle to hostile bidders (see Chapter 5).

Table 7.4.   Examples of Post-Nabisco Poison Put Bond Insurance

Company	Issue	Issue Amount ($ millions)	Bondholder Gets Date Principal Back If-
Becton Dickinson	3/13/89	100	20% of stock bought and ratings downgraded
Federal Express	4/18/89	100	30% of stock bought and ratings downgraded
Long Island Lighting	4/10/89	375	Acquired by government body
RJR Nabisco	5/12/89	4,110	KKR's state reduced to less than 40%
Vons Companies	4/25/89	100	50% of stock bought and ratings downgraded

Source: "Investors Are Developing a Taste for this Poison," *Business Week,* July 10, 1989, p. 78. Reprinted from July 10, 1989 issue of *Business Week* by special permission, copyright © 1989 by Mc-Graw-Hill, Inc.

SUMMARY

An LBO is a financing technique in which the equity of a public corporation is purchased mostly with debt. After the purchase, the public company is taken private. The 1980s witnessed the widespread use of this technique and the participation in the financing of LBOs by many groups of institutional investors. The deals grew larger and larger and were structured by many different layers of secured and unsecured debt as well as by equity. Leveraged buyouts were first known as asset-based lending deals that usually involved firms with significant fixed assets and much unused borrowing capacity. As the major LBO dealmakers heavily promoted the financing technique in the 1980s, cash flow LBOs of firms that did not have significant assets to be used as collateral but had sizable and steady cash flows became popular. Higher buyout premiums caused more deals to rely on cash flow coverage rather than on the more traditional asset-based lending.

Stockholders of companies that were taken private reaped large gains, but some of these gains came at the expense of the firms' debt holders, who saw the value of the debt they held decline dramatically. The market value of debt usually fell after the buyout as the debt rating agencies lowered the ratings they gave these securities. Bondholders then sought protection in future debt offerings such as through put options, which allowed the debt to be sold back to the issuer at a specific price after the buyout.

Several of the companies that went private in the 1980s failed by the 1990s. The reasons for their failure were the combined effect of high debt service pressures and the 1990–91 recession and anemic recovery that followed. Large-scale megadeals disappeared from the financial scene, even though LBO investors remained interested in trying to enjoy the high returns that these risky deals may provide. The rising stock market also made going private transactions more expensive.

The LBOs of the 1990s are smaller transactions that use less debt and more equity. Investors scrutinize them more carefully and are mindful not to rely on aggressive sales projections or overly optimistic prices for asset sales. Many institutions that previously were active participants in this market no longer support these deals. Thus, the LBO market is a smaller and, it is hoped, wiser market in the 1990s.

REFERENCES

Anderson, Gary B. "Defining the Board Game." In Stephen C. Diamond, ed. *Leveraged Buyouts* (Homewood, Ill.: Dow Jones Irwin, 1985).

Blasi, Joseph. *Employee Ownership* (Cambridge, Mass.: Ballinger Publishing Co., 1988).

Block, Stanley B., and Geoffrey A. Hirt. *Foundations of Financial Management,* 7th ed. (Blue Ridge, Ill.: Irwin Publishing Co., 1994).

"Bondholders Are As Mad As Hell—And No Wonder." *Business Week,* 5 December 1988.

Borden, Arthur M. *Going Private* (New York: Law Journal Seminar Press, 1987).

Brancato, Carolyn, and Kevin Winch. *Merger Activity and Leveraged Buyouts: Sound Corporate Restructuring or Wall Street Alchemy.* Report prepared for the Committee on Energy and Commerce, U.S. House of Representatives, November 1984.

Brancato, Carolyn, and Kevin Winch. *Leveraged Buyouts and the Pot of Gold: Trends, Public Policy, and Case Studies.* Congressional Research Service, Library of Congress, September 15, 1987.

Brigham, Eugene F., and Louis C. Gapinski. *Intermediate Financial Management,* 3rd ed. (Chicago: Dryden Press, 1990).

Brudney, Victor, and Marvin A. Chirelstein. "A Restatement of Corporate Freezeouts." *Yale Law Journal* 87 (June 1978).

Bull, Ivan. "Management Performance in Leveraged Buyouts." Paper presented at the New York University Conference on Management Buyouts, May 20, 1988.

Burrough, Bryan, and John Helyar. *Barbarians at the Gate: The Fall of RJR Nabisco* (New York: Harper & Row, 1988).

Dabney, Michael R. "Asset Based Financing." In Milton Rock, ed. *Mergers and Acquisitions* (New York: McGraw-Hill, 1987).

DeAngelo, Harry, Linda DeAngelo, and Edward Rice. "Going Private: Minority Freezeouts and Stockholder Wealth." *Journal of Law and Economics* (October 1984), pp. 367–402.

Diamond, Stephen C., ed. *Leveraged Buyouts* (Homewood, Ill.: Dow Jones Irwin, 1985).

Edelman v. Fruehauf, F. 2d 882, 886–87 (6th Cir. 1986).

Fama, Eugene. "Agency Problems and the Theory of the Firm." *Journal of Political Economy* 88 no. 2 (April 1980).

Fama, Eugene, and Michael Jensen. "Separation of Ownership Control." *Journal of Law and Economics* 26 (1983).

Frisch, Robert A. *The Magic of ESOP's and LBO's* (New York: Farnsworth Publishing, 1985).

Gargiulo, Albert F., and Steven J. Levine. *The Leveraged Buyout* (New York: American Management Association, 1982).

Graham, Benjamin. *The Interpretation of Financial Statements* (New York: Harper & Row, 1987).

Greve, J. Terrance. "Management Buyouts and LBO's." In Milton Rock, ed. *Mergers and Acquisitions* (New York: McGraw-Hill, 1987).

Grunfest, Joseph. "Management Buyouts and Leveraged Buyouts: Are the Critics Right?" In Yakov Amihud, ed. *Leveraged Buyouts.* pp. (Homewood, Ill.: Dow Jones Irwin, 1989), pp. 241–261.

Hanson Trust PLC v. SCM Corporation, 781 F. 2d 264 (2d Cir. 1986).

Hite, Gailen L., and Michael R. Vetsuypens. "Management Buyouts of Divisions and Stockholder Wealth." *Journal of Finance* 44, no. 4 (September 1989).

Holthausen, Robert W., and David F. Larker. "The Financial Performance of Reverse Leveraged Buyouts." *Journal of Financial Economics,* 42, no. 3 (November 1996).

Industry Norms and Key Business Ratios (Murray Hill, N.J.: Dun & Bradstreet).

"Investors Are Developing a Taste for This Poison." *Business Week,* 10 July 1989.

Jensen, Michael. "The Eclipse of the Public Corporation." *Harvard Business Review* 5 (1989).

Jensen, Michael, and William Meckling. "Theory of the Firm: Managerial Behavior, Agency Costs and Ownership Structure." *Journal of Financial Economics* 3 (October 1976).

Jereski, Laura. "Buyout Funds Have Lots of Money, But Few Deals." *Wall Street Journal,* 26 April 1995.

Kaplan, Steven. "Management Buyouts: Efficiency Gains or Value Transfers." University of Chicago Working Paper No. 244, October 1988.

Kaplan, Steven. "Management Buyouts: Evidence on Taxes As a Source of Value." *Journal of Finance* 3 (July 1989).

Kaplan, Steven. "A Summary of Sources of Value in Management Buyouts." Paper presented at the New York University Conference on Management Buyouts, May 20, 1988.

Kaplan, Steven. "The Staying Power of Leveraged Buyouts." *Journal of Financial Economics* 29 (October 1991).

Kieschnick, Robert L. "Management Buyouts of Public Corporations: An Analysis of Prior Characteristics." In Yakov Amihud, ed. *Leveraged Management Buyouts* (Homewood, Ill.: Dow Jones Irwin, 1989), pp. 35–38.

Kitching, James. "Early Returns on LBOs." *Harvard Business Review* (November/December 1989).

Kohlberg Kravis & Roberts. "Presentation on Leveraged Buyouts." January 1989.

Kolb, Robert W., and Ricardo J. Gonzalez. *Principles of Finance* (Denver, Colorado: Kolb Publishing Co., 1995).

Lederman, Lawrence, and Barry B. Bryer. "Representing a Public Company in a Leveraged Transaction." In Yakov Amihud, ed. *Leveraged Management Buyouts* (Homewood, Ill.: Dow Jones Irwin, 1989), pp. 111–174.

Lehn, K., and A. Poulsen. "Leveraged Buyouts: Wealth Created or Wealth Distributed." In M. Weidenbaum and K. Chilton, eds. *Public Policy Towards Corporate Takeovers* (New Brunswick, N.J.: Transaction Publishers, 1988).

Lehn, K., and A. Poulsen. "Free Cash Flow and Stockholder Gains in Going Private Transactions." *Journal of Finance* 3 (July 1989).

Lichtenberg, Frank, and Donald Siegel. "The Effects of Takeovers on Employment and Wages of Central Office and Other Personnel." Columbia Graduate School Working Paper No. FB-89–05, 1989.

Long, William F., and David J. Ravenscraft. "The Record of LBO Performance." Paper presented at the New York University Conference on Corporate Governance, May 17, 1989.

Lowenstein, Louis. *What's Wrong with Wall Street* (Reading, Mass.: Addison-Wesley, 1988).

Marais, L., K. Schipper, and A. Smith. "Wealth Effects of Going Private on Senior Securities." *Journal of Financial Economics* 23, no. 1 (June 1989).

Moyer, R. Charles, James R. McGuigan, and William Kretlow. *Contemporary Financial Management,* 5th ed. (St. Paul, Minn.: West Publishing Co., 1992).

Mueller, Dennis. "A Theory of Conglomerate Mergers." *Quarterly Journal of Economics* 83 (1969).

Muscarella, Chris J., and Michael R. Vetsuypens. "Efficiency and Organizational Structure: A Study of Reverse LBOs." *Journal of Finance* 45, no. 5 (December 1990).

National Science Foundation. *An Assessment of the Impact of Recent Leveraged Buyouts and Other Restructurings on Industrial Research and Development Expenditures.* Prepared for the House of Representatives Committee on Energy and Commerce, 1989.

Prentice-Hall's Almanac of Business and Financial Ratios (Englewood Cliffs, N.J.: Prentice-Hall, 1989).

Rappaport, Albert. "The Staying Power of the Public Corporation." *Harvard Business Review* 1 (1990).

"Revco: The Anatomy of a Failed Buyout." *Business Week,* 3 October 1988.

Revlon, Inc. v. MacAndrews & Forbes Holdings, Inc., 506 A. 2d 173 (Del. Sup. 1986).

Schuchert, Joseph S. "The Art of the ESOP Leveraged Buyout." In Stephen C. Diamond, ed. *Leveraged Buyouts* (Homewood, Ill.: Dow Jones Irwin, 1985), p. 94.

Shleifer, Andrei, and Robert W. Vishny. "Management's Buyouts as a Response to Market Pressure." In Alan Auerbach, ed. *Mergers and Acquisitions* (Chicago: University of Chicago Press, 1988), pp. 87–103.

Stocks, Bills, Bonds and Inflation: 1994 Yearbook. Chicago: Ibbotson Associates.

Steinmetz, Greg. "LBO Funds Lure Investors But Returns Worry Some." *Wall Street Journal,* 29 June 1994.

"Takeovers and Buyouts Clobber Blue Chip Bondholders." *Business Week,* 11 November 1985.

Travlos, Nicholas, and M. M. Cornett. "Going Private Buyouts and Determinants of Shareholder Returns." *Journal of Accounting, Auditing and Finance* 8, no. 8 (Winter 1993).

U.S. Industrial Outlook, U.S. Department of Commerce, Washington, D.C.

Waine, Leslie. "Reverse LBOs Bring Riches." *New York Times,* 23 April 1987.

Waite, S., and M. Fridson. "The Credit Quality of Leveraged Buyouts." In *High Performance* (New York: Morgan Stanley, 1989).

Weston, Fred J., and Thomas E. Copeland. *Managerial Finance,* 9th ed. (Orlando, Fla.: Dryden Press, 1992).

8

JUNK BONDS

The junk bond market and the use of junk bonds as a financing tool for mergers and acquisitions and leveraged buyouts (LBOs) was a very important factor in the fourth merger wave. The availability of very large amounts of capital through the junk bond market made possible the participation of many people who would never have considered participating otherwise. The access to such large amounts of capital also made even the largest and most established firms potentially vulnerable to a takeover by much smaller suitors. The collapse of the junk bond market in the late 1980s was one of the main factors responsible for the slowdown in the pace of mergers in the fourth merger wave. Although this market has rebounded in the 1990s, its growth in the 1990s is not associated with hostile takeovers as much as it was in the past. Rather, it has become an integral component of modern corporate finance providing needed financing for less creditworthy companies. Nonetheless, it remains a smaller but still important part of the merger and acquisition business.

HISTORY

Contrary to popular belief, junk bonds are not a recent innovation. Junk bonds, or high-yield bonds, as many of their proponents would prefer to call them, have been around for decades. What is new is that takeover specialists helped pioneer their use as a financing tool for mergers and LBOs. One reason many people think junk bonds are an innovation is that they have had many different names in the past. They went by the term *low-grade bonds* for decades. In the 1930s and 1940s they were called "Fallen Angels." In the 1960s some of the lower grade debt that was issued to help finance conglomerate acquisitions was referred to as "Chinese Paper." Financier Meshulam Riklis, Chief Executive Officer (CEO) of Rapid American Corporation, states that the term *junk bonds* first originated in a conversation he had with Michael Milken, the former head of Drexel Burnham Lambert's junk bond operation. Riklis claims that when Milken surveyed some of the bonds that Riklis had issued, he exclaimed, "Rik, these are junk!"[1] In the 1920s and 1930s approximately 17% of all new corporate bond offerings were low-grade/high-yield bonds. A broader range of firms used these securities to finance their growth. The ranks of the high-yield bonds swelled during the 1930s as the Great Depression took its toll on many of America's companies. In 1928 13% of all outstanding corporate bonds were low-grade bonds; in

---

1. Connie Bruck, *The Predators' Ball* (New York: Simon & Schuster, 1988), p. 39.

1940 this percentage had risen to 42%.[2] Many of the bonds had entered the low-grade class through downgradings from rating agencies. (The rating process is discussed later in this chapter.) As the economy fell deeper and deeper into the depression and firms suffered the impact of declining demand for their goods and services, their ability to service the payments on their outstanding bonds was called into question. This led to a downgrading of the debt. As the overall level of economic demand fell, the revenues of some firms declined so much that they could no longer service the interest and principal payments on the outstanding bonds. As a result, the default rate on these bonds rose to 10%. Investors became disappointed by the rising default rate in a category of securities that they believed was generally low risk. These investors were previously attracted to the bond market by investment characteristics such as dependability of income coupled with low risk of default. As the risk of default rose, low-grade bonds became quite unpopular.

By the 1940s the low-grade bond market started to decline as old issues were retired or the issuing corporations entered into some form of bankruptcy. The declining popularity of the low-grade bond market made new issues difficult to market. Between 1944 and 1965 high-yield bonds accounted for only 6.5% of total corporate bond issues. This percentage declined even further as the 1970s began; by the beginning of the decade only 4% of all corporate bonds were low-grade bonds. The low-grade/high-yield bond market's declining popularity preempted access to one form of debt financing to certain groups of borrowers. Many corporations that would have preferred to issue long-term bonds were now forced to borrow from banks in the form of term loans that were generally of shorter maturity than 20– and 30–year corporate bonds. Those that could not borrow from a bank on acceptable terms were forced to forsake expansion or to issue more equity, which had the adverse effect of diluting the shares of ownership for outstanding equity holders. In addition, the rate of return on equity is generally higher than debt. Therefore, equity is a more costly source of capital.

The high-yield/low-grade market began to change in the late 1970s. Lehman Brothers, an investment bank that was itself acquired in the 1980s by Shearson, underwrote a series of new issues of high-yield corporate debt. These bonds were offered by Ling-Temco-Vought (LTV) ($75 million), Zapata Corporation ($75 million), Fuqua Industries ($60 million), and Pan American World Airways ($53 million).[3] This was followed by the entrance of a relatively smaller investment bank, Drexel Burnham Lambert, which started to underwrite issues of low-grade/high-yield debt on a larger scale. The first such issue that Drexel underwrote was a $30 million issue of bonds on Texas International, Inc. in April 1977.[4] Drexel Burnham Lambert's role in the development was the key to the growth of the low-grade/high-yield bond market. It served as a market maker for junk bonds, as they had begun to be called, which was crucial to the dramatic growth of the market.

By 1982 junk bond issuance had grown to $2 billion per year. Just three years later, in 1985, this total had risen to $14.1 billion and then jumped to $31.9 billion in the following year. This was the highest level the market reached in the fourth merger wave. It maintained similar levels until it collapsed in the second half of 1989. After falling to $1.4 billion in

---

2. Kevin J. Perry, "The Growing Role of Junk Bonds," *Journal of Applied Corporate Finance* 1, no. 1 (Spring 1988), pp. 37–45.

3. Ibid., p. 44.

4. Harlan D. Platt, *The First Junk Bond Market* (Armonk, N.Y.: M. E. Sharpe, 1994), p. xiii.

1990, the market rebounded in 1992 and rose to new heights in the first half of the 1990s. Although the market thrived in the 1990s, it took a different form from being the merger and LBO financing source that accounted for its growth in the fourth merger wave.

Why the Junk Bond Market Grew

The junk bond market experienced dramatic and rapid growth for several reasons, none of which by itself accounted for the precipitous increase that this market experienced. Some of these factors are:

1. *Privately placed bonds.* Bonds that are sold not publicly but to a small group of investors had become less popular. In such private sales the investment banker serves as an intermediary rather than as an underwriter, which is a riskier role. There were two reasons for this declining popularity. First, restrictive covenants associated with the indenture contract placed uncomfortable restrictions on the issuing firm. The *indenture contract* is the agreement between the bond issuer and the bond purchasers. *Restrictive covenants* are those restrictions that the purchasers require from the issuer before they purchase the securities. These restrictions limit the actions that the issuing firm may take in the course of its business activities. The restrictions are designed to lower the risk to the lender. An example of such restrictions would be a limitation on the additional debt the firm could assume in the future.

    Second, there was no standardization in the contracts for the bonds, thereby making sales in a secondary market more difficult. Buyers have to investigate the terms of each contract more carefully before purchasing, an additional time cost that many investors believe is not worth the added return. The lack of standardization meant that this market had limited liquidity, which is another risk factor that makes privately placed low-grade/high-yield bonds more difficult to market. The declining popularity of the privately placed market for low-grade/high-yield bonds created an opportunity for public issues of these bonds. This opportunity was not lost on investment bankers such as Drexel Burnham Lambert.

2. *Development of market makers.* A major factor leading to the growth of this market was the existence of an active market maker—an entity who serves as an agent of liquidity in facilitating sales between buyers and sellers. Drexel Burnham Lambert became a very active market maker in the junk bond market. Rather than have an issue lose its marketability by not having buyers in times when the issuing firm is experiencing more difficulty, Drexel had been known to become a buyer of last resort. It had also been known to provide financial assistance in the form of refinancing when an issuer appeared to be on the verge of default. This assistance, of course, comes at a price, such as an equity interest in the issuing firm. Drexel's growth in the 1980s was attributable largely to its involvement in the junk bond market. Therefore, the firm went to great lengths to ensure the growth and vitality of the market.

3. *Changing risk perceptions.* Another factor has been the changing risk perceptions of investors toward junk bonds. Investors began to believe that the risks associated with junk bond investments were less than what they once believed. The altered risk

perceptions came as a result of active promotion of this financing vehicle by interested parties such as Drexel Burnham Lambert and through academic research. Certain research studies examined the riskiness of junk bonds and reported that the risk
of default was far less than was popularly believed. Some of these findings would
later be challenged by other studies.

4. *Merger demand.* Yet another factor was the expansion of the field of mergers and
   acquisitions. As the targets of mergers and acquisitions as well as LBOs became increasingly larger, the demand for capital to fund these purchases grew. Investors increasingly relied on the junk bond market to provide a large part of this funding.

Historical Role of Drexel Burnham Lambert

Drexel Burnham Lambert was one of the first investment banks to underwrite new-issue
junk bonds and was unique in its efforts to promote the junk bond market as an attractive
investment alternative. These efforts were spearheaded by the former manager of Drexel's
Beverly Hills office, Michael Milken. Drexel's unique role as a market maker became
most apparent in 1986 when bondholders accused Morgan Stanley of failing to make a
market for the junk bonds of People Express, which it had previously underwritten. When
the price of the bonds fell significantly, Morgan Stanley was reported to have done little to
support them.

Morgan Stanley's reported passive stance contrasts strongly with Drexel's aggressive
market making in the 1980s. As a result of its involvement in the junk bond market, Drexel
progressed from a second-tier investment banking firm to a major first-tier firm. The firm's
dominance in the junk bond field during the 1980s made Drexel second only to Salomon
Brothers as an underwriting firm.

Drexel made a market for the junk bonds it had underwritten by cultivating a number of
buyers who could be depended on to purchase a new offering of junk bonds. The network
of buyers for new issues often consisted of previous issuers whose junk bonds were underwritten by Drexel Burnham Lambert. Drexel and Michael Milken used this network to
guarantee a demand for new issues of junk bonds. This guarantee often came in the form of
a *commitment letter* indicating that the buyer would buy a specific amount of a given issue
of junk bonds when they were issued. The commitment fees that the investor might receive
were usually less than 1% (i.e., three quarters of 1%) of the total capital committed. In
riskier deals, however, it ranged as high as 2%. The network of committed buyers is illustrated in Connie Bruck's *The Predators' Ball,* in which she describes how Norman Peltz
and his company, Triangle Industries, were eager participants in the "Drexel club" that
bought and sold junk bonds. Although these club members included financial institutions,
such as saving and loans associations (S&Ls), they also included nonfinancial companies
that may have used Drexel's junk-financing facilities to acquire their current concern and
now were being called upon to become buyers of another issuer's debt obligations.

Moreover, Peltz had already shown himself as pliant, someone who understood how to play
the Drexel game. A dues-paying member of the club, he had put up his Drexel-raised cash for
each of the new junk bond–financed takeovers as it came down the pike: $20 million for
Phillips, $25 million for Coastal. Indeed, in the next month, even after his own deal had
closed and he no longer had over $100 million burning a hole in his pocket, he would still find

$35 million to commit to Unocal. And he knew he had to give up equity, both to Milken and to those buyers who took the riskiest pieces of his paper. Drexel already owned 12% of Triangle from the warrants it had received as part of its earlier financing, and it would cut another 4% piece of the pie for itself here.[5]

Drexel commanded a dominant 57% of the total market share of new public issues of junk bonds in 1983 and 40% to 50% from 1984 through the beginning of 1987, when its market share began to steadily decline. This was mainly the result of the energetic efforts of other large investment banks, especially Goldman Sachs, Merrill Lynch, First Boston, and Morgan Stanley, to capture part of the lucrative junk bond market They increased their junk bond resources by expanding their trading, research, and sales staffs. The investment apparently paid off; by the late 1980s each of these banks had captured a significant part of the new public issue junk bond market. Drexel's dominant role in the junk bond market appeared to loosen in 1989 after Milken's indictment. Some firms, hesitant to do business with Drexel, turned to other underwriters. Drexel's end came ingloriously with its Chapter 11 filing in February 1990.

INVESTMENT BANKERS

The investment banker assists the issuer in picking the most opportune time to put the newly issued junk bonds on the market. This is facilitated by a *shelf registration* of the bonds with the Securities and Exchange Commission (SEC). Shelf registration allows the issuer to register the securities it may want to issue in advance and to wait for the most favorable time to bring the securities to the market. The investment banker is attuned to the market and will advise the issuer when it will receive the highest price for the securities. The investment banker often provides *bridge financing* to the issuer, which allows the issuing firm the time to select the best moment to bring the junk bonds to market. For example, First Boston Corporation, once the leading investment bank in mergers and acquisitions, committed $900 million to the Campeau Corporation, which enabled Campeau to buy Allied Stores in 1986. The combination of bridge financing and advisory services was reported to have earned First Boston $100 million in fees.[6]

The riskiness of some of these bridge loans became apparent when some investment bankers, such as First Boston, were unable to arrange refinancing in the junk bond market when it declined in the late 1980s. In November 1990 First Boston was eventually forced to sell some of its troubled "bridges," such as the $247 million bridge loan to Federated Stores and the $230 million bridge loan to Ohio Mattress Company to its owners, the Credit Suisse Bank and Metropolitan Life Insurance Company.[7] The failure of First Boston to be able to refinance its bridge loans committed to the Campeau Corporation was a watershed event in that it signaled the seriousness of the decline in the demand for high-yield bonds.

---

5. Bruck, *The Predator's Ball,* p. 127.

6. Gregory Miller, "Wall Street Money Wars," *Institutional Investor* (March 1987), p.169.

7. Michael Siconolfi, "First Boston to Sell Bridges to Its Owners," *Wall Street Journal,* 6 November 1990, p. C1.

Investment Bankers and Highly Confident Letters

As the size and complexity of the financing packages associated with the deals of the fourth merger wave increased, the need to demonstrate an ability to raise the requisite capital became more important, particularly for bidders who were significantly smaller than their targets. This process was facilitated by the use of a *Highly Confident Letter,* in which the bidder's investment bank states that, based on market conditions and its analysis of the deal, it is highly confident that it can raise the necessary capital to complete the deal. This letter is often attached to tender offer filing documents such as the Schedule 14D-1.

The genesis of the Highly Confident Letter can be traced to Carl Icahn's $4.5 billion bid for Phillips Petroleum in 1985. Icahn's investment banker, Drexel Burnham Lambert, issued a Highly Confident Letter in which it stated, "We are highly confident we can arrange the financing."[8] The letter gave Icahn instant credibility and was a major contributing factor in his success in selling the shares he had acquired back to Phillips without testing the strength of Drexel's letter. Thereafter the Highly Confident Letter became an important part of the takeover business.

Icahn later used the Highly Confident Letter as an essential part of his "takeover tool kit." Armed with the letter and the resulting increased credibility produced by this investment banker's ability to marshal the vast financial resources of the then-strong junk bond market, Icahn had to be taken more seriously. Targets responded to threats from hostile bidders armed with their letters with offers of greenmail. This was the case in Icahn's August 1986 bid for USX Corporation. In his letter to the board of directors of USX, Icahn included references to the high degree of confidence of his investment banker, Drexel Burnham Lambert, and outlined his plans to make a $31 per share offer for the steel company.

> As holders of 25,349,800 shares of the common stock of USX, constituting approximately 9.83% of the outstanding shares, we share your belief [made public by the board in a statement it issued dated September 22, 1986] that USX has been undervalued in the market place. After reflecting on your additional statements that USX's pension fund is not significantly overfunded and noting USX's larger debt burden, it appears that an alternative to a restructuring might be the optimal way to "enhance shareholder value." We are prepared to offer just such an alternative and hereby propose a "friendly" cash merger transaction of USX with a corporation to be formed by our group for that purpose....
>
> Of the approximately $8 million in cash required to fund the acquisition of the USX common stock, ACF Industries, Incorporated and other of my affiliates would be prepared to contribute approximately $1 billion in cash and USX stock for this purpose. Our financial advisor, Drexel Burnham Lambert Incorporated, has advised us that, based upon current market conditions, it is highly confident that it can obtain commitments for the placement of the new corporation's debt and equity securities sufficient for the balance of the acquisition.[9]

An example of a Highly Confident Letter is presented in Figure 8.1. It is a letter issued by Merrill Lynch Capital Markets to Smith-Vasiliou Management Company, Inc. for the bid for the Revere Copper and Brass, Inc. on May 13, 1986.

---

8. Moira Johnson, *Takeover* (New York: Penguin Books, 1987), p. 147.

9. Letter from Carl Icahn to the Board of Directors, USX Corporation, October 6, 1986, contained in the Schedule 13D filing to the Securities and Exchange Commission. As cited in Carolyn Brancato, *Takeover Bids and Highly Confident Letters,* Congressional Research Service, Library of Congress, Report 87–724 E, August 28, 1987.

Merrill Lynch Capital Markets
Investment Banking

One Liberty Plaza
165 Broadway
New York, New York 10080
212 637 7455

May 13, 1986

Smith-Vasilou Management Co., Inc.
19 Rector Street
New York, NY   10006

Gentlemen:

You have advised us of your intention to acquire Revere Copper and
Brass Incorporated ("Revere"), a Maryland corporation, in a
negotiated cash merger transaction pursuant to which one of your
subsidiaries will be merged with Revere and Revere's shareholders
will receive $23.00 per share in cash for each share of common
stock owned by them (the "Acquisition Transaction"). You have
retained us to assist you in raising the funds required to
consummate the Acquisition Transaction.

We are highly confident of our ability to finance the Acquisition
Transaction subject to (i) no material adverse change in the
financial condition, results of operations or business of Revere
since March 31, 1986, (ii) market conditions similar to those
currently existing, (iii) execution of customary underwriting or
placement agreements, (iv) the execution of an acquisition
agreement and approval of the Acquisition Transaction by the board
of directors and shareholders of Revere, (v) completion of the
divestiture of Revere's 34% equity interest in Ormet Corporation
on terms similar to those contained in draft agreements relating
to such divestiture and furnished to Merrill Lynch Capital Markets
prior to the date hereof, (vi) the arrangement of a revolving
credit facility and a senior term loan, both on terms and
conditions reasonably similar to those contained in a letter to
Smith-Vasiliou Management Co., Inc. from Bankers Trust Company
dated May 13, 1986 and appended hereto, and (vii) placement of
$7.0 million of common stock in Newco, a corporation to be formed
for the purpose of acquiring the stock of Revere.

In the last four years, Merrill Lynch has acted as book-running
manager or placement agent in completing over $8.0 billion of debt
and preferred stock financings rated BB or below.

                              Very truly yours,

                              MERRILL LYNCH CAPITAL MARKETS
                              Merrill Lynch, Pierce, Fenner & Smith
                                 Incorporated

                              By

                              Managing Director

Figure 8.1.   Example of a highly confident letter.

Investment Banks and Liquidity of Junk Bond Investments

As noted previously, investment banks, led by the trailblazing role of Drexel Burnham Lambert in the 1980s, served as a market maker for junk bonds. In doing so, they became buyers when holders wanted to sell and sellers when investors wanted to buy. This gave the market liquidity it otherwise would not have had. The enhanced liquidity lowered the risk of these investments and made them more marketable. Another way in which investment banks enhanced the liquidity of these investments was to work with troubled issuers when they appeared to be in danger of defaulting. At one time Drexel prided itself that issues underwritten by that bank did not default. Drexel would go to great lengths to ensure that these troubled issuers would not be technically declared in default. Sometimes the default might be prevented by the issuance of a new offering that would be exchanged for the troubled outstanding issue.

In cases of more serious liquidity problems, very different types of bonds might be offered in exchange for the bonds that investors were holding. Such bonds might not pay cash interest payments for a period of time while the issuer takes steps to improve its financial condition. One version of such securities are *PIK,* or *payment-in-kind* securities. These bonds do not make cash payments for an initial period, which might range from 3 to 10 years. These bonds came under sharp criticism as the junk bond market began to falter in the late 1980s and investors were being presented with the alternative of exchanging their interest-paying bonds that were about to default for other bonds that would not pay cash interest payments for an extended period of time. Given the poor prospects that security holders with an inferior position in the bankruptcy liquidation hierarchy have, many bondholders reluctantly accepted the exchanges.

THE EVOLUTIONARY GROWTH OF THE JUNK BOND MARKET

Figure 8.2 shows the dramatic growth in the new-issue junk bond market during the 1980s. The market peaked in 1986 but maintained a high level until it collapsed in the second half of 1989. The growth was largely due to the strong demand by institutional investors. Although the market collapsed dramatically in 1990, it rebounded strongly later in the 1990s.

Institutional Investors and the Growth of the Junk Bond Market

The largest categories of junk bond buyers are insurance companies and mutual funds, each of which accounts for 30% of total junk bond demand. Mutual funds have found that junk bonds can significantly enhance the return of their securities portfolio. Separate funds, which invest exclusively in junk bonds, have been established and successfully marketed.

Insurance companies initially found junk bonds to be a rewarding avenue for the large investment capital they attracted from policyholders. When the market turned downward in the late 1980s, however, many came to regret their high-yield investments. It became an even greater source of concern when the value of junk bond investments rose; for some insurers they rose two to four times the firm's capital. For example, Ohio Casualty held $169 million worth of junk bonds, which accounted for 481% of its statutory surplus capital, and

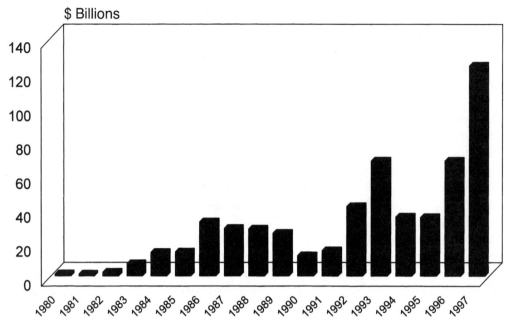

Figure 8.2. Growth of the junk bond market, 1980–97.

Source: Securities Data Company.

Transamerica held $780 in junk bond investments, which represented 223% of its statutory surplus capital.[10]

Pension funds accounted for 15% of total junk bond demand. The investment of pension funds, particularly state and local government pension funds, in junk bonds became a controversial issue in the late 1980s. Some people argued that these investments were too risky and could endanger the value of the retirees' capital in the event of a major economic downturn. Opponents of this view contended that, even though they fell in value, junk bonds withstood the stock market crash in 1987 and gave every sign of being a stable, high-yielding investment. The rebound of the market in the 1990s helped allay these concerns.

Another controversial group of investors has been the S&Ls, whose investment strategies came under intense criticism after the failure of a large number of them. Many economists blame these failures on overall mismanagement and poor investments. Some S&Ls, such as the Columbia Savings and Loan of Beverly Hills, California—which is referred to as the thrift institution that junk bonds built—appeared to be quite healthy before the junk bond market crash in 1989.[11] At that time Columbia Savings held $3.8 billion worth of junk bonds, which amounted to nearly 40% of its assets. After the junk bond market decline, its high-yield portfolio declined $320 million in the months of October and November alone.[12]

Foreign investors were another significant group of junk bond buyers. The increase in demand by these buyers was partly due to the lower costs of U.S. dollar-denominated junk

10. Linda Sandler, "Insurers Getting Queasy Over Junk Bond Holdings," *Wall Street Journal,* 12 February 1990, p. C1.

11. "Columbia S&L Charts Two-Way Course," *Wall Street Journal,* 9 February 1989, p. A8.

12. "A Savings Resignation Over 'Junk'," *New York Times,* 12 December 1989, p. D1.

bonds as a result of the fall in the dollar relative to other currencies such as the Japanese yen. As of 1988 these foreign investor junk bonds constituted 5% of the total junk bond market (Figure 8.3). Like other investors, their appetite for junk bonds decreased when the market turned down at the end of the 1980s.

Major Events in the Collapse of the Junk Bond Market

Certain major events rocked the junk bond market in the 1980s. They include the bankruptcy of the LTV Corporation and Integrated Resources, and the legal problems of Michael Milken and his investment bank, Drexel Burnham Lambert. These events are discussed in the following sections.

The LTV Bankruptcy
The resiliency of the junk bond market was called into question in 1986 when the LTV Corporation defaulted on the high-yield bonds it had issued. The LTV bankruptcy was the largest corporate bankruptcy at that time and represented 56% of the total debt defaulting in 1986.[13] Ma, Rao, and Peterson showed that this event caused a temporary six-month revision in the market's probabilities for default, as reflected by the risk-premium yields on junk bonds. This effect proved transitory, and the market more than fully rebounded afterward.

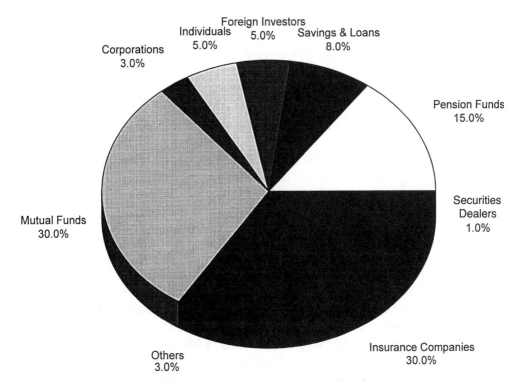

Figure 8.3. Participation of institutional investors in junk bond market.

---

13. Christopher K. Ma, Ramesh P. Rao, and Richard L. Peterson, "The Resiliency of the High-Yield Bond Market," *Journal of Finance* 44, no. 4 (September 1989), pp. 1085–1097.

The Ma study indicates that the junk bond market was at that time quite resilient and more than capable of withstanding the shock of a major default.

Financing Failures of 1989

In addition to the bankruptcy of LTV, the junk market was jolted by other critical events. Large offerings by issuers, such as Campeau Corporation, swelled the market with increased supply. In the first half of 1989, $20 billion worth of junk bonds were offered compared with $9.2 billion for the same period in 1988. Issuers had to offer higher and higher rates to attract investors to buy the risky securities. Campeau Corporation's offering of junk bonds in 1988, led by the investment bank First Boston Corporation, was poorly received even though it provided 16% coupon payments on 12–year bonds and 17.75% coupons on 16–year bonds. In October 1988 First Boston had to withdraw a $1.15 billion junk bond offering as investor demand for the debt-laden concern's securities failed to materialize. The investment bank responded with a $750 million offering that provided higher yields.

The secondary market also responded with decreased demand reflecting the falloff that was occurring in the primary market. For example, junk bonds issued by Resorts International, Tracor, and Interco declined significantly during this year. The lack of a strong, reliable secondary market made it even more difficult to offer new high-yield bonds. This downturn was a contributing factor to the unraveling of the financing for the buyout of United Airlines in October 1989. Even when reputable issuers, such as Ohio Mattress— maker of Sealy, Stearns, and Foster mattresses—offered 15% interest rates for a proposed $475 million issue in 1989, the market refused to respond.

Default of Integrated Resources

Integrated Resources, a company built on junk bonds and the most prominent buyer of junk bonds among insurance companies, defaulted in June 1989 and filed for bankruptcy in early 1990. This sent shock waves through the ranks of institutional investors who had helped fuel the growth of the junk bond market. This default is not discussed further here because it is covered at length in the case study at the end of this chapter.

Bankruptcy of Drexel Burnham Lambert

In its heyday in 1986 Drexel reported pretax annual profits of $1 billion. Only two years later, in late 1988, it pleaded guilty to criminal charges and paid more than $40 million in fines. In 1989 Drexel showed a loss of $40 million.[14]

The immediate cause of Drexel's Chapter 11 bankruptcy filing was a liquidity crisis resulting from the firm's inability to pay short-term loans and commercial paper financing that came due. Securities firms generally rely on short-term capital to finance their securities holdings. Drexel had been the issuer of more than $700 million in commercial paper.[15] When the commercial paper market contracted in 1989, Drexel was forced to pay off more than $575 million, which could not be refinanced through the issues of new commercial

---

14. "Junk Bond King Files for Bankruptcy," *Newark Star Ledger,* 14 February 1990, p. 39.

15. Affidavit filed by Frederick H. Joseph in Drexel Bankruptcy Filing, printed by the *New York Times,* 15 February 1990, p. D5.

paper. Closing the commercial paper market effectively wiped out Drexel's liquidity. With the prior collapse of the junk bond market, Drexel could not seek long-term financing as a substitute. The firm had no recourse but to file for Chapter 11 protection.

Fate of the Big Junk Bond Issuers

As of the end of the 1990s, we have the opportunity to consider the fate of the major junk bond issuers of the fourth merger wave. According to a study conducted by KDP Investment Advisors, of the 25 largest issuers of junk bond debt between the years 1985 and 1989 and who each had issued a minimum of $1 million in junk bond debt, almost half had defaulted. As Table 8.1 shows, 16 of the 25 were acquired. Clearly many of them took on too much debt to withstand the economic downturn that followed at the end of the decade.

Decline in the Use of Junk Bonds as a Source of Merger and Acquisition Financing

The growth of the junk bond market has added a highly combustible fuel to the fires of the fourth merger wave. As described previously, one of the first hostile takeover attempts financed by junk bonds was the attempted bid for Gulf Oil Co. by the celebrated raider

Table 8.1. Junk Bond's Toll, 25 Companies Issued High-Yield Bonds Between 1985–89

Company	High-Yield Debit Issued (Billions)
Allied Stores*[†]	1.0
American Standard	1.0
BCI Holdings (Beatrice)[†]	2.5
Burlington Industries	1.0
Charter Medical*[†]	1.0
Container Corp. of America[†]	1.5
Duracell[†]	1.1
E-II Holdings*[†]	1.5
Federated Department Stores*	1.5
Fort Howard	1.9
Gillette Holdings*[†]	1.0
Harcourt Brace Jovanovich[†]	1.9
Holiday Inns[†]	1.4
Kroger	1.4
R. H. Macy*[†]	2.0
National Gypsum*[†]	1.5
Owens Corning	1.0
Owens-Illinois	3.0
Quantum Chemical[†]	1.5
RJR Nabisco	15.0
SCI Holdings*[†]	2.6
Southland*[†]	1.9
USG*[†]	1.4
Viacom	1.3
Wickets[†]	2.0

* Filed for bankruptcy protection and defaulted on bonds, [†] was acquired.

Source: KDP Investment Advices (buyouts), Securities Data Company, New Generation Research.

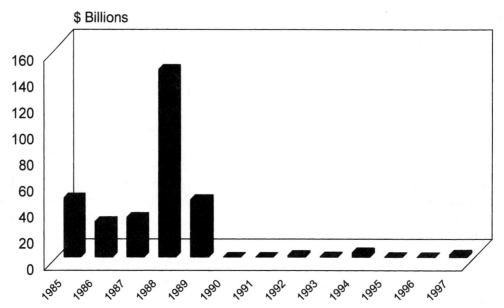

Figure 8.4. Junk bonds used for merger and acquisition financing.

Source: Securities Data Company.

T. Boone Pickens. Pickens was president of a relatively small company, Mesa Petroleum. A small oil company by Seven Sisters standards, Mesa was not a serious threat. When Pickens arranged a $2 billion commitment from Drexel Burnham Lambert, as set forth in a Highly Confident Letter, the smaller oil company gained instant credibility. The monies were ultimately to be raised by an offering of junk bonds. The access to such large amounts of financing instantly made Mesa a credible threat. Gulf took the offer seriously and finally agreed to be bought out by a white knight—Chevron. Ironically, Chevron's acquisition of Gulf appeared to have overextended Chevron's resources and caused its stock price to fall, making it vulnerable to a takeover.

Junk bond financing was particularly important for bidders that lacked the internal capital and access to traditional financing sources such as bank loans. The use of junk bond financing to finance acquisitions grew dramatically in 1988 and dramatically collapsed in the years that followed (Figure 8.4). Although the junk bond market recovered in the 1990s, the use of junk bonds to finance larger megadeals did not.

RATING SYSTEM FOR BONDS

A rating system for bonds was first published by John Moody in 1909. Since then, several services have also published ratings, the more well known being Standard & Poor's and Moody's. Ratings are also provided by Fitch Investors Service and Duff and Phelps. In addition to bonds, ratings of other types of securities, such as preferred stock, are also published. Ratings provide a gauge whereby an investor can judge the degree of default risk associated with the bond. Default risk refers to the likelihood that the issuer will not pay the periodic interest or principal payments. A breakdown of the ratings offered by the ratings services is provided in Table 8.2.

Table 8.2.   Meaning of Bond Ratings

Moody's Rating	S&P Rating	Interpretation
Aaa	AAA	Highest rating. Extremely strong ability to pay interest and principal.
Aa	AA	Almost as high quality as the triple A firms. Strong capacity to pay interest and principal.
A	A	Good capacity to pay interest and principal. These bonds possess many favorable attributes but may be susceptible to economic downturns.
Baa	BBB	Interest and principal protection is adequate, but adverse economic conditions could weaken ability to pay interest and principal.
Ba	BB	Only moderate protection for principal and interest payments in good economic conditions and even worse in economic downturns.
B	B	Limited long-term assurance of principal and principal interest payments. Default risk is considered moderate.
Caa	CCC	High default risk. These bonds may be currently near default.
Ca	CC	These bonds are considered highly speculative investments. They are often already in default.
C		This is Moody's lowest rating. This rating is generally given to bonds that are paying no interest.
	C	S & P generally gives this rating when the issuer is in bankruptcy but is making interest payments on the issue.
	D	These bonds are in default. The interest or principal payments, or both, are in arrears.

Source: Standard & Poor's Bond Guide and Moody's Bond Record, Moody's Investor's Service.

The investment community widely accepts the idea that ratings are a useful predictor of default risk. This concept is reported to have originated in a well-known study by W. B. Hickman, entitled *Corporate Bond Quality and Investor Experience* (1958), and showed that a significantly higher rate of default occurred among those securities that received lower quality ratings. The Hickman study, which is discussed further later in this chapter, used nine rating categories.

Determinants of Bond Ratings

Bond rating agencies examine a broad range of information when they are preparing a rating for a firm, especially financial ratios. This was underscored in August 1990, when Moody's acknowledged the market's concern about the quality of junk bonds by forming a separate unit within its industrials group to focus on the day-to-day analysis of junk bond companies. A set of financial ratios are generally used that give the analyst an overall picture of the risk of default for the issuer of the bonds. These ratios are described in detail in Chapter 12. Prime among these ratios are coverage ratios, such as the times interest earned, fixed charge, and cash flow coverage ratios. These ratios measure the ability of the firm to cover its interest charges and fixed obligations with operating income and cash flows. The higher the value of these ratios, the more likely the bonds of the firm will receive a better quality rating. When the ratios show a comparatively high level of debt, as reflected by the high values of the leverage ratios, with limited ability to meet the debt service and other fixed charges, along with possible low liquidity, as reflected by the liquidity ratios, the firm will receive a lower bond rating.

One prime factor in evaluating default risk is the relationship between cash flow and total debt. The greater the cash flow, the less likely the firm will default on its interest payments. A study by William Beaver on the use of financial ratios to predict default showed a very good predictive relationship between cash flow relative to debt and the probability of default.[16]

Consistency of Ratings

The consistency of bond ratings among the different rating services is a reliable indicator of default risk. If, for example, the two major rating services, Standard and Poor's and Moody's, were to give consistently different ratings for the same bonds, confusion would reign as to which service was more reliable. Fortunately, this does not happen very often, and when it does occur, the difference often is insignificant. When the same bond receives a different rating from two rating agencies, it is referred to as a *split rating.* This would be the case if, for example, Moody's gave a particular corporate bond an AA rating while Standard and Poor's gave it an A rating. "Louis Brand, former head of Standard and Poor's bond department, indicates that the two agencies disagreed on about 1 in 20 utility bonds and 1 in 10 industrial bonds."[17] It would be most unlikely, however, for one service to give a rating that is radically different from that of another service. Services tend to be consistent in their ratings because they use the same financial information and apply similar financial analysis techniques.

---

16. William H. Beaver, "Financial Ratios As Predictor of Failure," *Empirical Research in Accounting Selected Studies* (Chicago: Graduate School of Business, University of Chicago, 1966), pp. 71–127.

17. H. C. Sherwood, "How They Rate Your Company's Bonds," *Business Management* 29 (March 1966), pp. 38–42.

CASE STUDY: W. T. GRANT'S—AN EXAMPLE OF THE PREDICTIVE POWER OF FINANCIAL RATIOS

A classic example of how financial ratios may be used to predict default is the bankruptcy of W. T. Grant's, a large retail chain more commonly known as a five-and-dime store. Quite popular at one time, these stores have been superseded in the retail world by more modern retail chains such as Wal-Mart and K-Mart. At its peak, W. T. Grant's had over 1,000 stores throughout the United States. Figure 1 traces the pattern of financial performance ratios from a steady decline in the mid-1960s through October 1975, when the firm went bankrupt. Profitability ratios, such as the return on stockholders' equity and the return on assets, consistently declined until they began a precipitous drop in 1973. Activity ratios such as the inventory turnover, accounts receivable turnover, and the total assets turnover ratio also showed a downslide, indicating that the firm was losing its ability to move its inventory. W. T. Grant's liquidity decreased, indicating that its current liabilities were increasing

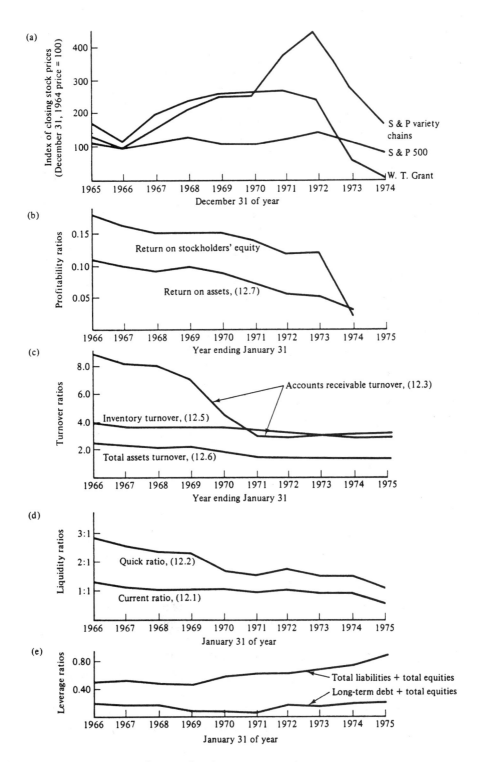

Figure 1. W. T. Grant's financial ratios.

Source: James A. Langay III and Clyde P. Stickney, "Cash Flows, Ratio Analysis and the W. T. Grant Company Bankruptcy," *Financial Analysts Journal* (July–August 1980): 52, exhibit 1.

faster than its current assets. The firm tried to take on debt to survive, as shown by the rise in the ratio of total liabilities to total equity or the ratio of long-term debt to total equity.

In the case of W. T. Grant's, the financial ratios provided a useful indication of the company's deteriorating financial condition. It therefore should have come as no surprise to stockholders and bondholders when the firm defaulted on its obligations. The market perceived the company's declining financial condition as reflected in the declining trend of its stock price. The price of W. T. Grant stock fell significantly more than the decline in the market as a whole or the other firms in that industry.

Z SCORES AND ZETA ANALYSIS: CREDIT EVALUATION ALTERNATIVE TO BOND RATINGS

The Altman Z Score, so-named after one of its developers, and the related Zeta Analysis were developed in the late 1970s.[18] They use a statistical technique known as discriminant analysis, a multivariate technique similar to regression analysis.[19] In this type of application, it allows the user to rate the bankruptcy risk of a corporation as a function of several indicator variables, such as financial ratios. The relationship is expressed as follows:

$$\text{Zeta} = a_0 + a_1 X_1 + a_2 X_2 + \ldots + a_6 X_6 \tag{8.1}$$

where
Zeta = a firm's credit score
  X_1 = a profitability measure such as operating profits (earnings before interest and taxes)
  X_2 = stability of earnings measure (standard deviation of earnings)
  X_3 = ability to service debt measure such as times interest earned or fixed charge coverage ratio
  X_4 = working capital measure to reflect liquidity
  X_5 = cumulative retained earnings to total assets
  X_6 = market value of equity to the book value of total liabilities that will reflect financial leverage $a_1 \ldots a_n$ = coefficients or weights for each indicator variable

The more the firm is "in distress," the more likely it will receive a lower Zeta score. The more creditworthy the company, the more likely it will receive a higher score.

Both the founders of the Zeta technique and Zeta's marketers, Zeta Services, Inc., claim a high degree of accuracy for the tool in predicting which firms may fall into bankruptcy. According to Altman and Namacher, 96% of bankrupt firms received a negative Zeta score

---

18. Edward Altman, R. Haldeman, and P. Narayanan, "Zeta Analysis: A Model to Identify Bankruptcy Risk of Corporations," *Journal of Banking and Finance* 1 no. 1 (June 1977), pp. 29–54.

19. Edward I. Altman, "Financial Ratios, Discriminant Analysis and the Prediction of Corporate Bankruptcy," *Journal of Finance* 23 (September 1968), pp. 568–609.

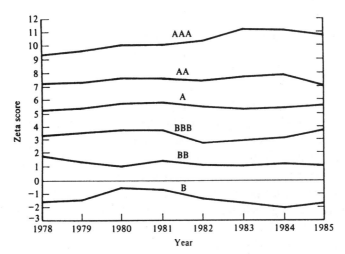

Figure 8.5.   Zeta score versus time.

Source: Edward Altman and Scott Namacher, Investing in Junk Bonds (New York: John & Sons, Inc., 1987)

one annual statement before bankruptcy, whereas 70% of bankrupt firms received a negative Zeta score five annual statements before bankruptcy.[20]

An evaluation of junk bonds reveals a good correlation between Zeta scores and the Standard & Poor's and Moody's bond ratings. Figure 8.5 shows that bonds rated BB received a Zeta rating between 1.75 and 1 between 1978 and 1985. Bonds with ratings below BB consistently received a negative Zeta rating. In contrast, the average single A company received a 5.6 Zeta score during the same time period.

JUNK BOND RESEARCH

Early Research

The most often cited research study of what are now known as junk bonds was the W. Braddock Hickman's National Bureau of Economic Research's study, which was published in 1958.[21] One of Hickman's main conclusions was that non–investment-grade bonds showed higher returns than investment-grade bonds, even after taking into account default losses. The time period of his study was from 1900 to 1943. These results were challenged by Harold Fraine, who pointed out that factors such as interest rate fluctuations may have biased Hickman's results.[22] Although Hickman's pro–junk bond results have been widely cited by the securities industry, the contradictory findings of Fraine failed to

---

20. Edward Altman and Scott Namacher, *Investing in Junk Bonds* (New York: John Wiley & Sons, 1987), p. 148.

21. W. B. Hickman, *Corporate Bond Quality and Investor Experience* (Princeton, N.J.: Princeton University Press), p. 195.

22. Harold G. Fraine and Robert H. Mills, "The Effects of Defaults and Credit Deterioration on Yields of Corporate Bonds," *Journal of Finance* (September 1961), pp. 423–434.

receive similar attention.[23] Indeed, Michael Milken used Hickman's findings to market high-yield bonds to conservative institutional investors.

Altman and Namacher's Study

The existence of the Hickman research notwithstanding, high-yield bonds remained a difficult sale until the late 1970s. Institutional investors were reluctant to add to their portfolio securities that they considered unduly risky. This attitude started to change with the publication of another major research study that seemed to lend support to the Hickman findings. The study by Edward I. Altman and Scott A. Namacher seemed to provide evidence that the default rates of low-rated firms were much lower than was believed (Table 8.3).[24]

The Altman and Namacher study showed that the average default rate for junk bonds was 2.1%, which was not significantly higher than the default rate on investment-grade securities, which was almost 0%. On an annual basis the default rate has been declining, as shown in the following figures. The slightly higher default rate does not account for the 3% to 5% higher yields of junk bonds.

Altman and Namacher also analyzed the number of firms that were originally given high ratings but subsequently defaulted. Of the 112 issues they examined, only 8% (9 of the 112 issues) were originally rated A. More than 30% (34), however, were originally rated investment-grade. This shows that a firm can achieve a high investment rating and later fall into bankruptcy. At first this finding would seem to imply that the ratings are not a valuable guide to the future performance of the bonds. As Altman and Namacher point out, however, a trail of declining ratings usually precedes the point of default.

Altman and Namacher's default figures are consistent with those reported in previous studies. Fitzpatrick and Severiens, for example, showed that the default rate on BB/Ba-rated and B-rated bonds for the period from 1965 to 1975 was 0.8%.[25] Another study, using a somewhat different methodology by Fridson and Monaghan, found a 1.07% default rate for a similar period.[26]

The Altman and Namacher study revealed that as the time of default approaches, the rating declines. They observed that 13 of 130 (10%) were rated as investment-grade one year before default, whereas only 4 out of 130 (3%) received such a rating six months before

Table 8.3. Percentage of Low-Rated Firms in Default, 1970–84

Year	Default Rate (%)
1970–84	2.1
1974–84	2.0
1978–84	1.8

Source: Edward I. Altman and Scott A. Namacher, "The Default Rate Experience on High Yield Corporate Debt" (New York: Morgan Stanley & Co., 1985).

---

23. Martin S. Fridson, "Fraine's Neglected Findings: Was Hickman Wrong?" *Financial Analysts Journal* (September/October 1994), pp. 43–53.

24. Edward I. Altman and Scott A. Namacher, *The Default Rate Experience on High Yield Corporate Debt* (New York: Morgan Stanley & Co., 1985).

25. J. D. Fitzpatrick and J. T. Severiens, "Hickman Revisited: The Case for Junk Bonds," New York, Salomon Brothers, March 1984.

26. Martin Fridson and Monaghan, "Default Experience of Corporate Bonds," New York, Salomon Brothers, March 1984.

default.[27] This implies that the bond rating can be used as a reliable indicator of the likelihood of default. In recent decades large bankruptcies have affected the junk bond market. For example, Penn Central's bankruptcy had a great impact on the 3.4% default rate for low-grade bonds in 1970. The June 17, 1986, bankruptcy of LTV Corporation had a profound impact on the bond market of the 1980s as a whole and the junk bond market in particular. LTV, the giant steel and oil firm, was the largest industrial corporation to declare bankruptcy. It was also one of the largest issuers of junk bonds at the time it filed Chapter 11. Not surprisingly, in response, LTV bonds fell 50% in value. The impact of the LTV bankruptcy on the junk bond market is discussed later in this chapter.

Recent updates of the Altman default rate analysis reveal similar values. As Table 8.4 shows, default rates for more recent years are similar with the exception of the 1990–1991 recession years, when the default rates rose to 10.140% and 10.273%, respectively.[28] Over a longer period, such as from 1985 to 1994, the impact of the economic downturn is lessened and the average (arithmetic) default rate equaled 2.613%.

Criticism of the Altman and Namacher Methodology

The Altman and Namacher study had been one of the dominant pieces of research on the default risk of junk bonds. Their results and those of other studies imply that the marketplace is inefficient and pays a return in excess of the risk on these securities.[29] (The return on junk bonds is discussed later in this chapter.) Their methodology is subject to a number of criticisms, however. First, in periods when the junk bond market is growing very rapidly, such as when the first Altman and Namacher studies were released, the ratio of the number of par value of defaulting issues in a given year divided by the par value of junk bonds outstanding may understate the true condition of the junk bond market.

$$\text{Altman's default rate} = \frac{\text{Par value of defaults in a given year}}{\text{Par value of junk bonds outstanding}}$$

The riskiness of a junk bond generally does not materialize until the junk bond has been on the market for several years. The firm is generally not going to default in the years immediately following the issuance. After several years, however, the risk factors affecting these junk bond issuers may take their toll and some may default. The impact of these defaults may not be noticed in the Altman index because the junk bond market was growing so rapidly. During parts of the 1980s the denominator was growing more rapidly than the numerator! When the growth of the junk bond market slows and some of the firms with greater risk begin to default, the Altman index should rise significantly.

---

27. Edward Altman and Scott A. Namacher, *The Default Rate Experience on High Yield Corporate Debt.* (New York: Morgan Stanley & Co., 1985).

28. Edward I. Altman and Joseph C. Bencivenga, "A Yield Premium Model for the High Yield Debt Market," *Financial Analysts Journal* (September/October 1995), pp. 49–56; and Edward I. Altman and Vellore M. Kishore, "Defaults and Returns on High Yield Bonds: Analysis Through 1997."

29. Mark I. Weinstein, "A Curmudgeon View of Junk Bonds," *Journal of Portfolio Management* (Spring 1987), pp. 76–80.

Table 8.4.   Historical Default Rates—Straight Debt Only Excluding Defaulted Issues from Par Value Outstanding, 1971–97

Year	Par Value Outstanding ($ millions)	Par Value Defaults ($ millions)	Default Rates (%)
1971	6,602	82	1.242
1972	6,928	193	2.786
1973	7,824	49	0.626
1974	10,894	123	1.129
1975	7,471	204	2.731
1976	7,735	30	0.388
1977	8,157	381	4.671
1978	8,946	119	1.330
1979	10,356	20	0.193
1980	14,935	224	1.500
1981	17,115	27	0.158
1982	18,109	577	3.186
1983	27,492	301	1.095
1984	40,939	344	0.840
1985	58,088	992	1.708
1986	90,243	3,156	3.497
1987	129,557	7,486	5.778
1988	148,187	3,944	2.662
1989	189,258	8,110	4.285
1990	181,000	18,354	10.140
1991	183,600	18,862	10.273
1992	163,000	5,545	3.402
1993	206,907	2,287	1.105
1994	235,000	3,418	1.454
1995	240,000	4,551	1.896
1996	271,000	3,336	1.231
1997	335,400	4,200	1.252

Arithmetic Average Default Rate

1971–97			2.613
			(2.554)
1978–97			2.849
			(2.808)
1985–97			3.745
			(3.059)

Weighted Average Default Rate

1971–97			3.311
			(3.452)
1978–97			3.342
			(3.066)
1985–97			3.465
			(3.100)

Median Annual Default Rate

| 1971–97 | | | 1.500 |

Source: Edward I. Altman and Vellore M. Kishore, "Defaults and Returns on High Yield Bonds: Analysis Through 1997."

Another criticism of the Altman and Namacher study is that it does not follow junk bonds over the course of their lifetime. It does not, for example, take a group of junk bonds that were issued in a given year and trace the number of defaults year after year. It merely aggregates new and old issues. It is the older issues, however, that have the higher degree of default risk and are a greater source of concern to investors. Altman, however, addressed the aging problem in a later study in which he used *cumulative bond mortality,* which measures the default rate on bonds that have been outstanding for an equal period of time.[30] Using this technique, Altman then finds significantly higher default rates for lower-rated bonds. For example, for bonds that have been outstanding for 10 years, he found cumulative mortality rates of 6.64% for BB-rated bonds, 31.91% for B-rated bonds, and 31.17% for CCC-rated bonds.

Asquith, Mullins, and Wolff Study

Many of the purported shortcomings of the Altman and Namacher study were addressed by the Asquith, Mullins, and Wolff research (hereafter referred to as Asquith) (Table 8.5).[31] Asquith considered the aging effect of junk bonds; he and his coresearchers followed the junk bonds that were issued in 1977 and 1978 until 1986. In doing so, they offset the impact of the rapidly growing junk bond market that pervaded the Altman and Namacher study.

Exchanges

The Asquith study also factored in the impact of exchanges on the default of junk bonds. When firms are in danger of defaulting, the creditors (including the junk bondholders) often engage in a voluntary reorganization agreement. Drexel Burnham Lambert was particularly skillful in this area. Through these agreements, new securities can be issued. These exchanges may involve the issuance of new bonds that have lower coupon payments, or they may involve the retirement of the original issue of junk bonds in exchange

Table 8.5. Frequency and Magnitude of Junk Bond Exchanges

Issue Year	Number Issued	Amount Issued ($ millions)	Average Issue Amount ($ millions)	N %	Average Coupon	N %	Average YTM	N %
1977	26	908	34.08	26	10.466	26	10.714	17
1978	51	1,442	28.28	51	11.416	51	11.631	34
1979	41	1,263	30.81	41	12.284	41	12.633	32
1980	37	1,223	33.05	37	13.596	36	14.709	28
1981	24	1,240	51.67	24	14.793	21	17.395	18
1982	41	2,490	60.73	41	13.772	40	16.832	29
1983	74	6,003	81.12	74	12.049	72	13.928	35
1984	104	11,552	113.26	102	14.349	74	15.577	61
1985	145	14,463	99.75	145	13.773	127	14.290	110
1986	200	30,949	154.75	200	12.471	188	12.636	73

High-yield bonds rated below investment grade at issue date by Moody's and Standard & Poor's. Par value is the customary method used to state the size of the high-yield market.

30. Edward Altman, "Measuring Corporate Bond Mortality and Performance," *Journal of Finance* 44 (September 1989), pp. 909–922.

31. Paul Asquith, David Mullins, and Eric Wolff, "Original Issue High Yield Bonds: Aging Analysis of Defaults, Exchanges and Calls," *Journal of Finance* 44, no. 4 (September 1989), pp. 923–952. Also in Patrick A. Gaughan, ed., *Readings in Mergers and Acquisitions* (Cambridge: Basil Blackwell, 1994), pp. 114–144; *Analysts Journal* (September/October 1995), pp. 49–56.

Table 8.6.   Junk Bond Defaults

Issue Year	Number of Issues Exchanged	Amount of Issues Exchanged ($ millions)	% of Total Issues Exchanged		% of Total Issues Exchanged with No Subsequent Default	
			Number	Amount	Number	Amount
1977	6	281	23.08	30.95	11.54	15.75
1978	10	290	19.61	20.11	7.84	9.02
1979	4	56	9.76	4.43	2.44	1.11
1980	7	212	18.92	17.33	8.11	6.13
1981	6	365	25.00	29.44	20.83	24.19
1982	4	180	9.76	7.23	4.88	0.80
1983	8	820	10.81	13.66	5.41	7.58
1984	7	555	6.86	4.80	6.86	4.80
1985	7	470	4.83	3.25	4.83	3.25
1986	3	480	1.50	1.55	1.00	3.48
Total	62	3,709	8.37	5.19	5.13	3.48

Source: Paul Asquith, David Mullins and Eric Wolff, "Original Issue High Yield Bonds: Aging Analysis of Defaults, Exchanges and Calls," *Journal of Finance* 44, no. 4 (September 1989), pp. 923–952.

for a new combination of bonds and stocks. In extreme cases, when the firm's cash flows are very limited, the bonds are exchanged for common stocks that carry no guarantee of regular dividend payments. When bondholders agree to such an exchange in advance of a formal default or declaration of bankruptcy, these securities are not normally counted in bond default statistics.

Table 8.6 shows the frequency and magnitude of the exchanges. In four of the first five years Asquith and coresearchers found cumulative exchange percentages in excess of 17%. In later years the cumulative exchange percentages were in the 2% to 14% range. This is important because a significant percentage (18% to 89%) of the exchanged securities defaulted.

Calls

Investors in junk bonds experience an additional element of call-related risks. Many firms that issued junk bonds with relatively higher interest rates took advantage of the decline in interest rates after they were issued. Many junk bonds have call protection for a limited period of time; during that period the bonds may not be called in. At the end of that period the bonds may be called in, as a result of which the bondholders may be deprived of a rate of return superior to other rates available in the market.

Asquith and his coworkers reported that 23% to 43% of the bonds issued during from 1977 to 1982 were called by November 1, 1988. These calls were a result of the decline in interest rates that started in 1982.

Defaults

The Asquith study defined defaults to be either a declaration of default by the bond trustee, a bankruptcy filing by the issuer, or the assignment of a D rating by Standard & Poor's. If the bonds were exchanged for other securities that eventually defaulted, this also was considered a default of the original issue. This study showed that, as expected, default rates were higher for "older" issues. For example, bonds issued in 1977 had a cumulative default rate of 33.92%, whereas bonds issued in 1978 had a cumulative default rate equal to 34.26% (Table 8.7 and Figure 8.6).

Table 8.7.   Cumulative Junk Bond Default Rate in Asquith Study

Issue Year	Total Issued		Total Defaulted		Cumulative % of Total Default	
	Number	Amount ($ millions)	Number	Amount ($ millions)	Number	Amount ($ millions)
1977	26	908	6	308	23.08	33.92
1978	51	1,442	17	494	33.33	34.26
1979	41	1,263	12	312	29.27	24.70

Defaults and Aging

The Asquith study also measured the relationship between defaults and aging. As noted, it showed that default rates were low in the early years after the issuance of a junk bond. They found, for example, that for 7 of the 10 issue years covered by their study, there were no defaults in the first year. Seven years after issue, however, defaults rose to between 17% and 26%. By 11 and 12 years, the default rates increased to greater than one-third for the two relevant issue years, 1977 and 1978. Altman, however, disputes the relationship between aging and defaults and fails to find a discernible pattern that would support this relationship.[32]

The Asquith study raises serious questions regarding the riskiness of junk bonds. It contradicts the Altman and Namacher findings, which downplay the riskiness of junk bonds. However, later research by Altman supports the aging factor. For example, Altman and Kishore show that low-rated bonds are less likely to default in the first year of their life but that this probability rises significantly by the third year.[33]

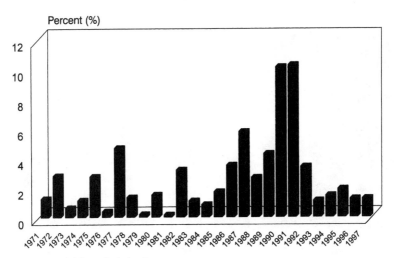

Figure 8.6.   High-yield bond default rates.

Source: Edward I. Altman and Vellore M. Kishore, "Defaults and Returns on High Yield Bonds: Analysis through 1997."

---

32. Edward Altman, "Setting the Record Straight on Junk Bonds: A Review of the Research on Default Rates and Returns," *Journal of Applied Corporate Finance* 3, no. 21 (Summer 1990): 82–95. Also in Patrick A. Gaughan, ed., *Readings in Mergers and Acquisitions* (Cambridge: Basil Blackwell, 1994), pp. 185–200.

33. Edward Altman and Vellore Kishore, "Report on Defaults and Returns on High Yield Bonds: Analysis through 1997, December 1997, Working Paper, New York University Salomon Center.

Barrie Wigmore's Study

Barrie Wigmore exposed further problems in the junk bond market.[34] Although the Asquith study pointed out the risk effects of junk bond aging, calls, and exchanges, it did not consider changes in the quality of bonds that were being issued as the junk bond market grew. Asquith focused on bonds that were originally issued in 1977 and 1978. Nonetheless, the consideration of these factors resulted in a high default rate of 34%. Many junk bond critics maintain that as the number of deals financed by junk bonds grew, the quality of junk bonds being issued deteriorated. This criticism was supported by Barrie Wigmore.

Wigmore examined a database of 694 publicly underwritten junk bonds issued between 1980 and 1988 (excluding financial institution issues). He measured the quality of the issues by considering ratios such as interest coverage, debt/net tangible assets, and cash flow as a percentage of debt. He found that earnings before interest and taxes (EBIT) coverage of interest charges fell from 1.99 in 1980 to 0.71 in 1988 (Figure 8.7). Debt as a percentage of net tangible assets presented a similar picture of deterioration. This ratio rose from 60% in 1980 to 202% in 1988 (Figure 8.8). Cash flow as a percentage of debt fell from 17% in 1980 to 3% in 1988 (Figure 8.9).

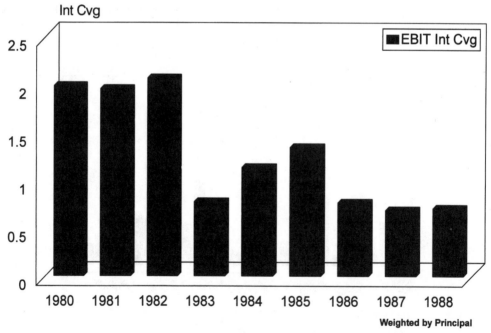

Figure 8.7. Pro forma credit ratios for junk bond EBIT coverage of interest, 1980–88.

Source: Barrie Wigmore, "The Decline in Credit Quality of Junk Bond Issues: 1980–1988," in *Readings in Mergers and Acquisitions,* edited by Patrick A. Gaughan (Cambridge: Basil Blackwell, 1994), pp. 171–184.

---

34. Barrie Wigmore, "The Decline in Credit Quality of Junk Bond Issues: 1980–1988," in Patrick A. Gaughan, ed., *Readings in Mergers and Acquisitions* (Cambridge: Basil Blackwell, 1994), pp. 171–184.

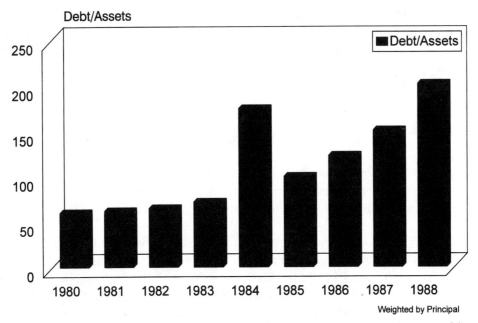

Figure 8.8. Pro forma credit ratios for junk bond debt as a percentage of net tangible assets, 1980–88.

Source: Barrie Wigmore, "The Decline in Credit Quality of Junk Bond Issues: 1980–1988," in *Readings in Mergers and Acquisitions,* edited by Patrick A. Gaughan (Cambridge: Basil Blackwell, 1994), pp. 171–184.

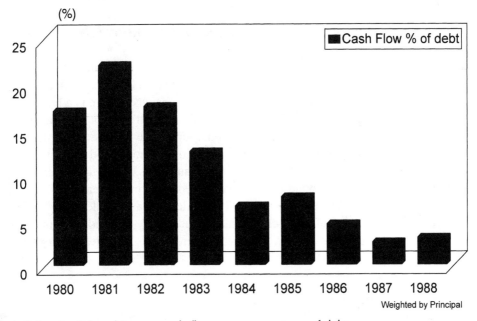

Figure 8.9. Junk bond issues: cash flow as a percentage of debt.

Source: Barrie Wigmore, "The Decline in Credit Quality of Junk Bond Issues: 1980–1988," in *Readings in Mergers and Acquisitions,* edited by Patrick A. Gaughan (Cambridge: Basil Blackwell, 1994), pp. 171–184.

Wigmore's financial ratios show that the quality of junk bonds issued during the 1980s deteriorated steadily. It is not surprising, therefore, that the junk bond market fell as we approached the late 1980s. The decline of the junk bond market (which is discussed later in this chapter) would be expected as the market rationally responded to a steadily lower quality of issues being offered.

Junk Bond Recovery Rates

It is important to remember that default does not mean a total loss of the investment. Defaulting issuers may renegotiate their obligations allowing security holders to receive a new payment stream in lieu of the payment they originally agreed to when they bought the bonds.

Researchers define recovery as the price of the bond relative to its issue value either at the time of default or at the end of the reorganization period. Altman and Namacher found an average recovery rate of $41.70 per $100 face value on 700 defaulting bonds from 1978 to 1995.[35] Altman and Kishore, in measuring the recovery rate on 696 defaulted bonds from 1971 to 1995, showed that this recovery rate varied by seniority with senior secured debt averaging 58% of face value, whereas less senior securities averaged lower values.[36] The lowest seniority category they considered, junior subordinated debt, averaged 31% of face value. They also showed significant variation across industry categories. The highest recovery occurred in the public utility sector (70%), whereas other sectors were considerably below that rate. For example, savings institutions showed an average recovery rate of only $9.25.

Conclusion of the Junk Bond Default Research

Even though the Altman research was the target of repeated criticism and opposing studies conducted by well-regarded researchers, the methodology and general conclusions have held up quite well. Altman openly concedes that in periods when there is a large issuance of junk bonds, the aging effect will tend to suppress the default rate. During the late 1980s and early 1990s the junk bond market suffered at the same time the criticizing studies were being released. Some people worried that the declining economy and collapsing market marked just the beginning of a trend toward rising default rates. As Figure 8.6 shows, however, the resiliency of the junk bond market manifested itself in the years 1992 and thereafter. From 1993 through 1997 the average junk bond default rate equaled 1.39%. The conclusion is that junk bond default rates clearly may be adversely affected by poor economic conditions and declines in this market, but over longer periods their default rates are generally low.

---

35. Edward Altman and Scott Namacher, *Investing in Junk Bonds* (New York: John Wiley & Sons, 1987.)

36. Edward Altman and Vellore M. Kishore, "Almost Everything You Wanted to Know about Recoveries on Defaulted Bonds," *Financial Analysts Journal* (November/December 1996), pp. 57–64.

Risk and Return on Junk Bonds

A well-established proposition in corporate finance is the direct relationship between risk and return. That is, with all other factors being constant, investors will demand a higher expected return before they purchase a riskier asset. Therefore, if firms are going to be able to market junk bonds, they must offer higher returns. This higher return is known as the *risk premium*. The risk premium associated with junk bonds is designed to compensate investors for two main categories of risk: default risk and liquidity risk. (Default risk was discussed at length in the previous section.) Liquidity risk means that junk bonds are not as liquid as other types of securities. An added element of risk to the investor is that there is no active secondary market for junk bonds as there is for other, lower risk securities such as U.S. Treasury bonds. Thus, if it became necessary to liquidate their junk bond investments, investors might not be able to do so or might only be able to sell them at a significant loss. For these reasons, junk bond yields have a distinct risk premium above the yields of higher quality and more liquid debt securities.

Blume, Keim, and Patel analyzed the returns on high-yield bonds for the period from January 1977 through December 1989.[37] During this period they found that high-yield bonds paid an average annual return of 10.2%, which was half a percent higher than high-grade bonds, 4.4% lower than the S&P 500, and 8.9% lower than small company stocks (Table 8.8). Looking at a shorter time period that coincided with the end of the fourth merger wave, low-grade bonds yielded a return that was significantly less than long-term government bonds and high-grade bonds.

Blume, Keim, and Patel also discovered that low-grade bonds had a lower volatility than high-grade corporates or equities as reflected by the standard deviation of monthly returns. The authors believed that this lower volatility could be explained by the fact that lower-grade bonds had higher coupons and lower durations than their high-grade counterparts. Low-grade bonds would, therefore, be less sensitive to interest rate fluctuations and theoretically would exhibit less price variability. They also believed that because much of the risk of lower grade bonds was firm-specific, this risk could be reduced through diversification of bond portfolios. They noted that a comparison of the correlation coefficients between the returns of low-grade bonds, high-grade bonds, and equities

Table 8.8. Annual Geometric Mean Return

Assets	1/77 to 12/89 (%)	1/77 to 12/88 (%)	1/82 to 12/89 (%)	1/82 to 12/85 (%)	1/86 to 12/89 (%)
Long-term government bonds	9.3	8.6	16.3	20.9	11.9
High-grade bonds	9.7	9.1	17.1	23.1	11.4
Low-grade bonds	10.2	11.3	14.0	20.9	7.5
S&P 500	14.6	13.3	18.9	20.2	17.6
Small stocks	19.1	19.4	13.4	20.1	7.0

Source: Blume et al.

---

37. Marshall E. Blume, Donald E. Keim, and Sandeep A. Patel, "Returns and Volatility of Low Grade Bonds: 1977–1989," *Journal of Finance* 46 (March 1991), pp. 49–74. Also in Patrick A. Gaughan, ed., *Readings in Mergers and Acquisitions* (Cambridge: Basil Blackwell, 1994), pp. 145–170.

showed a low correlation. This would mean that low-grade bonds might be effective diversification vehicles for a portfolio containing these different securities.

JUNK BOND RETURNS: 1980–94

Using data for a longer time period than that covered by the Blume, Keim, and Patel study, it may be seen that junk bonds provide a full percentage point higher return than high-grade bonds, while yielding a two percentage point lower return than stocks as measured by the S&P 500 (Table 8.9). There still appear to be some asymmetries in the risk-return rankings of the broad investment categories. High-yield bonds yielded a full two percentage points lower return and significantly lower risk as reflected by a standard deviation in their return of 10.5, whereas the standard deviation of the return on the S&P 500 is 17.5. However, high-yield bonds offer a full percentage point higher return but a lower standard deviation than the high quality bonds. These statistics seem to support the notion that investors can "have their cake and eat it too." That is, they can realize higher returns while incurring lower risk when they select high-yield bonds over investment-grade bonds.

Investment Grade versus Junk Bonds

Having discussed the ratings given to various categories of bonds, the return on the securities, and the risk-return relationship, the obvious question arises: Do bond yields reflect ratings? Martin Fridson has tested the extent to which the correlation between risk and return applies to junk bonds in the same way that it applies to investment-grade securities.[38] In a comparison of a sample of investment-grade securities with high-yield bonds, he found that the correlation between ratings and yields was higher in the investment-grade sector than in the high-yield sector. For investment-grade issues, the R^2 factor (squared correlation coefficient) was 0.891, versus 0.573 for the high-yield bonds (Figure 8.10). These results were significant at the 98.1% and 85.4% levels, respectively.

In his study Fridson cited the limited range of factors that rating agencies took into account (Figure 8.11). He showed that they principally considered default risk and seniority. In his view, they fail to consider other relevant factors such as the potential for recovery in bankruptcy, liquidity, issue terms, price, and rumors about restructuring.

Table 8.9. Comparative Securities Return and Risk: 1980-1998

Investment Category	Average Annual Return	Standard Deviation
S&P 500	14.5%	17.5
Salomon Brothers high-yield index	12.4%	10.5
High-grade corporate bonds	17.7%	12.0
Long-term treasuries	11.8%	12.6
Intermediate-term treasuries	10.2%	6.8

Sources: Salomon Brothers, Standard & Poors, *SBBI 1999 Yearbook* (Ibbotson Associates).

---

38. Martin S. Fridson, *High Yield Bonds* (Chicago: Probus Publishing Co., 1989), pp. 37–38.

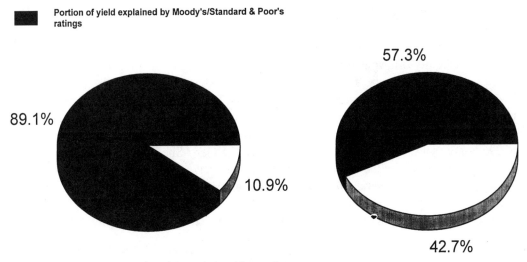

Figure 8.10.   Percent of yield explained by ratings.

The Fridson study raises questions regarding the reliance on bond ratings when investing in junk bonds. The R^2 in his study showed a much looser relationship between the ratings and yields for high-yield securities than for investment-grade bonds. These results indicate that although ratings are a useful guide to the risk and required rates of return for bonds, the high-yield bond investor should not blindly rely on the information content of bond ratings to determine the appropriate yield. Junk bond investors must carefully analyze the issuer to determine whether the expected yield is consistent with the investor's perceived level of risk.

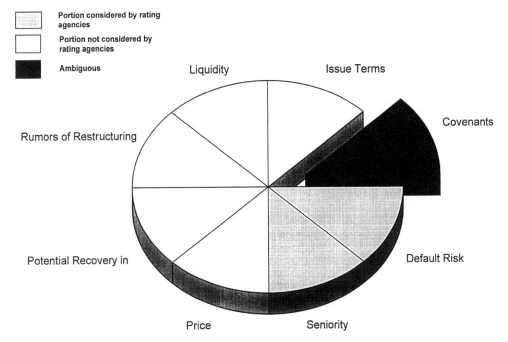

Figure 8.11.   Risk factors considered by rating agencies.

Junk Bonds Returns and Subsequent Equity Offerings

Several issuers of junk bonds issued equity in the years after they had issued the high-yield debt. These equity offerings often reversed some of the highly leveraged transactions that took place in earlier years. The 1990s was a period when many of these equity offerings took place, reversing debt-laden deals of the 1980s. Bondholders who held securities after the equity offerings benefited from a greater equity cushion, which lowered the default risk of the company. Jean Helwege analyzed the impact of this deleveraging activity in a study of 295 bond issues, including 113 bonds issued in LBOs.[39] She found that returns to bonds that issued equity exceeded those that did not by an average of 64 basis points over a two-month announcement period. However, bonds that were callable did not perform well and many showed negative returns. When the callable bonds were eliminated, the difference in returns compared with the nonequity issuing group rose to 150 basis points.

DIVERSIFICATION OF JUNK BOND INVESTMENTS

Diversifying junk bond investments enables investors to enjoy the higher average returns provided by junk bond yields without the higher degree of risk normally associated with individual junk bond issues. The risk-reduction benefits of diversification and the formation of portfolios has attracted much attention. The bulk of the research has focused on the market for equities rather than bonds. They show that as the number of securities in a portfolio increases, the total risk declines and approaches the level of systematic risk, which is the undiversifiable risk that results from broad market-based movements. As the number of securities rises, there are few, if any, risk-reduction benefits.[40]

Wagner and Lau analyzed the risk-reduction effects of diversifying across randomly selected equity securities.[41] Their results show lower risk, reflected by the lower standard deviation of monthly stock returns, as the number of securities in a portfolio increased from 1 to 20. They showed that the greatest risk-reduction benefits were achieved before the tenth security was added to the portfolio. These findings imply that investors may enjoy significant risk-reduction benefits without having to have a very large portfolio.

RISK OF A JUNK BOND PORTFOLIO

In the 1980s junk bond investors began to tout the risk-reduction benefits of portfolio formation as a means of lowering the firm-specific default risk. The risk-reduction benefits of portfolio formation had been well established before the dramatic growth of the junk bond market in the 1980s. As previously noted, most of this research focused on applying portfolio analysis to equity securities. Bond investors, however, soon began to make the obvious extension and applied this research to the junk bond market.

---

39. Jean Helwege, "High Yield Bonds Returns and Equity Offerings in the Early 1990s," *Fixed Income Research,* 1995.

40. J. H. Evans and S. H. Archer, "Diversification and the Reduction of Dispersion: An Empirical Analysis," *Journal of Finance* (December 1968), pp. 761–767.

41. W. H. Wagner and S. C. Lau, "The Effects of Diversification on Risk," *Financial Analysts Journal* (November-December 1971), pp. 49–51.

Junk Bond Funds

Diversification may be easily accomplished through the use of junk bond funds. Several funds, which operate like the more common stock mutual funds, pool investment capital and invest in a portfolio of junk bonds. As noted previously, these funds provide the appeal of the higher yields of junk bonds while reducing risk through the process of diversification. Diversification lowers the impact on the fund's portfolio of any single junk bond issue's default risk. Some of these funds are listed in Table 8.10.

UNDERWRITING SPREADS

Underwriters receive higher spreads from underwriting junk bond offerings than from offerings of other less risky securities. Underwriting is the process whereby an investment bank guarantees an issuer of securities a given percentage of the value of the offering. The underwriter then bears the risk that the issue will be sold for a certain expected price.

The average gross underwriting spread is approximately 1%.[42] Gross underwriting spreads for junk bonds, however, average approximately 3%, with some as high as 4% or 5%. Altman and Namacher conducted a study of the determinants of underwriting spreads for junk bonds based on a regression analysis that had the following specification:[43]

$$GS = f\,(IS,\ TA,\ S\&P,\ Z) \tag{8.2}$$

where

GS = gross underwriting spread
IS = issue size
TA = total assets
$S\&P$ = Standard & Poor's rating
Z = Zeta score

Table 8.10. Selected High-Yield Bond Funds

Name of Mutual Fund	Date Fund Established	Minimum Investment	Total Assets ($ millions)	Ten-Year Return
AIM-High-Fund A	1978	$500	550.8	13.4
Dean Witter High Yield	1979	1,000	556.1	9.3
Franklin AGE High Income Fund	1969	100	2,050.6	10.8
Kemper High Yield Fund	1978	1,000	2,299.5	13.6
Merrill Lynch High Income Port A	1978	1,000	923.1	132.4
Price T Rowe High-Yield Fund	1984	2,500	1,613.9	—
Prudential High Yield B	1979	1,000	3,745.9	10.8
Putnam High Yield Tr A	1978	500	3,285.9	12.2
Smith Bny Shears High Income B	1986	1,000	242.4	—
Transamerica Special High-Yield B	1987	1,000	139.9	—
Vanguard F/I High Yield Corporate	1978	3,000	2,508.6	11.6

---

42. Ernest Bloch, *Inside Investment Banking* (Homewood, Ill.: Dow Jones Irwin, 1989), p. 323.
43. Altman and Namacher, *Investing in Junk Bonds,* p. 47.

They reported the following results for the 1983–84 period:

$$GS = 1.6193 - 0.00016(IS) - 0.000044(TA) + 0.2640(SP) - 0.0691(Z)$$
$$(5.22) \ (-0.30) \ (-0.89) \qquad (4.63) \quad (-2.34)$$

$R^2 = 38.1\%, N = 109$
Durban Watson Statistic $= 1.72$

Thus, we see an inverse relationship between the size of the issue and the underwriting spread. The terms in the brackets under each coefficient are t-statistics and indicate the level of statistical significance. Values greater than 1.96 indicate that there is a 95% probability that the true value of the coefficient is within a confidence interval that is constructed around the coefficient itself. In other words, the higher the t-statistics, the more confident we may feel about the coefficient.

The signs of the coefficients are consistent with other studies of underwriting commissions. The signs of the S&P and Zeta variables show that the higher the risk of the issue, the greater the underwriting spread. Similarly, as the size of the firm increases, the gross underwriting spreads decline, revealing that underwriters generally consider the larger firms to be less risky.

Typical Junk Bond Takeover Process

Listed here is a generalized step-by-step junk bond takeover process. It should be noted, however, that because junk bond–financed takeovers were more of a 1980s phenomenon, they are not as relevant to the takeovers of the 1990s.

Step 1. The takeover process involving junk bonds usually begins with the acquirer establishing a shell corporation as a subsidiary. This shell serves as the acquisition vehicle for the target's takeover.

Step 2. The shell company makes a tender offer for the target. The offer is usually conditional on the arrangement of financing. The acquiring firm's investment bank issues a Highly Confident Letter indicating that the bank believes it can raise the requisite financing. The fall of the junk bond market made it more difficult for investment banks to be highly confident.

Step 3. At this point, the investment bank secures commitments from investors who will buy the junk bonds when the shell corporation eventually issues them. Investors receive a guaranteed amount of money or commitment fee for agreeing to the commitment of their funds. This fee is not usually refundable even if the takeover is aborted.

Step 4. The investment bank may also arrange bridge financing to provide the necessary capital to complete the deal. The bridge loan will be refinanced after the sale of the junk bonds issued by the shell corporation. The advantage to using bridge financing is that the investment bank is able to choose the most opportune time to issue the junk bonds. If the junk bond market is temporarily depressed, such as immediately after several other large junk bond offerings, the investment bank may choose to wait until the rates decline. Investment banks consider the following factors:

a. Recent and future junk bond offerings

b. Recent performance of the junk bond market

c. The current level of interest rates

Many bridge financing commitments were left in suspended animation when the junk bond market collapsed and investment bankers could not refinance the bridge loans through an offering of junk bonds.

Step 5. Once the financing is arranged, the bonds are sold and the cash is used to buy the stock tendered. If the offer is a two-tiered bid, the cash is used to purchase the stock tendered in the first tier. The purchase of the first tier, which may amount to 51% of the target's outstanding common stock, gives the acquirer control of the target.

Step 6. Assuming a two-tiered transaction, once the acquirer attains control of the first tier, another set of junk bonds is issued to purchase remaining stock in the second tier. It should be pointed out, however, that the double issue of junk bonds is not always necessary. Indeed, many takeovers financed by junk bonds involved only one junk bond offering.

Step 7. At this point the acquiring firm and its shell subsidiary are beset with large interest payments associated with the junk bonds offered. The acquirer seeks to reduce these debt payments as soon as possible. This process usually involves the sale of the target's assets. The proceeds are used to retire the debt assumed in the takeover. This is why many heavily leveraged takeovers and LBOs have been referred to as bustup takeovers.

The preceding takeover process was common in the mid-1980s but became increasingly less common toward the end of the 1980s as it became more and more difficult to find buyers for junk bonds. However, when the junk bond market rebounded in the 1990s, this process became more feasible. Nonetheless, junk bond–financed takeovers are still less common even though the pace of mergers resumed strongly in the mid-1990s.

Small versus Large Hostile Raiders

The growth of the junk bond market has strengthened the credibility of small companies as raiders. Smaller companies do not usually have as much access to bank financing as larger, more creditworthy companies do. Before the junk bond market developed, these small companies would not be taken seriously if they made an offer to take over a much larger target.

As noted earlier in this chapter, when an investment bank provides a smaller bidder with a Highly Confident Letter, it gives the bidder instant credibility. The investment bank knows the bonds will be marketable inasmuch as the substantial assets of the target will serve as collateral for the junk bonds that will be offered. A classic example of such instant credibility was Triangle Industries' offer for the National Can Company. In April 1985 Triangle Industries, led by CEO Nelson Peltz, made a $430 million all-cash offer for National Can. In terms of sales, National Can (1.9 billion) was more than six times larger than Triangle ($291 million). Triangle's investment bankers arranged the financing through agreements with 36 different large investors.[44] This was made possible through Triangle's investment banker, Drexel Burnham Lambert.

---

44. *New York Times,* 14 April 1985, p. 8.

CASE STUDY: REPACKING JUNK BONDS

As the junk bond market turned downward in the late 1980s, market participants used certain innovations to rekindle the dwindling demand. Principal among these was the *collateralization* of junk bonds, which allows junk bond holders to package their junk bond portfolio and reissue new, higher rated securities backed by the low rated junk bond debt. The technique, first applied to junk bonds in November 1988, is an adaptation of a technique used in the mortgage-backed securities market.

As noted earlier in this chapter, a diversified portfolio of high-yield debt may provide a high average yield with a reduced degree of risk. The reduced risk allows the securities to receive a higher quality debt rating.

The way in which the transactions are structured may be complicated. A typical transaction process for a collateralized deal is structured through a combination of sections called *tranches.* The first tranche, usually about three quarters of the issue, is senior to the others. The so-called Class A investors receive their interest payments before any other creditors, and the yield is typically about two percentage points higher than other A-rated bonds. For instance, a recent $300 million collateralized obligation offered by Duff & Phelps, an investment firm in Chicago, included a senior tranche of $240 million with a 10.05 yield, according to Timothy P. Norman, a vice president of the firm. Investors in the second and third tranches—known as Class B and Class C holders—receive a much higher interest rate but their securities have a lower rating. In the Duff & Phelps issue, the $45 million Class B tranche is a zero coupon yielding 15.29 percent. The yield on these units is much higher than the Class A tranche because of the risk that a higher than expected default rate will wipe out these investors' expected interest payments, but this tranche also has a great opportunity for appreciation.

The capital structure of the collateralized obligation also includes a group of equity holders. In many cases, the issuing companies put their own capital into the equity and the third tranche. In exchange, they receive whatever interest is left over when all the bondholders have received their principal and interest. Their goals are to realize cash flow from the sale of the top tranches and to profit from the unusually wide yield spread between the average interest rate of the underlying bonds and the interest rate on the new bonds.[a]

Institutions that have larger junk bond portfolios but that want to divest themselves of these high-risk investments use the collateralization technique. Large savings and loans have larger high-yield investments and want to reduce their exposure to this risky market. Buyers of these securities also tend to be institutions, particularly European institutional investors.

---

a. Anise Wallace, "Making Junk Bonds Respectable," *New York Times,* 15 December 1989, p. D1.

BANK LOAN FINANCING VERSUS JUNK BOND FINANCING

As noted previously, smaller companies may have access to large-scale bank financing. Their size and lesser credit standing do not make them attractive candidates for bank loans of the magnitude that was often necessary in the takeovers of the 1980s. Banks look for lower debt-equity ratios and other financial measures more stringent than those offered by smaller companies. The junk bond investor is not as demanding as the bank lender, not because he or she does not care about the risk of the borrower, but because the junk bond investor is better able to lower risk through diversification. A buyer may purchase a diversified portfolio of junk bonds that will have lower risk because of diversification. Because of the limited amount of capital (relative to the junk bond market as a whole), banks invest in loans to a limited number of borrowers. Therefore, a bank cannot easily maintain a well-diversified portfolio and thereby assume a higher degree of event risk. For these reasons, direct-issue high-yield securities are concentrated in the low quality end of the risk spectrum.[45]

Bank loan financing terms are generally inferior to junk bond financing terms. Bank loans typically have a term of less than 7 years, whereas junk bonds may have 10– to 20–year maturities. Junk bonds also have call options that allow the issuer to retire the issue more quickly if the opportunity arises.

JUNK BONDS AND GREENMAIL

With the advent of the junk bond–financed takeovers, smaller, less well financed companies became credible raiders in the 1980s. This created new opportunities for greenmail. With the growth of the junk bond market, less ubstantial bidders had to be taken seriously, and more bidders were able to extract greenmail from targets. Targets, fearing they might eventually be taken over, were now more willing to pay greenmail. For example, in 1984 Saul Steinberg and his company, Reliance, sought to acquire the relatively larger Walt Disney. Steinberg needed $2.4 billion for the acquisition, some of which would come from Reliance's own

---

45. Arie L. Melnik and Steven E. Plant, "High Yield Debt as a Substitute for Bank Loans," in Edward Altman, ed., *The High Yield Debt Market* (New York: Salomon Brother Center for the Study of Financial Institutions, New York University, 1990), pp. 206–225.

resources and the banks it controlled. But Reliance was depending on Drexel Burnham Lambert to provide $1.5 billion in mezzanine layer financing, most of which would be raised through the sale of junk bonds. The greenmail offer to Steinberg was as follows:

> Disney would pay Reliance $325.5 million ($77.50 per share) for its 4.2 million shares. That included $297.3 million ($70.83 a share) for the Steinberg stock, plus $28 million ($6.67 a share) to cover Steinberg's expenses, including his legal bills and the commitment fees he would have to pay Kirk Kerkorian, the Fishers, Irwin Jacobs, and the rest of the investors. Excluding those expenses, Steinberg would make a profit of $31.7 million on the buyback, the difference between the price he had paid for his stock over the last 90 days and the price Disney would pay for it.[46]

Without the credibility of the junk bond financing and Drexel's ability to raise this capital in the junk bond market, the greenmail offer might not have been made as quickly. Disney might have tried to wait out the offer in the hope that it could get away without having to incur the expense of greenmail. Given Steinberg's access to junk bond financing, he was a credible threat.

As discussed in Chapter 5, greenmail payments declined and are an infrequent occurrence in the 1990s. Both junk bonds and greenmail tend not to be part of the 1990s merger landscape.

REGULATIONS AFFECTING JUNK BOND FINANCING

On December 6, 1985, the Federal Reserve, through Regulation G, established margin requirements that affect the use of junk bonds to finance takeovers. In the 1930s the Federal Reserve was empowered to establish margin requirements for the purchase of stock. The maximum value of a loan that uses stock as collateral is set at 50%. If the stock of a target corporation is used as collateral for a loan, this transaction is governed by the Federal Reserve's margin requirements.

As noted previously, the acquisition process financed by junk bonds usually features a shell corporation, which is a wholly owned subsidiary of the original acquiring corporation. The shell corporation issues the junk bonds and uses the proceeds to purchase the stock in the target. The target is then acquired by the shell corporation. As of January 1986, however, shell corporations set up as acquisition vehicles were prohibited from purchasing more than 50% of a target corporation's stock with financing secured by junk bonds. At the time the Federal Reserve believed that this regulation would limit takeovers financed by junk bonds.

This reasoning proved to be quite shortsighted and underestimated the innovativeness of an investment banking community motivated by the desire to continue earning great profits.

The following exceptions to Regulation G apply:

1. Operating companies with substantial assets are not governed by this regulation, but shell corporations used as acquisition vehicles are.

---

46. John Taylor, *Storming the Magic Kingdom* (New York: Ballantine Books, 1987), pp. 128–129.

2. A shell corporation may still issue an unrestricted amount of junk bonds if a corporation with substantial assets and cash flows, such as the shell's parent company, guarantees the junk bond issue.

3. If the target agrees to the merger, Regulation G does not apply. The regulation is designed to limit hostile takeovers financed by junk bonds.

4. If the sources of financing are foreign leaders, Regulation G may not apply. This is another gray area of the law.[47] A legal decision in the *Metro-Goldwyn-Mayer v. Transamerica Corporation* case held that foreign financing was not governed by Regulation G.[48]

Takeovers financed by junk bonds slowed down during the first nine months of 1986. Late that year, however, the number of such takeovers increased. The marketplace discovered an easy way around Regulation G. The regulation placed limits on the total financing that could be raised by shell corporations issuing junk bonds and using the stock of the target as collateral. The rule did not restrict the acquiring corporation itself from issuing the junk bonds directly rather than relying on the shell to issue the bonds.

The market also circumvented the restriction imposed by Regulation G by issuing *rising rate preferred stock* instead of junk bonds. This stock was used in the 1988 attempted takeover of Interco by the Rales Brothers. Although rising rate preferred stock is technically equity, it is actually more like junk bonds in disguise. The disadvantage of using these securities instead of junk bonds is that the investment criteria of some high-yield bond funds preclude their investing in these securities. This tends to reduce their marketability.

From the latter part of 1986 through 1988, corporations issued large amounts of junk bonds, using the capital as a "war chest" that could later be used to take over a suitable target. For example, in 1986 the Wickes Companies raised over $1 billion in the junk bond market for "acquisition purposes." At the time of the sale of the junk bonds, the Wickes Companies did not have any specific target in mind. This situation underscored the fact that the increased regulation did not place any permanent and meaningful limits on the growth of the junk bond market. Changing preferences of buyers, however, accomplished this objective.

---

47. Martin Lipton and Erica H. Steinberger, *Takeovers and Freezeouts* (New York: Law Journal Seminar Press, 1987), pp. 2.12(3)–2.12(4).

48. *Metro-Goldwyn-Mayer, Inc. v. Transamerica Corporation,* 303 F. Supp. 1354 (S.D.N.Y. 1969).

CASE STUDY: INTEGRATED RESOURCES

In April 1991 First Executive Corporation's main subsidiaries, its Executive Life Insurance Company (ELIC) in California and Executive Life Insurance of New York (ELNY), were seized by their respective state regulators. The parent company, First Executive Corporation, being dependent on upstream cash flow from its subsidiaries, was unable to service its debt and was forced to declare bankruptcy. This marked the end of the high-flying performer of the staid insurance industry.

First Executive can trace its phenomenal growth to CEO Fred Carr's aggressive use of junk bonds to generate high returns for its policyholders. Armed with the high yields of junk bonds, First Executive was able to offer high-yield products that enabled it to capture market share from its conservative competitors. For example, it offered interest rate–sensitive products that forced competitor insurance companies, who were locked into long-term low-yield investments, to compete on yield. At that time most insurance companies invested heavily in comparatively lower return government bonds (15.4% of their portfolio on average) and corporate bonds (36.5%) and mortgages (20.6%).[a] First Executive, on the other hand, had almost $11 billion of junk bonds by the end of 1989, when the entire junk bond market was valued at $205 billion.[b]

The rest of the insurance industry was highly critical of Fred Carr and high aggressive junk bond investment strategy. They defended their conservative portfolio strategy by claiming that it was designed out of concerns about the safety of policyholders. Carr claimed that through diversification, safety was achieved while affording high returns for policyholders.

With the collapse of the junk bond market, First Executive announced in January 1990 that the value of its junk bond portfolio had declined by $968 million in the fourth quarter of 1989. The company took a $515 million after-tax charge on its 1989 earnings. At this time many major junk bond issuers fell into default. First Executive held a disproportionate amount of defaulted issues. The company held the securities of 62 junk bond issuers, of which three defaulted in 1989 (carrying a value of $343 million), 11 defaulted in 1990 (carrying a value of $806 million), and five more defaulted in 1991 (carrying a value of $591 million).[c] By the end of 1990, 20% of First Executive's junk bond portfolio was in default while the overall average for the junk bond market was 10%.[d]

The collapse of First Executive confirmed the need for a life insurance company to pursue an investment strategy that is not filled with volatile fluctuations in the return on its investments. The public profile of a life insurance company is almost as important to it as it is to a bank. Life insurance policies and annuity products are similar to other debt obligations except that they have a put option associated with them, which enables the holder to sell or surrender them back to the company. Therefore, the company is always susceptible to a damaging cash drain that may create a liquidity crisis, as it did at First Executive. Banks have the federal government's FDIC insurance to stave off such depositor runs. Without such federal government backing, life insurance companies are dependent on the public perception of their net worth and ability to pay the returns it promised.

[a] Carolyn Kay Brancato and Patrick A. Gaughan, "The Growth of Institutional Investors in U.S. Capital Markets," *The Institutional Investor Project,* Columbia University School of Law, November 1988.

[b] Harry DeAngelo, Linda DeAngelo, and Stuart Gilson, *First Executive Corporation,* Harvard Business School, 9–294–105, July 15, 1994.

[c] Harry DeAngelo, Linda DeAngelo, and Stuart Gilson, "The Collapse of First Executive Corporation: Junk Bonds, Adverse Publicity and the 'Run on the Bank' Phenomena," *Journal of Financial Economics* 36, no. 3 (December 1994), pp. 287–336.

[d] DeAngelo, DeAngelo, and Gilson, *First Executive Corporation,* p. 5.

First Executive pursued an aggressive strategy that won market share from its rivals by relying on the high returns from the junk bond market. As this market grew in the 1980s, more conservative competitors lost market share to First Executive. When the junk bond market collapsed, First Executive was one of the first to go with it.

Alarmed policyholders, hearing the bad news, besieged the company to surrender annuity investments or policies or to request loans against policies. The massive surrenders were similar to a run on a bank where depositors lose confidence and withdraw their money. This created a cash flow crisis for the firm, which it could not survive.

SUMMARY

The junk bond market grew dramatically during the fourth merger wave and fell precipitously by the end of the 1980s. Its growth enabled the fourth wave to be fundamentally different from any of the previous merger periods. Using the junk bond market, relatively smaller firms were able to make hostile bids for far larger companies. Investors came to regard the junk bond debt used to finance these takeovers as a means to enjoy high returns while they diversified their junk bond holdings to try to lower their risk. The high returns provided by these securities made them quite popular among a variety of investors, including large institutions such as pension funds, insurance companies, and savings and loan associations.

The market's view of junk bonds turned downward toward the end of the 1980s. Research studies conducted at the end of that decade contradicted the view of earlier studies, which implied that junk bonds were a relatively safe investment vehicle that provided relatively high yields. These later studies showed that high-yield bonds had high default risk and were of questionable quality. The junk bond market was also rocked by several large defaults and the eventual collapse of its leading market maker, Drexel Burnham Lambert. The absence of Drexel's aggressive market making reduced the liquidity of these securities. In addition, regulatory changes forced some institutions to decrease or eliminate their holdings of high-yield bonds. The big buyouts of the 1980s left a large supply of junk bonds on a market that showed falling demand.

The fall of the junk bond market slowed the pace of mergers and LBOs. The deals that occurred in 1990 relied much more on equity and less on debt. The mergers and acquisitions business was increasingly conducted by well-financed bidders and less by junk bond raiders.

One important by-product of the use of junk bonds to finance many of the mergers of the fourth merger wave was the introduction of original issue junk bonds to the everyday world of corporate finance. Investors grew accustomed to the high returns these securities offered and quickly learned how to lower their default risk through proper diversification. As a result, less creditworthy corporations now have access to a component of the capital markets that did not exist before. The junk bond market of the 1990s remains vibrant and an important part of the world of corporate finance. It is still relevant to the field of mergers and acquisitions but much less important than it was in the 1980s.

REFERENCES

Altman, Edward, and Scott Namacher, *Investing in Junk Bonds* (New York: John Wiley & Sons, 1987).

Altman, Edward, and Vellore M. Kishore. "Almost Everything You Wanted to Know about Recoveries on Defaulted Bonds. *Financial Analysts Journal* (November/December 1996).

Altman, Edward, and Vellore Kishore. "Report on Defaults and Returns on High Yield Bonds: Analysis through 1994. Working Paper, New York University Salomon Center.

Altman, Edward I. "Financial Ratios, Discriminant Analysis and the Prediction of Corporate Bankruptcy." *Journal of Finance* 23 (September 1968).

Altman, Edward. "Setting the Record Straight in Junk Bonds." *Journal of Applied Corporate Finance* 3, no. 2 (Summer 1990).

Altman, Edward I., R. Haldeman, and P. Narayanan. "Zeta Analysis: A Model to Identify Bankruptcy Risk of Corporations." *Journal of Banking and Finance* 1, no. 1 (June 1977).

Altman, Edward I., and Scott A. Namacher. *The Default Rate Experience on High Yield Corporate Debt* (New York: Morgan Stanley & Co., 1985).

Altman, Edward I., and Scott A. Namacher. *Investing in Junk Bonds: Inside the High Yield Debt Market* (New York: John Wiley & Sons, 1987).

Asquith, Paul, David Mullins, and Eric Wolff. "Original Issue High Yield Bonds: Aging Analysis of Defaults, Exchanges and Calls." *Journal of Finance* 44 (September 1989).

Beaver, William H. "Financial Ratios as Predictors of Failure." In *Empirical Research in Accounting Selected Studies* (Chicago: Graduate School of Business, University of Chicago, 1966).

Blume, Marshall E., and Donald E. Keim. "Risk and Return Characteristics of Lower Grade Bonds." Working Paper, Rodney L. White Center for Financial Research. Wharton School, University of Pennsylvania.

Brancato, Carolyn Kay. *Takeover Bids and Highly Confident Letters.* Congressional Research Service, August 28, 1987.

Bruck, Connie. *The Predators' Ball* (New York: Simon & Schuster, 1988).

DeAngelo, Harry, Linda DeAngelo, and Stuart Gilson. *First Executive Corporation,* Harvard Business School, 9–294–105, July 15, 1994.

DeAngelo, Harry, Linda DeAngelo, and Stuart Gilson. "The Collapse of First Executive Corporation: Junk Bonds, Adverse Publicity and the 'Run on the Bank' Phenomena." *Journal of Financial Economics* 36, no. (December 1994).

Drexel Burnham Lambert. "The Case for High Yield Bonds." 1985.

Evans, J. H., and S. H. Archer. "Diversification and the Reduction of Dispersion: An Empirical Analysis." *Journal of Finance* (December 1968).

Fitzpatrick, J. D., and J. T. Severiens. "Hickman Revisited: The Case for Junk Bonds." Salomon Brothers, March 1984.

Francis, Jack Clark. *Investments* (New York: McGraw-Hill, 1986).

Fridson, Martin S., and Monaghan. "Default Experience of Corporate Bonds." Salomon Brothers, March 1984.

Fridson, Martin S. *High Yield Bonds* (Chicago: Probus Publishing Co., 1989).

Helwege, Jean. "High Yield Bonds Returns and Equity Offerings in the Early 1990s." *Fixed Income Research,* 1995.

Hickman, W. B. *Corporate Bond Quality and Investor Experience* (Princeton, N.J.: Princeton University Press, 1958).

Lintner, John. "The Valuation of Risk Assets and the Selection of Risky Investments in Stock Portfolio and Capital Budget." *Review of Economics and Statistics* 47 (February 1965).

Lipton, Martin, and Erica H. Steinberger. *Takeovers and Freezeouts* (New York: Law Journal Seminar Press, 1987).

Mishkin, Frederic. *The Economics of Money, Banking and Financial Markets* (Glenview, Ill.: Scott, Foresman, 1988).

Perry, Kevin J. "The Growing Role of Junk Bonds on Corporate Finance." *Journal of Applied Corporate Finance* 1, no. 1 (Spring 1988).

Platt, Harlan D. *The First Junk Bond* (Armonk, N.Y.: M. E. Sharpe, 1994).

Pye, Gordon. "Gauging the Default Risk Premium." *Financial Analysts Journal* 30, no. 1 (January–February 1974).

Radcliffe, Robert C. *Investments* (Glenview, Ill.: Scott, Foresman, 1982).

Rosenberg, Hilary. "The Unsinkable Junk Bond." *Institutional Investor,* vol. 23, no. 1 (January 1989).

Sharpe, William F. "Capital Asset Prices: A Theory of Market Equilibrium Under Conditions of Risk." *Journal of Finance* 19 (September 1964).

Sharpe, William F. *Investments* (Englewood Cliffs, N.J.: Prentice-Hall, 1985).

Sherwood, H. C. "How They Rate Your Company's Bonds." *Business Management* 29 (March 1966).

Siconolfi, Michael. "First Boston to Sell Bridges to Its Owners." *Wall Street Journal,* 6 November 1990.

Taylor, John. *Storming the Magic Kingdom* (New York: Ballantine Books, 1987).

Van Horne, James. *Financial Management and Policy* (Englewood Cliffs, N.J.: Prentice-Hall, 1989).

Wagner, W. H., and S. C. Lau. "The Effects of Diversification on Risk." *Financial Analysts Journal* (November-December 1971).

Weinstein, Mark. "A Curmudgeon View of Junk Bonds." *Journal of Portfolio Management,* vol. 13, no. 3 (Spring 1987).

Wigmore, Barrie. "The Decline in Credit Quality of Junk Bond Issues: 1980." In Patrick A. Gaughan, ed. *Readings in Mergers and Acquisitions* (Cambridge: Basil Blackwell, 1994).

Yugo, Glenn. *Junk Bonds* (New York: Oxford University Press, 1991).

9

EMPLOYEE STOCK OWNERSHIP PLANS*

A large component of the dramatic growth of employee stock ownership plans (ESOPs) that occurred in the United States in the 1980s is attributable to their role in mergers, acquisitions, and leveraged buyouts (LBOs). Employee stock ownership plans are involved in mergers and LBOs in two main ways: as a financing vehicle for the acquisition of companies, including through LBOs, and as an antitakeover defense. Bidders and employees discovered that they could make a bid for a firm through an ESOP and realize significant tax benefits that would help lower the cost of the buyout. For their part, targets learned that ESOPs could provide them with an effective antitakeover defense.

Employee stock ownership plans are allowable under the Employee Retirement Income Security Act of 1974 (ERISA), a law that governs the administration and structure of corporate pension plans. The Employee Retirement Income Security Act specified how corporations could utilize ESOPs to provide employee benefits. An ESOP provides a vehicle whereby the employer corporation may make tax deductible contributions of cash or stock into a trust. These trust assets are then allocated in some predetermined manner to the employee participants in the trust. The corporation's contributions to the ESOP are tax-deductible. Moreover, the employees are not taxed on the contributions they are entitled to receive until they withdraw them from the ESOP. The contributions are made in direct proportion to each plan participant's compensation. The proportion is based on the ratio of the employee's compensation divided by total compensation. Thus all employees are paid the same percentage but different absolute amounts.

Participants in an ESOP are required to invest in the employer's stock. They may buy stock in subsidiaries of the employer's corporation if the employer corporation owns more than 50% of the subsidiary's stock. Unlike pension plans, ESOPs do not try to lower the risk level of their assets by diversifying. Although pension plans seek to invest in a variety of assets to lower risk, ESOPs are designed to hold only cash, cash equivalents, or the stock of the employer corporation.

HISTORICAL GROWTH OF ESOPs

Employee stock ownership plans were very popular in the United States during the 1920s, when the stock market was rising and Americans widely owned stock. The stock market

*The author would like to express special thanks to Robert E. Massengill, vice president and principal of Menke & Associates, Inc., for his helpful comments and advice on employee stock ownership plans.

crash of 1929 and the economic downturn that followed caused the stockholdings of employees to decline dramatically. After the decline in the value of the firm's stock, employees were less willing to take shares in the company as compensation, given the added risk that this form of compensation brought.

In 1974 tax laws were enacted that allowed a qualified retirement plan to borrow for the purpose of purchasing stock. This set the stage for the eventual development of the leveraged ESOPs that would become more common years later. Nonetheless, ESOP activity was not very significant until the 1980s, when the tax benefits and other advantages of ESOPs began to be explored.

The popularity of ESOPs was also particularly high in the 1980s, especially toward the end of the decade. This increased interest in ESOPs was partly due to improved tax incentives that were enacted in the Tax Reform Act of 1984 and the use of ESOPs as an antitakeover defense. These plans became more relevant in antitakeover strategy after the passage of the Delaware antitakeover statute, which, as discussed in Chapter 3, imposed a three-year delay in actions such as asset sales after takeovers unless the bidder acquired 85% of the target shares. The use of ESOPs as an antitakeover defense, particularly as it relates to the Delaware antitakeover statute, is discussed further later in this chapter.

Table 9.1 and Figure 9.1 show the growth in the number of ESOP plans from 1975 to 1997. They show that the number of ESOPs has been steadily rising over this period. However, the use of ESOPs as a financing vehicle for leveraged buyouts has varied.

Table 9.1. Number of ESOP Plans and Number of Employees Covered, 1975–97

Year	Number of Plans
1975	1,601
1976	2,331
1977	3,137
1978	4,028
1979	4,551
1980	5,009
1981	5,680
1982	6,082
1983	6,456
1984	6,904
1985	7,402
1986	8,046
1987	8,514
1988	8,862
1989	9,385
1990	9,870
1991	9,888
1992	9,762
1993	9,226
1994	9,670
1995	10,170
1996	10,670
1997	11,090

Source: National Center for Employee Ownership and the Statistical Abstract of the United States, U.S. Department of Commerce, Washington, D.C.

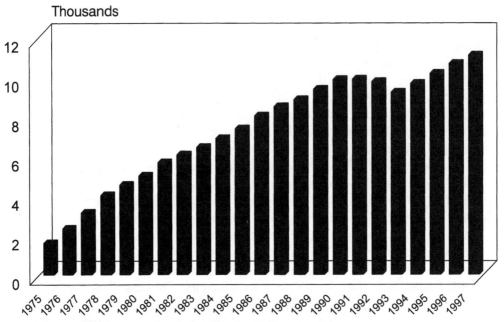

Figure 9.1.   Growth in the number of ESOP plans, 1975–97.

Sources: National Center for Employee Ownership and the *Statistical Abstract of the United States,* U.S. Department of Commerce, Washington, D.C.

TYPES OF PLANS

The two main types of pension plans are defined benefit plans and defined contribution plans.

Defined Benefit Plans

In a defined benefit plan, an employer agrees to pay employees specific benefits upon retirement. These benefits may be defined in terms of a dollar amount per month or a percentage of the previous year's salary, or several years' salary, according to a preset formula. Government workers often have such plans.

Defined Contribution Plans

Employers commit to making a substantial and recurring contribution rather than a specific benefit in a defined contribution plan. The employees' benefits depend on the investment performance of the benefit fund. These funds may be managed by a union that oversees the investment of the funds. Defined contribution plans can be riskier for employees, since their benefits will depend on the investment performance of the fund, which is not guaranteed by the employer. Defined contribution plans include Money Purchased Pension Plans,

Profit Sharing Plans, 401(K) Plans, and ESOPs. ESOPs are a type of defined contribution plan in which the employer contributions are used to invest primarily in employer securities.

CHARACTERISTICS OF ESOPs

In 1986 the General Accounting Office (GAO) conducted a survey of firms that had ESOPs in place. It found that 91% of the respondents indicated that the primary reason for starting an ESOP was to provide benefits to employees; 74% cited tax incentives; and 70% mentioned improved productivity.[1]

Using data derived from the GAO as well as from other sources, however, Corey Rosen found that half the plans were used to buy the company. In approximately one-third of ESOPs, employees owned a majority of the company, and in almost another one-third they owned less than 25% of the firm.[2] Menke & Associates report that approximately 80% of ESOPs own a minority position. Of the 1,500 plans they have installed, the average ESOP ownership was just under 40%. In sum, ESOPs generally own a minority position in the company.

Average Contribution

Employers with ESOPs contribute approximately 8% to 10% of their payroll to the ESOP each year. This is less than the maximum contribution allowable as a tax deduction under the law.[3] For some ESOP firms, such as Menke & Associates, the contributions into ESOPs they form are higher. They report that their average contribution equals 16% of participants' pay, which is significantly higher than the 4% to 5% range for non–ESOP-defined contribution plans.

LEVERAGED VERSUS UNLEVERAGED ESOPs

Employee stock ownership plans can be divided into two groups: leveraged and unleveraged. Leveraged ESOPs are those that borrow, whereas unleveraged ESOPs do not borrow. Leveraged ESOPs are of more interest as a vehicle for LBOs.

The size of the contribution that the corporation may make to the ESOP depends on whether it is a leveraged ESOP. The contribution limitation for leveraged ESOPs is up to 25% of payroll compared with 15% for unleveraged ESOPs. With leveraged ESOPs, the corporation borrows to buy its own stock. The company then makes a contribution to the ESOP that is used to pay the principal and interest on the loan.

---

1. U.S. General Accounting Office, *Employee Stock Ownership Plans: Benefits and Costs of ESOP Tax Incentives for Broadening Stock Ownership* (Washington, D.C.: 1987).

2. Corey Rosen, "The Record of Employee Ownership," *Financial Management* 19, no. 1 (Spring 1990), pp. 39–47.

3. Ibid.

CORPORATE FINANCE USES OF ESOPs

The world of corporate finance has developed several innovative uses for ESOPs. Some of these uses are discussed in the following sections.[4]

Buyouts

Employee stock ownership plans have been widely used as a vehicle to purchase companies. This technique has been used for both private and public firms. Robert Bruner reports that 59% of leveraged ESOPs have been used to buy out owners of private companies.

Divestitures

Employee stock ownership plans have also been widely used as divestiture and sell-off vehicles. Bruner reports that 37% of the leveraged ESOPs have been used as divestiture vehicles. For example, the Hospitals Corporation of America sold off 104 of its 180 hospitals to a new corporation, HealthTrust, which was owned by its employees through a leveraged ESOP.[5]

Rescue of Failing Companies

The employees of a failing company may use an ESOP as an alternative to bankruptcy. Several examples of this have occurred in the troubled steel industry. The employees of McLouth Steel, for example, exchanged wage concessions for stock in the company in an effort to avoid bankruptcy proceedings. Weirton Steel's 1983 rescue is another example.

Raising Capital

An ESOP may also be used to raise new capital for the corporation. The use of an ESOP as an alternative to a public offering of stock is discussed later in this chapter. Bruner reports that 11% of ESOPs have been used for this purpose.

VOTING OF ESOP SHARES

Voting the ESOP shares may be an important issue when the ESOP is used as a tool in mergers and leveraged acquisitions. As noted in Chapter 5, a target corporation may try to use the ESOP as a white squire by placing stock in the plan. It then hopes that the ESOP

---

4. This outline is based partially on Bruner, Robert F, "Leveraged ESOPs and Corporate Re-structuring," *Journal of Applied Corporate Finance* 1, no. 1 (Spring 1988), pp. 54–66.

5. Ibid.

shares will vote with management on major decisions such as approving mergers and other major transactions. Use of ESOPs as an antitakeover defense is discussed in greater detail later in this chapter. We will see that the voting rights of the shares is an important determinant of the use of the ESOP as an antitakeover defense.

Shares owned by an ESOP are in an Employee Stock Ownership Trust (ESOT) and are not controlled directly by employees compared with shares they might purchase from a broker. The company stock owned by the ESOT is controlled by the board of directors who appoint the ESOP trustees. Thus the voting power is really with the board of directors, not with the employees. In private companies ESOP shareholders generally have even less voting power. Whether the ESOP employee participants in private corporations retain the right to vote their shares depends on the prevailing state laws, which vary from state to state. Some states provide for limited voting rights, which do not allow full voting privileges for the individual employee shareholders. Employees in private company ESOPs usually do not have the right to vote on major issues, such as elections of the board of directors, unless the owners of the company set up the plan that way.

Approval for the Establishment of an ESOP

Shareholder approval may not always be necessary to establish an ESOP. Companies traded on the New York Stock Exchange, however, are required to receive stockholder approval when an ESOP that will acquire more than 18.5% of the firm's stock is established.

CASH FLOW IMPLICATIONS

As noted previously, cash flows are critically important to the success of an LBO. Employee stock ownership plan contributions positively affect the cash flow of all corporations whether they are involved in an LBO or not.

Let us assume that a corporation makes a $1,000 stock contribution to an ESOP. Because the contribution is in the form of stock, there is no cash outlay. Tax laws allow the corporation a $1,000 tax deduction, which improves the firm's cash flow by the amount of the tax savings. We should not conclude, however, that these cash flow benefits are costless. The benefits may be partially or completely offset by a dilution in the equity holdings of the non-ESOP stockholders. This may be reflected in lower earnings per share.

VALUATION OF STOCK CONTRIBUTED INTO AN ESOP

The cash flow of the corporation may be significantly improved by the tax benefits of the ESOP contribution. In deciding the size of the stock contribution, the company must first determine its value. For public corporations this is clear because there is a readily available market value to use. The problem is less clear for private corporations. It becomes necessary to rely on the various techniques of securities valuation for privately held companies. These methods are discussed in Chapter 14. The services of a business appraiser or an expert in business valuations may be used to determine the securities value. A valuation is particularly important in a LESOP to determine that accurate consideration was paid for the ESOP shares.[6] Stock held in an ESOP must be appraised annually by an independent outside appraiser.

ELIGIBILITY OF ESOPs

The ESOP must fulfill certain requirements to qualify for tax deductibility benefits. It must include all employees 21 years old and over with one year of service during which they have worked 1,000 hours.[7] One exception to this requirement is seasonal industries. The plan should include at least 80% of the eligible employees.

PUT OPTIONS OF ESOPs

Employees may receive a put option to sell their stock back to the employer corporation within 60 days of receiving it. If they do not choose to exercise this option in 60 days, they may receive another 60–day option the following year. Put options may even have a life of up to five years.

The put option is particularly important for departing employees. When employees exercise this option, they almost always ask to be paid in cash as opposed to stock. In S Corporation ESOPs, departing employees may receive only cash and may not receive stock. If a private company with an ESOP decides to go public in the future, the put option may be terminated. This is the case when the ESOP shares are included in the registration statement for going public. The reason for terminating the put option is that it is not necessary given that there is a public market for departing employees to liquidate their holdings.

DIVIDENDS PAID

Dividends paid by the employer corporation on the ESOP shares are charged against retained earnings. These dividend payments are a tax-deductible expense if they are paid in the following manner:

- Dividends are paid directly to ESOP participants.
- Dividends are paid directly to the ESOP, which distributes them to the ESOP participants within 90 days of the close of the plan year.
- Dividends on the ESOP are used to make payments on an ESOP loan.[8]
- Dividends paid by S Corporation ESOPs are not tax-deductible.

---

6. Robert Macris, "Leveraged Buyouts: Federal Income Tax Considerations," in Amihud Yikov, ed., *Leveraged Management Buyouts: Causes and Consequences* (Homewood, Ill.: Dow Jones Irwin, 1989).

7. Robert A. Frisch, *The Magic of ESOPs and LBOs* (New York: Farnsworth Publishing, 1985).

8. Myron Scholes and Mark Wolfson, "Employee Stock Ownership Plans and Corporate Restructuring: Myths and Realities," *Financial Management* 19, no. 1 (Spring 1990), pp. 12–28.

ESOPs VERSUS A PUBLIC OFFERING OF STOCK

Let us compare the relative benefit of an ESOP to a public offering of stock. Consider the example of a public offering of stock of $1 million that brings in $1 million, less investment banking fees, legal charges, and other costs associated with the issuance and sale of equity. These costs are often referred to as *floatation costs.* Employee compensation and benefits generally are not affected by such a transaction.

A sale of stock to an ESOP may bring in $1 million without the normal floatation costs of a public offering. However, employee compensation and benefits usually decline because the contributed stock takes the place of some of the compensation and benefits. For example, pension plan contributions could be eliminated. The firm receives a tax deduction on the ESOP contribution, although the pension plan contributions and wages that were paid before the ESOP was established were already tax-deductible. If the ESOP incurs interest costs for borrowing the capital needed to purchase the stock, the tax deduction should more than offset the interest payments.

The substitution of an ESOP for parts of the employee benefits package that was in effect before the ESOP was established may present an employee relations problem for the firm. If the pension plan is eliminated, employees may not be eligible to receive the same defined benefits at the time of retirement. With the ESOP, their postretirement income will be a function of the company's financial performance. Employees may not prefer this increase in the uncertainty of their retirement compensation. The employer may have to convince the employees that the company will make substantial contributions to the ESOP. The size of the proposed contributions, plus a favorable track record of financial performance, may persuade employees that they will be better off with the ESOP. Employees may also be favorably impressed by the fact that when stock paid to an ESOP is substituted for wage income, employees enjoy the benefits of a tax shield.

Some privately held companies are reluctant to repurchase the ESOP shares from employee shareholders. Although they have a legal obligation to do so, they may lead employees to understand that such sales are considered a sign of corporate disloyalty and may reflect badly on the employee who is seeking advancement within the company. This practice reduces the liquidity of part of this employee's compensation. The employee will then have to weigh the increased compensation against this reduced liquidity.

In addition to eliminating pension obligations, corporations such as Ralston Purina and Boise Cascade have substituted ESOPs for postretirement health care plans. The corporation will then make contributions of stock into an ESOP. The ESOP, in turn, will fund the provision of health care benefits to employees. Given the rising cost of health care and the resulting uncertainty vis-à-vis the corporation's future cost structure, firms are eager to find ways to avoid these potential liabilities. Employee stock ownership plans offer them one alternative.

Although this section compares ESOPs with initial public offerings (IPOs), it is important to bear in mind that most ESOPs are private stock transactions in which the owner is seeking personal liquidity and is not intent on accessing capital markets. Many of these companies are not of a sufficiently high profile to be able to go public. The owner uses the ESOP alternative to liquidate part of his holdings in the business while also providing ownership to employees. However, privately held companies that are on the IPO track sometimes use a leveraged ESOP as a way to liquidate part of their interest in the business, such as a one-third holding, and then go public at a later date. When the company goes public, some of the proceeds of the public offering may be used to pay off the debt incurred by the leveraged ESOP.

EMPLOYEE RISK AND ESOPs

By accepting part of their compensation in the form of stock in the employer corporation, workers take on an increased risk. They are, in effect, "putting more of their eggs in one basket." If the company fails, employees will lose not only their regular source of income but also perhaps the value of their pension. This occurred in January 1990, when the South Bend Lathe Company was forced to file for bankruptcy under Chapter 7 of the bankruptcy law. Chapter 7 is the part of the law that regulates firms in liquidation. South Bend Lathe, a manufacturing firm established in 1906, was purchased in 1976 by its employees, who owned 100% of the stock. The creditors, who initiated the bankruptcy filing, sought to seize 100% of the firm's stock, which was used as collateral for a loan to one creditor.[9]

Corporations may offset some of this risk by contributing convertible preferred shares instead of shares of common stock. The law requires that the shares be convertible in common stock to be eligible for the plan. Preferred shares have a higher priority than common stock in bankruptcy. If the value of the firm's stock increases, the employees will be able to participate in this growth by converting to shares of common stock. The risk-reduction benefits of using preferred stock instead of common stock are limited, given that both preferred stockholders and common stockholders tend to suffer significant losses in bankruptcy proceedings, although preferred stockholders do a little better than common stockholders.

The law does allow employee/shareholders to diversify some of their holdings as they become older. They may diversify from 25% to 100% as they advance in age between the years 55 and 65.[10]

It is important to bear in mind that many successful proponents of ESOPs disagree with this assessment of the risks of ESOPs. For example, Robert Massengill of Menke & Associates indicates that in most of the ESOPs their firm forms, employees do not use any of their own money and do not have their compensation reduced in exchange for the ESOP benefit. When this is combined with the fact that most ESOPs have higher contribution rates than other defined contribution plans, employees are ahead of where they would be without the ESOP and have not incurred more risk.

SECURITIES LAWS AND ESOPs

Under federal securities laws, the sale of stock to an ESOP is not considered an issuance of securities to the public. When this stock is issued, it generally comes with a letter stating that it is not subject to a sale to a third party. State corporation laws differ in their treatment of ESOPs. For example, New York laws do not require the registration of the donated securities.

---

9. Paul Dodson, "Creditors Seek Bankruptcy for S. B. Lathe," *Indiana Tribune,* 18 January 1990, p. 19.

10. Robert A. Frisch, *ESOP: The Ultimate Instrument of Corporate Finance* (Los Angeles: Margate Associates, 1990), pp. 34–35.

TAX BENEFITS OF LEVERAGED ESOPs

One of the more valuable characteristics of leveraged ESOPs is their unique tax benefits. These benefits are described in the following sections.

Deductibility of Interest and Principal Payments

If a corporation borrows directly from a bank, only the interest payments are tax-deductible. However, if the leveraged ESOP borrows from a bank or other lender such as an insurance company, both the interest and the principal payments are tax-deductible. This significantly lowers the costs of debt capital.

Other Tax Benefits of ESOPs

Some additional tax benefits of ESOPs are discussed in the following sections.

Employee/Shareholder Benefits
Like other types of pension plans, employee participants in an ESOP are not taxed on the benefits they receive until they actually receive distributions from the ESOP. In a merger or an acquisition, if the target is not a public company, the target shareholders who tender their shares to an acquiring firm's leveraged ESOP may elect to defer the gain from the sale of the stock. Target shareholders are eligible for this deferment if certain conditions are met, such as the ESOP holding at least 30% of the value of the outstanding shares after the sale.[11]

Employer Corporation Benefits: Dividend Deduction
In addition to the benefits discussed, an additional tax benefit of ESOPs is that dividends paid to the ESOP generally are tax-deductible. This helps avoid the double taxation of corporate income and gives this component of equity some of the same tax benefits that are enjoyed by debt financing.

It is even possible to pay no dividends on non-ESOP shares while paying dividends on ESOP stock. This may be done by creating a separate class of stock just for the ESOP that will receive these dividends.

Ability to Use Loss Carryforwards
The changes in the tax law that took place in 1986 limited the ability of corporations to carry forward losses after control changes. However, this limitation does not apply if an ESOP purchases at least 50% of the equity in the target.

BALANCE SHEET EFFECTS OF ESOPs

The debt that a leveraged ESOP incurs must be recorded on the firm's balance sheet. This corresponding reduction in shareholder equity must also be reflected on the firm's financial

---

11. Coopers & Lybrand, *Business Acquisitions and Leveraged Buyouts* (New York: Coopers & Lybrand, 1989), pp. 181–240.

statements.[12] The shares issued to the ESOP must be counted as outstanding shares for the purpose of computing earnings per share. In doing so, the post-ESOP earnings per share measure captures the equity dilution effects.

DRAWBACKS OF LEVERAGED ESOPs

There are certain drawbacks that offset the advantages that have been previously cited. These benefits are discussed in the following sections.

Equity Dilution Effects

The ability of ESOPs to borrow while providing the borrower with attractive tax advantages that lower the ultimate borrowing costs is a clear advantage. However, to compare the after-tax effects of borrowing directly from a bank with those of borrowing through an ESOP would be misleading. When a firm borrows through an ESOP, the employer firm is issuing equity while it is borrowing. From the original stockholders' viewpoint, the result is a dilution of equity. These new equity holders, the firm's employees, will share in any gains that the new debt capital can generate. They will still be expecting to receive returns on their stock even after the loan has been repaid. Therefore, a true analysis of the costs of borrowing through an ESOP is accurate only if the equity dilution effects are considered. This is more difficult to do because the equity dilution costs depend on the firm's future performance, which may be difficult to predict. The true equity dilution effects are based on the productivity of the new "capital," which derives from the ESOP's cost-savings effects.

To reverse the equity dilution effects, the firm must repurchase the newly issued shares at a later date. When it does so, the discounted value of this expenditure may be used to derive a measure of the true costs of borrowing.

The ESOP may be structured so that there are smaller equity dilution effects. If the ESOP purchases currently outstanding shares instead of issuing new shares, equity is not diluted.[13]

Distributional Effects of ESOPs

Depending on the price the ESOP pays for the firm's shares, there may be distributional effects associated with the formation of the ESOP. If employees receive shares in the company at a below–market price, a redistribution of wealth may occur. Employees gain wealth at the expense of nonemployee shareholders. If employees make other sacrifices, such as lower wages or benefits, which offset the gain on the below–market price shares, there may not be any distributional effects.

In a survey of 192 publicly held firms with ESOPs, Susan Chaplinsky and Greg Niehaus found that 48.2% of the firms reported an increase in employee compensation as a result of

---

12. Ibid.
13. Joseph Blasi, *Employee Ownership* (Cambridge, Mass.: Ballinger Publishing Co., 1988), p. 70.

the ESOP and that 39.3% did not change their compensation. Only 6% reported a decline in employee compensation when the ESOP was adopted.[14]

Because almost half the cases in the Chaplinsky-Niehaus sample reported increases in employee compensation, there may be a redistribution of wealth from nonemployee shareholders to employees. It would be shortsighted, however, to conclude that the total net effect is that nonemployee shareholders lose. Some of the higher employees' compensation may be necessary to offset the increased risk of their total compensation package. In addition, productivity gains may be associated with the fact that employees are now owners of shares in the company.

Loss of Control

Another disadvantage of ESOPs, which is related to the equity dilution effects, is the loss of control by the non-ESOP stockholders. After shares have been issued to the ESOP, the non-ESOP stockholders experience reduced ownership and control of the corporation.

It is more difficult for management to expand its control when an ESOP owns much of the firm's stock. The Tax Reform Act of 1986 contained antidiscrimination provisions requiring that an ESOP's benefits may not be controlled by a small group of managers. This law requires that the percentage of employees who are not highly compensated must comprise at least 70% of the shareholdings controlled by highly compensated employees. Highly compensated employees are defined as those who earn more than $75,000 or those who earn more than $50,000 and who are in the top 20% employee compensation bracket for that company.

Although there may be some loss of control by management, it is important to bear in mind that the shares are held by an ESOP whose trustees hold the voting rights. As noted previously, these trustees are appointed by the board of directors, so the board usually still controls the voting rights. When this is the case, the loss of control may not be very significant.

ESOPs AND CORPORATE PERFORMANCE

Some proponents of ESOPs contend that ESOPs are beneficial for corporations because they help finance capital expenditures and facilitate improvements in labor productivity. Employee stock ownership plans may also enhance worker productivity if the workers view their ownership position as a reason to take a greater interest in their performance. With sufficient financial incentives, workers may be less resistant to productivity-enhancing changes such as mechanization or more efficient work procedures.

In a report to the chairman of the U.S. Senate Finance Committee, the GAO found little evidence of such benefits.[15] The study failed to find a perceptible difference in profitability between firms that had ESOPs and those that did not. Apparently, in the first year after

---

14. Susan Chaplinsky and Greg Niehaus, "The Role of ESOPs in Takeover Contests," *Journal of Finance* 49, no. 4 (September 1994), pp. 1451–1470.

15. U.S. General Accounting Office, Employment Stock Ownership Effects: Little Evidence of Effects on Corporate Performance, Report to the Committee on Finance, U.S. Senate, October 1987.

adopting an ESOP, firms experienced a temporary increase in profitability; there were no noticeable long-term increases in profitability. The GAO study also compared labor productivity, as measured by the ratio of real value added to real compensation of ESOP firms, with non-ESOP firms. An examination of the productivity trend for ESOP firms appears to show an increase after the adoption of the ESOP. A statistical analysis of this relationship fails to reveal a significant relationship, however.

The GAO findings were contradicted by more recent research. Sangsoo Park and Moon Song examined the long-term performance of firms with ESOPs and found that there was a significant improvement in performance after the adoption of an ESOP.[16] Their analysis of a sample of 232 firms from 1979 to 1989 showed higher market-book ratios and returns on assets. For example, the market-book ratio increased 10.3% in the year the plan was adopted, whereas it increased 24.8% three years after adoption. It is interesting that Park and Song found that the performance improvements were limited to those firms that had large outside blockholders. This is consistent with the thesis that ESOPs have antitakeover attributes that may serve to entrench managers. These researchers theorize that outside blockholders keep management honest, offsetting the management entrenchment effects of ESOPs while allowing the firm to realize the performance-enhancing benefits of the greater employee incentives available with ESOPs.

Employee Stock Ownership and Corporate Stability

Margaret Blair, Douglas Kruse, and Joseph Blasi studied 27 publicly traded firms which had at least 20% of their stock held by employees in 1983 and compared their performance from that year through 1997 with a control group of 45 firms of similar size and industry classification.[17] They found that the companies with significant employee ownership had more stable management, and were less likely to be acquired, taken private, or fall into bankruptcy. They also failed to find any adverse effects on productivity or firm performance.

Fiduciary Responsibilities and ESOPs

A fiduciary of an ESOP is an individual or other entity that exercises discretionary authority in managing and overseeing the plan. The investment in the employer stock must be "prudent." This is particularly relevant to LBO transactions. The Department of Labor may scrutinize a transaction if a company terminates a pension plan to finance a buyout in which employees receive shares in a now highly leveraged company. It is acceptable that parties other than the employee, such as the employer corporation, receive benefits from formation of the ESOP. If, however, employee welfare is reduced by the transaction in an indisputable manner, the Labor Department may disallow the ESOP.

---

16. Sangsoo Park and Moon H. Song, "Employee Stock Ownership Plans, Firm Performance, and Monitoring by Outside Blockholders," *Financial Management* 24, no. 4 (Winter 1995), pp. 52–65.

17. Margaret Blair, Douglas Kruse, and Joseph Blasi, "Is Employee Ownership an Unstable Form or a Stabilizing Force?" Bookings Institute (ongoing paper), November 1998.

CASE STUDY: DAN RIVER, INC.—CASE OF A FAILED ESOP[a]

Dan River, Inc., a textile manufacturer in Danville, Virginia, went private in 1983 to prevent being taken over by corporate raider Carl Icahn. As part of the going-private transaction, workers agreed to give up their pensions in return for an ESOP. The ESOP gave workers 70% of the stock in the company. The company adopted the ESOP in part to achieve the tax advantages associated with this type of benefit package while avoiding being taken over.

Media reports soon documented workers' disenchantment with their failure to achieve greater voice in the company's affairs even though they were majority owners of the firm. The company did not perform well after the buyout. It incurred the following losses in the three years after the buyout:

Year	Losses
1984	$8.4 million
1985	$32.9 million
1986	$8.1 million

Dan River, Inc. had planned to offer the public 34% of total equity in the company in an effort to reduce the $181 million debt the firm had accumulated. The offering of stock would lower the employees' percentage of ownership. Management, however, owned a separate class of stock, Class B, which, according to a formula designed at the time of the buyout, appreciated faster than the employees' shares. Employees, who owned Class A shares, would sacrifice the potential to achieve greater appreciation while retaining higher priority in the event of liquidation.

Gains in worker productivity are often cited as one of the potential benefits of ESOPs. Dan River's workers, however, reportedly did not experience any increase in their involvement in determining the company's direction. The public stock offering, for example, did not require the employees' approval even though it would affect their ownership shares. The Dan River case illustrates that employee ownership is not necessarily synonymous with increases in employee morale.

---

a. This account is partially based on Dean Foust, "How Dan River Misses the Boat," *Business Week,* 26 October 1987, pp. 34–35.

ESOPs AS AS ANTITAKEOVER DEFENSE

Much of the rising popularity of ESOPs is related to the use of this compensation vehicle as an antitakeover defense rather than because of its tax advantages. Although the antitakeover implications of ESOPs have been discussed in Chapter 5, in the interest of completeness they are reviewed and expanded on here.

A large percentage of American corporations are incorporated in Delaware, where an antitakeover law became effective December 27, 1987 (see Chapter 3). As noted previously, this law provided that if a bidder purchases more than 15% of a firm's stock, the bidder may not complete the takeover for three years unless:

- The bidder purchases as much as 85% of the target's shares
- Two-thirds of the shareholders approve the acquisition (excluding the bidder's shares)
- The board of directors and the shareholders decide to exempt themselves from the provisions of the law

A Delaware corporation can establish an ESOP, which may act as its own white squire. The combined holdings of stock in the ESOP plus other "loyal" blocks of stock may prevent a bidder from ever reaching the 85% level necessary to complete the takeover. This defense was used most effectively in the Polaroid–Shamrock Holdings takeover battle in 1988.

In January 1989 the Polaroid court ruling imposed certain qualifications that restrict the indiscriminate use of ESOPs in takeover contests. The court ruled that the ESOP must be planned before the takeover contest. Employee stock ownership plans that are quickly constructed in the midst of a takeover battle, such as in the AT&T–NCR takeover, may be blocked.

Effectiveness of ESOPs as an Antitakeover Defense

Susan Chaplinsky and Greg Niehaus analyzed takeover incidence for targets with and without ESOPs.[18] After controlling for the effects of other relevant factors, such as state takeover laws and other antitakeover defenses, they found that ESOPs significantly reduce the probability of a takeover. Their results show that the defensive attributes of ESOPs compare favorably even with poison pills.

Park and Song noticed that the frequency of adoption of antitakeover defenses dropped dramatically after ESOPs were created or expanded.[19] They found that some ESOPs were used as substitutes for other antitakeover defenses such as poison pills.

ESOPs AND SHAREHOLDER WEALTH

Theoretically, ESOPs may have an impact on shareholder wealth in two opposing ways. On the one hand, ESOPs may provide tax benefits to corporations, which can lower their tax liabilities. If tax liabilities are lowered, after-tax profitability is greater and larger distributions can be made to shareholders. On the other hand, if the ESOP is used as an antitakeover defense, the probability that shareholders might receive a takeover premium may be reduced because the firm's stock price could decline.

---

18. Susan Chaplinsky and Greg Niehaus, "The Role of ESOPs in Takeover Contests," *Journal of Finance* 49, no. 4 (September 1994), pp. 1451–1470.

19. Sangsoo Park and Moon H. Song, "Employee Stock Ownership Plans, Firm Performance, and Monitoring by Outside Blockholders," *Financial Management* 24, no. 4 (Winter 1995), pp. 52–65.

In a study of 165 announcements of the formation of an ESOP, Saeyoung Chang found that 65% of the firms showed positive abnormal returns for a two-day period around the announcement. The average abnormal two-day return was 3.66%.[20] Chang then analyzed the different motives for adopting an ESOP, such as financing an LBO or adopting an anti-takeover defense. The impact on shareholder wealth for each of these separate subsamples of ESOP adoptions was considered. For firms that adopted an ESOP to facilitate the financing of an LBO, the average abnormal two-day return was 11.45%. Firms that adopted an ESOP to achieve wage concessions from employees, and thereby improve cash flow, showed an abnormal two-day return of 4.19%. When an ESOP was adopted as an anti-takeover defense, a 22.34% average abnormal return was shown.

Chang's results suggest that ESOPs may increase shareholder wealth except when they are used as an antitakeover defense. These results were supported in later research. Upinder Dhillon and Gabriel Ramirez reported that before the Polaroid court ruling, which found that the antitakeover use of ESOPs were legal, ESOPs were associated with positive shareholder wealth effects.[21] After the Polaroid ruling, however, a negative market response was found. The negative effect of the antitakeover defense on shareholder wealth might not be apparent if a longer time period than the two-day window around the announcement were used. If the ESOP results in a better negotiating position for a target, which, in turn, results in a higher takeover premium, this might not be apparent in the short two-day window. Therefore, although ESOPs that are used as an antitakeover defense may reduce shareholder wealth, further analysis is necessary to prove it.

Not all research studies found statistically significant shareholder wealth effects. Chaplinsky and Niehaus failed to detect a statistically significant stock price reaction to the announcement of the formation of an ESOP.[22] However, they interpret this result, along with their other finding in this study (that ESOPs were an effective defense), as testimony to the beneficial effects of ESOPs because the institution of a potent defense reduces the probability that shareholders will receive a takeover premium. They surmise that this must be offset by higher premiums received by shareholders of companies that have ESOPs and are eventually taken over.

ESOPs AND LBOs

One of the more dynamic ways in which LBOs may be structured involves the innovative use of ESOPs.[23] Louis Kelso of Kelso and Company pioneered the use of this technique to purchase firms. (Kelso was also active in convincing legislators, such as Senator Russell Long, former chairman of the Senate Finance Committee, to support provisions of ERISA that would enhance the powers of ESOPs.) Using an ESOP as a corporate finance tool, Kelso

20. Saeyoung Chang, "Employee Stock Ownership Plans and Shareholder Wealth: An Empirical Investigation," *Financial Management* 19, no. 1 (Spring 1990), pp. 48–58.

21. Upinder S. Dhillon and Gabriel G. Ramirez, "Employee Stock Ownership and Corporate Control: An Empirical Study," *Journal of Banking and Finance* 18 (1994), pp. 9–26.

22. Susan Chaplinsky and Greg Niehaus, "The Role of ESOPs in Takeover Contests," *Journal of Finance* 49, no. 4 (September 1994), pp. 1451–1470.

23. Robert A. Frisch, *The Magic of ESOPs and LBOs* (New York: Farnsworth Publishing, 1985), p.12. This book provides a comprehensive treatment of the use of ESOPs to finance LBOs.

helped the employees of a small newspaper chain in Palo Alto, California, Peninsula Newspapers, to buy this business from the retiring owner of the chain.[24] The plan enabled them to buy the company while enjoying significant tax benefits that lowered the cost of the purchase.

In helping to finance an LBO, the ESOP, or more appropriately the leveraged ESOP, arranges to borrow funds that will be used to finance the LBO. This may be done through a bank or a group of lenders. The larger the amount of funds required, the more likely the capital will come from a group of lenders. The leveraged ESOP borrows a certain amount of money from a bank (or group of lenders). The collateral for this loan will be the stock in the borrowing corporation. The loan may also be guaranteed by the parent corporation in the case of an LBO of a division of a company. The employer corporation makes tax-deductible contributions to the leveraged ESOP for the payment of the loan and principal.

Leveraged ESOP-LBO Process

All LBOs are somewhat different but tend to share many common characteristics. For the purposes of exposition, consider the case of a sell-off of a division in which the management of the parent company seeks to buy the division through an LBO. The steps by which this transaction could take place, using a LESOP, are as follows:

Step 1. A new company is formed, which will be the division in an independent form.

Step 2. The management of the division, which will constitute the new owners of that part of the parent company, may make an equity investment in the division. Up to this point, the division may be a corporate shell without assets.

Step 3. An ESOP for the new company is established. The ESOP negotiates with a bank or other lenders for a loan.

Step 4. Then the ESOP uses its loan proceeds to purchase newly issued stock of the new company.

Step 5. The new company agrees to make tax deductible contributions to the ESOP for the repayment of the ESOP's debt. This loan can be guaranteed by the original corporation, if that becomes a condition of the lenders. When the risk level of the new company is perceived to be high, a guarantee is often required.

The deal may also be structured so that the leveraged ESOP uses the loan proceeds to purchase stock in the new corporation rather than to purchase assets. Under this scenario, the new corporation uses the proceeds of the sale to buy the assets of the parent corporation.

Employee stock ownership plans may be used to lower the cost of the LBO by taking advantage of the tax deductions allowable under the law. In this way, they are an innovative means of completing an LBO. In a leveraged ESOP, the securities that are purchased are placed in a *suspense account*. Shares that are in the suspense account are referred to as unallocated shares. These securities are allocated to the participants in the ESOP as the

---

24. Joseph S. Schuchert, "The Art of the ESOP Leveraged Buyout," in Stephen C. Diamond, ed., *Leveraged Buyouts* (Homewood, Ill.: Dow Jones Irwin, 1985), p.94.

CASE STUDY: POLAROID—
AN ESOP AS AN ANTITAKEOVER DEFENSE

Polaroid made the first use of an ESOP as an antitakeover defense in response to an unsolicited $40 per share bid from Shamrock Holdings on July 20, 1988. The ESOP did not provide additional compensation to Polaroid employees. The ESOP was funded through a 5% pay cut and a reduction in certain other employee benefits. The ESOP was structured so that all employees would participate.

> The ESOP borrowed a total of $285 million and received a total of $15 million in cash from Polaroid to purchase 9.7166 million new shares at $30.875. . . . The share price to the ESOP was determined more by legal reference than from financial analysis. Legal precedent suggested three possible pricing rules: (i) closing price on the date of the plan approval by the board (July 12); (ii) average between the high and low price on July 12; and (iii) the average share price over a longer time period. Polaroid adopted the lowest price consistent with these rules, rule (ii).[a]

The sale of shares to the ESOP was followed by a share repurchase program that was implemented through a self-tender. A total of 24.5 million shares were repurchased at an average price of $45.918 per share, which resulted in a decline in the number of Polaroid shares outstanding and left the ESOP holding approximately 20% of the firm's stock.[b]

Shamrock Holdings attempted to dismantle the ESOP defense through legal action in the Delaware courts. They took the position that the ESOP was discriminatory in that it was established to prevent Shamrock from purchasing Polaroid. As noted previously, however, the court found that Polaroid's board of directors had considered establishing an ESOP as early as 1985. The court failed to agree with Shamrock's position that the ESOP shares not be considered in computing total shares according to Delaware's antitakeover law. The court thought that because the Polaroid ESOP plan allowed the employees holding shares through the ESOP to vote those shares in the tender offer, these shares should be considered with the other outstanding shares in computing the 85%. Judge Berger stated that the ESOP was "fundamentally fair" and did not advance management's interest over those of the employees.[c] This made it almost impossible for Shamrock to acquire the 85% of total shares necessary to complete the takeover under this law.

Many corporations realized that the cost of establishing a defensive ESOP might be far less than the 14% shareholding that Polaroid used for its ESOP. Many firms already have shares in various pension, savings, and employee benefit plans. These shares may be used as part, if not all, of the necessary 15% to achieve protection under the Delaware law. Chevron, for example, only had to place 5% of its shares in

a. Robert F. Bruner and E. Richard Brownlee II, "Leveraged ESOPs, Wealth Transfers and 'Shareholder Neutrality': The Case of Polaroid," *Financial Management* 19, no. 1 (Spring 1990), p. 63.

b. Ibid., p. 64.

c. Keith Hammonds, John Hoerr, and Zachary Schiller, "A New Way to Keep Raiders at Bay," *Business Week,* 23 January 1989, p. 39.

an ESOP because it already had 11% of its stock in company employee benefit plans. Some firms already have 15% of their shares in employee benefit plans, which means that an ESOP may be established without the usual dilution of equity. The firm may be required to alter the voting rights of the shares already in employee benefit plans to allow for the shares to have voting rights if they do not already possess these rights.

Shamrock Holdings was forced to drop its bid and entered into a 10–year stand-still agreement with Polaroid. Shamrock, in turn, was compensated by Polaroid for some of the expenses it incurred through the bidding process. Polaroid also paid Shamrock Holdings for advertising time on some of the radio stations owned by Shamrock as part of the reimbursement agreement.

loan is repaid. The allocation is based on the compensation relevant to each participating employee.

ESOPs versus MBOs

A study by Chaplinsky, Niehaus, and Van de Gucht compared employee buyouts with management buyouts (MBOs).[25] One of their major findings was that employees played a key role in the financing of the acquisition. Employee stock ownership plans allow the company to gain access to pension assets when the employee-defined benefit plans are converted to equity claims. These assets then become part of the overall financing package to fund the buyout. They also showed how the positive cash flow effects derived from sub-stituting equity claims for a certain amount of future cash payouts in the form of wages re-ductions increased the amount of money that may be raised to pay for the acquisition. They also noted that before the buyout, employee buyout firms tended to have poorer stock price performance, were more often under takeover pressure, and were more likely to have over-funded pension plans. In addition, they noticed that cash-reducing compensation changes were reported in only 2.6% of MBOs but were present in 56% of employee buyouts.

SUMMARY

Employee stock ownership plans were originally developed to provide benefits to employ-ees. Finance practitioners have discovered, however, that they may also be a highly innov-ative corporate finance tool. When used as borrowing vehicles by corporations, ESOPs may provide the company with significant cash flow and tax benefits. These cash flow benefits may be enhanced when the company combines the tax benefits with a reduction in outstanding contributions to other benefits programs. Buyers of corporations have realized that this financing tool may give bidders cost advantages in raising the debt capital neces-sary to finance leveraged acquisitions. Employee stock ownership plans, therefore, may be

25. Susan Chaplinsky, Greg Niehaus, and Linda Van de Gucht, "Employee Buyouts: Causes, Structure, and Consequences," *Journal of Financial Economics* 48 (3) June, 1998, pp. 283–332.

used by hostile bidders as well as by employee groups interested in acquiring their company.

Although ESOPs may be of great financing benefit to buyers of companies, they also have been instrumental in creating a potent antitakeover defense for corporations. The value of this defense has been underscored by the fact that it has successfully withstood legal challenges. In the Polaroid–Shamrock Holdings decision, the court concluded that, subject to certain qualifications such as the ESOP being planned before the takeover contest, ESOPs are valid when used as an takeover defense.

In addition to providing benefits to buyers of companies and defending corporations in hostile contests, ESOPs also seem to generate positive shareholder wealth effects. Research studies support this conclusion, even though they also find that ESOPs are an effective antitakeover deterrent. This implies that there must be significant benefits that more than offset the lower probability of a takeover when this defense is instituted.

CASE STUDY: KASEY MANUFACTURING— ESOP & MANAGEMENT-LED LBO

by Robert E. Massengill, Menke & Associates, Inc.

Kasey Manufacturing is a closely held manufacturer and distributor of electrical components based in Cary, North Carolina. The company was founded in 1968 and has been run by its sole shareholder and president since that time. By 1997 sales exceeded $65 million and pretax income was $1.9 million for the same period. The company was debt-free and its book value was $4.7 million.

Over the years the owner had developed a strong management team and reached the point where his daily operating responsibilities were largely delegated. As time went by and the business became larger, he began to spend more time planning his transition from the company. He knew that his retirement would have important management and financial implications that not only required careful preparation but also had to be handled "his way." He decided that the buyout of his stock, which was worth $10 million, would have to be accomplished in a way that met four important conditions: (1) he wanted to maximize his personal proceeds, (2) he wanted his key managers to have the equity opportunity he had, (3) he wanted to reward all his employees for their contribution to his success, and (4) he did not want the cost of the buyout to compromise the financial health of the business.

In reviewing his options, he decided with his key management group to pursue a management-led ESOP buyout. The ESOP would ultimately own 70% of the company and the key management group would own 30%. The key managers would have to purchase a portion of their stock, but they would also have the opportunity to earn a sizable portion. The owner would appoint the key managers to the ESOP committee so they would be responsible for making certain the plan was run for the benefit of the employees. By structuring his buyout in this manner, the owner was able to achieve several important goals. The first was that the owner would be able to indefinitely defer paying any capital gains taxes due on the sale of stock to the ESOP. Because the proceeds from the sale of stock to the ESOP were $7 million, he would "save" over $2 million by not having to pay the capital gains taxes when the deal closed. Stock set aside for the management group was set up as a purchase and option plan. In this way, the managers had to commit some capital but also had the opportunity to realize additional equity if the company reached certain financial performance targets. The company's primary benefit was the ability to repay the ESOP debt on a completely pretax basis, which is unique to ESOPs. Thus the $7 million ESOP debt was nearly $3 million less expensive than the cost of "regular debt" because the company would be eligible to deduct from taxes the principal repayments and the interest expense. Last but not least, all of the company's employees would receive $7 million worth of company stock for their retirement—at no cost to them—as participants in the ESOP. The company had approximately 150 employees at the time the transaction closed. Thus, assuming the price of the company stock did not change over time, the average employee would receive over $45,000 upon retirement.

REFERENCES

Beatty, Anne. "The Cash Flow and Information Effects of Employee Stock Ownership Plans." *Journal of Financial Economics* 38, no. 2 (June 1995).

Blasi, Joseph. *Employee Ownership* (Cambridge, Mass.: Ballinger Publishing Co., 1988).

Brigham, Eugene F., and Louis C. Gapenski. *Intermediate Financial Management,* 3rd ed. (Chicago: Dryden Press, 1990).

Bruner, Robert F. "Leveraged ESOPs and Corporate Restructuring." *Journal of Applied Corporate Finance* 1, no. 1 (Spring 1988).

Bruner, Robert F., and E. Richard Brownlee II. "Leveraged ESOPs, Wealth Transfers and 'Shareholder Neutrality': The Case of Polaroid." *Financial Management* 19, no. 1 (Spring 1990).

Chang, Saeyoung. "Employee Stock Ownership Plans and Shareholder Wealth: An Empirical Investigation." *Financial Management* 19, no. 1 (Spring 1990).

Chaplinsky, Susan, and Greg Niehaus. "The Role of ESOPs in Takeover Contests." *Journal of Finance* 49, no. 4 (September 1994).

Chaplinsky, Susan, Greg Niehaus, and Linda Van de Gucht. "Employee Buyouts: Causes, Structure, and Consequences." *Journal of Financial Economics* 48, no. 3 (June 1998).

Chen, Andrew H. "Beyond the Tax Benefits of ESOPs." *Journal of Applied Corporate Finance* 1, no. 1 (Spring 1988).

Coopers & Lybrand. *Business Acquisitions and Leveraged Buyouts* (New York: Coopers & Lybrand, 1989).

Dhillon, Upinder S., and Gabriel G. Ramirez. "Employee Stock Ownership and Corporate Control: An Empirical Study." *Journal of Banking and Finance* 18 (1994).

Dodson, Paul. "Creditors Seek Bankruptcy for S. B. Lathe." *Indiana Tribune,* 18 January 1990.

Foust, Dean. "How Dan River Misses the Boat." *Business Week,* 26 October 1987.

Frisch, Robert A. *The Magic of ESOPs and LBOs* (New York: Farnsworth Publishing, 1985).

Frisch, Robert A. *ESOP: The Ultimate Instrument of Corporate Finance* (Los Angeles: Margate Associates, 1990).

Hammonds, Keith, John Hoerr, and Zachary Schiller. "A New Way to Keep Raiders at Bay." *Business Week,* 23 January 1989.

Macris, Robert. "Leveraged Buyouts: Federal Income Tax Considerations." In Yikov, Amihud, ed. *Leveraged Management Buyouts: Causes and Consequences* (Homewood, Ill.: Dow Jones Irwin, 1989).

Park, Sangsoo, and Moon H. Song. "Employee Stock Ownership Plans, Firm Performance, and Monitoring by Outside Blockholders." *Financial Management* 24, no. 4 (Winter 1995).

Rosen, Corey. "The Record of Employee Ownership." *Financial Management* 19, no. 1 (Spring 1990).

Scholes, Myron, and Mark Wolfson. "Employee Stock Ownership Plans and Corporate Restructuring: Myths and Realities." *Financial Management* 19, no. 1 (Spring 1990).

Schuchert, Joseph S. "The Art of the ESOP Leveraged Buyout." In Stephen C. Diamond, ed. *Leveraged Buyouts* (Homewood, Ill.: Dow Jones Irwin, 1985).

U.S. General Accounting Office. *Employee Stock Ownership Plans: Benefits and Costs of ESOP Tax Incentives for Broadening Stock Ownership.* Washington, D.C.: 1987.

Part Four

CORPORATE RESTRUCTURING

10

CORPORATE RESTRUCTURING

Although the field of mergers and acquisitions tends to focus on corporate expansion, companies often have to contract and downsize their operations. This need may arise because a division of the company is performing poorly or simply because it no longer fits into the firm's plans. Restructuring may also be necessary to undo a previous merger or acquisition that was unsuccessful. As the pace of the fourth merger wave slowed toward the end of the 1980s, divestitures and sell-offs increased as firms began to reconsider prior expansionary strategies. The pressures of large interest payments that were incurred to finance acquisitions or leveraged buyouts (LBOs) began to take their toll. For some of these companies, divestitures and sell-offs were among the few alternatives available to corporations to help pay down debt. Even companies that were not burdened by the pressure of debt or poor performance considered sell-offs and divestitures as a way of increasing shareholder values.

In this chapter, the different types of corporate contraction are considered, and a decision-making methodology for reaching the divestiture decision is developed. The methods used to value acquisition targets are also used by companies to determine whether a particular component of the firm is worth retaining. Both the divesting and the acquiring firm commonly go through a similar type of analysis as they view the transaction from opposite sides. Even though the methods are similar, the two parties may come up with different values because they use different assumptions or have different needs.

This chapter considers the shareholder wealth effects of several forms of corporate restructuring. Corporate contraction may have positive stock price effects when the divested component fails to yield a value to the corporation that is commensurate with its market value. In such instances the corporation may be able to enhance the value of shareholder investments by pursuing a policy of corporate restructuring.

Corporate restructuring can take several different forms: *divestitures,* equity carve-outs, spin-offs, split-offs, and split-ups. A divestiture is a sale of a portion of the firm to an outside party. The selling firm is usually paid in cash, marketable securities, or a combination of the two. An *equity carve-out* is a variation of a divestiture that involves the sale of an equity interest in a subsidiary to outsiders. The sale may not necessarily leave the parent company in control of the subsidiary. The new equity gives the investors shares of ownership in the portion of the selling company that is being divested. In an equity carve-out, a new legal entity is created with a stockholder base that may be different from that of the parent selling company. The divested company has a different management team and is run as a separate firm.

A new legal entity is also created in a standard *spin-off.* Once again, new shares are issued, but here they are distributed to stockholders on a pro rata basis. As a result of the proportional distribution of shares, the stockholder base in the new company is the same as that of the old company. Although the stockholders are initially the same, the spun-off firm has its own management and is run as a separate company. Another difference between a spin-off and a divestiture is that a divestiture involves an infusion of funds into the parent corporation, whereas a spin-off normally does not provide the parent with a cash infusion.[1]

In a *split-off,* some of the stockholders in the parent company are given shares in a division of the parent company, which is split off *in exchange* for their shares in the parent company. A variation on a split-off occurred in 1981 when Dome Petroleum, which had purchased an equity interest in Conoco, exchanged its shares in Conoco for Conoco's Hudson Bay oil and gas fields.

Finally, in a *split-up,* the entire firm is broken up into a series of spin-offs. The end result of this process is that the parent company no longer exists, leaving only the newly formed companies. The stockholders in the companies may be different because stockholders exchange their shares in the parent company for shares in one or more of the units that are spun off.

Sometimes a combination of a divestiture and a spin-off may occur. For example, Trans World Airlines, Inc. (TWA) sold shares in TWA to the public equal to approximately 20% of the ownership of the airline. This is also referred to as a *partial public offering.* The remaining shares were distributed to existing TWA stockholders.

DIVESTITURES

Most sell-offs are simple divestitures. Companies pursue other forms of sell-offs, such as a spin-off or an equity carve-out, to achieve other objectives in addition to getting rid of a particular division. These objectives may be to make the transaction tax-free, which may call for a spin-off.

The most common form of divestiture involves the sale of a division of the parent company to another firm. The process is a form of contraction for the selling company but a means of expansion for the purchasing corporation. The number of divestitures that took place between 1965 and 1997 is listed in Table 10.1.

Historical Trends

In the late 1960s, during the third merger wave, the number of divestitures and sell-offs was relatively small as a percentage of the total number of transactions. Companies were engaging in major expansions at this time, widely using the acquisition of other firms to increase the acquiring company's stock price. This expansion came to an abrupt end following changes in the tax laws and other regulatory measures, along with the stock market decline. Companies then began to reconsider some of the acquisitions that had proved to be poor combinations—a need intensified by the 1974–75 recession. Under the pressure of falling economic demand, companies were forced to sell off divisions to raise funds and improve cash flow. International competition also pressured some of the 1960s conglom-

---

1. Joel Stern, "A Discussion of Corporate Restructuring, Comments of Gailen Hite," *Midland Corporate Finance Journal* 2, no. 2 (Summer 1984), p. 69.

Table 10.1. Number of Divestitures, 1965–1998

Year	Number	Percent of All Transactions	Year	Number	Percent of All Transactions
1965	191	9	1982	875	37
1966	264	11	1983	932	37
1967	328	11	1984	900	36
1968	557	12	1985	1,218	41
1969	801	13	1986	1,259	38
1970	1,401	27	1987	807	40
1971	1,920	42	1988	894	40
1972	1,770	37	1989	1,055	45
1973	1,557	39	1990	940	45
1974	1,331	47	1991	849	45
1975	1,236	54	1992	1,026	40
1976	1,204	53	1993	1,134	43
1977	1,002	45	1994	1,134	38
1978	820	39	1995	1,199	34
1979	752	35	1996	1,702	29
1980	666	35	1997	2,086	27
1981	830	35	1998	1,705	22

Source: Mergerstat Review, 1989, 1998.

erates to become more efficient by selling off prior acquisitions that were not competitive in a world market.

This reversal of the acquisition trend was visible as early as 1971, when divestitures jumped to 42% of total transactions. The trend peaked in 1975, a period of economic recession, when the number of divestitures constituted 54% of all transactions. They remained between 35% and 40% throughout the 1980s. In the 1990s, however, the number of divestitures rose again as downsizing and refocusing became prominent business strategies.

Many divestitures are the result of sell-offs of previous acquisitions. The relationship between acquisitions and subsequent divestitures is shown in Figure 10.1. The belief that many divestitures are the undoing of previous acquisitions is seen in the leading trend in the acquisitions curve relative to the divestiture curve. The intense period of merger activity of the late 1960s is reflected in a pronounced peak at this time, followed by a peak in the divestiture curve in the early 1970s. The stock market performance seemed to play a determining role in the volume of divestitures. Linn and Rozeff used regression analysis to show that in years when the stock market fell, such as 1966, 1969, and 1973–74, the rate of divestiture fell below what one would have predicted given the previous merger rates. When the market performed well, the number of divestitures increased.[2] This research is also consistent with the rising stock market and increased number of divestitures of the 1990s. Figures 10.1 and 10.2 show that when merger and acquisition activity slowed in the late 1980s, the pace of spin-offs and divestitures increased. However, as the fifth merger wave accelerated in the 1990s, the number of selloffs continued to increase athough as a percent of total transactions they declined.

---

2. Scott C. Linn and Michael S. Rozeff, "The Corporate Selloff," *Midland Corporate Finance Journal* 2, no. 2 (Summer 1984), p. 24.

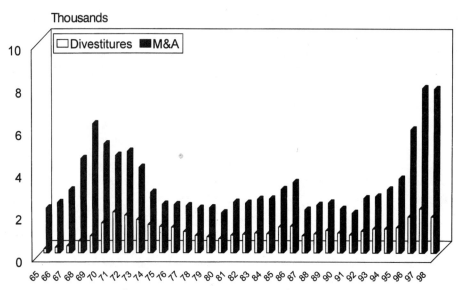

Figure 10.1. Mergers and acquisitions versus divestitures, 1965–98.

Source: Mergerstat Review, 1994–98.

Many critics of corporate acquisitions use the record of the divestitures following poor acquisitions as evidence of ill-conceived expansion planning. Using a sample of 33 companies during the period from 1950 to 1986, Michael Porter shows that these firms divested 53% of the acquisitions that brought the acquiring companies into new industries.[3] Based on this evidence, he concludes that the corporate acquisition record is "dismal."

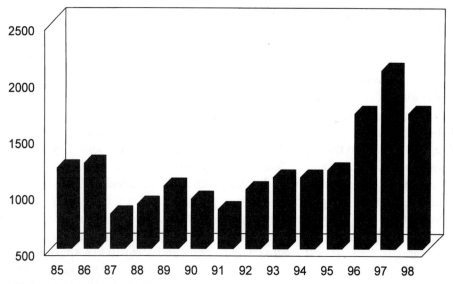

Figure 10.2. Divestitures, 1985–98.

Source: Mergerstat Review, 1994–98.

---

3. Michael Porter, "From Competitive Advantage to Corporate Strategy," *Harvard Business Review* (May-June 1987), pp. 43–59.

These results were somewhat supported by Ravenscraft and Scherer, who found that 33% of acquisitions made during the 1960s and 1970s were later divested.[4]

Others take a less harsh view than Michael Porter of the divesting companies. Fred Weston, for example, points out that divestitures tend to increase shareholder value and thus have wealth-increasing effects for shareholders.[5] He observes that divestitures occur for a variety of reasons, not just to remedy poor acquisitions. For instance, divestitures may be motivated by the firm's desire to pursue a new strategy made possible by the development of new opportunities in the marketplace that did not exist at the time of the original acquisition.

Divestiture Likelihood and Prior Acquisitions

Steven Kaplan and Michael Weisbach analyzed 271 large acquisitions completed between 1971 and 1982.[6] A total of 43.9%, or 119, of these acquisitions were divested by 1982 (Table 10.2). The divested entities were held for an average of seven years.

Kaplan and Weisbach investigated the pattern of the divestitures in search for a common motive for some of the sell-offs. They found that diversifying acquisitions are four times more likely to be divested than nondiversifying acquisitions. This result supports other evidence, discussed in Chapter 4, that questioned the benefits of acquisition programs. The motives for divestitures, which are discussed in subsequent sections, are summarized in Table 10.3.

Table 10.2. Acquisitions and Divestitures

Year	Number of Acquisitions	Median Target Value as Percentage of Acquirer Value	Number Divested	Percentage Divested	Median Years Held
1971	8	36.0	5	62.5	15.6
1972	4	28.9	1	25.0	15.6
1973	9	22.3	7	77.8	11.6
1974	7	19.6	2	28.6	7.7
1975	7	34.1	4	57.1	11.5
1976	16	19.8	8	50.0	8.3
1977	30	26.1	12	40.0	8.8
1978	39	28.0	16	41.0	7.6
1979	45	28.1	23	51.1	6.5
1980	30	25.7	12	40.0	6.3
1981	34	28.4	17	50.0	6.5
1982	42	24.6	12	28.6	4.5
Total	272	25.6	119	43.9	7.0

Source: Kaplan and Weisbach, 1992.

4. David Ravenscraft and Frederic Scherer, *Mergers, Selloffs and Economic Efficiency* (Washington, D.C.: Brookings Institution, 1987).

5. J. Fred Weston, "Divestitures: Mistakes or Learnings," *Journal of Applied Corporate Finance* 2, no. 2 (Summer 1989), pp. 68–76.

6. Steven N. Kaplan and Michael N. Weisbach, "The Success of Acquisitions: Evidence from Divestitures," *Journal of Finance* 47, no. 1 (March 1992), pp. 107–138.

Table 10.3. Reasons for Divestitures

Reason	Number of Divestitures
Change of focus or corporate strategy	43
Unit unprofitable or mistake	22
Sale to finance acquisition or leveraged restructuring	29
Antitrust	2
Need cash	3
To defend against takeover	1
Good Price	3
Divestitures with reasons	103

Source: Kaplan and Weisbach

Involuntary versus Voluntary Divestitures

A divestiture may be either voluntary or involuntary. An involuntary divestiture may occur when a company receives an unfavorable review by the Justice Department or the Federal Trade Commission (FTC), requiring the company to divest itself of a particular division. For example, in June 1987, in a 4 to 1 vote, the Interstate Commerce Commission (ICC) ruled that the merger of the Santa Fe and Southern Pacific railway systems might reduce competition. Santa Fe had merged with Southern Pacific in 1983 in one of the biggest mergers in railway history. The combined railway was operated together while awaiting an antitrust analysis and ruling from the ICC, which had antitrust jurisdiction for this type of merger. After the ruling, the ICC required Santa Fe–Southern Pacific to submit a divestiture plan within 90 days. The adverse ruling had a depressing effect on Santa Fe's stock price and made the firm a target of a bid by the Henley Group

Reasons for Voluntary Divestitures

Poor Fit of Division
Voluntary divestitures are more common than involuntary divestitures and are motivated by a variety of reasons. For example, the parent company may want to move out of a particular line of business that it feels no longer fits into its plans or in which it is unable to operate profitably. This does not mean that another firm, with greater expertise in this line of business, could not profitably manage the division's assets. Divestitures then become part of an efficient market process that reallocates assets to those who will allow them to reach their greatest gain.

Reverse Synergy
One motive that is often ascribed to mergers and acquisitions is synergy. As described in Chapter 4, synergy refers to the additional gains that may be derived when two forms combine. When synergy exists, the combined entity is worth more than the sum of the parts valued separately. In other words, $2 + 2 = 5$. *Reverse synergy* means that the parts are worth more separately than they are within the parent company's corporate structure. In other words, $4 - 1 = 5$. In such cases, an outside bidder might be able to pay more for a division than what the division is worth to the parent company. For instance, a large parent

company is not able to operate a division profitably, whereas a smaller firm, or even the division by itself, might operate more efficiently and therefore earn a higher rate of return.

Reverse synergy occurred in the late 1980s when the Allegis Corporation was forced to sell off its previously acquired companies, Hertz Rent A Car and the Weston and Hilton International hotel chains. Allegis had paid a high price for these acquisitions based on the belief that the synergistic benefits of combining the travel industry companies with United Airlines, its main asset, would more than justify the high prices. When the synergistic benefits failed to materialize, the stock price fell, setting the stage for a hostile bid from the New York investment firm Coniston Partners. Coniston made a bid based on its analysis that the separate parts of Allegis were worth more than the combined entity.

Poor Performance

Companies may want to divest divisions simply because they are not sufficiently profitable. The division could fail to pay a rate of return that exceeds the parent company's *hurdle rate*—the minimum return threshold that a company will use to evaluate projects or the performance of parts of the overall company. A typical hurdle rate could be the firm's cost of capital.

A division could decline for many reasons. The industry as a whole might be in a state of decline. For example, high labor costs, caused by a unionized labor force, may make the division uncompetitive in the world market. This occurred when Swift and Company decided that it would have to sell its fresh meats division. (See the case study later in this chapter.) Beset with a high-cost, unionized labor force, this division could not compete with its nonunionized competitors, and Swift and Company decided to sell it off.

Management may be reluctant to sell a poorly performing division because they may have to admit that they did a poor job of managing it or, in the case of a prior acquisition, that the purchase was a mistake. They may then hold on to the division for a longer time than would be dictated by its performance.[7]

Capital Market Factors

A divestiture may also take place because the postdivestiture firm, as well as the divested division, has greater access to capital markets. The combined corporate structure may be more difficult for investors to categorize. Certain providers of capital might be looking to invest in steel companies but not in pharmaceutical firms. Other investors might seek to invest capital in pharmaceutical companies but may think that the steel industry is too cyclical and has low growth potential. These two groups of investors might not want to invest in a combined steel and pharmaceutical company, but each group might separately invest in a stand-alone steel or pharmaceutical firm. Divestitures might provide greater access to capital markets for the two firms as separate companies than as a combined corporation.

Similarly, divestitures may create companies in which investors would like to invest but that do not exist in the marketplace. Such companies are sometimes referred to as *pure plays*. Many analysts argue that the market is incomplete and that there is a demand for certain types of firms, which is not matched by a supply of securities in the market. The sale of those parts of the parent company that become pure plays helps complete the market.

---

7. Arnoud W. A. Boot, "Why Hang on to Losers? Divestitures and Takeovers," *Journal of Finance* 47, no. 4 (September 1992), pp. 1401–1423.

The separation of divisions facilitates clearer identification and market segmentation for the investment community. New investment dollars may then be attracted. Ronald Kudla and Thomas McInish give the following example of enhanced capital access:

> An example of a capital market induced spin-off involves Koger Properties, Inc. which historically consisted of two distinct businesses. These two businesses were development and construction and property ownership and management. The development and construction business traditionally had provided investors with relatively volatile, high risk opportunities. As a result, earnings were quite sensitive to the availability and cost of capital for real estate development, and to the strength of the national and local economies. But the ownership and management of the rental office properties, while also involving risks to the investor, was not as sensitive to those factors because completed, leased properties have established rental income and generally are financed through long term mortgage indebtedness having fixed equal monthly payments of principal and interest. Koger Properties, Inc.'s management felt that the development aspect of the company was never fully reflected in the marketplace. Accordingly, management believed that it was in the interest of stockholders for the firm's two business activities to be conducted by separate and independent companies.[8]

Cash Flow Factors

A sell-off produces the immediate benefits of an infusion of cash from the sale. The selling firm is selling a long-term asset, which generated a certain cash flow per period, in exchange for a larger payment in the short run. Companies that are under financial duress are often forced to sell off valuable assets to enhance cash flows. Beset with the threat of bankruptcy in the early 1980s, Chrysler Corporation was forced to sell off its prized tank division in an effort to stave off bankruptcy. International Harvester (now known as Navistar) sold its profitable Solar Turbines International Division to Caterpillar Tractor Company, Inc. to realize the immediate proceeds of $505 million. These funds were used to cut Harvester's short-term debt in half.

Abandoning the Core Business

The sale of a company's core business is a less common reason for a sell-off. An example of the sale of a core business was the 1987 sale by Greyhound of its bus business. The sale of a core business is often motivated by management's desire to leave an area that it believes has matured and presents few growth opportunities. The firm usually has already diversified into other more profitable areas, and the sale of the core business may help finance the expansion of these more productive activities.

DIVESTITURE AND SPIN-OFF PROCESS

Each divestiture is unique and takes place in a different sequence of events. A generalized process is described here.

Step 1. *Divestitures or the Spin-Off Decision.* The management of the parent company must decide whether a divestiture is the appropriate course of action. This decision

---

8. Ronald J. Kudla and Thomas H. McInish, *Corporate Spin-Offs: Strategy for the 1980s* (Westport, Conn.: Quorum Books, 1984), p. 18.

can be made only after a thorough financial analysis of the various alternatives has been completed. The method of conducting the financial analysis for a divestiture or spin-off is discussed later in this chapter.

Step 2. *Formulation of a Restructuring Plan.* A restructuring or reorganization plan must be formulated, and an agreement between the parent and the subsidiary may be negotiated. This plan is necessary in the case of a spin-off that will feature a continuing relationship between the parent and the subsidiary. The plan should cover such details as the disposition of the subsidiary's assets and liabilities. In cases in which the subsidiary is to keep certain of its assets while others are to be transferred back to the parent company, the plan may provide a detailed breakdown of the asset disposition. Other issues, such as the retention of employees and the funding of their pension and, possibly, health care liabilities should also be addressed.

Step 3. *Approval of the Plan by Shareholders.* The extent to which approval of the plan is necessary depends on the significance of the transaction and the relevant state laws. In cases such as a spin-off of a major division of the parent company, stockholder approval may be required. If so, the plan is submitted to the stockholders at a stockholders' meeting, which may be the normally scheduled shareholders' meeting or a special meeting called to consider only this issue. A proxy statement requesting approval of the spin-off is also sent to stockholders. The materials submitted to stockholders may address other issues related to the meeting, such as the amendment of the articles of incorporation.

Step 4. *Registration of Shares.* Shares issued in a spin-off must be registered with the Securities and Exchange Commission (SEC). As part of the normal registration process, a prospectus, which is part of the registration statement, must be produced. The prospectus must be distributed to all shareholders who receive stock in the spun-off entity.

Step 5. *Completion of the Deal.* After these preliminary steps have been taken, the deal may be consummated. Consideration is exchanged, and the division is separated from the parent company according to a prearranged timetable.

CASE STUDY: SWIFT AND COMPANY

Swift and Company was a food products concern with a long record of success.[a] Its profitability began declining in the 1960s as a result of competition from more efficient producers. Of particular concern was the fresh meats division. The meat-packing business was characterized by low profit margins and high labor costs for companies, like Swift, that had a unionized workforce. The union stead-

---

[a] The discussion of the case is based on several sources, especially Hope Lambert, *Behind Closed Doors* (New York: Atheneum, 1986), pp. 277–324.

fastly objected to wage concessions that would have helped make Swift's fresh meats division more competitive and threatened to strike if Swift tried to force the concessions on the union. A strike would mean that Swift would be unable to deliver its meat products to the supermarkets. Their shelf space would then be taken by other aggressive competitors, who might not relinquish it easily after the strike was over.

Through broad acquisitions of firms such as Playtex, Jensen Stereos, STP Oil, and Danskin leotards, Swift, under the leadership of Chief Executive Officer Donald Kelly, had been shifting toward a diversified consumer products concern. During the early 1980s Swift and Company was only one part of Kelly's growing conglomerate that traded under the name Esmark. Kelly believed that the strategy of continued acquisitions of consumer products companies would strengthen the company. He simply considered the fresh meats division a thorn in the parent company's side. The newly acquired companies were generally performing up to expectations, whereas the Swift and Company part of Esmark was subject to erratic income swings and low profitability.

The union contract made Swift and Company an unattractive target. Although Kelly tried to sell the division through his investment bank, Salomon Brothers, no takers were found. The situation was troubling for Kelly because Swift's poor performance was hurting Esmark's stock price, making the parent company vulnerable to a takeover.

Esmark, in association with Salomon Brothers, conducted a valuation analysis of each Esmark subsidiary. Such an analysis is a standard first step when a divestiture is being contemplated. The firm determined the value of each division of the parent company as if it were a separate company and then compared it with their market values. Divisional profits were used to compute their going concern values and to compare this value with each division's liquidation value (Table 1). The final tabulation of the combined firm showed Esmark's total value as $1,220 to $1,580 million, or $55 to $71 per share.

The focus of the analysis was the poorly performing Swift division. The weakest component of Swift, the fresh meats division, was burdened with noncompetitive wage rates enforced by an inflexible union. Esmark reevaluated the fresh meats component, based on the assumption of wage concessions from the unions. It tried to sell the fresh meats division to the union but to no avail, at which point Esmark decided to sell the division to the public in an equity carve-out. A total of 2.75 million shares were sold for $15 per share, and Esmark raised $41.25 million from the sale. This was greater than the sales projection by Salomon Brothers.

Table 1. Esmark's Divisional Valuation Analysis

Division	Value ($ millions)
Estech	350–400
International Jensen	125–150
International Playtex	500–600
Vickers Petroleum Corporation	610–700
STP Corporation	50–75
Swift and Company	300

Source: Hope Lambert, *Behind Closed Doors* (New York: Atheneum, 1986), pp. 293–294,

The postdivestiture Swift proved to be economically viable. The scaled-down company was able to wrest wage concessions from the union, something Esmark could not do. Some plants were renovated and others were sold. In addition, the price of Esmark's stock rose as the stock market signaled that the postdivestiture Esmark was more valuable than its predivestiture company.

Financial Evaluation of Divestitures

Financial evaluation techniques are discussed in Chapters 13 and 14. The financial evaluation of a subsidiary by a parent company that is contemplating divestiture should proceed in a logical fashion. The following steps form a basis for a general process of evaluation.

Step 1. *Estimation of After-Tax Cash Flows.* The parent company needs to estimate the after-tax cash flows of the division. This analysis should consider the interrelationship between the subsidiary's and the parent company's respective capabilities to generate cash flow. If, for example, the subsidiary's operations are closely related to the parent company's activities, the parent company's cash flows may be positively or negatively affected after the divestiture. Thus, this needs to be factored into the analysis at the beginning of the evaluation process.

Step 2. *Determination of the Division's Discount Rate.* The present value of the division's after-tax cash flows needs to be calculated. To do so, a division-specific discount rate must be derived, taking into account the risk characteristics of the division on a stand-alone basis. The cost of capital of other firms that are in the same business and approximately the same size may be a good proxy for this discount rate.

Step 3. *Present Value Calculation.* Using the discount rate derived in step 2, we can calculate the present value of each projected after-tax cash flow. The sum of these terms will represent the present value of the income-generating capability of the division by itself.

Step 4. *Deduction of the Market Value of the Division's Liabilities.* Step 3 of this process did not take into account the division's liabilities. The market value of these liabilities needs to be deducted from the present value of the after-tax cash flows. The market value is used because the market has in effect already computed the present value calculation in its determination of the current value of these obligations. This results in a net of liability value of the division, which is the value of the division as part of the parent company, assuming it maintains ownership of the division.

$$NOL = \sum_{i=1}^{n} \frac{ATCF_i}{(1 + k)^i} - MVL$$

where
NOL = the net of liabilities value of the present value of the after-tax cash flows
$ATCF$ = the after-tax cash flows

k = the division-specific discount rate
MVL = the market value of the liabilities

Step 5. *Deduction of the Divestiture Proceeds.* The proceeds that the parent can derive from a sale of the division *(DP)* are then compared with the value developed in step 4. If the divestiture proceeds, net of selling costs, are higher than the value of keeping the division, the unit should be sold.

$DP > NOL$ Sell division.
$DP = NOL$ Other factors will control decision.
$DP < NOL$ Keep division.

Spin-Offs

Spin-offs have become one of the more popular forms of corporate downsizing.

Recent Trends

Spin-offs have grown in popularity since 1992. This growth was partly fueled by investors' pressure to release internal values that are unrealized in the company's stock price (Figure 10.3). A record number of spin-offs occurred in 1996, with a $93.4 billion volume being recorded. The number of spin-offs remained at relatively high levels in 1997.

The classic example of a large-scale spin-off is the 1995 ITT $12.4 billion spin-off of the international conglomerate's assets into three separate entities. This spin-off was the culmination of decades of acquisitions that the conglomerate had engaged in, followed by

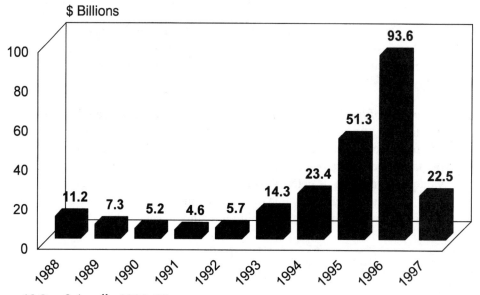

Figure 10.3. Spin-offs, 1988–97.

Note: At the end of 1997 transactions valued $14.6 billion were pending.
Source: J. P. Morgan.

years in which the company's stock price failed to reach the levels that its management hoped to realize. The ITT spin-off is discussed in detail as a case study at the end of this chapter.

Involuntary Spin-Offs

When faced with an adverse regulatory ruling, a firm may decide that a spin-off is the only viable way to comply. The classic example of such an involuntary spin-off was the mammoth spin-off of AT&T's operating companies in 1984. As a result of an antitrust suit originally filed in 1974 by the Justice Department, the government and AT&T reached an agreement providing for the breakup of the large telecommunications company. The agreement, which became effective January 1, 1984, provided for the reorganization of the 22 operating companies within AT&T into seven regional holding companies. These holding companies would be responsible for local telecommunications service, and the new AT&T would maintain responsibility for long-distance communications.

The spin-off of the 22 operating companies would still allow AT&T shareholders to have the same number of shares in the post–spin-off company. These shares represented ownership rights in a much smaller telecommunications company. For every 10 shares that each shareholder had in the original AT&T, shareholders received one share in each of the seven regional holding companies. Those shareholders who had fewer than 10 shares received a cash value for their shares rather than shares in the regional holding companies.[9] They would still be shareholders in the post–spin-off AT&T. The spin-off created a major administrative problem. Thousands of workers were hired to process the stock transfers and to handle record keeping. A special administrative center was established in Jacksonville, Florida, to coordinate the paperwork and share distribution.[10]

The 1984 AT&T spin-off is an extreme form of an involuntary spin-off, given the sheer size of the transaction. The spin-off resulted in a dramatic change in the nature of the telecommunications industry in the United States. Most spin-offs, however, are not of this magnitude and are not a response to a regulatory mandate. AT&T made history again in 1995, when it engaged in a three-way split-off that separated the company into three separate firms.

Defensive Spin-Offs

Chapter 5 discussed the use of corporate restructuring to defend against hostile takeovers. Companies may choose to spin off divisions to make them less attractive to the bidder. For example, in January 1987 Diamond Shamrock's board of directors approved a restructuring plan that provided for spinning off two core businesses and forming a new entity, called Diamond Shamrock R&M, and distributing R&M stock to its shareholders.[11]

Defensive spin-offs, or other types of sell-offs, constitute a drastic takeover defense. They may be challenged in the courts by the bidder and possibly by shareholders. If they are determined to limit the auction process and reduce shareholder value, they may be voided. The wealth effects of these defensive sell-offs are discussed later in this chapter.

---

9. *AT&T Shareholders Newsletter* (Fourth Quarter, 1982).

10. Kudla and McInish, *Corporate Spin-Offs,* p. 8.

11. James L. Bicksler and Andrew H. Chen, "The Economics of Corporate Restructuring: An Overview," In *The Battle for Corporate Control* (Homewood, Ill.: Business One Irwin, 1991), pp. 386–387.

Tax Consequences of Spin-Offs

One of the advantages a spin-off has over other types of sell-offs is that the transaction may be structured so that it is tax-free. For example, the shares in the regional Bells that stockholders received did not result in additional tax liabilities for those shareholders. The Internal Revenue Service treated the distribution of shares in the AT&T spin-off as neither a gain nor a loss. Voluntary spin-offs are also often treated as nontaxable transactions. If the spin-off occurs for valid business reasons, rather than for the purpose of tax avoidance, Section 355 of the Tax Code allows for the transaction to be nontaxable. Among the Tax Code's requirements for a tax-free spin-off are:

- Both the parent company and the spun-off entity must be in business for at least five years before the restructuring.
- The subsidiary must also be at least 80% owned by the parent company.

When the General Utilities Doctrine was in effect, companies could sell off assets without incurring capital gains taxes. With its repeal in the mid-1980s, spin-offs became more popular because they were an alternative that provided a tax-free way to shed assets.

Treatment of Warrants and Convertible Securities

When the parent company has issued warrants or convertible securities, such as convertible debentures, the conversion ratio may have to be adjusted when shares are issued in a spin-off. The spin-off may cause the common stock in the parent company to be less valuable. If the deal is so structured that current common stockholders gain through the distribution of proceeds in the form of a special dividend, warrant holders and convertible security holders may not participate in this gain. After the distribution, the stock price of the parent company may fall, making the expected conversion more difficult because it will be less likely that the price will rise high enough to enable the securities to be converted. If this is the case, the conversion prices may need to be adjusted as part of the terms of the deal.

Employee Stock Option Plans

For employees holding shares under an employee stock option plan (ESOP), the number of shares obtainable by option holders may also need to be adjusted after a spin-off. The adjustment is designed to leave the market value of shares that could be obtained after the spin-off at the same level. This is usually done by increasing the number of shares that may be obtained with a given option. Those option-holding employees in the parent company who become employees in the spun-off entity have their stock options changed to become options in the new company. Here again, the goal is to maintain the market value of the shares that may be obtained through conversion of the employee stock options.

WEALTH EFFECTS OF SELL-OFFS

A major motivating factor for divestitures and spin-offs is the belief that reverse synergy may exist. Divestitures, spin-offs, and equity carve-outs are basically a "downsizing" of the parent firm. Therefore, the smaller firm must be economically more viable by itself than as a part of its parent company. Several research studies have analyzed the impact of spin-offs by examining the effect on the stock prices of both the parent company and the spun-off entity. This effect is then compared with a market index to determine whether the stocks experience extranormal performance that cannot be explained by market movements alone. Spin-offs are a unique opportunity to analyze the effects of the separation because a market exists for both the stock of the parent company and the spun-off entity.

The research in the field of sell-offs, whether they are spin-offs or other forms of asset sales such as equity carve-outs, presents a picture of clear benefits for shareholders. This is the case in early studies such as Oppenheimer (1981), Kudla and McInish (1983), and Miles and Rosenfeld (1984), or later studies such as Schipper and Smith (1986), Cusatis and co-researchers (1993), or J. P. Morgan (1995, 1997). Research from the 1970s through the early 1990s presents a clear pattern of positive shareholder wealth effects from corporate sell-offs. This leads to strong conclusions that are not just dependent on trends that prevailed in any one time period (such as in one decade).

Oppenheimer (1981)

In 1981 Oppenheimer and Company conducted a study of 19 major spin-offs in the 1970s.[12] It was reported that the combined value of the parent company and the spun-off entity was greater than the market value of the parent company before the spin-off in the majority of the cases considered. Of the 19 spun-off companies, 14 companies outperformed the Standard & Poor's 400 index for six months after the spin-off. In addition, a portfolio of these spun-off firms yielded a 440% return during the 1970s. This exceeds a 364% return generated by small company stocks during that decade.[13]

Kudla-McInish (1983)

Kudla and McInish, in a study of six major spin-offs in the 1970s, used residuals as the measure of market-adjusted returns (Table 10.4).[14] Their results showed a positive market reaction to the spin-offs. It is interesting that Kudla and McInish showed that the pronounced positive reaction occurred between 15 and 40 weeks before the spin-off (Figure 10.4). This indicates that the market correctly anticipated the spin-offs long before the actual event. Because the performance of a division may be actively debated in the media or the market well in advance of a decision to sever the division from the parent company, it is not surprising that the market would anticipate the parent company's reaction.

Miles and Rosenfeld (1983)

James Miles and James Rosenfeld conducted a study of 59 spin-offs between 1963 and 1980, focusing on the impact of the spin-off on the difference between predicted and actual

12. "The Sum of the Parts" (New York, Oppenheimer and Co., January 14, 1981).

13. *Stocks, Bills, Bonds and Inflation: 1994* (Chicago: Ibbotson Associates).

14. Ronald Kudla and Thomas McInish, "Valuation Consequences of Corporate Spin-Offs," *Review of Economics and Business Research* (March 1983), pp. 71–77.

Table 10.4.   Kudla and McInish Sample Characteristics

Parent Firm	Spun-Off Firm	Size of Spin-Off (%)
Browning-Ferris Industries	Consolidated Fibres	22
Easco Corporation	Eastmet Corporation	47
Olin Corporation	Olinkraft Corporation	12
Tandy Corporation	Tandycraft Corporation	18
Tandy Corporation	Tandy Brands	6
Valmac Corporation	Distribuco, Inc.	10

Source: Ronald Kudla and Thomas McInish, "Valuation Consequences of Corporate Spin-Offs," *Review of Economics and Business Research* (March 1983), pp. 71–77.

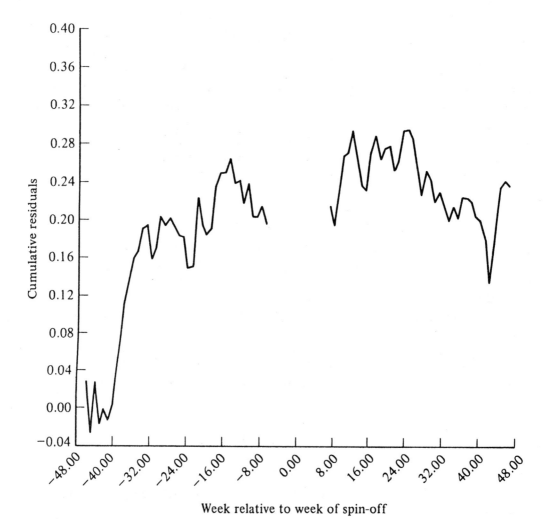

Week relative to week of spin-off

Figure 10.4.   Plot of cumulative residuals for six voluntary corporate spin-offs.

Source: Ronald Kudla and Thomas McInish, "Valuation Consequences of Corporate Spin-offs," *Review of Economics and Business Research* (March 1983): 71–77.

returns.[15] Using this method, they filtered out the influence of the market. As did Kudla and McInish, Miles and Rosenfeld found that the effect of the spin-off was positive and internalized in the stock price before the actual spin-off date.

The Miles-Rosenfeld study also revealed that the positive stock price reaction was accompanied by a negative price reaction by the parent company's bonds. In effect, it seems that the wealth-increasing effects for stockholders comes at the expense of the bondholders. Some analysts have interpreted this to be the result of the fact that the cash flow from the spun-off entity may no longer be relied on to meet the debt service payments. Another explanation is that, all other factors being constant, larger firms tend to receive higher bond ratings.

Price Effects of Voluntary Sell-Offs: Summary of Later Research

The Kudla-McInish and Miles-Rosenfeld studies of the early 1980s demonstrate the positive stock price reaction to corporate sell-offs. This reaction is supported in later studies. These research findings have been summarized using an expanded version of a table originally compiled by Linn and Rozeff but with the addition of other more recent studies (Table 10.5). The table shows an increase in stockholder wealth resulting from corporate sell-offs, with the positive impact on equity values ranging from 0.17% to 2.33%. The equity market clearly concludes that the voluntary selling of a division is a positive development that will result in an increase in the value of the firm's stock.

Shareholder Wealth Effects of Spin-Offs: Recent Evidence

Cusatis, Miles, and Woolridge examined the common stock returns of both spin-offs and their former parent companies. Unlike some prior research studies, which mainly examined the shareholder returns leading up to and including the announcement of the spin-off, the study by Cusatis and co-researchers tracked the companies after the spin-off to determine

Table 10.5. Average Stock Price Effects of Voluntary Sell-Offs

Study	Days	Average Abnormal Returns (%)	Period Sampled	Sample Size
Alexander, Benson, and Kampmeyer (1984)	−1 through 0	0.17	1964–73	53
Hite and Owers (1984)	−1 through 0	1.50	1963–79	56
Hite, Owers, and Rogers (1987)	−50 through -5	0.69	1963–81	55
Jain (1985)	−5 through -1	0.70	1976–78	1,107
Klein (1983)	−2 through 0	1.12	1970–79	202
Linn and Rozeff (1984)	−1 through 0	1.45	1977–82	77
Loh, Bezjak, and Toms (1995)	−1 through 0	1.50	1982–87	59
Rosenfeld (1984)	−1 through 0	2.33	1963–81	62

15. James Miles and James Rosenfeld, "An Empirical Analysis of the Effects of Spin-Off Announcements on Shareholder Wealth," *Journal of Finance* 38, no. 5 (December 1983), pp. 1597–1606.

what the more long-term wealth effects were. These researchers examined 815 distributions of stock in spun-off firms from 1965 to 1988.

The Cusatis, Miles, and Woolridge research presents a very favorable picture of the postevent performance of spin-offs. Both spin-offs and their parent companies showed positive abnormal returns over a period that ranged between 6 months before and 36 months after the stock distribution date.[16] Another interesting finding of Cusatis and colleagues was that both the spin-off and the parent company *were more active in takeovers* than the control group of comparable firms. This takeover activity may help explain some of the positive shareholder wealth effects. When the firms that were involved in takeovers were removed from the sample, the returns were still positive but not statistically different from zero. This suggests that spin-offs and their parent company are more likely to be involved in takeovers, and when they are they enable their shareholders to realize takeover premiums.

J. P. Morgan Study (1997)

In 1995 J. P. Morgan conducted an event study of 77 spin-offs using more recent spin-offs than prior academic studies.[17] This was followed by a second study in 1997 that added another 27 spin-offs to their data set.[18] This research is useful because it tests whether the shareholder wealth effects that have been reported in many prior studies covering the 1970s and 1980s also persist through the 1990s. The findings confirm those reported in the prior work. Figure 10.5 shows a sharply positive stock price reaction for the parent company around the announcement date. Figure 10.6 indicates that the larger the size of the spin-off as a percentage of the parent company, the greater this positive effect. That is, bigger spin-offs have relatively greater positive shareholder wealth effects.

The 1997 J. P. Morgan study also analyzed the stock price performance of spun-off subsidiaries relative to the market as a whole. Figure 10.7 shows the average cumulative market-adjusted return up to 18 months after the spin-off. The spin-off subsidiary outperformed the market by greater than 20% during this 18–month period.

The study also analyzed the shareholder wealth effects as a function of the size of the spin-off. Smaller spinoffs, those with an initial market capitalization of less than $200 million, showed significantly better performance than larger spin-offs—those with a capitalization in excess of $200 million (Figure 10.8). The J. P. Morgan researchers who conducted this study attribute the strong performance of the smaller spin-offs to underpricing. This explanation is similar to the one that is sometimes used to account for why initial public offerings (IPOs) outperform the market. In turn, the researchers attribute the underpricing to a lack of knowledge on the part of the market regarding the subsidiary. Given that financial reporting on divisions may be somewhat limited, particularly when the division is a relatively small part of the parent company, this seems like a reasonable explanation.

16. Patrick J. Cusatis, James A. Miles, and J. Randall Woolridge, "Restructuring Through Spin-offs—The Stock Market Evidence," *Journal of Financial Economics* 33, no. 3 (June 1993), pp. 293–311.

17. *J. P. Morgan's Spinoffs Study,* June 6, 1995.

18. *J. P. Morgan's Spinoffs Study,* August 20, 1997.

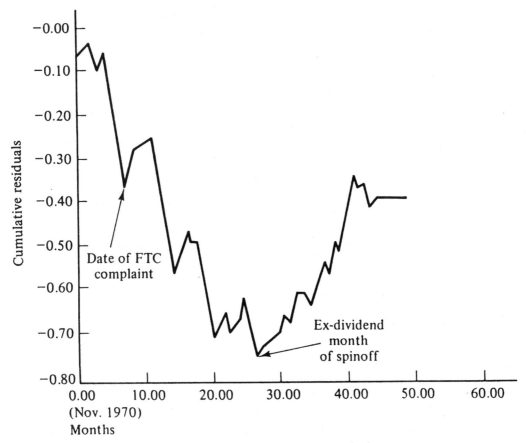

Figure 10.5. Georgia-Pacific Corporation's cumulative residuals versus time.

Source: Reprinted from "The Microeconomic Consequences of an Involuntary Corporate Spin-off," Ronald J. Kudla and Thomas H. McInish, *Sloan Management Review* 22, no. 4 (1981): 45. By permission of the publisher. Copyright © 1981 by The Sloan Management Review Association. All rights reserved.

Rationale for a Positive Stock Price Reaction to Sell-Offs

When a firm decides to sell off a poorly performing division, this asset goes to another owner, who presumably will value it more highly because he or she can utilize this asset more advantageously than the seller. The seller receives cash (or sometimes other compensation) in place of the asset. When the market responds positively to this asset reallocation, it is expressing a belief that the firm will use this cash more efficiently than it was utilizing the asset that was sold. Moreover, the asset that was sold may have attracted a premium above market value, which should also cause the market to respond positively.

The selling firm has a few options at its disposal when it is contemplating the disposition of the newly acquired cash. The firm may pay the cash to stockholders in the form of a dividend, or it may repurchase its own shares at a premium. Either option is a way for the selling corporation to give its stockholders an immediate payout. If the seller retains the cash, it will be used for internal investment to expand in one of its current areas of activity or for an acquisition. The choice of another acquisition may give stockholders cause for

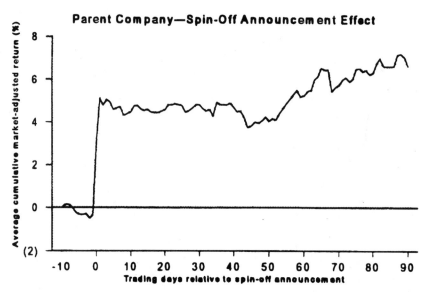

Figure 10.6.   Parent company stock price effects of spin-offs.

Source: J. P. Morgan's Spinoffs Study, June 6, 1995.

concern. The fact that acquisitions may have a dampening effect on stock prices has been documented in some financial research. (See Chapter 4.)

Another argument in favor of the value-increasing effects of sell-offs is that the market might find it difficult to evaluate highly diversified companies. The validity of this argument is a matter of considerable debate because it implies that the market is somewhat inefficient. If the market is inefficient in evaluating these types of firms, the sale of one or

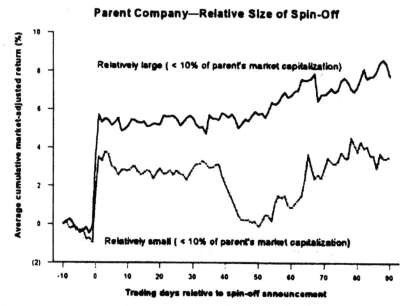

Figure 10.7.   Parent company stock price effects of spin-offs, by size of transaction.

Source: J. P. Morgan's Spinoffs Study, June 6, 1995.

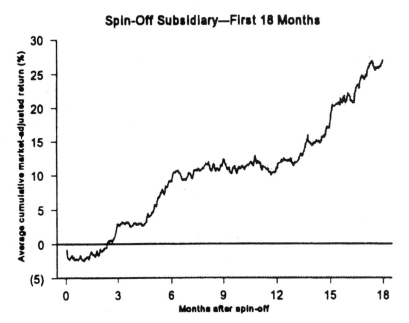

Figure 10.8.   Spun-off subsidiary stock price effects.

Source: J. P. Morgan's Spinoffs Study, June 6, 1995.

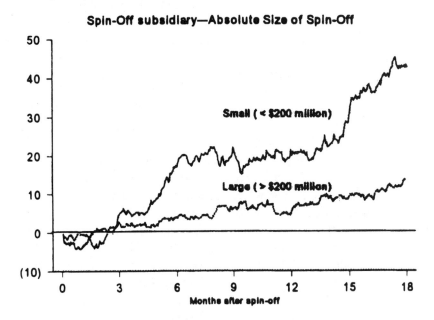

Figure 10.9.   Performance of spin-off subsidiary by size of spin-off.

Source: J. P. Morgan's Spinoffs Study, June 6, 1995.

more divisions might facilitate categorization of the parent company. The greater ease of categorization and evaluation would encourage investors who are looking to invest in certain types of companies.

Wealth Effects of Voluntary Defensive Sell-Offs

We discussed in previous sections the positive wealth effects of voluntary sell-offs. There is some evidence that when these voluntary sell-offs are used as an antitakeover defense, positive effects may not exist. Loh, Bezjak, and Toms found positive shareholder wealth effects to voluntary sell-offs that are consistent with the other research that has been discussed.[19] However, they found that this positive response was not present when companies used sell-offs as an antitakeover defense.

In a sample of 59 firms from 1980 to 1987, 13 of which featured takeover speculation, Loh, Bezjak, and Toms found cumulative average abnormal return equal to 1.5% over a one-day period up to the sell-off date. However, when they divided their sample into two subsamples—those with and without takeover speculation, the 13 firms that were the targets of takeover speculation failed to show any significant changes in shareholder wealth. These results suggest that when firms engage in sell-offs to prevent themselves from being taken over, the market treats the transactions differently and does not consider it a positive change.

Wealth Effects of Involuntary Sell-Offs

Most research studies on the effects of sell-offs on stockholder wealth conclude that sell-offs increase the wealth of parent company stockholders and that the market is somewhat efficient in anticipating the event. Therefore, the stock price reaction occurs in advance of the actual sell-off date. The wealth-increasing effects of a sell-off of an unwanted or poorly performing subsidiary should be different from those of a parent company being forced to divest itself of a profitable division. This was the case when Santa Fe–Southern Pacific received its unfavorable ruling requiring it to divest itself of the Southern Pacific Railway. As noted previously, the stock price declined and Santa Fe became a takeover target.

In 1981 Kudla and McInish conducted a case study of the effects of the required spin-off of the Louisiana-Pacific Corporation by Georgia-Pacific, the parent company.[20] The spin-off was required by the FTC, which concluded that the acquisition of 16 companies in the southern part of the United States, which accounted for a total of 673,000 acres of pine trees, would result in an anticompetitive concentration in the plywood industry. Using cumulative residuals to adjust for market effects, Kudla and McInish showed that the price of Georgia-Pacific stock had been declining before the formal filing of the FTC complaint. Louisiana-Pacific was spun off in 1972. Figure 10.9 shows that the downward movement of the stock price ended with the spin-off, after which the stock price rebounded. Although the stock price rebound was significant, the cumulative residuals did not fully recover to the start of the 1971 level, even as late as March 1974.

The Miles-Rosenfeld study showed that the wealth of bondholders declined after the spin-off even while the wealth of stockholders increased. This was believed to have been

19. Charmen Loh, Jennifer Russell Bezjak, and Harrison Toms, "Voluntary Corporate Divestitures as Antitakeover Mechanisms," *The Financial Review* 30, no. 1, (February 1995), pp. 41–60.

20. Ronald Kudla and Thomas McInish, "The Microeconomic Consequences of an Involuntary Corporate Spin-Off," *Sloan Management Review* 22, no. 4 (1981), pp. 41–46.

attributed to the lower cash flows after the spin-off and the resulting increase in risk to bondholders. Kudla and McInish attempted to measure the risk effects of the involuntary Louisiana-Pacific spin-off by examining the betas of Georgia-Pacific before and after the spin-off. The betas would then reflect any change in the systematic or undiversifiable risk associated with Georgia-Pacific stock. Kudla and McInish found a large, statistically significant increase in the betas of Georgia-Pacific after the spin-off. They attributed this increase to the market's perception that Georgia-Pacific incurred a decrease in monopoly power after the spin-off and that this caused the firm to be riskier.

The finance research community seems to have reached a consensus that a divestiture that is forced by government mandate, as opposed to a voluntary sell-off, will have an adverse effect on the divesting firm's stock price. James Ellert's review of 205 defendants in antitrust merger lawsuits showed a 21.86% decline in the value of the equity of these firms during the month the complaint was filed.[21] The issue that the Kudla-McInish study addresses is the timing of that impact and the reversal of the declining trend.

If the antitrust enforcement is effective in reducing the selling firm's monopoly power, this should be reflected in an *increase* in the value of the equity of that firm's competitors. Unfortunately, the antitrust authorities can find little support for their actions in the stock prices of the competitors of divesting firms.[22] The value of the equity of competitors of divesting firms failed to show a significant positive response to mandated sell-offs.

Wealth Effects of Sell-Offs on Buyers

The preceding discussion focused on the wealth effects to stockholders and bondholders of the selling companies. Prem Jain also analyzed the shareholder wealth effects for the buying company.[23] In his large sample event study, which included 304 buyers and 1,062 sellers (not all the buyers were known), he found that buyers earn a statistically significant positive excess return of 0.34%.

Jain's results show that sell-offs are good news for both sellers and buyers, although sellers gain more than buyers. It is also interesting that the sales did not seem to take place in an active auction process. In most instances, Jain failed to find more than one bidder coming forward to try to buy the sold-off entity. This raises the question of what the shareholder wealth effects would be if the units were sold in a more auction-like environment.

Corporate Focus and Spin-Offs

A study of 85 spinoffs between 1975 and 1991 by Daley, Mehrotra, and Sivakumar examined the relationship between spin-offs and corporate focus by comparing the performance

21. James C. Ellert, "Mergers, Antitrust Law Enforcement and the Behavior of Stock Prices," *Journal of Finance* 31 (1976), pp. 715–732.

22. Robert Stillman, "Examining Antitrust Policy Towards Horizontal Mergers," *Journal of Financial Economics* 11 (1983), pp. 225–240; Bjorn E. Eckbo, "Horizontal Mergers, Collusion and Stockholder Wealth," *Journal of Financial Economics* 11 (1983), pp. 241–274.

23. Prem C. Jain, "Sell-Off Announcements and Shareholder Wealth," *Journal of Finance* 40, no. 1 (March 1985), pp. 209–224.

of spin-off firms when the parent company and the spun-off entity were in two different Standard Industrial Classification (SIC) codes (cross-industry spin-offs) relative to instances in which both were in the same SIC code (own industry spin-offs).[24] They found improvements in various measures of performance, such as the return on assets, for cross-industry spin-offs but not for own industry deals. They conclude that cross-industry spin-offs only create value when they result in an increase in corporate focus. They attribute the performance improvements to companies removing unrelated businesses and allowing managers to concentrate their efforts on the core business and removing the distraction of noncore entities.

EQUITY CARVE-OUTS

Equity carve-outs became a popular financing technique in the late 1980s, even though the market for public offerings was poor. Companies such as Enron Corporation, W. R. Grace, Hanson Trust, and Macmillan decided that equity carve-outs provided significant financial advantages over other forms of restructuring. Between 1987 and 1989, the 10 largest equity carve-outs totaled $13.92 billion, even though the IPO market was depressed.[25]

The parent company may sell a 100% interest in the subsidiary, or it may choose to remain in the subsidiary's line of business by selling only a partial interest and keeping the remaining percentage of ownership. This was the case, for example, when the Neoax Corporation chose to sell a 53% ownership in a trucking business that it had acquired in March 1988 in a highly leveraged transaction.[26] Neoax sold this ownership interest in the trucking company, which it had renamed Landstar, for $94 million. The transaction enabled Neoax to maintain a reduced total debt load while providing the firm with the option to regain control of the trucking company in the future. Neoax also received a value for the division that was consistent with its internal valuation analysis, which showed that the entire division was worth $200 million. Efforts to sell the division outright failed to attract offers near this value.

Many firms look to equity carve-outs as a means of reducing their exposure to a riskier line of business. For example, American Express bought the brokerage firm Shearson in 1981. It later acquired the investment bank Lehman Brothers to form Shearson Lehman. This is a riskier line of business than American Express's traditional credit card operations. American Express later decided that, although it liked the synergy that came with being a diversified financial services company, it wanted to reduce its exposure to the risks of the securities business. In 1987 Amexco, its holding company, sold off a 39% interest in Shearson Lehman. This proved to be fortuitous because the sale preceded the stock market crash, an event that securities firms still had not recovered from by the end of the 1980s. The company would later completely undo these acquisitions.

---

24. Lane Daley, Vikas Mehrotra, and Ranjini Sivakumar, "Corporate Focus and Value Creation: Evidence from Spinoffs," *Journal of Financial Economics* 45, no. 2 (August 1997), pp. 257–281.

25. Susan Jarzombek, "A Way to Put a Spotlight on Unseen Value," *Corporate Finance* (December 1989), pp. 62–64.

26. Ibid.

Equity Carve-Out Transactions Data: J. P. Morgan 1998 Study

In 1998 J. P. Morgan conducted a study of equity carve-out transactions in 1998.[27] They found the market to be quite robust, with equity carve-outs constituting 23% of the total IPO market or a total of $9 billion in 1997. Consistent with the research in this field, they also found a positive stock price reaction for parent companies. This effect was greater for larger carve-outs relative to smaller transactions (see Figure 10.10). One interesting finding of this study was that carve-outs tended not to remain public very long after the transaction. Only approximately 37% remained in their original form three years after the carve-out. Approximately 15% were required by the parent company, whereas 11% were sold to a third party.

Characteristics of Equity Carve-Out Firms and the Disposition of Carve-Out Proceeds

Allen and McConnell conducted a study of the financial characteristics of firms that undertook equity carve-outs. They analyzed 188 carve-outs between 1978 and 1993.[28] They found that carve-out subsidiaries tended to have poorer operating performance and higher leverage than their industry counterparts. As Table 10.6 shows, pre–carve-out firms have

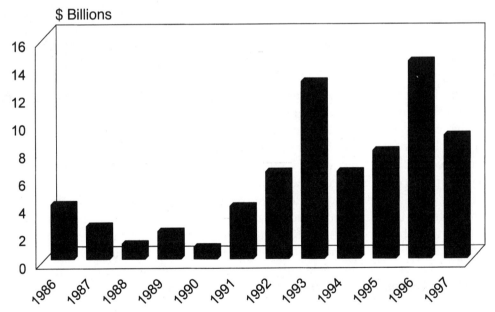

Figure 10.10.   Carve-out volume, 1986–97.

Source: J. P. Morgan's Equity Carve-outs and Shareholder Value Study, July 17, 1998.

---

27. *J. P. Morgan Equity Carve Out Study,* July 17, 1998.

28. Jeffrey Allen and John J. McConnell, "Equity Carve Outs and Managerial Discretion," *Journal of Finance* 53. no. 1 (February 1998), pp. 163–186.

Table 10.6.　Comparison of Pre–Carve-Out Firms with Industry Peers

Performance Measure	Pre–Carve-Out Firms	Industry Peers
EBDIT/Interest	2.29	5.42
Long-term debt/Total assets	0.260	0.220
Total debt/Total assets	0.331	0.285
EBDIT/Sales	0.070	0.103

Source: Jeffrey Allen and John J. McConnell, "Equity Carve Outs and Managerial Discretion." *Journal of Finance* 53 (1) February 1998, pp.163–186.

lower interest coverage and higher ratios of long-term debt and total debt to total assets. They also had lower ratios of EBDIT (earnings before depreciation, interest, and taxes) to sales and total assets. Allen and McConnell also traced the use of the carve-out proceeds. They found that when the funds were used to pay down debt, the company showed an average excess return of +6.63%, whereas when the funds were retained for investment purposes, the company experienced a –0.01% return.

Equity Carve-Outs versus Public Offerings

An equity carve-out, as opposed to a spin-off, brings in new capital to the parent company. Because the acquisition of capital is obviously a motivating factor for this type of sell-off, we must investigate why the equity carve-out option may be chosen over a public offering of stock. Katherine Schipper and Abbie Smith conducted a study of equity carve-outs that examined the share price reactions to 76 carve-out announcements. They compared these reactions with previous studies documenting the stock price reactions to public equity offerings.[29] Previous studies have shown that the announcement of seasoned equity offerings results in an abnormal stock return of between 22% and 23% in the periods around the equity offering.[30] In contrast to other equity financing arrangements, Schipper and Smith found that equity carve-outs increase shareholder wealth. Schipper and Smith found that the shareholders of the parent firms experienced average gains of 1.8%. They compared this positive stock price effect with a 23% shareholder loss for a subset of parent firms that engaged in public offerings of common stock or debt.

Schipper and Smith propose that the positive stock price reactions are due to a combination of effects, including better and more defined information available about both the parent and the subsidiary. This is clear to those who have attempted to evaluate the subsidiaries of a publicly held company. The annual reports and other publicly available documents may be very brief and yield little of the data necessary to value the components of a company. When the subsidiary becomes a stand-alone public company, it publishes more detailed information about its operations because its activities are its only line of business, as opposed to merely being a part of a larger parent company.

29. Katherine Schipper and Abbie Smith, "A Comparison of Equity Carve-Outs and Seasonized Equity Offerings," *Journal of Financial Economics* 15 (January-February 1986), pp. 153–186.

30. For a review of some of this literature and additional research showing that the effects of stock offerings are more negative for industrial firms than for public utilities, see Ronald W. Masulis and Ashok N. Korwar, "Seasonized Equity Offerings," *Journal of Financial Economics* 15, no. 11 (January-February 1986), pp. 91–118.

Schipper and Smith also point out other possible factors responsible for the positive stock price reaction to equity carve-outs, such as the restructuring and asset management that tend to be associated with equity carve-outs. In addition, divisions may be consolidated into a more efficient form, and managers may work with new compensation incentives. The combination of these and other changes may make the subsidiary a more viable entity as a separate public company. The market's perception of this value may be a source of a premium for the selling company. The parent company, no longer encumbered by a subsidiary that it could not manage as well as another owner might, becomes more valuable when it converts this asset into cash, which it can, it is hoped, invest in more productive areas.

Equity Carve-Outs versus Spin-Offs

There are a number of important differences between spin-offs and equity carve-outs. A carve-out results in a new set of shareholders, whereas the same shareholders hold stock in the spun-off entity as in the parent company. There are positive cash flow effects in carve-outs, but spin-offs do not result in initial changes in parent company cash flows. Carve-outs are more expensive to implement and are subject to greater securities law disclosure requirements.

In a study of 91 master limited partnerships (MLPs) that were created between 1981 and 1989, Michaely and Shaw found that for their sample riskier and more highly leveraged firms chose to go the spin-off route rather than to opt for a carve-out.[31] They show in their study that bigger, less leveraged, and more profitable firms chose the carve-out option. They conclude that the equity carve-out versus spin-off decision is determined by access to capital markets. Those companies that have better access, that is, more desirable firms in better financial condition, will choose to market themselves to public markets and enjoy the positive cash flow effects of an equity carve-out. Less desirable firms will be forced to choose the spin-off route. It should be noted that although it may seem that the Michaely and Shaw results contradict those of Allen and McConnell reported earlier, this is not the case. The Allen and McConnell results show a comparison of carve-out firms with industry peers, whereas the Michaely and Shaw study compares firms that did carve-outs with those that did spin-offs.

This study clearly does not explain all spin-off versus equity carve-out decisions. It does not address, for example, the large spin-offs of 1995, such as the ITT and AT&T deals. On the other hand, the Michaely and Shaw research results provide much useful insight into other types of transactions.

VOLUNTARY LIQUIDATIONS, OR BUSTUPS

Voluntary liquidations, or bustups, are the most extreme form of corporate restructuring. Corporate liquidations are more often associated with bankruptcy. A company may be liquidated in bankruptcy when all parties concerned recognize that the continuation of the firm in a reorganized form will not enhance its value. The outlook, however, is not as negative

---

31. Roni Michaely and Wayne H. Shaw, "The Choice of Going Public: Spinoffs vs. Carve Outs," *Financial Management* 24, no. 3 (Autumn 1995), pp. 5–21.

for voluntary liquidations. In a voluntary liquidation, the general criterion applied is as follows: If the market value of the firm's assets significantly exceeds the value of the firm's equity, a liquidation may need to be seriously considered. This is not to imply that liquidation should be an alternative in instances of a temporary downturn of the firm's stock. The liquidation option becomes viable only when the firm's stock has been depressed for an extended time. The liquidation option becomes even more likely when the stock prices of other firms in the same industry are not also depressed. In addition, low price-earnings (P/E) ratios may sometimes point to a need to consider the liquidation option. Managers are often reluctant to consider such a drastic step, which would result in their loss of position. They may prefer to sell the entire firm to a single acquirer rather than pursue liquidation. Stockholders sometimes try to force management's hand by threatening a proxy battle to decide the issue.

Voluntary liquidations may be contrasted with divestitures. A divestiture is generally a single transaction in which a certain part of the firm is sold, whereas a voluntary liquidation is a series of transactions in which all the firm's assets are sold in separate parcels.

Tax motives may make a liquidation more attractive than a divestiture. Divestitures may be subject to capital gains taxes, whereas voluntary liquidations may often be structured to receive more preferential tax treatment.

Shareholder Wealth Effects of Voluntary Bustups

Skantz and Marchesini's study of liquidation announcements made by 37 firms from 1970 to 1982 showed an average excess return of 21.4% during the month of the announcement.[32] Hite, Owers, and Rogers found similar positive shareholder wealth effects during the month of the announcement of voluntary liquidations made by the 49 firms in their sample, which covered the years 1966 to 1975.[33] They showed a positive abnormal return in the announcement month equal to 13.62%. Almost half the firms in their sample had been the object of a bid for control within two years of the announcement of the liquidation plan. These bids included a wide range of actions, including LBOs, tender offers, and proxy contests. Moreover, more than 80% of the firms in their sample showed positive abnormal returns. This suggests that the stock market agreed that continued operation of the firm under its prior operating policy will reduce shareholder wealth.

The positive stock market reaction was affirmed by two other studies. Kim and Schatzberg found a 14% positive return for 73 liquidating firms during a three-day period associated with the liquidation announcement.[34] They revealed that a 3% return was added when shareholders confirmed the transaction. Kim and Schatzberg failed to detect any significant wealth effect, either positive or negative, for the shareholders of the acquiring firms. In a study of 61 publicly traded firms that completed voluntary liquidations between 1970 and 1991, Erwin and McConnell found that voluntary liquidations were associated

32. Terrence Skantz and Roberto Marchesini, "The Effect of Voluntary Corporate Liquidation on Shareholder Wealth," *Journal of Financial Research* 10 (Spring 1987), pp. 65–75.

33. Gailen Hite, James Owers, and Ronald Rogers, "The Market for Interfirm Asset Sales: Partial Selloffs and Total Liquidations," *Journal of Financial Economics* 18 (June 1987), pp. 229–252.

34. E. Han Kim and John Schatzberg, "Voluntary Corporate Liquidations," *Journal of Financial Economics* 19, no. 2 (December 1987), pp. 311–328.

with an even higher average excess stock return of 20%.[35] They also confirmed the intuitive expectation that firms that decide to voluntarily liquidate face limited growth prospects. The liquidation decision is the rational one because it releases financial resources to be applied to higher yielding alternatives. As suggested previously, these research studies imply that the stock market often agrees that the continued operation of the firm under its prior operating policy will reduce shareholder wealth. This is not surprising because most firms that are considering liquidation are suffering serious problems. Liquidation then releases the firm's assets to other companies that might be able to realize a higher return on them.

MASTER LIMITED PARTNERSHIPS

Master limited partnerships (MLPs) are limited partnerships in which the shares are publicly traded. A limited partnership consists of a general partner and one or more limited partners. The general partner runs the business and bears unlimited liability. This is one of the major disadvantages of this form of business organization compared with a corporation. In a corporation, the owners—the stockholders—are insulated from the company's liabilities. The limited partners in the MLP, however, do not incur the liability exposure of the general partner.

The key advantage of the MLP is its elimination of the corporate layer of taxation. Stockholders in a corporation are taxed twice on their investments: first at the corporate level and then, as distributions in the form of dividends, at the individual level. Master limited partnerships are not taxed as a separate business entity, and the returns to the business flow through to the owners just as they do in other partnerships. This advantage was strengthened by the 1986 Tax Reform Act, which lowered the highest personal income tax bracket to 28% (which is less than the top corporate rate of 34%). This advantage was reduced when the tax law was changed in later years to raise the rate charged in the upper tax bracket.

Corporations have used MLPs to redistribute assets so that their returns are not subject to double taxation. In a *roll-out* MLP, corporations may transfer assets or divisions in separate MLPs.[36] Stockholders in the corporation are then given units of ownership in the MLP while maintaining their shares in the corporation. The income distributed by the MLP is not subject to double taxation.

Master limited partnerships may be involved in either spin-offs or equity carve-outs. In a spin-off, assets are directly transferred from the parent company to the MLP. Parent company shareholders receive MLP units on a pro rata basis. In an equity carve-out, the MLP raises cash through a public offering. This cash is then used to purchase assets of the division of the parent company that is being sold off.

Master limited partnerships have been popular in the petroleum industry. Oil companies have distributed oil and gas assets into MLPs, allowing the returns to flow through directly to stockholders without double taxation. Initially, start-up businesses may also be structured as MLPs. The MLP may be run by a general partner who receives an income from

---

35. Gayle R. Erwin and John J. McConnell, "To Live or Die? An Empirical Analysis of Piecemeal Voluntary Liquidations," *Journal of Corporate Finance* 3, no. 4 (December 1997), pp. 325–354.

36. J. Fred Weston, Kwang S. Chung, and Susan E. Hoag, *Mergers, Restructuring and Corporate Control* (Englewood Cliffs, N.J.: Prentice Hall, 1990), pp. 384–385.

managing the business. The general partner may or may not own a unit in the MLP. Capital is raised through an initial sale of MLP units to investors.

Master limited partnerships are generally held by individuals as opposed to corporations, which are predominantly owned by institutional investors. This trend may be explained by observing several differences between corporations and MLPs. Limited partners in MLPs do not have control, which is an attribute that institutions are starting to value more. Moreover, corporate shareholders are normally taxed on their MLP income as opposed to the exclusion they would qualify for if they were receiving dividends from another corporation. In addition, even institutions that are normally tax-exempt may have their MLP income taxed. For these reasons, MLPs are not very attractive to institutions.

RESTRUCTURING OF THE 1990s

The 1990s featured another type of corporate restructuring as companies responded to the effects of the 1990–91 recession and the weak recovery that followed. Companies sought to reduce their overhead, particularly with respect to their employment levels, and they began to *downsize*. The 1990s therefore featured a regular pattern of major layoff announcements, in which major companies engaged in large-scale layoffs that often affected thousands of employees. The impact of this downsizing may be seen in a rise in productivity statistics, where output per man-hour rose as output increased and manufacturing employment fell. As companies became more efficient, they positioned themselves to weather another economic downturn while enabling themselves to more effectively compete in international markets. Companies in the United States, particularly manufacturing firms with their high labor costs, found themselves in a difficult competitive position vis-à-vis certain foreign manufacturers, such as Asian companies. (This situation changed in 1998 when the "Asian Crisis" took hold.) The workforce restructuring was a response to the competitive and cyclical fluctuations.

One example of the use of workforce restructuring to accomplish the twin goals of becoming more efficient and becoming internationally competitive is the response of heavy equipment manufacturer Caterpillar, Inc. In 1979 Caterpillar had 90,000 employees, but in 1994 the workforce had been reduced to 54,000.[37] In addition, the company not only had too many workers but also had a significant number of unionized workers who command above-average compensation and sizable benefits packages, which equal an average of 41.1% of income for manufacturing firms.[38] In addition to reducing the number of employees, Caterpillar substituted lower paid nonunion workers to lower the average costs of its workforce. It combined these efforts with other modernizing efforts in its factories. These structural changes positioned the company not only to weather a possible future recession but also to better compete with the international heavy equipment manufacturers.

Workforce restructuring and other cost restructuring attempt to lower the *break-even point* of companies. With a lower break-even point, the risk of revenues being insufficient to cover costs is less. This is particularly important for capital-intensive companies such as heavy equipment manufacturers and automobile manufacturers.

---

37. James Sterngold, "Facing the Next Recession Without Fear," *New York Times,* 9 May 1995, p. D1.

38. *Employee Benefits as a Percent of Income* (Washington, D.C.: U.S. Chamber of Commerce, 1993).

The irony of the cost restructuring of the 1990s is that it came at a time when many of the companies engaging in the practice were experiencing significant increases in profits. For example, corporate profits as reported by DRI/McGraw-Hill rose 13% in 1993, following an 11% increase in 1992.[39] These years featured many significant layoffs. In prior years, companies were reluctant to lay off employees and only did so as a last resort. In the early 1990s, however, firms continually took steps to improve their efficiency, even when they were not motivated by the immediate prospect of turning losses. This key difference contrasts with other periods of restructuring that have taken place in the U.S. economy. It also came at a time when companies were expanding through acquisitions and mergers. This is why the unemployment rate declined even though many companies were engaging in large-scale layoffs. As the economy expands, it creates more employment opportunities, which offset the adverse effects of corporate downsizing. It is for this reason that the corporate downsizing movement did not cause net unemployment, although it did cause some firm-specific unemployment.[40]

---

39. Matt Murray, "Amid Record Profits Companies Continue to Lay Off Employees," *Wall Street Journal,* 4 May 1995, p. 1.

40. Christopher Vaz and Patrick A. Gaughan, "Do Mergers and Acquisitions Really Cause Net Unemployment?" New York/New Jersey Economic Research Center Report, Fairleigh Dickinson University, June, 1998.

CASE STUDY: ITT—THE DISSOLUTION OF THE QUINTESSENTIAL CONGLOMERATE

On June 13, 1995, the ITT Corporation announced that it would split the giant conglomerate that was constructed during the third merger wave through the acquisition of many dissimilar businesses throughout the world. The transaction was one of the largest of its kind in history. It involved the creation of three separate public companies, each with its own board of directors and each listed on the New York Stock Exchange. Holders of ITT stock received one share of stock in each of the new companies.

The breakup of ITT, once known as the International Telephone and Telegraph company, was an endorsement of the belief that the sum of the parts of the company, as stand-alone entities, was worth more than the value of them combined under the ITT umbrella. It was difficult to find many commonalities or synergies in ITT's diverse business interests; that is, it is a stretch to say that casinos and hockey teams have much in common with casualty insurance or the hotel business.

One of the clear benefits of splitting the company up was better access to capital.

We just think that having these three companies acting and operating and being evaluated in their own business environment will provide investors, analysts and those who deploy debt a simpler, more clear way to evaluate us," the chairman president and chief executive of ITT, Rand V. Araskog . . .[a]

---

[a] Stephanie Storm, "ITT the Quintessential Conglomerate, Plans to Split Up," *New York Times,* 14 June 1995, D1.

The $25 billion conglomerate that was built by Harold Geneen was split into three companies: an insurance company, ITT Hartford; an industrial products firm, ITT Industries; and a casino, hotel, and sports company, ITT Corporation. During the 1960s and 1970s, ITT had acquired more than 250 companies, including Avis Rent a Car, Continental Baking Company, Canteen, Rayonier, Sheraton Hotels, Hartford Insurance Company, and others.[b] ITT sold what was originally its core business in 1986. At that time, it sold its telecommunications operations to Alcatel Alsthom (CGE France).

The three new companies each included divisions that shared common elements for which there might be some synergies. For example, many of the managerial skills and administrative systems necessary to run a hotel are somewhat similar to those of casinos. Within the new ITT Corporation, Sheraton and Ciga hotels were combined. Also included in this company is the Madison Square Garden (MSG) sports arena, along with two of the major users of the arena, the New York Knickerbockers and the New York Rangers. In addition, the company has a partnership arrangement with Cablevision System Corporation—the New York cable television company that offers the MSG cable programming that televises the games of these teams. However, each company still contains many dissimilar elements that require some imagination to understand how shareholders are better off to have them within the now smaller but still somewhat diverse umbrellas. For example, the ITT Corporation still contains ITT World Directories, the world's largest producer of telephone directories outside the United States, and ITT Educational Services, which operates the ITT Technical Institutes.

The breakup of ITT was typical of the transactions that took place in the mid-1990s, when the pressure to increase efficiency rather than pursue convoluted acquisitions strategies was the way of the day. Whereas the third and fourth merger waves featured many questionable acquisitions, the early to mid-1990s featured more strategic acquisitions, which were closer to two merging companies' core businesses, in addition to the unraveling of many of the poorly conceived deals of earlier periods.

[b] ITT Company Press Release, June 13, 1995.

SUMMARY

Corporate restructuring is often warranted when the current structure of the corporation is not yielding values that are consistent with market or management's expectations. It may occur when a given part of a company no longer fits into management's plans. Other restructuring may be necessary when a prior acquisition has not performed up to management's expectations. The decision to sell may be difficult because it requires management to admit that the firm made a mistake when it acquired the asset that is being sold. Once the decision to sell has been made, management must decide how the sale will be implemented.

Managers may consider several of the different options discussed in this chapter, such as a straightforward sale, or divestiture, or the sale of an equity interest in a subsidiary to outsiders, which is an equity carve-out. In both cases, a separate legal entity is created and the divested entity is run by a new management team as a stand-alone company. An alternative that also results in the creation of a separate legal entity is a spin-off. In a spin-off, shares are issued on a pro rata basis and distributed to the parent company's shareholders, also on a pro rata basis. When the transaction is structured so that shares in the original company are exchanged for shares in the parent firm, the deal is called a split-off. A split-up occurs when the entire firm is broken up and shareholders exchange their shares in the parent company according to a predetermined formula.

Empirical research has found that a significant number of sell-offs are associated with positive shareholder wealth effects for parent company shareholders. This implies that the market agrees that the sale of part of the company will yield a higher return than the continued operation of the division under current operating policies. The market is indicating that the proceeds of the sale of the firm may be used more advantageously than the division that is being sold. The market also has responded with a positive stock price response for shareholders in the divested or spun-off entities. Even the price performance of buyers of divested firms enjoy positive wealth effects. Research results also show positive stock price effects for announcements of voluntary liquidations.

The positive market response to restructuring paints this form of corporate change in a favorable light. Other forms of corporate downsizing, such as large-scale employee lay-offs, also are quite common in the 1990s. Although this type of restructuring has been criticized because it is often associated with employee duress, it is partially responsible for the improvement in U.S. productivity in the 1990s. The declining unemployment rate in the economy at a time when the corporate downsizing was ongoing confirms the fact that the firm-specific unemployment associated with downsizing does not result in net unemployment.

REFERENCES

Allen, Jeffrey, and John J. McConnell. "Equity Carve Outs and Managerial Discretion." *Journal of Finance* 53, no. 1 (February 1998).

AT&T Shareholders Newsletter (Fourth Quarter, 1982).

Bicksler, James L., and Andrew H. Chen. "The Economics of Corporate Restructuring: An Overview." In Arnold W. Sametz, ed. *The Battle for Corporate Control* (Homewood, Ill.: Business One Irwin, 1991), pp. 386–387.

Boot, Arnoud W. A. "Why Hang on to Losers? Divestitures and Takeovers." *Journal of Finance* 47, no. 4 (September 1992).

Cusatis, Patrick J., James A. Miles, and J. Randall Woolridge. "Restructuring through Spinoffs, The Stock Market Evidence." *Journal of Financial Economics* 33, no. 3 (June 1993).

Daley, Lane, Vikas Mehrotra, and Ranjini Sivakumar. "Corporate Focus and Value Creation: Evidence from Spinoffs." *Journal of Financial Economics* 45, no. 2 (August 1997).

Eckbo, Bjorn E. "Horizontal Mergers, Collusion and Stockholders Wealth." *Journal of Financial Economics* 11 (1983).

Ellert, James C. "Mergers, Antitrust Law Enforcement and the Behavior of Stock Prices." *Journal of Finance* 31 (1976).

Employee Benefits as a Percent of Income. (Washington, D.C.: U.S. Chamber of Commerce, 1993).

Erwin, Gayle R., and John J. McConnell. "To Live or Die? An Empirical Analysis of Piecemeal Voluntary Liquidations." *Journal of Corporate Finance* 3, no. 4 (December 1997).

Hite, Gailen, and James Owers. "Security Price Reactions Around Corporate Spinoff Announcements." *Journal of Financial Economics* 12, no. 4 (December 1983).

Hite, Gailen, James Owers, and Ronald Rogers. "The Market for Interfirm Asset Sales: Partial Selloffs and Total Liquidations." *Journal of Financial Economics* 18 (June 1987).

ITT Company Press Release, June 13, 1995.

J. P. Morgan Equity Carve Out Study, July 17, 1998.

J. P. Morgan's Spinoffs Study, June 6, 1995.

J. P. Morgan's Spinoffs Study, August 20, 1997.

Jain, Prem C. "Sell-Off Announcements and Shareholder Wealth." *Journal of Finance* 40, no. 1 (March 1985).

Jarzombek, Susan. "A Way to Put a Spotlight on Unseen Value." *Corporate Finance* (December 1989).

Kaplan, Steven N., and Michael N. Weisbach. "The Success of Acquisitions: Evidence from Divestitures." *Journal of Finance* 47, no. 1, (March 1992).

Kim, E. Han, and John Schatzberg. "Voluntary Corporate Liquidations." *Journal of Financial Economics* 19, no. 2 (December 1987).

Kudla, Ronald J., and Thomas H. McInish. "The Microeconomic Consequences of an Involuntary Corporate Spin-Off." *Sloan Management Review* 22, no. 4 (1981).

Kudla, Ronald J., and Thomas H. McInish. "Valuation Consequences of Corporate Spin-Offs." *Review of Economics and Business Research* (March 1983).

Kudla, Ronald J., and Thomas H. McInish. *Corporate Spin-Offs: Strategy for the 1980s* (Westport, Conn.: Quorum Books, 1984).

Lambert, Hope. *Behind Closed Doors* (New York: Atheneum, 1986).

Linn, Scott C., and Michael S. Rozeff. "The Corporate Selloff." *Midland Corporate Finance Journal* 2, no. 2 (Summer 1984).

Loh, Charmen, Jennifer Russell Bezjak, and Harrison Toms. "Voluntary Corporate Divestitures as Antitakeover Mechanism." *The Financial Review* 30, no. 1 (February 1995).

McGinley, Laurie, Judith Valente, and Daniel Machalaba. "ICC Reaffirms Its Rejection of Merger of Santa Fe, Southern Pacific Railroads." *Wall Street Journal,* July 1, 1987.

Masulis, Ronald W., and Ashok N. Korwar. "Seasonized Equity Offerings." *Journal of Financial Economics* 15, no. 1/2 (January/February 1986).

Miles, James, and James Rosenfeld. "An Empirical Analysis of the Effects of Spin-Off Announcements on Shareholder Wealth." *Journal of Finance* 38, no. 5 (December 1983).

Murray, Matt. "Amid Record Profits Companies Continue to Lay Off Employees." *Wall Street Journal,* May 4, 1995, p. 1.

Pipin, Steven, and Randall Smith. "Spinoffs Burgeon, Fueled by Tax Status, Investor Pressure and Stock Performance." *Wall Street Journal,* June 15, 1995.

Porter, Michael. "From Competitive Advantage to Corporate Strategy." *Harvard Business Review* 65, no. 3 (May-June 1987).

Ravenscraft, David, and Frederic Scherer. *Mergers, Selloffs and Economic Efficiency* (Washington D.C.: Brookings Institution, 1987).

Schipper, Katherine, and Abbie Smith. "A Comparison of Equity Carve-Outs and Seasonized Equity Offerings." *Journal of Financial Economics* 15 (January-February 1986).

Skantz, Terrence, and Roberto Marchesini. "The Effect of Voluntary Corporate Liquidation on Shareholder Wealth." *Journal of Financial Research* 10 (Spring 1987).

Stern, Joel. "A Discussion of Corporate Restructuring, Comments of Gailen Hite." *Midland Corporate Finance Journal* 2, no. 2 (Summer 1984).

Sterngold, James. "Facing the Next Recession Without Fear." *New York Times,* 9 May 1995.

Stillman, Robert. "Examining Antitrust Policy Towards Horizontal Mergers." *Journal of Financial Economics* 11 (1983).

Stocks, Bills, Bonds and Inflation: 1994 (Chicago: Ibbotson Associates).

Storm, Stephanie. "ITT the Quintessential Conglomerate, Plans to Split Up." *New York Times,* 14 June 1995.

"The Sum of the Parts." Oppenheimer and Company, New York, January 14, 1981.

Vaz, Christopher, and Patrick A. Gaughan. "Do Mergers and Acquisitions Really Cause Net Unemployment?" New York/New Jersey Economic Research Center Report, Fairleigh Dickinson University, June 1998.

Weston, J. Fred. "Divestitures: Mistakes or Learnings." *Journal of Applied Corporate Finance* 2, no. 2 (Summer 1989).

Weston, J. Fred, Kwang S. Chung, and Susan E. Hoag. *Mergers, Restructuring and Corporate Control* (Englewood Cliffs, N.J.: Prentice Hall, 1990).

11

RESTRUCTURING IN BANKRUPTCY

The 1990–91 recession, combined with the unraveling of many of the leveraged transactions of the fourth merger wave, called attention to the creative corporate finance uses of bankruptcy. Reorganization through the bankruptcy process is a tool of corporate finance that in certain instances provides unique benefits that are unattainable through other means. This chapter explores the different forms of bankruptcy and discusses the circumstances in which a company would use either of the two broad forms of corporate bankruptcy that are available: Chapter 7 and Chapter 11. Chapter 7, liquidation, is appropriate for more severely distressed companies. Chapter 11, reorganization, however, is the more flexible corporate finance tool that allows the company to continue to operate while it explores other forms of restructuring. In addition, Chapter 11 allows companies to continue to operate while a reorganization plan is being developed and approved.

TYPES OF BUSINESS FAILURE

Clearly, bankruptcy is a drastic step that is only pursued when other more favorable options are unavailable. A bankruptcy filing is an admission that a company has in some way failed to achieve certain goals. The term *business failure* is somewhat ambiguous and has different meanings, depending on the context and the users. There are two main forms of business failure: economic failure and financial failure. Each has a very different meaning.

Economic Failure

Of the two broad types of business failure, economic failure is the more ambiguous. For example, economic failure could mean that the firm is generating losses; that is, revenues are less than costs. However, depending on the users and the context, economic failure could also mean that the rate of return on investment is less than the cost of capital. It could also mean that the actual returns earned by a firm are less than those that were forecast. These uses of the term are very different and cover situations in which a company could be unprofitable as well as cases in which the company is profitable but not as profitable as was expected.

Financial Failure

Financial failure is less ambiguous than economic failure. Financial failure means that a company cannot meet its current obligations as they come due. The company does not have sufficient liquidity to satisfy its current liabilities. This may occur even when the company has a positive net worth, with the value of its assets exceeding its liabilities.

Costs of Financial Distress

Andrade and Kaplan conducted a study of 31 distressed highly leveraged transactions (HLTs) consisting of management buyouts (MBOs) and leveraged recapitalizations.[1] They focused on firms that were financially but not economically distressed. They traced the causes of the distress to a pre- versus post-HLT leverage, as measured by the median ratio of book value of debt to total capital, 0.21 versus 0.91, and median ratios of EBITDA-interest coverage of 7.95 versus 1.16. Their analysis points to the higher leverage as the cause of the financial distress. They then compared the value of the company over a period two months before the HLT until the resolution of the distress. The resolution was defined as the date they either exited Chapter 11, were sold, issued new equity, or were liquidated. They conclude that the changes brought about by the HLTs and the subsequent distress result in an *increase* in value. It is important to note that their conclusions are only relevant to financial distress, not to economic distress.

CAUSES OF BUSINESS FAILURE

Dun and Bradstreet conducted a study of the causes of business failure. They found that the three most common factors, in order of frequency, were economic factors, such as weakness in the industry; financial factors, such as insufficient capitalization; and weaknesses in managerial experience, such as insufficient managerial knowledge (Table 11.1). The last factor highlights the role of management skills in preventing bankruptcy and is one reason workout specialists focus so strongly on managerial skills when they are working on a company turnaround.

Dun and Bradstreet also analyzed the average ages of the businesses that failed (Table 11.2). They found only 10.7% of the failures were in business for one year or less. Just under one-third of the companies were in business for three years or less, whereas 44.3% existed for up to five years.

Causes of Financial Distress Following Leveraged Recapitalizations

Financial distress and bankruptcy have been linked to many of the highly leveraged deals that took place in the 1980s. As discussed in Chapter 7, leveraged buyouts (LBOs) became popular during this period, along with the use of leveraged recapitalization as an anti-takeover defense. Denis and Denis conducted a study of 29 leveraged recapitalizations that took place between 1984 and 1988.[2] They define leveraged recapitalizations as transactions

---

1. Gregor Andrade and Steven N. Kaplan, "How Costly is Financial (Not Economic) Distress? Evidence from Highly Leveraged Transactions that Became Distressed," *Journal of Finance* 53, no. 5 (October 1998), pp.1443–1493.

2. David J. Denis and Diane K. Denis, "Causes of Financial Distress Following Leveraged Recapitalizations," *Journal of Financial Economics* 37 (1995), pp. 129–157.

Table 11.1.   Causes of Business Failure

Underlying Causes	Percentage (%)*
Economic factors (e.g., industry weakness, insufficient profits)	41.0
Financial factors (e.g., heavy operating expenses, insufficient capital)	32.5
Experience factors (e.g., lack of business knowledge, lack of line experience, lack of managerial experience)	20.6
Neglect (e.g., poor work habits, business conflicts)	2.5
Fraud	1.2
Disaster	1.1
Strategy factors (e.g., receivable difficulties, overexpansion)	1.1
	100.0

*Results are based on primary reason for failure.

that use proceeds from new debt obligations to make a payout to shareholders. Their results show that 31% of the firms that completed leveraged recapitalizations encountered financial distress. Contrary to what had been hypothesized by other researchers, such as Kaplan and Stein, who had asserted that failures of leveraged transactions were due to overpricing and poor financial structure, Denis and Denis conclude that although these factors are important, the 1990–91 recession and the regulatory factors were the reason some leveraged recapitalizations failed and others did not.[3] They did find that distressed firms had similar but somewhat higher debt levels and lower interest coverages. However, distressed firms required more postdeal cash than nondistressed firms. For example, the cash needs of distressed firms required them to sell an average of 6.3% of their assets, whereas nondistressed firms would only have had to sell 3.6% of their assets. Distressed firms also had to achieve greater postdeal performance improvements. For example, in order to meet the postdeal debt service, distressed firms would have had to have a median increase in operating income of 41.8% compared with 18.9% for nondistressed firms.

Given the reliance on postdeal assets sales, regulatory changes and the recession of 1990–91 played a key role in the failure of the leveraged recapitalizations. These regulatory factors are related to the collapse of the junk bond market. Following the difficulties

Table 11.2.   Failure by Age of Business

Number of Years in Business	Percentage (%)
One year or less	10.7
Two years	10.1
Three years	8.7
Total three years or less	29.5
Four years	7.8
Five years	7.0
Total five years or less	44.3
Total six to ten years	23.9
Total over ten years	31.8
	100.0

Source: The Dun & Bradstreet Corporation, Business Failure Record, 1997.

3. Steven Kaplan and Jeremy Stein, "The Evolution of Buyout Pricing and the Financial Structure of the 1980s," *Quarterly Journal of Economics* (May 1993), pp. 313–357.

Table 11.3. A Comparison of the Total Cash Shortfall from Asset Sales and the Additional Cash Required to Avoid Default in the Year of the First Indication of Financial Distress for the Nine Distressed Firms

Firm name	Total asset sale shortfall* ($ millions)	Additional cash required in year of distress ($ millions)
Carter Hawley Hale	$612.6	$38.6
Goodyear	489.1	139.5
Harcourt Brace Jovanovich	924.9	243.6
Holiday	35.2	−33.7
Interco	288.5	223.1
Quantum Chemical	140.7	164.4
Standard Brands Paint	0.0	164.4
Swank	0.0	8.3
USG	54.5	351.0
Median	140.7	139.5

The total asset sale shortfall is the sum of the shortfall from completed asset sales and the shortfall from sales not completed. We measure both shortfalls as the difference between the price received for the asset (zero in the case of an asset sale that was not completed) and the expected price as stated in press reports. When this quantity is unavailable, we measure the shortfall as the abnormal return over the three days centered on the announcement of the sale multiplied by the market value of the firm's equity. The additional cash required in the first year of distress is the difference between the firm's interest and principal obligations and its net cash flow (operating income less capital expenditures) for that year.

* Carter Hawley Hale's total shortfall includes $650 million from asset sales not completed. Similarly, Goodyear's total includes $750 million, and Harcourt Brace Jovanovich's includes $33.9 million from sales not completed

Source: David J. Denis and Diane K. Denis, "Causes of Financial Distress Following Leveraged Recapitalizations," *Journal of Financial Economics* 37 (1995), pp. 129–157.

of this market, certain financial institutions were forced to sell off their junk bond holdings, which hurt the ability of potential junk bond issuers to sell new bonds. This, in turn, limited the resources available to buyers of assets of companies that engaged in leveraged recapitalizations. The limited resources lower the values that leveraged recap firms could realize from asset sales (Table 11.3). Many of these firms overestimated the prices they would receive for assets, such as divisions. This error was partially related to not being able to anticipate the dramatic changes that occurred in the junk bond market. The difficulties of the market for assets were compounded by the recession of 1990–91, which made performance improvement more difficult to achieve.

BANKRUPTCY DATA

Total bankruptcies rose significantly toward the end of the 1980s in direct relation to the performance of the overall economy (Figure 11.1). As the economic growth slowed toward the end of the 1980s, bankruptcies, both personal and business, increased. Business bankruptcies increased steadily during this period, hit a 1980s' peak in 1986, declined through 1989, and then rose again as the economy slowed (Figure 11.2).

Table 11.4 shows that the value of LBOs peaked in 1989 and declined dramatically by 1991, whereas Chapter 11 filings, which included some of the firms that participated in

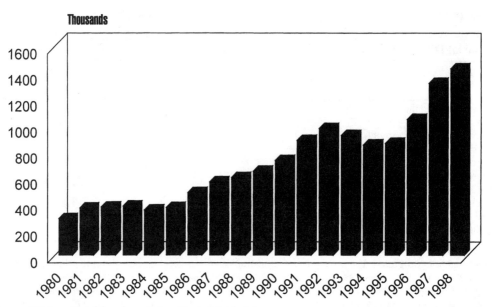

Figure 11.1.   Total bankruptcies filed, 1980–98.

Source: Haver Analytics.

LBOs in the 1980s, remained high through the recession of 1990–91 and declined slowly as the economy recovered in the first half of the 1990s (Table 11.4 and Figure 11.3).

By far the largest business bankruptcy in history was the Chapter 11 filing of Texaco (Table 11.5). Interestingly, the bankruptcy filing of this healthy company was the result of a judgment entered against it in a lawsuit filed by Pennzoil *(Pennzoil Co. v. Texaco, Inc.)* as a result of Texaco's acquisition of Getty. Getty and Pennzoil had reached an agreement to

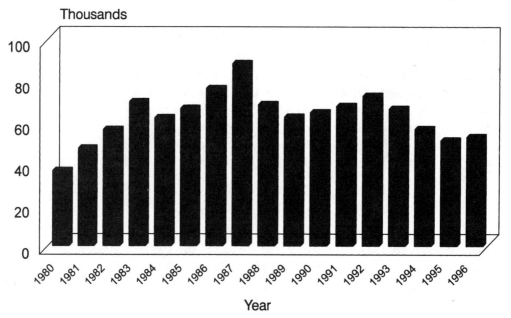

Figure 11.2.   Total business bankruptcies filed, 1980–98.

Source: Haver Analytics.

Table 11.4.   Frequency and Size of Chapter 11 Filings and other Corporate Restructuring Transactions by Publicly Traded Firms, 1981–94

Year	Number of Transactions				Total Value of Transactions ($ billions)*			
	Chapter 11 Filings	Hostile Tender Offers	LBOs	Spin-Offs	Chapter 11 Filngs	Hostile Tender Offers	LBOs	Spin-Offs
1980	62							
1981	74	10	14	2	6.0	8.6	2.7	1.3
1982	84	8	15	3	11.3	3.4	2.1	0.2
1983	89	9	47	17	15.4	2.5	3.1	3.6
1984	121	9	113	13	7.9	3.3	18.7	1.3
1985	149	12	156	19	6.9	20.3	18.9	1.5
1986	149	17	238	26	15.9	20.6	56.6	4.4
1987	112	16	214	20	49.5	6.1	51.5	3.5
1988	122	28	300	34	49.9	50.0	66.7	12.8
1989	135	15	305	25	78.0	50.0	82.9	8.0
1990	116	5	201	27	85.7	9.0	18.6	5.4
1991	125	3	193	18	86.1	2.8	7.4	4.8
1992	91	1	223	19	55.4	0.5	8.2	5.8
1993	86	1	176	26	17.1	0.0**	10.2	14.4
1994	70	7	159	28	8.3	12.4	8.3	23.4
1995	84							
1996	84							
1997	82							
Total	1,834	141	2,354	277	$493.3	$189.4	$355.8	$90.5

*All dollar values are converted into constant 1994 dollars using the producer price index. For a Chapter 11 filing, "Total Value of Transaction" equals the book value of total assets of the filing firm. For a hostile tender offer and an LBO, "Total Value of Transaction" equals the total value of consideration paid by the acquirer (including assumption of debt), excluding fees and expenses. For a spin-off, "Total Value of Transaction" equals the market value of the common stock of the spun-off entity evaluated at the first non-when-issued stock price available after the spin-off.

**Less than $0.1 billion.

Source: The 1995 *Bankruptcy Yearbook and Almanac* and Securities Data Corporation as cited in Stuart C. Gilson, "Investing in Distressed Situations: A Market Survey," *Financial Analyst Journal* (November–December 1995), p. 9; the 1998 *Bankruptcy Yearbook and Almanac.*

merge and a Houston, Texas, jury found that Texaco wrongfully interfered with a handshake agreement between Getty and Pennzoil. The $10 billion award to Pennzoil was the largest judgment in legal history.[4] The overwhelming pressures of this obligation forced Texaco to file Chapter 11 bankruptcy.

BANKRUPTCY LAWS

The Bankruptcy Act of 1978, also known as the Bankruptcy Code, is the main bankruptcy law of the United States. It organized bankruptcy laws under eight odd-numbered chapters. These are shown in Table 11.6.

---

4. James Shannon, *Texaco and the $10 Billion Jury* (Englewood Cliffs, N.J.: Prentice-Hall, 1988).

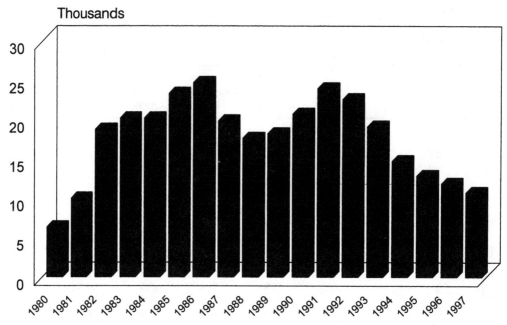

Figure 11.3.   Chapter 11 bankruptcy filings, 1980–97.

Source: 1998 Bankruptcy Yearbook and Almanac.

Table 11.5.   Large U.S. Bankruptcies

Company	Total Assets ($ billions)	Date Filed
Texaco	35.9	04/12/87
Financial Corp. of America	33.9	09/09/88
M Corp.	20.2	03/31/89
First Executive Corp.	15.3	05/13/91
Gibraltar Financial Corp.	15.0	02/08/90
HomeFed Corp.	13.9	10/22/92
Imperial Corp. of America	12.3	02/28/90
First Capital Holdings	9.8	05/30/91
Baldwin-United	9.4	09/26/83
Southmark Corp.	9.2	07/14/89
Federated Dept. Stores	7.9	01/15/90
Integrated Resources, Inc.	7.9	02/13/90
Continental Airlines Holdings	7.7	12/03/90
Home Holdings, Inc.	7.6	01/15/98
Olympia & York Devel. Ltd.	7.0	05/14/92
Penn Central	6.9	06/21/70
Lomas Financial Corp.	6.7	09/24/89
Maxwell Communication Corp.	6.4	12/16/91
LTV Corp.	6.3	07/17/86
Columbia Gas System, Inc.	6.2	07/31/91

Source: Moyer, McGuigan, and Kretlow, in Dominic DiNapoli, Sanford C. Sigoloff, and Robert F. Cushman, eds., *Contemporary Financial Management Workouts and Turnarounds* (Homewood, Ill.: Business Irwin One, 1991).

Table 11.6.   Bankruptcy Act of 1978

Chapter	Subject
1	General provisions and definitions
3	Case administration
5	Creditors, debtors, and estates
7	Liquidation
9	Bankruptcies of municipalities
11	Reorganization
13	Bankruptcies of individuals
15	U.S. trustees system

1984 and 1994 Bankruptcy Laws

The Bankruptcy Act of 1978 has been enhanced by later bankruptcy laws. In 1984 the Bankruptcy Amendments and Federal Judgeship Act established the jurisdiction of the bankruptcy court as a unit of the district courts. This law was in response to a Supreme Court ruling that challenged the jurisdiction of bankruptcy courts. The 1984 law also made it more difficult to immediately void labor contracts in bankruptcy. This was in response to a Supreme Court ruling in the Wilson Foods case, in which the court decided that companies could abrogate existing labor contracts as soon as they filed for bankruptcy. The revised law, which was passed partly because of labor union pressure, requires that a company try to work out a labor agreement before going to the bankruptcy courts. If the sincerity of the efforts of the parties is an issue, a bankruptcy will decide whether each party acted in good faith and under compliance with the law.

The Bankruptcy Reform Act of 1994 enhanced the powers of the bankruptcy courts. The act gave these courts the right to issue orders that they deem necessary or appropriate to carry out the provisions of the Bankruptcy Code.

REORGANIZATION VERSUS LIQUIDATION

The purpose of the reorganization section of the Bankruptcy Code is to allow a *reorganization plan* to be developed that will allow the company to continue to operate. This plan will contain the changes in the company that its designers believe are necessary to convert it to a profitable entity. If a plan to allow the profitable operation of the business cannot be formulated, the company may have to be liquidated, with its assets sold and the proceeds used to satisfy the company's liabilities.

CHAPTER 11 REORGANIZATION PROCESS

Although the Chapter 11 process varies somewhat depending on the particular circumstances of the bankruptcy, most Chapter 11 bankruptcies have certain important common characteristics. These are highlighted next.

Bankruptcy Petition and the Filing

The reorganization process starts with the filing of a bankruptcy *petition for relief* with the bankruptcy court. In the petition, the debtor lists its creditors and security holders. Standard financial statements, including an income statement and balance sheet, are also included. The court then sets a date when the creditors may file their *proofs of claim*. The company then attempts to put together a reorganization plan while it continues its operations. Contrary to what a layperson might think, there is no financial test that is performed by the court at this time to determine whether the debtor is truly financially insolvent.

The petition is usually filed in the federal district in which the debtor has its home office. After the petition is filed, a case number is assigned, a court file is opened, and a bankruptcy judge is assigned to the case.

Debtor in Possession

After the bankruptcy filing, the bankrupt company is referred to as the *debtor in possession*. This is a new legal entity; however, for all practical purposes, it usually is the same company with the same management and the same employees. From the creditors' point of view, this is one of the problems of the bankruptcy process; that is, the same management that led the company into its financial troubles usually is still running the business while a reorganization plan is being developed.

If the creditors strongly oppose the management of the debtor staying in control of the business, they may petition the court and ask that a trustee and examiner be appointed. For example, if concerns exist about fraudulent actions or incompetence of the debtor's directors or management, the court may agree. A trustee is charged with overseeing the operations of the company while it is in bankruptcy. An examiner may be appointed to investigate specific issues. If the court denies a request for a trustee, an examiner is usually appointed.

Automatic Stay

When the petition is accepted by the court, an automatic stay is granted. This is one of the main benefits the debtor receives in the Chapter 11 process. During the automatic stay, a halt is placed on any prepetition legal proceedings as well as on the enforcement of any prefiling judgment. Creditors are unable to pursue a lien on the debtor's assets or to collect money from the debtor. Parties seeking relief from the stay may petition the court and request a hearing. If the creditors can convince the court that the assets that are being used as collateral for obligations due them are not necessary for the continued operation of the company, or the debtor has no equity interest in the assets, they may be able to get relief from the stay.

Time Line in the Reorganization Process

Table 11.7 shows some of the key events and dates in the Chapter 11 process. Within 10 days of the filing of the Chapter 11 bankruptcy petition, the debtor is required to file a schedule of assets and liabilities with the court. This schedule must include the name and

Table 11.7.   Time Line of Key Events and Dates in a Chapter 11 Reorganization

1. Filing of the Chapter 11 petition
2. Filing a schedule of assets and liabilities
3. Bar date
4. Filing a reorganization plan and disclosure statement
5. Hearing on the disclosure statement
6. Voting on the plan
7. Plan confirmation hearing
8. Effective date of plan/distribution of new claims under the plan

address of each creditor. The next important date is the *bar date,* which is the date when those creditors who have disputed or contingent claims must file a *proof of claim.* A proof of claim is a written statement that sets forth what is owed by the debtor to the particular creditor. Failure to file by the bar date results in forfeiture of the claim. It is automatically assumed, however, that other claimholders have filed a proof of claim. Following the bar date, the next important dates are those associated with the filing and approval of the reorganization plan.

Use of Secured Creditors' Collateral

The Chapter 11 process allows for the use of the security creditors' collateral by the debtor in possession. Creditors are barred from seizing assets while the stay is in effect. This does not mean that the debtor has free use of the property. The debtor must make some accommodation to the creditors, such as periodic payments (i.e., monthly), for continued use of the assets.

Duties of the Debtor in Possession

After the filing of the petition, the court establishes certain schedules, which feature various reporting requirements. For example, the debtor has to file monthly financial statements 15 days after the end of each calendar month. In addition to the court rules as set forth in the federal law, each federal district may have additional reporting requirements. For example, the southern district of New York has local rules that relate to further reporting requirements and the opening of bank accounts.

Creditors' Committees

A creditors' meeting is usually held within 20 to 40 days of the bankruptcy filing. The meeting is called by the U.S. Trustee and is usually held at his or her office. The debtor and its principal officers must be present at this meeting. All creditors may attend this meeting and may ask the debtor specific questions that are of concern to them.

In larger lawsuits, a creditors' committee is formed. This committee is usually composed of the largest creditors, assuming they are interested in being represented. Along with the U.S. Trustee, the creditors' committee monitors the actions of the debtor, ensuring that it does not do anything that would adversely affect the creditors' interests. The creditors' committee may retain counsel, accountants, and other financial experts to represent the creditors' interests during the reorganization process. The fees of professionals are borne by the debtor.

The bigger the bankruptcy, the more likely it is that there may be more committees, such as an equity holders' committee, or different types of creditors' committees, such as a bondholders' committee, representing the various forms of debt that might exist. One example of a megabankruptcy that had several committees was the bankruptcy of the Campeau Corporation, which featured the bankruptcy of Campeau's two major subunits, Federated Department Stores, Inc. and Allied Stores Corp. In this proceeding, there were several committees, including a bondholders' committee and two trade creditors' committees. The court attempted to appoint a cross section of similarly situated creditors on each committee. In smaller bankruptcies, creditors may have little interest in the committees. In the Campeau bankruptcy, the office of U.S. Trustee Conrad J. Morgenstern was flooded with bondholders who were interested in serving on the committee.

Debtor's Actions and Its Supervision

The debtor may continue to operate the business during the reorganization process. The law requires that the debtor obtain the approval of the bankruptcy court before its takes any extraordinary action that is not part of the normal business operations, such as selling assets or property.

Technically, the supervision of the debtor is the responsibility of the judge and the creditors. They may acquire resources, such as legal and accounting or other financial expert assistance, to help them. Practically, neither the judge nor the creditors usually have the resources or time to closely supervise the debtor. Even if the debtor does something that the creditors do not approve of, the debtor may be able to convince the judge that some actions are necessary for the survival of the company; that is, if the court does not allow the debtor to take these actions, the company may go under. Thus, the judge is put in the difficult position of making this decision with limited information. If the judge rules against the debtor and is wrong, he risks the company's going out of business and all the duress and employee suffering this might cause. For this reason, the debtor is usually granted significant leeway and will only be opposed when its proposed actions are clearly objectionable.

Exclusivity Period

After the filing of the bankruptcy petition and the granting of the automatic stay, only the debtor has the right to file a reorganization plan. This period, which is initially 120 days, is known as the *exclusivity period*. It is rare, however, particularly in larger bankruptcies, to have the plan submitted during that time frame. It is common for the debtor to ask for one or more extensions. Extensions are only granted for cause, but they are not difficult to obtain.

Under early versions of the bankruptcy law, only the debtor could file a reorganization plan. Later versions of the code, however, allow the creditors to prepare and file their own reorganization plan if they do not approve of the one the debtor put forward.

The end of the exclusivity period signals that control in the bankruptcy process is shifting from the debtor to the creditors. Contrary to what one might think, there is no specific time limit on when the Chapter 11 process must come to an end. If the judge determines that sufficient progress toward the submission and approval of a plan is not being made, however, he or she may try to take steps to move the process along.

Obtaining Postpetition Credit

One of the problems a near-bankrupt company has is difficulty obtaining credit. If trade creditors are concerned that a company may become bankrupt, they may cut off all additional credit. For companies that are dependent on such credit to survive, this may mean that a bankruptcy filing is accelerated.

To assist bankrupt companies in acquiring essential credit, the code has given postpetition creditors an elevated priority in the bankruptcy process. That is, postpetition claims have an elevated priority over prepetition claims. It is ironic that creditors may be unwilling to extend credit unless the debtor files for bankruptcy so that the creditor can obtain the elevated priority.

Reorganization Plan

The reorganization plan, which is part of a larger document called the *disclosure statement,* looks like a prospectus. For larger bankruptcies, it is a long document that contains the plans for the turnaround of the company. The plan is submitted to all the creditors and equity holders' committees. The plan is approved when each class of creditor and equity holder approves it. Approval is granted if one-half in number and two-thirds in dollar amount of a given class approve the plan. Once the plan is approved, the dissenters are bound by the details of the plan.

A confirmation hearing follows the attainment of the approval of the plan. The hearing is not intended to be a pro forma proceeding, even if the vote is unanimous. The presiding judge must make a determination that the plan meets the standards set forth by the Bankruptcy Code. After the plan is confirmed, the debtor is discharged of all prepetition claims and other claims up to the date of the confirmation hearing. This does not mean that the reorganized company is a debt-free entity. It simply means that it has new obligations that are different from the prior obligations. Ideally, the postconfirmation capital structure is one that will allow the company to remain sufficiently liquid to meet its new obligations and generate a profit.

Cramdown

The plan may be made binding on all classes of security holders, even if they all do not approve it. This is known as a *cramdown.* The judge may conduct a cramdown if at least one class of creditors approves the plan and the "crammed down" class is not being treated unfairly. In this context, "unfairly" means that no class with inferior claims in the bankruptcy hierarchy is receiving compensation without the higher-up class being paid 100% of its claims. This order of claims is known as the *absolute priority rule,* which states that claims must be settled in full before any junior claims can receive any compensation.

The concept of a cramdown comes from the concern by lawmakers that a small group of creditors could block the approval of a plan to the detriment of the majority of the creditors.[5] By giving the court the ability to cram down a plan, the law reduces the potential for a holdout problem.

Fairness and Feasibility of the Plan

The reorganization plan must be both fair and feasible. Fairness refers to the satisfaction of claims in order of priority, as discussed in the previous section. Feasibility refers to the probability that the postconfirmation company has a reasonable chance of survival. The plan must provide for certain essential features, such as adequate working capital and a reasonable capital structure that does not contain too much debt. Projected revenues must be sufficient to adequately cover the fixed charges associated with the postconfirmation liabilities and other operating expenses.

Partial Satisfaction of Prepetition Claims

The plan will provide a new capital structure that, it is hoped, will be one that the company can adequately service. This will typically feature payment of less than the full amount that was due the claimholders. For example, the Penn Central Railroad, in a bankruptcy process that lasted eight years, produced a confirmed plan that gave holders of secured bonds 10% of their claims in cash. The cash was generated by the sale of assets. The remaining 90% was satisfied by 30% each in new mortgage bonds, preferred stock, and common stock. This provided Penn Central with a lower amount of financial leverage because the secured bond debt was 10% discharged by the cash payment, and 60% was converted to preferred and common equity.

BENEFITS OF THE CHAPTER 11 PROCESS FOR THE DEBTOR

The U.S. Bankruptcy Code provides great benefits to debtors, some of which are listed in Table 11.8. The debtor is left in charge of the business and allowed to operate relatively free of close control. Some people are critical of what they perceive as a process that overly favors the debtor at the expense of the creditors' interests.[6] The law, however, seeks to rehabilitate the debtor so that it may become a viable business and a productive member of the business community.

---

5. Rosemary E. Williams and Daniel P. Jakala, *Bankruptcy Practice Handbook* (Deerfield, Ill.: Callaghan & Company, 1990), p. 11:54.

6. Lawrence H. Kallen, *Corporate Welfare: The Mega-Bankruptcies of the 80s and 90s* (New York: Lyle Stuart, 1991).

Table 11.8.   Benefits of Chapter 11 for Debtors

- The ability to restrain creditors from seizing the debtor's property or canceling beneficial contracts and to stay judicial actions against the debtor
- The ability to continue to operate the business effectively without interference from creditors
- The ability to borrow money by granting liens on debtor's assets equal to or superior to the liens of the existing creditors
- The ability to avoid certain transfers that occurred before the filing of the bankruptcy petition
- The cessation of interest accrual on debts that were unsecured as of the filing date
- The ability to propose and negotiate a single plan with all of the debtor's creditors
- The power to bind dissenting creditors to a reorganization plan that meets the Bankruptcy Code standard
- The receipt of a discharge by the bankruptcy court of all prepetition claims treated under the reorganization plan

Source: William A. Slaughter and Linda G. Worton, "Workout or Bankruptcy?" in Dominic DiNapoli, Sanford C. Sigoloff, and Robert F. Cushman, eds., *Workouts and Turnarounds* (Homewood, Ill.: Business One Irwin, 1991), pp. 72–96.

COMPANY SIZE AND CHAPTER 11 BENEFITS

The fact that debtors enjoy unique benefits while operating under the protection of the bankruptcy process is clear. Smaller companies, however, may not enjoy the same benefits that the process bestows on larger counterparts. A study by Turnaround Management Associates showed that the probability of surviving the Chapter 11 process is directly related to the size of the company.[7] Figure 11.4 shows that 69% of the larger companies, those with revenues in excess of $100 million, survived the process and were viable afterward, whereas only 30% of the smaller firms, those with revenues under $25 million, were able to do so.

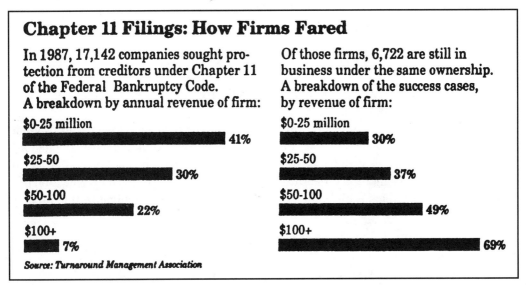

Figure 11.4.   How Chapter 11 firms fared by company size.

7. *Wall Street Journal,* 14 July 1988, p. 29.

The reason for the size differential in survival rates is that larger companies are in a better position to handle the additional unique demands placed on a Chapter 11 debtor. For example, the bankruptcy process is very demanding on management time. Before the bankruptcy, management presumably was devoting all its time to managing the business, and the business still was not successful. Now management has to devote its time to managing the business and dealing with the time demands that the bankruptcy litigation imposes. This task may be more difficult for smaller companies, where management is not as deep as in larger firms.

Although the additional expenses of the bankruptcy process may be relatively small compared with a larger company's revenue base, such expenses may be an additional burden that a smaller business cannot handle. For example, Lawrence A. Weiss reports that direct costs average 3.1% of the book value of the debt, plus the market value of the equity.[8] Professional fees may be very high—particularly in larger bankruptcies. For example, in the Johns Manville bankruptcy, professional fees were almost $200 million.[9] For a small firm with a thin capitalization, percentages may be much higher than the average reported by Weiss. For these reasons, Chapter 11 may be an excellent choice for some large companies but may not be a good idea for smaller businesses.

Projections Done in Chapter 11

Before emerging from Chapter 11, a company is required to put forward certain financial and operational projections as part of its reorganization plan. These projections include balance sheets, income statements, and cash flow statements. Michel, Shaked, and McHugh followed 35 Chapter 11 companies from 1989 to 1995.[10] They found that these projections were frequently overstated—sometimes significantly so. For example, they found that actual sales generally lagged projected sales in the first year after emerging from Chapter 11. In some cases the overstatement was as much as 20%.

PREPACKAGED BANKRUPTCY

A new type of bankruptcy emerged in the late 1980s. By 1993 it accounted for one-fifth of all distressed restructurings (Table 11.9).

In a prepackaged bankruptcy, the firm negotiates the reorganization plan with its creditors before an actual Chapter 11 filing. Ideally, the debtor would like to have solicited and received an understanding with the creditors that the plan would be approved after the filing. In a prepackaged bankruptcy, the parties try to have the terms of the reorganization plan approved in advance. This is different from the typical Chapter 11 reorganization process,

---

8. Lawrence A. Weiss, "Bankruptcy Resolution: Direct Costs and Violation of Priority of Claims," *Journal of Financial Economics* 27, no. 2 (October 1990), pp. 285–314.

9. William Slaughter and Linda Worton, "Workout or Bankruptcy?" in Dominic DiNapoli, Sanford C. Sigoloff, and Robert F. Cushman, eds., *Workouts and Turnarounds* (Homewood, Ill.: Business One Irwin, 1991), p. 87.

10. Allen Michel, Isreal Shaked, and Christopher McHugh, "After Bankruptcy: Can Ugly Ducklings Turn into Swans?" *Financial Analysts Journal* 54, no. 3 (May-June 1998), pp. 31–40.

Table 11.9.   Distressed Restructurings, 1986–93

Year[a]	Traditional Chapter 11 Prepacks/Total Filings by Public Firms[b]	Distressed Exchange Offers for Public Debt[c]	Filings	Prepackaged Chapter 11 Restructurings(%)[d]
1986	148	10	1	0.6
1987	112	15	0	0.0
1988	121	17	1	0.7
1989	132	15	3	2.0
1990	113	25	5	3.5
1991	120	25	10	6.5
1992	78	16	17	15.3
1993	71	12	20	19.4

[a]Year is the year the restructuring was initiated.

[b]Traditional Chapter 11 filings are identified from *The Bankruptcy Yearbook and Almanac* (1993).

[c]Distressed exchange offers are identified from First Boston's *High Yield Handbook,* the Nexis database, and Standard & Poor's *Creditweek.*

[d]Prepackaged bankruptcies are identified from *The Bankruptcy Yearbook and Almanac* (1993), The Bankruptcy DataSource, and the Nexis database.

Source: Brian Betker, "An Empirical Examination of Prepackaged Bankruptcy," *Financial Management* 24, no. 1 (Spring 1995), pp. 3–18.

which may feature a time-consuming and expensive plan development and approval process in which the terms and conditions of the plan are agreed to only after a painstaking negotiation process.

The first major prepackaged bankruptcy was the Crystal Oil Company, an oil and natural gas exploration company located in Louisiana.[11] The total time between the bankruptcy filing in 1986 and the company's emergence was only three months. During this time the company negotiated a new capital structure in which it reduced its total indebtedness from $277 million to $129 million.[12] As is typical of such debt restructurings, the creditors received other securities, such as equity and convertible debt and warrants, in exchange for the reduction in the original debt.

Benefits of Prepackaged Bankruptcy

The completion of the bankruptcy process is usually dramatically shorter in a prepackaged bankruptcy than in the typical Chapter 11 process. Both time and financial resources are saved. This is of great benefit to the distressed debtor, who would prefer to conserve financial resources and spend as little time as possible in the suspended Chapter 11 state.[13]

---

11. John J. McConnell, "The Economics of Prepackaged Bankruptcy," *Journal of Applied Corporate Finance* 4, no. 2 (September 1991), pp. 93–97.

12. Ibid.

13. Critics of the Chapter 11 debtor benefits would disagree. They would contend that some Chapter 11 companies prefer the benefits that protection of the Bankruptcy Code gives them and try to exploit these advantages over their creditors for as long as possible. Therefore, they are not in a hurry to leave the Chapter 11 protection.

In addition, a prepackaged bankruptcy reduces the holdout problem associated with voluntary nonbankruptcy agreements. In such agreements, the debtor often needs to receive the approval of all the creditors. This is difficult when there are many creditors, particularly many small creditors. One of the ways a voluntary agreement is accomplished is to pay all the small creditors 100% of what they are owed and pay the main creditors, who hold the bulk of the debt, an agreed upon lower amount.

It was noted previously that approval of a Chapter 11 reorganization plan requires creditors' approval equal to one-half in number and two-thirds in dollar amount. With the imminent threat of a Chapter 11 filing, creditors know that after the filing is made, these voting percentages, as opposed to unanimity, will apply. Therefore, if the threat of a Chapter 11 filing is real, the postbankruptcy voting threshold will become the operative one during the prepackaged negotiation process.

Pre-Voted versus Post-Voted PrePacks

The voting approval for the prepackaged bankruptcy may take place before or after the plan is filed. In a "pre-voted prepack" the results of the voting process are filed with the bankruptcy petition and reorganization plan. In a "post-voted prepack" the voting process is overseen by the bankruptcy court after the Chapter 11 filing. In a study of 49 prepackaged bankruptcies, Tashjian, Lease, and McConnell found that pre-voted prepacks spend less time in bankruptcy court but devote more time in prefiling negotiations.[14] Pre-voted prepacks also had lower direct costs as a fraction of assets and had higher recovery rates for non-equity obligations.

Tax Advantages of Prepackaged Bankruptcy

A prepackaged bankruptcy may also provide tax benefits because net operating losses are treated differently in a workout than in a bankruptcy. For example, if a company enters into a voluntary negotiated agreement with debt holders whereby debt holders exchange their debt for equity and the original equity holders now own less than 50% of the company, the company may lose its right to claim net operating losses in its tax filings. The forfeiture of these tax-loss carryforwards may have adverse future cash flow consequences. In bankruptcy, however, if the court rules that the firm was insolvent, as defined by a negative net asset value, the right to claim loss carryforwards may be preserved. Brian Betker estimates that the present value of future taxes saved by restructuring through a prepackaged bankruptcy, as opposed to a workout, is equal to 3% of total assets.

If a debtor company reaches a voluntary agreement whereby creditors agree to cancel a certain percentage of the debt—say, one-third—this amount is treated as income for tax purposes, thus creating a tax liability. A similar debt restructuring in bankruptcy, however, does not create such a tax liability.[15]

---

14. Elizabeth Tashjian, Ronald Lease, and John J. McConnell, "Prepacks: An Empirical Analysis of Prepackaged Bankruptcies," *Journal of Financial Economics* 40, no. 1 (January 1996), pp. 135–162.

15. McConnell, "The Economics of Prepackaged Bankruptcy," pp. 93–97.

WORKOUTS

A *workout* refers to a negotiated agreement between the debtors and its creditors outside the bankruptcy process. The debtor may try to extend the payment terms, which is called *extension,* or convince creditors to agree to accept a lesser amount than they are owed, which is called *composition.* A workout differs from a prepackaged bankruptcy in that in a workout the debtor either has already violated the terms of the debt agreements or is about to. In a workout, the debtor tries to convince creditors that they would be financially better off with the new terms of a workout agreement than with the terms of a formal bankruptcy.

Benefits of Workouts

The main benefits of workouts are cost savings and flexibility.[16] Workout agreements generally cost less to both the debtor and the creditors in terms of the resources the participants need to devote to the agreement process. In addition, participants in a workout are not burdened by the rules and regulations of Chapter 11 of the Bankruptcy Code. They are free to create their own rules as long as the parties agree to them. They also avoid the public scrutiny, such as from opening accounting records to the public, that would occur in a bankruptcy filing. Workouts may also help the debtor avoid any business disruption and loss of employees and overall morale that might occur in a bankruptcy. With these benefits come certain risks. The key risk is the holdout problem discussed previously. If this problem cannot be circumvented, a bankruptcy filing may be the only viable alternative.

Recognizing Better Workout Candidates

Depending on the particular financial circumstances of the company and the personal makeup of the parties involved, a negotiated private settlement outside the bankruptcy process may or may not be possible. Gilson, John, and Lang analyzed 169 debt restructurings from 1978 to 1987 and found that 52.7% of them ended up in bankruptcy.[17] They found that two-day average stock returns around the restructuring announcement equaled 21.6% for successful firms, whereas they were 26.3% for those firms that were not successful in reaching a nonbankruptcy restructuring agreement. This suggests that the market is capable of determining in advance which firms will be able to reach such an agreement.

Evidence on Role of Transactions Costs in Voluntary Restructuring versus Chapter 11 Decision

Stuart Gilson analyzed 108 publicly traded companies between 1980 and 1989 that either restructured their debt out of court (57 companies) or reorganized under Chapter 11 (51

16. Slaughter and Worton, "Workout or Bankruptcy?" pp. 72–96.
17. Stuart C. Gilson, Kose John, and Larry H. P. Lang, "Troubled Debt Restructurings: An Empirical Study of Private Reorganization of Firms in Default," *Journal of Financial Economics* 27, no. 2 (October 1990), pp. 315–354.

companies).[18] He found that the firms that attempt voluntary restructuring outside Chapter 11 were less able to reduce their leverage compared with Chapter 11 firms. He traced the problem to higher transactions costs of voluntary restructuring. Examples of these costs include the credit holdout problem, which makes it difficult to get all creditors to participate in the agreement. This problem is greater for holders of smaller claims who have an incentive to hold up transactions until they receive preferential treatment. Although a small number of such creditors may not be as much of a problem, the situation becomes very difficult if there are numerous creditors with similar motivations. Other difficulties of voluntary restructuring include the fact that creditors may be less willing to exchange their debt for equity when managers of the company have a significant informational advantage over them. This disadvantage renders creditors less able to assess the value of the equity they would receive in exchange for their debt claims. One additional factor is that institutional holders of debt may simply prefer debt to equity and may not want to voluntarily become an equity holder. These issues become moot when the process moves into Chapter 11 and the position of the debtor improves.

CORPORATE CONTROL AND DEFAULT

When a firm defaults, it typically loses control, which is passed to its creditors. Creditors may then acquire seats on the defaulting firm's board of directors and may even require that there be a change in management. Creditors may also receive an ownership position in the debtor in exchange for other consideration, such as a reduction in the amount owed. Stuart Gilson analyzed a sample of 111 publicly held companies that experienced significant financial distress between 1979 and 1985.[19] Of this sample, 61 filed for Chapter 11 and 50 restructured their debt privately. He found that banks received an average of 36% of the distressed firm's stock. Of this sample, Gilson found that only 46% and 43% of the pre-distress directors and chief executive officers (CEOs), respectively, remained in place two years later, when they had either emerged from bankruptcy or reached a negotiated restructuring agreement. It is interesting that directors who resign from distressed boards serve less often than other directors on other boards. As might be expected, very few of the distressed firms were involved in acquisition-related activity during this period.

LIQUIDATION

Liquidation is a distressed firm's most drastic alternative, and it is usually pursued only when voluntary agreement and reorganization cannot be successfully implemented. In a liquidation, the company's assets are sold and the proceeds are used to satisfy claims. The sales are made pursuant to the regulations that are set forth under Chapter 7 of the Bankruptcy Code. The priority of satisfaction of claims is as follows:

---

18. Stuart Gilson, "Transactions Costs and Capital Structure Choice: Evidence from Financially Distressed Firms," *Journal of Finance* 52, no. 1 (March 1997), pp. 161–196.

19. Stuart C. Gilson, "Bankruptcy, Boards, Banks, and Blockholders: Evidence on Changes in Corporate Ownership and Control When Firms Default," *Journal of Financial Economics* 27, no. 2 (October 1990), pp. 355–388.

- Secured creditors. If the amount owed exceeds the proceeds from the sale of the asset, the remainder becomes an unsecured claim.
- Bankruptcy administrative costs
- Postpetition bankruptcy expenses
- Wages of workers owed for three months before the filing (limit $2,000 per employee)
- Employee benefit plan contributions owed for six months before the filing (limit $2,000 per employee)
- Unsecured customer deposits (limit $900)
- Federal, state, and local taxes
- Unfunded pension liabilities (limit 30% book value of preferred and common equity; any remainder becomes an unsecured claim)
- Unsecured claims
- Preferred stockholders (up to the par value of their stock)
- Common stockholders

Liquidation Example: Eastern Packaging Company

Eastern Packaging Company Balance Sheet

Current assets	50,000	Accounts payable	15,000
		Bank notes payable	15,000
		Accrued wages 750 @ $800 per/worker	600
		Taxes	5,400
		Total current assets	36,000
Fixed assets	50,000	First mortgage	10,000
		Second mortgage	5,000
		Subordinated debentures	15,000[a]
		Total long-term debt	30,000
		Preferred stock	4,000
		Common stock	20,000
		Retained earnings	10,000
		Total equity	34,000
Total assets	100,00	Total claims	100,000

[a]Subordinated to notes payable

Let us assume that the assets of the company are sold, and liquidation proceeds are equal to $60 million.

Distribution of Priority Claims

Liquidation proceeds	$40,000,000
Proceeds from sale of first mortgage assets	5,000,000
Administrative bankruptcy expenses	3,000,000
Wages due for 3 months prior to bankruptcy	600,000
Taxes	5,400,000
Available to general creditors	26,000,000
Unadjusted general creditor percentage	65.0%

General Creditor Claims	Claim Amount	65.0%	After Subordination Adjustment	% of Original Claim Received
Unsatisfied 1st mortgage	5,000,000	3,250,000	3,250,000	82.5
2nd mortgage	5,000,000	3,250,000	3,250,000	65.0
Notes payable	15,000,000	9,750,000	15,000,000	100
Accounts payable	15,000,000	9,750,000	9,750,000	65.0
Subordinated debentures	15,000,000	9,750,000	4,500,000	30.0

INVESTING IN THE SECURITIES OF DISTRESSED COMPANIES

Investing in the securities of distressed companies may offer great profit potential, but only if the buyer is willing to assume significant risks. Distressed securities are defined as the bonds or stocks of companies that have defaulted on their debt obligations or have filed for Chapter 11. The market for these securities grew significantly in the late 1980s through the 1990s. In the early 1970s it was uncommon to find quotes for the securities of bankrupt firms.[20] This changed in the 1980s, when such quotes were common. Investment firms dedicated to the distressed securities field began to actively manage distressed securities portfolios.

The prices of bonds of a distressed company decline significantly as the company defaults on these obligations. Table 11.10 shows that this price decline is greater when the claim is less senior.

Returns on Distressed Debt Securities

Returns on distressed debt securities have a unique profile. Hradsky and Long found that returns start to become negative approximately 18 months before default as the market internalizes information on the weak condition of the issuer.[21] These returns start to turn sharply negative five months before default and bottom out at approximately –40% around five months after default (Figure 11.5). If investors were to buy after default, returns would equal 7.5% over the two-year postdefault period.

Edward Altman created an index of defaulted debt securities covering the period January 1987 through July 1990.[22] As expected, he found highly variable returns, which were as high as 37.9% in 1987 and 26.5% in 1988 but as low as 223.0% in 1989. He found an average annual rate of return over this period of 10%. This exceeded the high-yield index return for the same period, which was equal to 6.7%. One must be careful drawing long-term conclusions from this short analysis period. However, there is some evidence to support the high-return but high-risk attributes of distressed debt securities.

20. Dale Morse and Wayne Shaw, "Investing in Bankrupt Companies," *Journal of Finance* 43, no. 5 (December 1988), pp. 1193–1206.

21. G. Hradsky and R. Long, "High Yield Default Losses and the Return Performance of Bankrupt Debt," *Financial Analysts Journal* (July-August 1989), p. 46.

22. Edward I. Altman, "Investing in Distressed Securities," in Dominic DiNapoli, Sanford C. Sigoloff, and Robert F. Cushman, eds., *Workouts and Turnarounds* (Homewood, Ill.: Business Irwin One, 1991), pp. 663–685.

Table 11.10.   Weighted Average Price of Defaulted Bonds at End of Default Month as Percent of Face Value, January 1, 1977–March 31, 1991

Bond Class	Price/Face Value (%)
Senior secured	54.6
Senior unsecured	40.6
Senior subordinated	31.3
Subordinated	30.1
Junior subordinated	23.0
All bonds	34.2

Source: Salomon Brothers Study (April 18, 1991) as cited in Stuart C. Gilson, "Investing in Distressed Situations: A Market Survey," *Financial Analysts Journal* (November- December 1995), pp. 8–27.

Altman also analyzed the correlation of the returns on debt securities to those on other major categories of investments. Portfolio theory shows that if there is a low correlation between returns on distressed securities and other potential investment portfolio components, these securities may provide diversification benefits.[23] He found a lower than expected correlation, 0.56, between the returns on distressed debt securities and high-yield bonds (Table 11.11). This suggests that managers of high-yield portfolios might want to consider adding distressed debt securities to this nondefaulted high-yield portfolio to increase their overall returns while obtaining some diversification benefits.

Control Opportunities Using Distressed Debt Securities

One of the typical changes that a reorganized company undergoes in the Chapter 11 process is to have its capital structure altered, with some debt being replaced by equity and

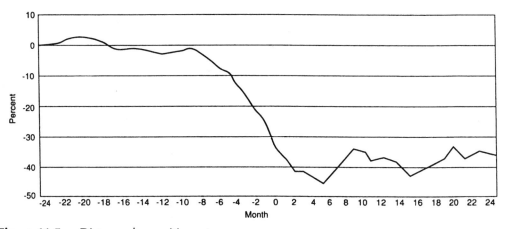

Figure 11.5.   Distressed securities returns.

Source: G. Hradsky and R. Long, "High Yield Default Losses and the Return Performance of Bankrupt Debt," *Financial Analysts Journal* (July–August 1989): 46.

23. For a good discussion of portfolio theory, see Sid Mittra and Chris Gassen, *Investment Analysis and Portfolio Management* (New York: Harcourt Brace Jovanovich, 1981).

Table 11.11.   Correlation Matrix between Defaulted Debt Security Returns and Various Equity and High-Yield Bond Returns

			Monthly Returns Observations, 1987–90	
	Defaulted Debt	S&P 500 Equity	Value Line Equity	Merrill Lynch High-Yield
Defaulted Debt	1.00	0.50	0.59	0.56
S&P 500 Equity	0.50	1.00	0.87	0.56
Value Line Equity	0.59	0.87	1.00	0.69
Merrill Lynch High-Yield	0.56	0.56	0.69	1.00

Source: Edward I. Altman, "Investing in Distressed Securities," in Dominic DiNapoli, Sanford C. Sigoloff, and Robert Cushman, eds., *Workouts and Turnarounds* (Homewood, Ill.: Business One Irwin, 1991), pp. 663–685.

some, possibly all, prepetition equity disappearing. Debt holders may become equity holders. Buyers of distressed debt securities may actually be seeking to obtain an equity stake in the distressed company when they purchase the debt securities. This has helped fuel the market for *claims trading.* Investors in Chapter 11 companies may buy the claims themselves or purchase components of the bankrupt company as the firm seeks to finance its turnaround or *fund its reorganization plan.*

The more aggressive of these opportunistic investors are sometimes referred to as *bankruptcy sharks* or *vultures.* They purchase the debt of bankrupt companies with a goal of taking control of the company. The strategy may yield high returns to those who are able to aggressively participate in the reorganization negotiation process to acquire the desired control. Although the securities may be purchased relatively inexpensively (Table 11.9), the outcome of the negotiation process, which may be quite lengthy, is very uncertain. For this reason, this type of takeover strategy is particularly risky.

CASE STUDY: CAMPEAU BANKRUPTCY

In January 1988 Campeau Corporation launched a takeover of Federated Stores. The company had a market value of $4.25, with $2.93 billion being equity and $1.33 billion being debt. The purchase price was double the market value of the company ($8.17 billion). The deal was a highly leveraged transaction, with 97% of the total value financed by debt.

In the beginning of 1990, after two years of troubled operations in which the company failed to refinance its takeover debt and bridge loans through the issuance of junk bonds, Campeau filed for Chapter 11 reorganization. Campeau's management of Federated Stores was poor. Under Campeau's reign the company suffered through a difficult Christmas season in 1990, which was also affected by the overall downturn in the economy as the country moved into a recession. In the period between the acquisition and the bankruptcy filing, earnings before interest, taxes, depreciation, and amortization (EBITDA) declined. The board of directors took away all operating responsibility from Robert Campeau. The company had excess inventories and had to lower prices in an effort to sell off these inventories while paying down the debt.

During bankruptcy, a management team composed of new CEO Allen Questrom, President James Zimmerman, and CFO Ronald Tysoe increased operating efficiency and raised capital through asset sales while managing to keep most of the management team of this large department store chain mainly intact. They sold off or closed unprofitable stores, streamlined operations, and remodeled stores that needed improvement.

Steven Kaplan concludes that the Chapter 11 process worked remarkably well.[a] The process was not costly in terms of a deterioration of value. He compared the value of the postbankrupt company with the preacquisition value. He measured the postbankruptcy value of Federated, net of bankruptcy costs and inclusive of interim cash flows earned during bankruptcy. As Table 1 shows, the value of the company increased with the acquisition from a preacquisition market value of $4.25 billion to the $8.17 billion value Campeau paid. Using the preceding definition of value, Kaplan computed a $7.81 billion value before an adjustment for market fluctuations. After taking into account market fluctuations, he arrived at a substantially higher value ($11.31).

a. Steven N. Kaplan, "Campeau's Acquisition of Federated Stores," *Journal of Financial Economics* 35, no. 1 (February 1994): 123–136.

Table 1. Post-Campeau Federated Value, Pre-Campeau Federated Value, and Campeau Purchase Price

Market-adjusted and nominal values[a] of Federated Department Stores (A) post-Campeau, post–Chapter 11, (B) pre-Campeau, and (C) purchase price paid by Campeau Corporation. Post-Campeau, post–Chapter 11 value of Federated equals the sum of asset sales, interim cash flows, and the value of remaining Federated assets. All sales are in billions of dollars.

	Market-Adjusted December 1987	Market-Adjusted February 1992	Nominal
(A) Post-Campeau, post-Chapter 11 Federated market value			
Asset sales[b]	3.77	7.31	4.04
Interim cash flows	0.79	1.52	1.29
Less direct costs of bankruptcy[c]	(0.14)	(0.27)	(0.27)
Value remaining assets	1.41	2.75	2.75
Total	5.85	11.31	7.81
(B) Pre-Campeau Federated market value[d]	4.25	8.25	4.25
(C) Price paid by Campeau for Federated[e]	7.67	14.89	8.17

[a]Market-adjusted values in December 1987 equal the actual values discounted from the month in which they occur to December 31, 1987, by the actual return on the S&P 500. If invested in the S&P 500 on January 1, 1988, the market-adjusted value would equal the actual value in the month the cash flow occurs. The market-adjusted values in February 1992 equal the actual values adjusted from the month in which they occur to February 1992, by the actual return on the S&P 500 over that period.

[b]Asset sales are the value of the divisions sold by Federated from May 1988 to February 1989. These values are detailed in Kaplan (1989).

[c]Interim cash flow equals EBITDA, less capital expenditures, less the increase in net working capital, plus the proceeds from asset sales, less taxes paid.

[d]Pre-Campeau Federated market value on December 31, 1987, equals the sum of the market value of Federated debt.

[e]Purchase price paid by Campeau is the sum of the market value paid for all equity and the fees paid in May 1988 and the book value of Federated debt outstanding on January 30, 1988.

Kaplan's analysis shows that a leveraged acquisition may increase value even if the company proves not to have sufficient cash flows to service its debt. Campeau's inability to service its debt led to its Chapter 11 filing. However, the Chapter 11 process did not result in a deterioration in value of the bankrupt company. Kaplan does not imply that this is the rule. Rather, he uses the Campeau Chapter 11 reorganization to illustrate that if the process is handled correctly, Chapter 11 does not necessarily result in a loss of company value.

Role of Vulture Investors and the Market for Control for Distressed Firms

Hotchkiss and Mooradian analyzed the role of vulture investors in the governance of 288 firms that defaulted on their debt between 1980 and 1993.[24] Contrary to the reputation that such investors have, Hotchkiss and Mooradian's research found that they had a positive effect on the post-debt operating performance. They found that post-restructuring operating performance was improved relative to the predefault level when the vulture investor becomes CEO or in some way gains control of the company. They attribute this improved performance to enhanced managerial discipline. It is interesting that they also found that a greater percentage of vulture firms were reorganized under Chapter 11 (70.3% for vulture firms versus 39% for non–vulture firms), indicating that these investors seek the benefits of the Chapter 11 process more then management.

SUMMARY

The world of bankruptcy changed dramatically in the 1980s as companies began to discover the creative corporate finance uses of Chapter 11 of the Bankruptcy Code. Chapter 11 reorganization became a method of corporate restructuring that under certain circumstances can bestow significant benefits to the distressed company. By formulating a reorganization plan, the company may restructure its liabilities and engage in other forms of restructuring, such as selling off assets to fund the plan. The Chapter 11 company obtains an automatic stay after entering Chapter 11, and creditors are held at bay by the court while the debtor and possibly the creditors structure a reorganization plan.

The reorganization plan must be approved by creditors before being approved by the court. Initially, only the debtor may propose a reorganization plan. This time period is called the exclusivity period. At the end of this period, which is initially 120 days but is often extended by the court, the creditors may propose an alternative plan if they oppose aspects of the debtor's plan. The plan must be fair and feasible as determined by the court. If all classes of creditors fail to approve the plan, it may be crammed down on the dissenting class, as long as there is one class that approves it.

Prepackaged bankruptcies became popular in the late 1980s. In a prepackaged bankruptcy, approval of a plan is obtained before entering bankruptcy. The bankruptcy process is

---

24. Edith S. Hotchkiss and Robert M. Mooradian, "Vulture Investors and the Market for Control of Distressed Firms," *Journal of Financial Economics* 43 (1997), pp. 401–432.

significantly shorter in a prepackaged bankruptcy. Therefore, there is less disruption to the debtor's business, and both debtors and creditors may gain from this form of reorganization. There also may be tax advantages that this alternative may pose that are not available in a workout. A workout is a voluntary agreement that does not involve a bankruptcy filing.

Trading in the securities of bankrupt companies, both bonds and equity, may be a high-risk way to implement a takeover. The purchasers of the securities may participate in the bankruptcy process in an effort to win control of the postbankrupt company. Although this method may enable a company to be taken over relatively inexpensively, it is highly unpredictable and fraught with risk for these investors.

REFERENCES

Altman, Edward I. "Investing in Distressed Securities." In Dominic DiNapoli, Sanford C. Sigoloff, and Robert Cushman, eds. *Workouts and Turnarounds* (Homewood, Ill.: Business One Irwin, 1991), pp. 663–685

Andrade, Gregor, and Steven N. Kaplan. "How Costly is Financial (Not Economic) Distress? Evidence from Highly Leveraged Transactions that Became Distressed." *Journal of Finance* 53, no. 5 (October 1998).

Betker, Brian. "An Empirical Examination of Prepackaged Bankruptcy." *Financial Management* 24, no. 1 (Spring 1995).

Denis, David J., and Diane K. Denis. "Causes of Financial Distress Following Leveraged Recapitalizations." *Journal of Financial Economics* 37 (1995).

Gilson, Stuart C. "Bankruptcy, Boards, Banks, and Blockholders: Evidence on Changes in Corporate Ownership and Control When Firms Default." *Journal of Financial Economics* 27, no. 2 (October 1990).

Gilson, Stuart C. "Investing in Distressed Situations: A Market Survey." *Financial Analysts Journal* (November–December 1995).

Gilson, Stuart C., John Kose, and Larry H. P. Lang. "Troubled Debt Restructurings: An Empirical Study of Private Reorganization of Firms in Default." *Journal of Financial Economics* 27, no. 2 (October 1990).

Gilson, Stuart C. "Transactions Costs and Capital Structure Choice: Evidence from Financially Distressed Firms." *Journal of Finance* 52, no. 1 (March 1997).

Harwood, Jeremy J. O. "Basics of Bankruptcy." *MAINBRACE Newsletter* 6, no. 2 (New York: Healy & Baillie Law Firm, July 1995).

Hotchkiss, Edith S., and Robert M. Mooradian. "Vulture Investors and the Market for Control of Distressed Firms." *Journal of Financial Economics* 43 (1997).

Hradsky, G., and R. Long. "High Yield Default Losses and the Return Performance of Bankrupt Debt." *Financial Analyst Journal* (July-August 1989).

Kallen, Lawrence H. *Corporate Welfare: The Mega-Bankruptcies of 80s and 90s* (New York: Lyle Stuart, 1991).

Kaplan, Steven, and Jeremy Stein. "The Evolution of Buyout Pricing and the Financial Structure of the 1980s." *Quarterly Journal of Economics* (May 1993).

McConnell, John J. "The Economics of Prepackaged Bankruptcy." *Journal of Applied Corporate Finance* 4, no. 2 (September 1991).

Mittra, Sid, and Chris Gassen. *Investment Analysis and Portfolio Management* (New York: Harcourt Brace Jovanovich, 1981).

Morse, Dale, and Wayne Shaw. "Investing in Bankrupt Companies." *Journal of Finance* 43, no. 5 (December 1988).

Slaughter, William A., and Linda G. Worton. "Workout or Bankruptcy?" In Dominic Di-Napoli, Sanford C. Sigoloff, and Robert F. Cushman, eds. *Workouts and Turnarounds* (Homewood, Ill.: Business One Irwin, 1991), pp. 72–96.

Tashjian, Elizabeth, Ronald Lease, and John J. McConnell. "Prepacks: An Empirical Analysis of Prepackaged Bankruptcies." *Journal of Financial Economics* 40, no. 1 (January 1996).

Weiss, Lawrence A. "Bankruptcy Resolution: Direct Costs and Violation of Priority of Claims" *Journal of Financial Economics* 27, no. 2 (October 1990).

Williams, Rosemary E., and Daniel P. Jakala. *Bankruptcy Practice Handbook* (Deerfield, Ill.: Callaghan & Company, 1990).

Part Five

VALUATION FOR MERGERS AND ACQUISITIONS

12

FINANCIAL ANALYSIS

Many financial documents need to be analyzed when conducting a valuation of a potential target. The analysis should focus on both the acquirer and the target. The acquirer needs to ascertain the value of the target to determine the proper offering price and whether the target meets the acquirer's financial standards. The target, in turn, needs to know what its company is worth. Presumably, this will tell the acquirer's management and board of directors whether the offer is in the stockholders' best interests. As part of this analysis, a series of key financial statements are examined. Each acquisition candidate has its own unique characteristics that make it different from other firms. These novel aspects may be discerned after considering information other than what is contained within the four corners of the standard financial statements. Therefore, the framework of financial statement analysis presented in this chapter is a basic model that may be followed in an analysis of a merger or an acquisition. It is a minimum and should be supplemented by additional analysis that is required because of the unique aspects of each transaction.

This chapter provides a review of financial statements and financial ratio analysis. The discussion of financial statement analysis is not meant to be comprehensive. Rather, it is designed to highlight some of the basic financial issues that need to be considered in business valuations for mergers and acquisitions. A more thorough and detailed discussion may be found in most good corporate finance textbooks. Suggested references are provided at the end of the chapter.

The three most basic financial statements are the balance sheet, the income statement, and the statement of cash flows. Publicly held companies prepare these statements on a quarterly and an annual basis. The quarterly statements are available in the 10Q quarterly reports that are filed with the Securities and Exchange Commission (SEC). The annual statements are available in the firm's 10K and Annual Report. These statements are available through many mediums. They may be readily downloaded on-line from various data sources such as the Edgar database.

The financial analysis of a merger or acquisition is one part of the overall due diligence process. Before a deal is completed, there is a legal and accounting due diligence process that is usually pursued. Attorneys and accountants usually run through a series of checklists of items that must be addressed or gathered. This process usually includes various informational items that must be verified before completing the deal. Many items are reviewed when doing due diligence. These items are far too numerous to be listed here but some of these items include leases, loan agreements, minutes of board of directors' meetings, employment contracts, other relevant contracts, and so forth. Various published acquisition checklists are available.[1]

---

1. Joseph Morris, *Mergers and Acquisitions: Business Strategies for Accountants* (New York: John Wiley & Sons, 1995), pp. 36–121.

HOSTILE VERSUS FRIENDLY DEALS: ACCESS TO FINANCIAL DATA

One of the significant differences between friendly deals and hostile deals is the bidder's access to detailed financial data. In a friendly transaction, the bidder and the target may work closely together to reach an agreement. This often involves the target releasing detailed internal financial data that the bidder requests. The target does this to be able to sell the company for a certain goal price. In a hostile deal, the target usually gives the bidder only the minimum information required by the law. This may mean that the bidder has to conduct its valuation analysis using publicly available information, such as the financial statements that are required to be disclosed by securities laws. This puts the bidder at a disadvantage, particularly when the offer is for a multidivisional target that may not disclose much detail on the performance of specific divisions. This may be important because the bidder may be planning on selling off some divisions and using the proceeds to reduce the takeover financing obligations. Without detailed internal financial data, the bidder may have to estimate the performance of the divisions.

The bidder may try to force the target to provide such data by trying to have the court compel it to do so. Sometimes the bidder may indicate that, without any supporting financial data, it is unwilling to pay a price that the target indicates it is worth. This puts pressure on the target's board to release the information, lest the bidder withdraw its offer and shareholders incur losses. Although the target's board and management may truly want the bidder to withdraw the offer, the target's position is made more difficult because if a bidder's offer is withdrawn, ostensibly because of the target's unwillingness to comply with "reasonable" information requests, the target could become the object of a shareholders' lawsuit.

CASE STUDY: TRUMP VERSUS GRIFFIN AND RESORTS INTERNATIONAL

Exclusive reliance on public data is a disadvantage for the bidder. The bidder must then depend on the accuracy of financial statements, which may not be sufficiently detailed to give an accurate picture of the company's financial condition. This problem of relying on public data was highlighted in the takeover battle between Merv Griffin and Donald Trump over Resorts International, Inc.[a] Merv Griffin took over Resorts in November 1988. As of July 1989 Resorts' $925 million worth of bonds had fallen 42% in value as the market responded to the declining fortunes of the gambling and hotel concern. The 1989 debt service amounted to $133.6 million, whereas net income plus depreciation were estimated to be between $55 million and $68 million. Part of the problem resulted from an inaccurate estimate of the cash flows of Resorts, as well as the underestimated cost of maintaining some of Resorts' assets. For example, renovation costs for the hotel-casino in Atlantic City and the company's facilities on Paradise Island in the Bahamas proved to be higher than anticipated. Griffin estimated that the renovation costs would run to $50 million, but after the takeover he discovered that at least $100 million would be necessary.

---

[a] Pauline Yoshihasi and Neil Barsky, "Merv Griffin's Plunge into Casino Gambling Could Prove a Loser," *Wall Street Journal*, 5 July 1989, pp. A1 and A7. This example draws on data supplied by the authors of this article.

According to the *Wall Street Journal,* Griffin's projection of the sale prices of Resorts' land assets was unreasonably optimistic. In a New Jersey Casino Control Commission hearing in October 1988, Griffin's real estate appraiser valued the Atlantic City land at between $145 and $161 million. Market conditions brought the value well below that after the merger. Given the competitive nature of the Atlantic City casino business, Resorts needed to upgrade its facilities to remain on a par with the competition. This placed added pressure on the firm's cash flows, which were already stretched thin with the high debt service payments. Part of the problem was the limited data available to Griffin. Resorts' president, David P. Hanlon, reportedly stated, "We found a surprising number of things about the company that were different than what we anticipated." Apparently, the value of Resorts' assets had been overestimated. Moreover, other assets proved to require greater maintenance investments than they were thought to have needed.

BALANCE SHEET

The balance sheet, sometimes called the statement of financial position, is basically a snapshot of a firm's financial position at a given moment in time. The statement constructed on a different date may present a very different picture of the firm's financial position. This may be important for an analyst to bear in mind if he or she suspects that the seller is attempting to present an inaccurate picture of value to inflate the purchase price. The seller may attempt to temporarily alter the makeup of the balance sheet to try to receive a higher purchase price for the firm. In such instances, buyers must critically scrutinize the balance sheet to detect inaccuracies or inconsistencies. The balance sheet reflects information about the resources and assets of the company along with the firm's various obligations. The name *balance sheet* comes from the equality between assets and liabilities and stockholder equity. These two parts of the balance sheet are, by definition, always in balance because the difference between assets and liabilities is the value of stockholders' equity.

$$\text{Assets} - \text{liabilities} = \text{stockholders' equity}$$

The balance sheet is constructed so that current items appear before noncurrent items. A review of the items that normally appear in a balance sheet follows.

Assets

Current assets can be converted into cash within a year. Among the assets included here are cash, marketable securities, accounts receivable, inventories, and prepaid expenses.

Cash. Obviously, cash is the seller's most liquid asset. Firms concerned about being the object of a hostile bid may attempt to keep their cash reserves as low as the normal operation of the business will allow to prevent the cash from being used to finance the offer. Therefore, potential targets need to monitor their liquidity position.

This became an issue in 1995 when Kirk Kerkorian, a substantial shareholder in Chrysler Corporation, tried to use Chrysler's large cash position to finance the takeover of the automobile manufacturer. Chrysler rebuffed his overtures, contending that such larger cash reserves were necessary because of the cyclical nature of the industry.

Marketable Securities. Marketable securities are short-term investments of excess cash. Typical investments are Treasury securities, certificates of deposit (CDs), or other money market securities. Like cash, these very liquid assets can also be used to finance the target's own acquisition.

Accounts Receivable. Accounts receivable items reflect the amount of money the company expects to collect from sales. They include an allowance for bad debts based on the firm's historical collection efforts. The accounts receivable and the allowance for bad debts are usually shown separately, with the net accounts receivable shown in the far-right column of the balance sheet. Acquirers may want to qualify the target's accounts receivable through an aging analysis and only include those receivables that have a reasonable likelihood of being collected.

Inventories. Inventories include items such as work in progress, raw materials, and finished goods. Inventories are typically the least liquid asset of the firm. Goods that are finished are naturally considered more liquid than work in progress. Only those inventories that are marketable should be included in a valuation analysis. That is, obsolete inventories should be identified and eliminated.

Prepaid Expenses. Prepaid expenses items have already been paid in advance. Examples are insurance premiums or rent.

Other Assets. This category consists of items such as long-term investments, including the stocks or bonds of other companies. For firms that are active in takeovers, this category may be an important one. The value of these investments will depend on their liquidity and the size of the holdings. The greater the liquidity, the more valuable the asset. If the company holds a large amount of the available stock of a company that is traded on the over-the-counter market with a relatively small daily trading volume, the value of this asset may be questionable.

Plant and Equipment. Plant and equipment consists of the tangible capital assets of the firm. They are usually valued at cost, minus accumulated depreciation, and include land, buildings, machinery, and other tangible assets the firm may own, such as computer equipment, vehicles, and furniture. A buyer may attempt to revalue these assets at market prices rather than the book values that the balance sheet reflects. Quick sales of some of these assets may enable a buyer to pay down some of the debt assumed in a leveraged transaction. An inaccurate valuation of the market value of such assets may cause a buyer to assume more debt than the combined firms can handle. Some investment banks were the object of criticism in the late 1980s for presenting an overly optimistic picture of the market value of the assets of merger partners and leveraged buyout (LBO) candidates.

Liabilities

Current liabilities consist of those obligations that the firm must pay within one year. Among the liabilities included here are accounts payable, notes payable, accrued expenses, and long-term debts.

Accounts Payable. Accounts payable are the amounts owed by the firm to suppliers for credit purchases. For each accounts payable, there should be a corresponding accounts receivable on the supplier's balance.

Notes Payable. Notes payable are outstanding obligations, such as loans to commercial banks or obligations to other creditors.

Accrued Expenses. Accrued expenses are expenses for items that have been used to generate sales for which the firm has not paid. The firm may or may not have been billed for these goods or services.

Long-Term Debts. Long-term debts are obligations for which payment does not have to be made within one year. This might be, for example, the value of the bonds that the firm may have issued or term loans from financial institutions. The balance sheet should include, where relevant, the long-term obligations of the company, such as capital lease obligations, pension liabilities, and estimated liabilities under warranty agreements. Some explanation of these items may be contained in footnotes. Depending on the company's accounting practices, there may also be a description of deferred federal income taxes. This will be affected by tax law changes that will determine the firm's ability to shelter income through accelerated depreciation write-offs and other tax-avoidance methods. Buyers should be careful to detect the presence of hidden liabilities. These are the potential obligations of the seller that may not be explicitly highlighted on the firm's balance sheet. Such liabilities might include future environmental liabilities or losses from pending litigation. These hidden liabilities have become a greater cause for concern in certain industries, such as the chemicals industry.

Stockholders' Equity

This part of the balance sheet shows the owner's claims on the firm's assets after taking into account the obligations to creditors who have a prior claim before equity holders. It includes the ownership interests of both preferred and common stockholders.

Preferred Stock. The company may or may not have issued preferred stock. Preferred stock is more like debt than equity in that it usually pays a fixed dividend that must be paid before dividends are paid to common stockholders. As noted in Chapter 5, preferred stock has been used as a poison pill defense. This defense is not used as much as poison pill warrants because preferred stock issued by the firm must be clearly displayed on the balance sheet. Given its debtlike characteristics, this does not enhance the company's financial appearance.

Common Stock. Common stock represents the claims of ownership of the corporation. In the event of bankruptcy, common stock–holders have the last claim on the corporation's assets. Several different classes of common stock may exist. The issuance of different classes of common stock with different voting rights is another anti-takeover defense. The common stock is listed on the balance sheet at par value, an arbitrarily assigned value for the common stock that is used primarily for accounting purposes. It may also be used as an indicator of the value of the stock in the event of liquidation. It does not, however, have a useful relationship to the market price of the stock of a publicly held company.

Paid in Capital in Excess of Par. This is the amount of money received for the sale of the common stock that was in excess of the par value.

Retained Earnings. Retained earnings represent the earnings of the corporation not paid out in dividends. The retained earnings on the balance sheet are not a supply of available cash that is put into a bank account and used to pay bills. They are monies that may be used to finance fixed assets such as plant and equipment.

Issues Related to Understanding Balance Sheets

The balance sheet is important in mergers because it provides an indication of what the company's assets and equity are worth while also showing what the business owes. However, the values of the assets, liabilities, and equity cannot be literally taken from the balance sheet without further scrutiny. A few of the issues that should be considered are as follows:

- *Time element.* As mentioned, balance sheets reflect the company's position at an instant in time. The time period chosen therefore affects the value reflected on the balance sheet.
- *Cash versus noncash assets.* The only item on the balance sheet that is actual cash is the one listed as cash. Although the other assets are denoted in dollars, they are not cash. They may be, for example, receivables or inventories, but they cannot be used at the moment to directly pay bills. (It is possible, however, to factor receivables, for a fee, and receive cash to pay bills.)
- *Inventory accounting.* The value of the inventory is affected by the type of accounting method used—FIFO (first-in, first-out) or LIFO (last-in, first-out). The FIFO method assumes that the items the firm uses from its inventory are the oldest items in the inventory, whereas LIFO assumes that the items used are the newest. In a world of rising prices, FIFO will show lower costs and higher profits and will also result in a higher tax bill.

Areas to Consider in Analyzing Balance Sheets

The merger analyst needs to focus on numerous areas when reviewing balance sheets. Following is a sample of a few of these. It is important to remember that each merger or acquisition presents its own unique issues. Therefore, the items mentioned here are merely provided as examples of some that may be relevant.

- *Understated liabilities.* Beware when the firm has the discretion to estimate its own liabilities. Firms that are offering themselves for sale may want to understate liabilities to increase the value of the firm. Companies may estimate the potential liabilities in various areas, such as litigation, health care, and pension liabilities. The bad debt policy of the firm should be examined, particularly if the firm has increased its sales by selling to a *riskier* category of customers while not increasing the allowances for bad debts.
- *Low-quality assets.* It should be determined that the valuation of all major assets on the balance sheet accurately reflects the value these assets might command in the marketplace or their value to an acquirer. Assets that may be affected by changing

government policies, such as pollution control equipment, or assets that are related to the sale of products that may become obsolete must be examined more closely. Unfortunately, publicly available documents, such as annual reports, lack the detail necessary to determine the market value of some assets. This may be a problem for hostile bidders who may have to rely solely on public documents.

- *Overstated receivables.* A receivable is only as good as its likelihood of being paid. Receivables from firms that are in financial difficulty or that are subject to return policies may have to be revalued. In the garment industry, for example, if retailers believe that a manufacturer may go out of business, they may not pay the receivables. Slow collection of receivables and deteriorating liquidity may cause factors, financing sources that many manufacturers depend on, to freeze credit. This may quickly bring an end to the company. Receivables from firms that are affiliated with the parent company may have been "manufactured" to overstate the parent's value. In general, transactions with affiliates usually merit closer scrutiny.

- *Inventory.* Changes in the level of inventory from period to period need to be considered. A rapid buildup of inventory may signal a decreased marketability for the product. This is often the case, for example, in the toy business. Toys may quickly go from being valuable to being near valueless.

- *Valuation of securities.* For firms that have substantial assets in marketable securities, an analysis of the firm's portfolio must be conducted. The marketability of each security in the portfolio should be determined. The increased volatility of the securities markets has heightened the need to be cautious in valuing such assets. Substantial holdings of the debt or common stock of firms that are traded in thin markets may be of questionable value unless ownership in these firms is one of the acquirer's goals. The riskiness of the securities portfolio should comport with the risk preferences of the acquirer. The more marketable the securities and the smaller the holdings, the more likely the acquirer can sell them without incurring a significant cost.

- *Intangible assets.* Intangible assets, such as goodwill, although it is difficult to value, may be quite valuable. The name of an established business with a sound reputation in the marketplace may be valuable even though it is intangible. Assets such as patents may only be as valuable as the company's ability and will to defend them through costly litigation. Patents may sometimes be copied without incurring significant legal liability. When this is likely, careful consideration must be given before paying a high price for these assets.

- *Real estate assets.* Real estate assets have been a motivation for many takeover battles, such as the recent Campeau takeover of Federated Stores and Olympia and York's attempted takeover of Santa Fe–Southern Pacific. The valuation of these assets is subject to the vicissitudes of the real estate market. The importance of an accurate valuation of these assets is one reason the real estate expert became a more important part of the takeover team in the fourth merger wave. The slowed pace of mergers in the late 1980s, combined with the collapse of the real estate market beginning in 1986, reduced the importance of these specialists in acquisition analysis. The rebound of the real estate market in the mid-1990s, however, returned real estate valuation to greater prominence in merger and acquisition valuation.

- *Valuation of divisions.* The valuation of divisions of companies became crucial in the highly leveraged takeovers of the 1980s. The value that a division, subsidiary, or major asset might bring in the market will only be known after it has actually been sold. This problem may be prevented if the sale of certain assets can be prearranged with a third party. One problem with working with public documents such as annual reports is that it is difficult to get a detailed breakdown of the performance of separate divisions. Such information is hard to acquire in a hostile takeover. Sometimes an acquirer will resist increasing its bid unless the target provides the detailed information necessary to do a full evaluation.

INCOME STATEMENT

The income statement measures the net results of the firm's operations over a specific time interval, such as a calendar year or a fiscal year. A fiscal year is an accounting year that ends on a day other than December 31. The balance sheet and income statement are usually presented together. Most large companies typically prepare monthly statements for management and quarterly statements for stockholders. The balance sheet is usually prepared for the last date of the time period covered by the income statement. The income statement is sometimes referred to as the profit and loss statement. Items that appear in an income statement include:

Net Sales. Net sales are usually listed first on the income statement. Net sales means the sales after returns on goods shipped and other factors such as breakage. Cost of goods sold is deducted from net sales to determine the net operating profit.

Cost of Goods Sold. Cost of goods sold refers to the company's cost for the goods and services sold. For manufacturing firms, this includes labor, materials, and other items, such as overhead.

Gross Profits. Gross profits are the difference between sales revenues and the cost of goods sold. Gross profit divided by sales revenues is the gross profit margin, or gross margin.

Operating Expenses. Operating expenses are deducted from gross profits to determine operating profit. The main categories of operating expenses are selling expense, general and administrative expense, and depreciation expense.

EBITDA. Earnings before interest, taxes, depreciation, and amortization is often used as a proxy for cash flows in valuation analysis. Companies are often quoted as being worth certain multiples of EBITDA. It is basically operating income (EBIT) with noncash charges such as depreciation and amortization added back.

Operating Profit. Operating profit is also called earnings before interest and taxes (EBIT). Operating profit is often considered a good measure of managerial success. It reflects the profit derived from management's operating activities, not financing decisions or governmental tax obligations. It is often considered a good indicator of the target management's performance. Operating profit may be placed in perspective by considering it as a percentage of sales and comparing it with similarly sized firms in the same industry.

Interest Expense. Interest expense is deducted from operating profit to determine earnings before taxes (EBT).

Taxes. Taxes are deducted from EBT at the relevant tax rate for the corporation. The result is earnings after taxes.

Earnings Available for Common Stockholders. Preferred stock dividends are deducted from earnings after taxes to determine the income available for distribution to common stock–holders as dividends.

Earnings per Share (EPS). EPS is calculated by dividing the earnings available to common stock–holders by the number of shares of common stock outstanding.

Issues Related to Understanding Income Statements

Although there are many issues that are important to focus on when reviewing income statements, two issues that very often are relevant to valuations are depreciation policies and inventory valuation.

Depreciation
Depreciation refers to the charging of a portion of the cost of certain capital assets against revenues. Different methods of depreciation will result in different levels of taxable income for the same revenue stream. More rapid depreciation will show a lower taxable income. The Generally Acceptable Accounting Principles (GAAP) set forth the accepted methods of writing off an asset. The two primary methods are straight-line depreciation and accelerated depreciation. The same amount of depreciation is allowed under each method, but the timing of the write-off is different.

Valuing Inventory
The valuation of inventory will affect the value of cost of goods sold in the income statement. This factor, which was discussed in the context of balance sheet analysis, will affect profitability on the income statement. If a firm wants to appear more profitable, it may do so by using FIFO rather than LIFO inventory accounting.

Areas to Consider in Analyzing Income Statements

As with the balance sheet, there are various areas that the merger analyst needs to focus on when reviewing income statements. Perhaps the most important area is earnings quality. Also important is the related area of revenue recognition.

Quality of Earnings
The quality of earnings may be suspect for a variety of reasons. Some firms in industries that have been experiencing hard times have resorted to accounting manipulations to generate income. An example of this occurred in the thrift industry in 1984. Savings and loan associations (S&Ls) treated as income a stock dividend paid to them by the Federal Home Loan Mortgage Association (Freddie Mac), an institution owned by the thrifts, as income. The Financial Accounting Standards Board (FASB) stated that this was like paying yourself money. In 1984 the total profits of the S&L industry were $2.1 billion, but the stock dividend accounted for $600 million of this amount. The financial difficulties of the thrift

industry motivated many mergers as the industry sought to consolidate. The acquiring and merging firms had to examine the earnings and expected earnings of their merger partners to ascertain whether they were truly of high quality.

Another example of such low quality earnings occurs in the utilities industries, where the firms are allowed to claim income from projects under construction and allowance for funds used during construction (AFUDC) as earnings, even though the cash from the projects that are not even completed may not be realized until future reporting periods. In some cases, such as the WPPSS bankruptcy, some of these revenues were never realized because some power plants were never built.

Generally, the greater the noncash component of earnings, the lower their quality. The concern about earnings quality has placed greater emphasis on the cash flow statement and less focus on the income statement.

Revenue Recognition

A related point is that firms may alter the income that appears on their income statement through various accounting manipulations. For example, companies may recognize revenues for services that have not been performed and, in fact, may be performed in later time periods. This has the effect of increasing the profits in the current time period.[2]

STATEMENT OF CASH FLOWS

In November 1987 the FASB issued Financial Accounting Standard 95 (FAS 95), which required that, effective for all fiscal years subsequent to July 15, 1988, firms issue a statement of cash flows instead of a statement of changes in financial position. This statement would provide analysts and investors with valuable information about the cash receipts and cash payments of the firm. It shows the impact of the firm's operations, investment, and financial decisions on its cash position. (This is depicted in Figure 12.1.) Analyzing the statement of cash flows enables the merger analyst to assess the firm's ability to generate future cash flows that may be used to service the debt that might result from a merger or an LBO. The ability to generate sufficient cash flows may determine whether the firm can survive a leveraged transaction. More basically, firms have been forced into bankruptcy when their cash position deteriorated, even though their net income remained positive.

The highly leveraged deals that occurred in the fourth merger wave made cash flows even more important for firms that assumed the pressure of high debt service to finance the transactions. These high interest payments heightened the need to accurately predict the firm's ability to generate stable cash flows.

A classic example was W. T. Grant and Company, which filed for bankruptcy in 1975. The firm had been profitable for the years before the bankruptcy filing and showed a positive net income in those years.[3] Deterioration in cash flows, however, brought about the demise of this established company.

2. Joel G. Siegel, *How to Analyze Business, Financial Statements and the Quality of Earnings* (Englewood Cliffs, N.J.: Prentice-Hall, 1982), pp. 101–103.

3. Dennis E. Logue, *Handbook of Modern Finance* (Boston: Warren, Gorham and Lamont, 1984), pp. 15–19.

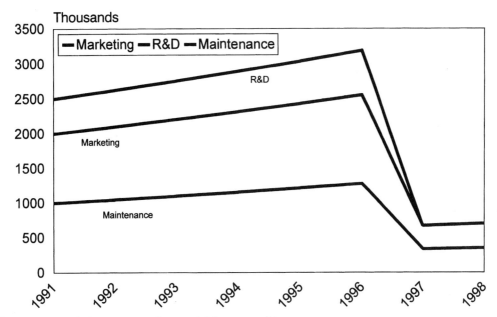

Figure 12.1.   Sales versus other variable expenditures.

The statement of cash flows adjusts net income to remove the noncash effects such as accruals of future cash receipts, gains and losses on sales of assets, and depreciation. In doing so, the statement of cash flows becomes a valuable measure of a firm's ability to generate cash, after taking into account the firm's cash needs. The difference between cash flows and net income may indicate the quality of earnings. The smaller this difference, the higher the quality of earnings. The ratio of cash flow to net income is often used as an indicator of earnings quality across different firms in the same industry.[4]

Depreciation and Cash Flows

The income statement and the statement of cash flows differ in how they treat depreciation. All noncash charges, those that do not involve a cash outlay, are added back to the net after-tax income to determine the cash flow. One of the major categories of noncash charges is depreciation. These charges are tax shields that minimize taxes but distort the firm's true cash flow. More basically, depreciation is neither a source nor a use of funds.

Free Cash Flows

Free cash flows became a buzzword in the fourth merger wave. It is defined differently by different users. One definition that is often used is:[5]

---

4. Joel Siegel and Anthony Akel, "A Financial Analysis and Evaluation of the Statement of Cash Flows," *The Practical Accountant* (June 1989), pp. 71–73.

5. R. Charles Moyer, James R. McGuigan, and William J. Kretlow, *Contemporary Financial Management,* 5th ed. (St. Paul: West, 1992), p. 66.

$$FCF = CF - I(1 - T) - Dp - Pf - B - Y \qquad (12.1)$$

where
FCF = free cash flow
  CF = after-tax operating cash flow
    I = before-tax interest payments
    T = firm's marginal tax rate
  Dp = preferred stock dividend payments
   Pf = required redemption of preferred stock
    B = required redemption of debt
    Y = investment in plant and equipment required to maintain cash flow

After-tax operating cash flows are defined as:

$$CF = (R - O - Dep)(1 - T) + Dep(T) - NWC \qquad (12.2)$$

where
    R = revenues
    O = operating expenses
  Dep = depreciation
NWC = net working capital

A firm is said to have free cash flows "when a firm is able to generate more cash flows from its ongoing operations than is needed to remain in business."[6]

Free cash flows can be projected into the future after taking into consideration the firm's future capital investment needs. Including capital investment enables free cash flows to be more than a short-term measure of the firm's health. Using free cash flows, as it is defined here, the analyst can measure both the quality of the firm's future earnings and the firm's ability to maintain its future competitive position.

ANALYSIS OF FINANCIAL STATEMENTS AND COMPUTER PROGRAMS

Having discussed the basics of financial statements, we will now analyze them to determine the firm's financial condition. The analyst's main tool is a spreadsheet program such as Lotus, Excel, or Quattro Pro, which allows the user to perform a great number of financial calculations very rapidly. It also permits a complete set of calculations to be redone instantly after certain changes have been enacted.

The various other software packages available are really large macro programs that use spreadsheet programs. The user loads the spreadsheet program and asks the program to use the financial programs written on this software package. One software package that provides good summary data for financial analysis, using Lotus, is Financial Calculator.[7] Among its many other functions, this package instantly provides a large array of financial

---

6. Kenneth Hackel and Joshua Livnat, *Cash Flow and Security Analysis* (New York: Business Irwin One, 1992), p. 167.

7. Sidney R. Finkel, *Financial Calculator* (Cincinnati: South-Western Publishing Co., 1987).

ratios after the user inputs the balance sheet and income statements. However, this package and others lack the flexibility to alter the framework to deal with the unique aspects of each merger. In effect, the user is locked into a standard framework that may not be very appropriate to the case at hand. Another such program is FINSOLVE,[8] which also uses Lotus to perform a variety of standard financial computations, such as financial statement analysis. In addition, Lotus offers various add-on templates to its Windows version 5.0 that compute financial ratios and even attempt to value businesses.

Software programs that do business valuations are available. One such program is Valu-Source.[9] This program does a complete valuation analysis that includes financial statement analysis but also goes so far as to do a complete valuation. It contains source data, such as comparable transaction data and risk premium data, using add-on data sets that are purchased separately. The advantage to using such a program is that the program will do a complete valuation and generate a report once the user inputs basic financial information. The disadvantage is that unless the user really understands valuation analysis, this process becomes a "black box." Therefore, it is important that the user thoroughly understand valuation analysis so that the valuation process and the resulting values can be explained and defended.

FINANCIAL RATIO ANALYSIS

Financial ratio analysis, one of the main tools of financial analysis, permits an easy comparison with similar firms, such as those in the same industry and of a similar size. Ratio analysis standardizes the financial data that help reduce the effect of factors such as sheer size. In doing so, the financial performance of acquisition candidates in the same industry that are of very different sizes may be better compared.

The more commonly used financial ratios are divided into the following categories:

- Liquidity ratios
- Activity ratios
- Financial leverage ratios
- Profitability ratios

Liquidity Ratios

Liquidity ratios measure the firm's ability to satisfy its current obligations as they come due. The two principal liquidity ratios are the current ratio and the quick ratio.

> Current ratio = Current assets/Current liabilities
> Quick ratio = (Current assets – Inventories)/Current liabilities
> Current assets = Cash plus all assets that can be converted into cash within a year. These include short-term marketable securities, accounts receivable, and inventories.

---

8. Allen Thompson, FINSOLVE (Cambridge: Basil Blackwell, 1996).
9. *ValuSource* (New York: John Wiley & Sons, 1998).

Current liabilities = All the financial obligations that are expected to be paid within a
                      year. These include accounts payable, notes payable, and the
                      current part of the long-term debt.
 Working capital = Current assets – Current liabilities

   The current ratio measures the firm's ability to meet its short-term obligations using assets that are expected to be converted into cash within a year. The quick ratio removes inventories from current assets because they may not be as liquid as some of the other current assets. The more liquid a firm, the higher the current and quick ratios. The greater the
liquidity of a firm, the lower the probability that it can become technically insolvent,
which means that the firm cannot meet its current obligations as they come due. The more
liquid the firm before a takeover, the more likely it is that it will not face liquidity problems
if it assumes additional postmerger costs, such as higher interest payments. If, however,
the firm is only marginally liquid at the time of the merger, it may experience liquidity
problems following the merger unless it can rely on the other merger partner for additional
liquidity. Generally, the more illiquid part of the current assets is the inventories. If the analyst would like to have a more stringent measure of liquidity, the quick ratio can be used.
When there are questions about the liquidity of the company's inventories, greater reliance
is placed on the quick ratio rather than the current ratio. In such circumstances, other measures, such as the activity ratios, need to be carefully examined.

Activity Ratios

Activity ratios reflect the speed with which various accounts are converted into cash. Activity ratios are an important supplement to liquidity ratios because liquidity ratios do not
provide information on the composition of the firm's various assets.

Average Collection Period

Average collection period = Accounts receivable/(Annual credit sales/360)

The average collection period indicates the number of days an account remains outstanding. For example, if the average collection period is 60 days, it takes the firm an average of
60 days to collect an account receivable.
   As with all financial ratios, activity ratios make sense only in relation to the firm's collection policy. If the firm requires customers to pay within 30 days and the average collection period is 60 days, the ratio is a negative indicator. But if the firm allows customers to
pay within 90 days and the average collection period is 60 days, the ratio looks good. Further analysis would have to be done to determine whether the early payment was a result of
cash discounts for early payment, which would cut into the company's profitability.
   In a merger, it is important to determine whether the collection and credit policies of the
two firms are similar. If they are not similar and if the acquirer plans to institute stricter
payment and credit policies, the impact of the policies on the target's sales needs to be projected. If the target has large sales only because it is extending credit to those customers
with weaker credit ratings, the compatibility of the two firms and their credit policies

needs to be examined further. This would be important in mergers of retail firms that have significant credit sales. Moreover, the profitability of the target, after the acquirer's credit policies are instituted, may be below what might be necessary to meet the cost of capital associated with the acquisition.

Inventory Turnover

Inventory turnover = Cost of goods sold/Average inventory

The inventory turnover ratio reveals how often the inventory of the firm turns over in a year. The cost of goods sold is derived from the income statement, whereas the average inventory is taken from the balance sheet. Given that the balance sheet reflects the firm's position on a specific day, it might be useful to derive the average inventory by taking the beginning year inventory from the previous year's balance sheet and averaging that with the current year's amount. A better way would be to determine the inventory levels on a monthly basis and average these amounts. This would help reduce the impact of seasonal influences. The more seasonal the business, the more care must be exercised in interpreting the inventory turnover ratio.

The appropriate amount of inventory turnover is highly dependent on industry norms. A ratio of 30 may be normal for a retail food store, whereas an aircraft manufacturer may be quite pleased with a value of 1.

Although the inventory turnover value should be compared with industry averages, care should be exercised not to place too much weight on the pure number without further analysis. A high inventory turnover is normally a good sign, but this need not always be the case. For example, a firm could have a very high inventory turnover level by holding smaller than appropriate inventories. A high inventory turnover could be a result of shortages, or it could be related to the firm's credit policies, whereby the firm is lowering its profit margins and is in effect "giving the product away" to move inventory. Therefore, inventory levels need to be placed in perspective with the firm's average inventory levels and the average for the industry.

Generally, a low inventory turnover is a bad sign for a potential target because it may be indicative of illiquid or inactive inventories. If the acquirer believes that the inventories are indeed marketable, it must also have an answer to the question, "Why was the manufacturer of the inventory unable to sell these goods in a manner that was comparable with competitors?" If the answer is mismanagement and if the acquirer believes it can solve this problem, the low inventory turnover should not be of as great a concern.

Fixed Asset Turnover

Fixed asset turnover = Sales/Net fixed assets

Fixed asset turnover reflects the extent to which a firm is utilizing its fixed assets to generate sales. This ratio is important to an acquirer who is contemplating acquiring a capital-intensive firm. However, the analyst should take great care when comparing this ratio with industry averages. The fixed asset turnover value derived from the ratio shown in the preceding equation is very sensitive to several factors that may vary by company.

The fixed asset ratio is based on the historical cost of assets. Firms that have acquired their assets more recently may show a lower fixed asset turnover because the dollar value of their fixed assets is higher, and this value enters into the denominator of the ratio. The greater the rate of inflation over the period of asset acquisition, the more this ratio may lead to deceptive results.

Other factors that may affect the fixed asset turnover are the firm's depreciation policies and the use of leased rather than purchased assets. If the assets were recently acquired, a lag may occur between the acquisition of the assets and the resulting generation of sales from the use of these assets. Therefore, a recent acquisition may increase the denominator of the ratio but have little immediate effect on the numerator. Consideration of the industry norms relating to the investment-sales lag should be given before any judgment is made with regard to a target's use of fixed assets. A fixed asset turnover of 1.90, for example, means that a firm turns over its fixed assets 1.9 times a year.

Total Asset Turnover

Total asset turnover = Sales/Total assets

This ratio shows how effectively a firm uses its total resources. The caveats that apply to the use of the fixed asset turnover also apply here. A total asset turnover ratio of 1.60, for example, means that the firm turns over its assets 1.60 times a year.

Financial Leverage Ratios

Given the large amounts of debt frequently associated with takeovers in the fourth merger wave, financial leverage ratios become a very useful financial analysis tool for the merger analyst. The financial leverage or debt ratios indicate the degree of financial leverage that the firm has assumed. Financial leverage refers to the amount of debt the firm has used relative to the equity in its total capitalization.

In takeovers, the analyst must compute the financial leverage ratios based on different assumptions regarding the total debt used to finance the acquisition. These resulting debt levels are then compared with industry norms and standards to reveal how the merged firm compares with other firms in the industry. A takeover often results in a firm's being well above the industry average.

When the acquirer has plans to "pay down" the debt following the acquisition by assets sales, the financial leverage ratios should be projected for several years to determine the impact of the debt retirement. In this case, the analyst would like to determine how long it takes until the leverage ratios return to industry norms.

Debt Ratio

Debt Ratio = Total debt/Total assets

The debt ratio is usually computed by adding together short-term debt and long-term debt. It is also sometimes computed by using total liabilities rather than only formal debt. The debt ratio indicates the firm's ability to service its debt. Obviously, creditors want this ratio to be low. An acquirer may consider a target firm with a relatively larger amount of marketable fixed assets and a low debt ratio to be an ideal takeover target. Such a firm may have much unused borrowing capacity and may be vulnerable to a takeover. Companies with low debt ratios relative to the industry, recognizing their own vulnerability, may load up on debt. This is ironic because doing so may adversely increase the risk level of the company.

A debt ratio of 0.65, for example, means that the firm has financed 65% of its assets by using debt.

Debt to Equity Ratio

$$\text{Debt to equity} = \text{Long-term debt/Total equity}$$

The debt-equity ratio is one of the more often quoted financial leverage ratios. Preferred stock is commonly added to long-term debt in the computation because preferred stock payments are somewhat fixed. A firm cannot be forced into receivership if preferred stock payments are not made. It is usually assumed, however, that the firm has every intention of making these payments when the debt is issued. Therefore, they usually are treated as fixed. This is why preferred stock is more like debt than equity and is often categorized with fixed income securities.

It is difficult to judge a good debt-equity ratio without analyzing the firm's cash flows. Firms with very stable cash flows can more predictably handle higher debt levels. If an acquirer is considering taking over a target and financing the acquisition primarily with debt, a cash flow analysis needs to be conducted. If the cash flows are volatile, an added element of risk is introduced. A debt-equity ratio of 0.67, for example, shows that the firm's long-term debt is only 67% as large as its equity.

Debt to Total Capitalization Ratio

$$\text{Debt to Total Capitalization} = \text{Long-term debt/Long-term debt} + \text{Stockholders' equity)}$$

This ratio determines the proportion of total capitalization, which is the firm's permanent financing, that long-term debt represents. A low debt–total capitalization ratio is usually taken to be a desirable attribute in a target. Generally, firms with lower debt–total capitalization ratios are considered better credit risks because a larger equity cushion exists to protect creditors. Such firms can become takeover targets because of a greater unused borrowing capacity.

In addition to the leverage ratios discussed, coverage ratios are often used to measure the firm's ability to meet its interest payments and other fixed payments. These ratios are the times interest earned ratio and the fixed charge coverage ratio.

Times Interest Earned

$$\text{Times interest earned} = \text{EBIT/Interest charges}$$

As noted previously, earnings before interest and taxes (EBIT) is also called operating profit. The times interest earned ratio is a good measure of the firm's ability to meet its debt obligations. It is a particularly important measure for creditors because it tells them how much operating profit can shrink and the firm still be able to meet its debt obligations. For this reason it has great relevance to firms that are planning to finance an acquisition through debt.

The premerger and the postmerger times interest earned ratios are calculated to determine whether earnings are sufficient to meet the expected debt payments. Generally, a ratio between 3 and 5 is considered good. Firms in more volatile or cyclical industries may need to have higher ratios.

Fixed Charge Coverage

Fixed charge coverage = EBIT/(Interest payments + Lease payments + Preferred stock dividends before tax + Before-tax sinking fund payments)

This ratio, along with variations, is used when there are other significant fixed payments in addition to interest payments. Because the inability to meet other fixed obligations could easily force the firm into receivership, the fixed charge coverage may be a better way to measure this type of risk.

Profitability Ratios

Profitability ratios allow the firm to measure profit in relation to sales volume. The purpose of an acquisition should be to generate profits. Profit-minded acquirers invest a given amount of capital to obtain the right to an expected future stream of profits. These profitability ratios allow the acquirer to determine the target's profitability relative to that of its competitors and other firms.

Gross profit margin = (Sales – Cost of goods sold)/Sales = Gross profit/Sales
Operating profit margin = EBIT/Sales
Net profit margin = Earning after taxes/Sales

The gross profit indicates how much is left, on a percentage basis, after payments are expended for goods. The operating profit margin measures what is left before the impact of the financing decisions and governmental tax liabilities. The net profit margin is an after-tax measure of the firm's profitability. It measures what is left after all payments, including taxes, are made. There is no standard net profit margin; there are great differences across industries. Although the net profit margin is often cited as a measure of a corporation's success, good net margins differ considerably across industries. A net margin as low as 1 may be considered acceptable for a high-volume business such as a retail food store, whereas a net profit margin of 10% would be low for a jewelry store.

The merger analyst should review the historical trend in the firm's gross, operating, and net profit margins. An upward trend is usually considered a sign of financial strength, whereas a decline generally signifies weakness. If a deterioration in those margins causes the stock price to sag, it may make a firm vulnerable to a hostile takeover. Falling stock prices combined with highly marketable assets may present an opportunity to leveraged buyers, who may be able to sell assets quickly to pay off the debt while keeping the remaining assets that they acquired at bargain prices.

Return on Investment

Return on investment = Earnings after taxes/Total assets

The return on investment ratio is sometimes also called the total asset ratio. This ratio measures how effectively management can generate after-tax profits by using the firm's available assets. It has a number of drawbacks, including the fact that it is a book value ratio. If the assets are not carried on the books at accurate values, the ratio may not be very meaningful. This was the same drawback of the total asset turnover ratio. Merger analysts are more concerned with market values than with book values. Therefore, this ratio may serve as a rough guide to the true return that the firm is receiving on its assets. If the market value of the assets is significantly greater than the book value, the return on investment may overstate the effectiveness of the firm's management. Buyers should understand that this high return does not mean that they could buy the target's assets and achieve a similar return. A low return on investment, however, does not mean that the target's assets could not be better utilized by the buyer.

Return on Equity

Return on equity = Earnings after taxes/Stockholders' equity

This ratio is usually calculated by including both preferred stock and common stock in the denominator. It is a measure of the kind of return the company's owners are earning. The return on equity is an often-cited measure of performance used by both investors and management. Because equity, like total assets, is a balance sheet item, it may not accurately reflect the value of equity during the full year. An average of quarterly values may help offset this drawback. The return on equity also suffers from the fact that it is a book value, not a market value. Ironically, a high return on equity does not mean that shareholders will receive a high return on their investment. This problem is greater when there is a larger divergence between the market value of the equity and the book value. One solution to this problem is for the analyst to reconstruct the return on equity by substituting the market value for the book value of equity.

The return on equity is greatly influenced by the degree of financial leverage the firm employs. For example, if a firm is willing to increase its level of debt by borrowing to purchase income-generating assets, it can increase after-tax earnings while stockholders' equity remains constant. A naive analyst might interpret this as an up-and-coming company and a good takeover target. The higher return on equity, however, does not come without a price. The cost of this higher return on equity is the additional risk the firm assumes when it increases its financial leverage.

Market-Based Ratios

If securities markets are relatively efficient, adverse information contained in the financial statements should be reflected in the market-based ratios. These ratios contain the market's assessment of the financial well-being of the firm as well as the market's projection of the company's future ability to provide stockholders a profitable return on their investment.

Price-Earnings Ratio

P/E = Market price per share/Current earnings per share = P/EPS

The price-earnings (P/E) ratio is discussed in greater detail in Chapter 14. This ratio is useful in determining the appropriate capitalization rate to value the firm's projected income stream. Generally, a higher P/E ratio indicates that investors have a greater degree of confidence in the firm's future prospects. The P/E ratio, however, is also affected by the performance of the market as a whole. For example, the P/E ratios of most firms fell dramatically after the October 1987 stock market crash. Some analysts believe that the very high precrash P/E ratios created a situation in which investors believed a correction was necessary to bring the P/E ratios of many firms back in line with their intrinsic earning power. However, the market grew strongly in the 1990s, elevating the ratios to levels that were difficult to sustain.

To offset short-term market fluctuations, the P/E ratio can be adjusted. One such adjustment would be to convert the numerator to a moving average of the past 30 days' stock prices. In cases of high-growth firms, where analysts want to measure the future prospects of the firm, the last quarter's earnings, as opposed to the past year's earnings, can be annualized by multiplying by four and inserting into the denominator of the ratio.

The P/E ratio is also affected by whether the firm has been subject to rumors of its eventual takeover. The P/E ratio of potential takeover targets normally rises as the market anticipates the possibility of receiving a takeover premium. The more likely the takeover seems, the greater the increase in the stock prices and the P/E ratio. If news is released that reduces the probability of a takeover, such as a likely antitrust conflict, the P/E ratio should decline.

Payout Ratio

Payout = Dividends/EPS

The dividend payout ratio reflects the percentage of earnings that are paid to stockholders as dividends. This measure, although it is important for investors, is not as relevant to potential acquirers because the buyer can set the dividend policy. Therefore, the payout ratio, although an often-cited ratio in financial analysis, does not play a role in merger and acquisition analysis.

Specialized Nonstandard Financial Ratios

The preceding ratios are often cited and industry data are available from a number of sources. However, sometimes a merger analyst may be concerned about specific issues for which these standard ratios provide little information. In such a case, the analyst may want to construct specialized ratios to address the areas of concern. For example, the efficiency with which a target uses its labor resources could be an area of concern. To address this, the ratio of employees to sales may be computed and compared with that of other firms in the industry. Other specialized ratios can be used to learn more about the quality of a firm's as-

Table 12.1. **Sales versus Other Variable Expenditures**

Year	Sales Growth (5%)	Marketing (4%–1%)	R&D (5%–1%)	Maintenance (2%–1/2%)	Net Income (10%)
1998	50,000,000	2,000,000	2,500,000	1,000,000	5,000,000
1999	52,500,000	2,100,000	2,625,000	1,050,000	5,250,000
2000	55,125,000	2,205,000	2,756,250	1,102,500	5,512,500
2001	57,881,250	2,315,250	2,894,062	1,157,625	5,788,125
2002	60,775,312	2,431,012	3,038,766	1,215,506	6,077,531
2003	63,814,078	2,552,563	3,190,704	1,276,282	6,381,408
2004	67,004,782	670,048	670,048	335,024	12,395,885
2005	70,355,021	703,550	703,550	351,775	13,015,679

sets or earnings. For example, a company could be reducing expenditures on the maintenance of its assets in an effort to attain a short-term improvement in earnings. Such expenditure reductions may have adverse consequences in the future after the company has been sold. Potential buyers who suspect this may want to compute the ratio of maintenance expenditures to sales. A decline may indicate a deteriorating asset quality. Once such a trend has been observed, other suspicious areas may be explored. For example, the ratios of marketing or research and development (R&D) expenditures to sales may be computed. A decline in these areas may not have an immediate adverse effect on revenues but may yield short-term improvements in profitability at the expense of deterioration in future profitability. Plotting the trend in these specialized ratios may provide valuable information for the buyer. An example of a company that was cutting back on these types of expenditures is shown in Table 12.1 and Figure 12.1.

One of the limitations of using these specialized ratios is that it is not easy to gather information on values of the ratios for comparable firms or the industry as a whole. The choice, then, is to simply compare the firm's own values with those of prior years to ascertain the trend in the values. That is, it may only be possible to do a time series comparison of the firm with itself, as opposed to a cross-sectional comparison that is typical of financial ratio analysis.

CASE STUDY: PHILIP MORRIS, INC.— GROWTH THROUGH ACQUISITIONS

The case of Philip Morris Companies, Inc., is a good example of how acquisitions may be used profitably to achieve growth. Before the acquisition of General Foods, Philip Morris's main lines of business were tobacco and beer. The company decided at the end of 1985 that the significant cash flows of the firm, which were generated by the tobacco business, could be used to diversify the company's operations into other growth areas. The company acquired General Foods in November 1985. This acquisition was the first in a series of three large acquisitions in the food industry between 1985 and 1990. The end result was a company that still had large and dependable cash flows but one that was not as dependent on the U.S. tobacco market, whose long-term outlook is not as optimistic as it once was. As of the beginning of 1990, the firm showed an impressive combination of economic strength and growth potential. Much of this may be attributed to major acquisitions it made during this time.

Three Major Food Market Acquisitions

Acquired Firm	Year	Price ($ billions)
General Foods	1985	5.6
Kraft	1988	12.9
Jacob Suchad[a]	1990	3.8

[a] The acquisition of $3.8 billion reflected the acquisition of 80% of the firm's outstanding shares.

Overview of the Philip Morris Companies, Inc.

The Philip Morris Companies, Inc., is a diversified firm with products in the following industry categories:

- Tobacco
- Food
- Beer
- Financial services and real estate

Tobacco

Philip Morris is the largest cigarette company in the world. The firm has been highly successful in this area. This success is partly attributed to the popularity of its leading brands such as Marlboro, which is the best-selling packaged cigarette in the world. The firm also markets other leading brands, such as Merit, Benson & Hedges, and Virginia Slims. Although the growth of the U.S. tobacco business has slowed, Philip Morris still appears strong. In addition, the company's brands have performed well in international markets, thereby offsetting the slowdown in the U.S. market and reinforcing the firm's globalization strategy.

Food

The 1988 acquisition of Kraft by Philip Morris and the eventual merger of this business into General Foods' operations resulted in the formation of one of the world's largest food manufacturers. Together these two divisions market a large variety of notable brands that have enjoyed considerable financial success. The move into the food business was reinforced by the subsequent acquisition of the Swiss coffee and chocolate maker Jacob Suchard. This acquisition not only increased Philip Morris's emphasis on food businesses but also firmly established the company's presence in the European market. With this last acquisition, tobacco sales accounted for less than 50% of the firm's total revenues.

Beer

The Miller Brewing Company of Philip Morris commands a rising 23.1% share of the U.S. market. This division markets several variations of the Miller brand name, including Miller Lite, which is the second best-selling beer in the United States. The firm has maintained its position in this highly competitive industry category through aggressive marketing, costs containment, and the development of new brands.

Financial Services and Real Estate

This category is clearly the smallest of the four business segments discussed here. Its performance is mixed, with financial services showing a profit and real estate causing losses. The combined effects, however, were positive, particularly in 1988, when the real estate segment made a positive contribution to earnings.

The contributions to revenues and profits for each of the aforementioned business segments are depicted in Figures 1 and 2. The high profitability of the tobacco segment is reflected by the fact that although 40% of the company's revenues are generated from tobacco, 72% of Philip Morris's profits in 1989 resulted from tobacco sales.

Leading Products of the Acquired Companies

A review of the list of a few of the major brands of the acquired companies shows that Philip Morris acquired established brands with leading market shares with each of the three acquisitions.

General Foods
Kool-Aid
Maxwell House coffee
Yuban coffee
Jell-O
Freihofer Baking Company
Entenmann's Baking Company

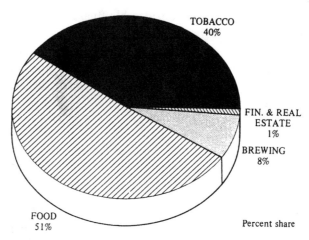

Figure 1. Revenues, Philip Morris Companies, Inc.

Kraft
Kraft cheese
Velveeta
Miracle Whip
Philadelphia brand cream cheese
Parkay margarine
Seven Seas salad dressing

Jacob Suchard
Jacob's Cafe brand coffee
Toblerone candy
Milka chocolate

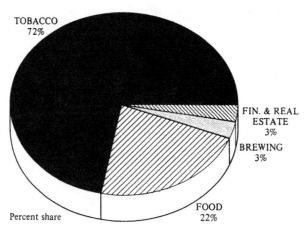

Figure 2. Profits, Philip Morris Companies, Inc.

Acquisition Strategy

Philip Morris used a well-designed acquisition strategy to reduce the company's dependence on an uncertain tobacco industry. The strategy featured transition of the firm from a tobacco company to one of the world's leading food producers. The move into the food business was fundamentally sound, given the fact that there is an inelastic demand for food in general. Although there is intense competition in many areas of the food business, the fact that Philip Morris purchased leading brand names through its acquisitions helped insulate the company from some of these competitive pressures. Many firms dramatically increased their financial leverage during the 1980s to finance acquisitions that proved to be poor investments, but Philip Morris carefully avoided such pitfalls in the acquisition game. Using the dependable cash flows that Philip Morris derived from the tobacco business, the company helped finance the acquisitions without excessive reliance on debt financing. The fact that the acquisitions improved Philip Morris's financial well-being is underscored by the financial analysis shown in Table 1. Table 1 and Figure 3 show a pattern of steadily increasing revenues. This trend was mirrored in the exponentially increasing operating and net income figures (Figures 4 and 5). One should bear in mind, however, that a significant component of these increases came from the addition of the General Foods and Kraft revenues and profits.

Financial Ratios

A review of selected financial ratios also depicts a growing company that maintained its financial well-being while aggressively pursuing a major acquisition strategy

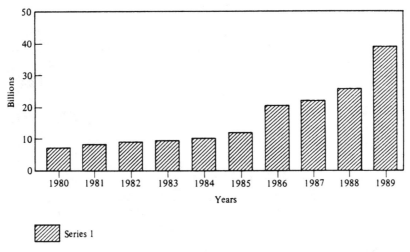

Figure 3.   Revenues, Philip Morris Companies, Inc.

Table 1.   Quarterly Financial Statements, Revenues, and Income, Philip Morris Companies, Inc.

Date	Sales ($ millions)	Income ($ millions)	Primary EPS	Dividends per Share	Shares Outstanding (000)
06/90	12,740	948	1.03	0.35	928,530
03/90	11,388	775	0.84	0.34	928,530
12/89	11,147	863	0.93	0.35	927,899
09/89	11,247	748	0.81	0.27	926,544
06/89	11,595	745	0.81	0.29	924,124
3/89	10,770	590	0.64	0.28	923,892
12/88	9,140	296	0.33	0.28	946,504
09/88	7,547	639	0.69	0.23	946,504
06/88	7,819	627	0.67	0.22	946,504
03/88	7,236	502	0.53	0.23	946,504
12/87	7,064	478	0.51	0.19	953,092
09/87	6,967	502	0.53	0.18	953,092
06/87	7,116	476	0.50	0.19	952,560
03/87	6,554	386	0.41	0.19	951,432
12/86	6,553	371	0.39	0.15	957,304
09/86	6,398	414	0.44	0.14	957,304

Five Year Growth Rates
Sales Growth Rate: 32%
EPS Growth Rate: 26%
Dividend Growth Rate: 25%

Source: Media general data.

(Table 2). Industry ratios were computed through a weighted average of the industry ratios for the food and tobacco industries. Because food sales account for 51% of revenues and tobacco accounts for 40%, a simple industry ratio is constructed by converting the industry ratios for each category into 100% equivalents, using weights of 0.56 and 0.44, respectively.

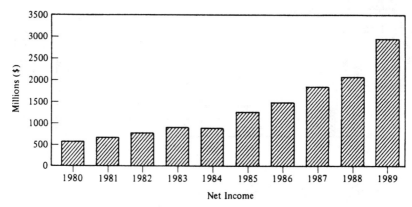

Figure 4.   Net income, Philip Morris Companies, Inc.

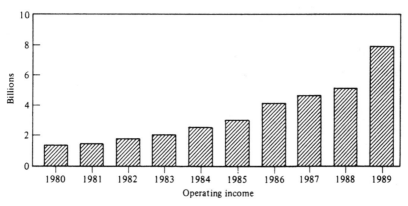

Figure 5. Operating income, Philip Morris Companies, Inc.

Table 2.   Financial Ratios, Philip Morris Companies, Inc.

Financial Ratios	Weighted Average (industry)	Philip Morris's Ratios				
		12/89	12/88	12/87	12/86	12/85
Profit margin, pretax (% of sales)	1.7	11.3	12.6	12.1	13.6	19.2
Current ratio	1.4	1.0	1.0	1.3	1.3	1.5
Quick ratio	0.8	0.3	0.3	0.4	0.4	0.5
Coverage ratio	3.3	2.7	4.5	3.7	3.0	4.6
Asset turnover	1.3	1.2	0.9	1.4	1.2	0.7
Total liabilities to net worth	1.0	1.6	2.1	0.8	1.1	1.5
Return on assets (%)	11.1	7.6	6.3	9.6	8.4	7.2
Return on equity	8.8	30.8	30.4	27.0	26.1	26.5

Interpretation of Selected Ratios

Pretax Profit Margin. Philip Morris's profit margin is significantly higher than the industry average.

Current Ratio. The current ratio of Philip Morris is lower than the industry average.

Quick Ratio. The quick ratio is also lower than the industry average.

Comment on the Liquidity Ratios. The lower liquidity ratios of Philip Morris do not present a problem because the firm is not in danger of becoming so illiquid that it would not be able to pay its bills as they come due.

Asset Turnover. There is little difference between the industry asset turnover average and the Philip Morris value.

Total Liabilities to Net Worth. Philip Morris increased its leverage in 1988. This is not surprising for firms that engage in major acquisitions. The financial leverage, however, as measured by this ratio, declined from 2.1 to 1.6 from 1988 to 1989. An examination of the return on equity, however, shows that this additional leverage was used to generate a higher rate of return on equity. The additional leverage does not represent a significant increase in the riskiness of the firm, given the great ability of the firm to generate cash flows.

Return on Assets. The return on assets for Philip Morris is less than the industry average.

Return on Equity. The return on equity for Philip Morris, in contrast to the return on assets, is significantly higher than the industry average.

Conclusion

The financial ratio analysis of the Philip Morris Companies, Inc., reflects a picture of financial health and high stockholder value relative to industry averages. This picture was reflected in the firm's stock market performance, which reflected a steady upward trend through the second half of the 1980s (Figure 6).

Philip Morris is a good example of how a company can effectively utilize acquisitions to pursue a strategy of low-risk growth. Many of the acquisitions that took place during the fourth merger wave involved firms that financed poorly conceived acquisition strategies through an excessive reliance on high-yield debt. The pursuit of some of these acquisition strategies damaged some firms' financial well-being while adding little to the future growth of the firm. The Philip Morris movement into the food industry through three major strategic acquisitions between the 1985 and 1990 period transformed this tobacco company into a company that does not rely excessively on a business segment that has an uncertain future. In doing so, Philip Mor-

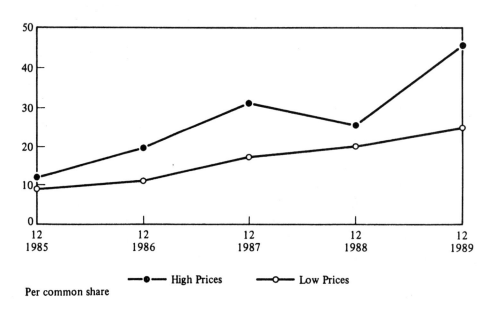

Figure 6.   High-low prices, Philip Morris Companies, Inc.

ris has demonstrated that a well-designed series of diversifications and acquisitions may lead to growth and increases in shareholder wealth. Whereas many other firms have unsuccessfully attempted to diversify, Philip Morris pursued a series of strategic acquisitions in the food industry involving leading firms with larger market shares. The stock market confirmed its approval of this strategy by continually bidding up the company's stock price. As of the start of the 1990s, Philip Morris had become a firm with strong cash flows from its tobacco business as well as a company that markets leading brands in both the food business and the tobacco business. The future of the company appears to have been significantly enhanced as a result of its strategic acquisitions.

SUMMARY

The analysis in this chapter is based on financial statements that are normally available publicly to the merger analyst by virtue of legal filing requirements for publicly held companies. A standard set of financial statements includes an income statement, a balance sheet, and a statement of cash flows. The merger analyst reviews these statements over a selected historical time period and derives various financial measures that are used in the valuation analysis. Among these measures are the various financial ratios commonly used to measure the financial well-being of a company. The standard ratios include four categories of ratios that measure liquidity, activity, leverage, and performance. To put them into proper perspective, these ratios are compared with industry averages, which are readily available from various data sources.

The value of much of this financial analysis depends on the quality of the available financial data. Friendly transactions tend to feature greater disclosure between the two parties. In a hostile takeover, however, the target will only disclose the minimum as required by federal disclosure laws and any other disclosure requirements imposed by litigation.

The financial analysis discussed in this chapter is one step in a valuation process. It is done to assess the financial well-being of the target. It may be used to discern potential problem areas. Once this has been done, the analyst can then proceed with the valuation process, which is discussed in the chapters that follow.

REFERENCES

Benoit, Ellen. "Real Money." *Financial World,* 20 September 1988.

Bowlin, Oswald, John Martin, and David Scott. *Guide to Financial Analysis* (New York: McGraw-Hill, 1980).

Brealey, Richard, Stewart Myers, and Alan Marcus. *Fundamentals of Corporate Finance,* 3rd ed (New York: McGraw-Hill, 1988).

Brigham, Eugene, and Louis Gapinski. *Intermediate Financial Management,* 3rd ed. (Chicago: Dryden Press, 1990).

Gitman, Lawrence J. *Principles of Managerial Finance,* 6th ed. (New York: Harper & Row, 1991).

Hackel, Kenneth, and Joshua Livnat. *Cash Flow and Security Analysis* (New York: Business Irwin One, 1992).

Helfert, Erich. *Techniques of Financial Analysis,* 6th ed. (New York: Richard D. Irwin, 1987).

Higgens, Robert. *Analysis for Financial Management,* 2nd ed. (Homewood, Ill.:. Dow Jones Irwin, 1989).

Jensen, Michael. "The Takeover Controversy: Analysis and Evidence." In John C. Coffee Jr., Louis Lowenstein, and Susan Rose Ackerman, eds. *Knights, Raiders, and Targets* (New York: Oxford University Press, 1988).

Logue, Dennis E. *Handbook of Modern Finance* (Boston: Warren, Gorham and Lamont, 1984).

Morris, Joseph. *Mergers and Acquisitions: Business Strategies for Accountants* (New York: John Wiley & Sons, 1995).

Moyer, R. Charles, James R. McGuigan, and William Kretlow. *Contemporary Financial Management,* 5th ed. (St. Paul: West, 1992).

Ross, Stephen, Randolph Westerfield, and Jeffrey Jaffe. *Fundamentals of Corporate Finance,* 3rd ed. (Homewood, IL: Dow Jones Irwin, 1991).

Siegel, Joel G. *How to Analyze Businesses, Financial Statements and the Quality of Earnings* (Englewood Cliffs, N.J.: Prentice-Hall, 1982).

Thomson, James, and Thomas Buttross. "Return to Cash Flow." *CPA Journal* (March 1988).

ValuSource (New York: John Wiley & Sons).

Weston, J. Fred, and Thomas Copeland. *Managerial Finance,* 9th ed. (Chicago: Dryden Press, 1992).

Yoshihasi, Pauline, and Neil Barsky. "Merv Griffin's Plunge into Casino Gambling Could Prove a Loser." *Wall Street Journal,* 5 July 1989.

13

VALUATION OF A PUBLICLY HELD COMPANY

The need for a systematic valuation process became more pronounced for corporate America during the fourth merger wave, when many companies found themselves the targets of friendly or unfriendly offers. Even companies that had not been targets had to determine their proper value in the event that such a bid might materialize. To exercise due diligence, the board of directors must fully and properly evaluate an offer and compare this price with its own internal valuation of the firm. The need to perform this evaluation as diligently as possible was emphasized in the 1980 bid for the Trans Union Corporation by Jay Pritzker and the Marmon Corporation.

In September 1980 Jerome Van Gorkom, chairman and chief executive officer of Trans Union, suggested to Jay Pritzker that Pritzker make a $55 a share merger bid for Trans Union, which would be merged with the Marmon Group, a company controlled by Pritzker. Van Gorkom called a board of directors meeting on September 20, 1980, on a one-day notice. Most of the directors had not been advised of the purpose of the meeting. The meeting featured a 20–minute presentation on the Pritzker bid and the terms of the offer. The offer allowed Trans Union to accept competing bids for 90 days. Some directors thought that the $55 offer would only be considered the beginning of the range of the value of the company. After a two-hour discussion, the directors agreed to the terms of the offer and a merger agreement was executed.

The Trans Union directors were sued by the stockholders, who considered the offer inadequate. A Delaware court found that the decision to sell the company for $55 was not an informed business judgment.

> The directors (1) did not adequately inform themselves as to Van Gorkom's role in forcing the "sale" of the Company and in the per share purchase price; (2) were uninformed as to the intrinsic value of the Company; and (3) given these circumstances, at a minimum, were grossly negligent in approving the "sale" of the Company upon two hours consideration, without prior notice, and without the exigency of a crisis or emergency.

The court was also impressed with other deficiencies in the board of directors' decision-making process. Among them was the fact that the board did not even have a copy of the merger agreement to review at a meeting convened for the explicit purpose of deciding on the merger. The board members therefore did not read the amendments to the agreement, and they did not request an outside valuation study of the merger offer.[1] Based on these

---

1. Stanley Foster Read and Alexandra Reed Lajoux, *The Art of M&A: A Merger Acquisition Buyout Guide,* 2nd ed. (New York: John Wiley & Sons, 1995), pp. 662–663.

facts, the case seems to be one of clear negligence on the part of the directors. However, there is evidence that the directors had conducted an analysis of the value of the firm before the meeting in which they approved the offer. In fact, the directors had been monitoring the firm's financial condition for several years before the Pritzker bid. Their defense also included the following factors:

> The directors' key defense was the "substantial" premium in Pritzker's $55 offer over Trans Union's market price of $38 per share. The merger price offered to the shareholders represented a premium of 62 percent over the average of the high and low prices at which Trans Union had traded in 1980, a premium of 48 percent over the last closing price, and a premium of 39 percent over the highest price at which the stock had traded at any time during the prior six years. They offered several other defenses as well. First, the market test period provided opportunity for other offers. Second, the board's collective experience was adequate to determine the reasonableness of the Pritzker offer. Third, their attorney, Brennan, advised them that they might be sued if they rejected the Pritzker proposal. Lastly, there was the stockholder's overwhelming vote approving the merger.[2]

The directors' defense clearly had some merit, as reflected in the opinions of the two dissenting justices, who saw adequate evidence that the directors had studied the value of Trans Union for an extended period of time before the directors' meeting and were in a position to determine whether the offer was inadequate.

The board of directors also considered the comments of Donald Romans, Trans Union's chief financial officer, who had stated that the $55 offer was at the beginning of the range within which an adequate value of Trans Union lay. Romans's analysis was prepared to determine whether Trans Union could service the necessary debt to fund the leveraged buyout (LBO) he was contemplating. The court had not, however, considered his analysis sufficient to approve a merger because it was not a valuation study. This ruling is significant because it affirms the need for a formal valuation analysis in all mergers, acquisitions, and LBOs. Ultimately, then, the *Smith v. Van Gorkom* decision is important because it set forth, under the business judgment rule, the responsibilities of directors of public companies to have a thorough and complete valuation analysis conducted by an objective party, such as an investment bank or valuation firm. Following *Smith v. Van Gorkom*, even the more financially adept directors seek to "take themselves off the hook" by having an outside valuation firm or investment bank issue a "fairness opinion" expressing their belief that the offer is adequate. What is also significant about the *Smith v. Van Gorkom* decision was that the court was more impressed with the decision-making process that the directors engaged in than with the ultimate decision that they made. When compared with the usual standards to which merger offers are held, such as the size of the merger premium relative to recent or industry averages or what the offer price was relative to historical stock prices, the offer seemed to be a good one for shareholders. The soundness of the decision was not enough for the court, however, when it was the result of a process that the court found to be deficient.

VALUATION METHODS: SCIENCE OR ART?

The methods and data considered in the valuation of businesses vary widely. In some respects, business valuation is as much of an art as it is a science. It is exact and scientific in

---

2. Arthur Fleisher, Geoffrey C. Hazard Jr., and Miriam Z. Klipper, *Board Games* (Boston: Little, Brown, 1988), pp. 31–32.

that there are standard methods and hard data to consider in the formulation of valuation. However, several different methods may be employed in a given evaluation. The methods may provide different business values and thus give the impression that the general methodology lacks systematic rigor.

The naive reader may infer that the valuation of businesses may be an overly subjective process. A closer examination of the methodology, however, reveals that objective valuations can be achieved. The variability of values is natural, given that we are considering the market for a business in which different participants may place variable values on the same business or collection of assets because the anticipated uses of these businesses or assets may be different in different hands.

This chapter and Chapter 14 discuss the methods of business valuation. This chapter focuses on the valuation of public companies, whereas Chapter 14 concerns the methods of valuation of closely held businesses. Many of the techniques are used for the valuation of both public firms and private firms. For example, while the selection of the discount rate and comparable multiples are discussed at greater length in Chapter 14, they are clearly relevant to valuing both public and private companies. Some techniques, such as the marketability discount, may be more relevant to the valuation of closely held businesses.

MANAGING VALUE AS AN ANTITAKEOVER DEFENSE

The intensified takeover pressures that managers experienced in the fourth merger wave gave them a great incentive to increase the value of their firms so as to reduce their vulnerability to a takeover. Firms with a falling stock price but marketable assets are vulnerable to a takeover. Managers have found that adopting a management strategy that will boost the stock price makes the firm a more expensive target. With an increased stock price, raiders have trouble convincing stockholders that management is doing a bad job and that there are more value-enhancing ways to run the company.

An increase in stock price reduces the effectiveness of several takeover tactics. It makes a tender offer more difficult by raising the cost of control, and it decreases the effectiveness of a proxy fight because it is harder to garner the requisite number of votes from other shareholders when management has increased the value of their investment. Some supporters of takeovers maintain that the pressures placed on management have benefited shareholders by forcing management to take actions that maximize the value of their investment. The stock price has become a report card of management performance. Managers now have to regularly monitor the market's valuation of their actions. This marks a significant change in the way corporations were run in earlier years, when managers kept the stock price in mind but did not make it a factor in most of their major decisions. For this reason, among others, valuation has been placed in the forefront of corporation management.

STOCK VALUATION METHODS

The most basic difference between the valuation of public firms and private corporations is that an active market exists for publicly held companies, whereas the stock of privately held corporations is not traded. The value of a public company's stock can be more readily discerned by considering the value for which the security trades in the market. Even this price, however, may not accurately reflect the value that would arise in a takeover. To fully understand this concept, it is necessary to consider the traditional stock valuation methods.

Gordon Stock Dividend Valuation Model

One of the most often cited models is the *Gordon Stock Dividend Valuation Model.* This model determines the value of common stock by considering the present value of the dividends that would be derived from the ownership of the security. The Gordon model can determine different values, depending on the assumptions about the expected growth of the dividends.

In the Gordon model, the share price is expressed as a positive additive function of anticipated dividends. The value of a share of common stock in a given company at time zero can be expressed as follows:

$$P_0 = \frac{D_1}{(1 + k_s)^1} + \frac{D_2}{(1 + k_s)^2} + \dots + \frac{D_\infty}{(1 + k_s)^\infty}$$

(13.1)

where

P_0 = the stock price at time zero
D_i = the dividend at time i
k_s = the capitalization rate for this firm's common stock

One of the first questions that arises from Equation 13.1 is: What will dividends D_1 through D_n equal? Presumably, the dividends would grow as a result of the effects of inflation and the earnings growth of the company. An accurate stock dividend valuation model should reflect this growth. One assumption that would simplify this process would be to have dividends growing at a constant rate. This assumption may be rationalized if the historical evidence indicates a certain rate of growth in dividends, which is apparent from the company's recent history. The constant growth rate model is often simply referred to as the Gordon model.[3]

This growth rate can be incorporated as follows:

$$P_0 = \frac{D_0(1 + g)^1}{(1 + k_s)^1} + \frac{D_0(1 + g)^2}{(1 + k_s)^2} + \dots + \frac{D_0(1 + g)^\infty}{(1 + k_s)^\infty}$$

(13.2)

Equation 13.2 can be simplified as follows:

$$P_0 = D_1/k_s - g$$

(13.3)

Equation 13.3 will yield accurate values for P_0 assuming that the capitalization rate, k, is greater than the growth rate, g. The growth rate of dividends can be determined by considering a reasonable historical period, such as the past 10 years. The average annual growth rate can be determined by applying the following expression:

$$D_{11} = D_1(1 + g)^{11}$$

(13.4)

---

3. Myron Gordon, *The Investment, Financing and Valuation of the Modern Corporation* (Homewood, Ill.: Richard D. Irwin, 1962).

Solving for g, we get

$$g = \sqrt[10]{\frac{D_{11}}{D_1}} - 1 \qquad (13.5)$$

Let us assume for simplicity's sake that dividends are paid annually. For the 10–year period shown in the accompanying tabulation, we can apply Equation 13.5 to determine the growth rate.

Year	Dividend ($)
1	1.00
2	1.10
3	1.20
4	1.35
5	1.45
6	1.60
7	1.90
8	1.90
9	2.00
10	2.10
11	2.15

$$g = \sqrt[10]{\frac{2.15}{1.00}} - 1 \qquad (13.6)$$

$$g = 7.95\%$$

The 10–year time period is somewhat arbitrary and is assumed to be a period in which there has been a stable dividends flow and one that will be indicative of future dividends flow. We have derived an average annual compounded rate of growth and have made the assumption that this average rate will apply in the future. Having derived the growth rate, we can apply it in an example. Let us assume that the capitalization rate for the company in question is 15%, or 0.15. Substituting this in Equation 13.3, we get a valuation as of the eleventh period.

$$P = \frac{\$2.15}{0.15 - 0.0795} \qquad (13.7)$$

$$P = \$30.50$$

Higher growth rates will yield higher stock valuations; lower growth rates will have the opposite effect. For example, if we were valuing the stock of a growing new company, a higher rate of growth might be anticipated for an initial period. As the firm matured and established itself in the marketplace, the growth rate would stabilize at some level. If we blindly applied the high initial growth rate, unrealistic stock prices would result.

Equation 13.3 can be adjusted to reflect a high initial rate of growth in dividends followed by a stable growth rate. This calculation can be conducted in two steps:

1. Calculate the present value of the dividends for the initial high-growth period. This can be done as follows:

$$P_0 = \sum_{t=1}^{m} \frac{D_0(1 + g_1)^t}{(1 + k_s)^t} \qquad (13.8)$$

where

g_1 = the high initial growth rate
m = the initial high-growth rate period

2. Calculate the present value of stock after the initial growth period. This is simply the value of the stock using Equation 13.3, which is its value at that time, and discounting the result back to time 0. The undiscounted part of this expression is the price that the stock should sell for at that time.

$$P_m = \frac{1}{(1 + k_s)^m} \left[\frac{D_{m+1}}{(k_s - g_2)} \right]$$

(13.9)

where

g_2 = the stabilized rate of growth

3. The value of the firm's stock is then calculated by adding the results of steps 1 and 2.

An obvious question arises: How do we determine what g_1 and g_2 should be equal to? One alternative would be to use the recent historical growth of dividends for the firm as an estimate of g_1. We can then approximate g_2 by using the industry growth rate of dividends.

Let us consider the following example of GrowMax Computer Technologies, a manufacturer of computer components for large computer companies that has been in existence for five years. Unlike many other high-growth companies, GrowMax has paid annual dividends that have been rising as fast as its earnings. Let us assume that these dividends have been paid in all five years of its brief existence. This would be unusual because many high-growth companies decide to put the earnings back into the company, where they can earn a higher return than the stockholders' could earn on alternative investments, particularly after the double corporation tax.

GrowMax's annual dividends for the years 1994 to 1998 are as follows:

Year	Dividends ($)
1994	1.50
1995	1.80
1996	2.30
1997	2.90
1998	3.65

The annual rate of growth in dividends is approximately 25%. Let us assume that this rate of growth is projected to continue for the next five years. After this period, it is assumed that the firm will pay the industry growth rate of dividends, which is assumed to be 5%.

The valuation of GrowMax stock encompasses three steps:

1. The 1999 dividend amount of $3.65 is used as the base. The discount rate is 17%. See Table 13.1 for the valuation figures for 2000 to 2004.
2. The value of the stock at the end of five years, 2004, is calculated by determining the dividend amount at the end of the sixth year, 2005. This value is:

$$\$3.65 \, (1.25)^5 \, (1.05) = \$11.70$$

(13.10)

Table 13.1. Valuation of GrowMax Stock, 2000–2004

Year	Dividend ($)	Growth Factor	Discount Factor	Value ($)
2000	3.65	1.25	0.850	3.87
2001	3.65	1.56	0.730	4.16
2002	3.65	1.95	0.624	4.44
2003	3.65	2.44	0.534	4.76
2004	3.65	3.05	0.456	5.08
				$22.31

Applying Equation 13.3,

$$P_5 = 11.70/(0.17 - 0.05) = \$97.50 = (97.50)(0.456) = \$44.46 \qquad (13.11)$$

3. Add steps 1 and 2.

$$P_0 = \$22.31 + \$44.46 = \$66.77 \qquad (13.12)$$

As is true of all financial analysis, we need to give the analysis and results a "sensibility check." The analysis was based on the assumption of a continued 25% growth in dividends for five years, based on the historical growth rate between 1996 and 2000. Is this realistic? The analysis then makes the assumption that the firm would approach the industry dividend growth rate in dividends of 5%. This is a simplifying assumption because it would be more reasonable to have an intermediate period with a different growth rate between 25% and 5%. A gradual reduction approaching the industry growth rate might be more realistic.

Step 3 shows a stock value of $66.77. The question that arises is: What are similar firms selling for? This, of course, assumes that you can find other firms with the impressive rate of annual dividend growth exhibited by GrowMax. If these other firms are selling for a fraction of what your analysis indicates GrowMax is worth, your assessment of the value of GrowMax differs dramatically from the market's assessment of similar firms. GrowMax's historical rate of growth in dividends is so high, however, that comparable firms may not exist. In this case, the company could possibly be worth the $66.77 value.

One obvious problem that arises from a consideration of this methodology concerns what to do for firms that do not pay out dividends. It might be more reasonable that such a high-growth firm like GrowMax would not pay out earnings in the form of dividends but would retain these earnings and reinvest them in the firm. This is one of the major drawbacks of the dividend stock valuation method.

Another major disadvantage of the Gordon model is that it considers only a small number of factors. It may be necessary to go beyond the historical growth rate of dividends and to examine many of the relevant factors that will affect the future dividend growth. The riskiness of the firm would need to be assessed in determining the appropriate discount rate. The risk of the company may be determined by a broad set of factors. Such important determining factors may be one reason the market arrives at a very different assessment of the appropriate value of the stock.

Another consideration in applying the Gordon model is that the analysis considers the flow of dividends for a given number of shares of stock outstanding. This valuation would be affected by a change in the number of shares that might result from the future issuance of equity and the earnings generated by this additional equity capital.

In sum, the Gordon stock dividend valuation formula is a convenient rule of thumb, but its requisite simplifying assumptions limit its use. It is a mainstay of most corporate finance textbooks, but the merger and acquisition analyst cannot put it to great use by itself.

MARKETABILITY OF THE STOCK

The marketability of common stock varies considerably. The equity of publicly held companies is traded on organized exchanges and on the over-the-counter (OTC) market. Securities that are traded on the New York Stock Exchange are generally considered quite liquid. Stocks that are traded on smaller exchanges, such as the regional exchanges, may not have the same liquidity. The *over-the-counter market* is a trading system wherein securities are bought and sold through a network of brokers and dealers who trade through the National Association of Security Dealers' Automated Quotations (NASDAQ) computerized network. In the past this market was for smaller companies, but in recent years NASD has grown in importance and features several large companies. Companies that trade on NASDAQ vary in size and trading volume. The over-the-market securities that are seldom traded are not kept on the NASDAQ computer network. Prices on these securities are available through the *pink sheets,* which appear daily and are made available through the National Quotation Bureau.

The market on which the security is traded is an important consideration in the valuation process. The broader the market and the greater the daily trading volume, the more liquid the security. This means that if you want to sell the stock, you have a better opportunity to sell a larger amount of stock without depressing the price significantly when it is actively traded on an organized exchange. If the stock is a seldom traded security on the OTC market, however, the price quoted may be less reliable. A seller may not be able to sell a large block of stock for anywhere near the last price quoted on the pink sheets. The exact value of the stock may not be determinable until offers for the block have been made.

The "thinness" of the market is a major determinant of the liquidity of the security. Lack of liquidity is another element of risk that must be factored into the stock price. This can be accomplished by adjusting the discount rate used to bring the dividends to present value. The greater the risk, the higher the discount rate and the lower the stock price. The issue of adjusting the discount rate is discussed later in this chapter and in Chapter 14.

The thinness of the market can be judged by looking at the number of *float shares*—the number of shares available for trading. Small companies on the OTC market may have only a small percentage of their shares traded, whereas most of the shares may be rarely traded. When the number of float shares is small compared with the total shares outstanding, the valuation provided by the market may not be very useful. Moreover, when the number of float shares is small, any sudden increase in trading volume can greatly affect the stock price. This is another element of risk that needs to be considered.

A related influence on the price a buyer may be willing to pay for an OTC-traded security is the concentration of securities in the hands of certain groups. The companies traded on the OTC market frequently have large blocks of stock concentrated in the hands of a small group of individuals. Some of these companies may be firms that have recently gone public and have large blocks of stock owned by family members. Such a concentration makes the likelihood of a successful takeover by an outside party less probable unless it is a friendly transaction. The greater the concentration of securities in the hands of parties opposed to a takeover, the more problematic and costly a takeover may be.

Target's Dividend Policy Not Relevant

The stock dividend valuation methodologies, which are usually applied from an investor's point of view, consider the value of a security in the investor's portfolio. This valuation is affected by the firm's dividend policy. The dividend policy is irrelevant to the acquirer who is considering buying 100% of the target. The acquirer can set the dividend policy to be whatever the acquirer chooses, within the limits of the firm's earnings and cash flows. Earnings and cash flows, not dividends, are what the acquirer is seeking. A firm that has a low dividend payout ratio, the percentage of earnings that are paid out in the form of dividends, would not be valued differently by an acquirer than a firm that was similar in all other respects but that had a high dividend payout ratio. For this reason, stock valuation for mergers and acquisitions should focus on cash flows and earnings rather than on dividends. The dividend flow is not irrelevant. It helps determine what the *market* is willing to pay for the stock. Cash flows and earnings reflect what the *acquirer* is willing to pay. If the market valuation, based on dividends, is higher than the acquirer's own subjective valuation, based on earnings, the acquirer may have to bypass the company because it is too costly relative to its earning power from the acquirer's viewpoint.

DEFINING THE EARNINGS BASE

Four commonly used ways to define earnings for the purposes of valuation of publicly held companies are:

EBITDA	Earnings before interest, taxes, depreciation, and amortization
EBIT	Earnings before interest or taxes
EBT	Earnings before taxes
Net income	Earnings after all operating expenses, depreciation, interest, taxes, and owners' compensation

The choice of the appropriate definition is a matter of the analyst's judgment based on his or her experience and the type of company being valued. Most valuations are done on the basis of cash flows and less attention is paid to earnings, which are more susceptible to accounting manipulations.

CASE STUDY: TIME-WARNER-PARAMOUNT—CASH FLOW versus EARNINGS VALUATIONS

In June 1989 Time, Inc. made a bid for Warner Communications, Inc., which was followed by a bid by Paramount Communications, Inc., for Time, Inc. Both combinations—Time-Warner and Paramount-Time—would result in a highly leveraged company that would generate few earnings. Paramount took on $8 billion in debt to complete a $14 billion acquisition of Warner. This, however, did not make the company valueless in the eyes of its bidders. Paramount offered $12.2 billion, or $200 per share, for Time, Inc. The key to the target's value was the cash-flow–generating capacity of the media assets that these communications giants commanded.

"What's significant is that Time, one of America's leading companies, is putting a stamp of approval on cash flow valuations as opposed to earnings valuations," said Bernard Gallagher, vice president and treasurer of the Philadelphia-based Comcast Corporation, the nation's third largest cable company. "Paramount, Time and Warner, all traditional earnings oriented companies, are now saying that earnings aren't nearly as important as combining and building assets that will generate cash in the future."[a]

The cash flow method of analyzing companies gained credence more than a decade ago with Denver-based cable giant Tele-Communications, Inc. Drexel Burnham Lambert analyst John Reidy says the company "made a decision years ago that it was foolish to generate a lot of earnings and pay taxes, when, by adding leverage, they could reduce taxes and add value by buying new cable systems." Adds Mr. Reidy, "Everyone else in the cable industry took a page out of their book."[b]

The presence of high cash flows is not enough to ensure profitability. The $8 billion Time borrowed to finance the merger with Warner left the combined firm, which became the world's largest media company, with $11 billion of debt. As with many of the leveraged transactions of the fourth merger wave, the pressure of interest payments on this debt took its toll on the firm's profitability. Time-Warner posted a $432 million loss for 1989.

It is ironic that Time turned down a substantial offer from Paramount, based on the belief of Time's management that the price of Time-Warner stock would eventually rise to $200 per share. This decision was questioned when in early 1990 Time-Warner's stock was trading as low as $96.125 per share, less than half management's projections.[c] This transaction, however, would prove to be one of many megaentertainment deals that would take place in the 1990s as this industry underwent significant restructuring.

a. "Time's Warner Bid Reflects Emphasis on Value of Cash Flow, Not Earnings," *Wall Street Journal,* 27 June 1989, p. A2.
b. Ibid.
c. David Hilder, "Time Warner Holders Fret As Stock Sinks," *Wall Street Journal,* 7 February 1990, p. 21.

Earnings versus Cash Flow

Many merger analysts do not choose to use earnings. Rather, they rely on free cash flows as a more dependable measure of the target's value. This is particularly important because earnings may be greatly influenced by the accounting methods used by the target. With different accounting methods, two otherwise identical firms may have very different earnings. An example of the importance of cash flows, as opposed to earnings, was shown in the 1989 Paramount bid for Time, Inc. (see the case study). The bids made in this takeover contest were based on multiples of cash flow, not on earnings. This is typical of buyout offers for these highly leveraged media companies.

Free cash flow is defined as after-tax income with various adjustments and addbacks included, such as depreciation and deferred taxes, as well deductions of certain necessary expenditures, such as net working capital or capital investment. Free cash flow is considered a more reliable measure of the value of a target corporation to a potential acquirer. An alternative statement of the definition of cash flow comes from Mike Jensen: "Free cash flow is cash flow in excess of that required to fund all projects that have positive net present values (NPVs) when discounted at the relevant cost of capital."[4]

One way to quickly construct a measure of future free cash flow is to examine the historical pattern of operating cash flows along with the capital expenditures over the same time period. Unless there are some anomalous capital expenditure amounts, the average from the historical period may be used as a proxy of future capital expenditure needs. These amounts can then be deducted from the projected operating cash flows. The method used to construct a projection of the operating cash flows is discussed later in this chapter.

Many investors and stock analysts pay less attention to reported income. Recognizing that reported earnings present a limited picture of a company's ability to generate cash, they focus instead on cash flows. Some use a ratio of stock price to free cash flow as opposed to the often-used price-earnings (P/E) ratio. This measure may present a very different picture of a given company's investment value.

Does the Market Value Net Income or Cash Flows?[5]

The issue of what the market follows—cash flow or net income—has drawn much attention in the corporate research going back to at least the 1960s. In early articles, researchers examined the impact on stock prices of variations in earnings that are derived from accounting changes that alter accounting income but that do not have economic significance.[6] Other studies have shown that changes in depreciation policies that have no cash flow significance, such as changes from accelerated depreciation to straight-line depreciation, which result in an increase in reported profits, failed to cause stock prices to increase.[7] Kaplan and Roll conducted an event study that found that the market was efficient in the processing of new information when it determined that accounting changes that did not have cash effects failed to receive a positive stock market response.[8] In fact, the typical stock price response was negative, leading the authors to conclude that because the firms that were engaging in the changes in depreciation policies were performing poorly, they were doing so to conceal this poor performance. In this case, the market

4. Michael C. Jensen, "The Takeover Controversy: Analysis and Evidence," in John C. Coffee, Louis Lowenstein, and Susan Rose Ackerman, eds., *Knights, Raiders and Targets* (New York: Oxford University Press, 1988), p. 321.

5. Patrick A. Gaughan, Henry Fuentes, and Laura Bonanomi, "Cash Flow versus Net Income in Commercial Litigation," *Litigation Economics Digest* (Fall 1995), pp. 13–24.

6. Philip Brown and Ray Ball, "An Empirical Evaluation of Accounting Income Numbers," *Journal of Accounting Research* 6, no. 2 (Autumn 1963), pp. 159–178.

7. T. Ross Archibald, "Stock Market Reaction to the Depreciation Switch-Back," *Accounting Review* 47, no. 1 (January 1972), pp. 22–30.

8. Robert S. Kaplan and Richard Roll, "Investor Evaluation of Accounting Information: Some Empirical Evidence," *Journal of Business* 45, no. 2 (April 1972), pp. 225–257.

was efficient in processing the new information on this apparent concealment by lowering stock prices.[9]

Other accounting policies changes, such as changes in inventory valuation from first in, first out (FIFO) to last in, first out (LIFO), which cause net income to *decline* but *increase* cash flows due to tax effects, were shown to increase stock prices.[10] The opposite was the case in switches from LIFO to FIFO (Figure 13.1). It was clear from the Sunder study that the market was not fooled by the accounting-motivated decreases in net income but perceived the improved cash position of the firm to warrant higher stock prices.

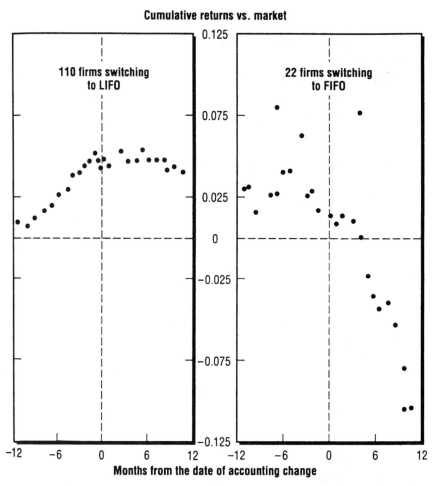

Figure 13.1.   Market returns in response to changes in inventory accounting policies.

Source: Tom Copeland, Tim Koller, and Jack Murrin, *Valuation: Measuring and Managing the Value of Companies* (New York: John Wiley & Sons, 1990), pp. 81–94.

9. For a review of this literature, see Frank Rielly, *Investment Analysis and Portfolio Management,* 2nd ed. (New York: Dryden Press, 1985), pp. 178–181.

10. Shyam Sunder, "Stock Price and Risk Related to Accounting Changes in Inventory Valuation," *Accounting Review* 50, no. 2 (April 1975), pp. 305–315.

Later studies have also confirmed that the stock market is not naive in its interpretation of accounting earnings.[11] For example, Copeland, Koller, and Murrin showed that there was a low 0.024 correlation between growth in earnings per share and the P/E ratio for the Standard & Poor's 400 (Figure 13.2). However, there was a high 0.94 correlation between the market value of companies and their discounted cash flows that were derived from Value Line forecasts.

There is some debate as to whether accounting earnings perform better in the long run than in the short run, where they clearly perform poorly.[12] Some analysts contend that

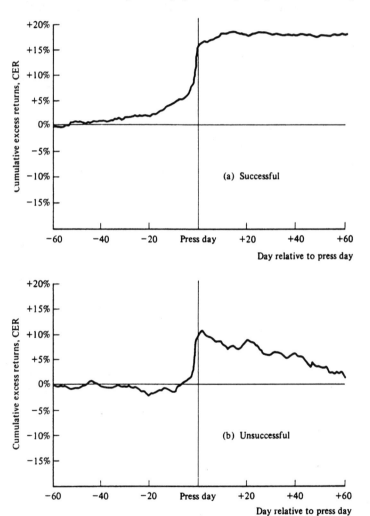

Figure 13.2. Average cumulative excess returns for (a) 211 successful and (b) 91 unsuccessful target firms from 60 days before until 60 days after the press day in the period 1962–76.

Source: Journal of Economics 20, no. 112 (April 1983): 62.

---

11. Tom Copeland, Tim Koller, and Jack Murrin, *Valuation: Measuring and Managing the Value of Companies* (New York: John Wiley & Sons, 1990), pp. 81–94.

12. Peter D. Easton, Trevor S. Harris, and James A. Ohlson, "Aggregating Accounting Earnings Can Explain Most Security Returns: The Case of Long Return Intervals," *Journal of Accounting and Economics* 15 (1992), pp. 119–142.

accounting earnings are a "major determinant over longer intervals" (such as 10 years) because earnings that are not distributed as dividends cause the book value of equity to rise, which in turn has a positive impact on stock prices.[13] The potential long-run rehabilitation of accounting earnings will be an area of empirical research in the future.

The preceding long-run caveats notwithstanding, the evidence covering decades of research is that the market values cash flows, and where it is possible to discriminate between events that have different accounting earnings and cash flow impacts, the market tends to focus on the cash flow effects. The relevance of this research to valuation is that less attention should be paid to net income and more attention paid to cash flows, particularly when there are significant deviations in the trends between the two.

Free Cash Flow Theory of Mergers, Acquisitions, and Leveraged Buyouts

Some researchers believe that a firm's amount of free cash flow may determine whether it is going to engage in takeovers.[14] The theory implies that managers of firms that have unused borrowing capacity and ample free cash flows are more likely to engage in takeovers. Managers use the cash resources to acquire other firms instead of paying the monies to stockholders in the form of higher dividends.

Michael Jensen contends that many of these mergers result in "low benefits or even value destroying mergers. Diversification programs generally fit this category and the theory predicts that they will generate lower total gains."[15] According to Jensen, these mergers are more likely to occur in industries that are in a period of retrenchment but that nonetheless have large cash flows. When the mergers are horizontal, they may create value because the payment of cash to the stockholders of the target firm is a way in which cash is leaving the company. However, in Jensen's view, mergers outside the industry may have low or even negative returns because the managers will be running a company in an industry that may be outside their area of managerial expertise. As an example, Jensen cites tobacco firms, which are experiencing a gradual decline in demand as society becomes more aware of the link between tobacco consumption and disease. The gradual decline in demand notwithstanding, tobacco companies still have large free cash flows to invest. Jensen's theory would then imply that the diversifying acquisitions, such as Philip Morris's acquisition of General Foods and R. J. Reynolds's acquisition of Nabisco, are more likely to have negative productivity effects. This was somewhat confirmed by the 1999 decision by RJR Nabisco to sell off its international tobacco operations and spin off its U.S. cigarette unit.

Industries that have high free cash flows and limited growth opportunities are sometimes considered good LBO candidates. This is supported by a study by Tim Opler and Sheridan Titman of 180 firms that undertook LBOs between 1980 and 1990.[16] They found

---

13. Michael Brennan, "A Perspective on Accounting and Stock Prices," *Journal of Applied Corporate Finance* 8, no. 1 (Spring 1995), pp. 43–52.

14. Michael Jensen, "The Takeover Controversy," pp. 333–337.

15. Ibid.

16. Tim Opler and Sheridan Titman, "The Determinants of Leveraged Buyout Activity: Free Cash Flow vs. Financial Distress Costs," *Journal of Finance* 48, no. 5 (December 1993), pp. 1985–2000.

that companies that did LBOs had relatively high cash flows and poor investment opportunities (as reflected by low Tobin's Qs). These results are consistent with those reported by Kenneth Lehn and Anne Poulsen, who investigated the role of free cash flows in going-private transactions.[17] They found that going-private companies had more free cash flows than a control group.

The presence of high free cash flows makes an LBO possible. Without such cash flows, the company cannot service the buyout debt. The anticipated existence of these cash flows was one of the motivating factors behind the RJR Nabisco LBO and buyouts of supermarkets and food-related businesses such as Supermarkets General and Beatrice.

The free cash flow theory of takeovers assumes that managers have the ability to use free cash flows for their own purposes. The greater the agency costs, the more likely this will occur. With high free cash flows and shielded by high monitoring and agency costs, managers may pursue their own corporate agenda as opposed to shareholder wealth maximization.[18] Robert Hanson investigated the free cash flow theory of takeovers and found that high cash flow target firms receive higher than average abnormal returns.[19] His research showed that during the 1970s, cash flow–rich bidding firms pursued low benefit takeovers. However, in the 1980s high free cash flow firms became targets of tender offers themselves as the market pursued the valuable free cash flows.

Reliability of Accounting Data

The reliability of earnings data has drawn much attention in recent years, particularly as it relates to mergers and acquisitions. The relevance to mergers and acquisitions has to do with not only the premerger valuation analysis but also the assessment of postmerger performance. Two areas of such manipulations that have received much attention in recent years are "in-process" research and development (R&D) charges and restructuring charges. Utilizing such charges has raised some concerns about the consistency of the accounting treatment of mergers. In addition, there is also the concern that the reported numbers may be fraudulently inaccurate.

In-Process Research and Development Charges

The classic example of such potential manipulations is the treatment of "in-process" R&D. Acquirers sometimes try to make postmerger earnings look more impressive by taking an initial charge for the in-process R&D expenses, which is allowable in light of the fact that the impact on future earnings is unknown and the investment in R&D could be worthless. As an example, when America Online (AOL) purchased NetChannel for $29 million in 1998, it wrote off $20 million of the purchase price for in-process R&D. When IBM acquired Lotus

17. Kenneth Lehn and Anne Poulsen, "Free Cash Flow and Shareholder Gains in Going Private Transactions," *Journal of Finance* 44 (July 1989), pp. 771–787.

18. Randall Morck, Andrei Shleifer, and Robert W. Vishny, "Do Managerial Objectives Drive Acquisitions?" *Journal of Finance* 45 (March 1990), pp. 31–48.

19. Robert C. Hanson, "Tender Offers and Free Cash Flow," *The Financial Review* 27, no. 2 (May 1992), pp. 185–209.

in 1995, 57% of the total purchase price of $3.24 billion was in-process R&D. IBM then expensed the entire R&D amount in the third quarter of 1995, which resulted in a reported loss of $538 million for that quarter compared with a profit of $710 million for the same quarter in the prior year.[20] Critics of such write-offs say that companies count on the market not focusing on such charges given that they are onetime events. However, when the positive effects of the acquisition on earnings materialize, the acquirer looks like it has improved its performance.

As of the date of this writing, there has been much discussion of changes in the accounting treatment of in process R&D. While some consider this likely, it has yet to take place.

Restructuring Charges

Sometimes referred to as "big-bath" write-offs, restructuring charges have also been the focus of much concern by critics of the current methods of treating write-offs. The reasoning is similar that for the R&D charges. Companies that may want future earnings to appear more impressive may want to collect expenses from current and future years and expense them in the current year. Companies that do this count on the market ignoring the adverse impact on the current year's performance because of the belief that it is a onetime event. The lower costs in future years will then result in higher earnings. Companies taking such write-offs hope the market considers the higher earnings to be the product of a restructuring program that paid off in the form of improved performance. Critics of such write-offs would say, however, that all the company did was collect future expenses and allocate them to one year so that future expenses are inaccurately low.

Pooling Accounting versus Purchase Accounting

The accounting treatment of acquisitions is discussed separately in Chapter 15. However, with respect to the charges discussed previously, there is some inconsistency in the use of one method over the other. Most acquirers prefer the pooling method because it avoids the recognition of goodwill, which has to be amortized in future years and thus reduces future reported earnings. However, by allowing companies to immediately write off large amounts of R&D, companies can use the purchase method and not have a lot of leftover goodwill to amortize. This then allows such companies to use purchase accounting and have a result similar to that which they would have in pooling accounting.

Fraudulent Inaccuracies

Perhaps the worst scenario is fraudulent misrepresentation of earnings. This was the case when Cendant Corp. reported in 1998 that its earnings were overstated. Cendant is a franchisor of Ramada hotels, Coldwell Banker real estate, and Avis Rent a Car, and a marketer

20. Zhen Deng and Baruch Lev, "The Valuation of Acquired R&D," April, 1998, Stern School of Business, New York University.

of membership clubs. It was formed with the December 1997 merger of HFS, Inc. and CUC International, Inc. The company was forced to report that CUC International deliberately inflated revenues and decreased expenses. Among the issues raised were the treatment of revenues from offered memberships for which customers may ask for a full refund. In its restated data, the company reported revenues reflecting a high 50% cancellation rate. Various estimates of the inflated profits ranged from $500 to $640 million. The deliberate falsification of financial statements is an acquisition nightmare scenario. The impact on the stock price can be seen in Figure 13.3.

FORECASTING METHODS

Forecasting methods vary from the most simple and straightforward to the highly sophisticated and complex econometric forecasting techniques. *Econometrics* is the highly specialized field of economics that uses statistical tools to analyze economic and financial variables. With regard to choosing between the simple techniques and the more sophisticated techniques, the general guiding principle is to use the simplest and least costly tools to develop a forecast. The problem often becomes moot when the analyst is not knowledgeable in sophisticated methodologies. The gains to be derived from employing these methods may also not be clear. The following discussion reviews some of the basic forecasting methods.

Extrapolating Historical Growth Rates

This method involves determining the historical growth rate for a selected time period and projecting it into the future. This calculation usually involves measuring the compounded annual rate of growth as opposed to using a simple average of the different annual growth

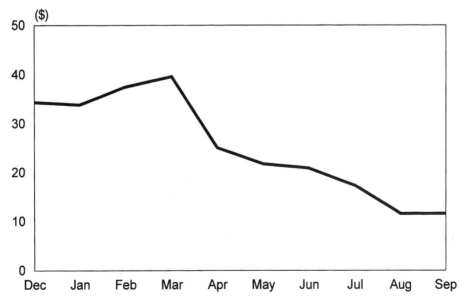

Figure 13.3.   Cendant stock price, 12/31/97–09/30/98.

rates. This can be derived using the same formula we used to derive the dividend compound growth rate (Equation 13.4).

$$Y = (1 + g)^n X \qquad (13.13)$$

where
    Y = the last cash flow value
    X = the first cash flow value
    n = the number of historical years or periods chosen
    g = the compounded annual growth rate

We have the values for Y, X, and n, and we have to solve for g. Rearranging the preceding equation to do that, we get the same type of equation as Equation 13.5.

$$g = \sqrt[n]{\frac{Y}{X}} - 1 \qquad (13.14)$$

The compounded annual rate of cash flows or earnings growth is then applied to the last value the firm recorded. This rate of annual growth is used to project the future annual sales growth. In its simplest form of application, costs are assumed to maintain their historical relationship with revenues. In this way, a balance sheet can be projected for each year into the future in which the analyst is interested. When specific information is available that would alter the level of a particular cost category, this information may be selectively applied to make a more accurate projection.

If the last time period used as the base in the projection is atypical, an average of several other years might have to be used. This process will help reduce the biased influence of the last year in formulating the base. When there is an upward trend in the cash flows or earnings, the averaging process will reduce the influence of the firm's own growth. The analyst must consider both factors and make a judgment on the costs and benefits of this trade-off.

Weighted Average Method

There may have been significant changes in either the firm being analyzed or the market as a whole, or both, that make the revenues earned in later years more relevant to the firm's future performance than revenues earned in earlier years. The difference, however, may not be so great that the analyst will want to discard the earlier years. The difference in the importance attributed to the various years can be accommodated by using a weighting process that places greater emphasis on more recent data. The choice of weights depends on the importance attributed to the different time periods. Larger weights are applied to more recent years when the analyst wants these years to play a greater role in the resulting forecasted values.

Table 13.2 presents an example of a weighted average forecasting process based on seven years of historical revenue data.

The weighted average method gives greater importance to recent years when revenues rose more quickly. In doing so, the sharp revenue increases in 1997 and 1998 play a greater

Table 13.2.   Weighted Average Method for 1992–98 ($ Millions)

Year	Revenues ($)	Weight	Weighted Revenues ($)
1992	1.05	1	1.05
1993	1.10	2	2.20
1994	1.20	3	3.60
1995	1.25	4	5.00
1996	1.50	5	7.50
1997	2.20	6	13.50
1998	3.10	7	21.70
Total	11.40	28	54.25

role in the final projected value of $1.94. This is why the weighted average value of $1.94 is greater than the simple average value of $1.63, which is derived from a process that places equal value on each year's revenues.

    Weighted average method   Simple average method
    $54.25/28.00 = $1.94 $11.40/7 = $1.63

    Both the weighted average and the simple average methods have serious drawbacks. In an inflationary environment, revenues tend to rise through the influence of the general increase in prices. Although the compounded average annual rate of growth takes this factor into account, the weighted and simple average methods fail to fully incorporate the upward annual increase brought on by inflation and other variables, such as industry and firm-specific growth. These methods are clearly inappropriate for newer and more rapidly growing businesses. They are somewhat more appropriate for mature firms in low-growth industries. If these industries have been keeping pace with inflation, however, the application of the relevant inflation factor to the most recent year's revenues may be a better forecasting method than either the weighted or the simple average method.

Linear Trend Analysis

A more sophisticated method of projecting future sales is to approximate the trend in the firm's revenues using a straight line. Although the firm's historical revenues vary in a non-linear manner, the trend can be approximated by assuming that the trend is approximately linear. The simplest way of accomplishing this is to plot the linear trend equation:

$$R = \alpha + \beta T \qquad (13.15)$$

where
R = the projected value of revenues for a selected time T
α = the revenue intercept
β = the slope of the line. This slope tells us how much revenues increase when T changes by one unit.
T = time

Time	Revenues ($ Millions)
1	1.05
2	1.10
3	1.20
4	1.25
5	1.50
6	2.20
7	3.10

The slope of the curve can be derived by the simple relationship

$$\beta = \frac{\Delta R}{\Delta T} = \frac{R_7 - R_1}{T_7 - T_1} = \frac{\$3.10 - \$1.05}{7 - 1} = \$0.34 \tag{13.16}$$

The value of β, the slope, tells us that the average annual increase in sales was $0.34 million. The straight line in Figure 13.4 has a slope of 0.34.

This analysis provides us with the following general equation:

$$Y = 0.76 + 0.34X \tag{13.17}$$

Y is the dependent variable (revenues in this example) and X is the independent variable (time in this example). This equation can be used to project revenues for future years.

Regression Analysis

The curve-fitting procedure can be made more precise by using the least squares method, a method that allows analysts to find the line that will exactly fit in the "middle" of the different points they have. It does so through a formula that minimizes the sum of the squared

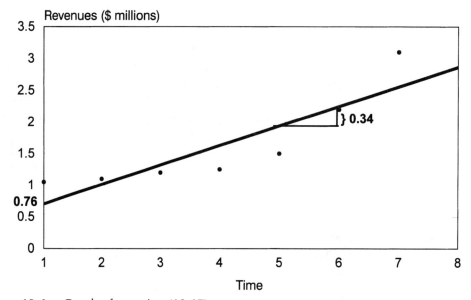

Figure 13.4. Graph of equation (13.17).

deviations from the actual data points for the variable that will be forecast and the values given by the line. Squaring the deviations prevents negative deviations from offsetting positive deviations. Moreover, through this method, the larger deviations receive greater weight in the forecasting process than smaller deviations because when small numbers become squared, they become bigger, but when larger numbers become squared, they become dramatically larger.

This method provides us with more precise estimates of the two parameters α and β. These two parameters, the intercept and the slope, define and place the curve on the graph. They can be determined using the least squares method, by means of the following general formula:

$$\beta = \frac{N(\Sigma XY) - (\Sigma X)(\Sigma Y)}{N(\Sigma X^2) - (\Sigma X)^2} \tag{13.18}$$

$$\alpha = \frac{\Sigma Y - \beta(\Sigma X)}{N}$$

$$\beta = \frac{7(54.25) - (28)(11.4)}{7(140) - (28^2)} = \frac{379.75 - 319.2}{980 - 784} = \frac{60.55}{196} = 0.31$$

$$\alpha = \frac{11.40 - 0.31(28)}{7} = \frac{11.40 - 8.4}{7} = \frac{3}{7} = 0.42$$

In the example we have been using regarding the annual revenues of the corporation, the years are denoted by X, and Y represents annual revenues (Table 13.3). Calculating the components of the intercept and slope terms, we get the following values:

$$Y = 0.42 + 0.31X \tag{13.19}$$

The regression equation derived can be used to forecast the firm's revenues for a given number of years into the future. For example, we can project revenues for years 8 and 9 by substituting 8 and 9 for X in the least squares equation, and we get:

Year 8 $\qquad R_8 = 0.42 + 0.31(8) = 2.90$

Year 9 $\qquad R_9 = 0.42 + 0.31(9) = 3.21$

Table 13.3. Regression Analysis of Revenues

Years (X)	Revenues	X	XY (N = 7)
1	1.05	1	1.05
2	1.10	4	2.20
3	1.20	9	3.60
4	1.25	16	5.00
5	1.50	25	7.50
6	2.20	36	13.20
7	3.10	49	21.70
28	11.40	140	54.25

The forecasted value of revenues for year 7 (2.59) is less than the actual value of 3.10 because, compared with previous years, the last year of data was atypical. It is not surprising, however, that the forecasted value for year 8 (2.90) is less than the actual value for year 7. Revenues for year 9 (3.21) are slightly higher than the actual value for year 7.

If the factors that caused the marked increases in revenues for years 6 and 7 are expected to prevail in the future, the least squares line will underestimate the revenues. But if the variations experienced in years 6 and 7 are normal cyclical variations in the industry, the least squares equation will provide more accurate forecasts.

Simple regression analysis using the least squares technique can provide fairly accurate projections of future revenues based on historical sales data. The disadvantage of this type of approach is that it does not consider the functional relationship between revenues and other deterministic variables, such as the overall level of economic activity or the price of inputs. These factors can be incorporated into the projection process through the use of multiple regression analysis. Multiple regression analysis allows the analyst to incorporate information on the principal determining factors that influence sales. The analyst then derives a multiple regression equation of the form:

$$R = \alpha_0 \, \alpha_1 X_1 + \alpha_2 X_2 + \alpha_3 X_3 + \ldots + \alpha_n X_n \tag{13.20}$$

This equation suggests that several factors determine revenues. The methodology necessary to calculate the regression coefficients is somewhat more involved than simple linear regression. The process may be tedious without the aid of a computer. The major complication, however, is not access to a computer because personal computers and the econometric software necessary to compute the regression equation are readily available. (One of the most popular is TSP, which is a high-quality econometric software package.) The complications may arise in the exact specification of the multiple regression equation: the determination of the appropriate functional form (i.e., linear or nonlinear) and the selection of the independent variables that best determine the dependent variable. This task may be very time-consuming and may lead to misleading or even erroneous results if the analyst does not know how to conduct the necessary econometric tests. Most merger analysts use simple trendfitting techniques or simple historical growth rate extrapolation.

FINANCIAL VALUATION METHODOLOGIES

The field of corporate finance employs various valuation techniques to determine the current value of an investment that will provide cash flows for different future time periods. These techniques are traditionally discussed in the framework of capital budgeting decisions, in which a firm is investing a certain amount of capital in a project that will generate net cash flows in the future. The analysis of an acquisition of a company is a similar type of analytical process. Instead of investing capital in a project, such as a new plant, the acquiring firm is investing capital in a complete company. The principal analytical techniques employed are net present value (NPV) and internal rate of return (IRR). The NPV of a proposed acquisition is the present value of the future cash flows of the target, discounted at the appropriate discount rate, minus the acquisition price. The IRR is the discount rate that equates the present value of the cash flows with the cost of the acquisition. This is the discount rate that gives the acquisition an NPV of zero.

Present Value and Discounting

The value of money varies over time; that is, a dollar next year is worth less than a dollar this year. This is because a dollar today can be invested and earn a return over the coming year and be worth more than a dollar by next year. How much less a dollar is worth next year depends on the rate of return that a dollar today could have earned. The longer funds are invested, the more income will be earned. This income-earning process is enhanced by the fact that the investor would earn interest on interest. This process is called *compounding*. The following equation indicates how the future value of a sum of money will grow if it is invested at an interest rate of r and invested for n time periods:

$$FV = PV(1 + r)^n \qquad (13.21)$$

where
FV = future value
PV = present value
  r = discount rate
  n = number of periods

From this equation we can see that if we wanted to determine what a certain value in the future is worth today, we could simply manipulate the preceding equation to see that

$$PV = FV/(1 + r)^n \qquad (13.22)$$

The process that allows us to determine the value today of a sum of money in the future is called *discounting*. This method can be applied not only to a single sum of money in the future but also to a stream of income generated at different time periods. Such a process is described in the following equation:

$$PV = \frac{FV_1}{(1 + r)} + \frac{FV_2}{(1 + r)^2} + \dots + \frac{FV_n}{(1 + r)^n} \qquad (13.23)$$

Net Present Value

The functional representation of net present value applied to free cash flows is shown in the following equation:

$$NPV = \frac{FCF_1}{(1 + R)} + \frac{FCF_2}{(1 + R)^2} + \dots + \frac{FCF_n}{(1 + r)^n} - P_A \qquad (13.24)$$

where
FCF_i = free cash flows generated in period i
  P_A = acquisition price
   r = discount rate
   n = number of periods the acquisition is projected to generate cash flows

The present value of each projected cash flow can be calculated by multiplying the cash flow by the appropriate present value factor that will bring this term to current dollars. These present value factors, which are referred to as *PVIF* factors, can be found in present value tables, which are readily available. For each discount rate chosen, there is a *PVIF* factor for each period that will convert the projected cash flows to current terms.

The calculation of the net present value of an acquisition was shown previously. A discount rate of 17% was used to bring the future cash flows to present value. The determination of the appropriate discount rate is discussed later in this chapter and in Chapter 14. The net present value was computed by performing the following calculation:

$$NPV = \frac{FCF_1}{(1 + 0.17)} + \frac{FCF_2}{(1 + 0.17)^2} + \cdots + \frac{FCF_5}{(1 + 0.17)^5} + \frac{SP_6}{(1 + 0.17)^6} - AP_0 \tag{13.25}$$

$$NPV = \frac{\$260}{(1.17)} + \frac{\$576}{(1.17)^2} + \frac{\$649}{(1.17)^3} + \frac{\$728}{(1.17)^4} + \frac{\$816}{(1.17)^5} + \frac{\$6,120}{(1.17)^6} - \$1500$$

where
AP_0 = acquisition price in year zero
SP_n = price company sells for in year n

In this example, it is assumed that the acquiring firm can confidently project the target's free cash flows for at least a five-year period. We can sidestep the problem of constructing longer projections by assuming that the target can be sold in the sixth year for the same multiple of its free cash flows as that for which it was acquired. It is therefore assumed that the target can be sold in the sixth year after the acquisition for 7.5 times its fifth year's cash flows, or $6,120,000 (*SP* = sales price).

$$NPV = \$260(PVIF_{1.17}) + \$576(PVIF_{2.17}) + \$649(PVIF_{3.17}) + \$728(PVIF_{4.17}) + \$816(PVIF_{5.17}) + \$6,120$$

$$NPV = \$260(0.8547) + \$576(0.7305) + \$649(0.6244) + \$728(0.5337) + \$816(0.4561) + \$6,120(0.3898) - \$1,500$$

$$= \$2,303$$

The general rule of capital budgeting is that if the net present value for a project, or in our case an acquisition, is greater than zero, the project should be accepted. This assumes that the acquisition is advisable based on all the other relevant criteria. If the acquiring firm is considering a choice among several potential acquisition candidates, the candidate with the highest net present value should be selected.

Accuracy of Discounted Cash Flows: Evidence from HLTs

Steven Kaplan and Richard Ruback conducted a study of 51 highly leveraged transactions (HLTs) between 1983 and 1989 in which they compared the market value of the transactions with the discounted used cash flow forecasts in an effort to ascertain the accuracy of the forecasts relative to the actual purchase price.[21] Of the 51 transactions, 43 were management

21. Steven N. Kaplan and Richard S. Ruback, "The Valuation of Cash Flow Forecasts: An Empirical Analysis," *Journal of Finance* 50, no. 4 (September 1995), pp. 1059–1093.

buyouts and 8 were recapitalizations. They found that the median estimates of the discounted cash flows were within 10% of the market values of the transactions. It is interesting that they compared the accuracy of the discounted cash flow forecasts with that of other valuation methods, such as comparable multiples from transactions in similar industries. The results showed that the discounted cash flow valuation performed at least as well, if not better, than comparable methods. When they added the comparable data to their model, however, the explanatory power of the discounted cash flow estimates improved. This suggests that using information from *both* methods would result in better valuations than using just one.

The import of the Kaplan and Ruback study is that it reinforces the superiority of discounted cash flow valuation to other valuation methods while recognizing the value of other methods, such as comparables, in enhancing a valuation. It further affirms the validity of discounted cash flows as they are currently used in the valuation of public and closely held firms.

Internal Rate of Return

The internal rate of return (IRR) is the discount rate that will equate the discounted free cash flows of the target to the acquisition price. In other words, it is the discount rate that equates the acquisition's net present value to zero.

$$P_A = \frac{FCF_1}{(1 + r)} + \frac{FCF_2}{(1 + r)^2} + \dots + \frac{FCF_n}{(1 + r)^n} \tag{13.27}$$

In the preceding analysis, we have the values of the free cash flows of the target, the potential sale value in the sixth year, and the acquisition price. The IRR can be computed by solving for the discount rate r.

$$\$1,500 = \frac{\$260}{(1 + r)} + \frac{\$576}{(1 + r)^2} + \frac{\$649}{(1 + r)^3} + \frac{\$728}{(1 + r)^4} + \frac{\$816}{(1 + r)^5} + \frac{\$6,120}{(1 + r)^6} \tag{13.28}$$

$$IRR = 47.7\%$$

The analysis for the IRR can be computed by hand through trial and error. The analyst simply tries different discount rates, starting with the best estimate of what the right rate might be. The correct rate is selected when the right side of the preceding equation equals the left side.

Although it is not very difficult to compute the IRR by trial and error, it is much easier to use a computer or at least one of the many financial calculators that compute IRR. Most analysts use spreadsheet programs to compute both the IRR and the NPV. These programs have convenient functions that allow both to be computed using one command. These packages also allow the analyst to perform many other necessary calculations on one spreadsheet.

Choice of the Discount Rate

The choice of the appropriate discount rate to calculate the NPV of the target requires that the riskiness of the target be determined. As is true of other forms of capital investment, an acquisition is a risky endeavor. The discounting process gives us a means of internalizing our judgments about the risk of a capital project or acquisition within the discount rate.

If a project were judged to be without risk, the appropriate discount rate would be the rate offered on Treasury bills, which are short-term government securities with a maturity of up to one year. Treasury bonds, the longer term version of U.S. government securities, may also have zero default risk, but they carry interest rate risk. Interest rate risk is the risk that interest rates may rise above the rate that the investor receives from the Treasury bond. Although the investor is guaranteed the predetermined coupon payments, these coupon payments will not necessarily be invested at the same rate of interest. If they are not, the investment's proceeds will not be compounded at the rate of interest offered on the Treasury bond.

The riskier the investment, the higher the discount rate that should be used; the higher the discount rate, the lower the present value of the projected cash flows. However, a firm methodology for matching the risk with the discount rate needs to be established.

Cost of Capital and the Discount Rate

One of the basic rules regarding the choice of the discount rate is to use the firm's cost of capital. This measure is useful in capital budgeting because only one firm is involved. The cost of capital for a given company can be generally derived through

$$CC = \sum_{i=1}^{n} w_i k_i$$

(13.29)

where
  CC = the firm's cost of capital
  w_i = the weight assigned to the particular k_i. This weight is the percentage of the total capital mix of the firm that this source of capital accounts for.
  k_i = the rate for this source of capital

Let us consider a simple example of a firm whose capital structure is composed of 50% debt and 50% equity. The weights for each source are 0.50. If the debt rate is 9% and the rate of return on equity is 15%, the cost of capital can be computed as follows:

$$CC = 0.50\,(0.09) + 0.50\,(0.15) = 0.045 + 0.075 = 0.12 \text{ or } 12\% \qquad (13.30)$$

The cost of capital can then be used as the discount rate for the firm when evaluating the *NPV* of an investment or acquisition. As the analysis is expanded to make the cost of capital reflect the true capital costs of the firm, all the various components of the capital mix must be considered. Therefore, if the firm has preferred stock outstanding as well as different forms of debt, such as secured bonds, unsecured debentures, and bank loans, each needs to be considered separately in the new expanded version of Equation 13.30.

Cost of Debt

The after-tax debt rate reflects the true cost of debt, given the fact that debt is a tax-deductible expense. The after-tax rate of debt can be determined as follows:

$$k^t = k_d(1 - t) \tag{13.31}$$

where

k^t_d = the after-tax cost of debt
k_d = the pretax cost of debt
t = the actual corporate tax rate for the firm

COST OF PREFERRED STOCK

Because preferred stock dividends are usually fixed, preferred stock shares some of the characteristics of debt securities. Therefore, preferred stock is also known as a fixed income security. The cost of preferred stock to the issuer can be determined by considering the dividends that have to be paid each period relative to the proceeds derived by the issuer. These proceeds should be net of floatation costs. Let us consider a firm that has issued 8% preferred stock with a par value of $100. Let us further assume that floatation costs are 2.0% of the par value. This suggests a net of proceeds value of $98. The annual dividends are $8, or 8% of the $100 par value. (Dividends are annualized for simplicity.) The cost can be determined as follows:

$$\text{Cost of preferred stock} = D_p/P_n = \$8/\$98 = 8.16\%$$

The consideration of floatation costs should also be applied to all publicly issued securities. For the sake of brevity, we consider only floatation costs for preferred stock.

COST OF COMMON STOCK

Many rules determine the cost to the corporation of the common stock it has issued. One of the simplest methods is to calculate the historical rate of return on equity for the stock over a given time period. A 5- to 10-year historical period is often chosen. The time period selected would have to be placed in perspective by considering the corporation's growth to see whether it represents the company's current and expected condition.

If the company is a start-up company with little available history, proxy firms should be used. Proxy firms are similar to the company being analyzed but they have more historical rate of return data available. The rate of return on equity for proxy firms is used in place of the company being analyzed.

Another method that is sometimes employed is the beta risk measure, which is derived from the capital asset pricing model. This measure allows us to consider the riskiness of the company and to use this risk level to determine the appropriate rate of return on the company's equity. The beta can be derived from the following expression:

$$R_i = R_{RF} + \beta_i (R_M - R_{RF}) \tag{13.32}$$

where

R_i = the rate of return on equity for security i
R_{RF} = the risk-free rate. The Treasury bill rate is typically used as the risk-free rate of interest.

β_i = the beta for security i
R_M = the rate of return for the market
$(R_M - R_{RF})$ = the market risk premium

Beta is derived from a regression analysis in which the variability of the market's return is compared with the variability of the security's return. From this analysis, a beta for the firm is derived, which can be used to weigh the risk premium. This weighed risk premium is then specific to the firm being analyzed. This method of measuring the cost of capital makes good conceptual sense but is not commonly used in daily merger analysis.

The rate of return on equity can also be measured by directly projecting the dividend flow. This calculation is easy in the case of preferred stock because the dividends are generally fixed. The following equation, derived from the Gordon model discussed previously, demonstrates the relationship between the stock price and dividends.

$$P_s = D_i/k_e - g \qquad (13.33)$$

where
P_s = the price of the firm's stock
D_i = the dividend paid in period i (i.e., the next quarter)
k_e = the capitalization rate for this stock
g = the growth rate of dividends

We can manipulate the preceding equation to solve for ke:

$$k_e = D_1/P_0 + g \qquad (13.34)$$

Consider the example of a firm whose common stock is currently selling for $40 per share. Annual dividends are $3, and the expected growth in dividends is 7% per year. (For simplicity's sake, dividends are considered annually, even though they may be paid quarterly.) The capitalization rate can be calculated as follows:

$$k_e = \$3 \ (1.07)/\$40 + 0.07 = 15\% \qquad (13.35)$$

The capitalization rate can be used as a measure of the firm's cost of equity capital.

A simple guideline in deriving the cost of equity is to consider that the rate on equity is generally 4% to 6% higher than the rate on debt. The rate of debt may be clear if the firm does not have many different types of debt. In this case, the debt rate is given, and 4% to 6% can simply be added to derive the rate for equity.

HOW THE MARKET DETERMINES DISCOUNT RATES

As should now be clear, no set discount rate exists; many different interest rates are available. The overall market for capital consists of many submarkets. The rate within each market is determined by that market's supply and demand for capital. Markets are differentiated on the basis of risk level. For example, the market for debt capital contains many different gradations of debt that vary according to their risk level. The market for secured

Table 13.4.   Rates of Return and Inflation, 1926–98

Category	Rate (%)
Inflation	3.1
Treasury bills	3.8
Long-term Treasury bonds	5.3
Long-term corporate bonds	5.8
Common stock of large corporations	11.2
Common stock of small corporations	12.7

Source: Stocks, Bonds, Bills, and Inflation (SBBI), 1999 Year-book, Ibbotson Associates, Chicago.

Table 13.5.   Rates of Return and Inflation, 1978–98

Category	Rate (%)
Inflation	4.7
Treasury bills	7.2
Long-term Treasury bonds	10.5
Long-term corporate bonds	10.3
Common stock of large corporations	17.2
Common stock of small corporations	16.4

Source: Stocks, Bonds, Bills, and Inflation (SBBI), 1999 Year-book, Ibbotson Associates, Chicago.

debt offers a lower rate of return than the market for unsecured debt. Within each of the secured and unsecured categories are other gradations, each of which has its own interest rate. The historical relationship between the broad categories of capital can be seen in Tables 13.4 and 13.5.

CONTROL PREMIUM

There is a major difference between the price of a single share quoted on an organized exchange and the price of a 51% block of stock that will give the buyer effective control of the company. When a buyer buys a controlling interest in a target company, he or she receives a combined package of two "goods" in one: the investment features normally associated with ownership of a share of stock and the right to control and change the company's direction. Control allows the buyer to use the target's assets in a manner that will maximize the value of the acquirer's stock. This additional control characteristic commands its own price. Therefore, the buyer of a controlling block of stock must pay a control premium.

The comparative value of a controlling interest relative to a minority interest can be seen by examining the data in Table 13.6 and Figure 13.5. In each of the years shown (1982–97), the controlling interest commanded a higher value.

The basis for the premium can also be found in the factors affecting supply and demand for the firm's stock. The amount of the target's stock is fixed at any moment in time. This assumes that the target is not going to take actions that will increase or decrease its outstanding shares in an effort to thwart an unwelcome bid. When a new bidder buys a large block of stock, the price of the target's stock may go up (Figure 13.6). Because the supply of the target's stock outstanding is fixed, at any moment in time the supply curve for those

Table 13.6. Average Percent Premium Paid: Controlling versus Minority, 1982–98

Year	Controlling Interest (%)	Base*	Minority Interest (%)	Base
1982	42.5	165	29.6	11
1983	37.8	160	35.9	8
1984	39.0	191	16.8	8
1985	37.3	310	34.2	21
1986	39.1	308	27.2	25
1987	38.2	228	39.8	9
1988	41.9	402	58.9	8
1989	41.8	303	26.5	15
1990	42.3	154	39.6	21
1991	35.4	125	32.6	12
1992	41.3	127	38.3	15
1993	38.7	151	38.3	22
1994	40.7	237	54.5	23
1995	44.1	313	61.7	11
1996	37.1	358	29.4	16
1997	35.9	480	22.4	7
1998	32.4	586	26.8	8

*Base: The number of transactions in which a price was reported and premium over market was paid.

Source: Mergerstat Review, 1994, 1999.

shares is vertical at the quantity denoting that number of shares. D_B represents the market demand for the target's shares before the acquirer's bid. The impact of the additional demand by the acquirer is shown by the shift of the demand curve to the right of D_A.

The analysis demonstrated in Figure 13.6 is not the complete story. In addition to the control feature, which by itself will add value to the target's share price, there may be some

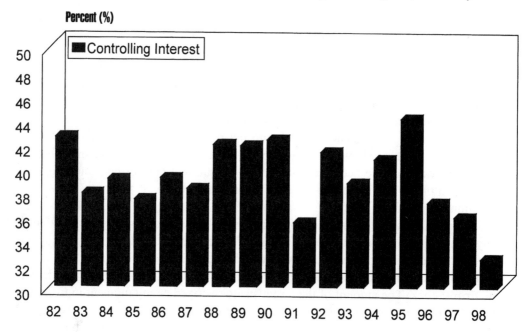

Figure 13.5. Average percent premium for controlling interest, 1982–98.

Source: Mergerstat Review, 1994, 1999.

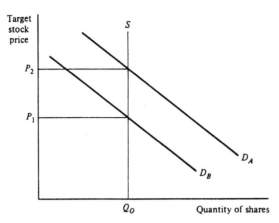

Figure 13.6. Demand-price effects of control bids. Assuming a fixed supply of shares, the increase in demand ($D_B \rightarrow D_A$) bids the share price up.

offsetting effects. These offsetting effects may come in the form of quantity-purchased discounts that often accompany large block purchases. When institutional investors purchase large blocks of stock, they are often able to negotiate a quantity discount from the seller, who may be another institution such as an insurance company or a pension fund.

Robert Holthausen, Richard Leftwich, and David Mayers found that for seller-initiated transactions, buyers receive temporary price concessions that are related to the size of the block.[22] For buyer-initiated transactions, the buyer is given a premium that is also a function of the size of the block. For cases in which the acquirer initiates the bid, the Holthausen, Leftwich, and Mayers study supports the demand-driven price adjustment shown in Figure 13.6. The offsetting effects discussed previously may come into play in cases in which the target is putting itself up for sale. Even when it does exist, this effect may not be observable because the control premium may more than totally offset it.

The Holthausen study does not focus on large blocks bought for mergers. Its focus is on block trading that is a normal part of securities markets. It is useful, however, because it indicates how the size of the block itself affects the purchase price.

Determinants of Acquisition Premiums

The magnitude of acquisition premiums are often attributed to a combination of the bidder's estimate of the acquisition gains and the strength of the target's bargaining position. The acquisition gains may come from a variety of sources, including anticipated synergistic benefits derived from combining the bidder and the target, or the target being underpriced or poorly managed. The bidder's bargaining position may also be affected by several factors, including the presence of other bidders and the strength of the target's antitakeover defenses. Nikhil Varaiya analyzed the role of these various factors in determining acquisition

---

22. Robert W. Holthausen, Richard W. Leftwich, and David Mayers, "The Effect of Larger Block Transactions on Security Prices," *Journal of Financial Economics* 19 (1987), pp. 237–267.

premiums in 77 deals between 1975 and 1980.[23] He found significant support for the role of competitive forces in the auction process and antitakeover measures in determining premiums but mixed results for the role of anticipated benefits.

Role of Arbitrageurs and Impact on Prices

When a company is rumored to be the object of a takeover, the target's stock becomes concentrated in the hands of risk arbitragers, which are institutions that gamble on the probability that a company will eventually be taken over. When this occurs, the holders of the shares, including the arbitragers, will receive a premium. As arbitragers accumulate stock, upward pressure is put on its price. This effect will tend to offset any large block discounts that institutions may receive. The net effect of the arbitrage buying is to increase the price while also increasing the probability that the company will be taken over. The likelihood of a takeover is increased because now more shares will be concentrated in the hands of fewer investors, making large block purchases easier. In addition, given that arbitragers are simply looking to realize a good return on their investment as quickly as possible, they are very willing sellers if the price is right. A committed buyer, therefore, can be aided by risk arbitrage activities.

Valuation Effects of Mergers and Acquisitions

Numerous studies have considered the valuation effects of mergers and acquisitions. Many of these studies were done in the early 1980s. Their results, however, also apply to later time periods. Some more recent research, such as that involving the magnitude of returns over longer time periods and how the returns vary by the medium of exchange, are discussed later in this chapter.[24] Most of these research studies consider the impact of bids over a relatively short-term window, which may be several months before and after a bid. Proponents of the positive effects of mergers contend that it takes many years for the bidder's acquisition plans to come to fruition. Researchers, however, respond that the market has the long-term experience of many prior acquisitions and that it draws on this information when evaluating bids. In addition, it is difficult to conduct long-term studies that filter out the effects of a specific transaction from many events and other transactions that may occur over a longer time period.

These studies have five general conclusions:

1. *Target shareholders earn positive returns from merger agreements.* Several studies have shown that for friendly, negotiated bids, target common stockholders earn sta-

---

23. Nikhil P. Varaiya, "Determinants of Premiums in Acquisition Transactions," *Managerial and Decision Economics* 8 (1987), pp.175–184.

24. It is important to note that the fact that research studies may be dated several years earlier does not mean that their findings no longer apply. It is difficult to publish research that uses a similar methodology and reaches the same conclusions as studies published a decade earlier. Generally, only if their findings differ in some significant aspect will journal referees and editors accept a new version of prior research.

tistically significant positive abnormal returns (Figure 13.7).[25] The source of this return can be traced to the premiums that target shareholders receive.

2. *Target shareholders may earn even higher significant positive returns from tender offers.* Target common shareholders of hostile bids that are tender offers also receive statistically significant positive returns.[26] The hostile bidding process may create a competitive environment, which may increase the acquiring firm's bid and cause

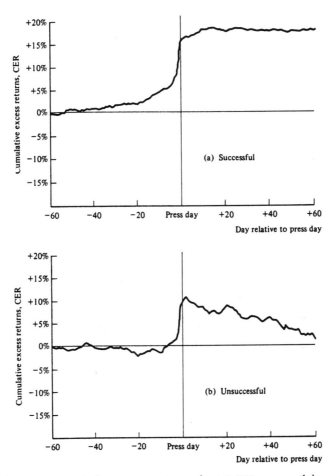

Figure 13.7. Average cumulative excess returns for (a) 211 successful and (b) 91 unsuccessful target firms from 60 days before until 60 days after the press day in the period 1962–76.

Source: Journal of Economics 20, no. 112 (April 1983): 62.

25. Debra K. Dennis and John J. McConnell, "Corporate Mergers and Security Returns," *Journal of Financial Economics* 16, no. 2 (June 1986), pp. 143–187; Paul Asquith, "Merger Bids, Uncertainty and Stockholder Returns," *Journal of Financial Economics* 11 (April 1983), pp. 51–83; Paul Asquith and E. Han Kim, "The Impact of Merger Bids on Participating Firm's Security Holders," *Journal of Finance* 37 (1982), pp. 121–139; Peter Dodd, "Merger Proposals, Management Discretion and Shareholder Wealth," *Journal of Financial Economics*, vol. 8(2), June 1980, pp.105–138.

26. Michael Bradley, Anand Desai, and E. Han Kim, "The Rationale Behind Interfirm Tender Offers," *Journal of Financial Economics* 11, no. 1–4 (April 1983), pp.183–206.

target shareholder returns to be even higher than what would have occurred in a friendly transactions.

3. *Target bondholders and preferred stockholders gain from takeovers.* Both target preferred stockholders and preferred bondholders gain from being acquired.[27] Given that bidders tend to be larger than targets, the addition of the bidder as another source of protection should lower the risk of preferred stocks and bonds, thus making them more valuable. Like the target common stockholder effects, this is an intuitive conclusion.

4. *Acquiring firm shareholders tend to earn zero or negative returns from mergers.* Acquiring firm stockholders tend not to do well when their companies engage in acquisitions.[28] These effects are either statistically insignificant or somewhat negative (Figure 13.8). Presumably, this reflects the fact that markets are skeptical that the bidder can enjoy synergistic gains that more than offset the fact that it is paying a premium for the target. The fact that the bidder's stock response is small compared with that of the target is due to the fact that bidders tend to be larger that targets.[29]

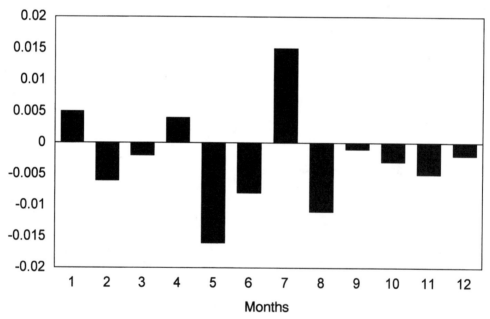

Figure 13.8.   Returns to acquiring firms.

Source: Paul H. Malatesta, "The Wealth Effect of Merger Activity and the Objecting Functions of Merging Firms," *Journal of Financial Economics,* April 1983, 11 (1-4), pp. 155–182.

---

27. Debra K. Dennis and John J. McConnell, "Corporate Mergers and Security Returns," *Journal of Financial Economics* 16, no. 2 (June 1986), pp.143–187.

28. Paul H. Malatesta, "The Wealth Effect of Merger Activity and the Objective Functions of Merging Firms," *Journal of Financial Economics* 11, no. 1–4 (April 1983), pp. 155–182; and Nikhil P. Varaiya, "An Empirical Investigation of the Bidding Firm's Gains from Corporate Takeovers," *Research in Finance* 6 (1986), pp.149–178.

29. Michael Jensen and Richard Ruback, "The Market for Corporate Control: The Scientific Evidence," *Journal of Financial Economics* 11, no. 1–4 (April 1983), pp. 5–50.

5. *Acquiring firm shareholders tend to little or no returns from tender offers.* Returns to acquiring firm shareholders following hostile bids are not impressive. There is some evidence that there may be a response that ranges from either mildly positive or zero.

What Types of Acquiring Firms Tend to Perform the Poorest?

Given that the acquiring firms tend to perform poorly in mergers and acquisitions, the question arises as to what types of firms do the worst and which do better? Rau and Vermaelen analyzed a sample of 3,169 mergers and 348 tender offers between 1980 and 1991.[30] They compared glamor firms, companies with low book to market ratios and high past earnings and cash flow growth, with value firms, companies that higher book to market ratios and poorer prior performance. The results of their research showed that glamor firms underperformed value companies. They attribute the relative poorer performance of glamor firms to factors such as hubris. They also noted that glamor firms tended to more frequently pay with stock. This is understandable because their stock is more valued than that of so-called value firms.

Control Premiums and Target Shareholder Returns

Given that the control premium is the source of the positive returns reported for target shareholders, it is useful to consider how these premiums vary under different circumstances. In the next section, we discuss the trends in these premiums over time, how they vary when the stock market varies, and how they may be different for strategic versus nonstrategic deals and for mergers of equals. Next we consider whether the market places a value of control independent of takeovers.

Historical Trends in Merger Premiums

Contrary to popular belief, the magnitude of merger premiums did not rise dramatically through the fourth merger wave. Indeed, the average merger premiums in the fourth merger wave were less than the average premiums that prevailed at the beginning of the 1980s. However, even in periods when mergers fell in the fourth merger wave, offer prices often rose. This is because offer premiums are greatly influenced by the level of stock market activity. Mergers and acquisitions, in turn, also lifted the stock market in the 1980s.

Merger premiums fell in 1991 with the overall slowdown in merger activity that occurred at that time. After a brief slowdown, however, premiums rose to their fourth merger wave levels in the years that followed. (See Table 13.7.)

---

30. P. Raghavendra Rau and Theo Vermaelen, "Glamor, Value and the Post-Acquisition Performance of Acquiring Firms," *Journal of Financial Economics* 49, no. 2 (August 1998), pp. 223–253.

Table 13.7.   Percent Premium Paid over Market Price,
1978–97

Year	DJIA	Average Premium
1978	805.0	46.2
1979	838.7	49.9
1980	964.0	49.9
1981	875.0	48.0
1982	1,046.5	47.4
1983	1,258.6	37.7
1984	1,211.6	37.9
1985	1,546.7	37.1
1986	1,896.0	38.2
1987	1,938.8	38.3
1988	2,168.6	41.9
1989	2,753.2	41.0
1990	2,633.7	42.0
1991	3,168.8	35.1
1992	3,301.1	41.0
1993	3,754.1	38.7
1994	3,834.4	41.9
1995	5,117.1	44.7
1996	6,448.3	36.6
1997	7,908.3	38.9
1998	9,181.4	41.3

Sources: Haver Analytics, 1998, and Mergerstat Review, 1998.

Stock Market Activity and Merger Premiums

The normal ups and downs of the stock market cause stock prices to rise and fall more than may be explained by variations in their earnings or dividends.[31] This causes some stock to be overpriced at times and underpriced at other times. Managers know that in a bear market their stock price may be below the long-term value of the firm. Believing that their stock price is only temporarily undervalued, managers are inclined to resist selling in bear markets unless a higher than average premium is forthcoming. Similarly, in bull markets, bidders are less inclined to pay the same average premium, knowing that the market has overpriced most stock already.

This relationship can be seen by considering the relationship between market performance and average premiums in rising markets. During the conglomerate merger wave of the late 1960s, which featured a bull market, the average premium ranged between 13% and 25% percent. When the market turned down in the 1970s, the average premium rose to between 33.1% and 50.1%. The highest premium, 50.1%, occurred in 1974 when the Dow Jones Industrial Average (DJIA) fell to 577.60, which was its lowest level in a decade.

---

31. Robert Shiller used this relationship to show that security markets are not perpetually efficient, as some researchers would like to believe. See Robert Shiller, "Do Stock Prices Move Too Much to Be Explained by Subsequent Changes in Dividends?" *American Economic Review* 71 (1981), pp. 421–426.

Premiums from Strategic Mergers

George Roach investigated whether the size of the control premium is greater for strategic mergers versus those transactions that lack such a strategic focus.[32] Nonstrategic acquisitions have been criticized as deals that add little value to the acquiring firm. In theory, if strategic deals are more valuable, the seller should be in a better position to demand higher premiums. In a study of 1,446 transactions between 1992 and 1997, Roach failed to find any difference in the control premium for those deals in which the merging companies have the same or different Standard Industrial Classification (SIC codes). This implies that strategic focus is not a determinant of merger premiums.

Premiums and Mergers of Equals

The findings of the Roach study are consistent with the absence of a significant premium in some of the large telecommunications megamergers that occurred in 1998. The deal between GTE Corp. and Bell Atlantic is a good example. If the transaction is considered an acquisition by Bell Atlantic, GTE shareholders were understandably disappointed when they only received 1.22 share of Bell Atlantic for each share of their company, as GTE shares closed at $55.13 shortly after the deal was announced whereas Bell Atlantic shares closed at $44.32. When one considers the fact that GTE had a higher P/E, a faster revenue growth rate, and a share price that was as high as $64, the offer is not impressive from GTE's point of view. GTE management, however, defended the deal as a "merger of equals." This view, however, is consistent with the Delaware court's position that stock-for-stock mergers are not changes in control. Based on this legal view, a control premium may not be in order. One lesson that was learned in the Time–Warner–Viacom–QVC takeover contest was that such deals can quickly turn into acquisitions if a third suitor enters the fray and makes an acquisition bid with an attractive premium.

Does the Market Value Control Independent of Takeovers?

Having cited the abundant evidence supporting the existence of a control premium in takeovers, we should determine whether control provides a premium in the absence of takeovers. In a study designed to measure the premium paid for control, Ronald Lease, John McConnell, and Wayne Mikkelson sought to determine whether capital markets place a separate value on control.[33]

The Lease study examined the market prices of common stocks of 30 companies with classes of common stock that pay identical dividends but differ significantly in their voting rights. One group had substantially greater voting rights on issues related to the control of the firm, such as the election of directors. The two groups of securities provided the same

32. George R. Roach, "Control Premiums and Strategic Mergers," *Business Valuation Review* (June 1998), pp. 42–49.

33. Ronald C. Lease, John J. McConnell, and Wayne H. Mikkelson, "The Market Value of Control in Publicly Traded Corporations," *Journal of Financial Economics* 11 (April 1983), pp. 439–471.

opportunities for financial gain and differed only in their voting rights and the opportunities to control the company's future. Their results showed that for 26 firms that had no voting preferred stock outstanding, the superior voting common stock graded at a premium relative to the other classes of common stock. The average premium they found was 5.44%. It is important to remember that this is not inconsistent with the premiums cited previously because these other premiums are found in takeovers. This is expected, however, because the companies included in the Lease study were not involved in takeovers.

Four of the 30 firms considered in the study showed that the superior voting rights common stock traded at a discount relative to the other class of common stock. These firms differed from the other 26, however, in that they had a more complex capital structure that featured preferred stock with voting rights. Given the existence of this type of voting preferred stock, these four firms are not as comparable to the other 26 clear-cut cases. Another study that focused on specific industries, such as the banking industry, found control premiums in the range of 50% to 70%.[34]

Long-Term Effects of Acquisitions

As previously noted, many of the early research studies on the valuation effects of mergers and acquisitions use the event study methodology to focus on a relatively short-term time period. More recently, researchers began to focus on the long-term effects of mergers. Franks, Harris, and Titman studied 399 takeovers in the United States covering the period from 1975 to 1984.[35] They found no evidence of significant abnormal returns over a three-year period after the acquisition date. Using an even larger sample of 765 mergers between New York Stock Exchange (NYSE) acquirers and NYSE and AMEX targets between 1955 and 1987, Agrawal, Jaffe, and Mandelker found that shareholders in acquiring firms suffered a loss of approximately 10% over a five-year period after the merger.[36] When subdivided by decades, their results held for the 1950s, 1960s, and 1980s, but not the 1970s. This suggests that any lessons learned by the 1970s were quickly forgotten when we entered the frenzy of the fourth takeover wave. Although they focused on a subsample of only tender offers, they failed to find significant returns.

The negative findings of the studies by Franks and colleagues and Agrawal and associates were supported by a more recent study by Loughran and Vijh, who analyzed 947 acquisitions between 1970 and 1989.[37] They found that companies that complete *stock financed mergers* earn negative excess returns equal to 25% over a five-year period after the deal. This finding contrasts sharply with the positive 61.7% returns they found for cash tender offers. They also found that target shareholders who held on to the stock that they

---

34. Larry G. Meeker and O. Maurice Joy, "Price Premiums for Controlling Shares of Closely Held Bank Stock," *Journal of Business* 53 (1980), pp. 297–314.

35. Julian Franks, Robert Harris, and Sheridan Titman, "The Post-Merger Share Price Performance of Acquiring Firms," *Journal of Financial Economics* 29, no. 1 (March 1991), pp. 81–96.

36. Anup Agrawal, Jeffrey F. Jaffe, and Gershon Mandelker, "The Post-Merger Performance of Acquiring Firms: A Re-examination of an Anomaly," *Journal of Finance* 47, no. 4 (September 1992), pp. 1605–1621.

37. Tim Loughran and Anand M. Vijh, "Do Long Term Shareholders Benefit from Corporate Acquisitions?" *Journal of Finance* 52, no. 5 (December 1997), pp. 1765–1790.

received in exchange for their shares failed to earn statistically significant positive returns. This suggests that target shareholders who receive stock in exchange for their holdings should sell these shares shortly after the deal.

The negative results on the long-term effects of mergers and acquisitions are not uniform. Healy, Palepu, and Ruback found significant improvements in asset productivity relative to industry averages for a sample of the 50 largest mergers that occurred between 1979 and 1984.[38] They found a strong positive relationship between those firms that experienced postmerger increases in cash flows and those that had experienced positive abnormal returns around the merger announcements. One other interesting result was that the positive performance improvements were more pronounced for overlapping businesses—those that had related business lines. This finding is consistent with some of the research on the success of related versus unrelated diversifications. However, the findings of the study by Healy and colleagues have recently come under criticism. Research by Aloke Ghosh shows that the positive effects may be simply a function of a biased comparison to industry medians. He found that when factors such as size are taken into account, the positive effects disappear.[39]

The negative results for many mergers and acquisitions raises concerns about the advisability of many of the takeovers that have taken place in the United States over the past several decades. The unimpressive returns to acquirers that are present in the short term and the long run should give reason for the management of prospective acquirers to reconsider their premerger analysis to make sure that it is well thought out. These findings also raise issues for boards of directors who may have to review a proposed acquisition. It certainly does not mean that companies should not engage in mergers and acquisitions. However, it does mean that the assumptions built into the premerger analysis need to be carefully reviewed before completing a deal. The findings underscore the need for better pre-merger analysis.

VALUATION OF STOCK-FOR-STOCK EXCHANGES

Most of the major acquisitions and hostile takeovers of the fourth merger wave were cash-for-stock exchanges. The acquirer generally determined the value of the target and offered a negotiated amount of cash for the target. Although the cash was raised through a variety of means, there was heavy reliance on debt.

Stock-for-stock swaps were often used in the third merger wave but were less common in the 1980s. As hostile mergers became more prevalent, managers became concerned that they might become targets of hostile bids. As a consequence, many managers became reluctant to make an offer for another firm lest their own firm be "put in play." It was believed that an acquisition offer for another firm might force both firms to be auctioned to the highest bidder. The mere announcement of an offer might bring other hostile bidders onto the scene with a demand for an auction in which they would attempt to offer the highest bid.

---

38. Paul M. Healy, Krishna G. Palepu, and Richard Ruback, "Does Corporate Performance Improve After Mergers?" *Journal of Financial Economics* 31, no. 2 (April 1992), pp.135–175.

39. Aloke Ghosh, "Does Operating Performance Really Improve Following Corporate Acquisitions?" Unpublished Baruch College, City University of New York working paper, November, 1998.

Stock-for-stock mergers sometimes take a longer time to complete, and during this interval, the participants in the merger are vulnerable to a takeover.

Such was the case in the 1989 Time, Inc. offer for Warner Communications. The announcement of a friendly stock-for-stock swap merger between Time and Warner Communications brought an unwanted bid by Paramount, Inc. Paramount demanded that the companies be put for sale to the highest bidder. Paramount's position was that the announcement of the bid by Time and Warner required an auction. The Delaware court ruling, however, failed to agree. The court's position was that an auction was not required. The Delaware decision has great significance for the future of friendly stock-for-stock mergers. Management and directors now have more leeway in agreeing to such transactions by relying on the business judgment rule. Managers and directors may take the position that they have a long-term plan for the corporation that is in the best interests of stockholders, and they may choose not to accept a hostile bid from another firm. This paves the way for more stock-financed friendly mergers and acquisitions.

Tax Incentives for Stock versus Cash Transactions

The tax laws provide that stock-for-stock exchanges may be treated as tax-free reorganizations.[40] This means the stock that target stockholders receive will *not* be taxed until the shares are sold. Target stockholders are thus able to postpone being taxed on the consideration that is received for the shares in the target company until the new shares in the acquirer are sold. One tax disadvantage of a reorganization is that the acquirer may not utilize other tax benefits that would be allowable if the transaction were not a reorganization, such as if it were financed by cash. If the transaction were not a reorganization, other tax advantages, such as the ability to step up the asset base or utilize unused tax credits that the target might possess, would be available. It is also possible to receive debt in exchange for the target's shares. For example, the target stockholders could receive debt as part of an installment sale of the target. In this case, the deferred payments are not taxed until they are actually received.[41] The seller can accumulate interest, tax-free, on the unreceived portions of the sale price.

Valuation Effects of the Medium of Exchange

The valuation effects tend to differ depending on whether the deal is a stock or cash deal.

Target Companies: Short-Term Effects of Method of Payment

Target companies research studies show that the target company valuation effects are greater for cash offers than for stock offers. For example, using a sample of 204 deals, Huang and

---

40. Alan J. Auerbach and David Reishus, "The Impact of Taxation on Mergers and Acquisitions," in *Mergers and Acquisitions,* edited by Alan J. Auerbach (Chicago: National Bureau of Economic Research, 1987), pp. 69–85.

41. Alan J. Auerbach and David Reishus, "Taxes and the Merger Decision," in *Knights, Raiders, and Targets,* edited by John C. Coffee Jr., Louis Lowenstein, and Susan Rose Ackerman (New York: Oxford University Press, 1988) pp. 300–313.

Walking find that cash offers are associated with substantially higher target returns before and after controlling for the type of acquisition and the amount of resistance.[42] They attribute the higher premiums of cash offers to tax effects. That is, they conclude that the higher premiums are caused by shareholders who demand them because they will be forced to incur the costs associated with cash-financed acquisitions. Huang and Walking's finding regarding the higher premiums of cash offers has been confirmed by later research.[43] It is interesting that in a sample of 84 target firms and 123 bidding firms between 1980 and 1988, Sullivan, Jensen, and Hudson found that the higher returns associated with cash offers persist even after offers were terminated. They interpret this as the market reevaluating firms that are targets of cash offers and placing a higher value on them as a result of the cash offer.

Acquiring Companies: Short-Term Effects of Method of Payment

As noted previously, acquiring companies tend to show zero or negative returns in response to announcements of takeovers. Saeyoung Chang analyzed the short-term announcement effects on acquiring firms of takeovers of public and privately held companies while also considering how these effects differed for cash versus stock offers.[44] Using a sample of 281 deals from 1981 to 1992, he found that abnormal returns were approximately zero and not statistically significant for cash takeovers of public companies, whereas returns were a positive and statistically significant 2.64% for stock offers. For private firm takeovers, returns were not statistically significant for cash offers but were a statistically significant −2.46% for stock deals. In conclusion, he found that for cash offers, returns were basically zero and did not vary depending on whether the deal was a public or private acquisition. However, the positive stock price reaction to takeovers of private companies is in sharp contrast to the negative response for public company takeovers. This study is discussed further in Chapter 14, as one theory that explains this result is that there may be more monitoring when stock is given to a few owners of the closely held company. This greater monitoring may reduce adverse agency effects and increase value. When the market perceives this, it reacts with a positive stock price response.

Acquiring Companies: Long-Term Effects of Method of Payment

The Chang finding of zero returns for cash offers was contradicted by Loughran and Vijh, who found positive abnormal long-term returns for cash acquisitions but negative abnormal return for stock deals.[45] In particular, they found that over the five-year period following the

42. Yen-Sheng Huang and Ralph A. Walking, "Target Abnormal Returns Associated with Acquisition Announcements," *Journal of Financial Economics* 19 (1987), 329–349.

43. Michael J. Sullivan, Marlin R. H. Johnson, and Carl D. Hudson, "The Role of Medium of Exchange in Merger Offers: Examination of Terminated Merger Proposals," *Financial Management* 23, no. 3 (Autumn 1994), 51–62.

44. Saeyoung Chang, "Takeovers of Privately Held Targets, Methods of Payment, and Bidder Returns, *Journal of Finance* 53, no. 2 (April 1998), pp. 773–784.

45. Tim Loughran and Anand M. Vijh, "Do Long Term Shareholders Benefit from Corporate Acquisitions?" *Journal of Finance* 52, no. 5 (December 1997), pp. 1765–1790.

acquisitions, stock deals averaged negative excess returns equal to –25%, whereas for cash tender offers the returns were an average abnormal return of a positive 61.7%! This is a sizable difference. Aloke Ghosh's research also provides some support for the long-term effects of the Loughran and Vijh study. He found that performance as measured by total asset turnover improved for cash acquisitions but performance measures such as cash flows declined for stock deals.[46] However, when he controlled for the size of the combined companies, which become larger after the deals, the performance difference of stock versus cash deals disappeared. In cash transactions the firms were larger than those in the stock deal subsample. Ghosh attributes improvements to the larger size of the postacquisition cash deals compared to stock transactions which involved relatively smaller combined companies.

Method of Payment, Managerial Ownership, and Executive Job Retention

Managers of acquiring companies who value control may want to avoid stock deals because such deals may dilute their control.[47] If this is the case, it may be reasonable to assume that the owners of target companies who value control may prefer stock instead of cash. In a study involving 212 acquisitions between 1981 and 1988, Ghosh and Ruland found a "strong positive association between managerial ownership of target firms and the likelihood of acquisitions for stock."[48] They also found that managers in target firms were more likely to retain their positions when they received stock as opposed to cash.

Legal Issues in Stock-Financed Transactions

Buyers seeking to finance an acquisition through the use of securities must be mindful of the registration requirements of the Securities and Exchange Commission (SEC) that are set forth in the Securities Act of 1933. Sellers prefer registered securities that can be readily sold in the market. However, buyers may prefer to offer unregistered securities. One reason buyers may prefer unregistered securities is the cost of the registration process, which is expensive in terms of both professional fees and management time. The registration process may also require the buyer to make public information it may not want to reveal to other parties, such as competitors. In addition, the registration process may impose impediments on the buyer that may inhibit its ability to take certain actions lest they necessitate an amendment in the registration statement filed with the SEC.

It may be possible for the parties to negotiate an agreement that allows the buyer to take advantage of certain exemptions to the registration requirements. The buyer may try to

---

46. Aloke Ghosh, "Does Operating Performance Really Improve Following Corporate Acquisitions?" Unpublished Baruch College, City University of New York working paper, November, 1998.

47. Yakov Amihud, Baruch Lev, and Nicholas Travlos, "Corporate Control and the Choice of Investment Financing: The Case of Corporate Acquisitions," *Journal of Finance,* vol. 45, no. 2, pp. 603–616.

48. Aloke Ghosh and William Ruland, "Managerial Ownership, the Method of Payment for Acquisitions, and Executive Job Retention," *Journal of Finance* 53, no. 2 (April 1998), pp. 785–798.

qualify for an exemption on the grounds that the securities being offered to purchase the target company do not constitute a public offering. Although the attainment of this non-public offering exemption is often not a certainty, it may have a significant effect on the costs of the total transaction from the buyer's viewpoint, as well as on the value the seller places on the consideration being offered by the buyer.

EXCHANGE RATIO

The exchange ratio is the number of the acquirer's shares that are offered for each share of the target. The number of shares offered depends on the valuation of the target by the acquirer. Both the acquirer and the target conduct a valuation of the target, and from this process the acquirer determines the maximum price it is willing to pay while the target determines the minimum it is willing to accept. Within this range, the actual agreement price will depend on each party's other investment opportunities and relative bargaining abilities. Based on a valuation of the target, the acquirer determines the per share price it is offering to pay. The exchange ratio is determined by dividing the per share offer price by the market price of the acquirer's shares. Let us consider the example of United Communications, which has made an offer for Dynamic Entertainment (Table 13.8).

Let us assume that, based on its valuation of Dynamic, United Communications has determined that it is willing to offer $65 per share for Dynamic. This is a 30% premium above the premerger market price of Dynamic. In terms of United's shares, the $65 offer is equivalent to United's $65/$150 share

$$\text{Exchange ratio} = \text{Offer price/Share price of acquirer} = \$65/\$150 = 0.43 \text{ shares}$$

Based on the preceding data, United Communications can calculate the total number of shares that it will have to offer to complete a bid for 100% of Dynamic Entertainment.

Total shares that United Communications will have to issue
= [(Offer price) (Total outstanding shares of target)]/Price of acquirer
= [($65)(2,000,000)]/$150 = 866,666.67

Earnings per Share of the Surviving Company

Calculating the earnings per share (EPS) of the surviving company reveals the impact of the merger on the acquirer's EPS.

Table 13.8. United Communications and Dynamic Entertainment: Comparative Financial Condition

	United Communications	Dynamic Entertainment
Present earnings	$50,000,000	$10,000,000
Shares outstanding	5,000,000	2,000,000
Earnings per share	10	5
Stock price	150	50
P/E ratio	15	10

Combined earnings = $50,000,000 + $10,000,000

Total shares outstanding = 5,000,000 + 866,666.67

United Communications' Impact on EPS-$65 Offer

Premerger EPS	Postmerger EPS
$10.00	$10.23

United Communications will experience an increase in its EPS if the deal is completed. Let us see the impact on earnings per share if a higher price is offered for Dynamic Entertainment.

Let us assume that Dynamic Entertainment rejects the first offer of $65 per share. Let us further assume that this rejection is based partly on Dynamic's own internal analysis showing the value of Dynamic to be at least $75. Dynamic also believes that its value to United is well in excess of $75. Based on some hard bargaining, United brings a $90 offer to the table.

To see the impact on the surviving company's earnings per share, we will have to redo the preceding analysis using this higher offer price.

$$\text{Exchange ratio} = \text{Offer price/Share price of acquirer}$$
$$= \$90/\$150 = 0.60 \text{ shares}$$

Total shares that United Communications will have to issue

$$= [(\text{Offer price })(\text{ Total outstanding shares of target})]/\text{Price of acquirer}$$
$$= [(\$90) (2,000,000)]/\$150 = 1,200,000$$

United Communications' Impact on EPS-$90 Offer

Premerger EPS	Postmerger EPS
$10.00	$9.68

United Communications' EPS declined following the higher offer of $90. This is an example of dilution in earnings per share.

Criteria for Dilution in EPS

Dilution in EPS will occur any time the P/E ratio paid for the target exceeds the P/E ratio of the company doing the acquiring. The P/E ratio paid is calculated by dividing the EPS of the target into the per share offer price. This is as follows:

$$\text{P/E ratio paid} = \$35/\$5 = \$13 < \$15$$

Offer price $65

In the case of the $65 offer, the P/E ratio paid was less than the P/E ratio of the acquirer, and there was no dilution in EPS. Table 13.9 shows that the median P/E paid is usually higher for acquisitions of public companies than for acquisitions of private firms.

Table 13.9.   Median P/E Paid, 1980–98

Year	Acquisition of Public Companies	Base	Acquisition of Private Companies	Base
1980	11.5	162	10.3	81
1981	14.0	160	11.5	70
1982	12.8	150	10.1	43
1983	15.5	141	11.5	48
1984	15.1	183	11.4	63
1985	16.4	240	12.3	187
1986	24.3	259	16.5	105
1987	21.7	191	15.2	25
1988	18.3	309	12.8	50
1989	18.4	222	12.7	42
1990	17.1	117	13.3	36
1991	15.9	93	8.5	23
1992	18.1	89	17.6	15
1993	19.7	113	22.0	14
1994	19.8	184	22.0	18
1995	19.4	239	15.5	16
1996	21.7	288	17.7	31
1997	25.0	389	17.0	83
1998	24.0	362	16.0	207

Source: Mergerstat Review, 1994, 1999.

Offer price $90

P/E ratio paid = $90/$5 = $18

In the case of the $90 offer, the P/E ratio paid was greater than the P/E ratio of the acquirer, and there was a dilution in EPS.

Example of Dilution in Earnings per Share

One example of anticipated dilution in earnings per share occurred in June 1995, when First Union Corporation of North Carolina acquired First Fidelity Bancorp of New Jersey in a $5.4 billion stock swap. Before the merger, First Union had forecasted that it would earn $6.55 per share but it lowered its postmerger forecast to $6.31 per share.[49] To counter the downward pressure on its stock, which fell $1.75 to $45.875 after the deal was publicly revealed, First Union announced a plan that featured a stock buyback and a 13% increase in its dividend. First Union believed so strongly in the synergistic benefits of being able to sell its various financial products to First Fidelity's customer base that it was willing to tolerate an initial dilution in EPS to be positioned to generate more rapid growth in the future.

---

49. Martha Brannigan and Timothy O'Brien, "First Union Is Viewed as Paying Dearly for First Fidelity," *Wall Street Journal,* 20 June 1995, p. B4.

Highest Offer Price without Dilution in EPS

We can determine the maximum offer price that will not result in a dilution in EPS by solving for P in the following expression:

Maximum nondilution offer price (P')

$$\$15 = P/\$5$$
$$P = \$75$$

Solving for P', we see that the maximum offer price that will not result in a dilution in EPS is \$75. This does not mean that the acquirer will not offer a price in excess of \$75 per share. A firm might be willing to incur an initial dilution in EPS to achieve certain benefits, such as synergies, which will result in an eventual increase in per share earnings. This can be seen in the trend in EPS in Table 13.10.

An examination of Table 13.10 reveals that although United Communications would incur an initial \$0.32 dilution in EPS, United would quickly surpass its premerger EPS level. Let us assume that United had a historical 4% growth in EPS before the merger. In other words, United's rate of growth in EPS was only equal to the rate of inflation. Presumably, United was interested in Dynamic Entertainment in order to achieve a higher rate of growth. Let us also assume that a premerger analysis convinced United that it would be able to achieve a 5% rate of growth after it acquired Dynamic Entertainment.

Based on a 5% rate of growth, it is clear that United Communications would achieve a higher EPS level by the fourth year. A more precise estimate of the break-even point can be determined as follows:

$$\$10 \, (1.04)t = \$9.68 \, (1.05)^t \tag{13.36}$$

where t = the break-even time period

Solving for t, we get

$$\frac{\$10}{\$9.68} = \frac{(1.05)^t}{(1.04)^t}$$

$$0.033 = (1.05/1.04)^t$$

Table 13.10.   Earnings per Share with and without Merger, United Communications

Years	Without Merger (4% growth) ($)	With Merger (5% growth) ($)
0	10.00	9.68
1	10.40	10.16
2	10.82	10.67
3	11.25	11.21
4	11.70	11.77
5	12.17	12.35
6	12.66	12.97
7	13.16	13.62
8	13.69	14.30

$$log\ (1.033) = t\ log\ (1.05/1.04)$$

$$0.01412 = (0.004156)$$

The firm may have a ceiling on the maximum amount of time it may be willing to wait until it breaks even with respect to EPS. If United Communications is willing to wait approximately 3.25 years to break even, it may agree to the merger at the higher price of $90. If United thinks that this is too long to wait, it may agree only at a lower price or it may look for other merger candidates.

Factors That Influence Initial Changes in Earnings per Share

The amount of change in EPS is a function of two main factors:[50]

1. *Differential in P/E Ratios.* Rule: The higher the P/E ratio of the acquirer relative to the target, the greater the increase in EPS of the acquirer.
2. *Relative Size of the Two Firms as Measured by Earnings.* Rule: The larger the earnings of the target relative to the acquirer, the greater the increase in the acquirer's EPS.

The first factor has already been explained, but the role of the relative size of the two firms needs to be explored. For the sake of this discussion, let us assume that earnings are an acceptable measure of value. Because EPS is the ratio of earnings divided by the number of outstanding shares, the greater the addition to the earnings of the surviving firm that is accounted for by the addition of the target's earnings, the greater the EPS of the surviving firm. This is a commonsense proposition.

We can combine the effect of both factors to say that the higher the P/E ratio of the acquirer relative to the target and the greater the earnings of the target relative to the acquirer, the greater the increase in the combined company's EPS. The opposite also follows. The combined effect of the P/E ratio differential and the relative earnings of the two firms can be seen in Figure 13.9.

Bootstrapping Earnings per Share

Bootstrapping EPS refers to the corporation's ability to increase its EPS through the purchase of other companies. These earnings were prevalent during the third merger wave of the late 1960s. During this time, the market was not efficient in its valuation of conglomerates. These conglomerates were able to experience an increase in EPS and stock prices simply by acquiring other firms.

In the case of United Communications' acquisition of Dynamic Entertainment, United issued 866,666.67 shares of stock based on a $65 offer price. This results in 5,866,667.67 total shares of United Communications outstanding (Table 13.11).

---

50. For an excellent discussion of these factors, see James C. Van Horne, *Fundamentals of Financial Management,* 9th ed. (Englewood Cliffs, N.J.: Prentice-Hall, 1995).

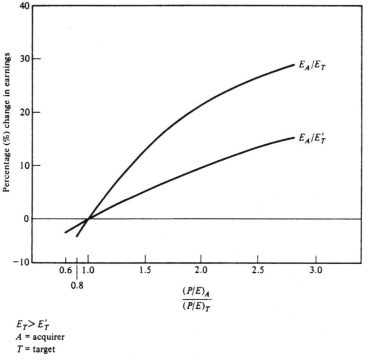

$E_T > E_T'$
A = acquirer
T = target

Figure 13.9.   Combined effect of P/E ratio differential and relative earnings.

With the offer price of $65 per share, United Communications can offer Dynamic Enter-
tainment a 30% percent premium above its premerger price of $50 and still experience an
increase in EPS. If we assume that the market will apply the same EPS to United before and
after the merger, the stock price has to rise. This can be seen from the following expression:

$$P/E = P/EPS$$
$$15 = P/\$10.23$$
$$P = \$153.45$$

United Communications' postmerger stock price has risen to $153.45 as a result of
bootstrapping EPS. Two conditions are necessary for bootstrapping EPS to occur:

1. *The P/E ratio must not decline following the merger.* This implies that the market
   must be willing to apply at least the premerger P/E ratio after the merger. If the market decides that the combined firm is not as valuable, per dollar of earnings, there may
   be a market correction and the P/E ratio may fall. In the third merger wave, the market
   was slow to reevaluate the growing conglomerates and apply a lower P/E ratio.

Table 13.11.   United Communications' Postmerger Financial Condition

Earnings	$60,000,000.00
Shares outstanding	5,866,666.67
EPS	10.23
P/E ratio	15.00
Stock price	153.45

2. *The acquirer must have a higher P/E ratio than the target.* If these two conditions prevail, companies with higher P/E ratios can acquire companies with lower P/E ratios and experience growth in EPS. This gives the acquiring company an incentive to continue with further acquisitions and have even greater increase in EPS. The process will continue to work as long as the stock market continues to value the acquiring company with the same P/E ratio. This occurred during the late 1960s. The movement came to an end when the market corrected itself as it questioned many of the acquisitions that appeared to lack synergistic benefits.

Postmerger P/E Ratio

If the market is efficient, bootstrapping EPS is not possible. The postmerger P/E ratio will be a weighted average of the premerger P/E ratios. This can be calculated using the following expression:

$$\frac{P}{E_{A+B}} = \frac{(P_A \times S_A) + (P_B \times S_B)}{E_A + E_B}$$

where

$\dfrac{P}{E_{A+B}}$ = the postmerger P/E ratio

P_A = the premerger stock price of Company A
P_B = the premerger stock price of Company B
S_A = the number of outstanding shares of Company A
S_B = the number of outstanding shares of Company B
E_A = the earnings of Company A
E_B = the earnings of Company B

Using the preceding expression, we can calculate United Communication's postmerger P/E ratio after the stock-for-stock acquisition of Dynamic Entertainment. We will calculate this ratio based on the $65 initial offer that required the issuance of 866,666.67 shares.

$$\frac{P}{E_{U+D}} = \frac{(P_U \times S_U) + (P_D \times S_U)}{E_U + E_D}$$

$$\frac{P}{E_{U+D}} = \frac{(\$150 \times 5,000,000) + (\$50 \times 2,000,000)}{\$50,000,000 + \$10,000,000}$$

$$= \frac{\$750,000,000 + \$100,000,000}{\$60,000,000} = \frac{\$850,000}{\$60,000} = 1$$

Without the bootstrapping effect, the P/E ratio of the combined firm falls relative to United Communications' premerger P/E ratio. The resulting P/E ratio is a blended combination of United's P/E ratio (15) and Dynamic's lower P/E ratio (10).

STOCK PRICE VARIABILITY AND COLLAR AGREEMENTS

Stock-for-stock exchanges may take a longer time to complete than all-cash acquisitions. The value of the respective shares may change between the time an agreed-on exchange ratio is determined and the acquisition date. One solution to this problem is to arrange to a *collar agreement*. This agreement usually stipulates that if the stock price goes above or below a certain value, there will be an adjustment in the exchange ratios. Such an agreement protects the acquiring firm in the event that its stock price is higher or the target's stock price is lower on the date of the merger than on the agreement date. If the merger were to be completed at the original exchange ratio, the acquirer would have overpaid. Similarly, the collar agreement protects the target when the acquirer's stock price has fallen since the agreement date or when the target's stock price has risen.

The collar agreement may tolerate small movements in the stock price without causing changes in the exchange ratio. A certain threshold is established beyond which the exchange ratio has to be adjusted. The existence of a collar agreement in a merger is usually a point of negotiation.[51] It is more important if the stock of one or both of the participants tends to be volatile. If both firms are in the same industry, market movements in each stock might offset each other.

Board Size and Valuation

A study by David Yermack analyzed the relationship between board size and market valuation.[52] In a study of 452 large U.S. corporations, Yermack found that companies with smaller boards had a higher market valuation. Most boards had between 6 and 24 members. As their size grows, firm values, as approximated by Tobin's Q, decline. Yermack attributed the findings to difficulties such as poorer communications and decision making when boards are bigger. He also found that smaller board firms had better financial ratios.

BENCHMARKS OF VALUE

The analysis presented in this chapter provides several different methods of valuing a company. Their accuracy can be tested through a basic sensibility check, which can be performed by comparing the resulting values with certain benchmarks that indicate the *floor value* of the company. The floor value is the normal minimum value that the company should command in the marketplace. Some of these benchmarks are described in the following sections.

---

51. In the Diamond Shamrock-Natomas merger in 1983, the existence of a collar agreement was an important point of negotiation between the two firms. See Dorman L. Commons, *Tender Offer* (New York: Penguin Books, 1986), pp. 103–104.

52. David Yermack, "Higher Market Valuation of Companies With a Small Board of Directors," *Journal of Financial Economics* 40, no. 2 (February 1996), pp. 185–211.

Book Value

Book value is the per share dollar value that would be received if the assets were liquidated for the values that the assets are kept on the books, minus the monies that must be paid to liquidate the liabilities and preferred stock. Book value is sometimes also called shareholders' equity or net worth. Book value tends not to be an accurate measure of a company's value. It tends merely to reflect the values for which the assets are held on the books. If these historical balance sheet values are not consistent with the true value of the company's assets, book value will not be as relevant to the company's valuation.

One use of book value is to provide a floor value, with the true value of the company being some amount higher. The evaluator's role is to determine how much higher the true value of the company is. In some cases, however, the company may be worth less than the book value. Although this is not common, a company may have many uncertain liabilities, such as pending litigation, which may make its value less than the book value.

Sales prices of companies can be expressed as multiples of book values. These multiples tend to vary by industry. Depending on the current trends in the industry, there is a certain average value that can be used to gauge the current market price of potential targets. If firms in the industry are priced at a certain average value, such as selling at six times the book value, and the firm in question is only selling for two times the book value, this might be an indicator of an undervalued situation. Book value is a preliminary indicator that takeover artists use to find undervalued firms.

Liquidation Value

Liquidation value is another benchmark of the company's floor value. It is a measure of the per share value that would be derived if the firm's assets were liquidated and all liabilities and preferred stock as well as liquidation costs were paid. Liquidation value may be a more realistic measure than book value. If accurately computed, it may be a more accurate indicator of the true value of the firm's assets in that to some extent it reflects the market value of the assets. However, it may underestimate the true market value because it considers this value in a liquidation when assets may sell at "fire sale" prices.

Liquidation value does not measure the earning power of the firm's assets. These assets may have different values depending on the user. If the firm is using its assets very efficiently, the company's value may be well in excess of the liquidation value.

DESIRABLE FINANCIAL CHARACTERISTICS OF TARGETS

Acquirers can use the following characteristics as financial screens.

Rapidly growing cash flows and earnings. A pattern of rising cash flows and earnings is the most desirable characteristic. The future cash flows are the most direct benefit the buyer derives from an acquisition. Therefore, a rising historical trend in these values may be an indicator of higher levels in the future.

Low price relative to earnings. A P/E that is low compared with its level over the past two to three years suggests that the company is relatively inexpensive. A low P/E ratio is generally considered a desirable characteristic in a target. The lower the P/E ratio, the lower the price that will be paid to acquire the target's earning power. Because of market fluctuations, the P/E ratio of a firm or an industry category may go up and down. In addition, the market fluctuates up and down. A falling stock price that is not caused by a reduction in the potential target's earning power may present a temporary undervaluation and an acquisition opportunity. An acquirer can measure the extent of the undervaluation by comparing the P/E ratio with the previous level over the preceding three years. A low level can mean undervaluation due to changes in investor preferences or it can reflect a change in the firm's ability to generate income in the future. The lowest value in three years is an indicator of one of the two; it is the analyst's job to decide which it is. (Although the prior discussion is framed in terms of a P/E ratio, it also applies to a pre-cash flow ratio.)

Market value less than book value. Book value is a more reliable measure of value in certain industries. Industries that tend to have more liquid assets also tend to have more useful book values. Finance companies and banks are examples of firms that have a large percentage of liquid assets. Even in industries in which assets may be less liquid, such as firms that have large real estate holdings, however, book value can be put to use as a floor value. This was the case in Campeau Corporation's acquisition of Federated Stores in 1988. Both firms had large real estate holdings and marketable divisions and store chains. The combined market value of these assets and the estimated market value of the divisions on a per share basis made Federated a vulnerable target. In retrospect, the estimated value of the divisions proved to be greater than their market value when they were offered for sale.

High liquidity. As mentioned in Chapter 12, a target company's own liquidity can be used to help finance its own acquisitions. High liquidity ratios relative to industry averages are a reflection of this condition. The additional liquidity is even more applicable for debt-financed takeovers, where the liquidity of the target may be an important factor in the target's ability to pay for its own financing after the merger.

Low leverage. Low leverage ratios, such as the debt ratio and debt-equity ratio, are desirable because this shows a lower level of risk as well as added debt capacity that can be used to finance the takeover. The more cyclical the industry, the more important it is to keep leverage within a manageable range.

CASE STUDY: DUNKIN' DONUTS[a]

Dunkin' Donuts is the largest coffee and donut chain in the United States. As of 1989, the company had 1,764 shops throughout the world. The firm, which was founded in 1950 in Quincy, Massachusetts, has expanded its product line over the years to include sandwiches and a wider selection of beverages so that it can cater to the breakfast and luncheon trade. Much of the firm's growth came between 1968 and 1973. Nonetheless, the firm posted a loss of approximately $1.5 million in 1973. It responded to the loss by slowing its rate of expansion.

After the falloff in profitability, Dunkin' Donuts changed its expansion emphasis from the number of units to sales at existing units. The company also began to make a more careful evaluation of individuals selected to own franchises, thereby enhanc-

---

a. This case study is a joint effort by Patrick Gaughan, Jamet Gabrielo, and Mona Shahad.

ing the quality of its franchise network. In 1985 the firm expanded beyond its traditional coffee and donut business, entering into an agreement with Chili's, Inc. to develop Chili's Bar & Grill restaurants. By 1989 it had opened nine such restaurants.

VALUATION OF INCOME BY SOURCE

The main sources of revenue of Dunkin' Donuts are its rental and franchise fee income.[b] The business is so structured that the company owns a small number of units and franchises the remaining ones, giving the company franchise fee income for the use of the company's name and know-how. The company's other major source of income—rental income—comes from a number of major real estate holdings (Table 1).

The rental income provides stable cash flow that can be used to service debt. A breakdown of the excess cash flow from the real estate part of the business, as represented by the difference between rental income and cash rental expenses, is shown in Table 2. The table shows that the ability of Dunkin' Donuts to service debt rose in the late 1980s. Based on a valuation multiple of eight times cash flow, the real estate division of the company was worth $216 million in 1988, or $34 per share. Its franchise fee income is approximately equal to 5% of sales. The company also receives between $20,000 and $40,000 for each new unit that is opened, resulting in the income stream shown in Table 3. Using the same eight times cash flow multiple that was used to value the real estate cash flow, we find that the franchise fee income equals $152 million, or approximately $24 per share. In addition to rental and franchise fee income, Dunkin' Donuts owned 29 shops in 1988, which produced approximately $4 million in cash flow. Using the cash flow multiple of eight, we observe that this is valued at $32 million, or approximately $5 per share.

Table 1. Real Estate Operations of Dunkin' Donuts

Status	Number of Units
Own land and building	215
Own building/lease land	345
Lease land and building	382
No real estate interest	727

Table 2. Real Estate Cash Flows, 1985–88 ($ millions)

Income/Expenditures	1988 (est.)	1987	1986	1985
Rental income	$41.0	$38.5	$35.4	$32.8
Cash rental expenses*	14.0	12.8	11.7	11.5

*Includes roughly $2 debt service on $10 in mortgages.

Source: Data provided by Amon Deshe.

---

b. Based on data provided by Arnon Deshe.

Table 3. Franchise Fee Income, 1985–88 ($ millions)

Income/Expenditures	1988 (est.)	1987	1986	1985
Fee income	$35.0	$32.7	$28.8	$25.6
Cash rental expenses	16.0	15.0	11.2	10.1

Source: Data provided by Amon Deshe.

Combined Cash Flow Valuation

The three sources of cash flow as of 1988 are shown in Table 4 and Figure 1.

Applying the cash flow multiple of eight to the combined cash flow of $50, we see that Dunkin' Donuts can be valued at $400 million, or approximately $63 per share. If the market were willing to apply a higher multiple, such as 10, the value would rise to $500 million or approximately $79.

MARKET VALUATION

During mid-1988 stock of Dunkin' Donuts traded in the mid-$20 range. Based on cash flow multiples of 8 to 10, Dunkin' Donuts was significantly undervalued in the mid-1980s, making the firm vulnerable for a takeover.

Table 4. Combined Cash Flows, 1988 ($ millions)

Source	Amount
Real estate	$27.0
Franchise fees	$19.0
Company-owned units	$4.0
Total	$50.0

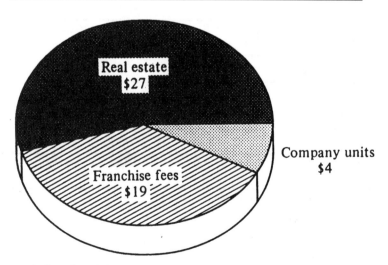

Figure 1.   Cash flow breakdown—Dunkin' Donuts, 1988 ($ millions).

The cash flows from the real estate assets could be used to service debt that a bidder might assume to finance the takeover. Moreover, the real estate assets could be used as security for creditors, thereby enhancing a bidder's ability to raise the necessary debt capital to finance the bid. It is important to note that the valuation year of 1988 precedes the major downturn in the real estate market. If the valuation year were 1990, the same multiple might not apply, given that the real estate market was severely depressed and real estate assets lost much of their marketability.

OFFSETTING FACTORS

Competition

The primary business of Dunkin' Donuts is fast food, a highly competitive business that is characterized by intense price and promotional competition. The industry appears to have reached maturity, as reflected in the rise in sales by fast-food restaurants in 1988 (only 1.7%, which was the smallest increase in any five-year period before 1988). Dunkin' Donuts was somewhat insulated from most of this competition, which was directed mainly at hamburger chains such as MacDonald's, Burger King, and Wendy's. Once these firms expanded their product lines, however, and entered into the breakfast market in the late 1980s, Dunkin' Donuts became more vulnerable to these competitive pressures.

Labor Costs

In the late 1980s the labor market became increasingly tight for employers. The unemployment rate hovered around 5.3%. Fast-food marketers were forced to raise wages to compete for workers. Moreover, the pool of young workers, which fast-food chains relies on for inexpensive labor, shrank in the 1980s. The U.S. Department of Labor showed that workers between 16 and 24 years of age represented only 16.3% of the civilian labor force in 1989, which was down from 19.8% in 1986. Much of the business of Dunkin' Donuts is concentrated in the northeastern United States, where the labor shortage is even worse. This points to higher labor costs and lower profit margins if conditions remain the same or worsen in the 1990s.

Chili's Restaurant Division Loss

The Chili's restaurant division lost approximately $2 million in 1987. In addition, Dunkin' Donuts had to invest $4 million for building two new Chili's restaurants. Seven more units were planned for 1988. This imposed a drain on the firm's capital and reduced its borrowing capacity.

ANTITAKEOVER MEASURES

During the late 1980s Dunkin' Donuts was undervalued by the market, making it vulnerable to a hostile takeover. As a preventative measure, the firm adopted various antitakeover measures. These measures, which were consistent with Delaware's corporation laws, included the supermajority position, classified board, Employee Stock Ownership Plan (ESOP) convertible preferred stock, and poison pills.

Supermajority Provision

Dunkin' Donuts amended its articles of incorporation so that a vote of 75% of the outstanding shares was required for approval of mergers.

Classified Board

Dunkin' Donuts adopted a classified board voting structure, whereby only one-third of the board may be replaced in any given election. According to this provision, a majority of the board could be achieved only after a second annual stockholders' meeting following a takeover.

Employee Stock Ownership Plan (ESOP)

Dunkin' Donuts adopted an ESOP on April 20, 1989, selling 1.1 million shares to the newly established ESOP for $35.25 per share. The ESOP was a leveraged ESOP funded by a loan from the company in the amount of $38,702,633.

Convertible Preferred Stock

On May 30, 1989, Dunkin' Donuts sold 28,000 shares of convertible preferred stock to General Electric Capital Corporation for $28 million. The preferred stock provided a 10% cash dividend that would increase semiannually up to a maximum of 11.5%. The preferred shares were convertible into common stock at $40 per share, at the holder's option, in the event that the company was taken over. Dunkin' Donuts could redeem these convertible preferred shares at any time at par plus an initial 10% premium. The redemption premium was set to decline each year until December 1993, when it would remain at a minimum of 2.5%. This defense is similar to a combination of a white squire and a poison pill.

Poison Pills

In October 1987 the company distributed as a dividend one right for each share outstanding. The rights were a poison pill that would allow the right holders to purchase shares at half price if a bidder were to announce an offer to acquire 20% of the firm's outstanding stock or to make a tender offer for 30% of the firm's outstanding stock. The rights were convertible into either participating preferred stock or common stock, depending on the occurrence of particular events. The poison pills could be re-deemed by a two-thirds vote of the board of directors for $0.01 per right.

EFFECT OF THE ANTITAKEOVER MEASURES

As discussed in Chapter 5, antitakeover measures do not guarantee a firm's indepen-dence, but they may improve a target's bargaining position, which, in turn, increases the premium offered by bidding firms.

Stock Ownership

As of the end of 1988, institutional investors owned 52% outstanding stock of Dunkin' Donuts, the five largest of these holdings, accounting for 28%. This larger concentration of shares in hands of institutions increases the firm's vulnerability to a takeover. At one point, insider shareholders accounted for as much as 13% of the outstanding stock. This declined to 9% toward the late 1980s.

As of October 1987, Dunkin' Donuts had approximately 7.78 million shares out-standing, a total that also included 0.4 million shares of Treasury stock. The com-pany later instituted a shares repurchase program at an average price of $25.44 per share. This reduced the total number of shares outstanding to 6.4 million shares. The large holdings by institutions, as well as the decline in insider holdings, increased the firm's vulnerability to a takeover.

Financial Ratio Analysis

A financial ratio analysis of Dunkin' Donuts is shown next. The ratios include liq-uidity, activity leverage, and performance ratios. In addition to the firm and industry average for each ratio, Table 5 also shows the degree of dispersion of the industry ra-tios that make up the average through the variance and standard deviation. These variability measures provide information on the degree of central tendency of the components that make up the industry average, thereby providing an indication of the reliability of the industry averages. Table 6 presents an analysis of various finan-cial ratios for five years ending 1988.

Liquidity Ratios
The liquidity ratios shown are quick and current ratios.

Quick Ratio	Actual	Industry
Ratio	0.7	0.4
Standard deviation	0.13	0.04

**Table 5. Statistical Analysis of Actual versus Industry Ratios
for Five Years Ending 1988**

	Mean		Variance		Standard Deviation	
	Firm	Industry	Firm	Industry	Firm	Industry
Quick ratio	0.7	0.4	0.0176	0.0016	0.133	0.040
Current ratio	0.8	0.6	0.0234	0.0016	0.153	0.040
Debt to equity	0.9	4.4	0.0192	1.6064	0.138	1.267
Net-fixed assets to equity	1.5	3.4	0.0087	0.5864	0.094	0.766
Sales to working capital	−321.5	−27.3	324299.5266	3.9904	569.473	1.998
Interest coverage	9.5	2.5	6.2654	0.0136	2.503	0.117
Inventory turnover	2.7	38.4	27.9955	6.2440	5.291	2.499
Return on equity (ROE)%	32.9	34.3	2.4707	10.7696	1.572	3.282

Current Ratio

	Firm	Industry
Ratio	1.0	0.5
Standard deviation	0.15	0.04

Because Dunkin' Donuts was quite liquid as of 1988, this suggests that the company should not have any difficulty meeting its current obligations as they become due.

Activity Ratios
The activity ratio selected here is inventory turnover.

Inventory Turnover

	Firm	Industry
Ratio	29.1	36.3
Standard deviation	5.29	2.50

Although this ratio is lower than the industry norm, this is not a source of concern given the nature of the firm's business.

Table 6. Dunkin' Donuts Capitalization Table ($ Thousands)

Percent Funded	Amount Funded	Method	Rate (%)	Derivation Rate as of 4/27/90
20%	$64,000	Revolver	12.06	3.5018.56 Labor
34%	$110,000	Senior notes (floating)	12.55	3.5019.50 5 yr.Treasury
29%	$95,000	Senior notes	12.55	3.5019.50 5 yr. Treasury
7%	$23,500	Jr. subordinated	13.84	4.7519.09 7 yr. Treasury
10%	$32,500	C.S. © $50	N/A	
100%	$325,000			

Leverage Ratios

The debt-equity ratio is used as an indicator of the degree of financial leverage of Dunkin' Donuts. The interest-coverage ratio is then used to measure the firm's ability to service this debt.

	Debt-Equity	
	Firm	Industry
Ratio	1.0	6.7
Standard deviation	0.14	1.27

	Interest Coverage	
	Firm	Industry
Ratio	9.7	0.24
Standard deviation	2.5	0.12

Dunkin' Donuts had a significantly lower level of debt than other firms in this industry. It also easily covers its interest charges. This suggests that it has much unused debt capacity that could make it vulnerable to a takeover.

Profitability Ratios

The performance of the firm is partly reflected in the return on equity and return on assets.

	Return on Equity	
	Firm	Industry
Ratio	31.2	37.4
Standard deviation	1.57	3.28

	Return on Assets	
	Firm	Industry
Ratio	15.6	6.8
Standard deviation	1.43	1.12

Although the return on equity is somewhat below industry norms, the return on assets is higher than the industry standard. Both measures, however, are of limited value; therefore, an analyst should not place too much emphasis on them. The industry average for the return on equity is skewed, as are most of the industry norms used in this section, by the larger fast-food chains that are not very similar to Dunkin' Donuts. The company's return on assets is also affected by the fact that the firm's real estate assets are not carried on its books at their appropriate market value.

FINANCING STRUCTURE AND CASH FLOW ANALYSIS

Based on the $50 per share, or $325 million total price shown in Table 6, we can construct a capital structure of the buyout. The capital structure and the payout schedule are shown in Table 6 and Table 7, respectively.

THE TAKEOVER PROCESS

Dunkin' Donuts became the target of a hostile bid in May 1989. For the chronology of the bidding process, see the following outline of events.

Chronological Order of Events

4/89*   Board of directors approves an ESOP plan; Dunkin's first takeover.
5/31/89   Kingsbridge purchases Dunkin's shares of 370,000 on the open market; owns 12% of the company and makes a $42 per share bid for Dunkin.
5/31/89   Dunkin' finds a white squire; sells 28,000 shares of preferred stock for $28 million to General Electric Capital, which are convertible into 700,000 shares of common stock at $40 per share in 1990.
6/12/89   Dunkin' authorizes the buyback of 1.4 million shares of stock on the open market to get the shares into friendly hands.
7/1/89 $43 per share bid; Value Line says the bid should be closer to $50 per share.
7/10/89   Dunkin' rejects $43 per share bid; the $43 per share offer is extended to 7/27.
7/26/89   Dunkin' obtains an injunction in the U.S. District Court against the pending tender offer by Kingsbridge.
8/8/89 $43 per share extended to 8/15.
8/22/89   Dunkin's acquisition is willing to increase its offer from $43 to $45 per share if takeover defenses are overturned.
8/29/89   Dunkin's $45 acquisition per share bid is conditional on at least 50.1% shares being tendered and on the removal of Dunkin's poison pill, which expires 9/15.
9/11/89   Dunkin' rejects $45 per share offer, saying it is inadequate.
9/12/89   Dunkin' will now explore the possibility of an LBO.
9/13/89   Dunkin' agrees to meet with DD acquiring executives (joint venture of Unicorp Canada and Cara Operations).
9/28/89   In an effort to explore possibilities, franchise owners offer to help finance the LBO.
9/29/89 $45 per share offer extended to 10/16.
10/16/89 $45 per share offer extended to 11/1.
10/24/89 Dunkin' is ready to accept proposals; November 10 is the last day for competing bids; DD acquisition is challenging Dunkin's takeover defenses in the Delaware court of chancery. They allege that Dunkin' has diverted a substantial portion of Dunkin's value to themselves in the form of "golden parachute" contracts. DD acquisition said these contracts will cost Dunkin' at least $16 million.
11/1/89   DD acquisition's $45 per share offer extended to 11/20. At the close of business 38.5% of the outstanding shares are tendered.
11/10/89 Dunkin's board extends the deadline for proposals to 11/15.
11/17/89 Allied-Lyons PLC, a major British beverage group, agrees to buy Dunkin' in a $325 million cash bid at $47.25 per share. Allied believes Dunkin' would be a good strategic fit. Allied-Lyons' proposal is subject to various conditions, including acquisition of at least 75% of Dunkin's outstanding shares. Their offer will expire 12/20.
11/20/89 DD acquisition extends its offer of $45 per share to 12/4.
12/4/89   DD acquisition extends its offer of $45 per share to 12/21.

---

*Dunkin' Donuts ("Dunkin") and the Kingsbridge Group had discussions prior to April 1989

Table 7. Prospective Debt Schedules for Dunkin' Donuts

Year	88	89	90	91	92	93	94	95	96	97	98	99	00	01	02	03
MAXIMUM FIXED CHARGES																
REVOLVER																
Balance (end of period)	$64,000	$64,000	$64,000	$64,000	$64,000	$64,000	$64,000	$64,000	$64,000	$64,000	$64,000	$64,000	$64,000	$64,000	$64,000	$64,000
Additional borrowings	$0	$0	$0	$0	$0	$0	$0	$0	$0	$0	$0	$0	$0	$0	$0	$0
Balance (end of period)	$64,000	$64,000	$64,000	$64,000	$64,000	$64,000	$64,000	$64,000	$64,000	$64,000	$64,000	$64,000	$64,000	$64,000	$64,000	$64,000
Additional borrowings	$0	$0	$0	$0	$0	$0	$0	$0	$0	$0	$0	$0	$0	$0	$0	$0
Principal repayments	$0	$0	$0	$0	$0	$0	$0	$0	$0	$0	$0	$0	$0	$0	$0	$0
Interest expense	$7,718	$7,718	$7,718	$7,718	$7,718	$7,718	$7,718									
Interest expense based on outs balance at beginning of period																
Balance-1/15th assmptn	$64,000	$59,733	$55,467	$51,200	$46,933	$42,667	$38,400	$34,133	$29,867	$25,600	$21,333	$17,087	$12,800	$8,533	$4,267	$0
Amortization-1/15 assmptn	$4,267	$4,267	$4,267	$4,267	$4,267	$4,267	$4,267	$4,267	$4,267	$4,267	$4,267	$4,267	$4,267	$4,267	$4,267	
Interest-1/15th assmptn	$7,461	$6,947	$6,432	$5,917	$5,403	$4,888	$4,374								$0	
TERM LOAN-FLOATING																
Balance (end of period)	$110,000	$94,300	$78,600	$62,900	$47,200	$31,500	$15,800	$0	$0	$0	$0	$0	$0	$0	$0	$0
Principal repayments	$15,700	$15,700	$15,700	$15,700	$15,700	$15,700	$15,800	$0	$0	$0	$0	$0	$0	$0	$0	$0
Interest expense	$0	$10,849	$8,879	$6,909	$4,938	$2,968	$991	$0	$0	$0	$0	$0	$0	$0	$0	$0
TERM LOAN-FIXED																
Balance (end of period)	$95,000	$81,400	$67,800	$54,200	$40,600	$27,000	$13,400	$0	$0	$0	$0	$0	$0	$0	$0	$0
Principal repayments	$13,600	$13,600	$13,600	$13,600	$13,600	$13,600	$13,400	$0	$0	$0	$0	$0	$0	$0	$0	$0
Interest expense	$11,069	$9,362	$7,656	$5,949	$4,242	$2,535	$841	$0	$0	$0	$0	$0	$0	$0	$0	$0
SUBORDINATED-FLOATING																
Balance (end of period)	$0	$0	$0	$0	$0	$0	$0	$0	$0	$0	$0	$0	$0	$0	$0	$0
Principal repayments	$0	$0	$0	$0	$0	$0	$0	$0	$0	$0	$0	$0	$0	$0	$0	$0
Interest expense	$0	$0	$0	$0	$0	$0	$0	$0	$0	$0	$0	$0	$0	$0	$0	$0
SUBORDINATED-FIXED																
Balance (end of period)	$23,500	$21,933	$20,367	$18,800	$17,233	$15,667	$14,100	$12,533	$10,967	$9,400	$7,833	$6,267	$4,700	$3,133	$1,567	$5
Principal repayments	$1,567	$1,567	$1,567	$1,567	$1,567	$1,567	$1,567	$1,567	$1,567	$1,567	$1,567	$1,567	$1,567	$1,567	$1,567	
Interest expense	$3,144	$2,927	$2,710	$2,494	$2,277	$2,060	$1,843	$1,626	$1,409	$1,193	$976	$759	$542	$325	$104	
THIRD PARTY DEBT																
Balance (end of period)	$0	$0	$0	$0	$0	$0	$0	$0	$0	$0	$0	$0	$0	$0	$0	$0
Principal repayments	$0	$0	$0	$0	$0	$0	$0	$0	$0	$0	$0	$0	$0	$0	$0	$0
Interest expense	$0	$0	$0	$0	$0	$0	$0	$0	$0	$0	$0	$0	$0	$0	$0	$0
ASSUMED PRE LBO																
EXISTING FINANCING																
Balance (end of period)	$0	$0	$0	$0	$0	$0	$0	$0	$0	$0	$0	$0	$0	$0	$0	$0
Principal payments	$0	$0	$0	$0	$0	$0	$0	$0	$0	$0	$0	$0	$0	$0	$0	$0
Interest expense	$0	$0	$0	$0	$0	$0	$0	$0	$0	$0	$0	$0	$0	$0	$0	$0
TOTAL FIXED CHARGES																
TOTAL BALANCE	$292,500	$261,633	$230,767	$199,900	$169,033	$138,167	$107,300	$76,533	$74,967	$73,400	$71,833	$70,267	$68,133	$67,133	$65,567	$64,005
Total principal repayments	$30,867	$30,867	$30,867	$30,867	$30,867	$30,867	$30,767	$1,567	$1,567	$1,567	$1,567	$1,567	$1,567	$1,567	$1,562	

Table 7. Continued

Year	88	89	90	91	92	93	94	95	96	97	98	99	00	01	02	03
Total interest expense	$21,931	$30,857	$26,963	$23,069	$19,175	$15,281	$11,394	$1,626	$1,409	$1,193	$976	$759	$542	$325	$109	
Rents	$0	$0	$0	$0	$0	$0	$0	$0	$0	$0	$0	$0	$0	$0	$0	
TOTAL FIXED CHARGES	52,798	$61,724	$57,830	$53,936	$50,042	$46,148	$42,160	$3,193	$2,976	$2,759	$2,542	$2,326	$2,109	$1,897	$1,670	
Reduction of Fixed Charges																
ADJ. TOTAL FIXED CHARGES	$56,808	$65,219	$60,810	$56,402	$51,993	$47,585	$43,082	$7,460	$7,243	$7,026	$6,809	$6,592	$6,375	$6,159	$5,937	

(uses 1/15 assumption):
MAX FIXED CHARGES (ADJ.):$65,219

PREFERRED																
Balance	$0	$0	$0	$0	$0	$0	$0	$0	$0	$0	$0	$0	$0	$0	$0	$0
Sinking Fund	$0	$0	$0	$0	$0	$0	$0	$0	$0	$0	$0	$0	$0	$0	$0	
Dividends	$0	$0	$0	$0	$0	$0	$0	$0	$0	$0	$0	$0	$0	$0	$0	

THIRD PARTY PREFERRED																
Balance	$0	$0	$0	$0	$0	$0	$0	$0	$0	$0	$0	$0	$0	$0	$0	$0
Sinking Fund	$0	$0	$0	$0	$0	$0	$0	$0	$0	$0	$0	$0	$0	$0	$0	
Dividends	$0	$0	$0	$0	$0	$0	$0	$0	$0	$0	$0	$0	$0	$0	$0	

AVERAGE LIFE:																
Term loan-floating	4.00	$15,700	$31,400	$47,100	$62,800	$78,500	$94,200	$0								
Term loan-fixed	3.99	$13,600	$27,200	$40,800	$54,400	$68,000	$81,600	$93,800								
Subordinated-floating	NA	$0	$0	$0	$0	$0	$0	$0								
Subordinated-fixed	800	$1,567	$3,133	$4,700	$6,267	$7,833	$9,400	$10,967	$12,533	$14,100	$15,667	$17,233	$18,800	$20,367	$21,933	$23,425

EPILOGUE

After an extended takeover battle, Dunkin' Donuts agreed to a takeover by the British food and beverage company, Allied-Lyons PLC.[c] The purchase price was $325 million in case per share. The number of shares outstanding changed during 1988–89. Based on the valuation cash-flow analysis that showed a total value of $400 million, Allied-Lyons appeared to have received a good price.

---

c. "Dunkin' Donuts Agrees to Sale," *New York Times,* 18 November 1989, p. 37.

SUMMARY

The variety of different financial techniques available to value publicly held companies were explored in this chapter. Some techniques that value the stock price of companies, such as the Gordon Stock Dividend Valuation Model, receive much attention in corporate finance textbooks but are of limited use in the valuation of a company. However, a similar type of computation using cash flows or earnings, as opposed to dividends, is used in the discounted cash flows method of valuation. A number of other factors not addressed by the Gordon model, such as the control premium and the depth of the market, need to be considered in determining the appropriate acquisition value. This value also depends on whether the deal was friendly or hostile. Hostile deals were shown to have higher premiums than friendly transactions.

Valuation analysis requires that the buyer forecast the free cash flows of the target. A variety of forecasting methods may be used, ranging from simple techniques to more complex econometric forecasts. Many of the same techniques that are used in capital budgeting, such as the NPV present value and IRR, are also applicable to the valuation of cash flows of public companies. This is reasonable because a merger valuation problem may be considered a capital budgeting exercise. The accuracy of the results of these methods depends on the discount rate selected. This rate may be adjusted to reflect the seller's risk characteristics. Higher risk firms tend to require a higher discount rate. An abundance of research studies have attempted to trace the valuations effects of mergers and acquisitions. These studies show that stockholders of target companies clearly earn statistically significant positive abnormal returns. Shareholders in bidding firms tend not to do as well. Research studies indicate that although they can earn slightly positive returns, they often realize zero or negative returns. Many of these studies are short term –oriented. However, research on the long-term effects of mergers and acquisitions on bidding shareholders, and shareholders who may have received stock in their shares of the target, also paint an unimpressive picture. Given the many benefits that may be derived from well-planned mergers, readers should not conclude that companies should avoid mergers and acquisitions. Rather, they should give rise to a need for greater caution and more thorough premerger planning.

Research studies also focused on the medium of payment. The analysis for stock-for-stock offers is different from that for cash offers. The relative value of the stock of both firms needs to be considered in stock-for-stock deals. Factors such as the dilution of EPS must be factored to do a thorough analysis. The agreed-upon relative stock values can then be "locked in" by a collar agreement that would adjust the stock amounts on either side of the deal according to market fluctuations in the stock prices of both firms.

Valuation analysis can be an intricate process that requires a well-rounded knowledge of finance and other related fields. To construct a reliable analysis, much due diligence analysis needs to be done. The lessons of some of the merger failures of the fourth merger wave point to deficiencies in this type of analysis.

REFERENCES

Agrawal, Anup, Jeffrey F. Jaffe, and Gershon Mandelker. "The Post-Merger Performance of Acquiring Firms: A Re-examination of an Anomaly." *Journal of Finance* 47, no. 4 (September 1992).

Amihud, Yakov, Baruch Lev, and Nicholas Travlos. "Corporate Control and the Choice of Investment Financing: The Case of Corporate Acquisitions." *Journal of Finance,* vol. 45, no. 2 (June 1990).

Archibald, T. Ross. "Stock Market Reaction to the Depreciation Switch-Back." *Accounting Review* 47, no. 1 (January 1972).

Asquith, Paul. "Merger Bids and Stockholder Returns." *Journal of Financial Economics* 11, no. 1–4 (April 1983).

Asquith, Paul, and E. Han Kim. "The Impact of Merger Bids on Participating Firm's Security Holders." *Journal of Finance* 37, (1982).

Auerbach, Alan J., and David Reishus. "The Impact of Taxation on Mergers and Acquisitions." In Alan J. Auerbach, ed. *Mergers and Acquisitions* (Chicago: National Bureau of Economic Research, 1987).

Auerbach, Alan J., and David Reishus. "Taxes and the Merger Decision." In John C. Coffee Jr., Louis Lowenstein, and Susan Rose Ackerman, eds. *Knights, Raiders and Targets* (New York: Oxford University Press, 1988).

Bierman, Harold, and Seymore Smidt. *The Capital Investment Decision,* 6th ed. (New York: Macmillan Publishing Co., 1984).

Block, Dennis J., Nancy E. Barton, and Stephen A. Radin. *The Business Judgement Rule* (Englewood Cliffs, N.J.: Prentice-Hall, 1988).

Brannigan, Martha, and Timothy O'Brien. "First Union Is Viewed as Paying Dearly for First Fidelity." *Wall Street Journal,* 20 June 1995.

Brennan, Michael. "A Perspective of Accounting and Stock Prices." *Journal of Applied Corporate Finance* 8, no. 1 (Spring 1995).

Brown, Philip, and Ray Ball. "An Empirical Evaluation of Accounting Income Numbers." *Journal of Accounting Research* 6, no. 2 (Autumn 1963).

Chang, Saeyoung. "Takeovers of Privately Held Targets, Methods of Payment, and Bidder Returns." *Journal of Finance* 53, no. 2 (April 1998).

Commons, Dorman L. *Tender Offer* (New York: Penguin Books, 1986).

Copeland, Tim, Tim Coller, and Jack Murrin. *Valuation: Measuring and Managing the Value of Companies* (New York: John Wiley & Sons, 1990).

Dennis, Debra K., and John J. McConnell. "Corporate Mergers and Security Returns." *Journal of Financial Economics* 16, no. 2, (June 1986).

Dodd, Peter. "Merger Proposals, Management Discretion and Shareholder Wealth." *Journal of Financial Economics*, vol. 8(2) June 1980, pp. 105–138.

Easton, Peter D., Trevor S. Harris, and James A. Ohlson. "Aggregating Accounting Earnings Can Explain Most Security Returns: The Case of Long Return Intervals." *Journal of Accounting and Economics* 15 (1992).

Fleisher, Arthur, Geoffrey C. Hazard Jr., and Miriam Z. Klipper. *Board Games* (Boston: Little, Brown, 1988).

Francis, Jack Clark. *Investments* (New York: McGraw-Hill, 1988).

Franks, Julian, Robert Harris, and Sheridan Titman. "The Post-Merger Share Price Performance of Acquiring Firms." *Journal of Financial Economics* 29, no. 1 (March 1995).

Gaughan, Patrick A., Henry Fuentes, and Laura Bonanomi. "Cash Flow versus Net Income in Commercial Litigation." *Litigation Economics Digest* (Fall 1995).

Ghosh, Aloke, and William Ruland. "Managerial Ownership, the Method of Payment for Acquisitions, and Executive Job Retention." *Journal of Finance* 53, no. 2 (April 1998).

Ghosh, Aloke. "Does Operating Performance Really Improve Following Corporate Acquisitions?" Unpublished Baruch College, City University of New York working paper, November 1998.

Gordon, Myron. *The Investment, Financing and Valuation of the Modern Corporation* (Homewood, Ill.: Richard D. Irwin, 1962).

Hanson, Robert C. "Tender Offers and Free Cash Flow." *The Financial Review* 27, no. 2 (May 1992).

Healy, Paul M., Krishna G. Palepu, and Richard Ruback. "Does Corporate Performance Improve After Mergers?" *Journal of Financial Economics* 31, no. 2 (April 1992), pp. 135–175.

Hilder, David. "Time Warner Holders Fret As Stock Sinks." *Wall Street Journal,* 7 February 1990

Holthausen, Robert W., Richard W. Leftwich, and David Mayers. "The Effect of Larger Block Transactions on Security Prices," *Journal of Financial Economics* 19 (1987).

Huang, Yen-Sheng, and Ralph A. Walking. "Target Abnormal Returns Associated with Acquisition Announcements." *Journal of Financial Economics* 19 (1987).

Jensen, Michael C. "The Takeover Controversy: Analysis and Evidence." In John C. Coffee Jr., Louis Lowenstein, and Susan Rose Ackerman, eds. *Knights, Raiders and Targets* (New York: Oxford University Press, 1988), p. 321.

Jensen, Michael, and Richard Ruback. "The Market for Corporate Control: The Scientific Evidence." *Journal of Financial Economics* 11, no. 1–4 (April 1983).

Kaplan, Steven N., and Richard S. Ruback. "The Valuation of Cash Flow Forecasts: An Empirical Analysis." *Journal of Finance* 50, no. 4, (September 1995).

Lease, Ronald C., John J. McConnell, and Wayne H. Mikkelson. "The Market Value of Control in Publicly Traded Corporations." *Journal of Financial Economics* 11 (April 1983).

Lehn, Kenneth, and Anne Poulsen. "Free Cash Flow and Shareholder Gains in Going Private Transactions." *Journal of Finance* 44 (July 1989).

Levy, Haim, and Marshall Salnat. *Capital Investment and Financial Decisions,* 3rd ed. (Englewood Cliffs, N.J.: Prentice-Hall, 1986).

Loughran, Tim, and Anand M. Vijh. "Do Long Term Shareholders Benefit from Corporate Acquisitions?" *Journal of Finance* 52, no. 5 (December 1997).

Malatesta, Paul H. "The Wealth Effect of Merger Activity and the Objective Functions of Merging Firms." *Journal of Financial Economics* 11, no. 1–4 (April 1983).

Meeker, Larry G., and O. Maurice Joy. "Price Premiums for Controlling Shares of Closely Held Bank Stock." *Journal of Business* 53 (1980).

Mergerstat Review, 1998.

Merrill Lynch, *Mergerstat Review,* 1994.

Morck, Randall, Andrei Shleifer, and Robert W. Vishny. "Do Managerial Objectives Drive Acquisitions?" *Journal of Finance* 45 (March 1990).

Opler, Tim, and Sheridan Titman. "The Determinants of Leveraged Buyout Activity: Free Cash Flow vs. Financial Distress Costs." *Journal of Finance* 48, no. 5 (December 1993).

Pratt, Shannon. *Valuing a Business,* 2nd ed. (Homewood, Ill.: Dow Jones Irwin, 1990).

Rau, P. Raghavendra, and Theo Vermaelen. "Glamor, Value and the Post-Acquisition Performance of Acquiring Firms." *Journal of Financial Economics* 49, no. 2 (August 1998), pp. 223–253.

Read, Stanley Foster, and Alexandra Reed Lajoux. *The Art of M&A: A Merger Acquisition Buyout Guide,* 2nd ed. (New York: John Wiley & Sons, 1995).

Rielly, Frank. *Investment Analysis and Portfolio Management,* 2nd ed. (New York, Dryden Press, 1985).

Shiller, Robert. "Do Stock Prices Move Too Much to Be Explained by Subsequent Changes in Dividends?" *American Economic Review* 71 (1981).

Stocks, Bills, Bonds, and Inflation: 1998,1995 Yearbook (Chicago: Ibbotson Associates).

Sullivan, Michael J., Marlin R. H. Johnson, and Carl D. Hudson. "The Role of Medium of Exchange in Merger Offers: Examination of Terminated Merger Proposals." *Financial Management* 23, no. 3 (Autumn 1994).

Sunder, Shyam. "Stock Price and Risk Related to Accounting Changes in Inventory Valuation." *Accounting Review* 50, no. 2 (April 1975).

"Time's Warner Bid Reflects Emphasis on Value of Cash Flow, Not Earnings." *Wall Street Journal,* 27 June 1989.

Van Horne, James C. *Fundamentals of Financial Management and Policy,* 9th ed. (Englewood Cliffs, N.J.: Prentice-Hall, 1995).

Varaiya, Nikhil P. "An Empirical Investigation of the Bidding Firm's Gains from Corporate Takeovers" *Research in Finance* 6 (1986).

Varaiya, Nikhil P. "Determinants of Premiums in Acquisition Transactions." *Managerial and Decision Economics* 8 (1987).

Yermack, David. "Higher Market Valuation of Companies With a Small Board of Directors." *Journal of Financial Economics* 40, np. 2 (February 1996).

14

VALUATION OF PRIVATELY HELD BUSINESSES

Of the myriad methods employed in business valuation, some are more appropriate to public firms and others to privately held concerns. Public companies often tend to be larger than privately held firms, a factor that greatly influences the method chosen. This chapter discusses the differences in the valuation methods used for public and privately held firms, followed by techniques used in private business valuation.

The analyst of a privately held firm often faces a more difficult task in valuing a business, given the general lack of data for private firms and the broadly circulated opinions that exist for public companies. A wide range of securities analysts often study public firms to determine the investment value of a firm's equity. The company reports of public firms are readily available. In addition, the various financial media publish a regular supply of articles about public firms. The analyst of a private firm, however, lacks the luxury of access to these information sources and must rely on more original sources.

The academic world places great emphasis on teaching the traditional methods of financial analysis as they apply to the large Fortune 500 public firms, but they often ignore the methods that are unique to valuing privately held concerns. These methods are found in only a small collection of specialized books that are designed for the practitioner in the field of valuation.[1] This chapter is designed to provide an overview of the valuation of closely held businesses. The reader may acquire a more detailed coverage of this topic through the various professional publications that are listed at the end of this chapter.

DIFFERENCES IN VALUATION OF PUBLIC AND PRIVATE BUSINESSES

A major difference between public and private business valuations centers on the availability and reliability of financial data.[2] Some of these differences are caused by the efforts

---

1. See, for example, Shannon Pratt, Robert F. Rielly, and Robert P. Schweihs, *Valuing a Business,* 3rd ed. (Chicago: Richard D. Irwin, 1996); Jay Fishman, Shannon Pratt, J. Clifford Griffith, and D. Keith Wilson, *Guide to Business Valuations,* 5th ed. (Fort Worth: Practitioners Publishing Co., 1995); and Robert Trout, "Reference Guide to Valuing a Closely Held Business," in *Expert Economic Testimony: Reference Guides for Judges and Attorneys* (Tucson: Lawyers and Judges Publishing Company, 1998), pp. 155–220.

2. This section is drawn from Patrick A. Gaughan and Henry Fuentes, "Taxable Income and Lost Profits Litigation," *Journal of Forensic Economics* IV, no. 1 (Winter 1990), pp. 55–64.

of firms, particularly private businesses, to minimize taxable income. Another factor is the requirement that public firms disclose certain financial data in a specific manner, whereas private firms do not face such requirements.

Reported Taxable Income

Public and private corporations are subject to different requirements with regard to the declaration of taxable income. Owners of closely held businesses take every opportunity to keep taxable income low and therefore have a lower tax obligation. Although public firms also want to minimize their taxes, privately held businesses have greater means available to do so than their public counterparts. Because of these efforts to minimize taxable income, private companies may issue less reliable financial data than public firms. Therefore, analysts may not be able to rely on the reported income of privately held firms to reflect their true profitability and earning power.

With regard to declaring income, public and private corporations have dramatically different objectives. Public corporations have several outside constraints that provide strong incentives to declare a higher taxable income. One of these constraints is the pressure applied by stockholders, the true "owners" of the corporation, to have a regular flow of dividends. Because dividends are paid out of taxable income, the public corporation's ability to minimize taxable income is limited.

Public Corporations and the Reporting of Income

Like their private counterparts, public corporations want to minimize taxes, but given their dividend obligations toward stockholders, public corporations have fewer opportunities to do so. They do not have as much ability to manipulate their reported income, primarily because of the accounting review requirements that the shareholder reporting process imposes on them.

In preparing financial statements, there are three levels of accounting reports: compilation, review, and audited statements. The compilation is the least rigorous of the three, whereas audited financial statements require an independent analysis of the company's financial records. Public corporations are required to prepare audited financial statements for their annual reports. These audit requirements are enforced by the Securities and Exchange Commission (SEC) subject to the requirements of the Securities and Exchange Act of 1934.[3] The SEC does not accept a review or a compilation statement for a 10K report. A review is acceptable for a 10Q quarterly report. However, a compilation is not acceptable for use in preparing either of these types of published financial reports. Because the reported income contained in published financial statements is subject to audit, the profit numbers tend to be more reliable than those that appear in the financial statements of private firms, which generally are not audited. The lack of required audit scrutiny is one rea-

---

3. Paul J. Wendell, *Corporate Controller's Manual* (Boston: Warren, Gorham and Lamont, 1989), pp. C214–C223.

son the reported profit levels may lack validity. The lack of an audit requirement allows private firms to manipulate their reported income levels to minimize taxable income. It is in this area that public and private corporations tend to have two very different agendas. Public firms may want to demonstrate higher reported profits to impress stockholders. Stockholders may become more impressed when these reported profits are translated into higher dividend payments or increased stock prices.

The need for higher reported income and dividends became even more important for public companies in the fourth merger wave when aggressively priced hostile bids were prevalent. Corporations that suffer a fall in profits or are forced to cut their dividends may sometimes become targets of unwanted hostile bids. An example of this phenomenon was the June 1984 decrease in ITT's quarterly dividend from $2.76 to $1.00 per share. This cut, and the resulting decline in the stock price, was one reason a group led by financier Jay Pritzker launched an unsuccessful hostile bid to take over the giant conglomerate.[4]

Higher reported dividends are a signal to securities markets that the company's performance has improved. In February 1989 General Motors announced a 2 for 1 stock split, a 20% increase in the quarterly dividend (on presplit shares) for its main class of shares, as well as increases in the dividends for its Class E and Class H shares. At that time, GM chairman, Roger Smith, stated: "This sends a message to our stockholders that we got a fundamental improvement in our earning power."[5] The stock price rose before and after the GM announcement in anticipation of the dividend increase.

Private corporations are subject to neither the government's public disclosure requirements nor the constraints and pressures of public securities markets. Free to utilize every opportunity to show a smaller taxable income, they therefore have a lower tax bill.

A private corporation can reduce taxable income in two ways. The first is to have lower reported revenues, and the second is to show higher costs. The first approach is more common for small businesses, particularly cash businesses, which sometimes show a smaller than actual level of reported income. This is occasionally done through deliberately inaccurate record keeping. In addition to being illegal, this practice creates obvious problems for the evaluators.

If there is a reason to believe that a company's revenues have been underreported, an estimate of the actual revenues may be reconstructed. This sometimes occurs in litigation involving minority stockholders who are suing for their share in a business. The actual revenue levels can be reconstructed from activity and volume measures, such as materials and inputs purchased, which can be translated into sales of final outputs.

The most common form of income manipulation for purposes of minimizing taxes is giving higher than normal compensation, benefits, and perquisites to officers. The entrepreneurs of closely held companies may withdraw a disproportionate amount of income from the company relative to total revenues. Furthermore, entrepreneurial owners may list a variety of extraordinary personal benefits on the corporation's books as expenses. Although these expenses may be legitimate tax deductions, they really are another form of compensation to the owner. Any measure of the closely held corporation's profitability that does not take into account these less overt forms of return to the owners will fall short of measuring the business's actual profitability.

---

4. Rand Araskog, *The ITT Wars* (New York: Henry Holt Co., 1989).

5. "GM Splits Its Basic Stock 2 for 1," *Wall Street Journal,* 7 February 1989, p. A3.

DIFFERENCES IN REPORTING OF INCOME

When income is inaccurately reported, it may be either understated or overstated. Income may be understated to lower tax liabilities. Overstatement of income, however, may occur when the owner of a company is trying to make the business appear more profitable than it really is. This may be done to try to increase the price that the company may be sold for. Examples of under and overstatement of income are provided in the case studies that follow.

CASE STUDY: UNDERSTATING INCOME

One example of underreported income comes from the food retail industry.[a] The client was a food broker—a business that arranges for the placement of brand name food products in major food retail chains. The broker is compensated through a commission on food shipments to the stores. The commission is a negotiated rate that varies between 1.5% and 4.0%. It is difficult for the food broker to know the level of current revenues at any one time. Orders are continually placed, but many are never actually shipped. Payment is usually made within 30 days of the actual shipments.

In the last month of the fiscal year, the food broker would tell his customers not to pay until the next month, which was another reporting year. The purpose was to minimize the current year's taxable income. The end result was a continual 30–day float on tax payments. For a business with monthly revenues of $2 million per month and a 12% cost of capital, this equals an annual value of $240,000. In a growing business, each year's profits are lower than the actual profits for that year. The float, which is clearly a benefit to the business, becomes larger every year.

---

a. Gaughan and Fuentes, "Taxable Income and Lost Profits Litigation."

CASE STUDY: OVERSTATING INCOME

Understating income is more common, but overstating also may occur. Specifically, companies tend to overstate their true income when the company is trying to give a more profitable appearance to prospective buyers of the company. One such case, encountered by Economatrix Research Associates, Inc., an economic and financial consulting firm, involved a paint manufacturer that would increase its sales and profits at the end of the fiscal year through an agreement with customers to accept higher than needed shipments during the last month of the fiscal year. Year-end sales and profits would be higher as a result of the last month's surge in sales. The higher sales, however, would be reversed by returns that occurred in the first month of the next fiscal year. The customers would simply return the paint and be issued credit memos.

This practice illustrates the difference between the reporting and audit requirements of public and private companies. A private company may prepare its financial statements through a noncertified review process. Accounting review or compilation standards and practices do not normally require that credit memos in the following period be examined.[a] Therefore, this practice would not be detected in the formation of the typical private firm's financial statements. It is hoped that public companies, adhering to stricter certified financial statement standards and normal audit procedures, would be confronted by a diligent auditor. Public firms should not be able to manipulate income in this manner.

---

a. SSARS No. 1

Costs of the Private Corporation

Inflating the private company's costs is the most often used approach to minimizing taxable income. The increase in costs tends to come through discretionary expenses. Common areas of overstatement are officers' compensation, travel and entertainment (T&E), pension contributions, automobile expenses, personal insurance, and excess rent paid.

One common area of inflation is compensation. Principals in closely held businesses generally enjoy far higher compensation relative to the firm's sales volume than the management of public companies. For example, a case study provided by Economatrix Research Associates, Inc. involves a company with annual revenues of $5.7 million. The company's five principals had a combined annual compensation of $1.8 to $2 million when all forms of compensation, including salary and pension, were considered. (This company is a service business with little overhead and fixed expenses.)

A telltale sign of this type of extraordinary compensation is to compare the growth in sales with the growth in officers' compensation. If, for example, the firm experiences a one-year increase in sales of $1 million in a service-oriented business and officers' compensation increases by $400,000, the officers' compensation needs to be more closely examined.

Travel and entertainment is another area in which considerable forms of personal compensation are hidden in seemingly legitimate expenses. Another instance reported by Economatrix Research Associates, Inc. is a company that lists as expenses two condominiums in Florida. A vast array of similar personal expenses, ranging from business and/or personal travel to other forms of entertainment, could be sources of income to a buyer. This area of expenses may contain many "costs" that are actually forms of compensation to the business owners; that is, they are truly discretionary expenditures that would be available to a buyer as profits. For this reason, an evaluator may treat them as income.

Reconstruction of True Profitability

This analysis reconstructs the true profitability of the privately held concern by means of addbacks to the taxable income. Reducing these excess expenditures, which are not necessary to achieve the projected cash flows, the true profitability can be derived.

In adjusting officers' and management's compensation, the analyst must differentiate between the appropriate compensation for the actual duties that the principal/manager performs and the excessive compensation withdrawn from the company because the manager has the discretion to set his or her compensation at an inordinately high level. Here it is necessary to critically examine what the principal/manager really does. Is he or she a truly innovative owner who would be very difficult to replace?

Whether agents rather than an active owner should manage the business is not an issue that should be ignored.[6] Agents cannot be expected to maximize income in the same way an owner would. However, perhaps the owner manages a business that runs itself through the direction of several departmental managers who report to the owner while he or she spends the bulk of the day on the golf course. In this case, from the potential buyer's viewpoint, the true compensation for the work done by the owner/manager should be minimal, with the excess compensation being put back in the company's bottom line.

RECASTING THE INCOME STATEMENT: AN EXAMPLE OF THE ADDBACK PROCESS

The example presented here is that of a service-oriented business and is taken from a case history provided by Economatrix Research Associates, Inc. A variety of addbacks are used to reconstruct the true profitability of this closely held company. The company, whose name is listed as XYZ Corporation, is a construction industry service company. The primary adjustments take place in the following areas: compensation, travel and entertainment, pension contributions, compensation of family members, and excessive rent payments to a family-run business.

A pro forma income statement for the past five years is shown in Table 14.1. The top half lists the main income and cost items as they appeared on financial statements prepared for tax purposes. The bottom half shows the reconstruction of profitability.

Explanation of Addback Items

Certain costs items are adjusted to create addbacks that increase XYZ's profitability. They are:

Officers' salaries. This adjustment was made after it was determined that the owner was performing the basic functions of a manager. After a consultation with a personnel specialist, it was determined that the market salary for such a manager was $75,000. To determine the appropriate addback, this amount was subtracted from the compensation that the owner was receiving. In the interest of accuracy, this replacement salary should be adjusted for inflation each year.[7]

---

6. Michael Jensen and William Meckling, "Theory of the Firm: Managerial Behavior, Agency Costs and Ownership Structure," *Journal of Financial Economics* 3 (October 1976), pp. 305–360; Eugene Fama, "Agency Problems and the Theory of the Firm," *Journal of Political Economy* 88, no. 2 (April 1980), pp. 288–307.

7. See also Executive Compensation Service, American Management Association, Karen Tracy, *Executive Compensation: Selected References* (Cambridge, Mass.: Harvard University Press, 1990).

Table 14.1. XYZ Service Corporation: Pro Forma Income Statement, 1998–2002

	1998	1999	2000	2001	2002
Sales	$3,590,000	$4,150,000	$4,750,000	$5,980,000	$7,220,000
Cost of sales	2,270,700	2,540,000	3,060,000	3,827,000	4,421,000
Gross profit	1,319,300	1,610,000	1,690,000	2,153,000	2,799,000
Other expenses	1,289,140	1,522,500	1,588,400	2,039,000	2,679,500
Net profit	30,160	87,500	101,600	114,000	119,500
Addbacks					
Officers' salaries	$225,000	$250,000	$325,000	$375,000	$425,000
Pension contributions	18,750	18,750	18,750	18,750	18,750
T&E	20,000	30,000	35,000	38,000	41,000
Automobile	20,000	20,000	25,000	25,000	35,000
Personal insurance	5,000	7,000	8,000	8,000	9,000
Family relations	30,000	45,000	50,000	50,000	50,000
Excess rent	60,000	60,000	60,000	75,000	75,000
True profits	408,910	518,250	623,000	703,750	773,250

Pension contributions. If officers' salaries are excessive, pension contributions, which often are computed as a percentage of compensation, also need to be adjusted.

Travel and entertainment. A buyer of a business must try to differentiate between the component of T&E that is truly necessary to generate the revenues and add back the excess component.

Automobile expenses. If more money than necessary is devoted to auto expenses, such as through the use of more expensive automobiles than would be necessary to provide to replacement management, these amounts need to be added back.

Personal insurance. Using similar reasoning, personal insurance may need to be adjusted.

Family relations. This is the compensation of a family member who did not really play a role in the business. The demonstration of this "nonrole," however, may present IRS problems.

Rent in excess of fair market rent. This was the excess rent paid by the business as rent to a family-owned business that owned the building the business was renting. The difference was computed by determining the market rental rates per square foot for similar commercial properties and deducting this total from the actual rent paid.

Examples of Other Individualistic Addbacks

To make a full and accurate adjustment of true profitability, the analyst must usually learn more about the business and the industry. A more detailed review of the industry norms will allow the analyst to spot unusual practices. The following sections discuss some unusual forms of indirect compensation that have appeared as costs in financial statements.

Excessive Professional Fees

When professionals are principals or owners of a business while still maintaining a professional practice as a separate business, two forms of compensation are available: direct compensation from the firm and indirect compensation derived from fees paid to the other firm. These fees may occur in many different ways. They may occur, for example, in a construction contracting company that pays fees to an engineering firm owned by one or more of the owners of the construction firm. Another example would be a computer hardware firm that uses the services of a software company that is owned by the principals of the hardware company.

Excessive Legal Fees

One relevant case of a business valuation, also reported by Economatrix Research Associates, Inc., involved an attorney who was a partner in a law firm while maintaining his position as managing partner in a medical research company. One unusual aspect of this medical research business was the large amount of legal fees it paid to the law firm. This was an indirect form of compensation to the attorney because his compensation at the law firm was proportionate to his billings. The true profitability of the medical research company had to be estimated without these legal fees when the nonattorney owner of the medical research company sued for the 50% value of the firm in a dispute with the attorney over the buyout purchase price that the attorney had previously paid.

Other Areas

Numerous other factors help determine the true profitability of the privately held firm. Depreciation policies, for example, may be used to understate or overstate profitability.[8] Ideally, the most appropriate depreciation schedule for the purposes of lost profit analysis should be one that best reflects the matching of revenue and expense. Depreciation is, in effect, a cost allocation.[9]

Accounting policies may greatly affect the profitability of the closely held firm. For example, a switch from a FIFO (first-in, first out) to a LIFO (last-in, first out) accounting method to reduce taxable income may result in understated reported income. These and other accounting practices may need to be considered before the true profitability of the firm can be determined. It is required that the income effects of changes in accounting practices be specifically disclosed on the firm's income statement.[10]

Factors to Consider When Valuing Closely Held Businesses

One set of factors that is often cited in valuing private firms is Revenue Ruling 59–60. This ruling sets forth various factors that tax courts consider in a valuation of the stock of closely held businesses for gift and estate purposes. These factors are:

- Nature and history of the business
- Condition of the economy and the industry
- Book value of the company and its financial condition

---

8. Joel Siegel, *How to Analyze Business, Financial Statements and the Quality of Earnings* (Englewood Cliffs, N.J.: Prentice-Hall, 1982), pp. 67–68.

9. Donald Kieso and Jerry Weygandt, *Intermediate Accounting* (New York: John Wiley & Sons, 1986).

10. "Accounting Changes," *Accounting Principles Board Opinion,* No. 20 (July 1971).

- Earnings capacity of the company
- Dividend-paying capacity
- Existence of goodwill or other intangibles
- Other sales of stock
- Prices of comparable stock

Evaluators of closely held businesses should be aware of the factors that are set forth in Revenue Ruling 59–60 because these are often-cited standards for the valuation of the stock of closely held companies. The inclusion of certain factors such as both earnings and dividend-paying capacity may be questionable because dividend-paying capacity presumably is a function of earnings capacity. Industry analysis and a macroeconomic and possibly regional economic analysis are important enough to be treated as separate components of the valuation process. Putting a lot of weight on book value, a measure that may not accurately reflect the value of the company, is questionable. Revenue Ruling 59–60 also fails to mention other benchmarks, such as liquidation value, which may be worth considering along with book value. Taking these issues into consideration, this revenue ruling is important to be aware of but should not be the exclusive list of factors that are considered.

MOST COMMONLY USED VALUATION METHODS

There are several techniques that are commonly used to value closely held businesses. Some of these methods, which are discussed below, are more appropriate than others depending on the particular circumstances surrounding the business being valued.

1. *Discounted future earnings.* This method, which is discussed in Chapter 13, requires a projection of future income and the selection of a discount rate. The method also depends on the particular definition of income chosen.
2. *Comparable multiples.* This is a very common approach to valuing both public and private businesses. Many business brokers, for example, simply use standard multiples of income or revenues as their basis for establishing the purchase price. Our discussion of the process of capitalization of earnings later in this chapter shows how the use of earnings multiples is tantamount to capitalizing earnings.
3. *Capitalization of earnings.* This valuation technique is similar to the discounted future earnings approach. Capitalization of future earnings also requires the calculation of the present value of a future income stream. The acquirer is considered to obtain the right to a future income stream of indefinite length. The usefulness of this method also hinges on the definition of income and the selection of the capitalization rate.
4. *Assets-oriented approaches.* There are several asset-oriented approaches; some are relevant to the valuation of both public and private businesses, whereas others are applied more frequently to privately held businesses. These approaches are fair market value, fair value, book value, and liquidation value.

Fair market value is the market value of the business. More specifically, it is the price a willing buyer would pay and what a willing seller would accept, each under no compulsion to buy or sell, and each being fully aware of the more important factors relating to the sale. It is easier to obtain the fair market value of a public company because a market exists for such a firm's stock. If there is an active market for similar private businesses, this method can be used. Generally, however, fair market value is difficult to obtain because data on the sales of similar businesses tend to be limited. For this reason, evaluators have to turn to *fair value*, a method used when there is no market for the business. Fair value is a dollar value that is derived through appraising the value of the tangible assets and determining the value of the intangible assets. These values are added together to determine the fair value of the business.

Book value is an accounting concept and may not be a good measure of value. As discussed in Chapter 13, book value is a function of the value of the assets as they are valued on the firm's books. It may or may not bear a close relationship to the market value of the firm's assets.

Finally, *liquidation value* is the estimated value of the firm's assets if they were sold off in liquidation. As discussed in Chapter 13, it may not be a good measure of a firm's value in an acquisition, but it may serve as a floor value for the valuation process.

Having provided an overview of the different valuation approaches, we will now detail some of the important issues related to these methods.

Discounted Future Cash Flows or Net Present Value Approach

When the investment that is required to purchase the target firm is deducted from the discounted future cash flows or earnings, this amount becomes the net present value. Therefore, the mechanics of using this approach will not be developed from the beginning. The methodology is the same as the net present value approach discussed in Chapter 13. However, its application and applicability to the valuation of a privately held firm may differ.

The discounted future cash flows approach to valuing a business is based on the projected magnitude of the future monetary benefits that it will generate. These annual benefits, which may be defined in terms of earnings or cash flows, are then discounted back to present value to determine the current value of the future benefits. Readers may be familiar with the discounting process from capital budgeting where net present value is used to determine whether a project is financially worth pursuing. In that context a computation such as is shown in Eq. 14.1 is used.

$$NPV = I_0 - \sum_{i=1}^{n} \frac{FB_1}{(1 + r)} + ... + \frac{FB_n}{(1 + r)^n}$$

(14.1)

where
FB_i = future benefit in year i
r = discount rate
I_0 = investment at time 0

When earnings are used instead of cash flows, the particular earnings measure utilized may differ depending on the user, but most earnings-oriented models use some version of adjusted operating income such as EBITDA, which is earnings before interest, taxes, depreciation, and amortization.

The cash flows or earnings must be adjusted before constructing a projection so that the projected benefits are equal to the value that a buyer would derive. For example, adjustments such as the elimination of excessive officers' compensation must be made to the base that is used for the projection.

One of the key decisions in using the discounted cash flows approach is to select the proper discount rate. This rate must be one that reflects the perceived level of risk in the target company.

In the context of discounted cash flows for valuing a business, the computation is quite similar, as shown in Eq. 14.2.

$$BV = \frac{FCF_1}{(1 + r)} + \frac{FCF_2}{(1 + r)^2} + \dots + \frac{FCF_5}{(1 + r)^5} + \frac{\dfrac{FCF_6}{(r - g)}}{(1 + r)^5} \qquad (14.2)$$

where:

BV = value of the business

FCF_i = free cash flows in the ith period

g = the growth rate in future cash flows after the fifth year

The numerators of all the fractions are free cash flows. Note that after the fifth year the values of all the future cash flows are measured by treating them as a perpetuity that is growing at a certain rate, g. This perpetuity or future stream of cash flows of indefinite length is valued using the process of capitalization. This process is explained subsequently because it is also used as a separate method of valuing businesses. However, the first step is to project free cash flows for the sixth year. This may be done by multiplying the fifth year's cash flows, FCF_5, by $(1 + g)$. The resulting value is then divided by the capitalization rate to obtain the present value of all cash flows from year six and thereafter. This is the value as of the beginning of year 6. We then compute the present value of that amount by dividing it by $(1 + r)^5$. This is the present value in year 0 of all future cash flows for year 6 and thereafter. This amount is sometimes referred to as the *residual*. It is then added to the other five present value amounts computed for the first five years to arrive at a value of the business.

Discount Rate and Risk

The greater the risk associated with a given earnings stream, the higher the discount rate that will be used. If the projected cash flow or income stream is considered highly likely, a lower discount rate should be used. For high-risk cash flow or income streams, a risk premium is added, which increases the discount rate. The use of a higher discount rate lowers the present value of each annual projected income amount.

Application of the Discounted Future Earnings Approach

Let us consider the case of a privately held company in which the owners are contemplating leaving the business and "cashing out" on their investment. Assume that the business is a family-owned company that has been in business for 15 years and has enjoyed a 5% average annual compounded rate of cash flow growth for the past 10 years.

Table 14.2.   Optimistic, Most Likely, and Pessimistic Projection Scenarios

		Optimistic Scenario (7.5% growth)			
Year	Projected Earnings ($ thousand)	Discount Rates			
		20%	25%	30%	35%
2000	10,750,000	$8,958,333	$8,600,000	$8,269,231	$7,962,963
2001	11,556,250	7,465,278	6,880,000	6,360,947	5,898,491
2002	12,422,969	6,221,065	5,504,000	4,893,036	4,369,253
2003	13,354,691	5,184,221	4,403,200	3,763,874	3,236,483
2004	14,356,293	4,320,184	3,522,560	2,895,288	2,397,395
2005	15,433,015	3,600,153	2,818,048	2,227,144	1,775,848
2006	16,590,491	3,000,128	2,254,438	1,713,188	1,315,443
Total		$38,749,361	$33,982,246	$30,122,707	$26,955,877
		Most Likely Scenario (5% growth)			
2000	10,500,000	$8,750,000	$8,400,000	$8,076,923	$7,777,778
2001	11,025,000	7,291,667	6,720,000	6,213,018	5,761,317
2002	11,576,250	6,076,389	5,376,000	4,779,244	4,267,642
2003	12,155,063	5,063,657	4,300,800	3,676,342	3,161,216
2004	12,762,816	4,219,715	3,440,640	2,827,955	2,341,642
2005	13,400,956	3,516,429	2,752,512	2,175,350	1,734,549
2006	14,071,004	2,930,357	2,202,010	1,673,346	1,284,851
Total		$37,848,214	$33,191,962	$29,422,179	$25,702,651
		Pessimistic Scenario (2.5% growth)			
2000	10,250,000	$8,541,667	$8,200,000	$7,884,615	$7,592,593
2001	10,506,250	7,118,056	6,560,000	6,065,089	5,624,143
2002	11,038,129	5,931,713	5,248,000	4,665,453	4,166,032
2003	11,314,082	4,943,094	4,198,400	3,588,810	3,085,949
2004	10,768,906	4,119,245	3,358,720	2,760,623	2,285,888
2005	11,596,934	3,432,704	2,686,976	2,123,556	1,693,251
2006	11,886,858	2,860,587	2,149,581	1,633,505	1,254,260
Total		$36,947,066	$32,401,677	$28,721,651	$25,702,115

We begin the analysis by constructing optimistic, most likely, and pessimistic projection scenarios (Table 14.2). Based on the acquirer's knowledge of the industry and the 10–year track record of steady 5% earnings growth, a 5% annual rate of growth is assumed to be very likely. It is possible that the target could benefit from the improved management and enhanced technology that would be available when the acquirer took over the target and provided an infusion of capital. Therefore, a 7.5% rate of growth is judged to be optimistic but possible.

The acquiring firm did have concerns about losing key personnel after the acquisition. There was also a concern that, although there was an agreement that some of the previous management would continue to work with the firm for at least two years following the takeover, they might not apply the same level of effort that they applied when they were owners. For this reason, the acquirer believed that a 2.5% annual rate of growth was also possible. This rate, then, is the pessimistic alternative.

The past year's earnings of $10 million is chosen as the base. The different rates of growth are applied to this dollar amount (Table 14.2). Some obvious trends are apparent in the table. The higher the discount rate, the lower the future value of the earnings stream that is generated. The greater the rate of growth of earnings, the greater the present value of the future earnings stream.

In the optimistic scenario, a maximum price between $26,955,877 and $38,749,361, depending on the discount rate, could be paid for the firm. At a lower growth rate, such as 5%

in the most likely scenario, the amount that could be paid would have a ceiling of $25,702,651 to $37,848,214. At a 2.5% rate of growth, in the pessimistic case, the range falls still further to between $25,702,115 and $36,947,066.

As is easily discernible, there is considerable room for disagreement among evaluators of businesses. Depending on the analyst's assumptions regarding the growth rate and the discount rate, different conclusions as to the value of the business may be developed. Therefore, it is critical to develop sound estimates of both the growth rate and the level of risk of the business, which, in turn, will provide guidance for selecting the appropriate discount rate. When the business has an extended earnings history in a mature industry, the growth rate assumptions may be relatively straightforward. If the earnings pattern has been stable, a low-risk discount rate should be chosen. When earnings have been high but volatile, however, the evaluator may have less confidence in the earnings growth rate assumptions, and a higher risk-adjusted discount rate will be used. The selection of a "customized" discount rate is discussed in a subsequent section.

Capitalization of Cash Flows or Earnings

The capitalization process allows the business analyst to determine the present value of a business's future income. There is no specific ending period in the capitalization process, unlike the forecasting of cash flows or earnings where a forecast for a specific time is used.

Some naive critics disparage the capitalization of earnings technique because in their view the process assumes that the business will be in existence for an infinite time. This is not a valid criticism inasmuch as monies that would be received an infinite number of years from now would be worth very little given the time value of money. Moreover, the present value of income that is received further into the future is worth less and less. The more distant the income that will be received, the less valuable it is to an acquirer.

The terms *capitalization rate* and *discount rate* are sometimes used interchangeably. When a specific projection of income per period has been developed for a certain time period, the term *discount rate* is used. When the task is to value a business that is capable of generating an income stream for an indefinite period of time, the term *capitalization rate* is used.

Students of corporate finance are already familiar with capitalization when calculating the value of preferred stock and common stock. Consider a share of preferred stock that pays annual dividends of $4 per share. If the appropriate capitalization rate is 0.15, the value of a single share of preferred stock that pays a constant $4 annual dividend for an indefinite period of time is

$$P_s = \$4/0.15 = \$26.67 \qquad (14.3)$$

Thus, $26.67 is the present value of a perpetual income stream that yields $4 per year. (This does not take into account the possibility that the preferred stock might be retired.) The capitalization rate is 0.15. This rate, used to capitalize the $4 income stream, might be the company's rate of return on equity.

Choice of Income Definition
The choice of the specific definition of income to be capitalized is crucial to the capitalization process. As we have already seen, several alternative definitions of income may be

used, including free cash flows; earnings before interest, taxes, depreciation, and amortization (EBITDA); earnings before interest and taxes (EBIT); and earnings after taxes (EAT). The capitalized value of the business will vary, depending on the definition chosen.

Selection of the Capitalization Rate

The capitalization rate should reflect the rate of return that is available in the marketplace on investments that are expected to produce a similar income stream. It therefore reflects the opportunity costs from investing the same amount of money (which is used to purchase the business) in a similar investment. The capitalization rate must be "tailor-made" for the type of income stream the firm is expected to generate.

Two possible guides to the capitalization rates are the rate of return on investment (ROI) and the rate of return on equity (ROE). The ROI is the rate of return provided by the total invested capital in the business—including both debt and equity. It may include only long-term debt or both short- and long-term debt. If the firm's debt capital consists of some long-term debt and some short-term debt that is "rolled over" each year, the short-term debt is actually disguised long-term debt. It should therefore be considered part of the firm's permanent debt capital. Short-term debt that is clearly short term may be left out.

The ROE refers to the rate of return provided by the ownership interest in the business. This return measure considers a more narrow definition of capital than the ROI. Both ROI and ROE can be computed on a pretax or posttax basis. Given the problems with the reliability of posttax income for privately held firms, pretax earnings should be used for closely held businesses and posttax earnings should be used for public companies.

Let us assume that a given privately held firm earns $2 million on a pretax basis. The total equity in the firm is $25 million, and the total borrowed capital is $20 million. The rate of return on investment and equity is computed as follows:

$$ROI= \$2,000,000/\$45,000,000 = 0.04 = 4\%$$

$$ROE = \$2,000,000/\$25,000,000 = 0.08 = 8\%$$

These two rates can then be used to capitalize the value of a business, which may yield a pretax income of $2 million.

Using the ROI as the capitalization rate, the value is

$$\$2,000,000/0.04 = \$5,000,000$$

Using the rate of return on equity as the capitalization rate, the value is

$$\$2,000,000/0.08 = \$2,500,000$$

Cost of Capital as the Capitalization Rate

In Chapter 13 we derived the cost of capital, which was then used to discount further income. The cost of capital is sometimes also used as a guide to the capitalization rate because it reflects the minimum acceptable rate of return for the firm. This includes a rate of return sufficient to meet the debt payments and to provide the expected ROE.

The Summation, or Buildup, Method

The capitalization rate can be determined by breaking the rate down into several component parts, a method termed the *summation*, or *buildup*, *method*. The three principal components are (1) risk-free rate, (2) risk premium, and (3) illiquidity premium.

1. *Risk-free rate.* The risk-free rate is the rate of return that an investor would receive from a risk-free investment. In other words, it is the rate of return provided when the investor parts with capital but has complete assurance of receiving it back along with a return to compensate for forsaking consumption.

    The rate of return on Treasury bills is considered the best proxy for a risk-free rate. Treasury bills have no default risk because the U.S. government is not expected to go out of business during the duration of this short-term investment. (They can have a maturity of up to one year.) The historical rate of return of T-bills bills is shown in Figure 14.1. Treasury bills are also somewhat free from interest rate risk, which is the risk that an adverse movement in interest rates will cause the value of the T-bills, which pay a fixed rate, to fall. In contrast, long-term Treasury securities are more influenced by interest rate movements and contain reinvestment risk.

2. *Risk premium.* At least two kinds of risk are relevant to acquiring a business: business risk and interest rate risk. Business risk is the risk that the company being acquired may not perform up to expectations set forth at the time of acquisition. This expectation is built into the acquisition price. Failure to live up to it will cause the investment to pay lower returns. In the extreme case, business risk may mean the default of the business. With a default, the return is considerably less than the level of expectations but not necessarily a zero return.

    Interest rate risk is the risk of adverse movements in interest rates. Specifically, it is the risk that other investments will provide a higher rate of return if rates rise, whereas the investment in question, the acquisition of a business, might pay a more or less constant return. The acquisition of a business does not contain as much interest rate risk as investments such as fixed income securities. As the name implies, fixed income securities, such as government or corporate bonds, usually offer a fixed rate. Increases in interest rates or inflation will erode the value of the fixed payment stream.

    The revenue and income of a business will normally adjust to increases in the rate of inflation unless the business is in an industry that tends to lag behind the movements in the inflationary process. Therefore, interest rate risk is a lesser concern to acquisitions of businesses than to investments in fixed income securities. It is relevant, however, to determining the appropriate risk premium because the analyst may use the rate of return on fixed income securities as a benchmark. The level of business and interest rate risk that is internalized into the market's determination of the rate on the security being used as a proxy for the capitalization rate needs to be considered.

    A variety of benchmarks can be considered as guides for the appropriate risk premium. The risk premium can be measured by the difference between the rate offered on another investment that has a similar level of risk. Among these benchmarks, long-term government bonds can be considered first. They contain virtually the same level of default risk as their short-term counterparts, T-bills, but they carry

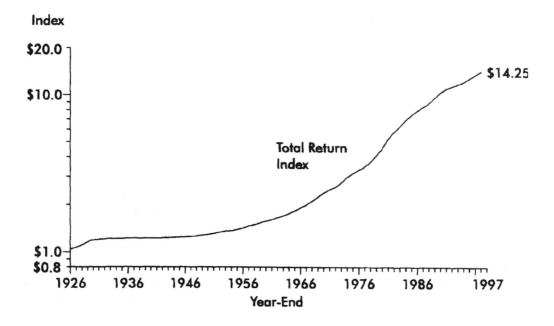

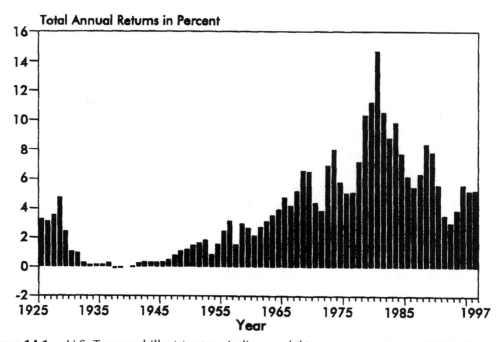

Figure 14.1.   U.S. Treasury bills: (a) return indices and (b) return percentages, 1926–97.

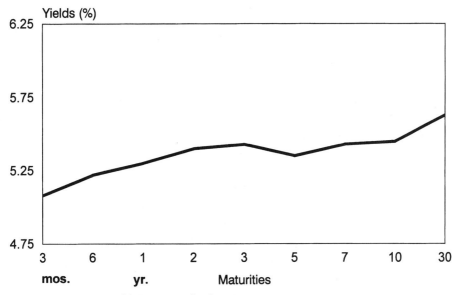

Figure 14.2. Treasury yield curve (08/09/1998).

greater interest rate risk. For this reason, it is not surprising that the normal shape of the Treasury securities' yield curve is upward sloping, reflecting the fact that longer-term securities normally command higher rates of return (Figure 14.2).[11]

The level of risk associated with long-term government securities is significantly less than that associated with the acquisition of a business. The historical rate of return of long-term government securities is shown in Table 14.3.

Table 14.3. Rates of Return on Selected Securities

Year	U.S. Treasury Bills	Long-Term Government Bonds	Long-Term Corporate Bonds	Large Company Stocks	Small Company Stocks
1950–98	5.2	5.9	6.3	13.5	14.7
1960–98	6.0	7.5	7.7	12.0	14.1
1970–98	6.8	9.6	9.8	13.5	13.6
1980–98	7.0	11.8	11.7	17.7	14.8
1990–98	5.0	11.0	10.3	17.9	13.6
1950–59	1.9	–0.01	1.0	19.4	16.9
1960–69	3.9	1.2	1.7	7.8	15.5
1970–79	6.3	5.5	6.2	5.9	11.5
1980–89	8.9	12.6	13.0	17.6	15.8
1990–98	5.0	11.0	10.3	17.9	13.6

Source: Stocks, Bonds, Bills, and Inflation, 1999 Yearbook, Ibbotson Associates.

---

11. Economic theory implies that long-term rates are a function of current short-term rates and expectations about future short-term rates. If short-term rates are expected to increase in the future, an average of current and expected short-term rates will be higher than current short-term rates. Therefore, the yield curve will be upward sloping.

The rates offered on *corporate bonds* reflect more business risk than those on government securities and are ranked according to default risk by the major rating agencies such as Standard & Poor's and Moody's. The historical rates of return on high-grade, long-term corporate bonds are shown in Table 14.3. The lower the security's rating, the higher the rate of return necessary to market the security. Most privately held businesses generally have significantly higher risk than the highly rated companies. Therefore, the rates offered on AAA-rated or AA-rated companies may not encompass the level of risk associated with smaller, privately held firms. The rates offered on high-yield junk bonds may be a more useful benchmark for the risk premium on private business acquisitions. At times these securities, rated BB or lower, offered rates of almost 20%. They contain both business risk and liquidity risk because the secondary market for junk bonds is not as strong as higher rated securities.

Numerous other securities can be used as benchmarks for the risk premium. Most of these contain less risk than junk bonds and, therefore, are not as useful. An example would be municipal bonds. Given that the income stream generated by a privately held firm may be even more risky than the income stream derived from a municipal bond investment, which may carry municipal bond insurance, less risky investments, such as many municipal bonds, may not warrant consideration.

We saw in Chapter 11 that bonds offer less default risk than equity investments, providing more protection for the investor in the event of default and bankruptcy because the bondholder will have access to the liquidation proceeds before equity investors will. Equity investors will usually get back a small percentage of their investment, if anything. Equities contain greater risk and reward potential than debt securities offered by the same company. For this reason, the difference between the rates offered on equities of comparable companies and on T-bills may be used as a partial measure of the risk premium. The historical rates of return on common stock are shown in Table 14.3

Although the privately held company may be comparable to some companies that are traded on the New York Stock Exchange, comparable companies will more likely be found on NASDAQ or regional exchanges. The over-the-counter (OTC) market contains companies that may not fulfill the requirements to be traded on an organized exchange. They are generally smaller and have a lower total capitalization. These firms are usually considered riskier.

The most generally available data sources are the *Wall Street Journal* and the *New York Times*. These publications provide daily quotes on the current rates offered on a variety of categories of securities described here. For historical data on rates of return, many sources are available, one of the more authoritative being the Ibbotson Associates' *Stocks, Bonds, Bills, and Inflation.* Ibbotson Associates makes these data available in a number of forms, including hard copy and on disk.

3. *Illiquidity premium.* Small capitalization stocks that are traded on the New York Stock Exchange are relatively liquid investments. This liquidity is provided by the reputation of the New York Stock Exchange and the Exchange's efforts to facilitate, through a system of specialists in each security, a liquid market that is somewhat free from sudden large swings in prices. The acquirer of a company does not have

the advantage of having a liquid investment. Some businesses are more marketable than others. The acquirer who wants to liquidate an investment might have to wait an extended time before selling or else suffer a large loss. For this reason, an illiquidity premium must be added to the risk premium derived previously.

One proxy for the illiquidity premium might be the rates offered on OTC stocks. Many of the stocks traded on the OTC market have thin markets with low daily trading volume. Because they have a small number of market makers, there is less protection from larger price swings. The sale of a large block of a firm's outstanding equity can greatly depress the stock prices. For this reason, some OTC stocks are considered less liquid investments. Therefore, the rates of return provided by firms that are in the same industry and of similar size can be regarded as a guide to the illiquidity premium. This premium might be part of the difference in the rate of return between the OTC company and a comparable company on the New York Stock Exchange. However, an investment in OTC equities may be more liquid than the acquisition of a privately held company. An even higher illiquidity premium therefore may need to be derived.

One benchmark that can be used is the rate of return demanded by venture capitalists who make equity investments in small start-up companies. They usually demand a markedly higher rate of return than that offered by the more conventional investments to compensate them for the risks associated with such investments. These rates incorporate both risks and illiquidity premiums. Venture capitalists look for 25% to 50% (or sometimes more) compounded annual rates of return, depending on the stage of development of the company and the degree of risk.

Implied Risk Premium of Highly Leveraged Transactions

In their 1995 study of 51 highly leveraged transactions (HLTs), Kaplan and Ruback derived the implied discount rate.[12] Although they used different growth rates, for a 4% growth rate assumption they found an average discount rate of 16.28%. They "backed their way" into the discount rate value using the cash flow forecasts and terminals values combined with the transaction values (see Panel A of Table 14.4). In effect, they used a methodology similar to one used to compute the internal rate of return for capital budgeting analysis. They then computed the implied risk premium as the difference between the implied discount rate and the rate of return on Treasury bonds that prevailed at the time of the cash flow forecast (see Panel B of Table 14.4). For the 4% growth rate assumption, they found an average risk premium of 7.08%.

For the evaluation of many closely held businesses, the discount rate and risk premium may have to be higher than the average for HLTs imputed by Kaplan and Ruback because all the transactions in their sample exceeded $100 million in transaction value. With smaller targets and transaction values, a higher discount rate may be in order, depending on the level of risk that is anticipated.

---

12. Steven N. Kaplan and Richard S. Ruback, "The Valuation of Cash Flow Forecasts," *Journal of Finance* 50, no. 4 (September 1995), pp.1059–1094.

Table 14.4.   Implied Discount Rates, Risk Premia, and Market Equity Risk Premia

Discount rates, risk premia, and market equity risk premia implied by projected capital cash flows in 51 HLTs completed between 1983 and 1989. Terminal growth rate assumed to grow at 4%, 6%, 2%, and 0%. The transaction value equals (1) the market value of the firm common stock; plus (2) the market value of firm preferred stock; plus (3) the value of the firm debt; plus (4) transaction fees; less (5) firm cash balances and marketable securities, all at the time of the transaction. Debt not repaid in the transaction is valued at book value; debt that is repaid is valued at repayment value. The implied discount rate discounts the capital cash flows to a value equal to the transaction value. The implied risk premium equals the difference between the implied discount rate and the yield on long-term Treasury bonds (from Ibbotson Associates) at the time of the projections. The implied market equity risk premium uses the value weighted capital structure for nonfinancial, nonutility firms in the S&P 500 in the fiscal year before the HLT announcement to transform the implied risk premium into the risk premium for an investment with a beta of one.

Terminal Value Growth Rate	Median	Mean	Standard Deviation	Interquartile Range	Minimum	Maximum	N
			Panel A: Implied Discount Rate				
0	15.77	16.28	2.69	3.06	10.37	24.16	51
6	16.77	17.32	2.64	2.80	11.55	25.39	51
2	14.85	15.29	2.75	3.24	9.29	23.16	51
0	13.79	14.36	2.83	3.50	8.29	22.46	51
			Panel B: Implied Risk Premium				
4	7.08	7.14	2.87	2.76	0.90	15.85	51
6	8.16	8.18	2.84	2.42	2.08	16.98	51
2	5.82	6.16	2.93	2.93	−0.00	14.75	51
0	5.00	5.22	2.99	2.76	−1.26	14.02	51
			Panel C: Implied Market Equity Risk Premium				
4	7.78	7.97	3.30	3.03	1.00	18.63	51
6	9.03	9.13	3.27	2.78	2.30	19.95	51
2	6.65	6.87	3.34	3.24	−0.02	17.34	51
0	5.60	5.83	3.41	3.05	−1.41	16.09	51

Source: Kaplan and Ruback, "The Valuation of Cash Flow Forecasts: An Empirical Analysis," *Journal of Finance* 50, no. 4, 1995, pp. 1059–1094.

Example of the Buildup Method

The buildup, or summation, method uses the risk-free rate as the base and adds various premiums that are determined by the risk characteristics of the company being evaluated. Consider the case of an athletic goods manufacturer that makes and markets under its own brand name. The firm has been in existence for six years and has experienced rapid growth during the past four years. Annual sales are $80 million. The industry is highly competitive but is also growing fairly rapidly. The company has received overtures from its larger rivals to sell the firm. The chief executive officer of this closely held company wants to know what value his company should command in the marketplace. Because there are no other comparable recent acquisitions, it is difficult to look to other recent transactions for guidance.

The following example of the use of the buildup method uses rates that prevailed in October 1998.

Buildup Rate Components	Rate
T-bill rate as of September 18, 1995	5.30
30–year Treasuries	6.74
Rates on Dow Jones 20 bonds	7.15
Rates on junk bonds of comparable maturity	10.00
Additional illiquidity and risk premium	10.00
Buildup rate	20.00

The preceding example uses an illiquidity premium of 10% to account for the fact that the investment in the closely held firm is less liquid than a junk bond investment. Depending on the size of the company and its risk characteristics, a risk premium even greater than 10% may be inappropriate.

Capitalization versus Discount Rate

The capitalization rate derived from the buildup method can be adjusted to reflect an expected high rate of growth in the target's earnings. This adjustment is made by subtracting the expected rate of growth from the capitalization rate.

Consider the example of a firm with $1 million in annual earnings. Let us assume that the buildup method suggested a capitalization rate of 30%. Let us also assume that the firm has exhibited a steady annual rate of growth in excess of 15%. A conservative evaluation might assume that a 10% rate of growth would be continued into the foreseeable future.

We then need to deduct the anticipated 10% growth from the rate we had to arrive at a growth adjusted rate of 15%. Using such a rate the evaluation would be as follows:

$$\text{Value of the firm} = \$1,000,000/(0.30 - 0.10) = \$5,000,000$$

This example illustrates the difference between a discount rate and a capitalization rate. The discount rate is the rate that might be derived from using the buildup method. It is the rate that is used to discount specifically projected future amounts. In the preceding example, the discount rate would have been 20% if we had actually made a projection of cash flows, as we did in Eq. 14.2. However, when we are valuing a perpetuity, we have to project only one period, the next period, and then divide by a growth-adjusted rate. This rate is the discount rate minus the rate of growth at which we expect the cash flow or earnings stream to grow. Deducting anticipated growth converts the discount rate to a capitalization rate.

Use of the Price-Earnings Ratio to Derive Capitalization Rate

The price-earnings (P/E) ratio can be used as a guide to the capitalization rate. Because the capitalization rate is the reciprocal of the P/E ratio, the higher the P/E ratio, the lower the capitalization rate.

$$\text{Capitalization rate} = 1/(\text{P/E ratio})$$

The P/E ratio can be calculated by using the current earnings or the most recent year's earnings, or by using projected earnings. It is more common to use current earnings or the most recent year's earnings.[13]

---

13. Sidney Cottle, Roger F. Murray, and Frank E. Block, *Graham and Dodd's Security Analysis,* 5th ed. (New York: McGraw-Hill, 1988), p. 346.

The P/E ratio reflects the amount an investor is willing to pay for the firm's earnings on a per share basis. For example, a company that has a P/E ratio of 16 suggests that the market is using a low capitalization rate of 6.75% to value that company's earnings. In a valuation of privately held firms, the analyst determines the P/E ratio of comparable public companies, or the industry average P/E ratio. Caution must be used in applying the P/E-derived capitalization rate. Simply because one company in a given industry group sells for 16 times its current earnings does not mean that the buyer of a privately held business in the same industry should use the same 6.75% capitalization rate of return. This capitalization rate needs to be adjusted to reflect the relevant types of risk for the firm being evaluated.

It is necessary to examine public companies in the same industry and to compare their P/E ratios. An industry P/E average should also be considered. In addition, market trends need to be factored into the analysis. If the P/E ratio of 16 came at a time when the market was reaching all-time highs, a more "average" market might show a lower P/E ratio and thus a higher capitalization rate.

The P/E ratio may not be useful if the expected rate of growth in earnings for the privately held company is very different from the P/E ratios of proxy firms. If the proxy firms and the industry as a whole are considered mature and have leveled off at a lower rate of growth, their P/E ratios will not be comparable to those of the privately held firm that might be growing at a rapid rate of growth. In this event, the analyst will need to look elsewhere, such as to the buildup method, for the appropriate capitalization rate.

The use of the P/E ratio is a market-based method of determining the capitalization rate because the ratios that are used are determined by a market process. It is also an earnings approach rather than an asset-oriented approach. This attribute may be attractive when the firm being valued has many assets of questionable market value. The use of the P/E ratio is also a future-oriented approach because buyers of the company's stock are concerned about the firm's future earning power, not just its current earnings.

Price-Earnings Ratio: Reflects Both the Risk and Growth of the Target

Given that the P/E ratio is the reciprocal of the capitalization rate, both the capitalization rate and the P/E ratios simultaneously take into account the risk of the business through the risk premium embodied in the discount rate and the expected growth of the enterprise. The more risky the business, the lower the P/E ratio. Conversely, the greater the anticipated growth of earnings, the higher the P/E ratio.

Price-Earnings Ratio and the Payback Method

The payback method indicates that a project should not be accepted if the expected cumulative net cash flows do not equal the purchase price within a predetermined time period. The P/E ratio is roughly equal to the number of years an acquisition is expected to take for the deal to pay for itself. For example, a buyer who pays a sum that is equal to eight times the target's earnings shows that the buyer is willing to wait eight years to have the acquisition pay for itself.

Capitalization Rate and the Payback Period

Because the P/E ratio can be equated to the payback period, the capitalization rate, which is the reciprocal of the P/E ratio, must be directly related to it. The capitalization rate must therefore also be equal to the reciprocal of the payback period.

$$\text{Capitalization rate} = 1/\text{Payback period}$$

For example, an acquirer with a four-year payback period would value a firm with $500,000 in earnings as follows:

$$\text{Capitalization rate} = 1/4 \text{ years} = 0.25$$

$$\text{Value of the company} = \$500,000/0.25 = \$2,000,000$$

Using the assumptions about the buyer's payback period as a guide to the capitalization rate has certain disadvantages. The payback period does not consider the time value of money. This method of evaluating projects would value two projects or acquisitions that have the same payback period as equally good purchases. One company, however, may return 65% of the total purchase price within the first three years, whereas the other might pay only 20% of the total purchase price within this time period, even though the payback period was the same. Given the time value of money, the discounted future earnings approach might reach a very different conclusion about the relative merits of these two approaches.

Changing Interest Rates and Acquisition Prices: Evidence from the Fifth Merger Wave

Lower interest rates tend to lower discount rates. Short-term fluctuations may not change the discount rate that one would use in a valuation, but changes in long-term rates that persist for an extended period of time should have an influence. Such was the case in the fifth merger wave where interest rates fell and the average price of acquisitions rose. This is shown in Figures 14.3 (a) and (b), which reveals that as the average yield on long-term Treasury bonds declined, the average acquisition prices rose. Long-term Treasuries are used as a base on which a risk premium is applied to arrive at a risk-adjusted discount rate. As interest rates fall for an extended period of time, evaluators lower their discount rates resulting in higher acquisition values. This is not to imply, however, that interest rates are the only factor determining acquisition prices. They are but one of several important factors that needs to be considered.

Marketability Discounts

The stock of closely held companies is distinctly different from that of public firms in that a market already exists for public stocks, whereas the stock of private companies has only limited marketability. Depending on where a public stock is traded, this investment may be quite liquid. Liquidity refers to the speed with which an asset can be sold without incurring a significant loss of value. Under normal conditions, the stocks of major companies that are traded on the New York Stock Exchange are liquid investments. Stocks of companies infrequently traded on the OTC market are not as liquid. However, even these stocks have a market maker who will endeavor to sell the shares. This is not the case for shares of closely held companies. Therefore, if the stock values of comparable public companies are used to value closely held shares, these derived values need to be reduced to reflect the relatively lower marketability of closely held shares.

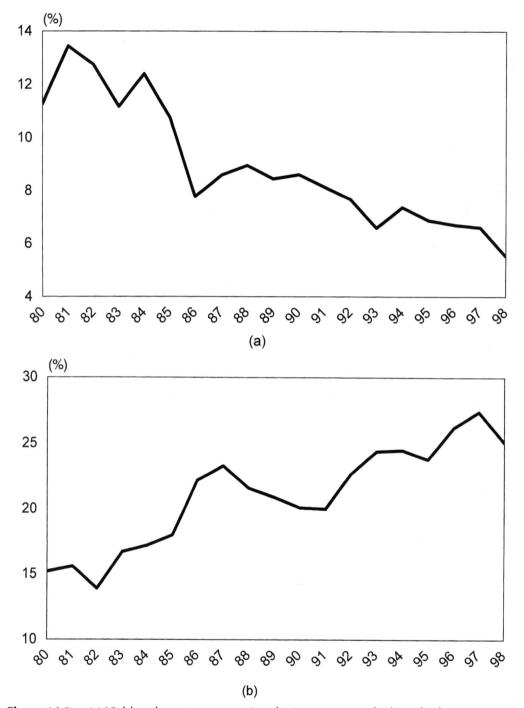

Figure 14.3.   (a) Yield on long-term treasuries; (b) Average annual P/E multiple.

There has been abundant research on marketability discounts. One body of research examined the prices of *letter stocks*. Letter stocks are shares of public companies that are identical to the company's shares that are actively traded except that letter stock is restricted and may not be traded for a specific time period. Companies issue restricted shares for a variety of reasons, including financing of mergers or for compensation of management. Because the letter stock may not be traded in public markets, although it may be exchanged privately, it lacks the marketability of the unrestricted shares. The price difference between those two categories of stock can be used as a guide to the value of this one attribute—marketability. Whatever discount is derived from this research, however, will underestimate the true marketability discount because letter stocks are usually restricted for a period of one to two years, at which point they become registered with the SEC and may be publicly traded. Therefore, this research will measure only the discount resulting from the temporary lack of marketability and the indefinite lack of marketability of closely held stock.

Marketability Discount Research

There have been a number of studies that have tried to measure the value of the discount that the market puts on a lack of marketability. These studies are categorized below according to the methodology that has been employed.

Restricted Stock Studies
One of the early studies on restricted stock discounts was the SEC's institutional investor study.[14] The SEC's researchers examined companies that were traded on the New York and American Stock Exchanges, as well as OTC companies, and found an average discount of 25.8%. Shortly after the SEC study, Milton Gelman examined 89 restricted stock transactions and found that the restricted shares sold at discounts equal to 33% of the unrestricted stock.[15] Similar results were found by Robert Moroney, who found a mean discount of 35.6% for 146 restricted stock transactions.[16] Robert Trout used a multiple regression model to estimate the marketability discount for 60 restricted stock purchases. He found an average discount of 33.45%.[17] Still another study, by J. Michael Maher, found a similar mean discount of 35.43%.[18]

In the 1980s, using data from 28 restricted stock private placements between 1978 and 1982, Standard Research Consultants found an average discount of 45%. Williamette Management Associates, using data on 33 restricted stock private placements between

14. *Institutional Investor Study Report of the Securities and Exchange Commission* (Washington, D.C.: U.S. Government Printing Office), Document No. 93–64, March 10, 1971.

15. Milton Gelman, "An Economist-Financial Analyst's Approach to Valuing Stock of a Closely Held Company," *Journal of Taxation* (June 1972).

16. Robert E. Moroney, "Most Courts Overvalue Closely Held Stocks," *Taxes,* vol. 51, no. 3 (March 1973), pp. 144–154.

17. Robert R. Trout, "Estimation of the Discount Associated with the Transfer of Restricted Securities," *Taxes,* vol. 55 (June 1977), pp. 381–385.

18. J. Michael Maher, "Discounts for Lack of Marketability for Closely Held Business Interests," *Taxes,* vol. 54, no. 9 (September 1976), pp. 562–571.

Table 14.5. Summary of Restricted Stock Studies

Study	Years Covered	Sample Size	Average Discount (%)
SEC	1966–69	398	25.80
German	1968–70	89	33.00
Trout	1968–72	60	33.45
Moroney	NA	146	35.60
Standard Research Consultants	1978–82	28	45.00
Williamette Management	1981–84	33	33.00

Source: Adapted from Shannon Pratt, *Valuing a Business,* 2nd ed. (Homewood, Ill.: Irwin Business One, 1989), p. 248.

1981 and 1984, found an average discount of 33%. The results of these studies are summarized in Table 14.5.

Research on Private Transactions Before Initial Public Offerings

An alternative methodology to deriving the marketability discount is to examine the difference between the prices of private securities transactions before initial public offerings (IPOs) and the IPO prices. Two such studies were conducted, one by John Emory of Baird & Company and another by Williamette Management Associates. Emory examined 97 offerings in the 1980–81 period and 130 offerings in the 1985–86 period.[19] He found that pre-IPO stock transactions, the prices of which were reported in SEC filings for five months before the IPO, trade at a mean discount of 60% from the IPO price.

Williamette Management Associates did a similar study covering parts of the period from 1975 to 1985.[20] Examining 665 transactions, they found discounts ranging from 41.7% to as high as 80%.

Conclusion of Restricted Stock and Pre-IPO Research

The research in this field shows that when public prices are used as a guide to the value of the stock of private companies, a marketability discount of at least one-third is appropriate. The various studies in this area support such a discount, if not an even higher one, from the public price.

Minority Discounts

A second discount might also be needed, depending on the percentage of ownership the privately held stock position constitutes. This is because control is an additional valuable characteristic that a majority position possesses that is not present in a minority holding. A minority shareholder is often at the mercy of majority shareholders. The holder of a minority position can only elect a minority of the directors, and possibly none of the direc-

19. John D. Emory, "The Value of Marketability as Illustrated in Initial Public Offerings of Common Stock," *Business Valuation News* (September 1985), pp. 21–24; and John D. Emory, "The Value of Marketability as Illustrated in Initial Public Offerings of Common Stock," *Business Valuation Review* (December 1986).

20. Shannon Pratt, *Valuing Business and Professional Practices* (Homewood, Ill.: Dow Jones Irwin, 1986), pp. 250–255.

tors, depending on whether the corporation is incorporated in a state that allows cumulative voting. Majority shareholders and minority shareholders each possess proportionate rights to dividends distribution, but a majority shareholder possesses the right to control the actions of the corporations in addition to these dividend claims. This is an additional valuable characteristic, and an additional premium must be paid for it. Looking at it from the minority shareholder's viewpoint, the minority position is valuable and will trade at a discount to account for the lack of control.

A guide to the appropriate minority discount is the magnitude of the average control premium. Table 14.6 shows that the average control premium between 1980 and 1998 was 40.7%. This premium can be used to compute the appropriate minority discount using the following formula:

$$\text{Minority discount} = 1 - [1/(1 + \text{Average premium})]$$

Using the average control premium of 40.7%, we get an implied minority discount of 28.8%.

Applying Marketability and Minority Discounts

Let us assume that a value of $50 per share has been computed for a 20% ownership position in a closely held firm. Assuming 33% marketability and minority discounts, the value of this stock position equals:

Unadjusted value:	$50/share
Less 33% marketability discount:	$33.50
Less 33% minority discount:	$22.45

Table 14.6.   Control Premiums and Implied Discounts

Year	Control Premium Offer (%)	Implied Minority Discount (%)
1980	49.9	33.3
1981	48.0	32.4
1982	47.4	32.2
1983	37.7	27.4
1984	37.9	27.5
1985	37.1	27.1
1986	38.2	27.6
1987	38.3	27.7
1988	41.9	29.5
1989	41.0	29.1
1990	42.0	29.6
1991	35.1	26.0
1992	41.0	29.1
1993	38.7	27.9
1994	41.9	29.5
1995	44.7	30.9
1996	36.6	26.8
1997	35.7	26.3
1998	40.7	26.8
Average	40.7	28.8

Source: Mergerstat Review, 1999.

The $22.45 per share value is the value of a nonmarketable minority position in this closely held business.

CASE STUDY: LDDS—ACQUISITION OF CLOSELY HELD LONG-DISTANCE TELECOMMUNICATIONS COMPANIES

The long-distance telecommunications business includes a few dominant companies, such as AT&T, MCI, and Sprint, followed by other smaller but rapidly growing companies, such as LDDS. This company, which is headquartered in Jackson, Mississippi, partially fueled its growth through the acquisition of small regional companies (Figure 1).

The industry contains many companies that buy long-distance services from the large companies at a volume discount and resell to local businesses, giving them back part of the discount and using the difference as a source of profit. These local resellers are typically closely held businesses whose primary asset is the customer base that they have built up through sales efforts. Some resellers own their own local switch, which they use to access the long-distance network, but many are "switchless resellers" who do not own any telecommunications hardware. Theirs is purely an arbitrage business.

Valuations of closely held businesses are often made through the use of multiples of performance variables such as revenues. The long-distance telecommunications industry is a good example of this. In this industry, acquisitions are often made at multiples of average monthly revenues. Table 1 shows the various multiples that LDDS paid in acquisitions they made from 1990 to 1992; LDDS also acquired one company in 1995.

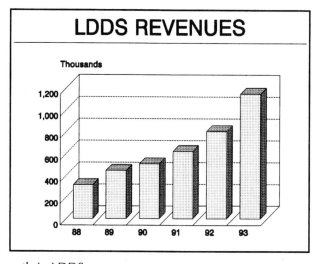

Figure 1.   Growth in LDDS revenues.

Source: LDDS Company reports.

Table 1. Acquisitions of LDDS, 1990–92

Company	Annual Revenue ($ millions)	Monthly Revenue ($ millions)	Price ($ millions)	Multiple
Advantage	20.4	1.7	11.6	6.8
Mercury	16.8	1.4	10.3	7.4
TMC of Louisiana	21.6	1.8	15.5	8.6
National Teleservices	35.0	2.9	33.2	11.4
Phone America	24.0	2.0	12.4	6.2
Mid-America	75.6	6.3	34.8	5.5
AmeriCall	69.6	5.8	31.8	5.5
Long Distance for Less	14.4	1.2	5.1	4.3

Source: Eric Petty, "Mergers and Acquisitions: Telecommunications Companies," presentation at the American Carriers Telecommunications Association Annual Meeting, San Francisco, 1995.

Although the deals cited in Table 1 were all fairly close to the average of seven times monthly net revenues, LDDS decided to significantly deviate from this average when it bought IDB in 1995. IDB was a much larger company than those listed in Table 1. It had annual revenues of $504 million and monthly revenues of $42 million. LDDS paid $870.2 million for IDB, which amounted to a multiple of 20.7. Such a multiple was high compared with what LDDS had paid in the past, but it was consistent with the multiples that other telecommunications companies sold for in 1995. Table 2 shows the multiples that Frontier Corporation, the fifth largest telecommunications company in the United States, paid for its 1995 acquisitions.

The 1995 multiples paid by Frontier and LDDS reflect the desire of these two companies to grow rapidly and become major players in the highly competitive and rapidly changing long-distance telecommunications business. Only time will tell whether the increase in multiples paid will provide a good return to shareholders.

LDDS Postscript: LDDS continued to grow through acquisitions and became Worldcom which, through a merger with MCI, became MCI Worldcom—one of the largest telecommunications companies in the United States.

Table 2. 1995 Acquisitions by Frontier Corporation

Company	Annual Revenue ($ millions)	Monthly Revenue ($ millions)	Price ($ millions)	Multiple
WCT	151	12.6	81	6.5
American Sharecom	125	10.4	198	19.0
ALC	612	51.0	1,804	35.4

Source: Eric Petty, "Mergers and Acquisitions: Telecommunications Companies," presentation at the American Carriers Telecommunications Association Annual Meeting, San Francisco, 1995.

Valuation Research on Takeovers of Private Held Companies

Although there is an abundance of published research on the valuation effects of takeovers of public companies, there is limited research for closely held businesses. This is because data are readily available on public companies but they are much harder to come by for private firms. One study by Saeyoung Chang analyzed the stock price reaction of public bidding firms when they acquire private companies.[21] In a study of 281 merger proposals between 1981 and 1992, which did not include any tender offers, Chang found that bidding firms did not experience any abnormal returns for cash offers but did show positive abnormal returns for stock offers. The positive returns for stock offers contrast with some research on stock acquisitions of public companies that feature negative returns. Chang compared the stock offers with private equity placements because the closely held targets typically were owned by a small number of shareholders. These positive returns are consistent with the research on the returns to companies that issue stock in private placements.[22]

As discussed in Chapter 13, one possible explanation for the positive stock response for public acquirers is that there may be more monitoring when stock is given to a few owners of the closely held company. This greater monitoring may reduce adverse agency effects and increase value. When the market perceives this, it reacts with a positive stock price response.

SUMMARY

Several of the more commonly used approaches to valuing a privately held business were described in this chapter. In addition to the asset-oriented approaches highlighted in Chapter 13, the use of the discounted future earnings and capitalization of future earnings methods were explained. These techniques are quite sensitive to the choice of discount rate or capitalization rate. The rate chosen must reflect the risk characteristics of the firm being evaluated. A market-derived proxy rate that has similar risk characteristics and a similar built-in risk premium can then be selected to serve as the capitalization rate. Many proxy rates are available, including the rates offered on Treasury securities, corporate bonds, and the equities of larger and smaller firms.

Analysts must be careful when using market-derived measures as a proxy for the capitalization rate for a privately held firm that lacks a public market in its equities. The lack of a public market may mean that the equity of the private firm is less liquid. Therefore, an illiquidity premium may have to be added to the proxy rate to derive a fuller risk adjustment. The use of the rate of return for junk bonds, which have equity characteristics and are less liquid than higher rated bonds and equities, may help account for some of this illiquidity.

In valuing closely held businesses, two discounts may be appropriate. A marketability discount to account for the fact that closely held shares lack a market may be applied. Numerous research studies have analyzed the magnitude of this discount using the difference in the prices of restricted or letter stocks and their unrestricted, more marketable counter-

---

21. Saeyoung Chang, "Takeovers of Privately Held Targets, Methods of Payment, and Bidder Returns," *Journal of Finance* 53, no. 2 (April 1998), pp. 773–784.

22. Michael Hertzel and Richard L. Smith, "Market Discounts and Shareholders Gains for Placing Private Equity," *Journal of Finance* 48, June 1993, pp. 459–485.

parts. Other studies have sought to measure the marketability discount by examining the difference between share prices of transaction in the stock of a closely held business before an IPO and the eventual IPO price.

Another discount may be appropriate when the stock position is a minority in a closely held business. This discount is due to the fact that a minority position lacks control, an attribute that a majority position possesses in addition to each having a proportionate claim on dividends. Control premiums are used as a guide to this discount.

Privately held businesses may be more difficult to value than public firms, primarily because the large supply of information and readily accessible reports that are available for large public firms are not available for their privately held counterparts. The analyst of a private firm may need to conduct a more original study than the public firm analyst. The methods and data used in valuing private firms may differ more across analysts than is true for public firms. For this reason, more care should be exercised when considering the results of these analyses.

REFERENCES

"Accounting Changes." *Accounting Principles Board Opinion,* no. 20 (July 1971).

Araskog, Rand. *The ITT Wars* (New York: Henry Holt & Co., 1989).

Chang, Saeyoung. "Takeovers of Privately Held Targets, Methods of Payment, and Bidder Returns." *Journal of Finance* 53, no. 2 (April 1998), pp. 773–784.

Cottle, Sidney, Roger F. Murray, and Frank E. Block. *Graham and Dood's Security Analysis,* 5th ed. (New York: McGraw-Hill, 1988).

Desmond, Glenn, and John Marcello. *Handbook of Small Business Valuation* (Marina Del Rey, Calif: Valuation Press, 1988).

Emory, John D. "The Valuation of Marketability as Illustrated in Initial Public Offerings of Common Stock." *Business Valuation News,* September 1985.

Emory, John D. "The Valuation of Marketability as Illustrated in Initial Public Offerings of Common Stock." *Business Valuation Review,* December 1986.

Executive Compensation Service, American Management Association, Karen Tracy. *Executive Compensation: Selected References* (Cambridge, Mass.: Harvard University Press, 1990).

Fama, Eugene. "Agency Problems and the Theory of the Firm." *Journal of Political Economy* 88, no. 2 (April 1980).

Fishman, Jay, Shannon Pratt, J. Clifford Griffith, and D. Keith Wilson. *Guide to Business Valuations,* 5th ed. (Fort Worth: Practitioners Publishing Co., 1995).

Gaughan, Patrick A., and Henry Fuentes. "Taxable Income and Lost Profits Litigation." *Journal of Forensic Economics* IV, no. 1 (Winter 1991).

Gelman, Milton. "An Economist-Financial Analyst's Approach to Valuing Stock of a Closely Held Company." *Journal of Taxation,* vol. 3, issue 6 (June 1972).

"GM Splits Its Basic Stock 2 for 1." *Wall Street Journal,* 7 February 1989.

Hertzel, Michael and Richard L. Smith. "Market Discounts and Shareholders Gains for Placing Private Equity." *Journal of Finance* 48, no. 2 (June 1993), pp. 459–485.

Ibbotson, Roger G., and Rex A. Sinquefield. *Stocks, Bonds, Bills, and Inflation, 1999 Yearbook* (Chicago: Ibbotson Associates, 1999).

Institutional Investor Study Report of the Securities and Exchange Commission (Washington, D.C.: U.S. Government Printing Office, Document No. 93–64, March 10, 1971).

Jensen, Michael, and William Meckling. "Theory of the Firm: Managerial Behavior, Agency Costs and Ownership Structure." *Journal of Financial Economics* 3 (October 1976).

Kaplan, Steven N., and Richard S. Ruback. "The Valuation of Cash Flow Forecasts: An Empirical Analysis." *Journal of Finance* 50, no. 4 (September 1995).

Kieso, Donald, and Jerry Weygandt. *Intermediate Accounting* (New York: John Wiley & Sons, 1986).

Maher, J. Michael. "Discounts for Lack of Marketability for Closely Held Business Interests." *Taxes,* vol. 54, no. 9 (September 1976).

Moroney, Robert E. "Most Courts Overvalue Closely Held Stocks." *Taxes,* vol. 51, no. 3 (March 1973).

Pratt, Shannon. *Valuing Businesses and Professional Practices* (Homewood, Ill.: Dow Jones Irwin, 1986).

Pratt, Shannon. *Valuing a Business,* 2nd ed. (Homewood, Ill.: Dow Jones Irwin, 1989).

Pratt, Shannon, Robert F. Rielly, and Robert P. Schweihs. *Valuing a Business,* 3rd ed. (Chicago: Richard D. Irwin, 1996).

Siegel, Joel. *How to Analyze Businesses, Financial Statements and the Quality of Earnings* (Englewood Cliffs, N.J.: Prentice-Hall, 1982).

Trout, Robert R. "Estimation of the Discount Associated with the Transfer of Restricted Securities." *Taxes,* vol. 55, no. 6 (June 1977).

Trout, Robert. "Reference Guide to Valuing a Closely Held Business." In *Expert Economic Testimony: Reference Guides for Judges and Attorneys* (Tucson: Lawyers and Judges Publishing Company, 1998).

Wendell, Paul J. *Corporate Controller's Manual* (Boston: Warren, Gorham and Lamont, 1989).

15

TAX ISSUES

Depending on the method used to finance the transaction, certain mergers, acquisitions, and restructuring may be tax-free. Some firms may use their tax benefits as assets in establishing the correct price that they might command in the marketplace. For this reason, tax considerations are important as both the motivation for a transaction and the valuation of a company. Part of the tax benefits from a transaction may derive from tax synergy, whereby one of the firms involved in a merger may not be able to fully utilize its tax shields. When combined with the merger partner, however, the tax shields may offset income. Some of these gains may come from unused net operating losses, which may be used by a more profitable merger partner. Tax reform, however, has limited the ability of firms to sell these net operating losses through mergers.

Other sources of tax benefits in mergers may arise from a market value of depreciable assets, which is greater than the value at which these assets are kept on the target's books. The acquiring firm that is able to step up the basis of these assets in accordance with the purchase price may finally realize tax savings.

This chapter discusses the mechanics of realizing some of the tax benefits through mergers. It also reviews the research studies that attempt to determine the importance of tax effects as a motivating factor for mergers and leveraged buyouts (LBOs) and examines the different accounting treatments that may be applied to a merger or an acquisition. These methods, which are regulated by tax laws, affect the importance of taxes in the overall merger valuation. It will be seen that various reforms in tax laws have diminished the role that taxes play in mergers and acquisitions. However, taxes may still be an important consideration that both the seller and buyer must carefully weigh before completing a transaction.

FINANCIAL ACCOUNTING

The two principal accounting methods used in mergers and acquisitions are the pooling of interests method and the purchase method. The main difference between them is the value that the combined firm's balance sheet places on the assets of the acquired firm, as well as the depreciation allowances and charges against income following the merger.

Pooling of Interests Method

For a transaction to qualify for the pooling of interests accounting treatment, it must satisfy certain accounting criteria. The most important are:[1]

1. The acquiring company must finance the acquisition with common stock that is the same as the outstanding common stock of the acquiring firm. This common stock must be used to purchase at least 90% of the common stock of the target corporation.
2. The common stock used to finance the acquisition may not be retired or repurchased later.
3. The target company's shareholders must retain an ownership position in the acquiring company.
4. The two firms must be autonomous for at least two years before pooling and must be independent of other firms as reflected by the fact that no more than 10% of the stock in either firm may be owned by another firm.
5. The transaction must be completed in a single transaction or according to a specific plan that is completed within one year.

In a pooling of interests transaction, the individual items on the two firms' balance sheets are added together. Assets are recorded at the values they held on the acquired firm's books. The end result of a pooling of interests transaction is that the total assets of the combined firm are equal to the sum of the assets of the individual firms. No goodwill is generated, and there are no charges against earnings. In effect, the stockholders in the two companies combine to form an entirely new entity. Each group of stockholders will share in the profits of the combined company according to the terms of exchange. No additional capital is involved in a pooling of interests transaction. Moreover, there is no change in the "basis" in such a transaction. Therefore, the assets, liabilities, and retainer earnings are combined at their recorded amounts.[2]

Purchase Method[3]

Under purchase method, the transaction is recorded at its fair market value. Fair market value is defined as the total amount paid for the acquisition, including related costs of the acquisition, such as legal and accounting fees, broker's commission, etc. If the acquisition is consummated with stock, then the acquisition price is based on the fair market value of the stock.

If the acquisition price, paid for with either stock or cash, is in excess of the underlying net book value of the company (total assets minus total liabilities), the excess of the pur-

---

1. *Opinions of the Accounting Principles of Board,* no. 16, American Institute of Certified Public Accountants, New York, August 1970.

2. Robert Levine and Richard P. Miller, "Accounting for Business Combinations," in Steven James Lee and Robert Douglas Coleman, eds. *Handbook of Mergers and Acquisitions* (Englewood Cliffs, N.J.: Prentice-Hall, 1981), pp. 251–292.

3. The author wishes to thank Professor Henry Fuentes for his helpful comments on this section.

chase price over underlying book value is allocated first to the difference between the fair market value of assets acquired and the book value of assets acquired. Any excess not allocated to fair value is assigned to goodwill. In effect, purchase accounting allows the purchaser to revalue the net assets of the acquired company at fair market value.

Goodwill is amortized over a period not exceeding 40 years by a charge against consolidated net earnings. Amortization of goodwill is deductible for tax purpose over a 15 year period if acquired after August 10, 1993. Amortization of goodwill for acquisition prior to August 10, 1993 is not deductible for tax purposes.

Under the purchase method the acquiring company is entitled to income of the acquired company only from the date of purchase. Prior retained earnings of the acquired company are not allowed to be brought forward to the consolidated entity.

In a pooling of interests acquisition the transaction is recorded at the net book value of the acquired company. Since a pooling of interest can only be consummated with the issuance of stock, the equity of the consolidated entity will be equal to the total equity of the consolidated entities. In a pooling of interests, the acquiring company is entitled to all historical profits of the acquired entity. Therefore, retained earnings of the acquired company prior to the acquisition is brought forward to the consolidated entity.

A comparison of the pooling and purchase methods pre- and post-merger is presented in Table 15.1. The table represents the effects of the following transaction. Company P (parent) acquires Company S (subsidiary) by issuing 100,000 shares of its $10 par value common stock which is currently selling at $45 per share in the open market. Condensed balance sheets of both companies prior to the acquisition and subsequent are shown in Table 15.1. The fair market value of the assets of S are $1 million higher than the book value ($6 million versus $5 million). Under the pooling method, the fair market value is ignored and we combine using the book value the subsidiary. Under the purchase method the $4.5 million purchase price, represented by 100,000 shares at $45 per share, is $1.5 million in excess of the book value of the subsidiary, $1.0 million is allocated to the fair value of assets and $0.5 million is allocated to goodwill.

Differences Pooling and Purchase Methods

Pooling
In a pooling of interests transaction all historical earnings of the acquired company are included in consolidated income. In addition all earnings of the pooled company for the current year are recognized in income regardless of the date acquired during the year. There is

Table 15.1. Comparison of Pooling Interests and Purchase Accounting ($ Thousands)

	Pre-merger Balance Sheet Company A	Pre-merger Balance Sheet Company B	Post-merger Consolidated Purchase	Post-merger Consolidated Pooling
Assets	20,000	5,000	26,000	25,000
Goodwill	0	0	500	0
Total assets	20,000	5,000	26,500	25,000
Total liabilities	9,000	2,000	11,000	11,000
Common stock	8,000	1,600	12,500	9,600
Retained earnings	3,000	1,400	3,000	4,400
Total liabilities	20,000	5,000	26,500	25,000

no write-up of assets or recognition of goodwill in a pooling. This results in higher consolidated income under pooling because there is no amortization of the face value of assets or goodwill. However the consolidated balance sheet will be reflected at historical value.

Purchase

Under purchase accounting the consolidated balance sheet reflects higher values than in a pooling-of-interests since the assets of the acquired company are written up to fair value and goodwill is recognized. However consolidated income will be lower due to amortization charges.

Effect of Accounting Treatment on Stock Prices

Although the purchase method does permit the creation of tax-deductible expenses, the choice of method does not itself create any value. The accounting treatment does not produce synergistic effects or other benefits that would affect the combined firm's cash flows. Therefore, if the securities markets are efficient with regard to accounting methods, these paper changes should not affect security prices. Hong, Mandelker, and Kaplan found that stock prices were unaffected by the choice of acquisition accounting.[4]

International Accounting Treatment of Mergers and Acquisitions

Nations differ in the allowable accounting treatment for mergers and acquisitions. Although both purchase accounting and pooling accounting are allowed in the United States, United Kingdom, Japan, and France, Germany and Italy permit only purchase accounting. Table 15.2 shows the varying international accounting treatments of mergers and acquisitions.

Table 15.2.   Different Ways Countries Account for Deals

Country	Methods
United States	Pooling and Purchase
United Kingdom	Pooling and Purchase
France	Pooling and Purchase
Germany	Purchase
Italy	Purchase
Netherlands	Purchase
Japan	Pooling and Purchase
Brazil	Purchase
Mexico	Pooling and Purchase

Source: Wall Street Journal, May 7, 1998, p. A10.

---

4. H. Hong, G. Mandelker, and R. S. Kaplan, "Pooling vs. Purchase: The Effects of Accounting for Mergers on Stock Prices," *Accounting Review* 53 (January 1978), pp. 31–47.

TAXABLE VERSUS TAX-FREE TRANSACTIONS

A merger or an acquisition may be either a taxable transaction or a tax-free transaction. The tax status of a transaction may affect the value of the transaction from the viewpoint of both the buyer and the seller. A tax-free transaction is known as a tax-free reorganization. The term *tax-free* is a misnomer because the tax is not eliminated but will be realized when a later taxable transaction occurs.

Tax-Free Reorganizations

There are several different types of tax-free reorganizations. Each is discussed below.

Type A Reorganization

For a transaction to qualify as a tax-free reorganization, it must be structured in certain ways.[5] One way is a type A reorganization, which is considered a more flexible tax-free reorganization technique than some of the others that are discussed in the following sections. In contrast to a type B reorganization, a type A reorganization allows the buyer to use either voting stock or nonvoting stock, common stock or preferred stock, or even other securities. It also permits the buyer to use more cash in the total consideration because the law does not stipulate a maximum amount of cash that may be used. At least 50% of the consideration, however, must be stock in the acquiring corporation. In addition, in a type A reorganization, the acquiring corporation may choose not to purchase all the target's assets. For example, the deal could be structured to allow the target to sell off certain assets separately and exclude them from this transaction.

In cases in which at least 50% of the bidder's stock is used as the consideration, but other considerations are used, such as cash, debt, or nonequity securities, the transaction may be partially taxable. Capital gains taxes must be paid on those shares that were exchanged for nonequity consideration, whereas taxes are deferred for those shares that were exchanged for stock. Rights and warrants that are convertible into the bidding firm's equity securities are generally classified as taxable.[6]

A type A reorganization must fulfill the continuity of interests requirement. That is, the shareholders in the acquired company must receive enough stock in the acquiring firm that they have a continuing financial interest in the buyer.[7]

Type B Reorganization

A type B merger or reorganization requires that the acquiring corporation use mainly its own voting common stock as the consideration for purchase of the target corporation's

5. For a good description of the tax-free reorganizations, see George Rodoff, "Tax Consequences to Shareholders in an Acquisitive Reorganization," in Steven James Lee and Robert Douglas Coleman, eds., *Handbook of Mergers, Acquisitions and Buyouts* (Englewood Cliffs, N.J.: Prentice-Hall, 1981), pp. 359–379.

6. Cathy M. Niden, "Acquisition Premia: Further Evidence on the Effects of Payment Method and Acquisition Method," paper presented at the American Economics Association annual meeting, December 1989.

7. Joseph Morris, *Mergers and Acquisitions: Business Strategies for Accountants* (New York: John Wiley & Sons, 1995), pp. 254–255.

common stock. Cash must constitute no more than 20% of the total consideration, and at least 80% of the target's stock must be paid for by voting stock in the acquirer. In this type of transaction, the acquiring corporation must buy at least 80% of the stock of the target, although the purchase of 100% is more common. Target company shareholders may not be given the option to opt for cash as opposed to stock, where the effect could be that less than 80% of stock could be used. The presentation of this option, even if at least 80% of stock is actually used, disallows the type B reorganization.

Following the purchase of the target's stock, the target becomes a subsidiary of the acquiring corporation. In both type A and type B reorganizations, the transactions are viewed, from a tax regulatory point of view, as merely a continuation of the original corporate entities in a reorganized form. Therefore, these transactions are not taxed because they are not considered true sales.

It is possible to have a *creeping type B reorganization,* in which the stock is purchased in several transactions over a period of time. To qualify as a type B reorganization, however, the stock purchases must be part of an overall plan to acquire the target company. The plan itself must be implemented over 12 months or less. In a creeping type B reorganization, only stock may be used as consideration. It is acceptable for the acquiring company to have bought some stock in the target with cash in the past as long as the purchases were not part of the acquisition plan.

Type C Reorganization

In a type C reorganization, the acquiring corporation must purchase 80% of the fair market value of the target's *assets.* Cash may be used only if at least 80% of the fair market value of the target's assets have been purchased using the voting stock of the acquiring corporation. As a result of the transaction, the target company usually must liquidate.

One advantage of a type C reorganization is that the acquiring company may not need to receive approval of its shareholders in such an asset purchase. Of course, target shareholders must approve this type of control transaction.

Type D Reorganization

There are two kinds of type D reorganization. One type covers acquisitions, and the other covers restructuring. In an acquisitive type D reorganization, the acquiring company receives 80% of the stock in the target in exchange for voting stock in the acquiring company. Shareholders in the acquiring company become controlling shareholders in the target.

Divisive type D reorganizations cover spin-offs, split-ups, and split-offs. As discussed in Chapter 10, one or more corporations are formed in a spin-off, with the stock in the new companies being distributed to the original company shareholders according to some predetermined formula. In a split-off, a component of the original company is separated from the parent company, and shareholders in the original company may exchange their shares for shares in the new entity. In a split-up, the original company ceases to exist, and one or more new companies are formed from the original business.

There are some additional requirements that a divisive type D reorganization must fulfill to qualify as tax-free. For example, the distribution of shares must not be for the purpose of tax avoidance. Both the parent company and the spun-off entity must be in business for at least five years before the spin-off.

TAX CONSEQUENCES OF A STOCK-FOR-STOCK EXCHANGE

Target stockholders who receive the stock of the acquiring corporation in exchange for their common stock are not immediately taxed on the consideration they receive. Taxes must be paid only if the stock is eventually sold. Given the time value of money, this postponement of tax payments clearly has value. If cash is included in the transaction, this cash may be taxed to the extent that it represents a gain on the sale of stock.

Taxable Purchases of Stock

As noted, consideration other than stock, such as cash or debt securities, may result in a tax liability for the target shareholders. This tax liability applies only to a gain that might be realized from sale of the stock. If the stock is sold at a loss, no tax liability results.

Taxable Purchases of Assets

A tax liability may also result when the acquiring corporation purchases the assets of the target using considerations other than stock in the acquiring corporation. The potential tax liability is measured by comparing the purchase price of the assets with the adjusted basis of these assets.

Taxable versus Partially Taxable Transactions

A transaction may be partially taxable if the consideration is a combination of stock and cash. The stock consideration may not be taxed but the cash is taxed. Therefore, the percentage of the transaction that is taxable depends on the relative percentages of stock and cash.

Tax Loss Carryforwards

A tax loss or tax credit carryover was a more important motive for mergers and acquisitions in prior years, such as the early 1980s, than it is today. In fact, at one time companies advertised the availability of such tax gains to motivate a sale. The Tax Code, however, has been changed to prevent such tax-motivated transactions.

The tax losses of target corporations can be used to offset a limited amount of the acquiring corporation's future income. These tax losses can be used to offset future income for a maximum of 15 years or until the tax loss is exhausted. Before 1981 the maximum period was five years. Only tax losses for the previous three years can be used to offset future income.

Tax loss carryforwards may motivate mergers and acquisitions in two ways. A company that has earned profits may find value in the tax losses of a target corporation that can be used to offset the income it plans to earn. However, the tax losses realized by a company that has lost money can be used in the purchase of a profitable company. Although tax benefits may be an important factor in determining whether a merger will take place, they may not be the sole motivating one. A merger may not be structured solely for tax purposes. The goal of the merger must be to maximize the profitability of the acquiring corporation.

An acquiring corporation may not make unrestricted use of the tax loss carryforwards that it receives through an acquisition. The primary restrictions include the requirements that the acquirer must continue to operate the preacquisition business of the company in a net loss position. The acquirer must also give up any tax savings from a change in the asset basis of the "loss company" that might otherwise have occurred in a taxable acquisition.[8] For an example of tax loss carryforwards, see Table 15.3.

As shown in Table 15.3, the acquiring corporation expects to earn $500 million in each of the next two years. (All dollar amounts shown in the table are in thousands of dollars.) It has acquired a company that has a tax loss of $600 million. The acquirer may use this tax loss to offset all the projected income for the year following the acquisition. In addition, $100 million is still available to offset income earned in the following year. The value of this tax loss is seen by the income after taxes in the first year of $500 million with the merger, as opposed to $300 million without the merger. In addition, income after taxes is $40 million higher in the second year after the merger. This income must be discounted to reflect the present value of these amounts. They are then used in the valuation process when the purchase price of the target is determined.

Tax Loss Carryforward Research

A number of research studies have sought to estimate the present value of tax loss carryforwards. These tax benefits may be less than their "face value," not only because of the time value of money but also because they might expire without being fully utilized. Estimates of these values have been developed by Alan Auerbach and James Poterba (1987) and by

Table 15.3.   Example of Tax Loss Carryforwards

Taxes and Income without the Merger ($ Thousands)

	Year I	Year II
Taxable income	500,000	500,000
Taxes (40%)	200,000	200,000
Income after taxes	300,000	300,000

Taxes and Income with the Merger ($ Thousands)

	Year I	Year II
Income before tax loss	500,000	500,000
Tax loss carryforward	500,000	100,000
Taxable income	0	400,000
Taxes (40%)	0	160,000
Income after taxes	500,000	340,000

8. Mark J. Warshawsky, Determinants of Corporate Merger Activity: A Review of the Literature, Staff Study No. 152, Board of Governors of the Federal Reserve System, April 1987, p. 5.

Roseanne Altshuler and Alan Auerbach (1987).[9] These research studies indicate that the two offsetting factors of deferral and expiration reduce the tax benefits to half their face value.

Acquiring Firm's Treatment of Target's Tax Benefits

In tax-free acquisitions, target firms may provide tax benefits through net operating loss carryforwards and unused investment and foreign tax credits. In taxable acquisitions, the acquiring firm may derive tax benefits in the form of depreciation deductions that are derived from a step-up in the basis of assets. The acquiring firm or target may be affected by the cost of the depreciation recapture tax, which reflects the accumulated depreciation for assets that are sold. The extent of this affect is a function of the negotiations between the acquirer and the target. Carla Hayn has summarized these effects in Table 15.4 according to the tax status of the acquisition.

Table 15.4.   Acquiring Firm's Treatment of Target Firm's Tax Attributes by Tax Status of Acquisition.

These are the tax provisions in effect before the Tax Reform Act of 1986. The relevant sections of the Internal Revenue Code are given in parentheses.

Target Firm's Tax Attribute	Tax Status of Acquisition	
	Tax-Free	Taxable
Tax basis on assets after acquisition	Basis transfers to acquiring firm unchanged [Secs. 358 and 362(b)]	Basis is revalued (stepped-up) at acquiring firm's cost [Sec. 1012]
Depreciation recapture taxes	The excess of cumulative accelerated depreciation over cumulative straight-line depreciation is deferred until a subsequent taxable transaction occurs [Secs. 354 and 361]	The excess of cumulative accelerated depreciation over cumulative straight-line depreciation is subject to tax at ordinary income rates, payable by the target firm [Secs. 1245 and 1250]
Net operating loss carryforward	Carryforward transfers to acquiring firm [Sec. 381], [Secs. 368(a)(1), 382, and 269]*	Carryforward ceases to exist upon acquisition and is not available to acquiring firm
Unused investment and foreign tax credits	Credit transfer to acquiring firm [Sec. 381], subject to restrictions [Secs. 368(a)(1), 382, and 269]*	Credits cease to exist upon acquisition and are not available to acquiring firm

*Section 381 does not apply to type B reorganizations, one of the types of tax-free acquisitions.

Source: C. Hayn, "Tax Attributes as Determinants of Shareholder Gains."

---

9. Alan Auerbach and James Poterba, "Tax Loss Carry Forwards and Corporate Tax Incentives," in Martin Feldstein, ed., *The Effect of Taxation on Capital Accumulation* (Chicago: University of Chicago Press, 1987); Roseanne Altshuler and Alan Auerbach, "The Importance of Tax Law Asymmetries: An Economic Analysis," National Bureau of Economic Research Working Paper No. 2279, National Bureau of Economic Research, Cambridge, Massachusetts, 1987.

ASSET BASIS STEP-UP

Tax advantages may arise in an acquisition when a target corporation carries assets on its books with a basis for tax purposes that is a fraction of the assets' replacement cost or market value. These assets could be more valuable for tax purposes if they were owned by another corporation, which could increase their tax basis after the acquisition and gain additional depreciation benefits. The tax basis for the acquiring corporation is the cost or purchase price of the assets. The acquiring corporation may use this higher asset basis to shelter income.

The Tax Reform Act of 1986 has also reduced some tax benefits. The selling corporation now incurs a greater tax liability on assets sales, which reduces the seller's incentive to participate in the transaction. Moreover, research seeking to find the existence of *asset basis step-up* as a motivating factor for mergers and acquisitions before the Tax Reform Act of 1986 did not find asset basis step-up to be a significant motivating factor.[10]

CHANGES IN THE TAX LAWS

General Utilities Doctrine

Until its repeal with the Tax Reform Act of 1986, the General Utilities Doctrine allowed preferential treatment for "disincorporating" or liquidating corporations.[11] According to this doctrine, the sale of corporate assets and a liquidating distribution to shareholders were exempt from capital gains taxation. These distributions could occur, for example, following the acquisition of one corporation by another. The acquiring corporation could then sell off the assets of the acquired corporation and distribute the proceeds to shareholders without incurring capital gains tax liability to the corporation. These tax-free liquidating distributions could also occur without an acquisition, such as when a firm chose to sell off certain assets and distribute the proceeds to shareholders.

Assets sales were often structured by establishing separate subsidiary corporations. An acquired corporation could be purchased and its assets distributed into one or more subsidiaries. These subsidiaries would contain the assets that the acquiring corporation was not interested in keeping.[12] The assets that would be retained would be put into the parent corporation or into a separate subsidiary. The stock of the subsidiaries containing the unwanted assets could then be sold without incurring a significant tax liability. With the repeal of the General Utilities Doctrine, the gains or losses from an acquisition must be attributed to the acquiring corporation. The opportunities to avoid such tax liabilities were narrowed with the passage of the Tax Reform Act of 1986. They were further narrowed by the 1987 and 1988 tax acts.

---

10. Alan J. Auerbach and David Reishus, "The Impact of Taxation on Mergers and Acquisitions," in Alan J. Auerbach, ed., *Mergers and Acquisitions* (Chicago: National Bureau of Economic Research, University of Chicago Press, 1988), pp. 69–88.

11. *General Utilities v. Helvering,* 296 U.S. 200 (1935).

12. George B. Pompa, "Federal Income Tax Considerations," in *Mergers and Acquisitions Back-to-Basics Techniques for the 90s,* 2nd ed. (New York: John Wiley & Sons, 1994), pp. 198–202.

Elimination of the Morris Trust

The Morris Trust is named after a 1966 tax court decision called the *Commissioner v. Morris Trust*. This decision established certain variants of spin-offs as tax-free. Using a Morris Trust, a company could spin off component businesses that it did not want to keep. In a second set preplanned transaction, the spun off business is merged into an acquirer's business in a tax-free stock transaction. The final result is that shareholders in the selling company end up with shares in both their own company and the company of the acquirer. Companies have creatively used these vehicles to borrow money through a subsidiary, spin it off, and later sell it while having the buyer agree to pay the loan. The selling parent company keeps the cash from the loan. The tax law was changed in 1997 to eliminate the tax-free status of a preplanned spin-off and subsequent sale, although if the deal is not preplanned it still may be possible to be tax-free.

Real Estate Investment Trusts

Real estate investment trusts (REITs) are publicly traded, passive investment vehicles that pay little or no federal taxes. The rebound of the real estate market in the mid-1990s enhanced the popularity of real REITs. A REIT consists of two entities in one: a management firm that manages real estate assets and an investment vehicle. Although they are supposed to be separate, their shares are paired and trade as one. Real estate investment trusts typically purchase property and rent it to a management firm. The management firm pays out its cash flow from properties to the investment vehicle, where it is treated as tax-free rent. Real estate investment trusts must distribute 95% of their earnings to shareholders, who then pay taxes on these monies at the individual level. Real estate assets such as hotels and shopping malls are often included in such investment vehicles. By combining them under a REIT umbrella, a real estate portfolio acquires tax benefits and liquidity. One of the more famous REITs is Starwood Hotels and Resorts Worldwide, Inc. There has been much debate about reducing the tax benefits of REITs but such discussions have not resulted in changes in the laws that relate to REITs.

Given that REITs are required to pay out 95% of their earnings, they are not considered good for companies that have good growth prospects. The market's confirmation of this came in April 1998, when Corrections Corporation of America, the nation's largest commercial operator of prisons, announced that it would merge into CCA Prison Realty Trust, which is a REIT that would be the surviving entity. In response to the announcement, the stock prices of both companies fell. Shareholders in Corrections Corporation of America were more interested in growth and believed that being in a REIT would limit growth prospects.

Tax Treatment of In-Process Research and Development and Restructuring Charges

In Chapter 13 we already discussed the impact of the current tax law treatment of in-process research and development charges and restructuring charges. Given the significant amount of attention this issue has attracted in the accounting profession, there is a reasonable probability that the law will be changed to eliminate some of the favorable aspects of this charges.

ROLE OF TAXES IN THE MERGER DECISION

Auerbach and Reishus examined a sample of 318 mergers and acquisitions that occurred between 1968 and 1983. Approximately two-thirds of these mergers were in the manufacturing sector, with the average acquiring firm approximately 10 times larger than the acquired company. They found that a significant percentage of the companies in their sample had various constraints on their ability to use their tax benefits. Nonetheless, many of the companies realized tax benefits as a result of merging. The average gain was 10.5% of the acquiring firm's market value.[13]

Myron Scholes and Mark Wolfson studied the number of mergers and acquisitions for various times, including the periods before 1981, between 1981 and 1986, and after 1986. The 1981 Tax Act provided various tax incentives for mergers and other forms of restructuring. Some of these were eliminated in the tax reforms that were part of the 1986 Tax Act. They attribute part of the intensified level of merger activity to tax motives that were put in place with the 1981 act and eliminated by the 1986 act. A similar type of comparative analysis is shown in Table 15.5.

Carla Hayn analyzed 640 successful acquisitions between 1970 and 1985.[14] In her sample she noted that 54% were taxable, 18% were partially taxable, and 28% were tax-free. There were 279 tender offers in her sample, and the majority of them (64%) were taxable. Mergers, however, varied in tax status. Of the 361 mergers in her sample, 39% were tax-free, whereas 46% were taxable and the remainder were partially taxable.

Hayn researched the role that the tax attributes of transactions played in determining abnormal returns for targets and acquirers. First, she noted that tax-free status is a prerequisite of certain deals. Targets that do not receive such a status may decline to continue with the deal and may look to other bidders who can structure the transaction so that such a status is attained. Specifically she found that "potential tax benefits stemming from net operating loss carryforwards and unused tax credits positively affect announcement period returns of firms involved in tax-free acquisitions, and capital gains and the step-up in the acquired assets basis affect returns of firms involved in taxable acquisitions."[15]

Effects of Increased Leverage

Interest payments on debt are a tax-deductible expense, whereas dividend payments from equity ownership are not. The existence of a tax advantage for debt is an incentive to have greater use of debt, as opposed to equity, as the means of exchange in mergers and acquisitions.

The leverage argument suggests that the acquiring firm has a suboptimal debt-equity ratio and has not sufficiently used debt in its capital mix. The argument goes on to put forward mergers and acquisitions as a means whereby companies can achieve greater utiliza-

---

13. Alan J. Auerbach and David Reishus, "Taxes and the Merger Decision," in John C. Coffee Jr., Louis Lowenstein, and Susan Rose Ackerman, eds., *Knights, Raiders and Targets* (New York: Oxford University Press, 1988), pp. 300–313.

14. Carla Hayn, "Tax Attributes as Determinants of Shareholder Gains in Corporate Acquisitions," *Journal of Financial Economics* 23 (1989), pp. 121–153.

15. Carla Hayn, p. 148.

Table 15.5. Merger and Acquisition Values: Nominal Dollar and Constant Dollar, Annual Figures 1968–97

Year	Nominal Dollar Value of M&A Activity ($ Billions)	Constant 1992 Dollar Value of M&A Activity ($ Billions)
1968	43.61	175.82
1969	23.71	90.64
1970	16.41	59.34
1971	12.62	43.72
1972	16.68	55.99
1973	16.66	52.64
1974	12.47	35.49
1975	11.80	30.77
1976	20.03	49.39
1977	21.94	50.80
1978	34.18	73.55
1979	43.54	84.14
1980	44.35	75.51
1981	82.62	127.52
1982	53.75	78.15
1983	73.08	102.94
1984	122.22	165.04
1985	179.77	234.40
1986	173.14	221.64
1987	163.69	202.16
1988	246.88	292.79
1989	221.09	250.15
1990	108.15	116.09
1991	71.16	73.30
1992	96.69	96.69
1993	176.40	171.27
1994	226.67	214.59
1995	356.02	327.75
1996	494.96	442.59
1997	657.06	574.36
AVG 1970–80	22.82	55.58
AVG 1975–80	29.31	60.69
AVG 1981–90	142.44	179.09
AVG 1985–90	182.12	219.54
AVG 1991–97	296.99	271.51
1991–97/1981–90	2.09	1.52
1991–97/1985–90	1.63	1.24

Source: Mergerstat for 1968–97 nominal values; Bureau of Labor Statistics, U.S. Dept. of Labor, Washington D.C., for consumer prices.

tion of debt. An overly simplistic "test" of this hypothesis would be to look at the debt-equity ratios before and after various mergers and acquisitions. This test is considered overly simplistic because the acquiring corporation might retain earnings for one or more years before an acquisition in anticipation of the takeover. After the takeover, which might be financed with internal funds and borrowed capital, there would be a sudden increase in the debt-equity ratio. This jump in the debt-equity ratio may be offset by a gradual reduction over the years following the acquisition as the firm moves to a long-term debt-equity ratio that it considers optimal.

The tax deductibility of interest payments is not an incentive to merge; rather, it is an incentive to increase the potential acquiring firm's borrowing. This may be done in a much more cost-effective manner by issuing bonds or directly borrowing from a lender than through the costly process of engaging in an acquisition.

Auerbach and Reishus found that, contrary to popular belief, firms that merge more frequently do not borrow more than firms that have exhibited less tendency to merge.[16] They also discovered that the long-term debt-equity ratios of firms in their sample increased from 25.4% to only 26.7% after the mergers that took place at a time when debt-equity ratios were increasing throughout the economy.

TAXES AS A SOURCE OF VALUE IN MANAGEMENT BUYOUTS

Taxes have quite a different role in management buyouts (MBOs) than they have in mergers and acquisitions. Steven Kaplan measured the value of tax benefits for 76 MBOs between 1980 and 1986.[17] In this sample of MBOs, the average premium was 42.3% above the market price two months before the initial announcement of the buyout. The median ratio of debt to total capital rose from 18.8% before the buyouts to 87.8% afterward. Kaplan found that the value of increased interest and depreciation deductions ranged between 21.0% and 142.6% of the premium paid to prebuyout shareholders. A regression analysis relating the total tax deductions generated by the buyout to the premium available to prebuyout shareholders suggested that total tax deductions are an important determining variable. t statistics equal to 5.9 indicated that total tax deductions were a highly significant explanatory variable. Kaplan's regression results were as follows.

$$\text{Buyout premiums} = f(\text{Total tax deductions}) \tag{15.1}$$
$$\text{MAP} = -0.13 + 0.76 \text{ x Total tax deductions}$$
$$(1.5) \qquad (5.9)$$

where
MAP = Market-adjusted premium (t statistics are in parentheses)
$R^2 = 0.31$
N = 75 (number of observations)

Leveraged Buyouts and Tax Revenues

Critics of leveraged buyouts (LBOs) contend that the tax deductibility of the debt used to finance these transactions causes a loss in tax revenues for the U.S. Treasury. These critics assert that, in effect, taxpayers are absorbing some of the financing costs of the LBOs. Michael Jensen, Steven Kaplan, and Laura Stiglin, however, argue that LBOs result in *positive* tax revenues for the U.S. Treasury. They cite factors such as the increased efficiency of post-LBO firms, which increases taxable income; tax payments on capital gains to shareholders; tax payments on the interest income; and capital gains taxes paid on post-LBO asset sales to support their position. Jensen and colleagues attempted to measure these factors for a typical LBO (Table 15.6).

16. Ibid., p. 80.
17. Steven Kaplan, "Management Buyouts: Evidence on Taxes as Source of Value," *Journal of Finance* 44, no. 3 (July 1989), pp. 611–632.

Table 15.6. Tax Revenue Implications of a Typical LBO ($ Millions)

I Typical LBO Features	
Prebuyout market value of equity	$360
Buyout purchase price	500
Incremental debt	400
Tax basis of selling shareholders' stock	290
Postbuyout value of equity (in 5 years)	750
Taxable capital gain to prebuyout shareholders (500–290)	210
Capital gain to buyout investors (750–500)	250

II Incremental Tax Revenues and Tax Losses to U.S. Treasury	
Incremental Revenues	
Capital gains taxes	$41.2
At buyout: $210 * 70\%^a * 28\%^b$	13.0
At subsequent restructuring: $250 * 30\%^c * 28\%^b * .62^d$	85.0
Taxes on increased operating income: $100^e * .25^f * .34^g * 10^h$	40.8
Taxes on LBO creditors' income: $400 * .6^i * .5^j * .34^g$	29.9
Taxes from increased capital efficiency: $44^k * .2^l * .1^m * .34^g * 10^n * 10^h$	17.0
Taxes to selling corporation on subsequent sale of assets: $500 * .2^o * .5^p * .34^g$	$226.9
Incremental Tax Losses	
Tax deductibility of interest payments on debt: $400 * .6^i * .34^g$	$–81.6
Taxes on foregone dividend payments: $2.05^q * \$360 * .7^a * .28^b * 10^h$	–35.3
Net Incremental Tax Revenues to U.S. Treasury	$110.0

[a]Percent of stock owned by taxable shareholders at buyout.

[b]Capital gains tax rate.

[c]Percent of stock owned by taxable shareholders at postbuyout sale.

[d]Present value factor for cash flows in 5 years discounted at 10% per year.

[e]Typical operating income prebuyout.

[f]Incremental operating income of 25% postbuyout due to increased efficiency.

[g]Corporate tax rate.

[h]The present value of a perpetuity of one dollar discounted at a rate of 10% per year is $10.

[i]Percent of incremental debt deemed to be permanent.

[j]Percent of debt held by taxable investors.

[k]Typical capital expenditure amount of prebuyout firm.

[l]Typical reduction in capital expenditures per year postbuyout.

[m]Reduced capital expenditures is assumed to be returned to shareholders where it earns this rate (10%) per year before tax, whereas the capital expenditure would have been a waste (earning 0% before tax).

[n]The 10% pretax income savings for each dollar of capital spending reduction is expected to recur in perpetuity, so this is the present value factor at a discount rate of 10%.

[o]Sale of 20% of the $500 million of LBO assets is assumed to take place within a year of the LBO.

[p]The basis of the assets sold within a year of the LBO is assumed to be equal to half the sales price, so the other half is a taxable gain.

[q]Reduction of dividend of 5% on $360 million worth of equity.

For a typical LBO of $500 million, Jensen and associates estimated that incremental tax revenues equal $226.9 million, with incremental tax losses equal to $116.9 million, resulting in a net positive incremental tax revenue equal to $110 million. Scholes and Wolfson criticized some of the assumptions used by Jensen and colleagues.[18] For example, they focused on the assumption that the LBO would cause an increased value of the company and its shares. They contend that it is reasonable that some of these gains would have occurred anyway. They also point out that some of the capital gains preceding the LBO would have resulted in capital gains for shareholders, some of whom would have sold their shares even without the LBO. These criticisms and others they point out would change the conclusions of the Jensen study. Scholes and Wolfson do not go so far as to say that their suggested refinements would have wiped out all the positive net incremental tax revenues noted by Jensen and colleagues. They simply state that the result would be different and probably lower, but that it remains an open and controversial issue.

SUMMARY

The various ways in which taxes may play a role in mergers and acquisitions were addressed in this chapter. It was seen that the tax impact of a transaction is a function of the accounting treatment applied to the deal, which, in turn, is regulated by tax laws. Tax law changes, such as those that occurred in 1986, have reduced the initiative to merge and acquire companies simply to realize tax gains.

Clearly, taxes must be carefully examined in any merger, acquisition, or LBO because they are important in evaluating the target firm and the overall cost of the acquisition. Some potential sellers will not sell unless they receive the desired tax consequence. Recent research has shown that tax benefits from net operating loss carryforwards and unused tax credits positively affect returns of companies involved in tax-free acquisitions. This research has also shown that capital gains and asset basis step-up also affect returns of companies involved in taxable acquisitions.

There is also evidence that taxes play an important role in LBOs. However, readers should be cautious in interpreting these research results. Simply demonstrating that taxes are a determinant of returns does not mean that tax effects are the prime reason for a deal. These studies have shown that taxes are one of several factors that influence returns. It would be reasonable to conclude that taxes normally play a secondary but still important role in determining mergers and acquisitions.

REFERENCES

Altshuler, Roseanne, and Alan Auerbach. "The Importance of Tax Law Asymmetries: An Economic Analysis." National Bureau of Economic Research Working Paper No. 2279, National Bureau of Economic Research, Cambridge, Massachusetts.

Auerbach, Alan, and James Poterba. "Tax Loss Carry Forwards and Corporate Tax Incentives." In Martin Feldstein, ed. *The Effect of Taxation on Capital Accumulation* (Chicago: University of Chicago Press, 1987).

---

18. Steven Kaplan, "Management Buyouts: Evidence on Taxes as Source of Value," *Journal of Finance* 44, no. 3 (July 1989), pp. 611–632.

Auerbach, Alan J., and David Reishus, "The Impact of Taxation on Mergers and Acquisitions." In Alan J. Auerbach, ed. *Mergers and Acquisitions* (Chicago: National Bureau of Economic Research, University of Chicago Press, 1988), pp. 69–88.

Auerbach, Alan J., and David Reishus. "Taxes and the Merger Decision." In John C. Coffee Jr., Louis Lowenstein, and Susan Rose Ackerman, eds. *Knights, Raiders and Targets* (New York: Oxford University Press, 1988), pp. 300–313.

Collins, J. Markham, and Roger P. Bey. "The Master Limited Partnership: An Alternative to the Corporation." *Financial Management* 15, no. 4 (Winter 1986).

General Utilities v. Helvering, 296 U.S. 200 (1935).

Hayn, Carla. "Tax Attributes as Determinants of Shareholder Gains in Corporate Acquisitions." *Journal of Financial Economics* 23 (1989), pp. 121–153.

Hong, H., G. Mandelker, and R. S. Kaplan. "Pooling vs. Purchase: The Effects of Accounting for Mergers on Stock Prices." *Accounting Review* 53 (January 1978).

Kaplan, Steven. "Management Buyouts: Evidence on Taxes as Source of Value." *Journal of Finance* 44, no. 3 (July 1989).

Levine, Robert, and Richard P. Miller. "Accounting for Business Combinations." In Steven James Lee and Robert Douglas Coleman, eds. *Handbook of Mergers and Acquisitions* (Englewood Cliffs, N.J.: Prentice-Hall, 1981).

Morris, Joseph. *Mergers and Acquisitions: Business Strategies for Accountants* (New York: John Wiley & Sons, 1995).

Niden, Cathy M. "Acquisition Premia: Further Evidence on the Effects of Payment Method and Acquisition Method." Paper presented at the American Economics Association annual meeting, December 1989.

Opinions of the Accounting Principles Board, no. 16 (New York: American Institute of Certified Public Accountants, August 1970).

Pompan, George B. "Federal Income Tax Considerations" In *Mergers and Acquisitions: Back to Basics Techniques for the 90s, 2nd ed.* (New York: John Wiley & Sons, 1994), pp. 212–213.

Rodoff, George. "Tax Consequences to Shareholders in an Acquisitive Reorganization." In Steven James Lee and Robert Douglas Coleman, eds. *Acquisitions and Buyouts* (Englewood Cliffs, N.J.: Prentice-Hall, 1981).

Scholes, Myron, and Mark A. Wolfson. *Taxes and Business Strategy* (Englewood Cliffs, N.J.: Prentice-Hall, 1992).

Wall Street Journal, May 17, 1998.

Warshawsky, Mark J. *Determinants of Corporate Merger Activity: A Review of the Literature.* Staff Study No. 152, Board of Governors of the Federal Reserve System, April 1987.

GLOSSARY

Abnormal return   In event studies, the part of the return that is not predicted by factors such as the market.

Absolute priority rule   The hierarchy whereby claims are satisfied in corporate liquidation.

Acquisition   The purchase of an entire company or a controlling interest in a company.

Agency problem   The conflict of interest that exists between owners of firms (shareholders) and their agents (management).

Antigreenmail amendment   A corporate charter amendment that prohibits targeted share purchases at a premium from an outside shareholder without the approval of nonparticipating shareholders.

Antitakeover amendment   A corporate charter amendment that is intended to make takeovers more difficult and/or expensive for an unwanted bidder.

Any-or-all tender offer   A tender offer for an unspecified number of shares in a target company.

Appraisal rights   The rights of shareholders to obtain an independent valuation of their shares to determine the appropriate value. Shareholders may pursue these rights in litigation.

Back-end rights plan   A type of poison pill antitakeover defense whereby shareholders are issued a rights dividend that is exercisable in the event that a hostile bidder purchases a certain number of shares. Upon the occurrence of that event, shareholders may then exchange their rights combined with their shares for a certain amount of cash and/or other securities equal to a value that is set by the target. In doing so, the target's board, in effect, establishes a minimum price for the company's stock.

Bear hug   An offer made directly to the board of directors of a target company. Usually made to increase the pressure on the target with the threat that a tender offer may follow.

Beta   A risk measure derived from the capital asset pricing model. It quantifies the systematic risk of a security.

Bidder   The acquiring firm.

Blended price   The weighted average price that is set in a two-tiered tender offer.

Board out clause   An antitakeover provision that allows the board of directors to decide when a supermajority provision is effective.

Business judgment rule   The legal principle that assumes the board of directors is acting in the best interests of shareholders unless it can be clearly established that it is not. If that is established, the board would be in violation of its fiduciary duty to shareholders.

Bustup fees   The payments that the target gives the bidder if the target decides to cancel the transaction.

Bustup takeover   A takeover in which an acquisition is followed by the sale of certain, or even all, of the assets of the target company. This is sometimes done to pay down the debt used to finance a leveraged acquisition.

Capital asset pricing model   A financial model that computes a security's rate of return as a function of the risk-free rate and a market premium that is weighted by the security's beta.

Capital budgeting   A project analysis in which a project's receipts and outlays are valued over a project's life.

Cash flow LBO   Leveraged buyout in which the debt financing relies more on the expectation of projected cash flows than on the collateral protection of the target's assets.

Casual pass   When a bidder makes an informal overture to the management of the target expressing interest in an acquisition.

Celler-Kefauver Act   A 1950 amendment to the Clayton Act that modified Section 7 of that act to make the acquisition of assets, not just the stock, of a company an antitrust violation when the deal has anticompetitive results. This amendment also made "anticompetitive" vertical and conglomerate mergers an antitrust violation.

Chapter 7   The part of the bankruptcy law that provides for the liquidation of corporations.

Chapter 11   The part of the bankruptcy law that provides for the reorganization of a bankrupt company.

Chinese wall   The imaginary barrier separating the investment banking, arbitrage, and securities trading activities within a financial institution such as an investment bank.

Classified board   Also called a **staggered board.** An antitakeover measure that separates the firm's board of directors into different classes with different voting rights. The goal is to make acquisition of voting rights more difficult.

Clayton Act   A federal antitrust law passed in 1914. Section 7, which is most relevant to mergers and acquisitions, prohibits the acquisition of stock and assets of a company when the effect is to lessen competition.

Coercive tender offer   A tender offer that exerts pressure on target shareholders to tender early. This pressure may come in the form of preferential compensation for early tendering shareholders. Changes in securities laws have limited the effectiveness of such tender offers.

Coinsurance effect   Where cash flows of two combining companies are not perfectly correlated so that the volatility of the combined firm's cash flows exhibits less variability.

Collar agreement   Agreed upon adjustments in the number of shares offered in a stock-for-stock exchange to account for fluctuations in stock prices before the completion of the deal.

Concentration ratios   Measures of the percentage of total industry revenues accounted for by a certain number of firms, usually the top four or eight.

Conglomerate   A combination of unrelated firms.

Cramdown   A situation that occurs when a reorganization plan is approved even when some classes of creditors do not approve it. At least one class of creditors needs to approve the plan for there to be a cramdown.

Cumulative abnormal return   The sum of daily abnormal returns over a certain period in an event study.

Cumulative voting rights   When shareholders have the right to pool their votes to concentrate them on the election of one or more directors rather than apply their votes to the election of all directors.

Dead hand provisions Antitakeover measure that gives the power to redeem a poison pill to the directors who were on the target's board of directors before the takeover attempt.

Debtor in possession   A term used to refer to a bankrupt company in a Chapter 11 proceeding.

Deconglomerization The process of taking apart a conglomerate through various sell-offs.

Dissident   A shareholder, or group of shareholders, who oppose current management and may try to use the proxy process to gain control of the company or to try to get the company to take certain actions, such as payment of certain dividends. Dissidents often try to have their representatives placed on the board of directors.

Diversification   In mergers and acquisitions, a term that refers to buying companies or assets outside the companies' current lines of business.

Divestiture   The sale of a component of the company, such as a division.

Dual classification   The creation of two classes of common stock, with the goal of concentrating more voting rights in the hands of management.

Economies of scale   The reduction of a company's average costs due to increasing output and spreading out fixed costs over higher output levels.

Economies of scope   The ability of a firm to utilize one set of inputs to provide a broader range of outputs or services.

Employee stock ownership plan (ESOP)   A type of pension plan in which the assets of the plan are the stock of the company.

Equity carve-out   The issuance of equity in a division or part of a parent company that then becomes a separate company.

ESOP   See **Employee stock ownership plan.**

Exclusivity period   The time period during the initial days after a Chapter 11 filing when only the debtor can put forward a reorganization plan. It is initially 120 days, but the time period is often extended.

Fair price provision   An antitakeover charter amendment that requires the payment of a certain minimum price for the shares of the target. It increases the bidder's cost of a takeover and makes coercive actions, such as two-tiered tender offers, less effective.

Fallen angel   A bond originally issued with an investment-grade rating that had its rating fall below the investment-grade level, BB or lower, into the junk bond category.

Flip-in poison pill plan   Shareholders are issued rights to acquire stock in the target at a significant discount, usually 50%.

Flip-over poison pill plan   The most commonly used poison pill antitakeover defense, in which shareholders are issued rights to purchase common stock in a bidding firm's company at a significant discount, usually 50%.

Free cash flow hypothesis   Theory put forward by Michael Jensen, which asserts that the assumption of debt used to finance leveraged takeovers will absorb discretionary cash flows and help eliminate the agency problem between management and shareholders. It is assumed that with the higher debt service obligations, management would apply the company's cash flows to activities that are in management's interest and not necessarily in shareholders' interests.

Front end-loaded tender offers   A tender offer in which the compensation of a first tier is superior to a later second tier. Such offers are designed to be coercive and cause shareholders to tender early.

General Utilities Doctrine   A component of the Tax Code that provided tax benefits for the sale of assets or liquidating distributions. It was repealed by the Tax Reform Act of 1986.

Going private   When a public corporation becomes privately held. This is usually done through a leveraged buyout.

Golden parachute   Employment contract of upper management that provides a larger payout upon the occurrence of certain control transactions, such as a certain percentage share purchase by an outside entity or when there is a tender offer for a certain percentage of the company's shares.

Greenmail   The payment of a premium above current market price for the shares held by a certain shareholder, with the goal of eliminating that shareholder as a threat to the company's independence.

Hart-Scott-Rodino Antitrust Improvements Act of 1976   A law that requires a bidding company to file with the Federal Trade Commission and the Justice Department and receive antitrust approval from one of these entities before completing a takeover.

Herfindahl-Hirschman (HH) Index   The sum of the squares of the market shares of companies in a given industry. It is a measure of industry concentration and is more sensitive to the effects of mergers than simple market shares.

Highly Confident Letter A letter issued by an investment bank indicating that it is confident that it can raise the necessary financing for a takeover.

High-yield bond   Another name for a junk bond.

Holding company   A company that owns the stock of other corporations. A holding company may not engage in actual operations of its own but merely manages various operating units that it owns an interest in.

Horizontal equity   A principle of equal treatment for all shareholders such as in tender offers. Front end-loaded tender offers violate this principle.

Horizontal integration   A merger of firms selling a similar product or service.

Hubris hypothesis   A theory by Richard Roll that asserts that managers in acquiring companies believe that their valuations of targets may be superior to the market. This hubris causes them to overpay and overestimate the gains from acquisitions.

Initial Public Offering (IPO)   The first offering of the common stock to the public by a closely held company.

In play   When the market believes that a company may be taken over. At this time, the stock becomes concentrated in the hands of arbitragers and the company becomes vulnerable to a takeover and the target of a bid.

Investment Company Act of 1940   One of several pieces of federal legislation passed after the October 1929 stock market crash and the Great Depression. This law regulated the activities and reporting requirements of investment companies, which are firms whose principal business is the trading and management of securities.

Joint venture   When companies jointly pursue a certain business activity.

Junk bond   High-yield bonds that receive a rating from Standard & Poor's (or other agency) of BB or below. Such bonds are riskier than investment-grade bonds, which have higher ratings.

LBO   See **Leveraged buyout.**

LBO funds   A pool of investment capital that invests in various leveraged buyouts seeking to realize the high returns potentially available in LBOs while lowering risk through diversification.

Lerner Index   Developed by Abba Lerner, the index measures market power as the difference between price and marginal cost relative to price.

Leveraged buyout (LBO)   The purchase of a company that is financed primarily by debt. However, the term is more often applied to debt-financed going-private transactions.

Leveraged ESOP   An employee stock ownership plan in which the purchase of shares is financed by debt. The principal and interest payments may be tax-deductible.

Liquidation   The sale of all of a company's assets whereby the firm ceases to exist.

Lockup option   An option to buy certain valuable assets or stock in the target, which it issues to a friendly party. If the option limits the bidding process, it could be legally challenged.

Management buyout (MBO)   A going-private transaction in which the management of a company or division of a company takes the company or division private.

Management entrenchment hypothesis   Proposes that nonparticipating shareholders experience reduced wealth when management takes actions to deter attempts to take control of the corporation.

Marketability discount   A discount applied to the value of some securities, such as securities in closely held companies, based on their comparatively lower liquidity.

Market model   A method that is used in event studies. Regression analysis is used to compute the return that is attributable to market forces. It is used to compute "excess returns" that may be attributable to the occurrence of an event.

Market power   Although this term is used differently in different contexts, one definition used in an industrial organization is the ability to set and maintain price above competitive levels.

Master limited partnership (MLP)   A limited partnership whose shares are publicly traded. Its key advantage is that it eliminates the layer of corporate taxation because MLPs are taxed like partnerships, not corporations.

Mezzanine layer financing   Subordinated debt financing that is often used in leveraged buyouts. It is debt but also has equity-like characteristics in that the debt securities are often accompanied by "equity kickers."

Minority discount A discount applied to the value of equity securities based on a lack of control.

MLP **See** Master limited partnership.

Monopoly An industry structure that is characterized by one seller.

Morris Trust Using a Morris Trust, a company could spin off component businesses that it did not want to keep while in a second set, preplanned transaction the spun-off business is merged into an acquirer's business in a tax-free stock transaction. The end result is that shareholders in the selling company end up with shares in both their own company and that of the acquirer.

NASDAQ National Association of Securities Dealers Automated Quotations. It is the trading system for the over-the-counter market.

Net operating loss carryover Tax benefits that allow companies to use net operating losses in certain years to offset taxable income in other years.

Net present value (NPV) A capital budgeting technique that combines the present value of cash inflows of a project with the present value of investment outlays.

No-shop provisions Where a seller agrees not to solicit or enter into sale agreements with any other bidders.

Note purchase rights Another name for back-end poison pill plans.

Oligopoly Industry structure characterized by a small number of sellers (i.e., 3-12).

Pac-Man defense One of the more extreme antitakeover defenses. It refers to a situation in which a target makes a counteroffer for the bidder.

Partial tender offer A tender offer for less than all of a target's outstanding shares.

Perfect competition An industry structure characterized by certain conditions, including many buyers and sellers, homogeneous products, perfect information, easy entry and exit, and no barriers to entry. The existence of these conditions implies that each seller is a price taker.

PIK debt securities Bonds that may pay bondholders compensation in a form other than cash.

Poison pill A right issued by a corporation as a preventative antitakeover defense. It allows right holders to purchase shares in either their own company or the combined target and bidder companies at a discount, usually 50%. This discount may make the takeover prohibitively expensive.

Poison put A provision added to bond indenture contracts that allows bondholders to sell or "put" their bonds back to the issuing corporation at a predetermined exercise price. Poison puts became popular in the leveraged buyout era of the 1980s, when bond prices plummeted in response to the increased debt loads of post-LBO companies and the subsequent downgrading of the debt.

Preferred stock plans Early version of poison pills that used preferred stock as opposed to rights.

Prepackaged bankruptcy In a prepackaged bankruptcy, the debtor negotiates the reorganization plan with its creditors before an actual Chapter 11 filing.

Proxy contest When a dissident shareholder or group of shareholders try to take control of the board of directors or use the process to enact certain changes in the activities of the company.

Pure plays Companies that operate within clearly defined market boundaries.

Rabbi trusts Where monies to fund golden parachutes are sometimes put.

Real estate investment trusts (REITs) are publicly traded, passive investment vehicles that pay little or no federal taxes.

Recapitalization plan The alteration of the capital structure of a company that adds debt and may reduce equity. It often is used as an antitakeover device when a target uses it as an alternative offer to a hostile bid. It often involves assuming considerable debt and paying a superdividend to target shareholders.

Restructuring charges Also referred to as big bath write-offs. In a merger context it refers to a company's taking large write-offs following an acquisition, which lowers current income but may carry the implication that future income may be higher.

Reverse LBO Companies that go public after having gone private in a leveraged buyout.

Reverse synergy $4 - 1 = 5$; where, following a sell-off, the remaining parts of a company are more valuable than the original parent business.

Revlon duties   Legal principle that actions, such as antitakeover measures, that promote a value maximizing auction process are allowable whereas those that thwart it are not.

Roll-up acquisitions   An acquisition program that features multiple acquisitions of smaller companies by a larger consolidator.

Schedule 13D   The document that is required by the Williams Act to be filed with the SEC within 10 days of acquiring 5% or more of a public company's outstanding shares. This filing discloses certain information, including the purchaser's identity and intentions, as well as other related information, such as financing sources, in the case of a planned takeover.

Schedule 14D   The document that, pursuant to the Williams Act, must be filed with the SEC by the initiator of a tender offer. This filing discloses information on the identity of the bidder, specifics of the offer, and other relevant information, such as sources of financing and postacquisition plans.

Scorched-earth defense   An antitakeover defense that has such an adverse effect on the target that it renders it undesirable to bidders.

Securities Act of 1933   The first of the federal securities laws of the 1930s. It provided for the registration of publicly traded securities.

Securities Exchange Act of 1934   The federal law that established the Securities and Exchange Commission. It also added further regulations for securities markets. The law has been amended several times since its initial passage. One of the amendments that is relevant to mergers is the Williams Act of 1968.

Sell-off   A general term describing a sale of a part of a company. It also includes other more specific transactions, such as divestitures or spin-offs.

Shareholder interests hypothesis   It implies that stockholder wealth rises when management takes actions to prevent changes in control.

Shark repellent   Another name for an antitakeover defense.

Shelf registration rule   SEC Rule 415 that allows companies to register, in advance, shares they may want to offer in the future.

Sherman Act of 1890   The major piece of federal antitrust legislation. It contains two principal sections: Section 1 prohibits all contracts and combinations in restraint of trade; Section 2 prohibits monopolization and attempts at monopolization.

Spin-off   A type of sell-off in which a parent company distributes shares on a pro rata basis to its shareholders. These new shares give shareholders ownership rights in a division or part of the parent company that is sold off.

Split-off   A type of sell-off in which shareholders of a parent company exchange their shares in the parent company for shares in the sold off entity.

Split-up   When the parent company spins off all of its component parts and ceases to exist.

Staggered board   Also called a **classified board.** This is an antitakeover measure in which the election of directors is split in separate periods so that only a percentage of the total number of directors come up for election in a given year. It is designed to make taking control of the board of directors more difficult.

Stakeholder   Any entity that is affected by the actions of a company, which may include shareholders, management, workers, communities, consumers, and so on.

Standstill agreement   An agreement that a potential hostile bidder enters into with the target corporation whereby the bidder agrees, in exchange for some consideration, not to purchase more than an agreed upon number of shares.

Strategic alliance   A more flexible alternative to a joint venture whereby certain companies agree to pursue certain common activities and interests.

Stock parking   The attempt to evade the disclosure requirements of securities law by keeping shares in names other than the true owner.

Street sweeps   Open-market purchases of a target's stock that are not tender offers and therefore are not subject to the requirements of the Williams Act.

Supermajority provision A preventative antitakeover defense that amends the corporate charter to require a higher majority, such as two-thirds or even more, to approve certain transactions such as mergers.

Synergy $2 + 2 = 5$; a combination of businesses in which the combined entity is more valuable than the sum of the parts.

Targeted share repurchase Refers to repurchase of stock of a large shareholder, such as a hostile bidder. It usually is done at a premium over market prices. This type of transaction is also referred to as **greenmail.**

Tax-free reorganizations Types of business combinations in which shareholders do not incur tax liabilities. There are four types-types, A, B, C, and D—which differ in various ways, including the amount of stock and/or cash that is offered.

Tender offer An offer made directly to shareholders. One of the more common ways hostile takeovers are implemented.

Two-tiered tender offer Tender offers in which the bidder offers a superior first-tier price for a maximum number of shares while it offers to acquire the remaining shares in the second tier at a lower price.

Unocal standard The legal principle that reasonable defensive measures that are consistent with the business judgment rule are legally acceptable.

Vertical merger A merger of companies that operate at different levels or stages of the production process in the same industry. For example, a company with large oil reserves buying a pipeline company for a gasoline retailer is an example of forward integration. A consumer electronics retail chain that buys a brand name manufacturer would be an example of backward integration.

Voting plans A variation on the poison pill defense theme. They allow preferred stockholders to have supervoting rights if a bidder acquires a certain percentage of the target's stock. They are designed to prevent a bidder from getting voting control of the target.

White knight A more acceptable buyer that a target of a hostile bid may approach.

White squire A friendly company or investor that purchases an interest in the target of a hostile bid. The target may do this to make a takeover more difficult.

Williams Act of 1968 An amendment of the Securities and Exchange Act of 1934 that regulates tender offers and other takeover-related actions, such as larger share purchases.

Winner's curse This is the ironic hypothesis that states that bidders who overestimate the value of a target will most likely win a contest. This is due to the fact that they will be more inclined to overpay and outbid rivals who more accurately value the target.

Workout A workout refers to a negotiated agreement between the debtors and its creditors outside the bankruptcy process.

INDEX

Abnormal returns, 259–260
Absolute priority rule, 444
Accelerated depreciation, 37, 465
Accounting manipulations, 35–36
Accounting methods, pooling *vs.* purchase, 506
Accounts payable, 465
Accounts receivable, 464, 467
Acquiring companies:
    method of payment:
        long-term effects, 531–532
        short-term effects, 531
    target's tax benefits and, 597
Acquisitions, generally:
    announcements, 4–5
    conglomerate, 35–36
    historical perspective, 138–139
    long-term effects of, 528–529
    P/E values and, 33–34
    premiums, 521–522
    sell-offs of, 399, 401
    small-scale, 12
    ten largest, 4
Activity ratios, 342, 474
Addback process:
    addback items, 562–563
    legal fees, excessive, 564
    professional fees, excessive, 563–564
Adham, Kamal, 279
Agee, William, 237
Agency theory, 294
Air Florida, 157
Airline industry, 156–158
Alcatel Alsthom, 428
All-cash offers, 91, 286
Allegis Corporation, 117–118, 403
Allen, William T., Chancellor, 215
Alley, William J., 235
Allied Chemical Corporation, 27
Allied Signal, 133, 221
Allied Stores Corporation, 266, 442
Alpha Beta, 109
Altman, Edward, 452
Altman Z score, *see* Z score
Altshuler, Roseanne, 597

Aluminum Company of America, 96
Aluminum industry, 156
Amanda Acquisition Corporation *vs.* Universal
    Foods Corporation, 106
Amended offer, 80
America Online (AOL), 505
American Brands, 235
American Can, 205
American Cottonseed Oil Trust, 24
American Express, 420
American General Corporation, 234, 275
American Stores Company, 109
American Sugar Refining Company, 23–24, 87
American Tobacco Inc., 22, 25, 96
Amerisource Corporation, 98
Ames Department Stores, 162
Ampco-Pittsburg, 214
Anderson Clayton *vs.* Gerber Products, 233–234
Anheuser-Busch, 210
Annual reports, 461
Antidiscrimination, 383
Antigreenmail provisions, 198
Antitakeover defenses, *see* Antitakeover measures
Antitakeover laws, state:
    Delaware, 106–107
    genesis of, 103–104
    passage of, 108
    Pennsylvania, 107–108
    second-generation laws, 104–106
    state actions, 109
    wealth effects of, 108–109
Antitakeover measures:
    active defenses:
        capital structure changes, 204–205, 217–231
        greenmail, 204, 205–209, 238
        "just say no," 236
        litigation, 205, 231–234
        managing value, 493
        overview, 204–205
        Pac-Man defense, 205, 213, 234–235
        standstill agreements, 204, 209–211
        white knights, 204, 211–213
        white squire defense, 204, 213–217
    antigreenmail provisions, 198

Antitakeover measures (*continued*)
 board of directors, staggered terms, 189–194
 companies with, 199
 corporate charter amendments, 188–189
 dual capitalization, 195–198
 elections, restriction ability, 198
 fair price provisions, 194–195
 golden parachutes, 199–203
 incorporation, changing the state of, 203–204
 information content of takeover resistance,
  236–238
 management entrenchment hypothesis, stockholder interests hypothesis
  vs.,176–177
 managerial ownership research, 198
 poison pills:
  flip-in, 182–183
  flip-over rights, 179–181
  legality of, 181–182
  limitations, recent court rulings, 184–185
  mechanics of, 183–184
  shareholder wealth, effects on, 188
  stock prices, impact on, 185–187
  types of, overview, 178–181
 preventative:
  back-end plans, 183
  blank check preferred stock, 184, 213
  dead hand provisions, 184
  early warning systems, 177
  flip-in poison pills, 182–183
  flip-over rights, 179–182
  preferred stock plans, 178
  types of, 177–178
  voting plans, 183
 shareholder wealth, 188–189, 212–213
Antitrust:
 advocates, 31
 regulations, 7. *See also* Antitrust laws
Antitrust laws:
 Celler-Kefauver Act of 1950, 89, 113
 Clayton Act, 88–89, 99
 enforcement of, 95–98
 Federal Trade Commission Act of 1914, 89, 113
 Hart-Scott-Rodino Antitrust Improvements Act
  of 1976, 89–95
 market share and, 99–103
 Sherman Antitrust Act, 87, 99
 significance of, 23–24, 28–29
Antitrust limbo, 95
Antitrust litigation, 232
Antitrust problems, holding companies and, 18
Any-and-all tender offers, 255, 257–258
Appraisal rights, shareholder, 15
Approval, merger:
 board of directors, special committees, 14

 fairness opinions, 14
 procedures, 13–14
 process, 12

Araskog, Rand V., 136, 427
Arbitrage, 48
Arbitrageurs, 48–49, 265, 267, 522
Archibald, T. Ross, 37
Armstrong World Industries, 167
Articles for merger or consolidation, 13–14
Articles of incorporation, 14
Arvida Corporation, 231
Ashe, Marvin, 75
Ashland Oil, 94
Asquith, Paul, 158, 258–259
Asset basis step-up, 598
Asset-based lending, 297, 299
Assets:
 acquisition of:
  advantages of, 16
  purchase of, 15
 book value, 298
 current, 463–464
 defined, 463–464
 intangible, 467
 low-quality, 466–467
 real estate, 467
 selloffs, 16–17
 taxable purchases of, 595
Assets-oriented valuation, 565
Assumption, of seller's liabilities, 15–16
Astor National Bank, 24
AT&T, 56, 409–410, 423, 584
Atlantic and Pacific Tea (A&P), 96–97
Attorneys, function of, 10, 254
Auction process, poison pills and, 187
Auerbach, Alan, 596–597
Automatic stay, 440
Average collection period, 474–475
Avis Rent a Car, 30, 428, 506
Avon Products, 270

Back-end plans, 183
Background:
 history of mergers, 18–59
 legal framework, 61–114
 merger strategy, 116–168
Bad bidders, 263–264
Bad deals, 160–161
Balance sheet:
 analysis of, 466–468
 assets, 463–464, 466
 ESOPs and, 381–382
 inventory accounting and, 466
 liabilities, 464–466

purpose of, 461, 463
stockholders' equity, 465–466
time frame, 466
Bally Manufacturing Corporation, 94
Banking industry, 53, 55
Banking Panic of 1907, 26
Bank loan financing, junk bonds *vs.*, 365
Bank mergers, 123
Bank of New York *vs.* Irving Bank, 185
Bank One, 55, 123
Bankruptcy:
    case study, 454–456
    Chapter 11 reorganization, 439–446
    corporate control, default and, 450
    data, 126, 435–437
    Drexel Burnham Lambert, 340–341
    ESOPs and, 380
    high-yield bonds and, 348
    laws, 437, 439
    LTV Corporation, 339–340, 343
    prepackaged, 446–448
    reorganization *vs.* liquidation, 439
    Revco, 325
    workouts, 449–450
Bankruptcy Act of 1978, 437, 439
Bankruptcy Amendments, 439
Bankruptcy Code, 437, 449–450
Bankruptcy Reform Act of 1994, 439
Bankrutpcy sharks/vultures, 454
Bar date, 441
Basic, Inc., 113
Bass Brothers, 207, 247
Bear hugs:
    case study, 246
    defined, 243, 246
    overview, 245–247
Beatrice, 308, 505
Becton Dickinson Company, 75–76, 247–248
Behavior argument, 96
Bell Atlantic, 112, 527
Benchmarks, 540–541, 571, 573–574
Bendix Corporation *vs.* Martin Marietta, 237–238
Beneficial owners, 67
Bergen Brunsweig Corporation, 98
Bergerac, Michael, 215
Berkshire Hathaway, 214
Best price rule, 80
Beta, 517–518
Betker, Brian, 448
Bilzerian, Paul, 46, 203
Black Thursday, 29
Blackstone Group, 307–308
Blair, Margaret, 384
Blank check preferred stock, 184, 213
Blasi, Joseph, 384

Blue Sky Laws, 251
Bluhdorn, Charles, 205, 246
Board of directors:
    elections, 198, 268–269
    proxy contests, 273
    size and valuation, 540
    special committees, 14
    staggered terms:
        board amendments, 191
        effectiveness as antitakeover defense,
            191–192
        operations, 189–191
        removal of directors, Delaware law, 191
        research, 192
        supermajority provisions, 192–193
    after successful tender offer, 83
Boeing Co., 95, 98, 108
Boesky, Ivan, 49, 64, 110
Boise Cascade, 379
Bondholders, leveraged buyouts (LBOs) and,
    319–322, 325
Bonds:
    junk, *see* Junk bonds
    rating system:
        consistency of, 344
        determinants of, 343–344
        overview, 342–343, 574
        Z score and zeta analysis, 346–347
Book value, 479, 541–542, 566, 591
Bootstrap effect, 36
Bootstrapping earnings per share, 537–538
Borden Corporation, 203
Bossidy, Lawrence, 133
Bradley, Michael, 259
Brass, Inc., 335
Break-even point, 426, 536
Breakup LBOs, 303
Bridge financing, 334, 362–363
Briloff, A. J., 35
British Petroleum, 50
Brokerage firms:
    proxy fights and, 278–280
    purchases by, 94
Brown Foreman, 178
Brown Shoe, 97
Bruck, Connie, 333
Buffalo Forge Company, 214
Buffett, Warren, 214
Buildup method, 571, 576–577
Bull, Ivan, 316
Bull market, historical perspective, 33–34, 53
Burroughs and Sperry, 7
Business broker, function of, 12
Business combination, 104–105
Business cycles, 136

Business failure, *see* Bankruptcy
  causes of, 433–435
  corporate control, default and, 450
  costs of, 423
  economic, 432
  financial, 432–433
  investment in distressed companies, 452–454, 456
  liquidation, 450–452
Business judgment rule:
  defined, 84–85, 201
  Revlon duties, 85–86
  Time-Warner-Paramount, 86
  Unocal standard, 85
Business risk, 310
Business Week, 142
Bustup fees, 216–217
Bustups, voluntary:
  defined, 423–424
  shareholder wealth effects, 424–425

California Public Employees Retirement System (CALPERS), 270
Calls, junk bonds and, 352
Campeau, Robert, 266, 454–455
Campeau Corporation:
  Allied Stores *vs.,* 266
  mergers, generally, 159, 302, 334, 340, 442, 454–456, 467, 542
Cannon Mills, 205
Canteen, 428
Capital Cities/ABC, 12
Capital, cost of, 516. *See also* Capital structure
Capitalization:
  cash flow, 569–575
  discount rate *vs.,* 577
  dual, 195–198
  of earnings, 565, 569–575
  rate, *see* Capitalization rate
Capitalization rate:
  cost of capital, 570–571
  defined, 569
  payback period, 578–579
  price-earnings ratio, derived from, 577–578
  selection of, 570
  significance of, generally, 517
Capital structure:
  changes, *see* Capital structure changes, antitakeover defenses
  junk bonds, 364–365
  post-buyout firms, 312–313
  unsecured LBO firms, 305–306
Capital structure changes, antitakeover defenses:
  corporate restructuring, 228–231
  debt assumption, 222, 224

recapitalization:
  case studies, 221–223
  leveraged buyouts compared with, 220
  overview, 217_220
  poison pill protection, 220–222
  problems with, 222–223
  share issuance, 224–226
  share repurchase, 226–228
Cardinal Health, Inc., 98
Carnegie, Andrew, 21
Carnegie Steel, 21
Carpet industry, 164–167
Carr, Fred, 367–368
Carter Hawley Hale, 214, 227, 252
Cash flow:
  analysis, 299, 499–500
  depreciation and, 471
  discounted, 514–515
  discounted future, 566–567
  divestitures and, 404, 407
  earnings *vs.,* 500–501
  employee stock ownership plans (ESOPs), 377
  free, 471–472, 504–505
  market value, 501–504
  statement of, 461, 470
Cash flow LBOs, 304–305
Cash-out statutes, 105
Cash tender offer, 61, 251
Cash transactions, 8, 530
Casual pass, 245
Caterpillar Tractor Company, 404, 426
Celler, Emmanuel, 36
Celler-Kefauver Act of 1950, 89, 97, 113
Cendant Corp., 506
Chambers, Raymond, 315
Champion International Corporation, 214
Chang, Saeyoung, 387
Chaplinsky, Susan, 382–383, 386
Chapter 11 reorganization:
  automatic stay, 440
  bankruptcy petition and filing, 440
  company size and, 445–446
  cramdown, 443–444
  creditors' committee, 441–442
  debtor:
    actions and supervision of, 442
    benefits for, 444
  debtor in possession, 440–441
  exclusivity period, 442–443
  obtaining postpetition credit, 443
  prepetition claims, partial satisfaction of, 444
  projections done in, 446
  reorganization plan, 443–444
  secured creditors' collateral, use of, 441
  time line, 440–441

transaction costs, 449–450
Chase Manhattan, 126
Chase National Bank, 24
Chemical Bank, 126
Chevalier, Judity, 150
Chevron Corporation, 153, 225, 342, 389
Chief executive officers (CEOs):
   antitakeover defense and, 189–190
   bankruptcy and, 450
   golden parachute agreements, 199–202
   share repurchase and, 226
Chili's, Inc., 543
Chili's Bar & Grill, 543, 545
Chinese Paper, 330
Chinese wall, 9
Chrysler Corporation, 19, 200, 404, 464
Citibank, 237
Citicorp Industrial Corporation, 210
Cities Service Oil Company, 212–213, 234
City Investing, 209
Civil Aeronautics Board (CAB), 157
Claims trading, 454
Classified board, 191
Clayton Act, 26, 30, 88–89, 99, 149
Closed-end investment companies, 17
Closely held businesses, valuation of:
   case study, 584–585
   overview, 564–565
Cluett, Peabody & Co., 258
Coastal Corporation, 234–235
Coca-Cola, 214
Code of ethics, 25
Code of Takeovers and Mergers, 84
Coefficient of variation (CV), 309
Coldwell Banker, 133–134
Colgate Palmolive, 210
Collar agreements, 540
Collateral:
   leveraged buyouts (LBOs), 297, 303
   secured creditors', use of, 441
Collateralization, junk bonds, 364
Colt Industries, Garlock Industries vs., 42–43
Columbia Savings and Loan of Beverly Hill, CA,
   338
Combustion Engineering, Inc., 113
Comcast Corporation, 112
Comment, Robert, 186
Commitment letter, 333
Commons, Dorman, 200
Common stock:
   cost of, 517–518
   defined, 8, 465
   voting rights, 190
Comparable multiples, 565
Compensation, executive, 161

Composition, defined, 449
Computer reservation systems (CRS), 157
Computer software, financial analysis programs,
   472–473
Comtronix, Corp., 111
Conglomerates:
   acquisition of, 35–37
   benefits of, 140–141
   merger, 8, 32
   performance of, 38
Coniston Partners:
   mergers, generally, 118, 210–211, 403
   T. W. Services vs., 77
Conoco, 398
Consolidation, 7, 14, 23, 150, 152
Continental Baking Company, 30, 428
Contributions, to ESOPs, 375
Control:
   after successful tender offer, 83
   employee stock ownership plans (ESOPs), 383
   holding companies and, 17
   merger premiums, 525–257
   premium:
      acquiring firms, performance of, 525
      acquisition premiums, determinants of,
         521–522
      arbitrageurs, role of, 522
   share, generally, 105
   target shareholder returns, 525
   valuation effects of mergers and acquisitions,
      522–525
Convertible securities:
   exception, 93–94
   spin-offs and, 410
Corporate acquisition decisions, 161
Corporate Bond Quality and Investor Experience
   (Hickman), 343
Corporate bonds, 574
Corporate charter amendments, 184, 188–189
Corporate culture, 125
Corporate finance theory, 136–139
Corporate performance, spin-offs and, 419–420
Corporate raiders, *see specific takeovers*
   antitakeover defenses and, *see* Antitakeover mea-
      sures
   role of, generally, 3, 46, 48–49, 175, 246
   small vs. large, 363–364
Corporate restructuring:
   bankruptcy, 432–457
   case study, 427–428
   divestitures, 398–408
   equity carve-outs, 420–423
   implications of, generally, 6, 11–12, 228–231
   master limited partnerships (MLPs), 425–426
   in the 1990s, 426–428

Corporate restructuring (*continued*)
overview, 397–429
sell-offs, wealth effects of, 410–420
spin-offs, 404–410
types of, overview, 397–398
voluntary liquidations/bustups, 423–425
Corrections Corporation of America, 599
Cost of goods sold, 468
Countercyclical firm, 136
Countersolicitations, 274
Cramdown, 443–444
Creason, William T., 179
Credit, postpetition, 443
Creditors, Chapter 11 reorganization and, 440–441
Credit Suisse Bank, 334
Creedon, John J., 319–320
Creeping tender offer, 248
Cross-marketing, 121
Crown Zellerbach Corporation, 179–181
Cruise mergers, 122
Crystal Oil Company, 447
CTS, 105
CUC International, Inc., 507
Current assets, 463–464, 473
Current liabilities, 464, 474
Current ratio, 473

Dan River, Inc., 385
Dan River Mills, 205
Dann, Larry, 210
Dayton-Hudson, 108
de facto merger, 16
Dead hand provisions, 184
Dean Witter Reynolds, 133–134
DeAngelo, Harry, 210
DeBartolo, Edward J., 266
Debentures, 8
Debt:
assumption of, 222, 224
coinsurance, 127
convertible, 36
cost of, 516
intermediate-term, 300–301
junior, 300
leveraged buyouts (LBOs), 49, 300–301
reduction strategies, 52
senior, 300, 303
subordinated, 300, 303–304
Debt-equity ratio, 127, 477, 600–602
Debtor, Chapter 11 reorganization, 440–442, 444
Debtor in possession:
defined, 440
duties of, 441
Debt ratio, 476–477
Debt to total capitalization ratio, 477

Deductions, taxation issues, 381, 601–602
Default risk, 342, 357, 360
Defaults, junk bonds and, 352–353
Defined benefit plans, 374
Defined contribution plans, 374–375
Delaware:
antitakeover law, 106–107
removal of directors, 191
Dependable source of supply, 154
Depository bank, 255, 273
Depository Trust Company, 273
Depreciation:
accelerated, 465
cash flows and, 471
defined, 37, 469
D. F. King and Company, 254, 271, 280
Desai, Anand, 258
Dhillon, Upinder, 387
Diamond Shamrock R&M, 409
Dickinson, Fairleigh S., Jr., 75–76, 247
Dingman, Michael, 221
Dingman's dogs, 221
Disclosure:
company obligations, 112–113
inadequate, litigation, 232
private corporations and, 559
Williams Act and, 13, 63, 68
Discount rate:
calculation of, 515–516
capital, cost of, 516
capitalization *vs.*, 577
divestitures, 407
implications of, 567
market determination of, 518–519
Discounted cash flows, 514–515
Discounted future earnings, 565, 567–568
Discounting, 513
Disney, Roy E., 229
Dissenting shareholders, 15
Dissidents, in proxy fight, 282
Distressed companies, investment in:
control, market for, 456
debt securities:
control opportunities, 453–454
returns on, 452–453
vulture investors, role of, 456
Distributions, employee stock ownership plans
(ESOPs), 382–383
Diversification:
acquisition of leading industry positions,
130–133
case study, 133–134
corporate finance theory and, 136–138
defined, 128
effects in firm value, 141

entering more profitable industries, 134–135
financial benefits of, 135–136
financing, bank loan *vs.* junk bonds, 365
free cash flow theory and, 50
positive evidence of benefits of, 140–141
related, unrelated *vs.*, 144
research, related *vs.* unrelated, 144
significance of, 128
stock market performance and, 139–140
Diversified Industries (DI), 297–298
Divestitures:
  acquisitions, likelihood of divestiture, 401
  employee stock ownership plans (ESOPs) and, 376
  financial evaluation of, 407–408
  historical trends, 398–401
  involuntary *vs.* voluntary, 402
  types of, generally, 12, 398
  voluntary, 402–404
Dividend policy, 499
Dividends, ESOPs, 378, 381
Divisional buyouts, 312
Divisions, valuation of, 467–468
Dodd, Peter, 280, 282
Dome Petroleum, 398
Dow Jones Industrial Average, 33, 291, 526
Downsizing, 11, 426
Drew, Daniel, 25
Drexel Burns Lambert:
  bankruptcy of, 340–341
  junk bonds and, 331–337
  role of, in mergers and acquisitions, 49, 110–111, 210, 258, 283, 366, 500
DRI/McGraw-Hill, 427
Dual capitalization, 195–198
Due diligence, 10, 461
Duff and Phelps, 342, 364
Dunkin' Donuts, 542–553
DuPont Inc., 22
Dworkin, Sidney, 322–324
Dynamic Entertainment, 533–534, 536–539
Dynamics *vs.* CTS, 105
Dyson-Kissner-Moran, Household International *vs.*, 181

E-II Holdings *vs.* American Brands, 235
Earnings:
  base, *see* Earnings base
  capitalization of, 565
  cash flow *vs.*, 500–501
  discounted future, 565, 567–568
  quality of, 469–470
  retained, 466
Earnings base:
  accounting:

data, reliability of, 505
  pooling *vs.* purchase, 506
calculation methods, 499
case study, 499–500
cash flow and, 501–504
earnings *vs.* cash flow, 500–501
fraudulent inaccuracies, 506–507
free cash flow theory, 504–505
net income, 501–504
research and development charges, in-process, 505–506
restructuring charges, 506
Earnings per share (EPS):
  bootstrapping, 537–539
  dilution criteria, 534–537
  implications of, generally, 33, 36, 469
  initial changes, influential factors, 537
  postmerger P/E ratio, 539
  surviving company, 533–534
Easterbrook, Frank, 253, 258
Eastman Kodak, 22
Easy Saver computer system, 118
EAT, 570
EBDIT (earnings before depreciation, interest, and taxes), 422
EBIT (earnings before interest and taxes), 354, 468, 477–478, 570
EBITDA (earnings before interest, taxes, depreciation, and amortization), 433, 454, 468, 566, 570
EBT (earnings before tax), 468
Eckbo, B. Epsen, 149
Eckerd Drug Stores, 323
Economatrix Research Associates, Inc., 564
Econometrics, 507
Economies of scale, 121–123, 127, 168
Economies of scope, 123, 168
Edelman, Asher, 229, 283, 318
Edgar *vs.* MITE, 103–104
EDS, 195
Edwards, William, 324
Efficient markets, 36–37
8K filing, 62
El Paso Electric, 178
Elasticity, 102
Electric Storage Battery (ESB) Corporation, 136, 249
Electronic Data Systems, 7
Ellert, James, 419
Emory, John, 582
Employee Retirement Income Security Act of 1974 (ERISA), 372
Employee stock ownership plans (ESOPs):
  as antitakeover defense, 192, 218, 224–226, 385–386, 389

Employee stock ownership plans (ESOPs) (*continued*)
   balance sheet effects of, 381–382
   case studies, 385, 389–392
   cash flow implications, 377
   characteristics of, 375
   corporate performance and, 383–385
   corporate uses of, 376
   dividends paid, 378
   eligibility of, 378
   employee risk, 380
   failure of, case study, 385
   historical growth of, 372–373
   leveraged:
      drawbacks of, 382–383
      tax benefits of, 381
      unleveraged vs., 375
   leveraged buyouts (LBOs) and, 376, 387–390
   public offering of stock *vs.,* 379–380
   put options, 378
   SEC regulation of, 68, 380
   shareholder wealth and, 386–387
   spin-offs and, 410
   taxation, 381
   types of plans, 374–375
   valuation of stock contributed to, 377–378
   voting of shares, 277–278, 376–377
Employee stock ownership trust (ESOT), 377
Enron Corpoation, 234, 420
Equity carve-outs:
   characteristics of, 421–422
   defined, 397
   public offerings vs., 422–423
   research studies, 421
   spin-offs *vs.,* 423
Equity dilution, 382, 390
Equity Funding Scandal, 294–295
Equity investment, leverged buyouts (LBOs), 299, 303
Equity kicker, 304
Equity rate of return, 517–518
Equity securities, 128
Erie Lackawanna Railroad, 224
Erie Railroad, 25
Ernst & Young, 94–95
ESB, 38–41
Escape clause, 193
Esmark, 406
Event studies, 37
Evergreen agreement, 200–201
Excel, 473
Exchange ratio, earnings per share (EPS):
   bootstrapping, 537–539
   dilution criteria, 534–537
   initial changes, influential factors, 537
   postmerger P/E ratio, 539
   surviving company, 533–534
Exchanges, junk bonds and, 351–352
Exclusivity period, 442–443
Executive Life Insurance Company (ELIC), 367
Executive Life Insurance of New York (ELNY), 367
Expansion:
   diversification and, 135, 138
   as motivation, 8, 51
Expected return, 258–259
Expected value (EV), leveraged buyouts, 309
Expenses:
   accrued, 465
   interest, 468
   operating, 468
   prepaid, 464
Extension, defined, 449
Exxon, 121

Failing companies, 376
Fair market value, 565–566, 590
Fairness opinions, 14
Fair price, defined, 104
Fair price provision:
   research, 195
   two-tiered tender offers, 194–195, 256
Fair value, defined, 566
Fallen Angels, 330
Farley, William, 258
Federal Home Loan Mortgage Association (Freddie Mac), 469
Federal Judgeship Act, 439
Federal Reserve, 26, 366
Federal Trade Commission (FTC), 28, 30–31, 73, 88, 92–95, 109, 230, 402, 418
Federal Trade Commission Act of 1914, 89, 113
Federated Department Stores, 159, 334, 442, 454, 467, 542
Ferris, Richard, 117–119
Fiduciary:
   misappropriation theory vs., 111
   responsibilities, 84–85, 384
   takeover tactics and, 245
FIFO (first-in, first-out), 466, 469, 502, 564
Fifth merger wave, 50–59, 202, 579
Financial Accounting Standard 95 (FAS 95), 470
Financial Accounting Standards Board (FASB), 469
Financial analysis:
   due diligence, 461
   computer programs, 472–473
   financial ratio analysis, 473–486
   financial statements, 461, 463–473
Financial data, accessibility to, 462
Financial General Bankshares, Inc., 279

Financial leverage ratios, 476
Financial ratio analysis:
    activity ratios, 474
    average collection period, 474–475
    case study, 482–486
    debt ratio, 476–477
    debt to equity ratio, 477
    debt to total capitalization ratio, 477
    financial leverage ratios, 476
    fixed asset turnover, 475–476
    fixed charge coverage, 478
    inventory turnover, 475
    leveraged buyouts, 311
    liquidity ratios, 473–474
    market-based ratios, 479
    payout ratio, 480
    price-earnings ratio, 480
    profitability ratio, 478
    purpose of, 473
    return on equity, 479
    return on investment, 479
    specialized nonstandard financial ratios, 480–482
    time interest earned, 477–478
    total asset turnover, 476
Financial ratios:
    analysis, *see* Financial ratio analysis
    nonstandard, 480–482
    W. T. Grant's, 344–346
Financial restructuring, 12
Financial synergy, 126–128
Financial valuation methodologies:
    capital, cost of, 516
    debt, cost of, 516
    discounted cash flows, 514–515
    discounting, 513
    discount rate, 515–516
    internal rate of return, 515
    net present value, 513–514
    present value, 513
Financing:
    fraudulent, 26
    leveraged buyouts (LBOs):
        candidates, financial analysis of, 298, 310–311
        funds, 307
        secured, 300–303
        sources of, 306
        unsecured, 303–305
    mezzanine layer, 304–305
FINSOLVE, 473
Firm value, 141
First Boston, 334, 339
First City Financial, 94
First Executive Corporation, 367–369
First Fidelity Bancorp of New Jersey, 150–152, 535
First merger wave (1897–1904), 21–26

First National Bank of Chicago, 24
First Nationwide Financial Corporation, 142
First Union Corporation, 123, 150–152, 535
Fischel, Daniel, 253, 258
Fisher Scientific, 247
Fisk, Jim, 25
Fitch Investors Service, 342
Fixed asset turnover, 475–476
Fixed charge coverage, 478
Fleisher, Arthur, 237
Flip-in poison pills, 182–183
Flip-over rights, 179–182
Float shares, 498
Floatation costs, 379, 517
Floor value, 540
FMC, 98
Forecasting methods:
    historical growth rates, extrapolation of, 507–508
    linear trend analysis, 509–510
    regression analysis, 510–512
    weighted average method, 508–509
Foreign mergers, 58–59
Foreign takeover(s), 50, 84
Forstmann, Ted, 310
Forstmann Little & Co., 210, 215–216, 307, 310, 318
Forwarding agent, 255
Forward integration, 153, 156
Fourth merger wave (1981–1989), 43–50, 525
Fox Meyer, 142–143
Fraine, Harold, 347
Fraud litigation, 232
Fraudulent financing, 26
Free cash flows, 471–472
Freezeouts, 15, 255
Fridson, Martin, 358
Front end-loaded tender offer, 255–256
Fruehauf, 283
Funeral home industry, 153
Fuqua Industries, 331

Gallagher, Bernard, 500
Garfinkel, Jon, 112
Garlock Industries, 42–43
Gary, E. H., Judge, 96
Gelman, Milton, 581
Geneen, Harold, 135, 310, 428
General Accounting Office (GAO), 375, 383–384
General American Oil, 178
General Cinema Corporation, 214, 227, 235
General Electric (GE), 22, 128–133
General Foods, 482, 485
General issue, 224
General Motors, 7, 27, 121, 195, 270

General Motors Acceptance Corporation (GMAC), 155–156
General Utilities Doctrine, 410, 598
Generally accepted accounting principles, 469
Georgeson and Company, 186, 254
Georgia-Pacific, 418–419
Gerber Products, 233–234
Getty, 205, 436
Ghosh, Aloke, 532
Gibbons Green & van Amerongen, 307
Gibson Greeting Cards, 315
Gillette, 163, 190, 210–211, 214
Gilson, Stuart, 449
Globalization, impact of, 12, 145
Go go years, 34
Going private, 10, 230
Golden handcuffs, 202
Golden parachutes:
    criticism of, 202
    legality of, 201–202
    mechanics of, 200–201
    overview, 199–200
    relevance in fifth merger wave, 202
Goldman Sachs, 334
Goldsmith, James, Sir, 179–181
Goodwill, amortization of, 591
Gordon stock dividend valuation model, 494–495
Gould, Jay, 25
Grand Metropolitan, 111
Gray, Henry, 41
Great Britain, takeover rules, 84
Great Depression, 25, 29, 330
Greenmail:
    case study, 206
    decline of, 208–209
    defined, 204–205, 238
    junk bonds and, 365–366
    legality, 206–207
    research, 207–208
Grey, Harry, 237
Griffin, Merv, 196, 462–463
Grimm and Company, 30
G. R. Kinney, 97
Gross profits, defined, 468
GrowMax, 496–497
Grumman, 7
GTE Corp., 527
Gulf & Western, 35, 136, 205
Gulf Oil Co., 153, 227, 341–342

Hammermill Paper Corporation, 206
Hanover National Bank, 24
Hanson, Robert, 505
Hanson Trust PLC, 265–265, 318, 420
Harsco-BMY, 98

Hartford Insruance Company, 35, 428
Hart-Scott-Rodino Antitrust Improvements Act of 1976:
    development of, 82, 89–90
    exemptions to, 93–94
    filing requirements, 90, 92, 265
    tender offers and, 94
    type of information to be filed, 90
    waiting periods, 251
Hayn, Carla, 164, 600
Healthdyne Technologies, Inc., 184
Henley Group, 221, 402
Hennessy, Edward, 41, 238
Herfindahl-Hirschman (HH) Index:
    applications, generally, 102–103
    defined, 100
    examples of, 101
    properties of, 100–101
Hertz Rent a Car, 118–119, 403
Heublein Corporation, 235
HFS, Inc., 507
Hickman, W. B., 343, 347–348
Highly Confident Letter, 335–336, 342, 362
Highly leveraged transactions (HLTs), 433, 575–579
High Voltage Engineering Corporation, 236
High-yield bonds, 347–348. See also Junk bonds
Hilton International, 118–119, 403
Historical growth rates, extrapolation of, 507–508
Historical perspective:
    fifth wave, 50–59, 579
    first wave (1897–1904), 21–26
    fourth wave (1981–1989), 43–50, 525
    the 1940s, 29–30
    the 1970s, 38–43
    second wave (1916–1929), 26–30
    third wave (1965–1969), 30–43
H. J. Heinz Co., 108
Holding companies:
    advantages, 17–18
    defined, 17
    disadvantages, 18
Holdout problem, 15, 267
Holiday Corporation, 94
Holthausen, Robert, 521
Hook, Harold, 275
Horizontal integration:
    case study, 150–152
    defined, 144–145, 168
    market power, 145, 150
    monopoly hypothesis, empircal evidence, 149–150
    social cost of increased concentration, 145–149
Horizontal mergers, 7, 23
Hostile deal, 61

Hostile mergers, implications of, 43
Hostile takeovers, *see specific takeovers*
  antitakeover measure, 175–239
  implications of, generally, 3, 42, 175
  takeover tactics, 243–287
Household International, 181–182
House of Morgan, 24
Houston Natural Gas Corporation, 234
Howe, Wesley, 75
Hubris hypothesis:
  defined, 158, 168
  empirical evidence, 158–159
Hughes Electric Corp., 98
Hurdle rate, 403

Ibbotson Associates, 574
IBM:
  Lotus *vs.*, 283–285
  mergers/acquisitions, generally, 27, 98, 505
Icahn, Carl, 163, 190–191, 205–206, 246–247,
    270–271, 335, 385
Illiquidity premiums, 574–575
Implied risk premium, 575–579
Improved management hypothesis, 161–163
INCO, *see* International Nickel Corporation
    (INCO)
Income, defined, 569–570
Income statement:
  analysis of, 469–470
  components of, 468–469
  defined, 461
  purpose of, 468
Incorporation, changing the state of, 203–204
Indenture contract, 332
Independent directors, 263
Independent Election Corporation of America
    (IECA), 277–278
Industry concentration, 32–33
Inflationary influences, 45
Information agent, 79, 254–255
Ingersoll Rand, 153
Initial public offerings (IPOs):
  equity carve-outs and, 421
  ESOPs *vs.*, 379–380
  research guidelines, 582
  spin-offs and, 414
Inside board, 190
Inside information, 9
Insider trading, regulation of:
  changing theory of, 111–112
  illegal, 109–110
  insiders, defined, 110
  trading scandals of the 1980s, 110–111
Insider Trading and Securities Fraud Enforcement
    Act of 1988, 109, 112

Insider Trading Sanctions Act of 1984, 110
Institutional investors, 188, 229, 278, 307, 337–339
Intangible assets, 467
Integrated Resources, 340, 367–369
Integration, after merger, 125
Interco, 185, 221–223
Interest expense, 468
Interest rate risk, 310, 571
Interest rates:
  acquisition prices and, 579
  leveraged buyouts and, 309
Internal rate of return (IRR), 515
International accounting, 592
International Harvester, 22, 404
International mergers, antitrust approval, 94–95
International Nickel Company (INCO):
  ESB *vs.*, 38–41
  mergers/acquisitions, generally, 136–137, 248
Interstate Commerce Commission (ICC), 402
Intuit, 98
Inventories, defined, 464
Inventory accounting, 466–467, 469
Inventory turnover, 475
Investment banks:
  aggressive role of, 49
  function of, 9, 14, 29, 254
  junk bonds and, 334, 362
Investment Company Act of 1940, 16
Investment exception, 93
Investment grade bonds, junk bonds *vs.*, 358–359
Investor Responsibility Research Center (IRRC), 199
Involuntary sell-offs, 418–419
Irving Bank, 185
ITT Corporation, 30–32, 35, 135–136, 152,
    408–409, 423, 427–428, 559

Jacob Suchard, 483
Jacobs, Irwin, 246
Jacobs, Jack, Judge, 184
Jain, Prem, 419
Jarrell, Gregg, 193, 195, 197, 232, 256–257
Jeffries, Boyd, 110
Jefferies and Company, 64
Jensen, Michael, 200, 312–313, 501, 504, 602
John Deere, 27
Johnson, Ross, 293
Joint ventures, 18–19
Jordan, Michael, 153
Josephson, Matthew, 224
J. P. Morgan, 414–415
J. P. Stevens, 215–216
Junior subordinated debt, 300
Junk bonds:
  bond rating system, 342–347
  case studies, 367–369

Junk bonds (*continued*)
  collapse of, major events in, 339–340
  decline in use as financial source, 341–342
  development of, 332–333
  diversification and, 360
  Drexel Burnham Lambert and, 333–334,
      340–341, 351
  evolutionary growth of, 337–342
  financing:
    bank loan *vs.,* 365
    regulations affecting, 366–367
  greenmail and, 365–366
  high-yield, 574
  history of, 107, 330–334
  hostile raiders, small *vs.* large, 363–364
  investment bankers, 334–337, 362
  investment grade *vs.,* 358–359
  issuers, fate of, 341
  recovery rate, 356
  repacking, 364–365
  research studies, 347–356
  returns on, 349, 357–360
  risk, 357, 360–361
  takeover process, 111, 255, 286, 319–320,
      362–363
  underwriting spreads, 361–364
Just-in-time inventory, 154

Kaiser Aluminum, 96
Kaplan, Robert, 37
Kaplan, Steven, 313–314, 316, 401, 455–456,
      514–515, 575, 602
Kay Jewelers, Inc., 188
KDP Investment Advisors, 341
Kekst, Gershon, 180
Kelly, Donald, 235, 406
Kelso, Louis, 387
Kerkorina, Kirk, 200, 464
Kidder, Peabody, 210
Kieschnick, Robert, 294
Kim, E. Han, 259
Kintner, Earl, 27
Kleinman, Robert, 220
K-Mart, 142, 162
Kohlberg Kravis & Roberts (KKR), 11, 41, 210,
      216, 293, 308, 315–316
KPMG, 94–95
Kraft, 483, 485
Kroger, 150
Kruse, Douglas, 384
Kudla, Ronald, 404, 411, 413, 418–419

Labor unions, 190
Lambert, Richard, 200–201
Larker, David, 200–201

Lawrence Pharmaceuticals, 142
LBO firms, 307–308
LBO funds, 307
LDDS, 56, 152, 584
Lease, Ronald, 527
Least squares method, 510
Leftwich, Richard, 521
Leg-up stock options, 214
Legal fees, 564
Legal framework:
  antitrust enforcement, changing pattern in the
      U.S., 96–99
  antitrust laws, 86–95
  business judgment rule, 84–86
  disclosure, of merger negotiations, 112–113
  insider trading, regulation of, 109–112
  laws governing mergers, acquisitions, and tender
      offers, 61–62
  market share, 99–103
  securities laws, 62–84
  state antitakeover laws, 103–109
Legislation, *see specific laws*
Lehman Brothers, 331
Lehn, Kenneth, 160, 263–264
Lenders, in leveraged buyouts (LBOs), 298–299
Lenox, 178
Lerner, Abba, 145
Lerner Index, 145
Letter of Transmittal, 76
Letter of withdrawal, 77
Letter stocks, 581
Leverage, generally:
  ratios, 542
  recapitalization, 217
  taxation and, 600–601
Leveraged buyouts (LBOs):
  bondholders, protection for, 322, 325
  candidates:
    desirable characteristics of, 301–303
    financial analysis of, 298, 310–311
  case study, 322–325
  data, 291–293
  debt holders, 319–321
  defined, 291
  divisional buyouts, 312
  efficiency gains from, 312–314
  employee stock ownership plans (ESOPs) and,
      376, 387–390
  financial distress following, 433–434
  financing:
    funds, 307
    secured, 300–303
    sources of, 306
    unsecured, 303–305
  firms, 307–308

free cash flow theory of, 504–505
implications of, generally, 3, 6, 10–11, 41, 49
management buyouts (MBO), 294–296, 304, 317–321
process, overview, 296–299
recapitalization plans compared with, 220
returns, to stockholders, 311–312
reverse, *see* Reverse LBOs
risk analysis, 308–310
samples, 150
tax revenues and, 602–604
unsecured firms, capital structure of, 305–306
wealth transfer effects, 321–322
white knights and, 319
Leveraged transactions:
    employee stock ownership plans (ESOPs), 372–392
    junk bonds, 330–369
    leveraged buyouts, 291–326

Levine, Dennis, 110
Liabilities:
    assumption of, 15–16
    divestitures, 407–408
    restructuring, 224
    successor, 15
Liberty Media, 112–113
Liberty National Bank, 24
Lichtenberg, Frank, 302
Liens, Chapter 11 reorganization and, 440
LIFO (last-in, first-out), 466, 469, 502, 564
Limited partners, in master limited partnerships (MLPs), 425–426
Linear trend analysis, 509–510
Ling, James Joseph, 53–54
Ling-Temco-Vought (LTV)
    bankruptcy, 339–340, 343, 349
    junk bonds and, 331
    mergers/acquisitions, generally, 30, 53–55, 136
Lintner, Carl, 246
Lipton, Martin, 178–180, 252, 258, 266
Liquidations:
    bankruptcy and, 450–451
    voluntary, 423–424
Liquidation value, 541, 566
Liquidity, generally:
    defined, 579
    high, 542
    ratios, 473–474
    risk, 357
Litigation:
    as antitakeover defense:
        case study, 233–234
        defined, 205
        overview, 231–232

research, 232–233
    management buyouts, 317–318
Litton Industries, 30
Lockheed Corporation, 278, 280
Lockheed Martin Corp., 98
Lockup options, 214
Lockup transactions, 214
Loewen Group, 153
Long, William, 315
Long-term debts, 465
Loss carryforwards, 381, 448
Lotus, 473, 505
Lotus Development Company, 283–285
Louisiana-Pacific Corporation, 418–419
Love, Howard, 141–142
Low-grade bonds, 330–331
Luce, Charles, 118–119
Lucky Stores, Inc., 109, 229

McConnell, John, 527
McDonnell Douglas Corp., 95, 98
McInish, Thomas, 404, 411, 413, 418–419
McLaren, Richard, 31–32, 36, 55
Macmillan Inc., 185, 216, 420
McWilliam, Victoria, 198
Maher, J. Michael, 581
Malatesta, Paul, 185
Management acquisition, 159
Management buyouts (MBOs):
    characteristics of, 10, 49, 294–296
    conflicts of interest in:
        overview, 317–318
        SEC Rule 13e-3, 318–319
        white knights, 319
    defined, 294
    employee stock ownership plans (ESOPs) vs., 390
    financing, unsecured, 304
    returns from, 311–312
    valuation, 602
Management entrenchment hypothesis, 176–177
Management proposals, 273
Management science, conglomerates and, 32
Managerial ownership, 198, 532
Managing (Geneen), 31
Manne, Henry, 282
Manufacturers Hanover Trust, 125–126
Manzi, James, 285
Marathon Oil, 215
Margolis, David, 42
Marketability discounts:
    applications, 583–584
    research studies, 581–582
    significance of, 579, 581
Marketable securities, 464

Market-based ratios, 479
Market efficiency, 36–37
Market makers, 332
Market power, 145, 150
Market timing, 140
Market value, 479, 542
Marmon Corporation, 491
Marshall Field & Co., 230, 252
Martin Marietta Corporation, 98, 234, 237–238
Massengill, Robert, 380
Master limited partnerships (MLPs):
    characteristics of, 425–426
    data, 423
    defined, 425
Maxwell, Robert, 185
Maxwell Communications Corporation vs.
        Macmillan Inc., 185, 216
Mayers, David, 521
MCI, 56, 152, 584
Medco Containment Services, Inc., 7, 144
MedPartners, 125
Megamergers, 56
Menke Associates, 375, 380
Merck, 7, 144
Meredith/Burdo Co., 95
Merger premiums:
    of equals, 527
    historical trends, 525–526
    stock market activity and, 526
    strategic mergers, 527
Mergers, generally:
    announcements, 4–5
    approval procedures, 13–14
    approval process, 12
    defined, 7
    financing, 8
    historical perspective, 21–59
    negotiations, 12–13
    professionals, 9–10
    reasons for, 8
    strategies, see Merger strategy
    ten largest, 4
    types of, 7–8, 18–19
Merger strategy:
    diversification:
        acquisition of leading industry positions,
            130–133
        corporate finance theory and, 136–138
        effects in firm value, 141
        entering more profitable industries, 134–135
        financial benefits of, 135–136
        positive evidence of benefits of, 140–141
        related, unrelated vs., 144
        research, related vs. unrelated, 144
        significance of, 128
        stock market performance and, 139–140

economic motives:
    consolidation, 150, 152
    horizontal integration, 144–151, 168
    monopoly hypothesis, empirical evidence of,
        149–150
    roll-up acquisition programs, 150, 152
    vertical integration, 153–157
growth, 116–117
hubris hypothesis of takeovers, 158–161
improved management hypothesis, 161–163
synergy:
    acquisition premiums and, 124
    case study, 117–118
    financial, 126–128
    operating, 120–124
    realizing gains, 124–126
    significance of, 117, 120
tax motives, 164–167
Merrill Lynch, 154, 318, 334
Merrill Lynch Capital Markets, 335
Mesa Partners II, 227–228, 234
Mesa Petroleum vs. Cities Service, 212–213, 342
Metromedia, 210
Metropolitan Life Insurance Company, 320, 334
Mezzanine layer financing, 304–305, 366
Microsoft, 92, 98, 285
Midway, 157
Mikkelson, Wayne, 208, 210, 527
Miles, James, 411, 418
Milken, Michael, 111, 330, 333–334, 339, 347
Miller Brewing Company, 483
Minimum offer period, 72–73
Minority discounts:
    applications, 583–584
    overview, 582–583
Minority shareholders, 15
Misappropriation theory, 111
Mitchell, John, 31
Mitchell, Mark, 160, 263–264
MITE, 103–104
Mitsubishi Motors, 19
Mobil Oil Corporation, 153–154, 215
Monopoly, antitrust legislation, 22–27
Monopoly hypothesis, empirical evidence of,
    149–150
Moody, John, 342
Moody's, 342, 344, 347, 574
Moore Corporation, 12
Moran, John, 181
Morgan, J. P., 21, 24
Morgan Bank, 24
Morgan Stanley, 40–41, 333–334
Morgenstern, 442
Morris Trust, elimination of, 599
Muelbroek, Lisa, 111
Mulherin, J. Harold, 280

Multimedia Corporation, 217–218
Murdock, David, 246
Mutual funds, 337

National Association of Securities Dealers (NASD), 13, 72, 196
National Association of Security Dealers' Automated Quotations (NASDAQ), 498, 574
National Bank of Commerce, 24
National Bureau of Economic Research, 21, 347
National Can Company, 364
National Car Rental, 181
National City Bank, 24
National Intergroup, 141–143
National Labor Relations Board, 16
National Lead Trust, 24
National Steel, 142
NationsBank, 55, 123
Navistar International, 22
NEC, 19
Negotiations:
  disclosure of, 13
  overview, 12–13
  prepackaged bankruptcy, 447
Nelson, Ralph, 21
Neoax Corporation, 420
NetChannel, 505
Net income, 501–504
Net present value (NPV), 501, 513–514, 566
Net sales, 468
Netter, Jeffrey, 204
Neutralized voting, 317
New Jersey Holding Company Act, 24
New offer, 79
New York Air, 157
New York Central Railroad, 224
New York Times, 42, 275, 574
Niehaus, Greg, 382–383, 386
Nippon Life Insurance Company, 307
Nixon, Richard M., 32
NKK Corporation, 141
NL Industries, 277–278, 280
NLT Corporation, 234–235
Northrop, 7
Northrop Grumman Corp., 98
No-shop provisions, 217
Notes payable, 465
Notes purchase rights plans, 183
Notice of guaranteed delivery, 78
NVF Company, 209
NYNEX, 112

Occidental Petroleum, 234
O'Connor, Sandra Day, Justice, 109
Odd Lot Trading Company, 323–324
Odyssey Partners, 215

Offer to Purchase, 76
Office Depot, 98
Ogden Corporation, 214
O'Hagan, James, 111
Ohio Casualty, 337
Ohio Mattress Company, 334, 340
Oligopoly, 26, 56–57
Open-end investment companies, 17
Open market purchases:
  case study, 266
  defined, 248
  street sweeps and, 264–266
  tender offers, compared with, 266–267
Operating profit, 468
Operating synergy:
  cost-reducing, 121–124
  revenue-enhancing (REO), 120–121
Opler, Tim,, 504
Option's premium, 93
Otis Elevator, 41–42
Outside board, 190
Over-the-counter (OTC) securities, 72, 498, 575, 579
Overstating income, 560
Ownership, generally:
  holding companies and, 18
  managerial, 198
  recapitalization plans and, 220
  voting rights and, 190

Packard Bell, 19
Pac-Man defense:
  case study, 235
  defined, 205, 234
  overview, 234–235, 238
Pan American Airways Pacific, 118
Pan American World Airways, 331
Pantry Pride, 215–216, 318
Paramount, Inc., 35, 112–113, 530
Paramount Communications, 217, 499–500
Park, Sangsoo, 384
Partially taxable transactions, 595
Partial public offering, defined, 398
Partial tender offers, 257–258
Payback method, 578
Payout ratio, 480
Pegram, 111
Peltz, Norman, 333–334

Penn Central Railroad, 444
Pennsylvania antitakeover law, 107
Pennzoil Corporation, 225, 436–437
Pension funds, 338
Pepsico, 210
Perelman, Ronald, 202, 210–211, 215–216
Perlmutter, Isaac, 324

Permian Oil, 142
Perot, Ross, 7, 270
Petition for relief, 440
Philadelphia Carpet Company, 166
Philadelphia Holding Company, 166
Philip Morris Companies, Inc., 8, 482–489
Phillips Petroleum, 335
PhyCor, 125
Pickens, Boone, 85, 212–213, 227–228, 234, 247, 342
PIK (payment-in-kind) securities, 337
Pillsbury, 111
Plant and equipment expenditures, 464
Poison puts, 188
Polaroid Corporation, 225, 229, 387, 389–390
Pooling of interests accounting, 35, 506, 590–592
Porter, Michael, 400–401
Portfolio theory, 453
Posner, Richard, 98
Posner, Victor, 246
Poterba, James, 596
Poulsen, Annette, 193, 195, 197, 204, 256–257, 280
Pound, John, 236, 274
Pownall, Thomas, 238
Predator's Bell, The (Bruck), 333
Prediction errors, 207
Preferred stock:
    cost of, 517
    defined, 465
    dividends, 469
    ESOPs and, 380
    implications of, generally, 8
    plans:
        as antitakeover prevention strategy, 178, 184
        blank check, 184, 213
        implications of, generally, 178
        rising rate, 367
Premiums, tender offer, 263. *See specific types of premiums*
Prepackaged bankruptcy:
    benefits of, 447
    defined, 446–447
    pre-voted *vs.* post-voted, 448
    tax advantages of, 448
Present value:
    divestitures, 407
    stock valuation, 496, 513
Press releases, 71
Price-earnings ratio (P/E):
    capitalization rate derived from, 577–578
    defined, 480
    implications of, generally, 33–34, 194
    payback method, 578
    target, risk and growth of, 578
    in targeted companies, 541–542

Prime rate, 303
Princess Cruises, 122
Pritzger, Jay, 135, 491
Privately held businesses:
    case studies, 560–561
    closely held businesses, 564–565
    costs of, 561
    income reports, 560–562
    income statement, addback process, 562–565
    profitability, reconstruction of, 561–562
    valuation:
        common methods of, 565–586
        public business compared with, 557–559
        research studies, 585–586
Procyclical sales, 136
Professional fees, 563
Profitability, 561–562
Profitability ratio, 478
Project Imperial, 222
Proofs of claim, 440–441
Proportionality test, 85
Proxy contest, *see* Proxy fight
Proxy fight(s):
    case studies, 271, 275
    corporate elections, 268–269
    costs of, 279–280
    data, 268
    defined, 268
    dissident campaigns, 282
    forms of, 273
    historical perspective, the 1990s, 283–285
    implications of, generally, 163, 190–191, 198, 210
    Independent Election Corporation of America (IECA), role of, 277
    insurgent's viewpoint, 274
    long-term effects of, 282
    management buyouts and, 296
    process, 275–277
    regulation of, 269, 273–274
    shareholder:
        activism, 274–275
        apathy, 269–270
        wealth, effects on, 280, 282
    tender offer, combination with, 283
    voting by proxy, 271–273
Proxy firms, 79, 517
Proxy solicitation, 84, 191–192
Public companies, cost of, 293–294. *See also* Publicly held companies
Public offerings, *see* Initial public offerings; Partial public offerings
Public utilities, 28
Public Utility Holding Company Act (PUHCA), 28–29

Publicly held companies, valuation of:
  as antitakeover defense, 493
  benchmarks, 540–541
  case studies, 542–553
  control premium, 519–529
  discount rates, 518–519
  earnings base, 499–507
  exchange ratio, 533–540
  financial methodologies, 512–517
  forecasting methods, 507–512
  methodology, 492–493
  overview, 491–492
  stock:
    common, cost of, 517–518
    marketability of, 498–499
    preferred, cost of, 517
    price variability and collar agreements, 540
    stock-for-stock exchanges, 529–533
    valuation methods, 493–498
  targets, desirable characteristics of, 541–542
Purchase accounting method, 35, 506, 590–592
Purchase price, in leveraged buyouts (LBOs), 298
Pure plays, 403
Put options,188, 378

Quattro Pro, 472
Questrom, Allen, 455
Quick ratio, 473
QVC, 112–113, 217

Rabbi trusts, 201
Radisson Diamond Cruises, 122
Rail transportation, national, 24–25, 27
Rales, Steven and Michael, 221–222
Rales vs. Interco, 185
Rales Brothers, 221–222, 367
Ralston Purina, 210, 379
Ramada, 506
Ramirez, Gabriel, 387
Rate of return, 517–518
Ratners Group P. L. C., 188
Ravenscraft, David, 139, 315
Rayonier, 428
Raytheon, 98
RCA, 118, 237
Real estate investment trusts (REITs), 599
Reasonableness test, 85
Recapitalization:
  case studies, 221–223
  leveraged, generally, 433–435
  leveraged buyouts compared with, 220
  overview, 217_220
  poison pill protection, 220–222
  problems with, 222–223
Regression analysis, 510–512

Regulation G, 366–367
Reidy, John, 500
Reincorporation, 203–204
Related diversification, 144
Related research, 144
Reliance Corporation, 207, 365–366
Reliance Group, 231
Reorganization plan:
  Chapter 11 reorganization, 443–444
  purpose of, generally, 439
Reorganizations, tax-free, 593–594
Research and development (R&D):
  charges, in-process, 599
  cost of, 505–506
  post-LBO firms, 316
Resolution, 13–14
Resorts International, 462–463
Resorts Worldwide, Inc., 599
Restricted stock, 581–582
Restrictive covenants, 332
Restructuring:
  corporate, see Corporate restructuring
  cost of, 506
  implications of, generally, 12
  spin-offs and, 405
Return on equity (ROE), 479, 570
Return on investment (ROI), 479
Returns, from leveraged buyouts, 311–312
Revco, leveraged buyout, 322–325
Revenues, income statement, 470
Revere Copper, 335
Reverse subsidiary merger, 7
Reverse LBOs:
  case study, 315
  defined, 314
  performance record, 315–317
  research, 314–315
Reverse synergy, divestitures and, 402–403
Revlon:
  mergers/acquisitions, generally, 210–211
  Pantry Pride vs., 215–216
Revlon duties, 85–86, 113
Reynolds Metals, 96
R. H. Macy & Co., 319
Riklis, Meshulam, 330
Rising rate preferred stock, 367
Risk, generally:
  arbitrage, 9, 64
  business, 310
  discount rate and, 567
  employee stock ownership plans (ESOPs), 380
  interest, 310
  junk bonds, 332–332
  leveraged buyouts (LBOs):
    business risk, 310

Risk, generally (*continued*)
    interest rate risk, 310
    risk analysis, 308–309
  premium, 357, 571–572
Risk-free rate, 571
Rite Aid Corporation, 322, 325
RJR Nabisco, 11, 159, 292, 308, 317, 319–321, 505
Roach, George, 527
Robber Barons, The (Josephson), 224
Rockefeller, J. D., 22, 24
Rocky Creek Mills, 166
Roll, Richard, 37, 158
Roll-up acquisition programs, 150, 152
Romans, Donald, 492
Roosevelt, Theodore, 26, 87
Rosenfeld, James, 411, 413, 418
R. R. Donnelly, 95
Ruback, Richard, 208, 210, 514–515, 575
Rule 14(d), Williams Act, 247
Rule of Reason, 96
Ryngaert, Michael, 185–186

Sabre Carpet, 166
Safeway, 150
Salem Carpet Mills, 167
Salomon Brothers, 210, 324
Sante Fe Corporation *vs.* Henley Group, 221
Sante Fe Railway, 402, 418
Sante Fe-Southern Pacific, 467
Saturday-night special, 42
Savings and loans associations, 333, 338, 469
Saxon Industries, 205
Schedule 13D filing, 64–67, 248, 265
Schedule 13G filing, 67
Schedule 14D-1, 68–70
Schedule 14D-9, 227
Scherer, Frederick, 139
Schipper, Katherine, 422–423
Scholes, Myron, 258, 600
Schwert, G., William, 186
SCM Corporation, 265, 318
S corporations, 378
Seagate Technology, 19
Sears Financial Services Center, 133
Sears Roebuck, 133–134
SEC Rule 13e-3, 318–319
Second merger wave (1916–1929), 26–30
Secretary of State, function of, 13
Secured creditors, Chapter 11 reorganization and, 441
Secured debt, 303
Secured financing, 303
Securities, valuation methods, 467
Securities Act of 1933, 251, 532
Securities and Exchange Act of 1934, 62, 84, 113, 227, 269, 318

Securities and Exchange Commission (SEC):
  function of, generally, 10
  regulations, generally, 16, 61–62, 67, 71, 84, 110, 128, 196–197, 224, 251, 266, 269, 273–274, 293, 334, 405, 461, 532, 558
Securities laws:
  8K filing, 62
  employee stock ownership plans (ESOPs), 68, 380
  Schedule 13D filing, 64–67
  Schedule 13G filing, 67
  Securities Exchange Act, 84
  Williams Act, 62–64, 68–84
Securities tender offers, 91–92, 251
Self-tender offers, 227
Seller's liabilities, assumption of, 15–16
Sell-offs:
  corporate focus and, 419–420
  defensive, 417
  involuntary, 418–419
  wealth effects, 410–410
Sensitivity analysis, leveraged buyouts and, 309–310
Service Corp., 153
Settlements, 15, 55, 208
7–Eleven, 301
Seven Seas Cruises, 122
Seven Sisters, 342
Seyhun, Nejat, 111
Shamrock Holdings *vs.* Polaroid Corporation, 225, 229, 389–390
Share issuance:
  case study, 225
  employee stock ownership plans (ESOPs), 224–226
  overview, 224
Share repurchase, 226–228, 246
Shareholder approval:
  employee stock ownership plans (ESOPs), 377
  spin-offs, 405
Shareholder votes, value in proxy fight, 282
Shareholder wealth:
  antitakeover measures and, 175–176, 188–189
  employee stock ownership plans (ESOPs) and, 386–387
  proxy contests, effects of, 280–281
  tender offers, 253, 257
  voluntary sell-offs and, 413–414
  white knight bids and, 212
Shareholders, generally:
  appraisal rights, 15
  dissenting, 15
  large-block, 206–207
  merger approval procedures, 13–14
  minority, 15

Shaw, Clarence, 165
Shaw Industries, 164–166
Shaw, Robert, 165
Shearson Lehman Brothers, 154, 420
Shelf registration, 224, 334
Sheraton Hotels, 30, 428
Sherman Antitrust Act, 22–23, 26, 87, 99
Shleifer, Andrei, 319
Shopping Bag Food, 97–98
Short-form merger, 14–15
Siegel, Donald, 302
Siemans AG, 152
Signature guarantee, 77
Simmons, Harold, 277–278
Simon, William, 315
Simple regression analysis, 512
Singer Corporation, 46, 48, 203
Sitmar Cruises, 122
Smiley, Robert, 267
Smith, Abbie, 422–423
Smith, Daniel T., 118
Smith, Roger, 270
Smith-Vasiliou Management Company, Inc., 335
Solicitation process, in proxy fight, 276
Song, Moon, 384
South Bend Lathe, 380
Southern Pacific railway, 402, 418
Southland Corporation, 301
Specialized inputs, 155
Spin-offs:
    case study, 405–407
    convertible securities, treatment of, 410
    defensive, 409
    defined, 397
    employee stock option plans and, 410
    equity carve-outs vs., 423
    involuntary, 409
    process overview, 404–405
    recent trends in, 408–409
    tax consequences of, 410
    warrants, treatment of, 410
Split rating, 344
Split-off, defined, 398
Split-up, defined, 398
Spreading overhead, 121
Spreadsheet programs, 472–473
Sprint, 56, 584
Stakeholders, antitakeover measures and, 175. See also Shareholders
Standard & Poor's, 342, 344, 347, 574
Standard deviations, 510–511
Standard Industrial Classification (SIC) codes, 90, 144, 420, 527
Standard Oil, 22, 24, 26, 50, 96
Standard Oil Trust, 25

Standstill agreement:
    case studies, 209, 210–211
    defined, 204
    overview, 209
    research, 210–211
    typical, 209
Staples, 98
Star Finishing Company, 166
Starwood Hotels, 599
Statement of cash flows, 461, 470
Statutory merger, 7
Steinberg, Saul, 205, 207–208, 231, 365–366
Steiner, Peter, 30, 35
Stevens, John Paul, Justic, 109
Stigler, George, 26
Stiglin, Laura, 602
Stillman, Robert S., 149
Stock, generally:
    common, see Common stock
    marketability of, 498–499
    parking, 64
    preferred, see Preferred stock
    prices:
        accounting treatment and, 592
        artificial manipulation of, 36–37
    purchase, 15, 595
    stock exchanges, see Stock-for-stock exchanges
    street names, 272
    tender offer, 61
    valuation methods, Gordon stock dividend valuation model, 494–495
Stock financed merger, 61, 528
Stock-for-stock exchanges:
    acquiring companies:
        long-term effects, 531–532
        short-term effects, 531
    collar agreements, 540
    executive job retention, 532
    historical perspective, 529
    legal issues, 532–533
    managerial ownership, 532
    medium of exchange, 530
    method of payment, 532
    target companies, short-term effects, 530–531
    tax incentives, 530
Stockholder interests hypothesis, 176–177
Stockholders, see Shareholders
    meetings, 272
    record date, 272
    wealth, see Shareholder wealth
Stock market crashes:
    of 1904, 26
    of 1929, 26, 63
    of 1987, 29
Stokley Van Camp, 233

Stop & Shop, 150
Straight-line depreciation, 37
Strategic alliances, 19–20
Strategic mergers, 527
Street sweeps, 264–266
Strichman, George, 42
Structure argument, 96
Subordinated debt, 300, 303–304
Subsidiaries, 405, 422–423, 467–468
Successor liability, 15
Summation method, 57
Sun Oil Co., 75–76, 108, 247–248
Superior Oil, 153–154
Supermajority provision:
    defined, 192
    legality of, 193
    overview, 192–193
    research studies, 193–194
Supermarkets General, 150, 505
Suspense account, 388
Swift and Company, 403, 405–407
Sync Research, 19
Synergy:
    acquisition premiums and, 124
    case study, 117–118
    defined, 8
    financial, 126–128
    operating, 120–124
    realizing gains, 124–126
    reverse, 402–403
    significance of, 117, 120

Taft, William Howard, 26, 87
Takeover, defined, 7
Takeover battle, 25
Takeover premiums, poison pill impact on, 186
Takeover tactics:
    bear hugs, 243, 245–247
    case study, 246
    casual pass, 245
    establishing a toe hold, 245
    preliminary steps, 245–247
    proxy fights, 244
    tender offers, 243–244
    types of, overview, 243–244
Target, generally:
    defined, 162
    dividend policy, 499
    method of payment, short-term effects, 530–531
Targeted share repurchases, 205
Taxable income, defined, 558
Tax Act (1981), 600
Taxation:
    asset basis step-up, 598
    bankruptcy, prepackaged, 448

employee stock ownership plans (ESOPs), 381
financial accounting and, 589–592
holding companies and, 18
management buyouts (MBOs), 602, 604
merger decision and, 600–602
as motivation, 8, 164
recapitalization plans, 220
spin-offs, 410
stock *vs.* cash transactions, 530
stock-for-stock exchanges, 530, 595–597
taxable *vs.* tax-free transactions, 593–594
tax laws, 598–599
tender offers, cash *vs.* securities, 251
voluntary liquidation, 424
Tax-free reorganizations, 593–594
Tax loss carryforwards:
    defined, 595–596
    research studies, 596–597
Tax Reform Act of 1969, 36
Tax Reform Act of 1984, 373
Tax Reform Act of 1986, 383, 425, 598
Technical insolvency, 126
Tele-Communications, Inc., 500
Telecommunications industry, 53, 56
Teledyne, 136, 139
Tender offer(s):
    any-and-all *vs.* partial, 257–258
    bad bidders as targets, 263–264
    best price rule, 80
    bidder purchase outside of, 81
    cash *vs.* securities, 251
    changes in, 79–80
    completion of, 83
    defined, 74–75
    effects of, empirical evidence, 258–259
    exemptions from rules, 81–82
    history of, 249
    honest management and, 254
    open market purchases and, 248, 264–267
    payment following completion of, 82–83
    premiums and director independence, 263
    proration period, 74
    proxy fight combined with, 283
    reasons for, 249–250
    response of target management, 252–254
    success rate, 250
    taking control after, 83
    team, creation of, 254–255
    10–day waiting period, 251
    tendering shares, 76–80
    time periods, 72–74
    two-tiered, 255–257
    unsuccessful, wealth effects of, 259–263
    under Williams Act, generally, 247–248, 251
10Q quarterly report, 461, 558

Texaco Corporation, 163, 190, 205, 270–271, 436–437
Texas Gulf Sulphur, 110
Texas International, 331
The Limited, 227
Thermo-King, 153
Third merger wave (1965–1969), 30–43
Thomas H. Lee & Co., 247
3Com Corporation, 19
Three-piece suitor, 258
Time, Inc., 154, 499–500, 530
Time interest earned, 477–478
Time-Warner-Paramount, 86
Time-Warner-Viacom-QVC, 527
Titman, Sheridan, 504
Toll Brothers, Inc., 184
Topping fees, 216–217
Torchmark Corporation vs. American General, 275
Total asset turnover ratio, 342, 476
Tracinda Corporation, 200
Tracor, Inc., 302
Tranches, defined, 364
Transaction costs, vertical integration, 155
Transcontinental Services Group, 324
Transportation system, national, 24–25, 27
Trans Union, Corporation, 491–492
t-statistic, 192, 362
Treasury bills, 571
Trendsetting mergers:
    Colt Industries versus Garlock Industries, 42–43
    INCO versus ESB merger, 38–41
    United Technologies versus Otis Elevator, 41–42
Triangle Industries, 364
Triple taxation, 18
Trump, Donald, 94, 196, 209
Trump vs. Griffin and Resorts International, 196, 462–463
Trust funds doctrine, 16
TSP, 512
Turnaround Management Associates, 445
Two-tiered tender offers:
    defined, 83, 255
    fair price provisions, 194–195
    overview, 255–256
    regulation of, 256–257
    stockholder wealth, effect on, 257
T. W. Services, 77
Type A reorganization, 593
Type B reorganization, 593–594
Type C reorganization, 594
Type D reorganization, 594
Tysoe, Ronald, 455

U.S. Air, 214
U.S. Steel, 21, 96, 215

U.S. Trustee, Chapter 11 reorganization, 441–442
Understating income, 560
Undervalued assets, 35
Underwriting spreads, junk bonds, 361–364
Unilever, 233
Union Carbide Corporation, 27
UNISYS, 7
United Airlines (UAL), 117–118
United Communications, 533–534, 536–539
United Technologies Corporation:
    mergers/acquisitions, generally, 237
    Otis Elevator vs., 41–42
Universal Foods Corporation, 106, 236
Unocal Corporation vs. Mesa Partners II, 227–228
Unocal standard, 85
Unrelated diversification, 144
Unrelated research, 144
Unsuccessful tender offer, wealth effects:
    on bidder, 261–263
    overview, 259–260
    on target, 260–261
USX Corporation, 22, 335

Valid business reasons, 206
Valuation:
    analyses, generally, 12
    ESOP shares, 377–378
    financial analysis, 461–489
    privately held businesses, 557–587
    publicly held companies, 491–556
    tax issues, 589–604
Valuation experts, 10
Value Line, 503
ValuSource, 473
Vanderbilt, Cornelius, 25, 224
Van Gorkom, Jerome, 491–492
Varaiya, Nikhil, 186, 521
Vertical integration:
    case study, 153–154
    competitive advantage and, 156
    defined, 153, 168
    motives for, 154–156
    as threat to competition, 156–157
Vertical mergers, 7
Vertical strips, 306
Viacom-Paramount-QVC, 112–113
Vishney, Robert, 319
Voluntary divestitures:
    involuntary vs., 402
    reasons for, 402–404
Vons Grocery Co., 97–98
Voting:
    neutralized, 317
    plans, 188–189
    proxy fights, 276–277

Voting (*continued*)
by proxy, 271–273
Voting Rights Policy, of the Securities and
Exchange Commission (SEC), 197
Vultures, bankruptcy, 454

Wahal, Sunil, 108
Waiting period, 92
Wal-Mart, 142–143, 162
Waldron, Hicks, 270
Walking, Ralph, 185
Wall Street Journal, 42, 222, 463, 574
Wallace Computer Services, Inc., 12
Walt Disney Co.:
Arvida acquisition, 231
mergers/acquisitions, generally, 12, 205,
207–208, 365
Warner, Jerrold, 280, 282
Warner Communications, Inc., 154, 499–500, 530
Warning systems, 177
Warrants:
exercise of, 304
spin-offs and, 410
Wasserstein-Perella, 222
Wealth transfer, in leveraged buyouts (LBOs),
321–322
Weighted average method, 508–509
Weirton Steel, 376
Weisbach, Michael, 401
Weiss, Lawrence A., 446
West Point-Pepperell, 167, 215–216, 258
Westin International, 118, 403
Westinghouse Electric Corp., 108, 152–153
White knights:
case studies, 212–213, 238
defined, 204, 211
leveraged buyouts and, 319
open market purchase and, 265
overview, 211–212
shareholder wealth, effect on bids, 212
White squire defense:
case study, 215–216
defined, 204, 213
lockup transactions, 214–216
merger agreement provision, 214
no-shop provisions, 217
overview, 213–214
stock options for bidders, 216
topping fees/bustup fees, 216–217

Wholly owned subsidiary, 17
Wickes Companies, 367
Wigmore, Barrie, 354
Wiles, Kenneth, 108
Williamette Management Associates, 581–582
Williams Act:
development of, 62–63, 113, 249
litigation and, 232
lockup transactions and, 215
merger tactics, 83–84
objectives of, 36, 42, 63
pro rata acceptance, 74
Schedule 13D, 64–67
Schedule 13G, 67–68
Section 14(d), 68–72
Section 13(d), 63–64
tender offer:
best price rule, 80
bidder purchase outside of, 81
changes in, 79–80
completion of, 83
defined, 74–75
exemptions from rules, 81–82
payment following completion of, 82–83
taking control after, 83
tendering shares, 76–80
time periods, 72–74
withdrawal rights, 74
Williams, Harrison, 62, 249
Winner's curse hypothesis, 159–160
Withdrawal rights, 72–74
Wolfson, Mark, 600
Working capital, 474
Workouts:
benefits of, 449
candidates, recognizing, 449
defined, 449
transaction costs, voluntary restructuring vs.
Chapter 11, 449–450
Worldcom, 152
W. R. Grace, 420
W. T. Grant, 344–346, 470

Zapata Corporation, 331
Zayre, 162
Zenner, Mark, 108
Zeta analysis, 346–347
Zimmerman, James, 455
Z score, 346–347